HANDBOOK OF
U.S. LATINO PSYCHOLOGY

The editors of this volume dedicate this book to our ancestors, our grandparents and parents, our spouses and children, and our future generations of families to come. We also honor those scholars who dedicated their careers to establishing the field of Latino psychology and who have passed into their next worlds, and those future scholars whom we hope will advance the scholarship of Latino psychology.

HANDBOOK OF
U.S. LATINO PSYCHOLOGY

DEVELOPMENTAL AND COMMUNITY-BASED PERSPECTIVES

EDITORS

Francisco A. Villarruel
Michigan State University

Gustavo Carlo
University of Nebraska–Lincoln

Josefina M. Grau
Kent State University

Margarita Azmitia
University of California, Santa Cruz

Natasha J. Cabrera
University of Maryland

T. Jaime Chahin
Texas State University

Los Angeles | London | New Delhi
Singapore | Washington DC

For information:

 SAGE Publications, Inc.
2455 Teller Road
Thousand Oaks, California 91320
E-mail: order@sagepub.com

SAGE Publications Ltd.
1 Oliver's Yard
55 City Road
London EC1Y 1SP
United Kingdom

SAGE Publications India Pvt. Ltd.
B 1/I 1 Mohan Cooperative Industrial Area
Mathura Road, New Delhi 110 044
India

SAGE Publications Asia-Pacific Pte. Ltd.
33 Pekin Street #02-01
Far East Square
Singapore 048763

Printed in the United States of America

Library of Congress Cataloging-in-Publication Data

Handbook of U.S. Latino psychology : developmental and community-based perspectives/Francisco A. Villarruel . . . [et al.].
   p. cm.
Includes bibliographical references and index.
ISBN 978-1-4129-5760-1 (cloth)
ISBN 978-1-4129-5761-8 (pbk.)

   1. Latin Americans—Mental Health—United States. 2. Hispanic Americans—Mental Health—United States. 3. Latin Americans–Psychology. 4. Hispanic Americans—Psychology. I. Villarruel, Francisco.

RC451.5.H57H36 2009
362.196′89008968073—dc22   2009003831

This book is printed on acid-free paper.

09   10   11   12   13   10   9   8   7   6   5   4   3   2   1

Acquisitions Editor:	Erik Evans
Editorial Assistant:	Sarita Sarak
Production Editor:	Astrid Virding
Copy Editor:	April Wells-Hayes
Typesetter:	C&M Digitals (P) Ltd.
Proofreader:	Joyce Li
Indexer:	J. Naomi Linzer Indexing Services
Cover Designer:	Bryan Fishman
Marketing Manager:	Stephanie Adams

CONTENTS

PREFACE

Latinos in the United States are a combination of diverse populations that differ on a range of factors, including mode of entry into the United States, length of time in the country, socioeconomic status, geographical location, level of acculturation, and so on. Some are colonized minorities, such as Chicanos/as and Puertorriqueños, while others came as war refugees (Mexicans, Salvadorians, Guatemalans), political refugees (Cubans), immigrants (Latin Americans and South Americans), and migrant and undocumented workers (Mexicans and other populations). It cannot be said that the experiences and challenges across these groups are the same, nor are their community and individual mental health needs. As Latino psychology comes of age, it must contend with the diversity of experiences across the subgroups.

In the young field of Latino psychology, one can still find a series of "first events," such as the delivery of the first graduate program, the formation of the first national organization, and the occurrence of the first annual national conference. This volume marks another important first in the field by being the first handbook on U.S. Latino psychology—an event that highlights the shift away from the concept of "Hispanic psychology" to one that is more self-referential, an interesting and important psychological turn in the development and dissemination of scholarship in the field. As Padilla and Olmedo note in Chapter 1, the origins of Latino psychology can be traced to the pre-Columbian era, but within the United States it has become more commonplace and widespread as the growth of the Latino population has propelled it to the status of the second-largest ethnic category in the nation. While Padilla and Olmedo describe and honor the legacy of many of the pioneers of Latino psychology, this volume articulates the evolution of the scholarship and the methodological contributions of the more recent generation of Latino scholars who have advanced the theoretical and practical understandings that contribute to the well-being of Latinos in the United States.

As in other areas of Latino scholarship, there is a unique importance associated with, and contribution to be made by, Latino psychology. Consider the legacy of one individual: Julian Samora, one of the pioneers of Mexican American studies. Dr. Samora firmly believed that the purpose of scientific knowledge was to improve the human condition—his focus was on improving the Mexican American community. In his effort to promote the production and application of knowledge about Mexican Americans, he ultimately contributed to the development of Latino psychology and other areas of study of Latino communities. Like Chicano studies and Latino studies, Latino psychology studies Latinos on their own terms; that is, as distinct population groups with their own histories, cultures, and trajectories in society. While their minority status cannot be ignored, it cannot be the only thing that defines them. This was also understood by George I. Sanchez, whom many regard as the father of Chicano psychology.

In addition to the "routine research" or "normal science" that must go on to develop the state of disciplinary knowledge, the work of Latino psychology today must address the psychological impacts of global change. Not only must it produce knowledge about the distinct cultures, mental processes, and needs of Latino populations, it must document the increasing diversity of Latinos in the United

States and develop mechanisms for meeting their mental health needs. For example, the global economy has been attended by the rise of transnational labor; people and communities have been displaced in their homelands and forced to become migrant workers on a global scale. In the United States, millions of undocumented workers have come to seek their fortunes in our economy. Their clandestine existence not only produces such psychological pressures as the fear of being exposed or detained, but nativistic movements that promote and legitimate raids by Immigration and Customs Enforcement (ICE) have engendered widespread terror in Latino communities across the nation. It is enough that the life of an undocumented migrant worker is often characterized by loneliness and depression, often without recourse to mental health services.

Community raids by ICE not only break up families, they strike fear in the lives of children, who worry that their parents will be arrested and deported or, worse yet, who come home from their days to be told that their parents are being held in deportation centers because of their immigrant status. In addition, many who are detained by ICE are held in centers where medical care is limited and women are subjected to sexual harassment by employees. Thus, not only must Latino psychology contribute to the development of effective multicultural competence within mainstream mental health agencies, it must explore ways by which those who exist "below the law" can access the services they need to improve their mental well-being. At the same time, related transnational labor issues include research questions about the sending societies, their economies and political climates, and the relations that transnational workers maintain with members of their families and networks in their societies of origin. The growing population of Latinos who are incarcerated, addicted to drugs, or suffering from illnesses with profound psychosocial consequences, such as cancer and AIDS, means that the field will also need to expand to serve the unique needs of a population that shies away from mental health services.

To a great extent, because of the impact of group domination dynamics and the great changes occurring in society today, Latino psychology goes beyond normal science by incorporating values as part of its work. Like postnormal science, it extends the boundaries of the work of scientists beyond the technical expertise provided within the policy arena, as well as the facts commonly circumscribed by a monolithic conception of science. Latino psychology accepts the injection of ethical considerations into the processes of knowledge production with Latino communities, and it recognizes and accepts that it stems from a plurality of knowledge, including ethnoscientific knowledge and practices.

The chapters in this volume reflect not only a history but also the evolution of Latino psychology. The contributors accepted the invitation to be a part of this volume as a way of disseminating knowledge in the field and because of the perceived need for a statement on the current status of key areas of the field. The editors did not seek to gather a comprehensive work on Latino psychology—that would be virtually impossible because of the broad scope of issues that have advanced knowledge on behalf of Latinos in the United States. Rather, strategic decisions were made to focus on issues of social, cultural, and policy importance for U.S. Latinos.

In the area of health, for example, two issues that adversely impact Latino health and the families of those dealing with health issues (i.e., breast cancer and HIV/AIDS) were selected because of their impact but also because of the scholarship that has evolved in these areas. Buki and Selem (Chapter 21, this volume) point out that the focus of scholarship in this area is critical, given the increased population and the prevalence of cancer that compromises the quality of life for cancer victims and their families. To provide optimal health prevention and intervention services, Buki and Selem assert that a pedagogical lens integrating the etiology of the cancers needs to build upon cultural mores that impact individual and familial responses to illness. Similarly, Singer and his colleagues (Chapter 5) underscore the importance of the study of Latino psychology given the realm of individual, social, and historical factors that increase their risk for adverse health issues and the individual understanding of health.

Similarly, three chapters focus on identity development among Latino populations (cf. Chapter 6, Quintana & Scull; Chapter 8, Gonzales, Fabrett, & Knight; Chapter 9, Umaña-Taylor & Alfaro). Collectively, the three chapters provide important insight into the normative development and challenges experienced by Latinos in the United States, which impact both identity formation and acculturative stress. Gonzales, Fabrett, and Knight advance the issues that underscore the development of identity by stressing the importance of context, whereas Quintana and Scull stress the importance of a strong ethnic identity in the adaptation and resiliency of Latino populations—an issue further elaborated upon by Kuperminc, Wilkins, Roche, and Alvarez-Jimenez (Chapter 13).

We also included chapters that focus on the intersection of family (Chapter 10, Grau, Azmitia, & Quattlebaum; Chapter 14, Applewhite, Garcia Biggs, & Herrera; Chapter 17, Zayas, Borrego, & Domenech Rodríguez; Chapter 18, Bernal, Sáez-Santiago, & Galloza-Carrero), education (Chapter 15, Cabrera, Shannon, Rodriguez, & Lubar; Chapter 16, García & Scribner), and intervention because family is centrally to Latinos and, as noted by Fuligni and Perreira (Chapter 7), education is an important motivator for immigration to the United States. The changing nature of Latino family values and socialization practices is evident in the chapters on prosocial behaviors and social competence (Chapter 12, Carlo & de Guzman); sexuality (Chapter 23, Raffaelli & Iturbide); risk, resiliency, and positive development (Chapter 13, Kuperminc, Wilkins, Roche, & Alvarez-Jimenez); and feminism (Chapter 11, Hurtado & Cervantez), which also point to the critical need for theory and research that focuses on the unique features of Latinos, as well as values and practices they share with other racial, ethnic, and socioeconomic groups in the United States. As with any handbook, this volume also provides scholarship that summarizes methodological contributions (Chapter 4, Knight, Roosa, Calderón-Tena, & Gonzales; Chapter 5, Singer,

Fisher, Hodge, Saleheen, & Mahadevan), as well as chapters that contextualize issues confronted by U.S. Latino populations in their lives (Chapter 2, Alegría & Woo; Chapter 3, Canino & Alegría; Chapter 19, Cardemil & Sarmiento; Chapter 20, Betancourt & Flynn; Chapter 22, Crockett & Zamboanga).

In short, each chapter in this volume offers a comprehensive summary of our knowledge to date, but the integration of and relationship between chapters illustrate the evolution of U.S. Latino psychology. Overall, the *Handbook of U.S. Latino Psychology* represents the great strides made in the field and the broad range of topics in which students, researchers, and practitioners can inform themselves and identify the challenges that remain. The handbook not only facilitates communication of the importance and relevance of the field, it provides evidence in the specific topic areas of rigorous research. As the field continues to move forward, translational research will become increasingly important. This is especially the case, given that more than 50% of Latino adults are foreign born and not integrated into the service delivery systems, and practitioners have limited professional experience with them.

We believe this volume provides important resources for students, researchers, policymakers, and practitioners.

Rubén O. Martinez, *Director, Julian Samora Research Institute*

Francisco A. Villarruel, *University Outreach and Engagement Senior Fellow and Professor, Family and Child Ecology*

ACKNOWLEDGMENTS

Pulling together a volume such as this is both a challenge and a unique opportunity. There is no doubt that, while it is an expansive work, some issues have not been included. We would first, and foremost, like to express our gratitude to the contributors of this volume and to those who declined our invitation to contribute due to their work and life challenges. They have all been supportive of this effort. Further appreciation is due to the past and current scholars in Latino psychology, whose work has inspired us and moved this important area of study forward to a place of prominence and relevance. We hope the present volume serves to continue their important work.

The editors of this volume would also like to express our gratitude to Jim Brace-Thompson for his vision and encouragement to produce this volume. During his tenure as the acquisitions editor at SAGE, Jim spoke to several of us individually and collectively about organizing and editing this volume. The editors made special efforts to gather at national meetings with him to plan the volume and to maintain the needed momentum and focus to the completion of this volume. His successors, Erik Evans and Sarita Sarak, have also been instrumental and supportive.

Gratitude is also extended to Lisa Y. Flores (University of Missouri–Columbia) and Miguel E. Gallardo (Pepperdine University Graduate School of Education and Psychology), whose initial review of the proposed volume was instrumental in defining the scope of the volume.

Finally, we also express our appreciation to Danny Layne and the Julian Samora Research Institute at Michigan State University for their generous support in developing a Web site to make the editorial work on this volume manageable. As with any project of this magnitude, many thanks are due to our families and to past and current students, colleagues, and mentors whose intellectual collaborations and emotional support provides the nourishing foundation for our work.

1

A HISTORY OF LATINO PSYCHOLOGY

AMADO M. PADILLA AND ESTEBAN L. OLMEDO

A HISTORY OF LATINO PSYCHOLOGY

The origins of Latino psychology can be traced to pre-Columbian times as well as to developments in Europe that were transported to Latin America (Padilla, 1980a, 1984, 2000; Padilla & Salgado de Snyder, 1988). Our purpose here is not to review the earliest developments in Latino psychology but to provide an overview of contemporary developments in the field between 1930 and 2000. We begin by briefly defining Latino psychology and placing it within the context of psychology in general and then present the careers of six pioneer Latino psychologists who contributed in significant ways to psychology in general and to Latino psychology in particular. These psychologists are deceased now, but all of them left a lasting imprint on Latino scholarship because of their research, their commitment to their cultural roots, and their advocacy on behalf of future generations of Latinos who walk in their footsteps as psychologists. In discussing each of these individuals, we place them in the context of their time and the struggles they overcame as Latino psychologists when there were no ethnic role models to emulate and when culture was not valued in the discourse of psychological inquiry.

In addition, we highlight several major developments that also contributed in unique ways to Latino psychology. The events in particular have

to do with the creation of professional associations that focus on professional training of Latinos in psychology. Our historical account is intended to be not comprehensive but rather heuristic; its goal is to encourage others to take up the study of the history of Latino psychology. Our perspective, too, is personal, since we knew most of the individuals whose names we give in this history.

WHAT IS LATINO PSYCHOLOGY?

A definition of Latino psychology is important because it sets the stage for the theoretical paradigms, research methodologies, and instruments used in our inquiry of Latinos and in the interpretations we give to our findings. We take the position that Latino psychology is a branch of ethnic psychology in which the population of interest is people of Latin American heritage who reside within the continental United States and Puerto Rico. Ethnic psychology, as we use the term, has as one of its focal points the study of Latinos within the context of majority-minority-group relations. Latinos are an ethnic group who historically have been oppressed and who can point to individual and group experiences of prejudice and discrimination in education, employment, and their communities of residence. Bernal, Trimble, Burlew, and Leong (2003),

1

in the *Handbook of Racial and Ethnic Minority Psychology*, make the point in the foreword to their book that until the 1970s American psychology was the study of the behavior of White persons. Thus, Latino psychologists, along with other ethnic psychologists, have worked to make psychology more inclusive of the multicultural context that is America.

Latino psychology also has a connection to cross-cultural psychology, but it is distinct in that it concentrates less on *inter*cultural group differences and more on *intra*cultural group variation. In other words, cross-cultural psychology is usually concerned with the systematic study of experience and behavior as they occur across cultures in different nation-states (e.g., Japan and the United States). Exceptions to this pattern often occur, of course, because the research approaches found in cross-cultural psychology can be used both within and across cultures.

In contrast, Latino psychology seeks to understand the influence of culture, language, and majority-minority-group status on people of Latin American origin who reside in the United States. The *intra*cultural comparison enters because Latinos, as mentioned above, maintain aspects of their culture of origin while also manifesting American cultural patterns of behavior. Latino psychology, then, seeks to learn how adaptation to the U.S. mainstream and acculturation influence a wide variety of behaviors, such as child-rearing practices, educational attainment of students, gender differences, and coping responses to stressful environments.

Also, Latino psychologists have had greater affinity for the applied areas, such as clinical, health, educational, and community psychology. This is due to social problems within the Latino community that call out for intervention and prevention programs of various types.

EARLY CONTRIBUTORS

George I. Sanchez

The first Latino psychologist was George I. Sanchez (1906–1972). Nathan Murillo wrote an excellent biography of Sanchez for the first volume of *Chicano Psychology* (Martinez, 1977). At the conclusion of editing *Chicano Psychology*, Joe Martinez dedicated the volume to George Sanchez and called him the father of Chicano psychology. Sanchez was born in New Mexico

and spent most of his professional career in his home state and in Texas. Thus, he was intimately familiar with the way of life of Latinos in the Southwest and with the social and educational exclusion they experienced because of their minority status. Throughout his life, Sanchez was an advocate of social justice and an activist for the rights of Chicanos. Sanchez received his doctorate from the University of California at Berkeley; for a time, he was on the faculty in education at the University of New Mexico and then became professor of Latin American education at the University of Texas at Austin. During his long career, Sanchez played a number of important professional roles—university professor, educational psychologist, social scientist, and frequent consultant to different Latin American countries on educational planning and policy.

The earliest contributions to Latino psychology are found in four articles Sanchez authored between 1932 and 1934 on the topic of intelligence testing of Mexican American children. In these four articles, Sanchez (1932a, b; 1934a, b) presented a series of cogent arguments for why standard intelligence tests lacked validity when used to assess Mexican American children. Considering the era in which he wrote, Sanchez provided exceptional insights into why IQ testing of Chicano children was inappropriate when these children did not have the same life experiences or level of English-language proficiency that majority-group children had and on whom the tests had been standardized. The four articles are as appropriate today as they were nearly 80 years ago. Importantly, mainstream psychologists at the time ignored Sanchez's call for caution in testing Mexican American children. Even today, there are concerns about high-stakes educational testing of Latino children on tests similar to those discussed by George Sanchez some 7 decades earlier.

Sanchez continued to contribute to the educational and social science literature for many years. His last publication was a keynote address entitled "Educational Change in Historical Perspective" given at a conference in the early 1970s on bilingual education, which appeared in the volume *Mexican Americans and Educational Change*, edited by Alfredo Castaneda, Manuel Ramirez III, Carlos E. Cortes, and Mario Barrera (1971). In this paper, Sanchez expressed his anger and disappointment with the poor academic progress that Latino students had made in education. He expressed his frustration in these words:

... While I have championed the cause of educational change for American children of Mexican descent for more than forty-five years, and while I have seen some changes and improvements in this long-standing dismal picture, I cannot, in conscience or as a professional educator, take any satisfaction in those developments. The picture is a shameful and an embarrassing one. (p. 14)

Sanchez, as he had done countless times before, placed the blame on an educational system that either failed to consider or chose to neglect the impact of poverty, cultural and linguistic differences, discrimination, and educational inequity on Mexican American students in public education.

Alfredo Castaneda

Another major figure in the history of Latino psychology is Alfredo Castaneda (1923–1981). Manuel Ramirez III (1981) eulogized Castaneda in the *Hispanic Journal of Behavioral Sciences* with these words: "With the passing of Alfredo Castaneda, the fields of psychology and education have lost an important leader and pioneer." As a leader in psychology, Castaneda was one of the most often cited and most prolific researchers in the area of child experimental psychology from the early 1950s to the mid-1970s. He earned his bachelor's degree from San Francisco State University in 1948 and received his master's (1951) and doctorate (1952) from Ohio State University. He began his career as an assistant professor at the State University of Iowa, where he remained until 1959. Castaneda then accepted the offer of a full professorship in clinical psychology at the University of Texas at Austin, where he also served as director of child research. He remained at the University of Texas at Austin through 1962 and subsequently relocated to New York City, where he held various teaching and research positions until 1968. During the period 1968–1970, he served as professor of psychology at the Ontario Institute for Studies in Education (OISE). At OISE, he was also a faculty member at the Institute for Child Study.

In 1970, Castaneda became professor of education and chairman of Mexican American studies at the University of California at Riverside. It was at this point that Castaneda broke with his earlier, more traditional experimental work and began an intense and productive period in which he concentrated his talents on bilingual and multicultural education.

Castaneda was likely the first Latino psychologist to recognize the importance of biculturalism from a psychological perspective and to call for inclusion of biculturalism in research, training, and services involving Latinos. This interest culminated in Castaneda's study of the cultural determinants of cognitive and motivational styles of learning and teaching. In 1972, Castaneda was appointed professor of educational psychology in the School of Education at Stanford University. At Stanford, he taught two very popular graduate seminars that were the cornerstone of his research interests: Cultural Pluralism and Educational Policy, and Bicultural Processes in Education. Today, courses with similar titles would be commonplace, but in the mid-1970s this was a bold step in the direction of multicultural instruction, especially at an elite institution of higher education.

It is difficult to summarize in a few lines the impact that Castaneda's research and writing had on psychology. For more than 2 decades, Castaneda was known for his creative laboratory experiments on such diverse topics as the development of word association norms for children, paired associate learning in children, development of the Children's Manifest Anxiety Scale, conflict behavior in children and adults, effects of anxiety on complex learning, and the relationship between anxiety and scholastic motivation. His papers were widely cited in the major research journals and handbooks of the time (see Reese & Lipsitt, 1970). In addition to his research and writing, he also served on the editorial board of the prestigious journal *Child Development* at a time when research on minority children was not being published in this or any other developmental journals (Padilla & Lindholm, 1992).

In addition to Castaneda's eminence as an experimental child psychologist, he also was an important contributor to the development of Chicano studies. While on the faculty at UC Riverside, Castaneda, with Manuel Ramirez, received a grant in 1973 from the National Institute of Mental Health to convene a conference that brought together Chicano psychologists for the first time. The theme of the conference was "Increasing Educational Opportunities for Chicanos in Psychology." At the conference, a series of recommendations was proposed having to do with admissions, recruitment, training, faculty and staff development, and supportive services for undergraduate and graduate Chicano students interested in pursuing careers in psychology. These recommendations were directed at departments of psychology, the American Psychological Association (APA), and the National Institute of Mental Health (NIMH).

Castaneda deserves to be recognized for his groundbreaking work in showing the need for cultural pluralism in education, for Latino biculturalism as a viable alternative to cultural assimilation, and for leading the way in advocating classroom instructional strategies that could enhance the learning potential of Latino students. His work on instructional strategies culminated in a 1974 book coauthored with Manuel Ramirez entitled *Cultural Democracy, Bicognitive Development, and Education*. The book offered a vision for multiculturalism in education (which was on the threshold of emerging as a recognizable field in education) that argued that language and culture shaped cognition and needed to be cornerstones of the instructional planning of Latino children.

Carlos Albizu Miranda

Few psychologists have had as profound an impact on the training of Latino psychologists as Carlos Albizu Miranda (1920–1984). Carlos Albizu Miranda was born in Ponce, Puerto Rico, and lived most of his life in Puerto Rico. He completed his bachelor's degree in psychology at the University of Puerto Rico. Following World War II, he worked for the Veterans Administration in the area of vocational rehabilitation. Seeing the need to broaden his training in psychology, Albizu traveled to the U.S. mainland to do graduate work at Purdue University. He completed his master's degree in experimental psychology in 1951 and his doctorate in clinical psychology in 1953.

Albizu returned to his native Puerto Rico and took a teaching position at the University of Puerto Rico, where he quickly rose to the rank of full professor. Increasingly, he saw the need to train a larger number of Puerto Rican students in psychology than was possible at the university. In addition, he was concerned that training failed to take into account the special circumstances of Puerto Ricans as Latinos who, because of Puerto Rico's commonwealth status with the United States, were U.S. citizens and could travel freely between the island and the mainland but who were marginalized on the mainland because of their culture, language, and skin color. Thus,

Albizu founded the Instituto Psicologico de Puerto Rico in 1966. The goal of the institute was to provide culturally appropriate training in clinical psychology. This bold step constituted the establishment of the first professional school of psychology. This was a remarkable feat, considering that the first freestanding school of professional psychology on the U.S. mainland was the California School of Professional Psychology, founded in 1969 by the California Psychological Association, whereas Albizu did not have the professional backing or support of an association of psychologists (Wikipedia, 2008).

In 1971, the institute changed its name to the Caribbean Center for Advanced Studies. A sister branch, the Miami Institute of Psychology, was opened in 1980. Together, these two professional schools have played a major role in the clinical and research training of Latino psychologists not only on the island of Puerto Rico but throughout the Caribbean, Latin America, and the United States. As the founder of the Caribbean Center for Advanced Studies, Albizu's vision and enthusiasm for psychology was infectious. He communicated the firm conviction that the science and practice of psychology could contribute to the social well-being of Puerto Ricans and other Latinos both on the island and on the mainland.

Carlos Albizu Miranda was active in the American Psychological Association. He received special recognition in 1980 from the American Psychological Foundation for his work in the professional development of psychologists in the Caribbean region. In recognition of his vision and pioneering spirit, on January 1, 2000, the Board of Trustees of the Caribbean Center for Advanced Studies officially changed the name of the institution in both Puerto Rico and Miami to the Carlos Albizu University. This was a fitting tribute to a man who had worked tirelessly to create an institution dedicated to training Latino psychologists to provide culturally appropriate services to the Latino community. Finally, in 1979 Albizu was also elected the first president of the National Hispanic Psychological Association.

Rene A. Ruiz

Another influential psychologist was Rene A. Ruiz (1929–1982), who was instrumental in drawing attention to the underrepresentation of Latinos in psychology. Like the other early Latino psychologists, Ruiz did not begin his career with the intent to focus on Latino issues. He was born and raised in the Los Angeles area and graduated from the University of Southern California in 1954 with a major in psychology. He completed his graduate training in clinical psychology in 1963 at the University of Nebraska. Early in his career, he held faculty appointments in the Department of Psychiatry at the University of Kansas Medical School and then at the University of Arizona. In 1970, he coauthored a popular text, *The Normal Personality*, with Robert Wrenn. However, the turning point came in a 1971 article Ruiz published in the *American Psychologist* entitled "Relative Frequency of Americans with Spanish Surnames in Associations of Psychology, Psychiatry, and Sociology," in which he reported that fewer than 1% of the total APA membership for the year 1970 had Spanish surnames. From that time forward, he worked in various ways and in numerous capacities to increase the number of Latino students in psychology and to show that minority-related content could be integrated into the graduate curriculum offered in departments of psychology.

Later academic appointments took Ruiz to the University of Missouri at Kansas City and to New Mexico State University, where he served as professor and chair of the Department of Counseling and Educational Psychology until he died unexpectedly from a heart attack in 1982. In addition to his academic appointments, Ruiz was also a visiting scholar (1979–1980) at the UCLA Spanish Speaking Mental Health Research Center. In conversations, Ruiz remarked that the circumstances that motivated him to advocate on behalf of Latinos in the profession was that he had spent the first 20 years of his university and postgraduate career as the only Latino psychologist on the staff, and he had no intention of allowing this to happen to other Latinos.

Like Carlos Albizu, Art Ruiz invested his time and talents in working with the American Psychological Association to bring minority issues to the attention of the membership. He was proudest of his work on the APA Committee for Equality of Opportunity in Psychology (1972–1976), of which he was a charter member and which he helped to bring to fruition through his insistence that the APA be responsive to minority concerns. He also served as an APA visiting psychologist on numerous occasions and traveled to different universities around the country, where he consulted and lectured on emerging themes in Latino psychology. In addition, he was often called on by the National Institute of Mental Health to consult on minority-group mental health. Ruiz was known among his friends for his quick wit and disarming humor, which allowed him to call attention to the plight of Latinos without seeming to also call attention to racist practices that segregated Latinos and resulted in their second-class status in schools, employment, social services, and housing.

In 1973, Ruiz collaborated with Amado Padilla on a volume titled *Latino Mental Health* (Padilla & Ruiz, 1973), which constituted the first state-of-the-art review of the literature on Latino mental health. The primary intent of the monograph was to serve as a catalyst for subsequent investigators interested in Latino mental health. Ruiz continued his research and writing on Latino mental health and authored many works on a variety of themes, including mental health services for Latinos, acculturation and mental health, ethnic identity among children, and issues of Latino aging and mental health.

Martha Bernal

Martha Bernal (1931–2001) was born in San Antonio, Texas. Her parents were immigrants from Mexico, and Bernal was educated in Texas, receiving her bachelor's degree in psychology from Texas Western University in El Paso (now known as the University of Texas at El Paso). She later earned her master's degree from Syracuse University and completed her doctorate in 1962 in clinical psychology at Indiana University. Bernal was the first Latina to receive a doctoral degree in psychology from an American university. From Indiana, she relocated to the University of Arizona, then moved to the UCLA Neuropsychiatric Institute and began work with behavior-problem children and autistic children. Her early publications were on behavioral techniques for eliminating "brat syndrome" behaviors in maladjusted children and on establishing desirable behaviors in autistic children. From UCLA, Martha Bernal moved on to academic appointments first at the University of Denver and then at Arizona State University.

In an autobiographical account, Martha Bernal describes how, after attending the 1973 Conference on Chicano Psychology organized by Castaneda and Ramirez, she turned increasingly in the direction of Latino research (Bernal, 2004). In her autobiography, she recounts her effort over a period of approximately 20 years to increase multicultural training in clinical and counseling psychology. Bernal's work in multicultural training (Bernal & Castro, 1994; Bernal & Padilla, 1982; Quintana & Bernal, 1995) has had important policy implications for the identification, recruitment, and training of Latino psychologists. Bernal coupled this interest with her advocacy on behalf of Latinos by serving on numerous APA boards and task forces addressing ethnic minority concerns in the profession (Vasquez & Lopez, 2002).

Martha Bernal received many awards for her professional contributions, among the more prestigious of which were the Distinguished Life Achievement Award from the Society for the Psychological Study of Ethnic Minority Issues (Division 45), the Carolyn Attneave Award for lifelong contributions to ethnic minority psychology, presented in 1999 at the first National Multicultural Conference and Summit, and in 2001 the APA Award for Distinguished Contributions to the Public Interest.

In her research, Bernal was a careful methodologist and student of child development. With her colleague George Knight, she investigated the developmental course of ethnic identity among Mexican-heritage children. In their seminal book, *Ethnic Identity: Formation and Transmission Among Hispanics and Other Minorities* (1993), Bernal and Knight provided a rich array of findings on the theme of ethnic socialization and the intergenerational transmission of ethnic identification. Bernal's research on ethnic identity development has been widely cited because of its groundbreaking approach to the study of how children process information about ethnicity through socialization by parents and contact with other adults and peers.

Finally, as the first Latina to receive a doctorate in psychology, Martha Bernal proved to be a shining beacon to younger Latinas in psychology. She was generous with her time, even though she was ill during most of the last 2 decades of her life. She was a role model and mentor (Vasquez & Lopez, 2002) who showed through her commitment to social issues affecting Latinos that it was possible to overcome racism and sexism and to excel in her chosen profession.

Edward Casavantes

Another early contributor to Latino psychology was Edward Casavantes (1927–1980). Casavantes was an educational psychologist who worked on Latino educational and civil rights issues. He worked for the U.S. Civil Rights Commission in Washington, D.C., for nearly a decade during the 1960s and 1970s. While with the Civil Rights Commission, Casavantes worked on its far-reaching study of the education of Mexican American students. The study resulted in the six-volume *Mexican American Education Study* (U.S. Commission on Civil Rights, 1974).

Casavantes was also the founder, in 1969, of the Association of Psychologists por la Raza. As a member of APA and Division 9 (the Society for the Psychological Study of Social Issues), Casavantes received a grant from Division 9 that funded some of the organizational work necessary for establishing the Association of Psychologists por la Raza. Casavantes played a critical role during this period in trying to identify other Latino psychologists when there were no established Latino professional networks to call upon for assistance. This is the reason why Rene Ruiz (1971) took it upon himself to do a manual search of the APA membership directory to identity individuals with Spanish surnames, which was the only method in those days for identifying possible Latino APA members.

Casavantes was also interested in showing how social scientists were often responsible for creating cultural stereotypes about Latinos. For instance, in an article called "Pride and Prejudice: A Mexican American Dilemma," published in the *Civil Rights Digest* (1970), Casavantes argued that the well-known anthropologist Oscar Lewis's culture of poverty was misdirected and that the observations made by Lewis were not really depictions of Puerto Rican and Mexican culture but rather observations of poor and oppressed people irrespective of their cultures. In addition, Casavantes was the first to comment on the diversity among Chicanos; he argued that Chicanos were not a homogeneous ethnic group but diverse in a number of respects ranging from skin color and social class to professed ethnic self-identification. In *El Tecato: Cultural and Sociological Factors Affecting Drug Use Among Chicanos,* Casavantes (1974) showed creativity and daring in his study of drug addiction among Latinos. One important theme taken up in *El Tecato* is the necessity of culturally relevant psychotherapeutic approaches in the treatment of drug abuse in Latinos. In his discussion of drug treatment, Casavantes argued that therapists needed to extend their treatments in culturally appropriate ways to be effective with Latino addicts. While this may appear to be common sense today, it was not 30 years ago. The National Coalition of

Spanish Speaking Mental Health Organizations published Casavantes's book. The book is the first contribution to the clinical literature on substance abuse and treatment of Chicanos.

SUMMARY

The six individuals whose lives and careers are described here are unique because in numerous ways each gave meaning to how psychology as a science and practice needed to be open to ethnocultural diversity. The six individuals, in their own independent and initially isolated ways, without mentors or intellectual guideposts, challenged traditional assumptions about the lack of importance given to culture and ethnicity in psychology. Unlike today, where there is an established body of literature on Latino psychology and where there are Latino symposia at professional meetings, none of the six individuals whose careers are presented here had any training or experience in Latino psychology. Each of them, because of cultural experience, saw the need to advance the cause of Latinos in psychology in his or her own way. In addition, each worked to broaden the goals of American psychology without the support of peers or professional organizations, by increasing the training of Latinos in psychology and by showing that psychology could be enriched by diversity. Moreover, these six individuals created an intellectual foundation for a Latino psychology of which younger psychologists may not be aware and which is the primary reason for writing historical essays such as this. We owe a special debt of appreciation to these six individuals because they took risks in their professional careers to open doors that others might pass through. Jones (1998), in reflecting on ethnic minority psychology in the 20th century, said it best:

> We all stand on others' shoulders to reach for new possibilities. We walk through doors that are now open where in the past no door existed at all. Our present is the cumulative consequence of our past, our collective past. Our predecessors worked in different venues in different times. We now reap what they have sown. (p. 206)

National Associations and Organizations

We turn now to early organizational efforts to bring Latino psychologists together. All the early psychologists except George Sanchez played key roles in activities to unite Latino psychologists. As mentioned earlier, Casavantes founded the Association of Psychologists por la Raza in 1969. The first meeting of Chicano psychologists was held in 1970 at the annual meeting of the APA in Miami. A handful of Chicano psychologists attended the meeting. Casavantes was elected president; Albert Ramirez, who was then at the University of Alabama, was elected vice president, and Manuel Ramirez III was elected secretary-treasurer.

A year later, a second meeting of Chicano psychologists was held at the APA meetings, this time in Washington, D.C. Casavantes also took the initiative at this meeting to organize a symposium on Chicano psychology entitled "The Effects of Cultural Variables on Mexican Americans." The panelists for the symposium were Casavantes, Manuel Ramirez, Albert Ramirez, Rene Ruiz, Ernest Bernal, and Amado Padilla. This was a historic symposium because it was the first time that Chicano psychologists had organized a symposium on Chicano psychology at an APA meeting. Since this first symposium in 1971, it has now become commonplace for Latinos to present their research at regional and national psychological conferences.

At the 1971 meeting, Alfredo Castaneda was elected president of the Association of Psychologists por la Raza, and Casavantes was elected executive director, since he worked in Washington, D.C., and could lobby the APA and the NIMH. The officers of the association remained unchanged until 1973. In the spring of 1973, Alfredo Castaneda and Manuel Ramirez organized a conference at the University of California at Riverside themed "Increasing Educational Opportunities for Chicanos in Psychology." The NIMH funded the conference, the purpose of which was to bring Latino psychologists together to discuss training, research, and service for Chicanos. Another goal was to make recommendations for increasing the number of Latinos in psychology. This objective was achieved, and recommendations for recruiting and training undergraduate and graduate students in psychology were written and disseminated widely to psychology departments, the APA, and the NIMH.

Although it is not possible to name all the individuals who attended this first conference of Chicano psychologists, the names of some individuals and their institutional affiliations at the time are presented for historical purposes. In attendance were Martha Bernal from the University of Denver; Ray Buriel, then a graduate student at UC Riverside and now professor of psychology at Pomona College; Ed DeAvila, who was with Bilingual Children's TV in Oakland, California; John Garcia, then at the University of Utah and now professor emeritus at UCLA; Richard Lopez, a postdoctoral fellow at Notre Dame University and later with the NIMH; Joe Martinez, then at California State University, San Bernardino, and later at UC Irvine; Albert Ramirez, University of Colorado; and Rene A. Ruiz from the University of Missouri at Kansas City. At this same meeting, the Association of Psychologists por la Raza elected Floyd Martinez as its second president. Martinez, a clinical psychologist who later worked for the NIMH, was instrumental in helping Latino psychologists throughout the United States obtain support for community mental health services programs, training programs, and research projects.

From the late 1960s through the mid-1980s, the NIMH was instrumental in assisting Latino psychologists to develop capacity in a variety of ways. Early efforts to organize Latino psychologists were facilitated by Juan Ramos, who held a doctorate in social policy from Brandeis University and who became chief of the Division for Special Mental Health Programs at NIMH. Among Ramos's early activities was organizing a conference in Washington, D.C., in July 1971, which was attended by a small number of Hispanic mental health professionals from around the country, with the agenda of prioritizing the mental health needs of Latinos. The attendees concluded that a national mental health organization was needed to advocate for the mental health service needs of Latinos as well as for the training of Latino professionals in the various mental health professions. The attendees named the new organization the Coalition of Spanish Speaking Mental Health Organizations (COSSMHO) and appointed a committee to draw up bylaws for the new organization to begin the process of incorporating the organization as a legal entity with an office in Washington, D.C. COSSMHO was established in 1974 with Rodolfo Sanchez, a former social worker, as its executive director. Several years later, Sanchez broadened COSSMHO's charter to include all human services; it is now known as the National Coalition of Hispanic Health and Human Services Organizations and maintains its office in Washington, D.C. Working through COSSMHO, Sanchez played a key role in bringing together Latino psychologists from different geographic areas to work on mutual interests involving families, substance abuse (especially among Latino adolescents), and services for the elderly.

In 1975, Joe Martinez, who was then a postdoctoral fellow in the Department of Psychobiology at the University of California at Irvine, secured funds from the Ford Foundation and a number of university offices to convene the First Symposium on Chicano Psychology, which was held in May 1976. Whereas the 1973 University of California at Riverside meeting addressed the training of Chicanos and Latinos in psychology, the 1975 meeting consisted of scientific presentations on Chicano psychology delivered over 2½ days. By this time, there was a cadre of young psychologists eager to present their burgeoning research on a wide variety of topics ranging from social to clinical psychology and from issues of psychological assessment to bilingualism. The meeting also served to establish networks for future collaboration among some participants and to reinforce the need for continued interest in Chicano psychology. Martinez proved to be an extremely capable editor of the symposium papers and published them in an edited volume entitled *Chicano Psychology* in 1977.

A second symposium on Chicano psychology was held in 1982 at the University of California at Riverside. Martinez and Mendoza (1984) edited a second volume of *Chicano Psychology* based on papers from this symposium and a few papers from the original volume. Following in the tradition of these two symposia on Chicano psychology, a meeting themed "Innovations in Chicana/o Psychology: Looking Toward the 21st Century" was held in the spring of 1998 at Michigan State University. Approximately 400 participants attended the meeting, and the fact that this was the first such conference held outside the western United States is significant. Some of the papers presented at the conference appear in *The Handbook of Chicana/o Psychology and Mental Health* (Velasquez, Arellano, & McNeill, 2004).

The 1978 Dulles Conference

As can be envisioned from this chronology of historical events, there was considerable excitement among Latino psychologists for the work they were doing and for the social networking that was bringing them together to meet and share their work. Similar excitement could also be found among African American, American Indian, and Asian American psychologists. There was a feeling in the air that at long last the door had been cracked open (some might argue that it had been forcibly opened) at the APA and at NIMH. Much more work needed to be done, but now, for the first time, ethnic psychologists were banging on the door with a single fist! Through the efforts of a few dedicated individuals, a joint conference of the leadership of psychologists from the different ethnic groups met with the leaderships of the APA at the Washington Dulles International Airport in 1978. This historic meeting, known as the Dulles Conference (Jones, 1998), resulted in several significant outcomes that were critical for Latinos in psychology and for the development of ethnic psychology in broader terms.

The recommendations that emerged from the Dulles Conference called for the establishment of an Office of Ethnic Minority Affairs, an APA Board of Ethnic Minority Affairs, a division, and a journal. All of these recommendations, as we know, have come to fruition; but the course of their development was not always easy, nor did it take place overnight (Jones, 1998). The first recommendation to be implemented was the opening of the Office of Ethnic Minority Affairs (OEMA). Moreover, at the insistence of the Hispanic Caucus at the conference, the final recommendation provided for representation on the Board of Ethnic Minority Affairs of the full spectrum of major Latino communities in the United States: Mexican Americans, Cuban Americans, and Puerto Ricans.

Esteban Olmedo assumed the directorship of OEMA in the latter part of 1978. Up until that time, Esteban Olmedo had been the associate director of the UCLA Spanish Speaking Mental Health Research Center. Olmedo was born in the United States of Argentinean parents but was raised in Argentina. He returned to the United States for his education and received his doctorate in experimental psychology at Baylor University. After Baylor, he took a teaching position at California State University, San Bernardino, was a colleague of Joe Martinez, and developed an interest in acculturation research. Although Olmedo was more adept initially in research methodology and statistics, he proved to be a solid administrator and guided OEMA for the next 6 years.

When Olmedo decided to leave the APA and OEMA for the California School of Professional Psychology, Lillian Comas Diaz, a Puerto Rican psychologist who had received her training in clinical psychology at Yale University, replaced him. Under the stewardship of Olmedo and Comas Diaz, the Board of Ethnic Minority Affairs and Division 45, the Society for the Psychological Study of Ethnic Minority Issues, were created. Comas Diaz also served as the inaugural editor of the APA journal *Cultural Diversity and Ethnic Minority Psychology*.

The UCLA Spanish Speaking Mental Health Research Center

Another noteworthy project during this era was the Spanish Speaking Mental Health Research Center (SSMHRC) at the University of California at Los Angeles (UCLA), funded by the NIMH Center for Minority Group Mental Health Programs. The UCLA center was the first minority research center funded by the NIMH and served as the prototype and testing ground for what became similar research centers for African Americans, American Indians, and Asian Americans, as well as the Hispanic Research Center at Fordham University. The original grant for the SSMHRC was awarded to Rodolfo Alvarez, professor of sociology at UCLA, who served as the first director of the project until October 1975, when Amado Padilla, professor of psychology at UCLA, became the principal investigator and director of the center. The activities of the SSMHRC continued with Padilla as director until funding ceased at the end of 1989.

Some of the Latino psychologists who began their professional careers at the SSMHRC include Gerardo Marin, Manuel Casas, Esteban Olmedo, Nelly Salgado de Snyder, Richard Cervantes, Steven Lopez, Hortensia Amaro, Felipe Castro, and Luis Moll. The SSMHRC was also responsible for the training of many undergraduate and graduate students during its 15 years. In addition to the large number of students who received research training, the

SSMHRC also sponsored 23 postdoctoral fellows and scholars from various parts of the United States and Spain, Mexico, Peru, and Brazil.

Although the SSMHRC was funded as a research project, it also served as a clearinghouse for information on Latino mental health and as a training center for students in psychology. In accordance with its training mandate, the center supported the work of approximately 50 graduate students over 15 years. Of these, about half received their doctoral degrees, and 10 completed their dissertations with direct center support. In addition, the SSMHRC sponsored the work of another 25 undergraduates, many of whom went on to graduate school in psychology.

The research agenda of the SSMHRC focused on acculturative stress and coping, mental health services, substance abuse among Latino youth, and children's school achievement. Critical in much of the research were concerns of poverty, language barriers, prejudice and discrimination, and issues of gender roles in mental health. Scholarly knowledge of the mental health needs of Latinos and the delivery of services was facilitated by the research and publications produced by the SSMHRC. The early research identified system barriers related to the low use of mental health services by Latinos. These barriers to effective treatment included availability and accessibility of services, language differences, scarcity of Latino mental health providers, and social class differences between clients and therapists (Padilla, Ruiz, & Alvarez, 1975). This was followed by research aimed at making available services more culturally relevant.

The importance of acculturation as it impacts the treatment process was also an area of research that aided service providers in developing a greater sensitivity to individual client differences. Along these lines were studies aimed at making clinical assessment tools more relevant for Latino clients. Numerous translation and validation studies of existing clinical instruments were conducted and reported on. In addition, Richard Cervantes took the lead in developing a culturally specific measure of psychosocial stress and coping for both Latino adults and children (Cervantes, Padilla, & Salgado de Snyder, 1988).

The research agenda of the SSMHRC between 1980 and 1988 was at times constricted by the Reagan administration's mandate to cut federal research funds for social-problem-oriented research. Because so much of Latino mental health research is social-problem oriented—especially because of the focus on the effects of oppression, poverty, prejudice, and discrimination on psychological well-being—there was always some tension in justifying SSMHRC's research agenda to NIMH. Despite this obstacle, tremendous gains were made by the SSMHRC in Latino mental health scholarship.

There is no easy way to judge the overall impact of any research enterprise; however, we can point to 5 books and approximately 120 journal articles and chapters authored by SSMHRC staff and students. In addition to this, the SSMHRC clearinghouse staff managed to publish 24 research reports, 4 special project reports, and 10 monographs, all of which were widely disseminated. The clearinghouse also developed a bibliographic database of more than 6,000 titles (Cota-Robles Newton, Olmedo, & Padilla, 1982). The database could be searched electronically and was widely used between 1977 and 1989. While the bibliographic database and the search capability may seem incredibly old-fashioned today, it should be remembered that electronic databases were limited and that this was before the creation of the Internet, which students today take for granted when searching the literature. The SSMHRC clearinghouse provided professionals and students alike with considerable information about all aspects of Latino mental health. Many SSMHRC publications were used as textbooks during this period in undergraduate and graduate classes and seminars. The bibliographic service was a mainstay of the SSMHRC, and staff members were called upon daily by students and professionals alike to assist in locating relevant research for literature reviews, grant proposals, and class work. The SSMHRC documents were also in frequent use for in-service workshops in community mental health settings, graduate programs, and university extension classes. In addition, SSMHRC staff gave literally hundreds of conference and workshop presentations over the years to organizations around the country.

Another area in which the SSMHRC had a national impact was in providing leadership regarding Latino priorities for President Carter's Commission on Mental Health. Esteban Olmedo and Pedro Lecca (a New York Puerto Rican mental health professional) were cochairs of the Hispanic Subpanel of the Special Populations Panel of the commission (President's Commission on Mental Health, 1978). Their report emphasized the at-risk status of the

Hispanic population in the United States as a result of low income, unemployment or underemployment, and lower socioeconomic status. Barriers to mental health services and the relative lack of culturally sensitive programs and service providers compounded this. The work of the commission ensured that Latino issues would become part of the national debate on the mental health needs of the U.S. population.

The SSMHRC was also a pioneer in contemporary psychological research on acculturation. In the early 1970s, it became clear to the staff of the center that acculturation was not only a worthwhile topic of research on its own but also played a key role in the relationships between ethnicity and psychological assessment and the implementation of culturally sensitive mental health services for Latino populations.

In addition to the work of Padilla and Olmedo, the contributions of Susan Keefe to acculturation research were very significant (Keefe, 1980). She broadened the research by introducing her anthropological perspectives, particularly with respect to the role of the extended family among urban Mexican Americans.

Our principal objective was to advance the dialogue on acculturation from theoretical (and, some would say, political) rhetoric to one more solidly grounded in science. Research by SSMHRC staff revealed that acculturation could be scientifically measured with a reasonable degree of validity and reliability and that it was a multidimensional construct (Olmedo, 1979). Moreover, we showed that such well-known constructs as cultural awareness and ethnic loyalty could be operationally defined with rigor and their role in acculturation determined by the use of proper statistical analyses (Padilla, 1980b).

Another contributing factor to Latino psychology was the *Hispanic Journal of Behavioral Sciences* (*HJBS*), which started with the SSMHRC clearinghouse. The *HJBS* first appeared in 1979 as a quarterly peer-reviewed journal and is still published through SAGE Publications (see Padilla, 2003). Even though the *HJBS* has always published articles in the behavioral and social sciences, not just psychology, over the years many of the leading research articles on Latino psychology and mental health have appeared in its pages.

Finally, through research, consultation, and technical assistance, the SSMHRC influenced mental health treatment policies and practices ranging from psychological assessment and psychotherapy to social-service delivery systems.

Active participation in conferences, professional associations, and symposia provided valuable linkages between researchers, policymakers, and service providers. In addition, SSMHRC staff participated in national policymaking panels organized by the National Research Council, the APA, the NIMH, the National Institute of Drug Abuse, and the National Institutes of Health. In sum, between 1975 and 1989, the SSMHRC led the way in shaping the future direction of Latino mental health research, training, and services.

The Spanish Family Guidance Center

Another center of major importance with a long-standing record of accomplishments in the area of Latino clinical research is the Spanish Family Guidance Center. The Spanish Family Guidance Center was established in 1972 as part of the Department of Psychiatry of the University of Miami. The center's original purpose was to investigate family-oriented prevention and treatment programs for Latino drug-abusing adolescents in the Miami area. In 1974, after completing his doctorate in clinical psychology from the University of Miami, Jose Szapocznik was appointed director of research at the center. Today, the center is known as the Center for Family Studies and is the largest family-oriented clinical intervention center for Latinos and other minority groups in the country.

With Szapocznik as director, the center has established a long track record of producing innovative clinical programs for Cuban Americans and other Latino families. The early work focused on acculturation and adjustment in Cuban families (e.g., Szapocznik & Herrera, 1978). As the work evolved, important contributions have been made in family therapy (Szapocznik, Rios, Perez-Vidal, Kurtines, Hervis, & Santisteban, 1982; Szapocznik, Santisteban, Kurtines, Hervis, & Spencer, 1982). The early work, known as bicultural effectiveness training, incorporated elements of structural family therapy but added ways in which the family members (parents, children, and adolescents) could identify cultural conflicts resulting in maladaptive patterns in family interaction. By using culture in family therapy, family members were trained in bicultural skills to more effectively handle cultural conflicts causing difficulties between family members who varied in level of acculturation.

The work of Latino psychologists at the Center for Family Studies has been widely praised over the years by many professional groups, including the APA, the American Family Therapy Academy, and the American Association of Marriage and Family Therapy. Further, the publications and training programs offered by Latino psychologists have inspired an entire generation of clinical psychologists who work with Latino families.

The Lake Arrowhead, California, Conference

We conclude with a description of the National Conference of Hispanic Psychologists held from November 29 to December 1, 1979, at the University of California Residential Conference Center and known as the Lake Arrowhead Conference (*Proceedings of the National Conference of Hispanic Psychologists,* n.d.). Plans for this conference were begun in the summer of 1978 after the SSMHRC received a grant from the Division of Manpower and Training and the Center for Minority Group Mental Health Programs of the NIMH to support a major meeting of Latino psychologists from across the country for the expressed purpose of sharing information on needed training, services, and research from a Latino perspective. A second goal was to determine whether there was universal agreement on the need to establish a national Latino psychological association. Sixty-five psychologists representing diverse Latino groups and interests attended the Lake Arrowhead Conference. Martha Bernal, Carlos Albizu Miranda, and Rene Ruiz, whose careers as pioneer Latino psychologists were presented in the first section of this paper, attended this historic meeting; they provided wisdom and much practical guidance to their younger colleagues. Other participants included Hortensia Amaro, Glorisa Canino, Lillian Comas-Diaz, Israel Cuellar, Oliva Espin, Angela Ginorio, Aida Hurtado, Richard Lopez, Steven Lopez, Gerardo Marin, Ricardo Munoz, Esteban Olmedo, Amado Padilla, Manuel Ramirez, Nelly Salgado, David Santisteban, Jose Szapocznik, and Melba Vasquez.

The Lake Arrowhead Conference was a landmark event in the history of Latino psychology because it was the first time that a significant number of Latinos representing different national origins, geographic regions, and disciplinary interests had come together to forge an alliance and speak with a single voice. At this meeting, too, the foundation for the establishment of a National Hispanic Psychological

Association was laid. Ricardo Munoz, from the University of California at San Francisco, served as the recorder for the conference, and the proceedings of the conference summarize the decisions made by the attendees regarding membership, governance, fiscal structure, and proportional representation of different Latino groups in leadership of the association. The detailed work of bringing to fruition a National Hispanic Psychological Association was left to a steering committee consisting of Floyd Martinez and Martha Bernal (Mexican American), Ana Alvarez and Luis Nieves (Puerto Rican), Dorita Marina and Angel Martinez (Cuban), and Jeannette Maluf and Gerardo Marin (Central and South American). The steering committee was charged with developing bylaws for the new organization. With Martha Bernal serving as the chair of the steering committee, the bylaws for the association were drafted in 1980, and the association was launched. In more recent years, the association has changed its name to the National Latino/a Psychological Association and has continued the work envisioned by the participants at the 1979 Lake Arrowhead Conference.

One of the more significant follow-up initiatives of the National Hispanic Psychological Association (NHPA) came during the 1990s. Under the auspices of Richard M. Suinn (former chair of the Board of Ethnic Minority Affairs and later member of the APA Board of Directors and president of the APA), a tradition was initiated whereby representatives of the various national ethnic minority psychological associations would participate in a breakfast meeting with the APA president during the APA annual convention. Thus, in addition to the NHPA, leaders of the Association of Black Psychologists, the Asian American Psychological Association, and the Society of Indian Psychologists now have the opportunity to periodically exchange ideas with the APA leadership and raise issues of concern to minority communities at large and psychologists of color in particular.

It is fair to say that a good number of minority psychologists continue to feel the need for a psychological association "of their own." Thus, although the (now) Committee on Ethnic Minority Affairs and Division 45 of the APA address many issues of import to minority communities, the independence provided by the ethnic minority associations is viewed by many as an important asset. The breakfast meetings offer the opportunity to complement and augment the work done inside and outside of APA and to ensure that those involved don't find themselves working at cross purposes.

Conclusion

In this history of Latino psychology, our goal first was to lay the intellectual foundation of Latino psychology by discussing the life and work of six Latino psychologists who, for 7 decades through their research, writings, and advocacy, sought to increase the visibility of Latinos in the profession. Often with little support from non-Latino colleagues and in the absence of other Latino psychologists, they sought through various means to encourage the leadership of the APA and the NIMH to support efforts to increase training opportunities for Latino students in psychology. In addition, we present a panoramic view of how the first Latino psychologists, in coordination with a second generation of Latino psychologists, organized conferences, associations, and research centers that shaped the contours of Latino psychology as we understand it today. In combination, the persons, events, and organizations all served to draw increased attention to the need to recruit and train undergraduate and graduate students in the discipline of psychology, and to bring people together with a common interest to advocate for broadening the base of American psychology through the recognition of a legitimate place for Latino psychology in research, training, and services.

A history can never be entirely comprehensive, because it is the story of people and events that represent the reflections and interpretations of the writer. Thus, the history of Latino psychology we offer here consists of our firsthand knowledge of many of the individuals and events mentioned; hopefully, our historical account will be of value to others who will use this work to expand on the history of Latino psychology and who will do so using different lenses and interpretations of the circumstances and developments surrounding Latino psychology.

References

Bernal, G., Trimble, J. E., Burlew, A. K., & Leong, F. T. (Eds.). (2003). *Handbook of racial and ethnic minority psychology.* Thousand Oaks, CA: Sage.

Bernal, M. E. (2004). Challenges and opportunities for Chicana/o psychologists: Past, present, and future. In R. J. Velasquez, L. M. Arellano, & B. W. McNeill (Eds.), *Handbook of Chicana/o psychology and mental health* (pp. 469–481). Mahwah, NJ: Lawrence Erlbaum.

Bernal, M. E., & Castro, F. G. (1994). Are clinical psychologists prepared for service and research with ethnic minorities? Report of a decade of progress. *American Psychologist, 49,* 797–805.

Bernal, M. E., & Knight, G. P. (1993). *Ethnic identity: Formation and transmission among Hispanics and other minorities.* Albany: State University of New York Press.

Bernal, M. E., & Padilla, A. M. (1982). Status of minority curriculum and training in clinical psychology. *American Psychologist, 37,* 780–787.

Casavantes, E. J. (1970). Pride and prejudice: A Mexican American dilemma. *Civil Rights Digest, 3,* 22–27.

Casavantes, E. J. (1974). *El Tecato: Social and cultural factors affecting drug use among Chicanos.* Washington, DC: National Coalition of Spanish Speaking Mental Health Organizations.

Castaneda, A., & Ramirez, M. (1974). *Cultural democracy, bicognitive development, and education.* New York: Academic Press.

Castaneda, A., Ramirez, M., Cortes, C., & Barrera, M. (Eds.). (1971). *Mexican Americans and educational change.* New York: Arno Press.

Cervantes, R. C., Padilla, A. M., & Salgado de Snyder, V. N. (1991). The Hispanic Stress Inventory: A culturally relevant approach to psychosocial assessment. *Psychological Assessment: Journal of Consulting and Clinical Psychology, 3,* 438–447.

Cota-Robles Newton, F., Olmedo, E., & Padilla, A. M. (1982). *Hispanic mental health research: A reference guide.* Los Angeles: University of California Press.

Jones, J. M. (1998). Ethnic minority psychology in the 20th century: Reflections and meditations on what has been and what is next. *Cultural Diversity and Mental Health, 4,* 203–211.

Keefe, S. E. (1980). Acculturation and the extended family among urban Mexican-Americans. In A. M. Padilla (Ed.), *Acculturation: Theory, models and some new findings* (pp. 85–105). Boulder, CO: Westview Press.

Martinez, J. L. (Ed.). (1977). *Chicano psychology.* New York: Academic Press.

Martinez, J. L., & Mendoza, R. H. (Eds.). (1984). *Chicano psychology* (2nd ed.). New York: Academic Press.

Murillo, N. (1974). The works of George I. Sanchez: An appreciation. In J. L. Martinez (Ed.), *Chicano psychology* (pp. 1–10). New York: Academic Press.

Olmedo, E. L. (1979). Acculturation: A psychometric perspective. *American Psychologist, 34,* 1061–1070.

Padilla, A. M. (1980a). Notes on the history of Hispanic psychology. *Hispanic Journal of Behavioral Sciences, 2,* 109–128.

Padilla, A. M. (1980b). The role of cultural awareness and ethnic loyalty in acculturation. In A. M. Padilla (Ed.), *Acculturation: Theory, models and some new findings* (pp. 47–84). Boulder, CO: Westview Press.

Padilla, A. M. (1984). Synopsis of the history of Chicano psychology. In J. L. Martinez & R. H. Mendoza (Eds.), *Chicano psychology* (2nd ed., pp. 1–19). New York: Academic Press.

Padilla, A. M. (1985). Obituary: Rene A. Ruiz (1929–1982). *American Psychologist, 40,* 367.

Padilla, A. M. (1988). Early psychological assessment of Mexican American children. *Journal of History of the Behavioral Sciences, 24,* 111–116.

Padilla, A. M. (1995). *Hispanic psychology: Critical issues in theory and research.* Thousand Oaks, CA: Sage.

Padilla, A. M. (2000). Hispanic psychology. In A. E. Kazdin (Ed.), *Encyclopedia of psychology* (pp. 126–131). New York: Oxford University Press.

Padilla, A. M. (2003). The origins of the *Hispanic Journal of Behavioral Sciences:* A personal memoir. *Hispanic Journal of Behavioral Sciences, 25,* 3–12.

Padilla, A. M., & Lindholm, K. (1992, August 14). *What do we know about culturally diverse children?* Paper presented at the Symposium on Racism in Developmental Research, American Psychological Association, Washington, DC.

Padilla, A. M., & Ruiz, R. A. (1973). *Latino mental health: A review of literature.* Washington, DC: U.S. Government Printing Office.

Padilla, A. M., Ruiz, R. A., & Alvarez, R. (1975). Community mental health services for the Spanish speaking/surnamed population. *American Psychologist, 30,* 892–905.

Padilla, A. M., & Salgado de Snyder, N. V. (1988). Psychology in pre-Columbian Mexico. *Hispanic Journal of Behavioral Sciences, 10,* 55–66.

President's Commission on Mental Health (1978). *Report of the task panel on special populations* (Vol. 3). Washington, DC: U.S. Government Printing Office.

Proceedings of the National Conference of Hispanic Psychologists, Lake Arrowhead, California, November 29–December 1, 1979. (n.d.). Los Angeles: UCLA Spanish Speaking Mental Health Research Center.

Quintana, S. M., & Bernal, M. E. (1995). Ethnic minority training in counseling psychology: Comparisons with clinical psychology and proposed standards. *The Counseling Psychologist, 23,* 102–121.

Ramirez, M. (1981). In memoriam—Alfredo Castaneda. *Hispanic Journal of Behavioral Sciences, 3,* 107–109.

Ramirez, M., & Castaneda, A. (1974). *Cultural democracy, bicognitive development and education.* New York: Academic Press.

Reese, H. W., & Lipsitt, L. P. (1970). *Experimental child psychology.* New York: Academic Press.

Ruiz, R. A. (1971). Relative frequency of Americans with Spanish surnames in associations of psychology, psychiatry, and sociology. *American Psychologist, 26,* 1022–1024.

Sanchez, G. I. (1932a). Group differences in Spanish-speaking children: A critical view. *Journal of Applied Psychology, 16,* 549–558.

Sanchez, G. I. (1932b). Scores of Spanish-speaking children on repeated tests. *Journal of Genetic Psychology, 40,* 223–231.

Sanchez, G. I. (1934a). Bilingualism and mental measures. *Journal of Applied Psychology, 18,* 765–772.

Sanchez, G. I. (1934b). The implications of a basal vocabulary to the measurement of abilities of bilingual children. *Journal of Social Psychology, 5,* 395–402.

Szapocznik, J., & Herrera, M. C. (1978). *Cuban Americans: Acculturation, adjustment and the family.* Washington, DC: The National Coalition of Hispanic Mental Health and Human Services Organizations.

Szapocznik, J., Rios, A., Perez-Vidal, A., Kurtines, W., Hervis, O., & Santisteban, D. (1986). Bicultural effectiveness training (BET): An experimental test of an intervention modality for families experiencing intergenerational/intercultural conflict. *Hispanic Journal of Behavioral Sciences, 8,* 303–330.

Szapocznik, J., Santisteban, D., Kurtines, W. M., Hervis, O., & Spencer, F. (1982). Life enhancement counseling and the treatment of depressed Cuban American elders. *Hispanic Journal of Behavioral Sciences, 4,* 487–502.

U.S. Commission on Civil Rights. (1974). *Mexican American education study* (Vols. 1–6). Washington, DC: U.S. Government Printing Office.

Vasquez, M. J. T., & Lopez, S. (2002). Martha E. Bernal (1931–2001). *American Psychologist, 57,* 362–363.

Velasquez, R. J., Arellano, L. M., & McNeill, B. W. (Eds.). (2004). *The handbook of Chicana/o psychology and mental health.* Mahwah, NJ: Lawrence Erlbaum.

Wrenn, R. L., & Ruiz, R. A. (1970). *The normal personality.* Belmont, CA: Brooks/Cole.

Wikipedia. (2008). California School of Professional Psychology. Retrieved February 3, 2009, from http://en.wikipedia.org/wiki/California_School_of_Professional_Psychology

2

Conceptual Issues in Latino Mental Health

Margarita Alegría and Meghan Woo

According to the U.S. Census Bureau, Latinos are currently the largest ethnic minority population, totaling 45.5 million, or 15.1% of the estimated total U.S. population (U.S. Census Bureau, 2008). During the period 2000–2004, Latino population growth represented half the total growth in the United States (The National Academies, 2007). Part of this considerable increase is a result of immigration from Latin America, which brings people who are culturally dissimilar from mainstream America and who confront challenges in integrating into U.S. society (Guarnaccia, Guevara-Ramos, González, Canino, & Bird, 2007). As a whole, members of the Latino population tend to sustain strong ties with families and friends in their home communities, which contributes to the maintenance of language and culture (Levitt, DeWind, & Vertovec, 2003; Viruell-Fuentes, 2006). These lasting relationships and transnational dynamics have posed complex challenges to understanding how circumstances of Latinos relate to their mental health and their need for services (U.S. Department of Health and Human Services [USDHHS], 2001b).

It is critical to understand the patterns of mental health needs as well as the challenges and barriers to services experienced by the growing Latino population in order to effectively plan services so that cities receiving an influx of Latinos can successfully respond to their distinct service needs. Not only is this group extremely heterogeneous in sociodemographic and contextual characteristics (Guarnaccia et al., 2007), but mental health disorder rates and service use profiles tend to vary across immigrant and U.S.-born Latino groups (Alegría, Mulvaney-Day, Torres, et al., 2007; Alegría, Mulvaney-Day, Woo, et al., 2007). Disparities in access to mental health services continue to pose significant concerns regarding equity among Latinos (USDHHS, 2001a). Although the prevalence of mental disorders for U.S. Latinos is similar to or lower than that for non-Latino whites (Alegría et al., 2008), Latinos have less access to mental health care, are less likely to receive needed services (USDHHS, 2001a), and are more likely to receive services that poorly match their needs (Vega & Alegría, 2001). Researchers and practitioners have also reported substantial difficulty engaging and retaining Latinos in mental health care (Diaz, Woods, & Rosenheck, 2005; Miranda & Cooper, 2004). In this chapter, we provide an overview of conceptual issues relevant to mental disorders among Latinos. We then discuss conceptual

15

issues in mental health service delivery that researchers and practitioners must consider when working with Latinos.

When examined in aggregate, findings from epidemiological studies suggest that Latinos in the United States are consistently at lower risk for all psychiatric disorders compared to non-Latino whites (Alegría et al., 2008; Breslau et al., 2006; Grant et al., 2004). However, when the Latino population is separated into subethnic groups, greater variability in the rates of disorder has been found. Puerto Ricans, in particular, report significantly higher rates of psychiatric disorders compared to other Latino groups; their rates approach those of non-Latino whites (Alegría et al., 2008). The similarity in disorder rates between Puerto Ricans and non-Latino whites could be attributed to the fact that in contrast to the other Latino groups, Puerto Ricans have lived with more than a century of U.S. influence and are more likely to be bilingual and to have adopted many lifestyle patterns of U.S. society (Guarnaccia, Martinez, Ramirez, & Canino, 2005). Higher degrees of family cultural conflict and family burden also appear associated with increased risk of mood disorders among Puerto Ricans (Alegría, Shrout, et al., 2007). Family cultural conflict might increase one's opportunities for loneliness and a reduced sense of belonging, since the family is no longer available to buffer stress.

In aggregate, findings have also been consistent with the immigrant paradox (in which foreign nativity seems protective against psychiatric disorders despite the stressful experiences and poverty often associated with immigration [Burnam, Hough, Karno, Escobar, & Telles, 1987]). Specifically, U.S.-born Latinos report higher risk than Latino immigrants for most lifetime and past-year disorders (Alegría et al., 2008; Grant et al., 2004). However, when disaggregated by subethnic group, the immigrant paradox was only consistently observed for depressive, anxiety, and substance-use disorders among Mexican respondents, while no evidence for the immigrant paradox was found among Puerto Rican respondents. Interestingly, the paradox was consistently observed among Mexican, Cuban, and Other Latino subjects for substance disorders (Alegría et al., 2008).

These findings suggest two different stories that are important to consider when discussing Latino mental health. On the one hand, the social tensions that U.S.-born Latinos face—whereby their socioeconomic profile has improved compared to those in their country of origin, and yet their social status is perceived as inferior to that of the majority culture—may lead to increased risk of substance disorder across generations. However, consistently lower rates for many mental health disorders point to sociocultural factors that persist across generational status (such as family cohesion and strong cultural norms), supplying a source of resiliency that has the effect of lowering risk of mental disorders for Latino groups (Alegría, Mulvaney-Day, Woo, & Viruell-Fuentes, in press; Salgado de Snyder, 1987). High levels of perceived family cohesion and support are thought to function as protective factors against external stressors (Sabogal, Marín, Otero-Sabogal, Vanoss Marín, & Pérez-Stable, 1987).

CONCEPTUAL ISSUES RELATED TO MENTAL HEALTH DISORDERS AMONG LATINOS

As evidenced by these study findings, the prevalence of mental illness appears to vary between Latinos and other racial/ethnic groups as well as within the Latino population. To facilitate the appropriate diagnosis and treatment of mental illness for Latinos, clinicians and practitioners should consider the following conceptual issues that may influence the expression of mental health disorders among Latinos as well the administration and success of treatment protocols for this population. Because many effectiveness trials have not included adequate representation of Latinos (Miranda et al., 2005), it is important to know if modifications in treatment protocols are needed to enhance effectiveness for Latino groups. The accumulated evidence questions the effectiveness of approaches that merely translate clinical interventions developed for Anglo populations into Spanish (Bernal, Bonilla, & Bellido, 1995). Findings also show that treatment effectiveness may vary depending on participants' needs and other factors (Clarke, 1995). Clients are likely to respond to the therapy in ways that are consistent with their cultural socialization regarding care. Culture most likely defines the options perceived as available, useful, and/or desirable manifestations of the therapist and client roles. To address disparities in access, development and integration of more culturally congruent services for Latinos will be necessary.

Differential Endorsement of Symptoms

Latino subgroups have divergent levels of exposure to U.S. culture—perceived discrimination, acculturation, ethnic identity, cultural factors, and human capital—and therefore may vary on which factors influence variations in mental illness. Literature on health disparities shows that symptom presentation for mental health disorders varies across racial and ethnic groups and can differ from what most clinicians are trained to expect, resulting in clinical misdiagnoses (Alegría & McGuire, 2003). For example, Latinos are more likely to somatize psychiatric distress or to express psychiatric illness through such cultural idioms of distress as *ataques de nervios* (Guarnaccia et al., 2005). For immigrant Latinos, *nervios* is an acceptable way to express psychological distress, but it is not captured well in standardized diagnostic instruments because its symptoms often reach across the spectrum of various psychiatric disorders (Guarnaccia, Lewis-Fernandez, & Rivera Marano, 2003). Furthermore, the relative underrepresentation of Latinos with eating disorders may be due to cultural differences in the presentation of eating disorder symptoms, Latinos being more inclined to exhibit binge eating than restricting (Alegría et al., 2007).

Practice guidelines that do not include common manifestations of symptoms among ethnocultural populations have been offered as possible explanations for the misdiagnoses observed. Another example is the expression of psychotic disorders among Latinos, which is particularly vulnerable to misdiagnosis (Lewis-Fernandez et al., in press). Data from epidemiological studies of Latino populations suggest high rates of endorsement of psychotic experiences in different community samples but significantly lower rates of actual psychotic disorder (Brugha et al., 2005; Van Os, Hanssen, Bijl, & Ravelli, 2000). Yet, endorsement of psychotic symptoms has clinical value for Latinos, as patients who endorse psychotic symptoms are more likely to have current suicidal ideation, overall impairment, and a history of psychiatric care than those who do not (Olfson et al., 2002).

Seeking comfort for emotional problems by religious means can also be associated with both lifetime and current risk of psychotic symptom endorsement. One potential explanation for this association is that Latinos who report greater participation in religious activities might relay to their clinicians spiritual experiences that may then be labeled as psychotic symptoms. For example, in more extreme cases, certain cultural or religious beliefs and practices common among Latinos accept and sometimes encourage visual and hearing perceptions of supernatural powers, which are often interpreted by professionals from another culture as pathological hallucinations. The relationship between religiosity and psychotic reports is useful to clinicians in terms of recognizing potential sources of support for patients suffering from a combination of psychiatric disorder and intense vulnerability. However, other study findings argue for the importance of thorough clinical assessment of Latino patients who describe symptoms that initially suggest the presence of psychosis (see Lewis-Fernandez et al., in press, for more details). Furthermore, psychotic symptom endorsement must be carefully considered, to avoid incorrectly diagnosing a psychotic disorder and potentially administering inappropriate and potentially risky antipsychotic medication. Alternative diagnoses must be carefully considered, particularly those related to traumatic exposure, dissociation, and anxiety.

Acculturation and Acculturative Stress

Acculturation is viewed as a multidimensional process that strengthens some aspects (e.g., ethnic identity) and/or potentially erodes other aspects (e.g., family cohesion) of the native culture as one becomes integrated with the host culture. The process of acculturation to the United States is thought to be associated with stressors that increase risk for mental health problems over time among immigrants and may partly explain the immigrant paradox. Acculturative stress can occur as a result of the acculturative process and includes such issues as language problems, perceived discrimination, perceived cultural incompatibilities, and commitment or lack of commitment to culturally prescribed protective values/behaviors, such as familism and cultural pride (Vega, Zimmerman, Gil, Warheit, & Apospori, 1993). As a result, level of acculturation and the influence of acculturative stress must be considered in the diagnosis and treatment of Latinos.

However, few studies have included the appropriate variables that might explain which aspects of acculturation influence the increased risk of psychiatric disorders. Studies examining acculturation and psychiatric disorders among immigrants report inconsistent findings with no clear causal pathway between immigration and higher or lower health and/or mental health risks. For instance, earlier researchers found that Mexican-born immigrants were significantly less likely than non-Hispanic whites to have a lifetime diagnosis of major depression, obsessive-compulsive disorder, or drug abuse or dependence (Burnam et al., 1987). Other studies report similar lifetime rates of psychiatric disorders for Mexicans in Mexico (Alderete, Vega, Kolody, & Aguilar-Gaxiola, 2000) and for Mexican immigrants entering the United States (Vega, Sribney, Aguilar-Gaxiola, & Kolody, 2004), rates that were lower than those of their U.S.-born counterparts. These findings have led to the notion that the "less acculturated" have better mental health (Karno et al., 1989; Vega et al., 1998). More recent findings have confirmed lower risk for immigrants when they are still in the country of origin for any depressive, any anxiety, and any substance disorders, compared to immigrants who have arrived in the United States (Alegría, Sribney, Woo, Guarnaccia, & Torres, 2007). However, the relationship between psychiatric disorders and acculturative stress may vary depending upon age at immigration; the U.S.-born and early-arrival immigrants (those who came to the United States before 7 years of age, a cutoff selected because it denotes the start of formal schooling) report similar high-risk profiles, while later-arrival immigrants report lower risk for disorders (Alegría et al., 2007). The cumulative evidence thus far points toward differential risk of psychopathology by nativity, Latino subgroup, and type of disorder.

These findings may be related to the wide variation between Latino subgroups on variables related to psychopathology risk, including sociostructural and family differences (Guarnaccia et al., 2007), factors that go beyond simple foreign nativity. For example, traditional family relationships seem to erode with increased number of years in the United States and are replaced with higher family intergenerational conflict, which has been associated with increased risk for substance use (Gil, Vega, & Dimas, 1994). A number of other studies have interpreted the

effect of acculturation as increased exposure to discrimination and bad environments in the host (U.S.) culture (Finch, Kolody, & Vega, 2000). Other explanations for the observed differences in risk among Latino subgroups may be related to the inconsistent measurement of acculturation and acculturative stress. Language, family, and contextual differences are crucial concepts in the measurement of the relationship between acculturation and psychiatric disorders (Alegría et al., in press), yet they are rarely included in Latino studies. Together, these findings suggest that researchers and clinicians must consider the effect of acculturation and acculturative stress on mental health when diagnosing Latinos, while treatment protocols that incorporate coping strategies for dealing with acculturative stress should be developed and tested.

Social Support and Social Connectedness

A frequent explanation for what appears to be better health for Latinos has been a higher degree of family support among Latino families. Studies have found positive mental and physical health benefits of family support for Latinos (Bird et al., 2001; Page, 2004). Disruption of family support networks (Rogler, Cortes, & Malgady, 1991), increased intergenerational conflict, and heightened family burden in the form of excessive demands by the extended family are associated with increased risk for depressive and anxiety disorders (Alegría, Mulvaney-Day, Torres, et al., 2007).

Studies of Latinos within poor ethnic enclaves have also found positive effects of dense relationships with friends through increased economic opportunities; however, negative effects have also been found due to lack of connections outside impoverished communities (Portes, 1998), which constrains opportunities for social mobility. The social support of unrelated close friends is thought to exert a positive impact on physical and mental health (Kawachi & Berkman, 2000) and has been found in some studies to have a more significant impact on mental health for Latinos than family support (Rodriguez, Mira, Myers, Morris, & Cardoza, 2003). The converse has also been found, with family conflict related to increased emotional distress and other health risk behaviors (McQueen, Getz, & Bray, 2003).

Social connectedness may also have a negative impact on mental health in economically and/or racially isolated or rural communities, where survival may depend on conformity to oppressive community norms that can hold back community development, such as the presence and acceptance of gangs (Caughy, O'Campo, & Mutaner, 2003; Wakefield & Poland, 2005). Higher levels of community social network density are associated with increased mortality and are more common in communities characterized by higher rates of crime with lower levels of socioeconomic status (SES; Wen, Cagney, & Christakis, 2005). In other words, social connectedness for impoverished Latinos in a community of violence, drug trafficking, and high crime might actually be conducive to an increased risk for substance disorders. In one study of women living in high-risk neighborhoods in metropolitan areas of Puerto Rico, social relations with partners and friends appeared central in predicting women's illicit drug use (Alegría et al., 2004). Women who reported having friends with drug problems were almost twice as likely to test positive for crack, cocaine, or heroine as those who did not. However, findings from a national mental health study on Latinos indicate that arrival in the United States after age 25 decreases the risk for substance disorders (Alegría et al., 2007), thereby offering insight into the context-dependent risk for substance disorders. Coming to the United States as an adult appears to hinder integration into risky social networks linked to drug use (Alegría, Shrout, et al., 2007). These findings indicate areas for prevention of mental illness as well as points of intervention. Researchers must further examine the positive and negative impact of social networks and social connectedness and how these factors can be incorporated into treatment and prevention programs.

Context of Exit and Neighborhood Context

A large proportion of Latinos in the United States are either immigrants or refugees (Fix, Passel, & Sucher, 2003). As a result, it is important to consider the impact of immigration and context of exit on mental health for this population. For immigrants, exit circumstances can have serious mental health consequences due to the added stressors associated with lost social supports and lost social status, acculturative stress, and displacement from home or country. For example, one study showed that those

exposed to political violence were more likely to report perceived need for mental health services and to feel that they should talk to a health professional about problems with their emotions, nerves, mental health, or use of alcohol or drugs (Fortuna, Porche, & Alegría, 2008).

Similarly, differences in experiences in the host neighborhood context may influence or present additive stressors for Latino immigrants. For example, Cuban immigrants who are able to access strong social, political, and economic networks within ethnic enclaves (U.S. Census Bureau, 2000) may experience, in integrating into their new neighborhood contexts, circumstances different from those experienced by immigrants from El Salvador, who may have less access to sociopolitical and economic resources in the United States. Neighborhood context can also be associated with the risk of psychiatric disorders when it captures important aspects of the physical and social contexts that may adversely affect or protect against mental health problems. Unsafe neighborhoods, where Latinos are more likely to live, in comparison to non-Latino whites (Martinez, 1996; Phillips, 2002), may increase the likelihood of psychiatric disorders (Singer, Baer, Scott, Horowitz, & Weinstein, 1998). For example, perceived neighborhood safety has been found to play a significant role in lowering the risk for substance disorders (Alegría, Mulvaney-Day, Torres, et al., 2007). This finding is consistent with other research (Cho, Park, & Echevarria-Cruz, 2005) that emphasizes the importance of the receiving context on mental health outcomes, particularly early exposure to neighborhood disadvantage and drug use, even after controlling for individual-level socioeconomic status (Boardman, Finch, Ellison, Williams, & Jackson, 2001). According to Sampson and Groves (1989), safe neighborhoods might represent the ability to sustain primary relationships and stable support networks willing to engage in guardianship behaviors and explore common solutions to problems.

Regardless of nativity, Latinos in the United States may face additional life stressors linked to contextual factors that can influence the risk for psychiatric disorders. Exposure to racially/ethnically based discrimination (Finch et al., 2000; Singh & Siahpush, 2001) has been associated with negative health outcomes. Because of their skin color and as a result of their culture and language, Latinos are exposed to discrimination upon migration to the U.S. mainland, which leaves them vulnerable to increased risk for poor mental health outcomes (Klonoff, Landrine, & Ullman, 1999). Specifically, exposure to discrimination has been found to be a positive correlate of last-year psychiatric disorders among Latinos (Alegría, Mulvaney-Day, Woo, et al., 2007); reporting increased as Latinos spent more time in the United States (Perez, Fortuna, & Alegría, 2008). Together, these findings emphasize the importance of understanding the living circumstances of newly arrived immigrants as well as screening for and addressing traumatic experiences that may have preceded immigration to the United States.

Socioeconomic Factors

Higher levels of SES have long been linked to better health outcomes (Syme, Lefkowitz, & Krimgold, 2002). Therefore, it is not surprising that factors related to the socioeconomic position of Latinos in the United States also appear to contribute to the differential expression of mental illness. For example, women of Puerto Rico who have less than an 8th-grade education and live in the inner city on the island have been found to be at significantly greater risk of using illicit drugs than those with higher levels of education (Alegría et al., 2004). In this same study, economic hardship was found to augment the odds of illicit drug use across time. It is possible that education provides protection from distress and mental health consequences through enhanced social status and access to resources. Education can also empower individuals, which may help buffer the emotional consequences of hardship (Ailinger, Dear, & Holley-Wilcox, 1993). In addition, it is believed that health decline among immigrants may relate to low social position (e.g., poverty, insufficient income [Marmot, 1999; Williams & Collins, 1995]) and to subjective perceptions of social status (Adler, Epel, Castellazzo, & Ickovics, 2000). Once again, these findings draw attention to the importance of addressing the great socioeconomic disparities that exist in this country as a means for improving the mental health status of Latinos.

Gender Roles

Latino men and women are exposed to very different cultural norms and expectations, which can augment risk for psychiatric disorders in very different ways. For example, Latina women have reported higher rates of 12-month depressive and anxiety disorders than their male counterparts (Alegría, Shrout, et al., 2007). The strong female gender effect for depressive and anxiety disorders in Latina immigrants suggests that changing gender roles may result in tensions between traditional role expectations of the native culture and U.S. cultural norms (Zayas, Lester, Cabassa, & Fortuna, 2005). In addition, female gender appears to be one of the most significant risk factors for suicide attempts among Latinos, even among women without a psychiatric disorder (Fortuna, Perez, Canino, Sribney, & Alegría, 2007). However, Latina women may also benefit from traditional cultural norms, as in the case of substance-use disorders, where immigrant women in particular report very low rates compared to men and the U.S. born (Alegría, Mulvaney-Day, Torres, et al., 2007). This is largely attributed to strong social controls against alcohol and drug use among women (Vega et al., 2002). Traditional Latino family values can also help support women's positive mental health by providing a healthy sense of cultural identity, a strong obligation to assist family and others, which can result in as sense of purpose, meaning, and belonging.

At the same time, understanding Latino men's social roles, supports, and stressors can provide insight into the social processes linked to their risk of mental illness, particularly increased risk for substance use. For example, Polo and Alegría (in press) found that relative to Latino men with at least 16 years of education, those with less than high school reported increased risk for any depressive disorder, any substance use disorder, and any psychiatric disorder. Latino men with disrupted marriages had higher risk for any 12-month depressive disorder, any 12-month anxiety disorder, any 12-month substance-use disorder, and any 12-month disorder than those who were married. Being out of the labor force or being unemployed also rendered men at increased risk for any depressive disorder, any anxiety disorder, and any disorder (Polo & Alegría, in press). However, subgroup comparisons underline the sharp differences in stressors, supports, and immigration characteristics across Latino subethnic groups, with Mexican men reporting higher acculturative stress and Puerto Rican men describing greater perceived discrimination. Yet, the importance of addressing Latino men's sociostructural risk profile, including their low educational achievement, high unemployment, elevated uninsurance rates, and soaring poverty, cannot be emphasized enough. These findings indicate the importance of understanding the specific gender and cultural norms that Latino men and women face, which augment their risk for psychiatric disorders. This understanding must be incorporated into diagnostic and treatment protocol.

Religiosity and Spirituality

Finally, religious attendance, common among low-income Latino groups, might help minorities cope with the hardship of these disadvantageous circumstances (Jarvis, Kirmayer, Weinfeld, & Lasry, 2005) by establishing socially protective ties that buffer stressors. Religious institutions have been shown to offer critical comfort to Latino immigrants by easing the transition to a new context and to serve as a link for immigrants to integrate into U.S. communities while remaining connected to the values and norms of their culture (Levitt, 1998; Menjivar, 2001). Religious attendance has emerged as a factor that facilitates social participation and integration into positive social networks that protect against the negative impact of disadvantageous neighborhoods (Alegría, Shrout, et al., 2007). This is consistent with evidence that religious involvement may be a protective factor against substance disorders (Miller, 1998) with the church functioning as a source of social control that discourages deviance. As a result, the positive impact of religious involvement on mental health should be further explored and examined as a potential complement to traditional psychiatric therapies.

CONCEPTUAL ISSUES RELATED TO MENTAL HEALTH SERVICE DELIVERY

Although efforts to decrease barriers to mental health care have been initiated, service use disparities persist and continue to pose significant equity concerns for many racial/ethnic minority groups (Agency for Health Research and Quality [AHRQ], 2006; USDHHS, 2001a). According to findings from the National Latino and Asian American Study (a nationally representative mental health study of U.S. Latinos), U.S.-born Latinos are far less likely to receive mental health services than non-Latino whites (Alegría, Mulvaney-Day, Woo, et al., 2007). However, rates of mental health service use are not consistent across Latino subethnic groups. Puerto Ricans are far more likely to have received past-year mental health services than Mexicans, Cubans, and Other Latinos (Alegría, Mulvaney-Day, Woo, et al., 2007). Such cultural factors as nativity, language, and number of years in the United States have also been associated with use of mental health services for Latinos; those who are U.S. born, speak English, and have the most number of years in the United States report higher rates of mental health service use. When stratified across those with and without a *Diagnostic and Statistical Manual of Mental Disorders, 4th ed.* (DSM-IV) diagnosis, these cultural differences remain only for those without a diagnosis. Thus, Latinos appear to be most vulnerable in preventive or discretionary use of mental health care. Access to mental health care among Latinos, particularly recent immigrants, also appears to be strongly related to policy restrictions regarding insurance coverage, with Latinos disproportionately uninsured compared to the overall U.S. population (Alegría, Mulvaney-Day, Woo, et al., 2007).

To decrease service-use disparities among Latinos has become a primary objective for practitioners, policymakers, and researchers alike. However, many key conceptual issues have been overlooked in the engagement and retention of Latinos in mental health services. We have failed to consider a variety of factors, such as family, sociostructural, contextual, and health system elements that are pertinent to understanding cross-cultural differences in risk of illness and lack of engagement in services. Traditional treatment services may be culturally mismatched for Latinos, resulting in poor treatment retention and adherence. For example, African American and Latino injection-drug users report that drug treatment programs are difficult to access and poorly designed to meet their needs (Walton, Blow, & Booth, 2001; Wells, Klap, Koike, & Sherbourne, 2001). We have also not assessed whether tailored treatments improve the likelihood of entering into care, such as Linehan's dialectical behavioral therapy (Linehan et al., 1999) or Interpersonal Psychotherapy (Roselló & Bernal, 1996), which appear better matched to the values and expectations for treatment of Latino populations. These factors not only limit access to mental health services but also influence patterns of engagement in services as well as the way in which Latinos interact with mental health providers and the health care system.

In addition, differential presentation of symptoms for Latinos compared to whites is another mechanism through which engagement in services may vary. If Latinos come to mental health services with limited health literacy, they might expect to solve some social problems that are in fact poorly addressed in mental health settings (e.g., insurance coverage or housing needs) and may be disappointed by the offerings of the specialty care setting. Latinos may also have culturally different expectations for provider behavior, such as warmth and more direct advice. Ethnic minority patients might not be as informed about diagnosis or prognosis (Schaafsma, Raynor, & de Jong-van den Berg, 2003) and may feel dissatisfied when they do not receive needed information (Levinson, Stiles, Inui, & Engle, 1993), which in turn may result in less compliance and retention in treatment (Kalichman, Catz, & Ramachandran, 1999) compared to white patients.

Finally, such sociocontextual factors as residential segregation and a community's social capital can work both to facilitate and to limit access to mental health services. For the remainder of this chapter, we delve more deeply into these mechanisms and others through which mental health service disparities occur. To this end, we present a series of conceptual issues that must be considered by practitioners and researchers alike in order to successfully engage and retain Latinos in mental health treatment.

Barriers to Care

Many of the barriers Latinos face in accessing mental health services result from federal and state policies. Access to mental health care among Latinos, particularly recent immigrants, is strongly related to public policy restrictions regarding insurance coverage. Policy changes in the Personal Work Opportunity and Reconciliation Act of 1996 limited Latino immigrants' ability to access outpatient mental health treatment services (Wang & Holahan, 2003). These changes in Medicaid laws require immigrants to be U.S. residents for at least 5 years before becoming eligible for health-care benefits. Implementation of this rule not only has eliminated enrollment of new immigrants, but

enrollment rates also dropped for those who had been in the country for many years and were, in fact, still eligible for the program (Kandula, Kersey, & Lurie, 2004). In February of 2009, the Children's Health Insurance Program Reauthorization Act (CHIPRA) was signed into law (Kaiser Family Foundation, 2009). This bill altered the Medicaid provisions for immigrants by allowing states the option to expand coverage to legal immigrant children and pregnant women during their first 5 years in the country. While this legislation has the potential to expand coverage for two very vulnerable groups, it is unclear how many individual states will actually expand coverage to their residents. Moreover, the legislation does not go far enough, given that the majority of legal Latino immigrant adults continue to face substantial barriers to mental health services.

Uninsurance

Recent studies have documented that uninsurance is more common among Latinos than among whites in the United States, particularly among recent (less than 5 years of residence) Latino immigrant populations (Alegría et al., 2006). Mexicans had the highest uninsured rate and a much lower rate of public insurance, compared with Puerto Ricans and Cubans. This is consistent with other work that has found that Latinos and African Americans have substantially lower rates of job-based insurance than their white counterparts (Zuvekas & Taliaferro, 2003).

Latino immigrants face additional barriers to securing coverage, such as learning to navigate a U.S. health-care system that differs substantially from the health-care systems in their native countries (Feld & Power, 2000). Unfortunately, even among Latino families who are eligible to enroll in Medicaid, underenrollment is observed due to misinterpretations of policy requirements as well as to persistent false rumors that receipt of Medicaid benefits may endanger immigrant residency status (Capps, Ku, & Fix, 2002). As a result, outreach programs must be established to inform immigrants about their rights, while existing policies should be reexamined.

Differential Referral to Mental Health and Substance Use Services

Differential pathways into services represent a key mechanism leading to service disparities among Latinos. For example, many ethnic and racial minorities receive alcohol or substance abuse treatment only after committing a criminal offense (Martin, Butzin, & Inciardi, 1995). Furthermore, ex-offenders are referred to labor market intermediaries that insist on treatment as a precondition for employment placement (Broome, Knight, Hiller, & Dwayne Simpson, 1996; Hiller, Knight, & Simpson, 1999). Adult Latinos are more likely to seek mental health care in primary-care clinics, even though this may lead to suboptimal mental health treatment for depression (Tai-Seale, McGuire, & Zhang, 2007). Disparities in mental health and substance-abuse service delivery could be explained by the differential interactions of minorities, compared to whites, with the medical and criminal justice systems. Given that minorities are less likely than whites to have a usual source of care and to have visited a doctor in the last year (Collins, Hall, & Neuhaus, 1999; Ross & Cox, 2004), they might have missed opportunities for referral to mental health treatment.

Limited Workforce Availability and Training of Service Providers to Treat Latinos

Communities with high proportions of black and Latino residents are 4 times more likely than non-Latino whites to have a shortage of physicians, regardless of community income (Morales, Lara, Kington, Valdez, & Escarce, 2002). This is primarily due to a disproportionately low geographic supply of providers, particularly multilingual service providers, in communities with ethnic and racial minorities. Health-care organization arrangements for distributing providers to minority Medicaid beneficiaries (Medicaid Access Study Group, 1994) are thought to be influential in service disparities. The implication is that Latinos might be unable to access high-quality bilingual providers who are already employed in the private health-care system. Minority physicians represent only 9% of all physicians in the United States (Association of American Medical Colleges, 2000), and most U.S. health-care providers tend to be monolingual English speakers (Fiscella & Franks, 2001). Medicaid beneficiaries, particularly those with limited English-language skills, may have a difficult time competing for physician services if physicians have high caseloads of privately insured patients (Tai-Seale, Freund, & LoSasso, 2001).

Problem Recognition

Disparities in health care among some ethnic minority children appear to be also linked to parental knowledge of mental health disorders and available treatments. For example, evidence suggests that different ethnic/cultural groups in the United States have varied perceptions of what is considered a mental health problem in their children. Roberts and colleagues (2005) compared non-Latino white, Latino, and African American parents' perception of their adolescents' mental health problems and life satisfaction. Even after adjusting for the clinical need profile of the child, the child's level of impairment, and the sociodemographic characteristics of the parents, minority parents perceived fewer emotional or behavioral problems in their children than did their white counterparts. Differing perceptions of mental health problems (see Canino & Alegría, in press) can lead to conflicting views over treatment and treatment need in general between parents and practitioners, resulting in inadequate care.

Poor Patient-Provider Interactions

Various studies have revealed that providers may hold preconceptions about patients based on their group membership, resulting in provider stereotypes (Balsa & McGuire, 2003). For example, overdiagnosis occurs when culturally appropriate behaviors are interpreted as pathological by a professional from another culture; for example, the overdiagnosis of psychotic disorders among Latinos (Guarnaccia, Guevara-Ramos, González, Canino, & Bird, 1992). Such misinterpretation can result in increasingly severe diagnoses of individuals as their social and cultural distance increases. Latinos also report feeling discriminated against when interacting with their mental health providers (Hughes, Doty, Ives, Edwards, & Tenney, 2002). Interestingly, Latinos are more likely to express the belief that unfair treatment was received due to race or spoken language, and a belief that better treatment would have been received had the clinician been of a different race or ethnicity. For example, Latino patients report being treated with disrespect or being looked down upon more often than white patients (19.4% of Latinos as compared to 9.4% of non-Latino whites [Blanchard & Lurie, 2004]). All of this might lead to lack of engagement and poor interaction in mental health care, which preclude receiving effective mental health and substance-use treatments.

Limited English Proficiency and Health Literacy

In general, Latinos have less access to mental health care, are less likely to receive needed services (USDHHS, 2001a), and are more likely to report lower levels of satisfaction with the care they do receive. This is particularly true of Latinos with limited English proficiency. Recent data show that insured Latinos with poor/fair English-language proficiency were more likely than those with good/excellent proficiency to report not having a regular source of care, long waits for appointments, and difficulty in getting information/advice by phone (Pippins, Alegría, & Haas, 2007). In addition, recent results looking specifically at the use of antidepressant medication among Latinos (Hodgkin, Volpe-Vartanian, & Alegría, 2007) found that whether respondents discontinued their antidepressant use was significantly associated with English-language proficiency. Those with good or excellent English proficiency were less likely to discontinue taking antidepressants. These findings emphasize the poor alignment of mental health services to fit the needs of non-English-speaking populations. Further efforts seem warranted to offer patient advocates or care managers who can facilitate navigating health-care delivery systems for non-English-speaking Latinos.

Health literacy includes the degree to which basic literacy skills can be applied within the health-care system in order to access health services and obtain and process health information (Safeer & Keenan, 2005). Low literacy skills create barriers to successful navigation and functioning within the U.S. health-care system. For Latinos, health literacy appears to contribute to service disparities (Gazmararian, Curran, Parker, Bernhardt, & DeBuono, 2005). Health literacy may indirectly create barriers to health-care use by inhibiting access to care due to a patient's inability to register for health insurance, difficulty in interpreting coverage benefits and rules, avoidance or delays in accessing health services due to the inability to adequately fill out forms in physician offices or difficulty following directions to service facilities. Even if

Latinos with poor health literacy enter care, they face disparities in health outcomes associated with literacy limitations; people who read at lower levels are at greater odds of experiencing adverse health outcomes than individuals with high literacy levels (Dewalt, Berkman, Sheridan, Lohr, & Pignone, 2004). For example, findings from The Commonwealth Fund 2001 Health Care Quality Survey (Johnson et al., 2004) reveal that 33% of Latinos, compared to 16% of whites, reported one or more of the following problems: The doctor did not listen to everything they said; they did not fully understand the doctor; or they had questions during the visit but did not ask them. Together, these findings highlight the great need to provide health information (both written and verbal) at a literacy level appropriate for all patients in an effort to improve health outcomes as well as the overall quality of care.

RECOMMENDATIONS AND DIRECTIONS FOR FUTURE RESEARCH

Based on the aforementioned findings, several recommendations are offered as strategies to reduce mental illness and increase access to mental health services among Latino adults in the United States.

1. High levels of unmet need are present across the U.S. Latino population. Adoption of interventions to improve entry into services should be prioritized for Latinos who do not recognize and attend to their own or their children's psychiatric illnesses but are in need of preventive treatment before they become disabled or impaired. Public symptom-recognition campaigns may be useful, as well as anti-stigma social marketing campaigns.

2. As discussed in this chapter, many barriers to accessing mental health services exist for Latinos. Therefore, it is necessary for mental health practitioners to explore nontraditional methods for delivering care. This includes collaborating with social service and community agencies in immigrant enclaves in order to facilitate the delivery of mental health services.

3. Given that symptom presentation for mental health disorders varies across racial/ethnic groups and can differ from what clinicians

are trained to expect, training programs must incorporate common symptom manifestations among Latinos and other groups into practice guidelines. We further argue for the importance of thorough clinical assessment of Latino patients who describe symptoms that initially suggest the presence of psychosis, due to the high rate of misdiagnosis for this disorder. Together, these strategies will work to decrease misdiagnosis and overpathologizing of mental health disorders among Latinos.

4. The effect of social networks and family support/conflict on Latino mental health has been touched on many times throughout this chapter. Effective strategies for improving Latino mental health should involve bolstering social support systems and social networks as well as resolving family conflict. Research studies should be conducted that examine the effectiveness of such interventions on improving mental health outcomes among Latinos.

5. Recent epidemiological findings emphasize the need to understand the role of context in the risk for mental health disorders, particularly the risk for substance-use disorders and access to services. Interventions should be developed to inform families and the larger community about the increased risk for disorders related to such contexts as disadvantaged neighborhoods. Furthermore, mental health interventions should focus on decreasing neighborhood violence and on increasing neighborhood safety and guardianship behaviors.

6. Interventions should also focus on improving the health literacy of Latinos in an effort to facilitate successful navigation and functioning within the U.S. health-care system. Conversely, it is also necessary to ensure that all forms, medical documentation, and even verbal instructions from clinicians are presented at an appropriate literacy level for patients. Moreover, interpreter services must be expanded so that they are readily available to all Spanish-speaking patients who require them.

7. Policymakers should explore policy interventions targeting poverty reduction and augmentation of educational achievement among Latinos and their families as a way of reducing mental health problems and disparities in access to care and increasing the political power of Latinos. Examples of potential policy interventions are the expansion of Title 1 programs in schools where poor Latino youth are overrepresented.

Conclusion

As Latinos continue to gain prominence in the demographic profile of the United States, understanding the patterns of mental health needs, as well as the challenges and barriers to services, is critical for developing effective services for this population. In this chapter, we presented a number of conceptual issues related to mental health disorders and service use that researchers and practitioners alike must consider when working with the Latino population. The findings highlighted in this chapter point to a number of key areas that must be addressed in order to facilitate the successful treatment of Latinos.

First, clinicians must be cognizant of the many mismatches that can occur in the treatment of Latinos. This includes the differential endorsement of psychiatric symptoms by Latinos, which must be acknowledged and incorporated into training programs for mental health professionals; poor patient-provider interactions, such as conflicting expectations for treatment visits, that could be addressed through cultural competency trainings; and mismatches in problem recognition, which could be prevented through media campaigns targeting mental health symptom recognition. Second, clinicians must consider the influence of family and such contextual factors as neighborhood disadvantage on risk for and prevention of mental illness when treating Latinos. Addressing these factors and incorporating them into treatment protocols may create powerful mechanisms for decreasing risk for disorders as well as for developing more effective treatments. Third and finally, practitioners must be aware of the many barriers that exist in access to mental health services for Latinos. These barriers include state and federal policies that directly limit access to health care, as well as more indirect pathways, such as limited training of service providers who treat Latinos and low levels of health literacy among the Latino population. Together, these findings highlight important areas for consideration as well as critical points for intervention. Addressing these issues will serve to push forward the field of mental health service research as well as improve mental health treatment and service delivery for Latinos.

References

Adler, N., Epel, E., Castellazzo, G., & Ickovics, J. (2000). Relationship of subjective and objective social status with psychological and physiological functioning: Preliminary data in healthy white women. *Health Psychology, 19*(6), 586–592.

Agency for Health Research and Quality (AHRQ). (2006). *National Healthcare Disparities Report* (No. AHRQ pub no 07–0012). Rockville, MD: U.S. Department of Health and Human Services.

Ailinger, R., Dear, M., & Holley-Wilcox, R. (1993). Predictors of function among older Hispanic immigrants: A five-year follow-up. *Nursing Research, 42*(4), 240–244.

Alderete, E., Vega, W., Kolody, B., & Aguilar-Gaxiola, S. (2000). Lifetime prevalence of and risk factors for psychiatric disorders among Mexican migrant farm workers in California. *American Journal of Public Health, 90*(4), 608–614.

Alegría, M., Canino, G., Shrout, P. E., Woo, M., Duan, N., Vila, D., et al. (2008). Prevalence of mental illness in immigrant and non-immigrant U.S. Latino groups. *American Journal of Psychiatry, 165*, 359–369.

Alegría, M., Cao, Z., McGuire, T., Ojeda, V., Sribney, W., Woo, M., et al. (2006). Health insurance coverage for vulnerable populations: Contrasting Asian Americans and Latinos in the U.S. *Inquiry, 43*(Fall), 231–254.

Alegría, M., & McGuire, T. (2003). Rethinking a universalist framework in the psychiatric symptom-disorder relationship. *Journal of Health and Social Behavior, 44*(3), 257–274.

Alegría, M., Mulvaney-Day, N., Torres, M., Polo, A., Cao, Z., & Canino, G. (2007). Prevalence of psychiatric disorders across Latino subgroups in the United States. *American Journal of Public Health, 97*, 68–75.

Alegría, M., Mulvaney-Day, N., Woo, M., Torres, M., Gao, S., & Oddo, V. (2007). Correlates of twelve-month mental health service use among Latinos: Results from the National Latino and Asian American Study (NLAAS). *American Journal of Public Health, 97*, 76–83.

Alegría, M., Mulvaney-Day, N., Woo, M., & Viruell-Fuentes, E. (in press). Psychology of Latino adults: Challenges and an agenda for action. In E. Chang & C. Downey (Eds.), *Mental health across racial groups: Lifespan perspectives.* New York: Springer.

Alegría, M., Shrout, P., Woo, M., Guarnaccia, P., Sribney, W., Vila, D., et al. (2007). Understanding differences in past year psychiatric disorders for Latinos living in the U.S. *Social Science and Medicine, 65*(2), 214–230.

Alegría, M., Sribney, W., Woo, M., Guarnaccia, P., & Torres, M. (2007). Looking beyond nativity: The relation of age of immigration, length of residence, and birth cohorts to the risk of onset of psychiatric disorders for Latinos. *Research on Human Development, 4*(1&2), 19–47.

Alegría, M., Vera, M., Shrout, P., Canino, G., Lai, S., Albizu, C., et al. (2004). Understanding hard-core drug use among urban Puerto Rican women in high-risk neighborhoods. *Addictive Behaviors, 29*(4), 643–664.

Alegría, M., Woo, M., Cao, Z., Torres, M., Meng, X., & Striegel-Moore, R. (2007). Prevalence and correlates of eating disorders in Latinos in the United States. *International Journal of Eating Disorders, 40*(S3), S15–S21.

Association of American Medical Colleges (AAMC). (2000). *Minority graduates of U.S. medical schools: Trends, 1950–1998.* Washington, DC: AAMC.

Balsa, A., & McGuire, T. (2003). Prejudice, clinical uncertainty and stereotypes as sources of health disparities. *Journal of Health Economics, 22*(1), 89–116.

Bernal, G., Bonilla, J., & Bellido, C. (1995). Ecological validity and cultural sensitivity for outcome research: Issues for the cultural adaptation and development of psychosocial treatments with Hispanics. *Journal of Abnormal Child Psychology, 23*(1), 67–82.

Bird, H., Canino, G., Davies, M., Zhang, H., Ramirez, R., & Lahey, B. (2001). Prevalence and correlates of antisocial behaviors among three ethnic groups. *Journal of Abnormal Child Psychology, 29*(6), 465–478.

Blanchard, J., & Lurie, N. (2004). R-E-S-P-E-C-T: Patient reports of disrespect in the health care setting and its impact on care. *The Journal of Family Practice, 53*(9), 721–730.

Boardman, J., Finch, B., Ellison, G., Williams, D., & Jackson, J. (2001). Neighborhood disadvantage, stress, and drug use among adults. *Journal of Health and Social Behavior, 42*(2), 151–165.

Breslau, J., Aguilar-Gaxiola, S., Kendler, K. S., Su, M., Williams, D., & Kessler, R. C. (2006). Specifying race-ethnic differences in risk for psychiatric disorder in a U.S.A. national sample. *Psychological Medicine, 36*(1), 57–68.

Broome, K. M., Knight, K., Hiller, M. L., & Dwayne Simpson, D. (1996). Drug treatment process indicators for probationers and prediction of recidivism. *Journal of Substance Abuse Treatment, 13*(6), 487–491.

Brugha, T., Singleton, N., Meltzer, H., Bebbington, P., Farrell, M., Jenkins, R., et al. (2005). Psychosis in the community and in prisons: A report from the British National Survey of Psychiatric Morbidity. *American Journal of Psychiatry, 162,* 774–780.

Burnam, M. A., Hough, R., Karno, M., Escobar, J., & Telles, C. (1987). Acculturation and lifetime prevalence of psychiatric disorders among Mexican Americans in Los Angeles. *Journal of Health and Social Behavior, 28,* 89–102.

Canino, G., & Alegría, M. (in press). Understanding psychopathology among the adult and child Latino population: An epidemiologic perspective. In J. Grau, M. Azmitia, N. Cabrera, G. Carlo, J. Chahin, & F. A. Villarruel (Eds.), *Handbook of Latino psychology: Community and developmental perspectives.* Thousand Oaks, CA: Sage.

Capps, R., Ku, L., & Fix, M. (2002). *How are immigrants faring after welfare reform? Preliminary evidence from Los Angeles and New York City.* Washington, DC: The Urban Institute.

Caughy, M. O., O'Campo, P. J., & Mutaner, C. (2003). When being alone might be better: Neighborhood poverty, social capital, and child mental health. *Social Science and Medicine, 57,* 227–237.

Cho, Y., Park, G.-S., & Echevarria-Cruz, S. (2005). Perceived neighborhood characteristics and the health of adult Koreans. *Social Science and Medicine, 60*(6), 1285–1297.

Clarke, G. N. (1995). Improving the transition from basic efficacy research to effectiveness studies: Methodology issues and procedures. *Journal of Consulting and Clinical Psychology, 63*(5), 718–725.

Collins, K. S., Hall, A. G., & Neuhaus, C. (1999). *U.S. minority health: A chartbook.* New York: The Commonwealth Fund.

Dewalt, D., Berkman, N., Sheridan, S., Lohr, K., & Pignone, M. (2004). Literacy and health outcomes: A systematic review of the literature. *Journal of General Internal Medicine, 19*(12), 1228–1239.

Diaz, E., Woods, S. W., & Rosenheck, R. A. (2005). Effects of ethnicity on psychotropic medications adherence. *Community Mental Health Journal, 41*(5), 521–537.

Feld, P., & Power, B. (2000). *Immigrants' access to health care after welfare reform: Findings from focus groups in four cities.* Washington, DC: Kaiser Commission on Medicaid and the Uninsured.

Finch, B., Kolody, B., & Vega, W. (2000). Perceived discrimination and depression among Mexican-origin adults in California. *Journal of Health and Social Behavior, 41,* 295–313.

Fiscella, K., & Franks, P. (2001). Impact of patient socioeconomic status on physician profiles: A comparison of census-derived and individual measures. *Medical Care, 39*(1), 8–14.

Fix, M., Passel, J., & Sucher, K. (2003). *Trends in naturalization.* Washington, DC: The Urban Institute.

Fortuna, L., Perez, D. J., Canino, G., Sribney, W., & Alegría, M. (2007). Prevalence and correlates of lifetime suicidal ideation and suicide attempts among Latino subgroups in the United States. *Journal of Clinical Psychiatry, 68*(4), 572–581.

Fortuna, L., Porche, M., & Alegría, M. (2008). Political violence, psychosocial trauma, and the context of mental health services use among immigrant Latinos in the United States. *Ethnicity and Health, 13*(5), 435–463.

Gazmararian, J. A., Curran, J. W., Parker, R. M., Bernhardt, J. M., & DeBuono, B. A. (2005). Public health literacy in America: An ethical imperative. *American Journal of Preventive Medicine, 28*(3), 317–322.

Gil, A. G., Vega, W. A., & Dimas, J. M. (1994). Acculturation stress and personal adjustment among Hispanic adolescent boys. *Journal of Community Psychology, 22,* 43–54.

Grant, B., Stinson, F., Dawson, D., Chou, P., Dufour, M., Compton, W., et al. (2004). Prevalence and co-occurrence of substance use disorders and independent mood and anxiety disorders: Results from the National Epidemiologic Survey on Alcohol and Related Conditions. *Archives of General Psychiatry, 61,* 807–816.

Guarnaccia, P., Guevara-Ramos, L., González, G., Canino, G., & Bird, H. (1992). Cross-cultural aspects of psychotic symptoms in Puerto Rico. *Research in Community and Mental Health, 7,* 99–110.

Guarnaccia, P., Martinez, I., Ramirez, R., & Canino, G. (2005). Are ataques de nervios in Puerto Rican children associated with psychiatric disorder? *Journal of the American Academy of Child and Adolescent Psychiatry, 44*(11), 1184–1192.

Guarnaccia, P., Pincay, I., Shrout, P., Alegría, M., Lewis-Fernandez, R., & Canino, G. (2007). Assessing diversity among Latinos: Results from the NLAAS. *Hispanic Journal of Behavioral Sciences, 29*(4), 510–534.

Guarnaccia, P. J., Lewis-Fernandez, R., & Rivera Marano, M. (2003). Toward a Puerto Rican popular nosology: Nervios and ataque de nervios. *Culture, Medicine and Psychiatry, 27*(3), 339–366.

Hiller, M. L., Knight, K., & Simpson, D. D. (1999). Prison-based substance abuse treatment, residential aftercare and recidivism. *Addiction, 94*(6), 833–842.

Hodgkin, D., Volpe-Vartanian, J., & Alegría, M. (2007). Discontinuation of antidepressant medication among Latinos in the USA. *The Journal of Behavioral Health Services and Research, 34*(3), 329–342.

Hughes, D. L., Doty, M. M., Ives, B. L., Edwards, J. N., & Tenney, K. (2002). *Diverse communities, common concerns: Assessing health care quality for minority Americans.* New York: The Commonwealth Fund.

Jarvis, E., Kirmayer, L., Weinfeld, M., & Lasry, J. (2005). Religious practice and psychological distress: The importance of gender, ethnicity and immigrant status. *Transcultural Psychiatry, 42*(4), 657–675.

Johnson, R. L., Saha, S., & Arbelaez, J. J. (2004). Racial and ethnic differences in patient perceptions of bias and cultural competence in health care. *Journal of General Internal Medicine, 19*(2), 101–110.

Kaiser Family Foundation. (2009). *State Children's Health Insurance Program (CHIP): Reauthorization history.* (Report of Kaiser Commission on Medicaid and the Uninsured). Retrieved February 20, 2009, from http://www.kff.org/medicaid/7863.cfm

Kalichman, S. C., Catz, S., & Ramachandran, B. (1999). Barriers to HIV/AIDS treatment and treatment adherence among African-American adults with disadvantaged education. *Journal of the National Medical Association 91*(8), 439–446.

Kandula, N., Kersey, M., & Lurie, N. (2004). Assuring the health of immigrants: What the leading health indicators tell us. *Annual Review of Public Health, 25,* 357–376.

Karno, M., Golding, J. M., Burnam, M. A., Hough, R. L., Escobar, J., Wells, K. M., et al. (1989). Anxiety disorders among Mexican Americans and non-Hispanic Whites in Los Angeles. *Journal of Nervous and Mental Disease, 177*(4), 202–209.

Kawachi, I., & Berkman, L. F. (2000). Social cohesion, social capital, and health. In L. F. Berkman & I. Kawachi (Eds.), *Social epidemiology* (pp. 174–190). New York: Oxford University Press.

Klonoff, E., Landrine, H., & Ullman, J. (1999). Racial discrimination and psychiatric symptoms among Blacks. *Cultural Diversity and Ethnic Minority Psychology, 5*(4), 329–339.

Levinson, W., Stiles, W., Inui, T., & Engle, R. (1993). Physician frustration in communicating with patients. *Medical Care, 31*(4), 285–295.

Levitt, P. (1998). Social remittances: Migration driven local-level forms of cultural diffusion. *International Migration Review, 32*(4), 926–948.

Levitt, P., DeWind, J., & Vertovec, S. (2003). International perspectives on transnational migration: An introduction. *International Migration Review, 37*(3), 565–575.

Lewis-Fernandez, R., Horvitz-Lenon, M., Blanco, C., Guarnaccia, P., Cao, Z., & Alegría, M. (in press). Significance of endorsement of psychotic symptoms by U.S. Latinos. *Journal of Nervous and Mental Disease.*

Linehan, M. M., Schmidt, H., Dimeff, L. A., Craft, J. C., Kanter, J., & Comtois, K. A. (1999). Dialectical behavior therapy for patients with borderline personality disorder and drug-dependence. *American Journal on Addictions, 8*(4), 279–292.

Marmot, M. (1999). Multi-level approaches to understanding social determinants. In L. Berkman & I. Kawachi (Eds.), *Social epidemiology.* New York: Oxford University Press.

Martin, S. S., Butzin, C. A., & Inciardi, J. A. (1995). Assessment of a multistage therapeutic community for drug-involved offenders. *Journal of Psychoactive Drugs, 27*(1), 109–116.

Martinez, R. (1996). Latinos and lethal violence: The impact of poverty and inequality. *Social Problems, 43*(2), 131–146.

McQueen, A., Getz, J. G., & Bray, J. H. (2003). Acculturation, substance use, and deviant behavior: Examining separation and family conflict as mediators. *Child Development, 74*(6), 1737–1750.

Medicaid Access Study Group. (1994). Access of Medicaid recipients to outpatient care. *New England Journal of Medicine, 330*(20), 1426–1430.

Menjivar, C. (2001). Latino immigrants and their perceptions of religious institutions: Cubans, Salvadorans, and Guatemalans in Phoenix, Arizona. *Migraciones Internacionales, 1*(1).

Miller, W. (1998). Researching the spiritual dimensions of alcohol and other drug problems. *Addiction, 93*(7), 979–990.

Miranda, J., Bernal, G., Lau, A., Kohn, L., Hwang, W., & LaFromboise, T. (2005). State of the science on psychosocial interventions for ethnic minorities. *Annual Review of Clinical Psychology, 1,* 113–142.

Miranda, J., & Cooper, L. (2004). Disparities in care for depression among primary care patients. *Journal of General Internal Medicine, 19*(2), 120–126.

Morales, L., Lara, M., Kington, R., Valdez, R., & Escarce, J. (2002). Socioeconomic, cultural and behavioral factors affecting Hispanic health outcomes. *Journal of Health Care for the Poor and Underserved, 13*(4), 477–503.

The National Academies. (2007). *Multiple origins, uncertain destinies: Hispanics and the American future.* Washington, DC: The National Academies. Retrieved February 5, 2009, from

http://www7.nationalacademies
.org/cpop/ADemographicDividend.pdf

Olfson, M., Lewis-Fernandez, R., Weissman, M. M., Feder, A., Gameroff, M. J., Pilowsky, D., et al. (2002). Psychotic symptoms in an urban general medicine practice. *American Journal of Psychiatry, 159*(8), 1412–1419.

Page, R. (2004). Positive pregnancy outcomes in Mexican immigrants: What can we learn? *Journal of Obstetric, Gynecologic, and Neonatal Nursing, 33*(6), 783–790.

Perez, D., Fortuna, L., & Alegría, M. (2008). Prevalence and correlates of everyday discrimination among U.S. Latinos. *Journal of Community Psychology, 36*(4), 321–333.

Phillips, J. (2002). White, Black, and Latino homicide rates: Why the difference? *Social Problems, 49*(3), 349–373.

Pippins, J., Alegría, M., & Haas, J. (2007). Association between language proficiency and the quality of primary care among a national sample of insured Latinos. *Medical Care, 45*(11), 1020–1025.

Polo, A., & Alegría, M. (in press). Psychiatric disorders and mental health service use profile of Latino men in the United States. In M. Aguirre-Molina, L. Borrell, & W. Vega (Eds.), *Social and structural factors affecting the health of Latino males.* New Brunswick, NJ: Rutgers University Press.

Portes, A. (1998). Social capital: Its origins and applications in modern sociology. *Annual Review of Sociology, 24*, 1–24.

Roberts, R. E., Alegría, M., Ramsay, R. C., & Chen, I. G. (2005). Mental health problems of adolescents as reported by their caregivers: A comparison of European, African and Latino Americans. *Journal of Behavioral Health Services and Research, 32*(1), 1–13.

Rodriguez, N., Mira, C., Myers, H., Morris, J., & Cardoza, D. (2003). Family or friends: Who plays a greater supportive role for Latino college students? *Cultural Diversity and Ethnic Minority Psychology, 9*(3), 236–250.

Rogler, L. H., Cortes, D. E., & Malgady, R. G. (1991). Acculturation and mental health status among Hispanics: Convergence and new directions in research. *American Psychologist, 46*, 584–597.

Roselló, J., & Bernal, G. (1996). Adaptation of cognitive-behavioral and interpersonal treatment for depression in Puerto Rican adolescents. In E. Hibbs & P. Jensen (Eds.), *Psychological treatments for child and adolescent disorders.* Washington, DC: American Psychological Association Press.

Ross, D. C., and Cox, L. (2004). *Beneath the surface: Barriers threaten to slow progress on expanding health coverage of children and families.* (Report of Kaiser Commission on Medicaid and the Uninsured). Kaiser Family Foundation. Retrieved February 5, 2009, from http://www .kff.org/medicaid/7191.cfm

Sabogal, F., Marín, G., Otero-Sabogal, R., Vanoss Marín, B., & Pérez-Stable, E. (1987). Hispanic familism and acculturation: What changes and what doesn't? *Hispanic Journal of Behavioral Sciences, 9*(4), 397–412.

Safeer, R. S., & Keenan, J. (2005). Health literacy: The gap between physicians and patients. *American Family Physician, 72*(3), 463–468.

Salgado de Snyder, V. N. (1987). Factors associated with acculturative stress and depressive symptomatology among married Mexican immigrant women. *Psychology of Women Quarterly, 11*(4), 475–488.

Sampson, R. J., & Groves, W. B. (1989). Community structure and crime: Testing social-disorganization theory. *American Journal of Sociology, 94*(4), 774–802.

Schaafsma, E. S., Raynor, T. D., & de Jong-van den Berg, L. T. (2003). Accessing medication information by ethnic minorities: Barriers and possible solutions. *Pharmacy World and Science, 25*(5), 185–190.

Singer, M., Baer, H., Scott, G., Horowitz, S., & Weinstein, B. (1998). Pharmacy access to syringes among injecting drug users: Follow-up findings from Hartford, Connecticut. *Public Health Reports, 113*(Supp. 1), 81–89.

Singh, G. K., & Siahpush, M. (2001). All-cause and cause-specific mortality of immigrants and native born in the United States. *American Journal of Public Health, 91*(3), 392–400.

Syme, L., Lefkowitz, B., & Krimgold, B. K. (2002). Incorporating socioeconomic factors into U.S. health policy: Addressing the barriers. *Health Affairs, 21*(2), 113–118.

Tai-Seale, M., Freund, D., & LoSasso, A. (2001). Racial disparities in service use among Medicaid beneficiaries after mandatory enrollment in managed care: A difference in differences approach. *Inquiry, 38*(1), 49–59.

Tai-Seale, M., McGuire, T., & Zhang, W. (2007). Time allocation in primary care office visits. *Health Services Research, 42*(5), 1871–1894.

U.S. Census Bureau. (2000). *Population profile of the United States.* Retrieved November 22, 2002, from www.census.gov/population/pop-profile/2000/chap09.pdf

U.S. Census Bureau. (2008). U.S. Hispanic population surpasses 45 million: Now 15 percent of total. *U.S. Census Bureau News.* Retrieved May 1, 2008, from http://www .census.gov/Press-Release/www/releases/ archives/population/011910.html

U. S. Department of Health and Human Services (USDHHS). (2001a). *Mental health: Culture, race, and ethnicity—A supplement to Mental health: A report of the surgeon general.* Rockville, MD: Author.

U.S. Department of Health and Human Services (USDHHS). (2001b). Mental health care for Hispanic Americans. In *Mental health: Culture, race, and ethnicity—A supplement to Mental health: A report of the surgeon general* (pp. 129–155). Rockville, MD: Author.

Van Os, J., Hanssen, M., Bijl, R. V., & Ravelli, A. (2000). Revisited: A psychosis continuum in the general population? *Schizophrenia Research, 45,* 11–20.

Vega, W., Aguilar-Gaxiola, S., Andrade, L., Bijl, R., Borges, G., Caraveo-Anduaga, J., et al. (2002). Prevalence and age of onset for drug use in seven international sites: Results from the International Consortium of Psychiatric Epidemiology. *Drug and Alcohol Dependence, 68*(3), 285–297.

Vega, W., & Alegría, M. (2001). Latino mental health and treatment in the United States. In M. Aguirre-Molina, C. Molina, & R. Zambrana (Eds.), *Health issues in the Latino community* (pp. 179–208). San Francisco: Jossey-Bass.

Vega, W., Kolody, B., Aguilar-Gaxiola, S., Alderete, E., Catalano, R., & Caraveo-Anduaga, J. (1998). Lifetime prevalence of DSM-III-R psychiatric disorders among urban and rural Mexican Americans in California. *Archives of General Psychiatry, 55*(9), 771–778.

Vega, W., Sribney, W., Aguilar-Gaxiola, S., & Kolody, B. (2004). 12-month prevalence of DSM-III-R psychiatric disorders among Mexican Americans: Nativity, social assimilation, and age determinants. *Journal of Nervous and Mental Disorders, 192*(8), 532–541.

Vega, W., Zimmerman, R., Gil, A., Warheit, G., & Apospori, E. (1993). Acculturation strain theory: Its application in explaining drug use behavior among Cuban and other Hispanic youth. In M. De La Rosa & J. L. Recio (Eds.), *Drug abuse among minority youth* (pp. 144–166). Rockville, MD: National Institute on Drug Abuse.

Viruell-Fuentes, E. (2006). "My heart is always there": The transnational practices of first-generation Mexican immigrant and second-generation Mexican American women. *Identities: Global Studies in Culture and Power, 13*(3), 335–362.

Wakefield, S. E., & Poland, B. (2005). Family, friend or foe? Critical reflections on the relevance and role of social capital in health promotion and community development. *Social Science and Medicine, 60*(12), 2819–2832.

Walton, M. A., Blow, F. C., & Booth, B. M. (2001). Diversity in relapse prevention needs: Gender and race comparisons among substance abuse treatment patients. *American Journal of Drug and Alcohol Abuse, 27*(2), 225–240.

Wang, M., & Holahan, J. (2003). *The decline in Medicaid use by noncitizens since welfare reform.* Washington, DC: The Urban Institute.

Wells, K., Klap, R., Koike, A., & Sherbourne, C. (2001). Ethnic disparities in unmet need for alcoholism, drug abuse and mental health care. *American Journal of Psychiatry, 158*(12), 2027–2032.

Wen, M., Cagney, K. A., & Christakis, N. A. (2005). Effect of specific aspects of community social environment on the morality of individuals diagnosed with serious illness. *Social Science and Medicine, 61*(6), 1119–1134.

Williams, R. B., & Collins, C. (1995). U.S. socioeconomic and racial differences in health: Patterns and explanations. *Annual Review of Sociology, 21,* 349–387.

Zayas, L. H., Lester, R. J., Cabassa, L. J., & Fortuna, L. R. (2005). Why do so many Latina teens attempt suicide? A conceptual model for research. *American Journal of Orthopsychiatry, 75*(2), 275–287.

Zuvekas, S., & Taliaferro, G. (2003). Pathways to access: Health insurance, the health care delivery system, and racial/ethnic disparities, 1996–1999. *Health Affairs, 22*(2), 139–153.

3

Understanding Psychopathology Among the Adult and Child Latino Population From the United States and Puerto Rico

An Epidemiologic Perspective

Glorisa Canino and Margarita Alegría

This chapter presents a literature review of the prevalence of psychiatric disorders and their associated correlates among Latino children and adults living in the United States and Puerto Rico as evidenced by psychiatric epidemiological studies; it also discusses future areas of research for this population. Psychiatric epidemiology is based on a medical model of disease and thus focuses on studying clinical disorders as ascertained by psychiatric nomenclatures such as the *Diagnostic Statistical Manual of Mental Disorders,* Fourth Edition (DSM-IV), of the American Psychiatric Association (American Psychiatric Association [APA], 1994). Thus, excluded from the review are studies that focus on symptom levels of psychopathology.

ADULT PSYCHIATRIC EPIDEMIOLOGY STUDIES

Over the past 3 decades, there have been several large, population-based epidemiologic studies examining the prevalence of psychiatric disorders among Latinos in the United States. At least eight studies have provided estimates of mental illness for Latinos: the Los Angeles Epidemiologic

Financial support for this chapter was obtained from P50 MH073469–01 (Alegría, PI) from the National Institute of Mental Health (NIMH) and from P60 MD002261–01 (Canino, PI) from the National Center for Minority Health and Health Disparities.

Catchment Area Study (LA-ECA), the Puerto Rico Epidemiologic Catchment Area Study (PR-ECA), the Hispanic Health and Nutrition Examination Survey (HHANES), the Mexican American Prevalence and Services Survey (MAPSS), the National Comorbidity Study (NCS), the National Comorbidity Survey–Replication (NCS-R), the National Epidemiological Survey on Alcohol and Related Conditions (NESARC), and the National Latino and Asian American Study (NLAAS). In what follows, we present the main findings of these studies.

The LA-ECA study (1983–1984; 68% response rate) determined the lifetime and 6-month prevalence rates of DSM-III psychiatric disorders among Mexican Americans and non-Hispanic whites 18 to 64 years of age for two Los Angeles, California, communities (Burnam, Hough, Karno, Escobar, & Telles, 1987). The total sample of 3,125 respondents included 1,243 Latinos of Mexican descent, 1,309 non-Latino whites, and 573 in the "Other" racial/ethnic category. Household interviews were conducted using the National Institute of Mental Health (NIMH) Diagnostic Interview Schedule (DIS). While the LA-ECA found that Mexican Americans and non-Latino whites had similar prevalence rates of psychiatric disorders, differences were found in the rates of substance-use disorders between these two groups. Mexican Americans had higher rates of alcohol abuse/dependence compared to non-Hispanic whites (17.3% compared to 14.8%) and lower rates of drug abuse/dependence (1.5% compared to 4.2%; Karno et al., 1987). Among the most important findings of the LA-ECA were that when Mexican Americans were separated into subgroups of Mexican born and U.S. born, the U.S.-born Mexicans had higher rates of depression and phobias than the Mexicans born in Mexico, a finding that has been termed the *immigrant paradox.* This seminal study was critical in raising awareness about the importance of studying Latino groups by nativity and thus establishing the immigrant paradox for mental health. However, data were not collected on other Latino subgroups, and although the interview was conducted in both English and Spanish, the sample was local to the Los Angeles area, restricting generalizability to the greater U.S. population and to other Latino subgroups.

The PR-ECA (1984–1987; 91% response rate) used a Spanish-language translation of the DIS in an island-wide study of Puerto Rican (N = 1,551) adults 17 to 64 years and had similar goals to the LA-ECA (Canino et al., 1987). Lifetime rates of 4.6% for major depressive episodes, 12.6% for alcohol abuse or dependence, 7.9% for affective disorders, and 13.6% for anxiety disorders were reported. The study demonstrated that with the exception of somatization, which was significantly higher on the island, the rates of overall psychiatric disorders on the island were similar to those reported for the U.S. ECA studies, particularly the rates of disorder reported for the Mexican American immigrants of the LA-ECA study (Shrout et al., 1992). In addition, *ataques de nervios* ("nerve attacks"), a cultural syndrome characterized by such symptoms as heart palpitations, crying, faintness, and seizure-like episodes, were measured for the first time in an island-wide study. The results showed that 16% of the adult population reported having experienced a nerve attack and having to seek services for it. The majority (60%) of respondents reporting an attack also met criteria for a psychiatric disorder, mostly depression or anxiety (Guarnaccia, Canino, Rubio-Stipec, & Bravo, 1993).

The MAPSS (1994–1996) utilized a stratified random sampling approach to study the prevalence of psychiatric disorders among noninstitutionalized Mexican American adults aged 18 to 59 years who were residents of Fresno County, California (Vega et al., 1998). Interviews were conducted in English and Spanish (N = 3,012; response rate 87.8% for urban areas, 92.3% for rural areas). DSM-III psychiatric disorders were ascertained with a modified version of the World Mental Health Composite International Diagnostic Interview (WMH-CIDI; World Health Organization, 1990). As in the LA-ECA study, results showed that foreign-born Mexicans experienced lower rates of any anxiety disorder than U.S.-born Mexicans (13.0% compared to 23.2%) and that being born in the United States and number of years living in the United States significantly increased lifetime use of illicit drugs for Mexican Americans. While the MAPSS was administered in both English and Spanish, the sample did not include other Latino subgroups and was restricted to one region of the country, limiting the generalizability of the findings.

The first national epidemiological survey that included a Latino sample was the NCS (1990–1992; 86% response rate; Kessler et al.,

1994). The goal of the NCS was to present data on lifetime and last-year prevalence rates of DSM-III-R disorders based on a modified version of the WMH-CIDI. The total sample for the NCS was 8,098 English-speaking respondents ages 15 to 54, including 733 Latinos. Results showed that Latinos had significantly lower risk than non-Latino whites for any anxiety, any mood, and any substance disorders. As in the LA-ECA and MAPSS studies, those born outside the United States had lower prevalence rates of any lifetime disorders than Mexicans born in the United States (Ortega, Rosenheck, Alegría, & Desai, 2000). Puerto Ricans did not differ from non-Latino whites in rates of lifetime prevalence disorders; however, the Puerto Rican sample had limited statistical power due to size (U.S. Department of Health and Human Services [USDHHS], 2001). Other investigators have posited that the lower risk of the Hispanics and other minorities found in the NCS data is attributable exclusively to differences in the lifetime risk of the disorders, since the course of illness tended to be more persistent among minorities as compared to the non-Hispanic whites (Breslau, Kendler, Su, Aguilar-Gaxiola, & Kessler, 2005).

While the NCS was designed to include a representative sample of the U.S. population, the Latino subset of the data was heterogeneous and not considered representative of specific Latino subcommunities. The prevalence estimates of psychiatric disorders from the LA-ECA and the MAPSS are considered similar, but they are lower than those from the NCS (Vega et al., 1998). Differences may be due to the lack of Spanish-language interviewing in the NCS, which may have excluded less acculturated Latinos and recent immigrants, who tend to have lower rates of psychiatric disorders.

The NCS-R (2001–2003; 70.9% response rate) had the same goals and eligibility criteria as the original NCS and was based on DSM-IV (APA, 1994) criteria (Kessler & Merikangas, 2004). The total sample size was 9,282 with 529 Latino respondents. As in the NCS, Latinos evidenced significantly lower risk of any anxiety and any depressive disorders compared to non-Latino whites. No difference was found in rates of substance-use disorders for Latinos compared to non-Latino whites (Kessler, Berglund, Demler, Jin, & Walters, 2005). The NCS-R had the same limitations as the NCS in that it did not include Spanish-speaking Latinos.

The NESARC (2000–2001; 81% response rate) is a national household survey that differs from the previously discussed surveys in that it presents nationally representative data on the prevalence of DSM-IV lifetime psychiatric disorders among English- and Spanish-speaking foreign born and U.S. born of three main Latino subgroups: Mexican Americans, Cubans, and Puerto Ricans (Grant, 1996). Non-Latino whites and African American were also included. Psychiatric disorders were ascertained with the Alcohol Use Disorder and Associated Disabilities Interview Schedule-IV (AUDADIS-IV) to respondents ages 18 and over (N = 43,093) in the populations of the United States (including Alaska and Hawaii). The Latino sample of the NESARC consisted of 4,558 respondents of Mexican descent, 450 Cubans, and 997 Puerto Ricans.

Grant and colleagues (2004) found that for Mexican Americans and non-Latino whites, foreign nativity was protective against most psychiatric disorders, with foreign-born respondents from both these groups reporting lower rates of any psychiatric disorder (any depressive, any anxiety, or any substance disorder) than their U.S.-born counterparts. However, U.S.-born Mexican Americans were at lower risk for disorder than U.S.-born non-Latino whites. Given these results, Grant and colleagues hypothesized that traditional Mexican American culture had a protective effect against psychiatric disorder.

Further analysis of the NESARC data by Alegría, Canino, Stinson, and Grant (2006) assessed the rates of disorder for Puerto Rican, Cuban American, and non-Latino whites. The prevalence rates of disorder for each of the ethnic/racial subgroups by nativity also showed that foreign nativity was protective for all groups but varied according to the assessed disorder. For non-Latino white immigrants, the protective effect was observed for most psychiatric disorders, whereas for Puerto Ricans and Cubans the protective effect was observed only for substance-use disorders. The importance of this study is that it established that the immigrant paradox did not generalize to all Latino ethnic groups or to all disorders. The advantages of this large national epidemiology study were the inclusion of the main Latino ethnic groups in greater quantity than in past surveys, the administration of the survey in both English and Spanish, and its generalizability to the Latino population of the United States. However, the NESARC did not include such important risk and protective factors of psychopathology for the Latino population as discrimination, cultural conflict, and social networks, which were included in the NLAAS survey.

The NLAAS (2000–2003; Alegría, Takeuchi, et al., 2004), a national household survey, was designed with a special emphasis on two ethnic minority groups: Latinos and Asian Americans living in the United States. Latino respondents (Mexican, N = 868; Cuban, N = 577; Puerto Rican, N = 495; Other Latino, N = 614) 18 years or older living in the coterminous United States or Hawaii were interviewed. All diagnoses were based on criteria of the DSM-IV ascertained by the WMH-CIDI administered in either English or Spanish (75% response rate).

An important contribution of the NLAAS study was the comparison of lifetime rates of disorder by Latino subgroup (Alegría, Mulvaney-Day, et al., 2007). Age- and gender-adjusted rates for any lifetime psychiatric disorder category showed significant differences in prevalence among Puerto Ricans (37.4%), Mexicans (29.5%), Cubans (28.2%), and Other Latinos (27.0%). Rates for any lifetime depressive disorder were not found to be statistically significant, but rates for any lifetime anxiety disorder were significantly different by subgroup, ranging from 21.7% for Puerto Ricans, 15.5% for Mexicans, 14.4% for Cubans, and 14.1% for Other Latinos. For any substance disorder, the prevalence estimates were significantly different for Puerto Ricans (13.8%), Mexicans (11.8%), Other Latinos (9.8%), and Cubans (6.6%). Puerto Ricans consistently showed higher rates of disorder, sometimes approaching the rates for the non-Latino white sample.

Another major contribution of the NLAAS study was the comparison of lifetime rates of disorders among the Latino population of the United States with that of the non-Latino white population of the NCS-R, since the same instruments and similar methods were used in both studies (Alegría et al., 2008). The results showed that after adjusting for age and gender, Latinos reported statistically significant lower rates for all disorder categories, compared to non-Latino whites. As in the NESARC and MAPPS studies, the NLAAS study also showed evidence of the immigrant paradox. After adjusting for age, gender, and socioeconomic status (SES), U.S.-born

Latinos were at significantly higher risk than immigrant Latinos for all lifetime disorders. When comparing U.S.-born non-Latino whites to U.S.-born Latinos, U.S.-born non-Latino whites reported higher rates for disorders.

The next step toward understanding the immigrant paradox was to stratify the Latino subgroups by nativity (Alegría et al., 2008). The age-, gender-, and SES-adjusted rates of disorder for the aggregate disorder categories, when stratified by nativity, revealed within-group differences. In the any psychiatric disorder category, a significant difference between U.S.-born and foreign-born Mexicans (39.2% vs. 23.9%) and U.S.-born and foreign-born Other Latinos (31.4% vs. 24.2%) was found. In the any depressive disorder category, only the U.S.-born and foreign-born Mexicans exhibited a significant difference (20.4% vs. 12.9%). This trend continued for the any anxiety disorder category, with U.S.-born Mexicans reporting 20.0% prevalence and foreign-born Mexicans, 14.2%. Lastly, the most striking results were reported in the any substance abuse disorder category. In this case, three of the four subgroups (Cubans, Mexicans, and Other Latinos) reported a significant difference in rates of disorder between U.S.-born respondents and foreign-born respondents, but U.S.-born Puerto Ricans were not significantly different from their island-born counterparts (15.9% vs. 11.1%). Thus, these results showed that the immigrant paradox holds true for some Latino groups (e.g., Mexicans) but not others (e.g., Puerto Ricans) and that the protection against psychiatric disorder observed in immigrants varies by specific disorder. Similar results were reported in the NESARC study (Alegría et al., 2006), suggesting that other factors besides nativity play a role in the likelihood of psychiatric disorders for Latinos.

An important contribution of the NLAAS that differed from the other epidemiologic studies was the inclusion of important protective or risk factors associated with psychiatric disorders specifically related to the Latino culture. Family support factors were associated with decreased likelihood of suicide attempts and ideation in the Latino population (Fortuna, Perez, Canino, Sribney, & Alegría, 2007). The generational status of the respondents or that of their families, the immigration experience, time in the United States, and the context of entry into the United States differed dramatically across and within

Latino subethnic groups and were differentially associated with the risk of psychiatric disorder. For example, the longer Latino immigrants remain in their country of origin, the lower their risk of psychiatric disorders, leading to lower lifetime rates of disorder (Alegría, Sribney, et al., 2007). Most of this lower risk for psychiatric illness is due to low risk in the country of origin, suggesting that protective familial and cultural values are most salient while in the country of origin and may lose their benefit following immigration to the United States. Thus, once an immigrant arrives in the United States, the risk of onset appears similar to that of U.S.-born Latinos of the same age, probably as a result of the erosion of these protective factors.

Given that Latino subgroups experience unique migratory patterns and social histories that often produce widely varying acculturation experiences, it is difficult to assess the relationship between mental health and acculturation for Latinos as an aggregate group (Guarnaccia et al., 2007). The NLAAS chose to measure the complex process of acculturation with a proxy variable related to language proficiency or the respondent's ability to speak, read, and write in English. Cultural stress was measured with the Family Cultural Conflict Scale. The results showed widely varying experiences of cultural stress among the Latino groups, with Mexicans reporting the highest acculturative distress and Puerto Ricans the lowest. However, Puerto Ricans also reported the highest level of family cultural conflict in this study, which has been shown to increase risk for mental disorders (Guarnaccia et al., 2007). The importance of more discretely considering this variability in measurement of acculturation is only beginning to become clear in recent research, due to limited sample sizes and subethnic composition in previous psychiatric epidemiologic studies (Alegría, Vila, et al., 2004).

Other analyses of the NLAAS showed that U.S.-born Latinos across all subgroups reported higher levels of perceived discrimination than immigrant Latinos (Perez, Fortuna, & Alegría, in press). It is possible that as immigrants assimilate over time and by generations, they may lose their idealized view of the United States and may have higher expectations for fair treatment. Furthermore, in the NLAAS sample as a whole, Latinos with higher education were more likely to report everyday discrimination, and higher levels of ethnic identity were associated with lower perceived discrimination. Given that other research (Finch, Kolody, & Vega, 2000) found that perceived discrimination was also related to depression, these relationships may play a role in the protective effect of low socioeconomic status found in some studies.

The NLAAS data showed elevated rates of any 12-month psychiatric disorder for Puerto Rican males and females, compared to other Latino subgroups (Alegría, Mulvaney-Day, et al., 2007), but the mechanisms involved in increasing the risk for psychiatric disorders of Puerto Ricans are not known. Although there have been suggestions that reverse selection bias (e.g., sicker Puerto Ricans come to the mainland for better health services) may explain these differences, current data do not support such an assumption. Future studies that contrast Puerto Ricans on the island with those on the mainland might facilitate a better understanding of the pathways for increased mental health risk, particularly if they focus on the role that perceived discrimination, relative poverty, and limited social opportunities might play.

The NLAAS data confirmed the results of many other studies that showed Latino immigrant women consistently reporting a lower rate of substance-use disorders than the U.S. born (Canino, Vega, Sribney, Warner, & Alegría, 2008). This could be due to strong cultural norms against alcohol and drug use, as well as proscribed gender roles (i.e., early marriage and pregnancy). It would be important for future research to disentangle what appears to be a normative behavior from a resilient trait, in order to affect intervention development. The same is true for the protective effect of foreign parental nativity against psychopathology. Foreign parental nativity could possibly be interpreted as a factor that enhances one's chances of retaining family ties, which diminish distress and reinstate equilibrium in the event of adversity. Future studies are needed to understand these possible intergenerational effects on health outcomes.

Findings indicate that Latino immigrants have lower risk of onset for some psychiatric disorders in their country of origin but similar risks to U.S.-born Latinos of the same age once in the United States. What do immigrants experience that rapidly changes their risk for psychiatric disorders? Conducting studies in different contexts might allow us to see how environmental factors interact with genetic or social vulnerabilities to augment the risk for mental illness.

CHILD PSYCHIATRIC EPIDEMIOLOGY STUDIES

At present, there are no psychiatric epidemiology studies of the child and adolescent (from now on referred to as *child*) population of the United States. The only psychiatric epidemiology data that can be generalized to the United States were focused on adolescents only and included a small number of adolescent Latinos as part of the National Comorbidity Survey Revised (NCS-R; Kessler & Merikangas, 2004), but the study has not been published. The only population-based studies of children identified in the United States that have included a sufficient number of Latinos were three studies carried out in Puerto Rico (Bird, Canino, Rubio-Stipec, & Ribera, 1987; Canino et al., 2004; Bird, Canino, et al., 2006), two in Texas (Roberts, Roberts, & Chen, 1997; Roberts, Roberts, & Xing, 2007a), and one in four urban areas of the United States, including Puerto Rico (Lahey et al., 1996). In what follows, we present the main findings of these studies.

The first psychiatric epidemiology study in Puerto Rico (1985–1987) used a probability sample of the population 4 to 17 years (N = 777; 92% response rate; Bird et al., 1987). The survey used the Child Behavior Checklist (CBCL; Achenbach & Edelbrock, 1983) as a screening instrument for determining emotional and behavioral problems, and those above the published cutoff in the CBCL were evaluated in a second stage by board-certified, indigenous child psychiatrists who used the parent and child versions of the Diagnostic Interview Schedule for Children (DISC) to structure the interview. Prevalence rates of psychiatric disorders were based on the clinical judgment of these clinicians, which in turn were based on the DSM-III and the administration of an impairment scale called the Child Global Assessment Scale (C-GAS; Bird et al., 1990).

The results of this island-wide survey showed that 49.5% of the population met DSM-III criteria if impairment in functioning was not considered. However, further analyses of the data showed that many children who met criteria for a diagnosis were functioning within the normal range (Bird et al., 1988, 1990). Prevalence rates fell to 17% when moderate to severe impairment was required for the definition of a case. The results of this study (and later on, the replication of these results in the next study carried out on the island) demonstrated the overinclusiveness of the DSM for classifying children and the need to revise the psychiatric nomenclature to include impairment in functioning as an important criterion for most child disorders (Canino, Costello, & Angold, 1999).

Other important findings from this study were that the correlates of disorder were similar in Puerto Rico to other international studies (Bird, Gould, Yager, Staghezza, & Canino, 1989), and that although the rates of specific disorders were similar to those obtained in other international studies, the rates of conduct disorder (1.5%) were significantly lower than in other studies, in which the prevalence was from 5% to 7% approximately (see Bauermeister, Canino, & Bird, 1994, for review). The main limitation of the study was that it referred only to island Puerto Ricans.

In the 1990s, a cross-sectional, probabilistic, population-based study of psychiatric disorders in children was carried out in San Juan, Puerto Rico (N = 312) and at three other sites in the United States: Chester County, New York (N = 360); New Haven, Connecticut (N = 314); and Emory, Georgia (N = 299), with children 9 to 17 years of age. The Methods for the Epidemiology of Child and Adolescents (MECA) had as its main goal the development of methods and instrumentation for a subsequent child epidemiological study, to be carried out in the United States and its territories (Lahey et al., 1996). The study provided a comparison of prevalence rates across different communities, since the same methods and instrumentation were used in this multi-site study. The results confirmed those obtained in the first island-wide survey (Bird et al., 1988), as the rates of DISC-ascertained DSM-III-R psychiatric disorder in all sites were very high (around 49%), and impairment in functioning needed to be added to the definition of a case in order to identify definite cases (Shaffer et al., 1996). As a result of these findings, the DSM-IV incorporated into most child psychiatric disorders an additional criterion that required the child to be impaired in functioning at school, in the family, or with peers. In addition, although the overall prevalence rate of disorders was similar across the different ethnic groups at the four sites, the rates of conduct disorder and antisocial behaviors were significantly lower in the San Juan, Puerto Rico, children (Bird et al., 2001). When the correlates of these conditions were compared across sites and ethnic groups, the results showed that the lower prevalence of conduct and oppositional disorders, as well as antisocial behaviors, found in San Juan were related to better family relations on the island as compared to the mainland Hispanic, African American, and non-Latino children at the other U.S. sites (Bird et al., 2001). Because the study was cross sectional, causality could not be established, but the findings suggested that in Puerto Rico, as in other Hispanic settings, close family attachments are fostered and seem to be protective against antisocial behaviors and disruptive behavior disorders in children.

The third Child Psychiatric Epidemiology and Mental Health Service Utilization Study in Puerto Rico (1999–2004) used two samples, one island-wide representative sample of children 4 to 17 years of age (N = 1,897; 90% response rate) and another of all children receiving mental health services in the public sector (N = 751; 71% response rate). The results of this study showed that 16.4% of the population met criteria for a DISC-ascertained DSM-IV disorder and that 6.9% were severely emotionally disturbed (SED), as evidenced by meeting criteria for any disorder and for substantial impairment in functioning (C-GAS < 69; Canino et al., 2004). Once more, the rates of conduct disorder were found to be very low in the population (1.4%), as were those of substance abuse/dependence (1.7%), compared to another DSM-IV epidemiologic survey conducted in the Great Smoky Mountains of South Carolina (Angold et al., 2002). Although this South Carolina study did not use the same instrument to assess psychiatric disorder, and the age range of the study was not the same, when special analyses were performed to equate the population age ranges, the results showed overall rates of disorder very similar to those found in the Puerto Rico study (17.7% in South Carolina and 17.3% in Puerto Rico; Canino et al., 2004). When comparative analyses were done between the rates of adolescent depression in Puerto Rico and another study in Australia that used the same instrument and time frame, the rates of last-year major depressive disorder in Puerto Rico (5.8%) did

not differ significantly from that study (4%; Costello, Foley, & Angold, 2006). Rates for children below the age of 13 (2.1%) did not differ either from those of either Australia (2.3%) or Germany (3.0%; Costello et al., 2006).

As found with the adult population, *ataques de nervios* were fairly common among Puerto Rican children and adolescents from the community (9%) and among children receiving mental health services (26%); these children were more likely to meet criteria for psychiatric disorders and impairment, compared to children without *ataques* (Guarnaccia, Martinez, Ramirez, & Canino, 2005). Like the results of other surveys, the results of the study showed attention-deficit disorder with hyperactivity (ADHD) and oppositional defiant disorder (ODD) to be the most prevalent disorders, and many of the expected correlates for most psychiatric disorders were also found (Bauermeister, Shrout, Chavez, et al., 2007; Bauermeister, Shrout, Ramirez, et al., 2007; Canino et al., 2004). However, unlike most other studies of mental disorders among children (Brooks-Gunn & Duncan, 1997; Costello, Keeler, & Angold, 2001) but like studies that involved mostly poor populations of African American and American Indian children (Costello, Farmer, Angold, Burns, & Erkanli, 1997), no association was found between rates of disorder and poverty, including relative or absolute poverty. When actual income was substituted for perception of poverty, disruptive behavior disorders, ADHD, and ODD were more frequently found among those who reported that they lived poorly. The findings suggested that absolute or relative poverty may not be the most appropriate indicator to use in populations where most people have low incomes. Further development of measures of perception of poverty or the use of measures of social capital that assess community resources may be more fruitful.

Other important results of this study showed that only 7% of children meeting criteria for ADHD were using stimulant medication in the community sample (Bauermeister et al., 2003). When comparing the use of stimulants in children who met criteria for ADHD and ADHD not otherwise specified (NOS) between Puerto Rican children in treatment and similar children in San Diego, the rates of stimulant use were also very low at both sites (for ADHD children, 32.9% in Puerto Rico and 38.8% in San Diego;

and for ADHD NOS, 20.2% in Puerto Rico and 17.8% in San Diego; Leslie et al., 2005). Despite demographic and cultural differences between the sites, the data were very similar, suggesting that stimulants were not overused in any of the public mental health sectors.

The fourth and last child psychiatric epidemiology study carried out in Puerto Rico (2000–2005) was motivated by the consistent finding in prior epidemiological studies that Puerto Rican children, compared to other ethnic groups or children from other international sites, had lower rates of conduct disorder (CD) and other behavior disruptive disorders (DBD) as well as antisocial behavior problems (ASB; Bird et al., 1988, 2001; Canino et al., 2004). It was hypothesized that important contextual and cultural factors would be related to the lower rates of these conditions among island children.

The study included two probability community samples of children 5 to 13 years of age (N = 2,491) from San Juan, Puerto Rico, and the South Bronx, New York (Bird, Davies, et al., 2006). The initial baseline results showed no significant age or site differences among males in the rates of DBD, but rates among females increased with age in the South Bronx and decreased with age in Puerto Rico. Multiple regression analyses showed that lack of parental warmth and approval, poor peer relationships, parental substance abuse, and parental report of aggressive behavior during the toddler years were the most significant correlates of DBD at both sites.

Because the investigators wanted to examine the precursors of DBD with longitudinal analyses, they developed scales of ASB that distinguished levels of ASB by severity, frequency of occurrence, and presence of multiple ASBs (Bird et al., 2005). Analyses of the 3-year longitudinal trajectories of DBD and ASB showed no difference at baseline for the overall levels of ASB and DBD in both samples (except for the females in the South Bronx, who showed an increase with age; Bird et al., 2007). However, with time ASB and DBD rates remained relatively the same in the South Bronx for both boys and girls and in both the younger and older age groups, yet in San Juan the rates decreased for both age groups and gender. At both sites, boys had higher rates of ASB and DBD. The decreased risk over time of ASB and DBD in Puerto Rico and not in the South Bronx seemed to be due to higher rates of risk factors of psychopathology in the South Bronx.

This same study examined the relationship between acculturation levels and acculturative stress of parent and child with ASB and internalizing symptoms (symptoms of depression and anxiety; Duarte et al., 2008). Acculturation, in this study, was defined as changes resulting from direct and continuous contact of individuals with a culture different from their own (Redfield, Linton, & Herskovits, 1936). It was measured with the Cultural Life Style Inventory (CLSI; Mendoza, 1989; Magaña, De la Rocha, Amsel, & Magaña, 1996), a multidimensional scale that assesses language preference, ethnic origin and pride, and preference for cultural activities. Acculturative stress was defined as the degree to which individuals become distressed by pressures to adapt to cultural norms and values other than their own. Cultural stress was measured using a scale derived from the Hispanic Stress Inventory (Cervantes, Padilla, Amado, & Salgado de Snyder, 1990) that taps different aspects of stress associated with the thrust toward acculturation. The results indicated that youth acculturation level was not significantly associated with ASB or internalizing symptoms, whereas parent acculturation was significantly associated with the youth ASB across the three waves but not with internalizing symptoms. On the other hand, youth acculturative stress in both sites was positively associated with ASB and internalizing symptoms at baseline, but in Puerto Rico ASB was associated with internalizing symptoms only 1 year after baseline. Parental acculturative stress was associated with the child outcomes at both sites and in the three waves. The results of these analyses suggested that it is not necessarily the level of involvement with another culture that might be associated with psychopathology in youth but the extent to which this involvement is experienced as distressing, and that this may vary over time and developmental stage in youth.

The Houston School Study included a representative sample (N = 5,496) of children 10 to 17 years of age from grades 6 to 8 from a school district. Major depressive disorder was ascertained with the DSM Scale for Depression (DSD), a self-administered checklist developed from the DISC-IV module of major depressive disorder (MDD) and based on DSM-IV (Roberts et al., 1997). This was the first study to ascertain major depression among adolescents from different ethnic groups in the United

States; all previous comparative studies had reported depressive symptoms and not clinical depression. Odds ratios for crude prevalence rates of MDD with and without impairment and adjusted for the effects of age, sex, and SES were presented. The results of the adjusted odds ratios showed elevated risk for MDD with and without impairment only for the Mexican American students (6.6%), compared with nine other ethnic groups. Girls and students who reported that their economic circumstances were somewhat or much worse than others also had significantly higher prevalence rates of MDD. Interaction analyses between ethnicity (European Americans, Mexican Americans, and African Americans) and SES were nonsignificant.

If the rate of 6.6% of MDD is compared with similar studies reported from Puerto Rico (5.6%) and Australia (4%), the rates among Mexican American adolescents are higher (Costello, Erkanli, & Angold, 2006). Unfortunately, confidence intervals were not reported for any of these rates, so it is not possible to ascertain whether the differences across studies are comparable or significantly different. The question that remains to be answered is why Mexican American youth have elevated risk for major depressive disorder as compared to other ethnic minority groups living in the United States. Roberts and colleagues (1997) suggest that the higher rates of MDD may be related to fatalistic attitudes and beliefs in external control common among persons of Mexican heritage. The stresses associated with acculturation and minority status were not analyzed in this study, although there is no reason to think that Mexican American youth would be subjected to more stress, compared to other minority youth living in the United States.

The Houston Household Survey measured DSM-IV psychiatric disorders in adolescents 11 to 17 years of age ascertained by the DISC-IV in a random sample of households from the Houston metropolitan area enrolled in local health maintenance organizations (HMOs). The study oversampled Mexican American (MA) and African American (AA) youth to ensure their representation in the sample (N = 4,175). The results showed that after adjusting for impairment, MA and AA had higher rates of anxiety disorders but not MDD, in which the European Americans (EA) had higher rates. For substance-use disorders, both the EA and the MA had higher rates than the AA. Overall, the

rates of any last-year DSM-IV disorder fluctuated from a lower bound of 7.4% to a higher bound of 13.7% in the three groups. However, when adjustments were made for gender, age, and SES, the results showed greater risk of psychiatric disorders for EA adolescents as compared to the two minority groups. As found in the Puerto Rico survey (Canino et al., 2004), as well as other surveys of low-income minority youth carried out in South Carolina (Angold et al., 2002; Costello et al., 1997), low income was not found to be a significant predictor of psychiatric disorders for either AA or MA youth. Other results of the same study showed that after adjustment for sex, gender, and SES, no differences in the rates of suicidal behaviors were observed among the three ethnic groups (Roberts, Roberts, & Xing, 2007b).

In an attempt to interpret these findings, Roberts and colleagues (2007b) compared the results of their study to a review of several studies (Costello, Angold, March, & Fairbank, 1998) that had compared rates of disorders between EA and AA and had stated no clear differences between ethnic groups once the rates were adjusted. However, it was interesting that no comparison was made between the results of this study and the previous school survey that had found MDD to be significantly higher among MA students even after adjusting for confounders (Roberts et al., 1997). It is possible that the differences in results may be related to the sample composition of both studies. The school sample is possibly more representative of MA youth, many of whom are low income or illegal and may not have been enrolled in HMOs.

The epidemiology studies carried out on the island of Puerto Rico and in various communities of the United States made several contributions to the field of child psychiatric epidemiology. The results of the first epidemiology study carried out on the island (Bird et al., 1987), as well as the MECA study (Lahey et al., 1996), demonstrated the overinclusiveness of the DSM for classifying children and the need to revise the psychiatric nomenclature to include impairment in functioning as an important criterion for most child disorders. In both studies, the rates of psychiatric disorder without impairment reached half of the population, but when impairment in functioning was considered in the definition, the rates fell to around 16% to 17% of the population. As a result of these studies, an important criterion for almost all DSM-IV disorders was added: The symptoms of the disorder must cause significant impairment in functioning. Another important contribution of these child studies was brought forth by the studies carried out in Texas, where the rates of disorder were compared across different racial/ethnic groups. These studies showed the importance of comparing with non-Latino whites while at the same time controlling for income or education. It is only by comparing with the non-Latino white majority population that we can determine the cultural influence in the manifestation of disorders.

Future child psychiatric epidemiology studies need to include other Latino subethnic groups in the United States. The data so far have compared MA children with other non-Latino ethnic groups, and it seems that MA adolescents have higher rates of MDD as compared to other groups. It is still not clear whether socioeconomic income is an explanation for these findings, because the data so far are equivocal. Several questions need to be answered: Do MA youth experience unique stress exposure or vulnerability not present in other minority groups? Are Mexican American youth truly at higher risk, or is this a sampling problem related to the region or sample of the United States in which the study was carried out? If they are at higher risk, what are some of the factors implicated in these risks, and what can be done to ameliorate them? The longitudinal data from Puerto Rico suggest the importance of protective familial factors in lowering the risk for externalizing disorders in children. The next step in research is to examine the ways in which this kind of information can be used for developing prevention and intervention strategies for populations at risk.

CONCLUSIONS

Most of the adult psychiatric epidemiology studies showed that overall, after adjusting for sociodemographic factors, Latinos in the United States seem to be at lower risk for most psychiatric disorders, compared to their U.S. counterparts. Puerto Ricans seem to be at greater risk for most disorders than any other Latino ethnic group, and the mechanisms involved for explaining this higher risk are unknown. Most studies also showed the existence of the immigrant paradox, whereby psychiatric disorders seem to be more prevalent among Latinos born in the United States, compared to those born in their countries of origin. However, the paradox was not observed in all Latino subgroups (e.g., Puerto Ricans) or for all specific psychiatric disorders. The risk for psychiatric disorder also seemed to vary according to the age of immigration and the time spent in the country of origin before immigration. The longer time spent in the country of origin, the lower the risk for disorders, which suggests the protective effect of traditional Latino values.

The child psychiatric epidemiology studies were fewer than the adult studies, but like the adult studies, they revealed the higher risk of certain disorders and behaviors (DBD and ASB) among children living in the United States, compared with those living in their country of origin. These studies also revealed that children on the island of Puerto Rico had significantly fewer risk factors and more protective factors than those on the mainland. Of interest was the finding that the level of involvement with the host culture (or level of acculturation) did not seem to be as closely related to DBD and ASB as the perceived stress associated with the process of acculturation. Although island and mainland differences were observed in the rates of DBD and ASB, no differences in rates of disorder were observed for other disorders in all of the studies quoted, but the explanation of this fact remains elusive. The Texas studies revealed that Mexican American youth seem to be at higher risk for MDD than any other disorder, but the reasons for this observation need to be further investigated. We hope that with the publication of the NCS-R adolescent survey in the near future, some of these questions can be better elucidated.

FUTURE STUDIES

Most of the adult and child studies were carried out by investigators indigenous to the culture studied, who ascertained psychiatric disorders with well-known, state-of-the-art instruments that were translated and tested with systematic methods geared to achieving cultural equivalence. However, all studies reviewed relied solely on self-report measures and evaluated mostly psychosocial correlates or risk factors. Yet, there is extensive evidence that environmental risk includes varying degrees of genetic mediation, indicating gene environment interactions (Carbonneau, Eaves, Silberg, Simonoff, & Rutter, 2002; Rutter, Pickles, Murray, & Eaves, 2001). A great many of the environmental risk factors of child and adult psychopathology involve some form of social interaction (e.g., divorce, family dysfunction, lack of social support) in which a person's own behavior plays an important role in the risk feature, and this behavior is subject to genetic influences (Rutter, 2000). There is a need for future studies of Latino populations that include designs that integrate molecular genetics and its interaction with environmental risk. In addition, of all the studies reviewed, only one (Bird, Canino, et al., 2006) included a three-wave design that permitted the analyses of developmental pathways or trajectories of psychopathology. Also needed are more longitudinal studies that examine gene-environment interactions within a developmental epidemiology design that examines how the trajectories of symptoms, environment, individual development, and genetics intertwine to produce psychopathology (Costello et al., 2006). Only with this type of design will we begin to answer the questions that remain regarding the role of culture in shaping psychopathology.

REFERENCES

Achenbach, T. M., & Edelbrock, C. (1983). *Manual for the child behavior checklist and revised child behavior profile.* Burlington: Department of Psychiatry, University of Vermont.

Alegría, M., Canino, G., Shrout, P. E., Woo, M., Duan, N., Vila, D., et al. (2008). Prevalence of mental illness in immigrant and non-immigrant U.S. Latino groups. *Am J Psychiatry, 165*(3), 359–369.

Alegría, M., Canino, G., Stinson, F. S., & Grant, B. F. (2006). Nativity and DSM-IV psychiatric disorders among Puerto Ricans, Cuban Americans, and non-Latino Whites in the United States: Results from the National Epidemiologic Survey on Alcohol and Related Conditions. *J Clin Psychiatry, 67*(1), 56–65.

Alegría, M., Mulvaney-Day, N., Torres, M., Polo, A., Cao, Z., & Canino, G. (2007). Prevalence of psychiatric disorders across Latino subgroups in the United States. *Am J Public Health, 97*(1), 68–75.

Alegría, M., Sribney, W., Woo, M., Guarnaccia, P., & Torres, M. (2007). Looking beyond nativity: The relation of age of immigration, length of residence, and birth cohorts to the risk of onset of psychiatric disorders for Latinos. *Res Human Develop, 4*(1&2), 19–47.

Alegría, M., Takeuchi, D., Canino, G., Duan, N., Shrout, P., Meng, X.-L., et al. (2004). Considering context, place and culture: The National Latino and Asian American Study. *Int J Methods Psychiatr Res, 13*(4), 208–220.

Alegría, M., Vila, D., Woo, M., Canino, G., Takeuchi, D., Vera, M., et al. (2004). Cultural relevance and equivalence in the NLAAS instrument: Integrating etic and emic in the development of cross-cultural measures for a psychiatric epidemiology and services study of Latinos. *Int J Methods Psychiatr Res, 13*(4), 270–288.

American Psychiatric Association (APA). (1994). *Diagnostic and statistical manual of mental disorders* (4th ed.). Washington, DC: Author.

Angold, A., Erkanli, A., Farmer, E. M., Fairbank, J. A., Burns, B. J., Keeler, G., et al. (2002). Psychiatric disorder, impairment, and service use in rural African American and white youth. *Arch Gen Psychiatry, 59*(10), 893–901.

Bauermeister, J. J., Canino, G., & Bird, H. (1994). Epidemiology of disruptive behavior disorders. In L. L. Greenhill (Ed.), *Child and adolescent psychiatry clinics of North America* (pp. 177–194). Philadelphia: Saunders.

Bauermeister, J. J., Canino, G., Bravo, M., Ramirez, R., Jensen, P. S., Chavez, L., et al. (2003). Stimulant and psychosocial treatment of ADHD in Latino/Hispanic children. *J Am Acad Child Adolesc Psychiatry, 42*(7), 851–855.

Bauermeister, J. J., Shrout, P. E., Chavez, L., Rubio-Stipec, M., Ramirez, R., Padilla, L., et al. (2007). ADHD and gender: Are risks and sequela of ADHD the same for boys and girls? *J Child Psychol Psychiatry, 48*(8), 831–839.

Bauermeister, J. J., Shrout, P. E., Ramirez, R., Bravo, M., Alegría, M., Martinez-Taboas, A., et al. (2007). ADHD correlates, comorbidity, and impairment in community and treated samples of children and adolescents. *J Abnorm Child Psychol, 35*(6), 883–898.

Bird, H. R., Canino, G. J., Davies, M., Duarte, C. S., Febo, V., Ramirez, R., et al. (2006). A study of disruptive behavior disorders in Puerto Rican youth: I. Background, design, and survey methods. *J Am Acad Child Adolesc Psychiatry, 45*(9), 1032–1041.

Bird, H. R., Canino, G. J., Davies, M., Ramirez, R., Chavez, L., Duarte, C., et al. (2005). The Brief Impairment Scale (BIS): A multidimensional scale of functional impairment for children and adolescents. *J Am Acad Child Adolesc Psychiatry, 44*(7), 699–707.

Bird, H. R., Canino, G. J., Davies, M., Zhang, H., Ramirez, R., & Lahey, B. B. (2001). Prevalence and correlates of antisocial behaviors among three ethnic groups. *J Abnorm Child Psychol, 29*(6), 465–478.

Bird, H. R., Canino, G., Rubio-Stipec, M., Gould, M. S., Ribera, J. C., Sesman, M., et al. (1988). Estimates of the prevalence of childhood maladjustment in a community survey in Puerto Rico. *Arch Gen Psychiatry, 45,* 1120–1126.

Bird, H. R., Canino, G., Rubio-Stipec, M., & Ribera, J. C. (1987). Further measures of the psychometric properties of the Children's Global Assessment Scale. *Arch Gen Psychiatry, 44*(9), 821–824.

Bird, H. R., Davies, M., Duarte, C. S., Shen, S., Loeber, R., & Canino, G. J. (2006). A study of disruptive behavior disorders in Puerto Rican youth: II. Baseline prevalence, comorbidity, and correlates in two sites. *J Am Acad Child Adolesc Psychiatry, 45*(9), 1042–1053.

Bird, H. R., Gould, M. S., Yager, T., Staghezza, B., & Canino, G. (1989). Risk factors for maladjustment in Puerto Rican children. *J Am Acad Child Adolesc Psychiatry, 28*(6), 847–850.

Bird, H. R., Shrout, P. E., Davies, M., Canino, G., Duarte, C. S., Shen, S., et al. (2007). Longitudinal development of antisocial behaviors in young and early adolescent Puerto Rican children at two sites. *J Am Acad Child Adolesc Psychiatry, 46*(1), 5–14.

Bird, H. R., Yager, T. J., Staghezza, B., Gould, M. S., Canino, G., & Rubio-Stipec, M. (1990). Impairment in the epidemiological measurement of childhood psychopathology in the community. *J Am Acad Child Adolesc Psychiatry, 29*(5), 796–803.

Breslau, J., Kendler, K. S., Su, M., Aguilar-Gaxiola, S., & Kessler, R. C. (2005). Lifetime risk and persistence of psychiatric disorders across ethnic groups in the United States. *Psychol Med, 35,* 317–327.

Brooks-Gunn, J., & Duncan, G. J. (1997). The effects of poverty on children. *The Future of Children: Children and Poverty, 7*(2), 55–71.

Burnam, M., Hough, R., Karno, M., Escobar, J., & Telles, C. (1987). Acculturation and lifetime prevalence of psychiatric disorders among Mexican Americans in Los Angeles. *J Health Soc Behav, 28*(1), 89–102.

Canino, G., Costello, E. J., & Angold, A. (1999). Assessing functional impairment and social adaptation for child mental health services research: A review of measures. *Ment Health Serv Res, 1*(2), 93–108.

Canino, G., Shrout, P. E., Rubio-Stipec, M., Bird, H. R., Bravo, M., Ramirez, R., et al. (2004). The DSM-IV rates of child and adolescent disorders in Puerto Rico: Prevalence, correlates, service use, and the effects of impairment. *Arch Gen Psychiatry, 61*(1), 85–93.

Canino, G., Vega, W. A., Sribney, W. M., Warner, L. A., & Alegría, M. (2008). Social relationships, social assimilation, and substance use disorder among adult Latinos in the US. *J Drug Issues, 38*(1), 69–102.

Canino, G. J., Bird, H. R., Shrout, P. E., Rubio-Stipec, M., Bravo, M., Martinez, R., et al. (1987). The prevalence of specific psychiatric disorders in Puerto Rico. *Arch Gen Psychiatry, 44*(8), 727–735.

Carbonneau, R., Eaves, L. J., Silberg, J. L., Simonoff, E., & Rutter, M. (2002). Assessment of the within-family environment in twins: Absolute versus differential ratings, and relationship with conduct problems. *J Child Psychol Psychiatry, 43*(8), 1064–1074.

Cervantes, R. C., Padilla, A. M., Amado, M., & Salgado de Snyder, N. (1990). Reliability and validity of the Hispanic Stress Inventory. *Hispanic J Beh Scs, 12,* 76–82.

Costello, E. J., Angold, A., March, J., & Fairbank, J. (1998). Life events and post-traumatic stress: The development of a new measure for children and adolescents. *Psychol Med, 28*(6), 1275–1288.

Costello, E. J., Erkanli, A., & Angold, A. (2006). Is there an epidemic of child or adolescent depression? *J Child Psychol Psychiatry, 47,* 1263–1271.

Costello, E. J., Farmer, E. M., Angold, A., Burns, B. J., & Erkanli, A. (1997). Psychiatric disorders among American Indian and white youth in Appalachia: The Great Smoky Mountains Study. *Am J Public Health, 87*(5), 827–832.

Costello, E. J., Foley, D. L., & Angold, A. (2006). 10-year research update review: The epidemiology of child and adolescent psychiatric disorders: II. Developmental epidemiology. *J Am Acad Child Adolesc Psychiatry, 45*(1), 8–25.

Costello, E. J., Keeler, G. P., & Angold, A. (2001). Poverty, race/ethnicity, and psychiatric disorder: A study of rural children. *Am J Public Health, 91*(9), 1494–1498.

Duarte, C., Bird, H., Shrout, P., Wu, P., Lewis-Fernandez, R., Shen, S., et al. (2008). Context, culture and psychiatric symptoms in children: Longitudinal results from one Latino population at two sites. *J Child Psychol Psychiatry, 49*(5), 563–572.

Finch, B., Kolody, B., & Vega, W. (2000). Perceived discrimination and depression among Mexican-origin adults in California. *J Health Soc Behv, 41,* 295–313.

Fortuna, L., Perez, D. J., Canino, G., Sribney, W. M., & Alegría, M. (2007). Prevalence and correlates of lifetime suicidal ideation and attempts among Latino subgroups in the United States. *J Clin Psychiatry, 68*(4), 572–581.

Grant, B. (1996). Prevalence and correlates of drug use and DSM-IV drug dependence in the United States: Results of the National Longitudinal Alcohol Epidemiologic Survey. *J Substance Abuse, 8*(2), 195–210.

Grant, B. F., Stinson, F., Hasin, D., Dawson, D., Chou, S., & Anderson, K. (2004). Immigration and lifetime prevalence of DSM-IV psychiatric disorders among Mexican Americans and non-Hispanic Whites in the United States. *Arch Gen Psychiatry, 61,* 1226–1233.

Guarnaccia, P. J., Canino, G., Rubio-Stipec, M., & Bravo, M. (1993). The prevalence of ataques de nervios in the Puerto Rican disaster study. *J Nerv Ment Dis, 181*(3), 157–165.

Guarnaccia, P. J., Martinez, I., Ramirez, R., & Canino, G. (2005). Are ataques de nervios in Puerto Rican children associated with psychiatric disorder? *J Am Acad Child Adolesc Psychiatry, 44*(11), 1184–1192.

Guarnaccia, P. J., Martinez-Pincay, I., Alegría, M., Shrout, P., Lewis-Fernandez, R., & Canino, G. (2007). Assessing diversity among Latinos: Results from the NLAAS. *Hispanic J Behav Sci, 29*(4), 510–534.

Karno, M., Hough, R., Burnam, M., Escobar, J., Timbers, D., Santana, F., et al. (1987). Lifetime prevalence of specific psychiatric disorders among Mexican Americans and non-Hispanic whites in Los Angeles. *Arch Gen Psychiatry, 44*(8), 695–701.

Kessler, R., Berglund, P., Demler, O., Jin, R., & Walters, E. (2005). Lifetime prevalence and age-of-onset distributions of DSM-IV disorders in the National Comorbidity Survey Replication. *Arch Gen Psychiatry, 62,* 593–602.

Kessler, R. C., McGonagle, K. A., Zhao, S., Nelson, C. B., Hughes, M., Eshleman, S., et al. (1994). Lifetime and 12-month prevalence of DSM-III-R psychiatric disorders in the United States: Results from the National Comorbidity Study. *Arch Gen Psychiatry, 51*(1), 8–19.

Kessler, R. C., & Merikangas, K. R. (2004). The National Comorbidity Survey Replication (NCS-R): Background and aims. *Int J Methods Psychiatr Res, 13*(2), 60–68.

Lahey, B. B., Flagg, E. W., Bird, H. R., Schwab-Stone, M. E., Canino, G., Dulcan, M. K., et al. (1996). The NIMH Methods for the Epidemiology of Child and Adolescent Mental Disorders (MECA) Study: Background and methodology. *J Am Acad Child Adolesc Psychiatry, 35*(7), 855–864.

Leslie, L. K., Canino, G., Landsverk, J., Wood, P. A., Chavez, L., Hough, R. L., et al. (2005). ADHD treatment patterns of youth served in public sectors in San Diego and Puerto Rico. *J Emot Behav Dis, 13*(4), 224–236.

Magaña, J. R., De La Rocha, O., Amsel, J. & Magaña, H. (1996). Revisiting the dimensions of acculturation: Cultural theory and psychometric practice. *Hispanic J Behav Sci, 18*(4), 444–468.

Mendoza, R. H. (1989). An empirical scale to measure type and degree of acculturation in Mexican-American adolescents and adults. *J Cross-Cultural Psychology, 20,* 372–385.

Ortega, A. N., Rosenheck, R., Alegría, M., & Desai, R. A. (2000). Acculturation and the lifetime risk of psychiatric and substance use disorders among Hispanics. *J Nerv Ment Dis, 188*(11), 728–735.

Perez, D., Fortuna, L., & Alegría, M. (in press). Prevalence and correlates of everyday discrimination among U.S. Latinos. *J Comm Psychology.*

Redfield, R., Linton, R., & Herskovits, M. (1936). Memorandum for the study of acculturation. *American Anthropologists, 38,* 149–150.

Roberts, R. E., Roberts, C. R., & Chen, Y. R. (1997). Ethnocultural differences in prevalence of adolescent depression. *Am J Comm Psychol, 25*(1), 95–110.

Roberts, R. E., Roberts, C. R., & Xing, Y. (2007a). Rates of DSM-IV psychiatric disorders among adolescents in a large metropolitan area. *J Psychiatr Res, 41*(11), 959–967.

Roberts, R. E., Roberts, C. R., & Xing, Y. (2007b). Are Mexican American adolescents at greater risk of suicidal behaviors? *Suicide Life Threat Behav, 37*(1), 10–21.

Rutter, M. (2000). Psychosocial influences: Critiques, findings, and research needs. *Develop Psychopath, 12*(03), 375–405.

Rutter, M., Pickles, A., Murray, R., & Eaves, L. (2001). Testing hypotheses on specific environmental causal effects on behavior. *Psychol Bull, 127*(3), 291–324.

Shaffer, D., Fisher, P., Dulcan, M. K., Davies, M., Piacentini, J., Schwab-Stone, M. E., et al. (1996). The NIMH Diagnostic Interview Schedule for Children Version 2.3 (DISC-2.3): Description, acceptability, prevalence rates, and performance in the MECA study. *J Am Acad Child Adolesc Psychiatry, 35*(7), 865–877.

Shrout, P., Canino, G., Bird, H., Rubio-Stipec, M., Bravo, M., & Burnam, A. (1992). Mental health status among Puerto Ricans, Mexican Americans, and Non-Hispanic Whites. *Am J Com Psychol, 20*(6), 729–752.

U. S. Department of Health and Human Services (USDHHS). (2001a). *Mental health: Culture, race, and ethnicity—A supplement to Mental health: A report of the surgeon general.* Rockville, MD: USDHHS, Substance Abuse and Mental Health Services Administration, Center for Mental Health Services.

Vega, W. A., Kolody, B., Aguilar-Gaxiola, S., Alderete, E., Catalano, R., & Caraveo-Anduaga, J. (1998). Lifetime prevalence of DSM-III-R psychiatric disorders among urban and rural Mexican Americans in California. *Arch Gen Psychiatry, 55*(9), 771–778.

World Health Organization. (1990). *Composite International Diagnostic Interview* (Version 1.0). Geneva: World Health Organization.

4

METHODOLOGICAL ISSUES IN RESEARCH ON LATINO POPULATIONS

GEORGE P. KNIGHT, MARK W. ROOSA, CARLOS O. CALDERÓN-TENA, AND NANCY A. GONZALES

The relatively rapid growth of Latino populations in the United States has resulted in an enhanced research focus on Latino individuals and families that will likely continue to expand over the next few decades. In this chapter, we hope to provide a constructive discussion of some of the methodological issues that represent serious challenges for researchers studying Latino populations. Specifically, we will discuss methodological issues associated with sampling, measurement, and translation because we believe that these key issues represent significant threats to the scientific inferences from the research literature on Latino populations.

Not only is the Latino population growing, but it is a diverse population that is becoming even more diverse over time. First, Latinos in the United States come from a broad range of countries of origin, including Mexico, Puerto Rico, Cuba, Central America, South America, and the Dominican Republic. Although these individuals are all considered Latino, they come from cultures that are discernibly different. Second, Latinos in the United States have a broad range of connection to the mainstream U.S. culture and their ethnic cultures. For example, 53% of

the increases in the Latino population are the result of immigration to the United States (U.S. Census Bureau, 2001). The remaining 47% of the increases are the result of the difference between birth and death rates among Latinos whose families have been in the United States for more than one generation. Regardless of their generation of immigration to the United States, these persons experience a process of dual cultural adaptation (see Gonzales, Fabrett, & Knight, Chapter 8, this volume) inherent in the processes of acculturation (adaptation to the mainstream culture of the United States) and enculturation (and adaptation to the ethnic culture). The variety of family histories, including differences in the circumstances or reasons leading to their families' immigration to the United States, differences in the length of time (i.e., years and generations) their families have been in the United States, and differences in the nature of the communities in which these families reside (i.e., from Latino ethnic enclaves to more integrated communities), enhance the diversity in the Latino population of the United States. One very limited but clear indication of this diversity pertains to the language use or capabilities of Latinos. In 2000, over

75% of Latinos reported speaking a language other than English (almost always Spanish) at home (U.S. Census Bureau, 2004). Although there is tremendous variability in the language use across Latinos from different countries of origin, generation since immigration, and age groups, approximately 40% of all Latino adults report speaking English less than "very well" (U.S. Census Bureau, 2004). Even though Latinos may share some characteristics (e.g., many are Catholic and come from countries where Spanish is spoken), there also are very large differences between some subgroups (e.g., cultural traditions, dominant language, reasons for immigration, treatment of immigrants). There are even phenotypic differences among Latino subgroups; significant portions of the Latinos from several countries have an African heritage, while most of the Latino population is *mestizo* (i.e., indigenous-European mixture).

Hence, there has been growth in the size and diversity of the Latino population associated with the burgeoning of Latino-focused research. This research has generally been either cross-group comparisons or within-group studies. But the lines between these two research strategies can sometimes be blurred. Cross-group comparisons have most often compared Latinos with European Americans. However, some forms of cross-group comparison research have focused on differences in constructs or processes between distinct Latino subgroups (i.e., individuals from different cultures of origin). Yet other research has focused on differences between Latinos who vary in their degree of connection to the mainstream and ethnic cultures (i.e., individuals who differ in acculturation status or ethnic identity). Of course, there is also research that examines processes of interest within a relatively homogenous Latino group but does not examine cultural variability within the group, whether that group is defined broadly (i.e., Latinos in general), more narrowly (i.e., Mexican Americans), or very narrowly (i.e., recently immigrated Mexican Americans). In this chapter, we describe several relevant methodological issues for these research strategies and provide recommendations that we hope will be useful to researchers studying Latinos.

SAMPLING, RECRUITMENT, AND RETENTION

Sampling is the process of selecting a sample from a population of interest to the researcher.

In quantitative research, the goal of sampling is to select members of the target population who are representative of (i.e., very similar to) the target population so that findings of research conducted with the sample can be generalized to the larger population. *Recruitment* is the process of trying to persuade those selected to participate in a study. Together, sampling and recruitment determine the initial quality of the sample studied, the degree to which the sample is representative of the target population and, therefore, the confidence with which researchers can *generalize* findings—that is, say that results obtained with the sample are the same results that would have been obtained if the entire population had been studied. Although researchers frequently think about sampling as key to establishing the external and ecological validity of research findings, for certain types of research questions sampling is critical in establishing the internal validity of the design as well. That is, in research that compares Latinos to other groups (e.g., Latinos vs. European Americans) or compares different Latino groups (e.g., Mexican Americans vs. Cuban Americans), sampling becomes the means of operationalizing the independent variable. In these cases, sampling strategies that do not generate equally representative comparison groups lead to bias in the observed findings that may be misleading. Thus, sampling and recruitment are basic processes in social science research that contribute to the overall quality of most research efforts. For longitudinal studies, sample *retention* becomes equally important. If researchers have managed to obtain a representative sample of the population of interest at the beginning of a study, the quality of the sample will deteriorate over time if large numbers of people or significant portions of particular subgroups (e.g., one subgroup of Latinos) drop out (i.e., *attrite*).

Sampling

Quantitative researchers studying Latinos can use any of the three general sampling designs: random sampling, stratified sampling, or convenience sampling. *Random sampling* is the most likely to generate a sample representative of the target Latino population and is the least often used of the three designs. In random sampling, every member of the target population has an equal probability of being selected for participation in the study. Except for telephone surveys or instances in which there is a sampling frame with names of all members of the target population, random sampling in studies of Latinos can be complex, time consuming, and costly. Even telephone surveys using random-digit dialing may not generate representative samples of Latinos. Low-income Latinos may not have telephones or may rely on pay-as-you-go cell phones that provide service only sporadically (i.e., when access time has been purchased). In addition, undocumented Latinos, a significant portion of some Latino groups, may be reluctant to respond to calls from strangers because of fears of immigration enforcement efforts. Internet sampling, which is growing in popularity, may be even more prone to these problems; computer and Internet access is limited among people of low income.

As desirable as random sampling studies are, some caveats exist for Latino research. Numerous data sets are available that are described as having nationally representative samples. Some of these data sets oversampled Latino (and other) populations to make the data set more attractive to those interested in comparing Latinos and others. Many of these data sets include large numbers of Latinos and, with similar data across multiple ethnic and racial groups, appear to represent quite an opportunity to researchers. However, these studies usually are limited to Latinos who speak English well, and so they rarely represent the overall Latino population. These national samples are particularly problematic for researchers interested in how cultural diversity or acculturation differences within Latino groups influence adjustment or school success, for instance, because by design these studies either underrepresent or do not represent those lowest in acculturation or highest in enculturation.

Stratified sampling is used when there are specific, well-defined subgroups in the target population, and researchers want to represent each in the final sample. Sometimes, stratified sampling is used is to make sure that small subgroups in the population are not underrepresented in the final sample. For example, in a study of Latinos generally, one might want to use stratified sampling to make sure that people from Central America or the Dominican Republic are represented. In addition, the researcher may use stratified sampling to ensure that all generations of immigration are represented in the sample. In these cases, the researcher would decide on a quota for these groups, often based on their proportion of the Latino population in the area where the study is being conducted, and continue sampling until the quota for each group is reached.

Another use of stratified sampling is to make cross-group comparisons possible. For example, in a study of the general Latino population, a researcher may decide to recruit equal numbers of people from Mexico, Cuba, and the Dominican Republic. In most parts of the United States, this would require oversampling at least one of these groups, depending upon which groups were less common in that area. It also is desirable to sample randomly within each stratum until the quota is reached (i.e., stratified random sampling).

Convenience sampling, because it is relatively easy, quick, and inexpensive, is the most common sampling design in research on Latinos. Convenience sampling usually involves identifying a community or part of a community in which the members of the target population reside in relatively large numbers, or identifying institutions (e.g., schools, churches) frequented by large numbers of the target Latino population. Convenience sampling, however, is very unlikely to generate a sample that is representative of any Latino population. When Latinos are concentrated in ethnic enclaves or barrios (common targets for researchers), any sample obtained is likely to overrepresent low-income and immigrant Latinos. Even if those sampled from Latino barrios were demographically similar to the general Latino population, the fact that they chose to live in barrios rather than in more diverse communities may indicate that they are more likely than others to adhere to traditional values and lifestyles. Similarly, studies of Latino adolescents often obtain samples from schools with large Latino enrollments. These schools are likely to serve ethnic enclaves and, again, to overrepresent those from low-income or immigrant families. In addition, studies of adolescents recruited exclusively from junior high and high schools will fail to represent those adolescents who have dropped out of school, a serious problem among some Latino groups, particularly Mexican Americans.

Although Latinos are a very diverse population, the bulk of research on Latinos is conducted with low-income residents of inner-city communities who speak English (Gonzales, Knight, Morgan-Lopez, Saenz, & Sirolli, 2002).

That is, most research on Latinos represents only a select portion of the Latino population. As long as researchers are aware of the limitations of their sampling plans, inform their readers of the procedures used and the associated limitations, and make appropriately limited generalizations, such studies can contribute to the growing science on Latino families and children. However, the use of random and stratified random sampling plans that target a broader range of the specific Latino populations is very desirable and may be necessary to address some research questions, such as the role of culture in family, developmental, and psychological processes (Roosa et al., 2008).

One way to increase the representativeness of Latino samples is to use a multistep process in which the first step involves sampling diverse communities in which Latinos live or diverse institutions that serve Latinos (Roosa et al., 2008). By sampling a range of residential communities or institutions, researchers should be able to increase the number of well-educated, middle-income Latinos in our studies at reasonable cost. Communities play a critical role in the socialization and adaptation of Latinos, particularly immigrants, to the larger community. For instance, speaking Spanish and adhering to traditions may be reinforced among those living in Latino enclaves, and there may be little social pressure for immigrants in these communities to learn English or adapt to mainstream lifestyles or values. For Latinos living in ethnically diverse communities, particularly those who are distinct minorities in their communities, it may be more difficult to maintain cultural traditions, and there may be more social pressure to acculturate toward mainstream attitudes, behaviors, and values.

Researchers interested in Latinos also need to consider one very broad sampling issue: Does the research question apply to all or multiple Latino subgroups, is it specific to one particular Latino group, or is the question about variations among Latino groups? Latinos are a very diverse population, and researchers should consider carefully whether their research questions are better answered with a pan-Latino sample or with a sample that targets a specific Latino subgroup. In addition, researchers need to make very deliberate choices about which Latino subgroups can be combined in studies based on the known similarities and differences among the subgroups and how these differences might affect the validity of the results of analyses that assume homogeneity within the sample. This issue generally has been ignored in the considerable pan-Latino literature to date.

Recruiting

Recruitment is the act of persuading selected members of the target population to participate in research. Obtaining a representative sample is not possible if large numbers of those selected refuse to participate. There is no research showing that Latinos per se are more difficult to recruit than other groups (see Cauce, Ryan, & Grove, 1998, for a review). However, several Latino subgroups are overrepresented among those who have low incomes and live in urban areas, two characteristics associated with below-average research participation rates (e.g., Capaldi & Patterson, 1987; Cauce, Ryan et al., 1998; Spoth, Goldberg, & Redman, 1999). Further, there are reasons to believe that some assumptions behind common recruitment strategies do not apply to some Latino subgroups (Knight, Roosa, & Umaña-Taylor, 2009). To improve recruitment response rates for Latinos, therefore, researchers need to focus on two sets of strategies, one for issues specific to Latinos and one for issues specific to low-income populations.

Recruitment Strategies for Latinos. To make the recruitment process more attractive to and relevant for Latinos, particularly immigrants and the less acculturated, researchers need to devise recruitment strategies that are consistent with the cultural values and lifestyles of the target Latino population. There are at least six significant steps researchers should consider to improve recruitment success with Latinos (Roosa et al., 2008). First, because a substantial portion of several Latino groups consists of relatively recent immigrants, all materials for recruitment must be available in Spanish (or, for some groups, French or Portuguese), and many or most recruiters must be bilingual and bicultural. Second, recruiters and interviewers should use formal modes of addressing adults, show respect during all parts of the research process, and follow culturally appropriate modes of interacting (e.g., informal talk about topics other than the research at the beginning) to develop rapport with potential participants. Third, researchers should emphasize the confidentiality of the research process, perhaps obtaining certificates of confidentiality to protect research data from police agencies, to improve recruitment rates among undocumented immigrants (Levkoff & Sanchez, 2003). Fourth, researchers should use culturally attractive symbols (e.g., brochures using colors from the Mexican flag) or labels (*La Familia*) to make a project more attractive on first appearance, thus reducing some potential resistance (Dumka, Lopez, & Jacobs Carter, 2002). Fifth, researchers should take a collectivist perspective when explaining the purposes of the research; that is, explain possible benefits of the research in terms of the target population (e.g., Latinos, Mexican Americans, community) rather than in terms of the individual or family being asked to participate. Finally, researchers should be aware of and respectful of traditional practices and beliefs (e.g., hierarchical power structures within families, exaggerated sense of respect toward authority figures) that can lead to misunderstandings. For instance, asking mothers in traditional households to give permission for them, their children, or family to participate in research without asking or consulting their husbands may be perceived as threatening the husbands' role as leader and protector. Although such power structures may not be consistent with a researcher's values, the researcher must respect them when they are displayed by potential research participants. Similarly, very traditional Latinos often feel that to say no to a direct request to participate in research made by authority figures (i.e., research staff) would be considered disrespectful. In our experience, when such families do not want to participate in research, many still will say yes to direct requests, will schedule interview appointments, and then repeatedly either break these appointments or not be home at the scheduled time (i.e., "soft refusals," Roosa et al., 2008). Further, it will be easier to devise culturally attractive recruitment processes using these strategies if researchers are focused on a specific Latino subgroup rather than on a pan-Latino sample because of subtle but critical differences in values, lifestyles, and Spanish (e.g., colloquialisms, accents, meanings of some words) across Latino subgroups.

Recruitment Strategies for Low-Income Latinos. There are at least four significant steps researchers can make to improve recruitment success among low-income Latinos (Roosa et al.,

2008). First, the recruitment process could educate potential participants about the research process and its possible benefits beyond the minimal information usually required by consent forms. Relative to most middle-class individuals, lower-income Latinos rarely have had any exposure to research or to institutions that conduct research. Second, developing collaborations with popular and trusted institutions or community leaders can help projects gain credibility and reduce participants' fears arising from a lack of familiarity with research or research institutions (Cauce et al., 1998; Roosa et al., 2008; Umaña-Taylor & Bámaca, 2004) This might mean developing partnerships with school systems, social service agencies, churches, or political action groups to gain credibility and trust in the eyes of the low-income Latino community. Note that researchers need to make sure in advance that institutions that seem appropriate for such partnerships actually do have strong positive reputations among Latinos, or these partnerships can backfire (Roosa et al., 2008). Developing a community advisory board made up of opinion leaders or other highly influential community members can be extremely helpful. Advisory boards also can help researchers identify institutions that have positive reputations in the local Latino community and are worth targeting as potential partners in the research process. Collaborative research between university researchers and community groups that involves the community group in identifying the research goals and procedures (sometimes called *community-based participatory research*) probably provides the strongest type of partnership for reducing barriers to participation in low-income Latino communities.

Third, researchers need to keep communication as personal as possible. Written communication in any language may not be the best way to communicate with potential low-income research participants or participants with lower levels of education and literacy. Low-income populations do most or all of their communication in person rather than by post or e-mail. Additionally, for low-income Latinos face-to-face communication may be a way of showing mutual respect, whereas formal, written communication may be perceived as impersonal and one sided.

Fourth, offer a concrete incentive whenever possible. Because of less experience with the research process and less understanding of what the research enterprise is about, low-income individuals may not feel a strong sense of obligation to participate in research (Knight et al., 2009). In addition, they may incorrectly classify researchers with those authority figures often associated with "bad news" for residents in low-income communities (i.e., police, social service agencies, landlords). Any concrete incentive (e.g., payment, coupons, and free services for families but particularly for children) will help grab a potential low-income participant's attention, differentiate researchers from other authority figures, and provide some motivation for paying attention and perhaps participating. Of course, incentives should not be so large as to limit a low-income individual's ability to refuse to participate. In addition, when monetary incentives are used with low-income participants, payments should be made with cash, gift cards, or the equivalent. Some low-income individuals do not have bank accounts and may have to pay a fee to cash checks. Furthermore, some immigrants may not be in the country legally and therefore may not have proper identification to get checks cashed; as a result, the businesses they use to cash checks charge them for this service.

These strategies for improving recruitment rates for Latinos are just the beginning. Local circumstances might offer unique opportunities (e.g., strong positive connections between researchers or research institutions and the local Latino community) or challenges (e.g., highly publicized instances of discrimination against Latinos) for recruiting. In addition, there is a great need for systematic study of recruitment rates for different groups of Latinos (e.g., differing national origins, degrees of acculturation and enculturation, social classes, or regions of the country) and for better documentation of the recruitment processes used in studies of Latinos and response rates to these efforts. Too many studies fail to provide this important information.

Retention

For longitudinal studies, successful recruitment is just the first step. Researchers in these studies also need a plan for retaining as many people as possible who enrolled in the study. Failure to retain participants for longitudinal studies creates problems in data analysis and in researchers' ability to interpret their results and generalize to the target population. Unfortunately, there has been little systematic research into retention techniques or strategies, less still

that has focused on any Latino population; in fact, relatively few researchers even report the retention techniques used in longitudinal studies or interventions (Scott, 2004).

In panel studies, researchers typically begin by recruiting a certain number of participants and conducting interviews or administering questionnaires immediately after successful recruitment. Then, the researchers want to re-interview all the original participants at one or more later times. The challenge in panel studies is to locate the original participants when study protocols say it is time for the next follow-up and to maintain positive relations with participants so that they are motivated to continue to participate. The good news is that *retention* rates of 90% or greater between assessments are not that unusual, even with high-risk populations (e.g., substance abusers; Scott, 2004).

Retaining participants requires, among many other things, keeping the lines of communication open. With a Latino sample, this often means maintaining the capability of communicating in Spanish or English, according to participants' preferences, and communicating in culturally respectful ways. More problems with mobility and literacy are likely to occur with the low-income portions of samples than with middle-class samples. Mobility issues are particularly challenging in longitudinal studies with some Latinos, particularly Puerto Ricans on the East Coast or Mexican Americans and Central Americans in the southwestern United States, because they can return to their families' country of origin so easily.

Longitudinal panel studies that use culturally sensitive recruitment methods like those described earlier are taking an important first step toward retaining participants. If Latino participants find the objectives of the research attractive, if they are treated with respect, do not find the research process threatening, and develop rapport with the research staff during interviews or other activities, they are likely to be more receptive to requests for continued participation in the research than if their initial experiences are negative. Researchers would do well to emphasize the importance of both (a) the research project's goals, particularly if the research might ultimately benefit the larger Latino population, not just the participant, and (b) the participant's contributions to the study during the recruitment and initial assessment stages to help develop the participant's commitment to the study. When possible, engaging members of Latino participants' families during the recruitment process (Miranda, Azocar, Organista, Munoz, & Lieberman, 1996) may be particularly helpful in gaining their support later to locate participants who change addresses. Still, retaining participants over the long term is a labor-intensive process that requires a well-developed multidimensional plan and careful coordination that builds on effective recruitment methods but cannot depend only on the successes at recruitment.

Intervention studies also need to retain participants for multiple-session or long-term interventions and long-term evaluation follow-ups. The use of culturally specific and attractive strategies may improve retention in studies with Latinos. For example, an intervention strategy used in one health promotion intervention specifically for Latinos was *promotoras,* lay workers who provided social support and encouragement to participants (Swider, 2002). The role of *promotora* probably has both practical and symbolic value to participants not only by having a supporter/cheerleader/coach to help a person stick with the intervention but also by showing that the intervention was designed specifically for that person or ethnic group. However, as attractive as this and similar strategies sound, none have been systematically tested (i.e., included in the processes with one group, left out of the processes with another group, and retention rates compared) to determine their effectiveness.

Most longitudinal studies use similar retention processes to keep in contact with study participants for future follow-ups (e.g., Coen, Patrick, & Shern, 1996; Hampson et al., 2001; Scott, 2004; Stephens, Thibodeaux, Sloboda, & Tonkin, 2007). There are five commonly recommended steps in the retention process. First, obtain *tracing information* either at first contact or during the assessment process. This means getting the names, addresses, and telephone numbers of several people (at least three) who will always know the participant's location. These tracers can include family, neighbors, friends, employers, and children's schools. Scott (2004) recommends verifying the names and addresses of tracers within 7–10 days after they are obtained. When working with relatively new Latino immigrants, we recommend not relying exclusively on family members as tracers because of the possibility that the extended family will move at the same time, even when

they live independently. In addition to gathering tracer information, it is incumbent upon researchers to obtain permission to contact these individuals in the event the researcher loses contact with the study participant. In addition, to overcome fears among the tracers about your intentions when you contact them for information about the participant, we recommend having the participant sign a letter addressed to the tracer that states that the participant is in a study and that the participant wants the tracer to provide contact information to the researcher. In our experience, such letters can be quite helpful in gaining the confidence of tracers if participants are low income, have had problems with police, or are undocumented.

Second, if the interval between interviews or assessments is more than a few months, systematically make contact in the interim to determine if the participant has changed addresses. All contacts with study participants should be done in ways that indicate how important they are to the study's success and attempt to strengthen the participant's commitment to continuing in the study. For instance, researchers can send out personalized birthday cards to participants and to participants' spouses or parents. A card or flyer can be included in this mailing to remind the participant of the study and upcoming interviews/assessments and to keep them engaged in the research (Scott, 2004). A toll-free telephone number and/or a postage-paid envelope will allow participants to respond with any address change almost painlessly. We recommend contacting participants at regular intervals of not more than 4–6 months, depending on the time between follow-ups and the social class of participants (i.e., shorter intervals for lower social class).

Third, follow up on mailings that do not generate a response. If there is no response within 2–4 weeks, depending upon the time between assessments, use other means (telephone, e-mail, home visits) to make contact. If the study participant has changed address and these processes are not successful in locating their new address, begin contacting tracers. It is important to follow up on study participants as soon as you discover that they have changed addresses without letting you know, because the longer they are in a new location, the more likely it is that tracers will also lose contact with them. It is not unusual for dozens of contact attempts to be necessary before successfully recontacting a relocated participant (Scott, 2004).

Fourth, when tracers are not able or willing to help you contact participants who have moved, using the Internet to search various public records may be helpful (although these methods usually are only useful within a limited geographic area). Potentially useful sources include municipal water customer records, electronic white pages directories, property tax records, police and court records, and drivers license records (Hampson et al., 2001; Stephens et al., 2007). There are commercial companies that will conduct such searches for you. Unfortunately, Internet sources are most likely to be successful with middle-class participants and probably least likely to be useful for immigrant participants.

Finally, prepare participants for the timing of upcoming assessments via mailings and direct contacts, and schedule their continued participation well in advance of the targeted assessment date. Then, remind them of the upcoming assessment a week in advance and again about 24 hours before the assessment.

MEASUREMENT AND MEASUREMENT EQUIVALENCE

The procedures for constructing and evaluating a reliable and valid measure of any underlying construct (cf. Cronbach, 1970; McDonald, 1999; Nunnally, 1967) start with a theory that specifies indicators of that construct. This theory defines the basic nature of the construct in the ethnic population of interest and provides the basis for identifying the items or observations that reflect the construct. Theory also describes how the underlying construct relates to other constructs, or fits into the nomological net of underlying constructs, in the ethnic populations in which the measure is to be administered. To obtain an unbiased assessment of this construct and the relation of this construct to other constructs, it is necessary to select a sample of items that is representative of the population of items defining the construct as it exists in the ethnic population being studied. As the set of items/observations used to assess the construct becomes less representative of the population of items in the ethnic population, it becomes less likely that the set of items accurately assesses the underlying construct in that ethnic group. For example, the potential indicators of family obligations could be substantially larger among Mexican Americans than among European Americans, and hence a measure developed in the latter population may not tap into the breadth of the construct for some Mexican Americans.

Furthermore, two other key premises have important implications for our understanding of measurement issues. First, the numerical score generated by a measure is an estimate of the degree to which a construct exists within the respondent and includes random errors in measurement. These random measurement errors, or unreliability in measurements, add random variance that cannot covary with other variables, thereby limiting the degree to which the scores produced by this measure can be correlated with scores produced by another measure (including the same measure administered at another time). This measurement error leads to underestimates of the magnitude of the relation of this construct to other constructs in the population by causing the observed correlations to be attenuated. Second, the items/observations on a measure may also be influenced by a construct other than the intended target construct. This measurement bias adds systematic variance that can covary with other constructs. The measurement bias resulting from an unintended second construct creates the possibility that the observed relations between the scores on the target measure and theoretically related constructs can either overestimate or underestimate the magnitude of the relation between these constructs in the population. Often, these secondary constructs are response biases or other methodological artifacts that are undesirable but often unavoidable. For example, there is evidence that Latinos, particularly less acculturated Latinos, more often endorse extreme responses than non-Latinos and more acculturated Latinos do (Hui & Triandis, 1989; Marín, Gamba, & Marín, 1992). Given the potential for measurement bias to produce systematic variance in a set of scores that is not a function of the target construct, and given the diversity of the Latino population, measurement equivalence becomes an important consideration (see Knight, Tein, Prost, & Gonzales, 2002).

The most obvious case in which measurement equivalence is important is when researchers make cross-ethnic comparisons among different Latino groups (or comparing a Latino group to a non-Latino group). Scalar equivalence, the degree to which any particular score on a measure reflects the same magnitude of the construct across groups, is essential if the comparison of different Latino groups is to accurately reflect any meaningful, real difference between these groups. This is because any measurement bias differentially associated with the different Latino groups being compared may exacerbate or reduce the observed differences between these Latino groups. For many researchers, the importance of measurement equivalence is clear in the case in which different groups are being compared. However, measurement equivalence is an important consideration even when a researcher is primarily interested in examining the relations among constructs within an ethnic group that is diverse. When studying a sample of Latinos that contains some representation of individuals with roots in different cultures of origin, measurement bias creates the possibility of nonequivalence of measures. Even if one is studying Latinos from one culture of origin, these individuals are likely to differ in their levels of acculturation and enculturation into the host and ethnic cultures or in their language use. These differences in acculturation and enculturation or language use allow measurement bias to create nonequivalence of measures. Further, when examining the relations among variables in a diverse population, the absence of measurement equivalence can bias observed relations and produce inaccurate findings (see Knight et al., 2002).

For example, when examining the relation between the scores on two measures in a diverse Latino sample when each measure uses a five-point Likert-type response scale, the observed correlation between these two sets of scores may be biased upward by the extreme-alternative response bias of less acculturated Latinos (Marín et al., 1992). In this case, the response bias adds systematic variance in each set of scores that represents additional shared variance beyond the shared variance based upon the true relation between the two constructs. In essence, the proportion of shared variance between the two sets of scores is increased by the common response bias. When the relation is examined between the scores on two measures, one of which uses a five-point Likert-type response scale and the other of which differs radically (perhaps behavioral observations by trained observers), the observed correlation between these two sets of scores may be biased downward by the extreme-alternative response bias of less acculturated Latinos (Marín et al., 1992). In this case, the response bias adds systematic variance to the Likert-type measure, but this additional variance is not shared with the other measure. In essence, the proportion of shared variance between the two sets of scores is decreased by the addition of variance to the Likert-type measure that is not shared with the other measure.

Measurement equivalence is also important when a researcher administers to members of a Latino population a measure developed in some other cultural group. That is, even if the researcher is studying a very homogenous Latino sample, if that researcher wished to use a measure of some construct developed in a different population, he or she would want to know that this measure was assessing the same construct in this particular Latino population. Perhaps the only research context in which measurement equivalence may not be directly relevant is that in which the researcher is investigating some phenomena in a homogeneous Latino population, and the researcher is specifically developing each measure for use in that population.

Given the importance of measurement equivalence and the premise that our understanding of the attribute being assessed with a measure is largely a function of the nature of the relations of the scores generated by that measure to scores produced by other measures, it is clear that measurement equivalence is largely a question of the comparability of reliability and construct validity of measures across diverse sets of Latino individuals. Hence, two elements are critical in the assessment of measurement equivalence: the degree of similarity of the internal structure of a measure across sets of diverse Latinos (measurement invariance or factorial invariance) and the degree of similarity in the construct validity of measures (construct validity equivalence). That is, the items/observations that compose a measure must be comparably related to one another across diverse Latino groups and based upon theory regarding the nature of the indicators of the construct in those diverse groups. Further, the scores generated by measures must be comparably related to scores produced by other measures in a manner consistent with the theory that specifies the nature of the construct in those diverse Latino groups. This does not necessarily suggest that these interrelations must be identical across groups. If the culturally informed theory indicates that the construct has some subtle differences in indicators or correlates across diverse sets of Latino individuals, then measurement equivalence may still exist, even when the interrelations among the items/observations or among the construct validity relations are not identical. Essentially, the observed pattern of interrelations among the items/observations or among the construct validity relations across the diverse sets of Latino individuals must conform to the expectations based upon the *culturally informed theory* if the measures are equivalent across these diverse populations.

Although there are several ways to examine the degree of factorial invariance (e.g., Knight & Hill, 1998; Labouvie & Ruetsch, 1995; McDonald, 1995; Widaman & Reise, 1997) in a set of items/observations, perhaps the most common approach is that described by Widaman and Reise (1997). These authors suggest the use of multigroup confirmatory factor analysis (CFA) to fit a series of hierarchically nested factor structures. The sequence of nested CFA models tested (configural, metric, strong, and strict) progresses from the least restrictive to the most restrictive model of invariance. Configural invariance exists if the same set of items forms a factor within each diverse Latino group, and one can conclude that the items are a good representation of the construct in each group. Metric invariance exists if the the relationship between each item and the latent factor (i.e., the factor loadings) is equally strong across diverse Latino groups. Strong invariance exists if the item intercepts are equal across groups. Finally, strict invariance exists if the unique error variances associated with each item are equal across groups. At all levels of invariance, a partially invariant model may be obtained if some but not all items are invariant on each element of the factor structure across groups (Byrne, Shavelson, & Muthén, 1989). Often, this evidence of partial invariance is associated with considerable dismay and attempts to use modification indices to "fix" the problem. Indeed, this may lead to the dropping of items/observations from the measure. Sometimes, the attempts to rectify the limited evidence of invariance (i.e., the so-called partial invariance) is misguided because very specific and selective partial invariance should exist if the theory that characterizes

the nature of the indicators of the construct is subtly different across sets of diverse Latino individuals (see Knight et al., 2002). Therefore, complete or partial measurement/factorial invariance may be the first indication of measurement equivalence.

Following the tests of measurement/factorial invariance, construct validity equivalence is established by examining the similarities of the slopes and intercepts of the relation of the latent construct to other theoretically related constructs across diverse Latino groups (see Knight & Hill, 1998). Equivalence in slopes can be tested by comparing the fit indices for a structural equations model in which the slopes are freely estimated across groups to a model that constrains slopes to be identical across diverse Latino groups. If the fit of the constrained slope model is satisfactory, and the fit indices are not substantially different between the constrained and unconstrained slope models, similar comparisons are made between models that allow the intercepts of the relations among constructs to vary with a model that constrains the intercepts to be identical across diverse Latino groups. If these comparisons of these hierarchically arranged structural equation models suggest that the slopes and intercepts are the same across diverse Latino groups, construct equivalence exists. However, partial construct validity equivalence may also be compatible with measurement equivalence if the theory regarding the nature of the construct being measured indicates that the construct should be related in a subtly different way to some other constructs among diverse Latino groups. Knight and colleagues (Knight & Hill, 1998; Knight et al., 2002) have suggested that the careful examination of measurement/factorial invariance and construct validity equivalence is the closest one can come to concluding that any scale score (or latent construct value) indicates the same degree, intensity, or magnitude of the construct across diverse sets of individuals (i.e., that scalar equivalence exists).

One of the biggest challenges in evaluating measurement equivalence across diverse Latino groups is developing the culturally informed theory that provides the basis for identifying the items or observations that reflect that psychological construct and how the construct relates to other constructs in the Latino population(s) in which the measure is to be administered. Qualitative research methodologies may be particularly useful in developing this culturally informed theory. In the initial stages of instrument development, qualitative research methods can be used to determine the breadth of the psychological construct across Latino populations and the accuracy of the operational definition of the construct. For example, qualitative methods may be instrumental in determining whether there are variants or culturally specific forms of the construct across diverse Latino groups. If a researcher wanted to develop a measure of familism that would be applicable to multiple Latino populations, or to individuals within a particular Latino population but who differ in their degree of acculturation and enculturation, the researcher could begin by conducting a series of focus groups with individuals from the appropriately representative Latino groups (Berg, 1995). The essence of these focus groups should be to elicit discussion from these representative participants that includes describing the nature of familism values and familistic behaviors in their families as well as how these values and behaviors function within their families. The focus group data can be examined for themes and important issues raised by the participants, and these themes can be compared and contrasted across diverse Latino groups (Bryman & Burgess, 1994; Feldman, 1995). Researchers may also conduct individual qualitative interviews with participants from diverse Latino populations to obtain clarification or more information about a theme discussed by a focus group (Fetterman, 1989). Themes regarding the breadth and nature of the familism values/behaviors can be used to generate items or observations appropriate for the measure of the familism construct as well as expectations regarding the construct validity relations in the diverse Latino groups being studied.

One of the difficult decisions researchers interested in studying Latino populations must make is whether to develop new measures of the psychological constructs they wish to study, or to rely upon and perhaps adapt existing measures that have been developed for use in other populations. Regardless of the decision, the evaluation of the equivalence of this measure across multiple Latino populations, or individuals within a particular Latino population who differ in their degree of acculturation and enculturation, is still important. Of course, if one is conducting research that compares Latinos broadly

defined or a more narrowly defined Latino group (i.e., Mexican Americans) with another ethnic group, then measurement equivalence, particularly scalar equivalence, across these groups is critically important. Here again, qualitative methods may also be useful. Focus groups or individual qualitative interviews can be used to have representative participants from the target Latino groups and other ethnic groups evaluate the familism items or observations and the operational definition of the construct to help determine where the familism measure may be equivalent or may need to be modified to become equivalent. The purpose of such panels or focus groups is to determine whether the familism items or observations make sense to the members of the target ethnic group(s) and whether important items or observations have been omitted from the measure.

Ultimately, the complementary use of qualitative and quantitative methodologies may lead to a better understanding of the sources of nonequivalence for measures and guidance for revising measures to achieve equivalence. In the development of new measures, qualitative methodologies may be used to determine which items or observations should be included to enhance the likelihood of achieving measurement equivalence across multiple Latino populations or across individuals within a particular Latino population who differ in their degree of acculturation and enculturation. Quantitative methodologies are useful for evaluating the degree of statistical success in creating new measures that are cross-group equivalent. For established measures, quantitative and qualitative methodologies may be used in conjunction to ferret out sources of nonequivalence. Quantitative methodologies may be useful in identifying which measures or parts of measures are nonequivalent, while qualitative methodologies may be useful in the confirmation of nonequivalences and modification of the measure, particularly when the nonequivalence is the result of the omission of relevant behaviors or items. A broader description of these measurement issues is available elsewhere (Knight et al., 2009).

TRANSLATION

The diversity of the Latino population and the need for representative sampling creates a research context in which the simultaneous construction of measures and protocols in Spanish and English, or the translation of existing measures and research protocols into Spanish, is almost always necessary to accurately study Latino populations. A substantial proportion of the Latino population is either not fluent in English or much more comfortable communicating in Spanish. This possibility creates a tremendous challenge for researchers interested in studying Latinos. Sampling the Latino population representatively requires being prepared to recruit and assess Latino research participants in Spanish as well as English. This means that all the kinds of communications between researchers and potential Latino participants need to be conducted in both English and Spanish. Without Spanish and English descriptions of the nature of the research project, informed consent forms, verbal scripts, and recruitment scripts, researchers may not be able to representatively entice individuals from the diverse Latino population to participate in the research. Without Spanish and English instructions to participants and measures, researchers may not be able to assess the necessary psychological constructs in individuals from across the range of diversity that exists within the Latino population. Without Spanish and English informed consent and debriefing forms and the associated verbal scripts, researchers cannot meet their ethical obligations when studying individuals across the range of diversity within the Latino population.

The need either to construct measures and protocols in two languages or to translate them into Spanish creates additional research demands and a potential methodological confound that poses a threat to the accuracy of the scientific inferences. That is, if translations are done poorly, the research context and assessments may not be comparable across multiple Latino groups or across individuals within a particular Latino population who differ in language preference or in their degree of acculturation and enculturation. It is essential that the entire research protocol and the measures are equivalent in Spanish and English to ensure that any mean differences or similarities across diverse Latino groups on a construct, or any observed differences or similarities in the relations between two psychological constructs, represent true differences in the nature of these groups rather than artifacts resulting from

differences in the degree to which the Spanish and English research protocols and measures assess the constructs of interest. That is, noncomparability of the Spanish and English research protocol and measures can lead to differences across diverse elements of the Latino population that are a function of differences in the research context or assessments introduced by the poor translation, rather than true differences in the psychological constructs of interests. Hence, the quality and accuracy of the translation of the research protocol and measures is critical.

Translation Approaches

Unfortunately, a wide variety of approaches to the translation of research protocols and measures have been reported in the literature, but no clear standard has emerged by which these approaches and the resulting translations are evaluated. Indeed, these translation processes have often been quite informal. For example, Brislin (1970) reported studies in which the full description of the translation processes was "a bilingual friend translated [the measure] from one language to another" (p. 187). These translation processes have varied from relatively *literal* translations to more *conceptual* translations. A literal translation process involves simple substitutions of Spanish words or phrases for each English word or phrase (or vice versa). A literal translation process is based upon two important assumptions. The first is that all *words* used in the original research protocol and measures have exact counterparts in Spanish, and the grammatical structures of the English and Spanish languages are the same. Hence, one can simply substitute Spanish words for English words and retain the ordering and punctuation of the original English version. The second is that the *ideas* expressed in the original research protocol and measures have relatively exact counterparts in the Spanish language, and the ways in which those ideas are expressed are identical across languages. For some very simple psychological constructs and research protocol ideas, literal translations may be somewhat acceptable. For example, an item to measure familism as "Children should always do things to make their parents happy" can be literally translated "Los niños deberían siempre hacer cosas para hacer a sus padres felices" with apparent equivalence of meaning.

However, the assumptions associated with a literal translation procedure are most often untenable (see Bracken & Barona, 1991; Van Widenfelt, Treffers, de Beurs, Siebelink, & Koudijs, 2005), and most ideas and items are not so amenable to a literal translation. Hence, literal translations can result in nonequivalent, nonsensical, or meaningless expressions when the source language (usually English) ideas have no exact counterpart or are expressed differently in the target language (usually Spanish). For example, it is not uncommon to use a Likert-type scale with anchors ranging from "strongly agree" to "strongly disagree" in English-language measures. There are a number of possible literal translations for these anchors in Spanish, such as "fuertemente *concuerdo*" to "fuertemente *discuerdo*," or "*convengo* fuertemente" to "*discrepo* fuertemente." There are two major problems with both of these literal translations. First, these verbs are used relatively infrequently among native Spanish speakers and usually then in a very formal context, such as a legal proceeding. Second, an adverb like *fuertemente* is commonly used to indicate the strength of a physical event (e.g., El terremoto sacudió la ciudad *fuertemente:* "The earthquake *strongly* shook the city") rather than the strength of a personal belief; in such a case, an adverb such as *firmemente* (literally "firmly") may be more adequate (e.g., Creo *firmemente:* "I firmly believe"). Hence, literal translations can often be problematic with regard to conveying the same information in Spanish and English.

A more *conceptual* translation approach involves the substitution of concepts and ideas expressed in English for the closest Spanish concepts or ideas (or vice versa), taking into consideration the cultural and sociolinguistic context (see Martinez, Marín, & Schoua-Glusberg, 2006; Van de Vijver & Tanzer, 2004). A conceptual translation process (or adaptation, as Van de Vijver calls it) may partially or completely modify original measures and research protocols by using different words, grammatical structures, and ways to express ideas across the English- and Spanish-language portions of the research protocol and measures. For example, a conceptual translation of "strongly agree" and "strongly disagree" must consider how these evaluative anchors are expressed in Latino cultures. The most likely conceptually translated alternatives are "muy de acuerdo" and "muy en desacuerdo,"

which, back-translated literally, correspond to "very much in agreement" and "very much in disagreement." Clearly, this conceptual translation is superior to the literal translations described earlier. However, conceptual translation, while adequate for most Latino populations, may not be for some. Some individuals may find the "muy en desacuerdo" anchor relatively awkward or unnatural because they do not typically express "disagreement." We observed such a difficulty expressing "disagreement" in a sample of Mexican American mothers who were not very highly educated. These mothers preferred to indicate, "No estoy de acuerdo para nada," which is translated "I am not in agreement at all." Of course, demonstrating the psychological equivalence of "strongly disagree" and "I am not in agreement at all" in this case represents a significant challenge. Educational and socioeconomic factors may influence the effectiveness of an anchor that uses a term rarely used in daily conversation.

Conceptual translations may also require that researchers consider the broader sociolinguistic context in which their participants exist, such as country/region of origin and educational background. For example, the item "You hardly ever praise your child for doing well" may be translated conceptually as "*Tú casi nunca elogias a tu niño por hacer algo bien*" and may be acceptable in some communities. However, among those who immigrate from more traditional communities, the use of the more informal pronoun *tú* with persons who are not close friends and relatives may seem inappropriate and disrespectful. The pronoun *usted* is typically used when communicating with a less familiar person or to show respect; hence, "*Usted* casi nunca elogia a su niño por hacer algo bien" may be a better alternative.

Similarly, "Usted casi nunca *felicita* a su niño por hacer algo bien" is another alternative for the item noted in the last paragraph. This item would be back-translated "You almost never congratulate your child for doing something good," and it may be a better choice when conducting research with Spanish speakers of diverse sociolinguistic and educational backgrounds. Although the former alternative is conceptually closer to the original English item, the verb *elogias* (i.e., "compliment" or "praise") may not seem as natural or as broadly understood as *felicita* among less educated Spanish speakers.

The implications associated with the need to consider the sociolinguistic context within which the Spanish-speaking Latino person exists are significant. In translating research protocols and measures, researchers need to avoid the presumption that "Spanish is Spanish" regardless of the backgrounds of the Spanish-speaking persons in the study. Spanish, like English, is a rich language with variants in the spoken form and the accents with which it is spoken, and it often differs substantially between immigrant families from different countries and different regions from within a country of origin. That is, the Spanish spoken by Cuban Americans, Mexican Americans, and Puerto Ricans is somewhat different, and adjustments to the translation process may usefully accommodate these differences. Similarly, the Spanish spoken by a Mexican immigrant from the Yucatán peninsula is richly different from the Spanish spoken by a Mexican immigrant from the Baja California peninsula, and sensitivity to the background of the participants in one's research may well be useful. That is, although most Latinos from a variety of countries of origin and from different regions within these countries may be able to communicate reasonably in generic Spanish, adaptations of the translation process to the specific nature of the Latino sample being studied may generate a more accurate (defined as faithful to the original) research protocol and set of measures, compared to those based on the presumptions that no regional and sociolinguistic differences exist.

Although conceptual translations may assume that the ideas expressed in the target language (usually Spanish) relate to relevant psychological constructs in the same way as in the original language (usually English), we need to consider the possibility that some ideas and items may not have equivalent counterparts in both English and Spanish. Further, some ideas that are easily expressible in one language may not be so easy to express in the other language. For example, the indicators of a particular psychological construct may be subtly different across persons with differing degrees of connection to the mainstream and Latino cultures. That is, Latino individuals with relatively strong connections to the Latino culture (i.e., highly enculturated Latinos) may interpret an item about social support from family members as referring to the extended family. In contrast, Latino individuals with relatively strong connections to the mainstream culture and relatively weak connections to the Latino culture (i.e., highly acculturated but not very enculturated) are more likely to interpret the term *family* as referring to the nuclear family. Since those Latinos completing this social support item in Spanish are likely to be more enculturated than those completing this item in English, differential responses may be a function of their differential interpretation of the meaning of the item. Many measures used to assess psychological constructs among Spanish-speaking Latinos are based upon the Spanish translation of a measure developed in English and may well have items that have different meaning, at least in part because of the translation. However, measures of target psychological constructs can also be developed simultaneously in English and Spanish. Van de Vijver and Tanzer (2004) note that when ideas do not exist across groups, one may want to *assemble* an instrument de novo, which is a comprehensive adaptation that results in the development of a totally new measure for use in both language groups.

Translation Procedures

Currently, three general sets of procedures are used for translating measures: one-way translation, back-translation, and committee translation. A *one-way translation* process is a one-directional translation of an existing measure by a bilingual person and is used primarily because it is quick, easy, and inexpensive (Weeks, Swerissen, & Belfrage, 2007). However, one-way translations are likely to produce translated instruments with low reliability and validity (Erkut, Alarcón, Coll, Tropp, & García, 1999) and provide no independent check of the accuracy of the translation. A *back-translation* process (originally proposed by Brislin, 1970) involves a bilingual person who translates the measure from English to Spanish and a second, independent bilingual person who translates the measure back into English. If the original English and the back-translated English measures are reasonably comparable, the translation is considered acceptable; otherwise, the process is repeated until the measures are reasonably comparable. In addition, *decentering*—resolving discrepancies by adjusting the original English-language measure to make it more comparable with the back-translated English measure—is sometimes used. The back-translation process with decentering is likely to produce more reliable and valid translated measures, in part because it includes some independent evaluation of the translation. A *committee translation* process involves a group of bilingual people who translate different measures and meet to review each others' translations, allowing an evaluation of the translations and the identification of inconsistencies or mistakes by committee members as the translation process occurs (Weeks et al., 2007). Bracken and Barona (1991) suggest using a combination of translation, back-translation, decentering, and committee approaches. Erkut et al. (1999) suggest including monolingual English speakers and monolingual Spanish speakers in the committee approach to ensure conceptually driven translations. Although significant advantages are associated with the use of committee approaches, these widely advocated but seldom used approaches are relatively costly (Weeks et al., 2007).

Although the combined use of these translation methods, particularly with an emphasis upon creating conceptually equivalent measures and research protocols, is likely to produce reasonably equivalent measures in both English and Spanish, these procedures can fail. There are at least two ways in which translation and back-translation by bilingual individuals and bilingual committees (particularly if Erkut and colleagues' suggestion of including monolingual committee members is not followed) may produce nonequivalent translations. First, very often the bilingual individuals involved in the translation and back-translation processes are substantially more educated than the target participants. These more educated translators are likely to be substantially more fluent in either English or Spanish (or both) than the target participants and perhaps less familiar with the more local nuances of the use of the Spanish language. Indeed, the individuals involved in the translation processes may not even be from the same country of origin as the target participants. Second, and perhaps even more difficult to address methodologically, the bilingual individuals involved in the translation processes may think differently and may be more cognitively flexible when it comes to understanding the nuances of selected content in the research protocol or measures than monolingual individuals

(see Knight et al., 2009). For example, evidence is emerging that bicultural individuals may "frame switch" given relatively simple and weak "priming" cues regarding the cultural nature of context (e.g., Hong, Morris, Chiu, & Benet-Martínez, 2000; Ramírez-Esparza, Gosling, Benet-Martínez, Potter, & Pennebaker, 2006). To the extent that simple primes may change the way in which a bicultural individual interprets the content presented subsequent to priming, and to the extent that the generally more educated bilingual individuals involved in the translation processes are more bicultural than the target respondents, these individuals may functionally switch the criteria they use for judging the meaning and meaningfulness of content included in the English- and Spanish-language research protocols and measures. Unfortunately, the limited means of checking the equivalence of translations, particularly translated measures, inherent in the translation process previously described provide little opportunity to search for translation problems that may result from the fundamental nature of the differences between the bilingual research team and the monolingual research participants. Too often, such errors are discovered only after the expense of gathering data from a complete sample and conducting analyses, which may result in a loss of potentially useful data. The inclusion of monolingual community members on the translation committee (Erkut et al., 1999) has some potential to find these translation failures; however, this procedure is rarely used, and even when it is used, it may not be sufficient in and of itself. Additional ways of examining the quality of the translated research protocols and measures are sorely needed to ensure that the scientific inferences are not simply a function of translation and measurement problems.

A strategy that may be useful for identifying the more complex translation failures in measures is to conduct the types of measurement equivalence analyses described earlier, including the more qualitative examinations. That is, once a combination translation approach has been used to produce English-language and Spanish-language measures of the target psychological construct, analyses of item functioning (i.e., factorial invariance tests) and scale functioning (i.e., construct validity equivalence tests) with a pilot sample, and focus group reviews by monolingual individuals representative of the target population, can be used to search for nonequivalencies that elude the bilingual translation team. In addition, the monolingual community members included in the translation team can assist in the generation of the culturally informed theory regarding the nature of the psychological constructs of interest and in examining the specific items and scales that are identified as potentially problematic in the more empirical analyses. A broader discussion of these translation issues is available elsewhere (Knight et al., 2009).

CONCLUSION

In conclusion, research on Latino psychology has come a long way. One need only compare this volume to the published volumes resulting from the first and second Chicano Psychology Conferences (Martinez, 1977; Martinez & Mendoza, 1984) to see the substantial advances in our understanding of a wealth of psychological processes as they apply to Latinos in the United States. However, we believe that future developments of Latino psychology may well depend upon advances in the types of methodological issues described herein. We believe that a better understanding of Latinos in the United States will require sampling procedures that clearly attract and retain participants who are representative of the broadly diverse Latino population. This will require careful attention to participants' particular countries of origin, length of time and number of generations in the United States, degree of acculturation and enculturation, language competence and preferences, and perhaps a host of other indicators of cultural orientation. In addition, we believe that a better understanding of Latinos in the United States will require measures that accurately assess the psychological constructs of interests within the broadly diverse Latino population. This will require careful attention to the nature of the psychological construct as it applies to the specific Latino population being studied and to the equivalence of that measure across the diverse elements of the Latino population of interest. Finally, these sampling and measurement issues will require careful attention to the translation of measures and research protocols to ensure that observed differences and similarities among subsets of the Latino population, as well as differences and similarities between the

Latino population and other ethnic groups in the United States, are fully representative of the broad diversity that exists within the Latino populations in the United States. We hope that the discussion of these methodological issues and challenges and the recommendations provided are helpful.

REFERENCES

Berg, B. L. (1995). *Qualitative research methods for the social sciences* (2nd ed.). Boston: Allyn & Bacon.

Bracken, B. A., & Barona, A. (1991). State of the art procedures for translating, validating and using psychoeducational tests in cross-cultural assessment. *School Psychology International, 12*, 119–132.

Brislin, R. W. (1970). Back-translation for cross-cultural research. *Journal of Cross-Cultural Psychology, 1*, 185–216.

Bryman, A., & Burgess, R. (Eds.). (1994). *Analyzing qualitative data.* New York: Routledge.

Byrne, B. M., Shavelson, R. J., & Muthén, B. (1989). Testing for the equivalence of factor covariance and mean structures: The issue of partial measurement invariance. *Psychological Bulletin, 105*, 456–466.

Capaldi, D., & Patterson, G. R. (1987). An approach to the problem of recruitment and retention rates for longitudinal research. *Behavioral Assessment, 9*, 169–177.

Cauce, A. M., Coronado, N., & Watson, J. (1998). Conceptual, methodological, and statistical issues in culturally competent research. In M. Hernandez & M. Isaacs (Eds.), *Promoting cultural competence in children's mental health services* (pp. 305–329). Baltimore: Paul H. Brookes.

Cauce, A. M., Ryan, K. D., & Grove, K. (1998). Children and adolescents of color, where are you? Participation, selection, recruitment, and retention in developmental research. In V. C. McLoyd & L. Steinberg (Eds.), *Studying minority adolescents: Conceptual, methodological, and theoretical issues* (pp. 147–166). Mahwah, NJ: Lawrence Erlbaum.

Coen, A. S., Patrick, D. C., & Shern, D. L. (1996). Minimizing attrition in longitudinal studies of special populations: An integrated management approach. *Evaluation and Program Planning, 19*, 309–319.

Cronbach, L. J. (1970). *Essentials of psychological testing* (3rd ed.). New York: Harper & Row.

Dumka, L. E., Lopez, V. A., & Jacobs Carter, S. (2002). Parenting interventions adapted for

Latino families: Progress and prospects. In J. M. Contreras, K. A. Kerns, & A. M. Neal-Barnett (Eds.), *Latino children and families in the United States* (pp. 203–231). Westport, CT: Greenwood.

Erkut, S., Alarcón, O., Coll, C. G., Tropp, L., & García, H. A. V. (1999). The dual-focus approach to creating bilingual measures. *Journal of Cross-Cultural Psychology, 30,* 206–218.

Feldman, M. S. (1995). *Strategies for interpreting qualitative data.* Thousand Oaks, CA: Sage.

Fetterman, D. M. (1989). *Ethnography: Step by step.* Newbury Park, CA: Sage.

Flaherty, J. A., Gaviria, M. F., Pathak, D., Mitchell, T., Wintrob, R., Richman, J. A., et al. (1988). Developing instruments for cross-cultural psychiatric research. *Journal of Nervous and Mental Disease, 176,* 257–263.

Gonzales, N. A., Knight, G. P., Morgan-Lopez, A., Saenz, D., & Sirolli, A. (2002). Acculturation and the mental health of Latino youths: An integration and critique of the literature. In J. M. Contreras, K. A. Kerns, & A. M. Neal-Barnett (Eds.), *Latino children and families in the United States.* Westport, CT: Greenwood.

Hampson, S. E., Dubanoski, J. P., Hamada, W., Marsella, A. J., Matsukawa, J., Suarez, E., et al. (2001). Where are they now? Locating former elementary-school students after nearly 40 years for a longitudinal study of personality and health. *Journal of Research in Personality, 35,* 375–387.

Hong, Y., Morris, M. W., Chiu, C., & Benet-Martínez, V. (2000). Multicultural minds: A dynamic constructivist approach to culture and cognition. *American Psychologist, 55,* 709–720.

Hui, C. H., & Triandis, H. C. (1989). Effects of culture and response format on extreme response style. *Journal of Cross-Cultural Psychology, 20,* 296–309.

Knight, G. P., & Hill, N. E. (1998). Measurement equivalence in research involving minority adolescents. In V. C. McLoyd & L. Steinberg (Eds.), *Studying minority adolescents: Conceptual, methodological, and theoretical issues* (pp. 183–210). Mahwah, NJ: Lawrence Erlbaum.

Knight, G. P., Roosa, M. W., & Umaña-Taylor, A. (2009). *Studying ethnic minority and economically disadvantaged populations: Methodological challenges and best practices.* Washington, DC: APA Books.

Knight, G. P., Tein, J.-Y., Prost, J., & Gonzales, N. A. (2002). Measurement equivalence and research on Latino children and families: The importance of culturally informed theory. In J. M. Contreras, K. A. Kerns, & A. M. Neal-Barnett (Eds.). *Latino children and families in*

the United States: Current research and future directions (pp. 181–201). Westport, CT: Praeger.

Labouvie, E., & Ruetsch, C. (1995). Testing the equivalence of measurement scales: Simple structure and metric invariance reconsidered. *Multivariate Behavioral Research, 30,* 63–70.

Levkoff, S., & Sanchez, H. (2003). Lessons learned about minority recruitment and retention from the Centers on Minority Aging and Health Promotion. *The Gerontologist, 43,* 18–26.

Luna, D., & Peracchio, L. A. (2002). Uncovering the cognitive duality of bilinguals through word association. *Psychology & Marketing, 19,* 457–475.

Marín, G., Gamba, R. J., & Marín, B. V. (1992). Extreme response style and acquiescence among Hispanics: The role of acculturation and education. *Journal of Cross-Cultural Psychology, 23,* 498–509.

Martinez, G., Marín, B. V., & Schoua-Glusberg, A. (2006). Translating from English to Spanish: The 2002 National Survey of Family Growth. *Hispanic Journal of Behavioral Sciences, 28,* 531–545.

Martinez, J. L., Jr. (Ed.). (1977). *Chicano psychology.* New York: Academic Press.

Martinez, J. L., Jr., & Mendoza, R. H. (Eds.). (1984). *Chicano psychology.* Orlando, FL: Academic Press.

Miranda, J., Azocar, F., Organista, K. C., Munoz, R. F., & Lieberman, A. (1996). Recruiting and retaining low-income Latinos in psychotherapy research. *Journal of Consulting and Clinical Psychology, 64,* 868–874.

McDonald, R. P. (1995). Testing for approximate dimensionality. In D. Laveault, B. D. Sumbo, M. E. Gessaroli, & M. W. Boss (Eds.), *Modern theories of measurement: Problems and issues* (pp. 63–86). Ottawa, Canada: Edumetric Research Group, University of Ottawa.

McDonald, R. P. (1999). *Test theory: A unified treatment.* Mahwah, NJ: Lawrence Erlbaum.

Nunnally, J. C. (1967). *Psychometric theory.* New York: McGraw-Hill.

Ramírez-Esparza, N., Gosling, S. D., Benet-Martínez, V., Potter, J. P., & Pennebaker, J. W. (2006). Do bilinguals have two personalities? A special case of cultural frame switching. *Journal of Research in Personality, 40,* 99–120.

Roosa, M. W., Liu, F., Torres, M., Gonzales, N., Knight, G. & Saenz, D. (2008). Sampling and recruitment in studies of cultural influences on adjustment: A case study with Mexican Americans. *Journal of Family Psychology, 22,* 293–302.

Scott, C. K. (2004). A replicable model for achieving over 90% follow-up rates in longitudinal studies of substance abusers. *Drug and Alcohol Dependence, 74,* 21–36.

Spoth, R., Goldberg, C., & Redmond, C. (1999). Engaging families in longitudinal prevention intervention research: Discrete-time survival analysis of socioeconomic and socio-emotional risk factors. *Journal of Consulting and Clinical Psychology, 67,* 157–163.

Stephens, R. C., Thibodeaux, L., Sloboda, Z., & Tonkin, P. (2007). Research note: An empirical study of adolescent student attrition. *The Journal of Drug Issues, 2,* 475–486.

Swider, S. M. (2002). Outcome effectiveness of community health workers: An integrative literature review. *Public Health Nursing, 19,* 11–20.

Umaña-Taylor, A. J., & Bámaca, M. Y. (2004). Conducting focus groups with Latino populations: Lessons from the field. *Family Relations, 53,* 261–272.

U.S. Census Bureau. (2001). *The Hispanic population: Census 2000 brief.* Washington, DC: U.S. Department of Commerce, Economics and Statistics Administration.

U.S. Census Bureau. (2004). *We the people: Hispanics in the United States. Census 2000 special reports.* Washington, DC: U.S. Department of Commerce, Economics and Statistics Administration.

Van de Vijver, F., & Tanzer, N. K. (2004). Bias and equivalence in cross-cultural assessment: An overview. *European Review of Applied Psychology/Revue Européenne de Psychologie Appliquée, 54,* 119–135.

Van Widenfelt, B., Treffers, P. D. A., de Beurs, E., Siebelink, B., & Koudijs, E. (2005). Translation and cross-cultural adaptation of assessment instruments used in psychological research with children and families. *Clinical Child and Family Psychology Review, 8,* 135–147.

Weeks, A., Swerissen, H., & Belfrage, J. (2007). Issues, challenges, and solutions in translating study instruments. *Evaluation Review, 31,* 153–165.

Widaman, K. F., & Reise, S. P. (1997). Exploring the measurement invariance of psychological instruments: Applicants in the substance use domain. In K. Bryant, M. Windle, & S. West (Eds.), *The science of prevention: Methodological advances from alcohol and substance abuse research* (pp. 281–324). Washington, DC: American Psychological Association.

5

Ethical Issues in Conducting Research With Latino Drug Users

Merrill Singer, Celia B. Fisher, G. Derrick Hodge,
Hassan N. Saleheen, and Meena Mahadevan

P ervasive inequalities, cultural differences, and significant dissimilarities in experience separate researchers from research subjects (Gold, 2003; Hoeyer, Dahlager, & Lynöe, 2005; Marshall, 2005; Turner, 2005). These distinctions raise important questions about how such issues as communication, trust, inclusion, and coercion impact research relationships, the quality of data collection, and the consequences of involvement in research for study participants and their respective communities (Alvidrez & Arean, 2002; Armstrong, Crum, Rieger, Bennett, & Edwards, 1999; Freimuth et al., 2001; Molyneux, Peshu, & Marsh, 2005). Although researchers have been increasingly active in the discussion of these issues in recent years, as Molyneux and colleagues (2005, p. 443) emphasize, "The voices of the

people likely to be the subjects of research have been notably absent from the debate." Only very recently have researchers begun to examine the views, attitudes, and concerns of prospective participants toward involvement in research (Brody, Gluck, & Aragon, 1997; Fisher, 2002; Fisher & Fyrberg, 1994; Fisher, Higgins-D'Allesandro, Rau, Kuther, & Belanger, 1996; Fisher & Wallace, 2000; Roberts, Warner, & Brody, 2000; Sugarman et al., 1998). Although progress has been made in the inclusion of participant perspectives in research on such issues as cancer, aging, and several other health-related conditions, much of this research has focused on white, middle-class participants. To the degree that ethnic minorities have been included in this kind of research, the bulk of the work has focused on assessing the attitudes

This chapter is based on the original article "Ethical Issues in Research With Hispanic Drug Users: Participant Perspectives on Risks and Benefits" by Merrill Singer, Greg Mirhej, G. Derrick Hodge, Hassan Saleheen, Celia B. Fisher, and Meena Mahadevan, published by the Florida State University (2008) in *Journal of Drug Issues*, 0022-0426/08/01, pp. 351–372. The research was supported by NIDA grant # 1 R01 DA015649-01A2 to Fordham University; Principal Investigators: Celia B. Fisher and Merrill Singer.

toward and understandings of research among African Americans (most notably in light of the Tuskegee syphilis study), with comparatively little examination of perspectives on research participation among Latinos (Corbie-Smith, Thomas, Williams, & Moody-Ayres, 1999; Napoles-Springer et al., 2000; Robinson, Ashley, & Haynes, 1996; Sengupta et al., 2000).

This pattern is noteworthy because within the realm of health research, Latinos constitute a vulnerable population in terms of several established criteria: (1) They are members of a marginalized ethnic minority population characterized by cultural and linguistic features that differentiate them from the dominant population; (2) they have difficulty accessing health care and health insurance; (3) they are disproportionately of lower socioeconomic status; (4) they have disproportionately high rates of immigration from other countries of origin, may therefore have little prior exposure to research, and may be dealing with immigration issues that increase their risk of being intimidated by researchers; (5) they have comparatively low levels of education and health literacy and high rates of school dropout; and (6) they are more likely than the dominant population to work in hazardous jobs or to be involved with the criminal justice system.

For all these reasons, it is extremely important to better understand the range of experiences in research of Latino participants. At the same time, investigators must be especially vigilant in protecting Latino research participants from various potential harms of research involvement and in ensuring that special ethical issues that arise in research with Latinos are identified and carefully addressed. To date, despite the recognized need for studies designed to elucidate how sociocultural factors among Latinos impact a range of ethical issues in research (e.g., recruitment, retention, informed consent, and safeguards against potential exploitation), very limited research has been conducted on the ethical dilemmas encountered in involving Latinos as research participants (Deren, Shedlin, Decena, & Mino, 2006; Miskimen, Marín, & Escobar, 2003); in particular, limited effort has been made to assess Latino perspectives on being research participants. In this light, the first goal of this chapter is to examine social, cultural, and linguistic features of the Latino population, as well as several notable social and health disparities that contribute to special ethical challenges in conducting research with Latinos. Within this framework, the second goal is to report findings from recent research that explores Latino participant perspectives on ethical issues encountered as a result of involvement in health-related research.

CULTURE AND RESEARCH AMONG LATINOS

As Rayna Rapp (2000, p. 44) has argued, the field of research ethics too often is "self-confidently unaware of its own sociocultural context" and fails to consider whether the standards it develops reflect the values of the world's diverse populations. Thus, like bioethics generally, discussion of research ethics has emphasized the importance of respecting individual autonomy, free will, and self-determination and thus has opposed forcing patients or research participants to do things against their will or without their full consent. While these are understandable concerns in the contemporary world, the problem is that the values emphasized reflect the Western celebration of individualism, a moral stance that is not necessarily shared or shared to the same degree by all cultural systems. While there is variation within Western and non-Western societies on individualist versus collectivist valuation, and these are in flux as a result of globalism and other social trends, the narrow application of Western ethical standards without sensitivity to alternative configurations of emphasis may be a form of unintended ethical imperialism. This is a concern that has been raised in research with Latino populations (Fisher et al., 2002; Fontes, 1998).

Latinos in the United States constitute a diverse group of people of varied national origin, generation, level of acculturation, socioeconomic class, region of residence, gender, sexual orientation, and preferred language. Too often, however, to the degree that they have been included in research—which in itself is an ethical issue of concern (Martinez, 1997; Naranjo & Dirksen, 1998)—Latino participants often have been aggregated into a single category or with African Americans and others as "ethnic minorities." As Birman (2006) stresses,

> Studies that include multiple ethnic subgroups must have sufficient participants in every cell to be able to conduct analyses that account for ethnocultural differences; however, the realities of most research projects prohibit such a focus and lead researchers either to concentrate on a single (generally larger) migrant group or to ignore specific cultural

variation and use a broader category, such as Latino or Black to describe them. (p. 156)

While it is possible to identify some important common cultural themes across Latino subgroups by country of national origin or in terms of other organizing criteria, all such generalizations are complicated by issues of age, acculturation, location, and other factors (Villa, Cuellar, Gamel, & Yeo, 1993). Latino cultures are not trait lists of immutable features; rather, they are dynamic systems that change over time and in response to various regional and situational contexts, including threats and opportunities in local environments.

Still, despite considerable variation by household, class status, country of origin, and generation—as well as recognition that in different contexts or in response to different challenges, the same person may place different emphasis on individualist versus collectivist values—some very general Latino differences from the dominant U.S. culture are identifiable. Broadly speaking, as contrasted with the high level of individualism commonly stressed in the dominant U.S. culture across multiple cultural domains, there tends to be a somewhat greater degree of emphasis on collectivist values among Latinos, especially with reference to the family, which may extend far beyond the nuclear unit. Thus, grandparents (*abuelitas/abuelos*), aunts and uncles (*tias* and *tios*) and cousins (*primos*) tend to be included as important and influential family members to whom an individual owes obligations. For example, traditionally it has been very common for the eldest child in a family to take responsibility for the care of aging parents, or for Latino individuals to put family priorities above personal needs or employment obligations (Marín & Marín, 1991; Sabogal, Marín, Otero-Sabogal, & Marín, 1987; Sue & Sue, 2003). Similarly, while success in the dominant U.S. culture is celebrated as an individual achievement, with associated benefits accruing to the individual, among Latinos greater emphasis traditionally has been placed on achievement as a means of bringing economic and emotional benefit to the family. Among Latino migrants to the United States, for example, family members already in residence can be expected to provide considerable assistance upon arrival and to help facilitate transition to the new social environment. At the same time, migrants are expected to return remittances to family members "back home" to improve their socioeconomic standing, as well as to assist additional family members to migrate (Falicov, 1995). Latino family pride and family honor endure as important cultural values even as Latino culture undergoes dramatic changes across generations.

These issues are of note because Latino family values may significantly influence involvement in and concerns about research, with family confidentiality, gender relations, and issues of sexual orientation being potentially quite sensitive topics among Latino research participants. Latino husbands, for example, may have strong concerns about the involvement of their spouses in research with unknown male researchers (Frias & Angel, 2005), and this has certainly been our experience over many years of multicultural research. Similarly, Latinos may be especially anxious about keeping knowledge about behaviors that violate family expectations (e.g., homosexuality) from reaching the awareness of family members, another force shaping the willingness of Latinos to participate in research or to disclose some types of personal information in this context (Singer et al., 2000).

One important reflection of differences between Latino and dominant cultural patterns has to do with school involvement. Tensions are common between the values to which Latinos are exposed at home and at school (especially in households with immigrant parents and American-born children), while the demands of school may be experienced as conflicting with a child's home responsibilities. This conflict appears to play some role in school dropout among Latinos, although socioeconomic status appears to be of greater consequence. Thus, as Hirschman (2001) reports, approximately 40% of foreign-born Latinos of school age are not enrolled in school. Overall rates of dropping out of school among Latinos 16 to 24 years old is 21.6%, compared to 11.5% for non-Latino whites (Hauser, Simmons, & Pager, 2000). Needless to say, educational achievement is a factor in various aspects of research involvement, including understanding both research risks and the nature of protections for research participants.

Further, existing research suggests that Latinos who try to assimilate with school culture, and as a result encounter conflict at home, experience more distress in life than those who maintain cultural ties to Latino cultural traditions (Vigil, 1999). A lower level of assimilation is expressed in various behaviors, such as exclusively watching Spanish-language television or speaking only

Spanish at home, routinely eating traditional Latino cultural foods, and participating in an annual round of family and community rituals. Needless to say, there is considerable variation in these behaviors across households, generations, and other characteristics, with most people mixing traditional and dominant cultural patterns in varying ways. At the same time, Latinos must contend with social rejection in the wider society. In their day-to-day lives, many Latinos report experiencing discrimination and prejudice (Sue & Sue, 2003). Expectation of discrimination may color Latino attitudes about involvement in research. Additionally, traditional Latino respect for medical authorities creates the opportunity for unintended coercion in health research.

Beyond the family, another critical cultural feature of Latinos involves the role of religion and spirituality in everyday life. Again, while this may be true of non-Latinos as well, the integration of religious motifs and practices (as well as the salience of particular symbols) remains a compelling feature of everyday Latino experience and behavior. Traditionally, many aspects of Latino culture were deeply rooted in the Catholic Church. Although this is changing as a result of the phenomenal growth of the Charismatic movement within Catholicism, Pentecostalism, and other Protestant denominations in Latin America and in U.S. Latino communities, traditional Catholic symbols and ritual practices are still widespread and influential in Latino populations. Recent research (Pew Research Center, 2007) indicates that most Latinos pray daily, most have at least one religious object in their homes, and most attend religious services at least once per month. While the issue has not been well studied, fear of a lack of sensitivity among researchers to values that are rooted in religious cultural traditions may be another influence on Latino involvement in research.

SOCIAL AND HEALTH DISPARITIES AMONG LATINOS

Latino cultural diversity notwithstanding, a number of health and social disparities stand out as prevailing features of the Latino population (although they certainly do not apply to all Latinos and are more characteristic of the social conditions faced by some Latino subgroups than others), and many of these disparities have implications for research ethics (Smedley, Stith,

& Nelson, 2002). Such disparities decrease the likelihood that Latinos will become research participants (raising issues of distributive justice) while also decreasing their access to the benefits of research.

Latinos now constitute the largest ethnic minority population in the country, 5 years earlier than had been projected by the U.S. Census Bureau (2000). This population continues to grow at an unprecedented rate of 5.7% each year nationally. It is estimated that 37 million Latinos reside in the United States, up almost 5% since the completion of the 2000 census. Latinos account for approximately 13% of the total U.S. population, or roughly one of every eight people in the country. The growing size of the Latino population underlines its importance as a focus of research. Yet, because Latinos are not reflective of average socioeconomic patterns in the country but rather suffer from a number vulnerabilities, studying this population, as discussed in the following paragraphs, raises various potential ethical dilemmas.

Most notable in this regard is the issue of poverty. Poverty has been found to be closely tied with health status and is generally considered a risk factor for poor health and disease, especially among children (LaVeist, 2005). Moreover, children who grow up in poverty are more likely to do poorly in school, to become teen parents, and to be unemployed as adults. The poverty rate among Latinos is 3 times the rate of non-Latino whites (approximately 26% vs. 8%) in the United States. Additionally, the median income for Latino households is about $15,000 a year below that of non-Latino white households (U.S. Census Bureau, 2000).

Rates of unemployment among Latinos are almost double those of non-Latino whites. Further, while there is a growing Latino middle class, the majority of employed Latinos are disproportionately concentrated in low-paid jobs with limited room for economic advancement; equally important, Latinos often hold jobs that do not provide health insurance. Several economic indicators show a drop in occupational status of Latinos and a growing gap in the respective occupational status of Latinos and non-Latino whites in recent years. Data from the 2000 census (U.S. Census Bureau, 2000) indicate that one quarter (27%) of Latino children under the age of 18 live in poverty, compared to only 9% of non-Latino white children. Poverty rates among Latinos, however, vary significantly by ethnic subgroup. While 16% of Cuban children live in poverty, the rate for Puerto Rican children is 44%. Although rates of poverty are especially high among immigrant Latinos, poverty rates are 2.5 times those of non-Latino white children, even among third- and fourth-generation children of Mexican origin,.

The 1998 report of the National Center for Health Statistics (Pamuk, Makuc, Heck, Reuben, & Lochner, 1998) reviewed available research and concluded that morbidity and mortality are related to socioeconomic status as measured by either income or educational achievement. Those with less than a high school education had higher rates of suicide, homicide, smoking, and heavy use of alcohol than did those with higher levels of education. The report, which is now supported by a considerable body of additional literature, concluded that on average, the lower one's income or educational attainment, the poorer one's health. Notably, Latinos reported lower levels of education as well as health literacy.

Health literacy is defined by Healthy People 2010 (2009, Ch. 11, Glossary) as "[t]he degree to which individuals have the capacity to obtain, process, and understand basic health information and services needed to make appropriate health decisions." Over the past several decades, numerous studies have analyzed the difficulty of health-related print materials and patients' ability to read health-related charts, tables, and text and to recognize common medical terms. The pattern of findings is seen, for example, on literacy proficiency scores produced by the Health Activities Literacy Scale (HALS), an instrument developed by the Educational Testing Service for the U.S. Department of Education, which uses a range of literacy tasks previously created for various large-scale national surveys of adult literacy (Rudd, Kirsch, & Yamamoto, 2004). Scores on the 191-item HALS range from 0 to 500 and are grouped in terms of five levels of literacy, with Level 1 (i.e., scores from 0 to 225) representing the lowest level of proficiency and Level 5 (i.e., scores from 376 to 500) the highest. The average proficiency score of white adults on the HALS was 285, significantly higher than the average for Latinos (217). The disparity was particularly significant between the percentage of white adults who were performing below Level 1, compared with Latinos. Among Latino adults, 30% were found to perform below Level 1. Moreover, Latinos born outside of the United States had an average HALS proficiency score of 170. This is

more than 100 points, or 1.75 standard deviations, below the average HALS score of all U.S.-born adults. These findings have immediate implications for Latino involvement in research, from understanding research questions to completing informed-consent procedures.

Additionally, existing research affirms that poverty and such related structural disadvantages as discrimination and racism affect health status in a number of direct and indirect ways, including unhealthy diet, increased exposure to physical and emotional stressors in the environment (e.g., street violence), heightened exposure to environmental toxins (e.g., lead paint, rodent infestation) and street violence, comparatively high rates of immune system impairment, and limitations on access to preventive care and treatment for existing conditions (LaVeist, 2005). For example, Latinos are 4 times as likely as non-Latino whites to suffer from tuberculosis. Rates of tuberculosis tend to reflect living conditions and residential crowding. Because of poverty, many Latino families live in substandard, poorly ventilated housing, with a higher number of people per square foot of living space than in non-Latino whites' homes. These are the conditions under which a communicable disease like tuberculosis is most likely to spread (Flores et al., 2003).

Moreover, Latinos are distinctive in having a comparatively young population. The median age of Latinos in the United States is 25 years, and nearly 40% of Latinos are under 20 years of age. Additionally, the proportion of the total number of children in the United States who are Latino has increased at a faster pace than that of any other ethnic group, growing from 9% of the child population in 1980 to 19% by 2000. If current trends continue, by 2050 one in four people living in the United States will be Latino (U.S. Census Bureau, 2000).

Nonetheless, the average life span of Latinos is 20 years shorter than for non-Latino whites. In terms of specific causes of death, Latinos are disproportionately likely to die of violence (homicide being the second leading cause of death for Latinos 15 to 24 years of age), to develop late-onset diabetes (11%, compared to 5% in the general population), to develop cervical cancer (with an incidence rate of 17 per 100,000 for Latinas, compared to just under 9 per 100,000 for non-Latinas), to suffer from asthma (hospitalization rates for Latino youth in some states are 5 times higher than for whites), to become infected with HIV/AIDS (although Latinos account for approximately 14% of the population of the United States and Puerto Rico, they constitute 18% of AIDS cases diagnosed since the beginning of the epidemic). Some Latino subgroups, especially Puerto Ricans and Mexican Americans, have comparatively high rates of illicit drug use and high rates of heavy drinking and report comparatively high levels of teen pregnancy. Indeed, Latinas have the highest teen birth rate of all ethnic populations in the United States (Interagency Forum on Child and Family Statistics, 2008; U.S. Centers for Disease Control and Prevention, 2002).

Equally significant is that Latinos are the least likely population in the United States to have health insurance and one of the most likely to encounter linguistic and cultural barriers in accessing effective and appropriate health care. For example, research has shown that although rates for English-speaking Latinos are similar to those of whites, monolingual Spanish-speaking Latino patients are significantly less likely than whites to have had a physician visit or an influenza vaccination during the year (Hispanic Health Council, 2006).

In assessing the health status of the Latino population, it must be stressed that public health researchers generally acknowledge that mortality rates among Latinos tend to be underestimated for several reasons, including misreporting of ethnicity on death certificates and other health-related documents used as health indicators in research, as well as the return migration of Latinos with life-threatening illnesses to their countries of origin (Aguirre-Molina et al., 2001). Similarly, morbidity rates for Latinos often are underestimated because of a failure to collect full ethnicity data in many studies or in surveillance monitoring; use of such methodologies as telephone interviewing, which does not effectively reach the lowest-income populations (because of geographic mobility, inability to pay telephone bills on time, doubling up of families in residential settings, homelessness, etc.); failure of survey research to reach segments of the Latino population; and lack of access to health care despite significant health problems. Moreover, because of diversity within the overall Latino population, national statistics on Latinos provide only a rough image of the sociodemographic characteristics and health profiles of Latinos in any particular state.

Country of origin (for individuals born outside the United States, or country of ancestors for those born in the United States), in particular, differentiates health patterns among Latino subgroups. For example, the frequency of female-headed households among Puerto Ricans is double that of Cubans; the percentage of Latinos of Mexican origin living in a nonmetropolitan area is more than double that of Puerto Ricans; the rate of asthma among Puerto Ricans is more than double that of Mexicans or Cubans; and the frequency of AIDS-related mortality among Puerto Ricans is more than 3 times the rate among Mexican Americans (U.S. Census Bureau, 2000). Moreover, for foreign-born Latinos in the United States who are undocumented, fear of deportation becomes another reason for avoiding research participation. Additionally, research by Calderón et al. (2006) has shown that in this subgroup of Latinos many fear being involved unwittingly in research experimentation (e.g., when entering health care).

While health disparities have been found to be strongly influenced by poverty, they are especially common among poor people who live in areas with a high percentage of poor people in the local population. Thus, poor people in cities with smaller impoverished populations are at lower risk of dying than those in cities with large impoverished populations. Comparisons of findings from the 1990 and 2000 census counts indicate that the size of the Latino population in big cities is increasing, especially in such large metropolitan areas as New York and Los Angeles, which already have large concentrations of Latinos. Thus, between 1990 and 2000, the number of Latinos who lived in neighborhoods in which a majority of residents were Latino grew faster (76%) than in neighborhoods in which Latinos constituted a minority of residents (51%). In many urban areas with Latino populations, Latinos are disproportionately found in more densely populated inner-city zones with comparatively high rates of poverty, places where disease syndemics involving multiple interacting diseases of diverse kinds are most common (Singer, 2006; U.S. Census Bureau, 2000).

Moreover, studies of differences by location among the poor show that the sociophysical environment in which people live—that is, their experience of their surrounding community, including issues of danger, stress, comfort, and appeal—is a critical determinant of their health.

Feelings of hopelessness and powerlessness in a community have been found to be good predictors of health risk and health status (Leon & Walt, 2001). These are precisely the kinds of sentiments that have been recorded in a number of studies of Latinos, particularly Latino youth (Grunbaum et al., 2004). These various vulnerabilities have direct implications for the conduct of research among Latinos.

In sum, although it is now a standard ethical principle that researchers seek to enhance the benefits of research for the individuals, communities, and populations being studied, they face difficult challenges in their efforts to select and define the ethnic group or subgroup membership of research participants and in knowing the often subtly varying issues raised in working with different vulnerable populations. At the same time, health and social disparities, not ethnic identification, may at times be the most critical challenges investigators confront in ensuring that their research is fair and beneficial.

A Case Study of Ethical Issues in Research Among Latino Drug Users

As part of the concern of our research team with ethical issues, particularly among ethnic minority subgroups—which we define as potential conflicts with prevailing ethical principles of research stemming from target group vulnerability—we initiated a study of ethical issues in research among drug users. We elaborate on the nature and findings of this study here for the following reasons. First, research of this kind, which intentionally included and analyzed perspectives on research participation among members of a delineated Latino subgroup (Puerto Ricans) is not common. Second, as noted previously, rates of substance abuse are comparatively high among some Latino groups, whereas shorter- and longer-term effects are particularly enhanced among Latinos compared to other U.S. populations. Although research on drug use began during the 1930s, efforts were limited until the 1960s and 1970s; and only with a significant rise in funding in the late 1980s and early 1990s, primarily as a result of the AIDS epidemic, did the study of active, not-in-treatment drug users become fully established as an important and active domain of scientific investigation (Singer, 1999). Third, although a

considerable body of research into causes, consequences, patterns, trends, risks, prevention, and treatment of drug use and abuse has accumulated over the last 25 years, most of this work proceeded without much direct input from drug users about their views of the costs and benefits of research involvement, their reasons and motivations for research participation, and the nature and quality of their experiences as research subjects (Fry & Dwyer, 2001). Finally, of special importance in this regard are the particularly silent voices of minority drug users, a result of the triple burden of class location, socially devalued ethnic identities, and demonization as illicit drug consumers. Those who also are infected with HIV/AIDS face a quadruple burden of social marginalization because of disease stigmatization. The lack of such research confirms the assertion by Anderson and DuBois (2007, p. 103) that "[w]hile the ethical issues that arise in research conducted with potentially vulnerable participants who abuse substances are numerous and well-documented, the evidentiary base for addressing these issues is clearly inadequate."

Design of the Study

The data presented in this chapter were collected as part of a larger, ongoing National Institute on Drug Abuse-funded project entitled *Participant Perspectives on Drug Use/HIV Research Ethics* (# 1 R01 DA015649–01A1). This mixed-method study was designed to address limitations in current understanding of the experiences and attitudes of vulnerable illicit drug users by examining participant points of view on a range of issues, including risks and benefits of participating in research, informed consent, confidentiality, and use of incentives in the social and clinical sciences.

The larger study is organized around three waves of data collection from each of the two sites (New York and Hartford) using both qualitative and quantitative methods. Data from a series of focus groups—structured by ethnicity, gender, and sexual orientation—were collected from January 11 to September 12, 2006. Here, we report findings from the Latino focus groups held in Hartford, although some comparisons with non-Latino participants are included to help describe the sociodemographic, health, and drug use characteristics of the Latino participants in the study. There were a small number of Latinos in the minority sexual orientation focus groups held in New York City, but because these groups included participants of diverse ethnic identities, comments specifically of Latino participants cannot be extracted from the taped focus group narratives, so they are not analyzed here.

In selecting a focus group approach, we were aware that participants would hold differing views and that individual perspectives might change in the course of group discussions (Fisher & Wallace, 2000). Indeed, it was the desire to capture participants' "opinions in progress" (ibid.) that led to our selection of the focus group format, as even heartfelt attitudes are often emergent and only achieve full coherence as they are articulated in social interaction. Focus groups are useful in ethics research because they have the potential to constitute quasi-ethnographic settings if participants feel comfortable and begin to partake in animated discussion with peers about meaningful issues of common concern. In Hartford, where all of the Latino participants discussed in this paper were recruited, focus group members were recruited through street outreach by experienced, bilingual staff. Outreach targeted public venues known from past research in the city to be higher-density areas for street-drug users, including illicit drug acquisition and use locations, sources of social services targeted to low-income populations, and sites of service provision specifically targeted to populations at high risk for HIV/AIDS (e.g., street locations visited by the local syringe-exchange program).

Focus groups with Latino participants were conducted in Spanish and facilitated by bilingual ethnographers. Discussions for the focus groups were stimulated by brief videotaped presentations of scenarios or "research vignettes" carefully designed to present participants with visual examples of ethical considerations and questions. Three vignettes of approximately 3–5 minutes each featured professional male and female actors portraying researchers and drug users conducting and participating in a survey, an ethnographic study, and a double-blind, placebo-controlled clinical trial. To account for the possibility that perceived differences in the versions might occur due to the ethnicity or gender of the actors, two versions were made of each vignette or research design: one version depicting a male researcher and a female drug user, the other a female researcher and a male user. Each version of the vignettes was also made available in Spanish, for a total of 12 vignettes. A male or female drug-user version was shown, depending on the gender of the focus group. The facilitator coordinating the focus group sessions introduced the vignettes to the participants one at a time, followed by guided focus group discussion of each vignette. Although participants were not asked about their own behaviors, they often framed their comments in terms of personal experiences.

Research Vignettes

The vignettes presented a range of research methodologies for which ethnically diverse street-drug users are recruited and about which ethical issues have been raised in the literature (Buchanan, Koshnood, Stopka, Santelices, & Singer, 2002; Charland, 2002) as well as in the experience of research team members (Singer et al., 1999). Descriptions of responses characteristic of the larger multigroup sample can be found in Oransky et al., in press, Fisher et al., 2009, and Fisher et al., 2008 for vignettes 1–3 respectively. The first vignette depicted a researcher engaged in street outreach recruitment to enroll a drug user in a survey about his or her sexual behavior and drug habits as well as attitudes and beliefs about what spreads HIV and other infectious diseases that affect drug users. The narrator in the video explains that this information will help researchers understand which sex practices and drug-sharing behaviors transmit HIV and hepatitis C in the community and that it will help policymakers improve services that help people stay healthy. The narrator encourages viewers to pay specific attention to the recruitment procedures employed in the scenario and the interactions between the researcher and the participant.

The second vignette illustrates participation in an ethnographic study of the transmission of HIV in illicit drug-using populations based on participant observation and street interviews. The narrator in this vignette explains to the focus group viewers that the ethnographer has spent several months with local drug users who have HIV/AIDS or are at risk of becoming infected with it, in order to gain an insider's perspective on the conditions that lead them to share syringes and other drug injection equipment. The narrator explains that the researcher usually gets to know one or two drug users very well, and these individuals are asked to introduce the researcher to other drug users in the community. The narrator encourages viewers to pay particular attention to the nature of the relationship between the researcher and the participant and to any ethical dilemmas they see that might arise in such a relationship.

The third vignette depicts recruitment of a drug user for a double-blind, placebo-controlled, randomized clinical trial to test the efficacy of a new drug for reducing cocaine cravings. The focus groups were introduced to this vignette with an explanation that the research was designed to compare a group that will receive the experimental drug with another group that will receive a placebo. The researcher in this video explains to the potential participant that although both groups will have the option to receive psychological therapy and counseling, neither the researcher nor the participant would know the specific group to which she would be assigned. Viewers are told to pay specific attention to the risks and benefits of participating in such a trial.

The total focus group sample comprised 100 participants. Within this larger sample, the Latino focus groups included 36 participants, the majority (64%) of whom were men and almost all of whom were Puerto Rican. The ages of participants ranged from 22 to 67 years (mean 43.3 years). Eighty-six percent of the Latino subsample self-identified as straight and 6% as bisexual, with the remaining participants declining to identify their sexual orientation. None had a full-time job; the majority (72%) were either unemployed or had been laid off. A minority (13%) worked part time. The remainder chose to not identify employment status. Forty-eight percent of participants in the Latino focus groups reported welfare or social security benefits as their only sources of income. Just over a quarter (28%) indicated that some form of hustling or selling drugs was a source of income. Notably, this compares to 9% for the non-Latinos in the total multiethnic focus group sample. As to their living situations, only 31% of participants in the Latino focus groups reported living in their own homes or apartments, compared to 47% of non-Latinos in the overall sample. Eleven percent of participants in the Latino focus groups reported that they were homeless, compared to 5% of non-Latinos in the overall sample. In short, Latino participants tended to live under less secure, riskier circumstances and as a

result may be more likely to face greater challenges of street life than their non-Latino counterparts in the study.

In the month prior to intake, participants in the Latino-specific focus groups reported drug use patterns that were noticeably different from and possibly more risky than those reported by non-Latinos in the overall sample. Prevalence rates of drug use for both groups during this period were as follows: heroin (Latinos, 81%; non-Latinos, 26%), powder cocaine (Latinos, 72%; non-Latinos, 28%), alcohol (Latinos, 31%; non-Latinos, 25%), crack (Latinos, 28%; non-Latinos, 37%), embalming fluid/marijuana mixtures (Latinos, 19%; non-Latinos, 0%), marijuana (Latinos, 17%; non-Latinos, 32%), and illicitly acquired antidepressant pills (Latinos, 14%; non-Latinos, 9%). While 67% of the participants in the Latino focus groups reported regular use of street drugs, this was true of only 35% of non-Latinos in the total sample. Almost 70% of participants in the Latino-specific focus groups reported injecting drugs in the last 30 days; among non-Latinos, this was the case for just over half (51%). Participants in the Latino-specific focus groups were much less likely to report an HIV/AIDS diagnosis (14%) than non-Latinos (49%) in the larger study. While most of the participants in the Latino subsample (81%) reported that they had previously participated in a drug/alcohol survey or interview study, 53% indicated participation in an HIV/AIDS-related survey or interview study, and 64% had participated in a clinical trial to test a new drug or HIV treatment.

FINDINGS

In the analysis of Latino focus group narratives, we identified a dynamic tension within and between participants about the dangers and appeals of involvement in drug use and HIV-risk research. In light of the prior discussion of special ethical challenges in research among Latinos, we found that participants in our Latino focus groups were particularly concerned about loss of confidentiality and resulting disruption of familial and community social support because of HIV/AIDS stigma. Yet, they also viewed research participation as an available means of acquiring health knowledge, health services, and hard-to-come-by sums of money.

HIV/AIDS Stigmatization: Fear of Family and Community Rejection

Participant fears about loss of confidentiality, especially in studies that include HIV testing, were a source of strong concerns among the Latino participants in our study. Indeed, this was seen as a primary risk of partaking in social science research among Latino participants. Participants seemed to be particularly concerned that taking part in research could lead to family members learning of their HIV status (or falsely believing they were infected just because of research participation). Worries about loss of confidentiality were closely tied by participants to their concerns over being marginalized or ostracized by their families, other kin and friends, and peers.

As expressed in the following comments by Latino focus group participants, the primary fear was not of the virus per se and the physical threats it presents to the health of infected individuals, but rather of that social stigma attached to HIV/AIDS infection, and the insensitivities and painful rejection that stigma can produce among significant others, especially family members. Participants felt that the period after learning about being HIV+ through a research project, when the need for family support would be greatest, would be the worst time for family members to "turn their backs" and leave the individual to suffer in isolation. Short of full rejection, unfounded family fear of contagion can lead to hurtful interactions with family members. One source of negative family reactions, according to participants, is a grave apprehension that the wider community might learn about the infection, subjecting the family to social disparagement and loss of dignity.

> The first thing . . . is your family. Because if you don't know what I am suffering, I cannot be important to you. The relatives are the first ones to say that you are sick, that you cannot come in [the house]. . . . They are the first one that say things that are hurtful to us.
>
> Well depending on, let me use a bad word here, if you have a f*cked-up family, they are going to only care about the stigma associated with knowing the fact that one of their relatives, especially if it is his son . . . that someone in their family has AIDS, and what this means for the family . . . you know, all this has to do with the

stigma because they may think, "my son or my daughter has AIDS," that is on the streets. There are families like that. These are families that don't think in the person but rather in the stigma.

Some of the rejection described by participants might be due to medical misconceptions in the Latino community regarding possible contagion. Such misconceptions can operate in conjunction with the physical abandonment concerns discussed in the preceding quotes; such treatment is viewed by participants as a form of emotional rejection even if the drug user has not been physically ejected from the household. Consider the following quote, in which a participant expresses fear of both kinds of rejection, followed by the statement of another participant, who is concerned that a family might allow its misunderstandings to impede a nurturing and supportive relationship.

> . . . with the situation they are referring to in the video, I think he will be helping his family [to find out his status], you know. That is, if they don't turn their back on him. Because very often the family is the one that turns its back on you, even when you need it the most. Because in a moment like that, when you find out that you are positive, that is when you really need support from all those 'round you . . . On the contrary, they turn their back on you; you go crazy because you learn that you are HIV positive and sometime you even feel like you want to commit suicide . . . and your family doesn't want to know anything about you. When you go to visit them and you want to drink water, let's say, they give it to you in a disposable paper cup. They don't want you to use the silverware; they don't want you to use nothing.
>
> For me, although she [actor in the vignette] is exposing her mother to risks, her mother may not have anything to do with that problem of drugs or whatever. Her mother may feel bad about it; she may be sorry because many families know it and they want to keep it covered. Because in some houses they only allow you to use certain things, because you may get things dirty, I mean, wherever you put your tongue. If you are going to serve yourself something, you have your own glass and whatever. Even today, there are some families that think that they can get infected by using your glass; they believe that. Those things still happen.

In addition to their fear of loss of family support as a result of unintended consequences of research participation, in the statements above there is expressed as well a degree of bitterness, perhaps reflecting participants' personal experiences with their own families.

Additionally, involvement with an organization that provides HIV/AIDS services or conducts HIV/AIDS research was seen as a cause for concern by participants because of erroneous conclusions some people in the community might draw. For instance, even though Hartford's Hispanic Health Council, the site at which the research was conducted, is a multiservice and research institute with various health education and support programs as well as research initiatives unrelated to HIV/AIDS, one participant stated that she was so concerned that her mother would think she had AIDS that she was even concerned about participating in the ethics research study:

> But if someone who knows you finds out and go tell your family, for them, in my case, for my mom, it would be terrible. Because we are here now, and after this interview anyone who will see us leaving this place . . . they may say, "Oh, they are sick because they were at the Hispanic Council."

Similarly, other participants commented:

> Eh, you know we face a risk . . . you know, because sometimes you are afraid . . . that if people get to know, if they find out, they are going to say . . . they are going to recognize you, and very quickly they are going to say, "Look, she does have AIDS."
>
> . . . when she [actor in the vignette] goes to an agency like this one and another person sees her entering, that person may say, "Ah, she was here the last time." And she may also say, "Oh that person has AIDS." And they will spread the word and tell other people. . . . It is like that. . . . There are many places where they are doing studies on AIDS, not just the Hispanic Health Council.

The consequences of family rejection are momentous, according to participants, leading possibly, as we have seen, to "going crazy" or contemplating suicide. Another participant noted,

> The thing is for the family to understand what he [participant in the vignette] is going through. . . . Because in the video you can see that he is afraid of explaining it to them. And he knows he has the virus. . . . And he doesn't know what to do . . . and not everyone in the family will understand. . . . If you don't know what it is about, you cannot help yourself. . . . You are alone in the world, you are lost.

As this comment suggests, without familial involvement and support, an individual lacks a social anchor or meaningful place in the world. This concern is magnified by possible rejection by the wider community, including fellow church members and coworkers, as indicated by the following participant:

> But you know I still have this issue today, going to my family's church and telling them that I have it, but then again I feel like I'm going to be shunned once I tell them I have it. Like nobody, not even people at work, gonna want to know me no more, like get away from me, like I don't want to shake your hand no more. Then they could fire me . . . it happened to my friend once.

Participants also were concerned about other ways their private information collected in a study could be exposed, subjecting them not only to consequent family or community rejection but to legal actions as well. As one participant stated,

> There is one thing and maybe I am wrong but I am going to say it. These [research] programs are good and they have their parts that are not that good too. I am going to explain why I see it this way. This information that we give to them, for example, something happens, the court may request this information and they will have it the moment they want it. That is what I say. They [the researchers] cannot say that this is private information. . . . It is not private, because with a warrant from the court, they come here and they take any information that they want and especially if it's federal. . . . So it is private because it is information they keep in their private files but at any moment that the Feds or any government person want this information, they will have to give it to them; they will give them the papers. They cannot refuse to give it to them because if they don't do so, they will be taken to

jail. . . . When we are doing these programs, we have to be very careful in the way in which we talk.

While it was explained to participants as part of the consent process that the ethics study, like many studies with drug users, was protected by a federal certificate of confidentiality from court order or police seizure of records, it is no doubt hard to believe that such certification could really stop a concerted law enforcement or court effort from gaining access to research files.

Health Benefits of Research Participation

Despite being worried that their families and others might find out their HIV status because of their involvement in research, the Latino drug users in our sample nonetheless tended to see participation in research as generally beneficial. Importantly, the benefits that they believed could be found in being a research subject appeared to reflect a lack of other access to needed health information and services. Research, in short, was seen by many participants as a means of overcoming structural barriers to prevention information, health screenings, and referral to care. As one participant commented, by participating in research it is possible to gain access to health "information that he doesn't have right now and information that is going to be good for him, information that will be beneficial for him and for his family . . . [and] tests . . . to know about his physical condition and how he is doing." Later, when assessing the risks of research participation, this individual added,

> Risks of what? Risks are the ones he [actor in the vignette] faces every day on the street, using drugs and doing other things. Those are the risks . . . but to participate in the program, I don't see any risk on that. . . . I mean, on the contrary, he is going to have knowledge that, most likely, he doesn't have right now.

Other participants commented,

> The benefit that if he [actor in vignette] ever finds himself in the situation of being HIV positive they can refer him to a doctor. . . . Also, the benefit that if he has hepatitis they will tell him, they will look for whatever disease he has, and if the disease is not too advanced, he will

have the benefit of receiving help. He can help himself with early detection.

> I think that it is beneficial [to participate] because in the same place you can get help if you are sick or any other type of help like clothing that one may need. They can offer that kind of help to us, you know. Because it's not only money . . . its help with medications.

> When you are using drugs on the streets, many times you engage in things that may put you in danger, so . . . if you submit to that . . . survey and the physical exam, and you know if you don't have any disease. So that is a relief and from there you can start protecting yourself. . . . He [actor in vignette] may say, "So far, this [HIV or other infection] has not happened to me so let me take better care of myself."

While many participants, as noted, fear that naïve family members could find out that they are HIV+, participation in a study and being tested for HIV were seen by others as a way to placate anxious and disgruntled family members who might falsely assume that their relative was infected (perhaps because they knew he or she was a drug user), as reflected in the following comments of a study participant:

> The benefit for the family is to know if he [actor in vignette] has any kind of disease or not, because sometimes our family, when they know that we are doing drugs and they have no orientation in regards to that . . . well they don't know anything about the drugs or anything. So many times they overwhelm you. They say, "You are lazy. You have this and that." In this case, they would get the benefit of knowing if he is clean [of HIV/AIDS infection].

In short, the Latino participants in our study see research participation as a two-edged sword, something that is simultaneously risky and potentially quite beneficial in light of other barriers to health knowledge and resources. Ultimately, all of the individuals decided to participate in the ethics study, presumably because risks were seen as manageable. That most had participated in previous research as well suggests they have reached this conclusion on more than one occasion. Given the scarcity of resources available to marginalized Latino drug users in the inner city, repeated research participation comes to be seen as a risk worth taking.

Without question, given their marginalized economic status, the financial incentives offered by research participation are an important motivator for not-in-treatment Latino drug users. As one participant explained,

Well I . . . think that forty dollars [the amount of the incentive mentioned in the vignette] is a million dollars. That's what that is, you know. Especially when you are sick and you have no money and you don't have a job. Forty dollars is a million dollars. . . . But . . . the money is just money. He has to do the blood test, they are going to do a bunch of other things, and he is going to be there for two hours. For me, I think that is enough money because he is getting a benefit too.

Other participants added,

Let me tell that for example if you say to me that you are going to pay me, I will go for the money. Let's be honest.

So [is] he [drug user in the vignette] doing it for the money or [is] he is doing it driven by his own will or for getting the money? That is difficult to answer from the point of view of the addict. Because one can believe that you are doing it on a volunteer basis but in reality you are doing it for the [money] . . . I am here, I can say I am here voluntarily, but I also came for the twenty bucks, do you understand?

Ultimately, however, many participants felt that receiving help with drug abuse and with other needs would be the best research incentive and the greatest benefit of involvement in research.

The best way to compensate John [name of the drug user in the vignette] is to help him with a program. They can send him to detox and then they can give him orientation to see if he can go to a long-term program so he can move on with his life. . . . And those forty dollars are gone in five minutes. But after that his life continues on. So for me it would be good if they offered a program, you know in-patient. You know, something that would benefit him.

I wanted to say the same, that . . . there is information about many of the programs that are available today and many times we are not aware they exist, programs that can help you stay clean if you want to be clean, they help you find a job,

they help you find a place to live. . . . So, the money is not the only thing. Sometimes the information helps you even more because you can get more than the forty dollars.

As these findings suggest, from the participants' perspectives there may be identified risks and benefits that are not always evident to researchers. That the level of concern about family response to a disclosure or even a presumption of HIV infection may be greater for a sample of long-term drug users—a group that often is portrayed as tending to be isolated from family members—is noteworthy and suggests the need to think through research procedures in community-based research in which research activities and participants may be open to public view. Similarly, the health knowledge some participants hope to gain from drug research participation may not be anticipated or adequately addressed by researchers as a benefit of research. Identification of these patterns underlines the importance of conducting participant-centered investigation of ethical issues in research.

Discussion of Case Study Findings

On the street, faced by multiple challenges and threats, drug users are forced to carefully sharpen their skills in assessing the costs and benefits of various courses of action. As described by Edward Preble and John Casey (1969) in their classic study of heroin addicts in New York, street drug users

are always on the move and must be alert, flexible, and resourceful. The surest way to identify heroin users in a slum neighborhood is to observe the way people walk. The heroin user walks with a fast, purposeful stride, as if he is late for an important appointment—indeed, he is. He is hustling (robbing or stealing), trying to sell stolen goods, avoiding the police, looking for a heroin dealer with a good bag (the street retail unit of heroin), coming back from copping (buying heroin), looking for a safe place to take the drug, or looking for someone who beat (cheated) him—among other things. (pp. 2–3)

In the shadow of the AIDS epidemic, with a significant jump in the number and kinds of research focused on drug-using individuals, participation in research emerged as new component of the street drug user's social environment.

Like other arenas in their world of concern, research was seen as presenting both threats and opportunities that had to be assessed in light of individual and group needs, sensitivities, understandings, and options.

It is evident from our focus group interviews with active Latino drug users that they are fully prepared and able to cogently evaluate the risks and benefits of research participation. In this, they do not appear to bring an "all or none" philosophy into play but rather to keenly recognize that life as a drug addict requires that they be prepared to accept significant risk in the pursuit of valued benefit. Among the Latino participants in our study, it is clear that underlying cultural values about the importance of family relations shape their cost/benefit assessment of research involvement. On the one hand, research participation is quite risky, not—as researchers might assume—primarily because the police or other institutions of social control might gain access to information about criminal activities (although this is certainly a concern), but because damaging personal information (e.g., HIV status, drug addiction) might reach an individual's family or wider community. Fearing that family members do not really understand AIDS, a loss of confidentiality was seen as possibly leading to rejection, an outcome that would be so frightening that it could push some participants to consider suicide.

On the other hand, because of the limited resources available to active street-drug users—both financial and in terms of access to health care—the risks of research participation routinely are outweighed by the benefits of participation (Hoffman, 2004). Benefit, in the eyes of our Latino focus group participants, includes gaining access to desired health information, learning about available drug-related services, receiving health screenings (including HIV testing), and being assisted to enter treatment or other intervention programs. Participants also see fiscal incentives as a valued benefit of taking part in research, given their limited options for income generation. Overall, the views of the benefits of research involvement appear among the Latino participants in our study to be strongly influenced by the significant barriers they face in gaining access to health, residential, and employment opportunities while tempered by fear of exposure and loss of one of the few sources of emotional support they possess.

CONCLUSIONS

The foregoing discussion and research findings suggest a number of key issues of concern in conducting research among Latinos. While stressing the importance of expanding the available research on Latinos, ethical challenges in conducting this work include

- The appropriateness of certain data collection methods with Latino populations (e.g., the limitations of telephone surveys because of economic barriers to access and maintaining a working telephone)

- The need to recruit and train bilingual and bicultural research staff who can recruit and communicate effectively and sensitively with Latino research participants in light of cultural factors and past experience with dominant institutions

- The need to assess literacy and language skills when adapting research instruments for Latino populations

- The need for awareness and sensitivity concerning family and gender issues as factors in research participation

- Preparation for research dropout and loss to follow-up due to economic issues and family obligations

- Recognition of the importance and responsibility to include communities in research designs and to return findings in understandable form to target communities through the development of an ethics framework to guide collaborative efforts and enhance trust

- Attention to the power differential between the researcher and participants, including the influence of health or other services made available in the research, or because participants, taught to be deferential to elders and social elites, may not fully understand that they have the right to say no to a "doctor"

- The need for an expanded research focus on the perspectives of Latinos on participation in various kinds of research

Insensitivity to the seriousness of these issues puts researchers at risk of producing biased results that can inaccurately represent the Latino population, their research-related concerns, their expressed needs, and their vulnerabilities, both in research and in the wider society (Lange, 2002). Moreover, given that Latinos often are under-recruited to research samples, findings on them are aggregated with other ethnic minority populations, or individuals from different subgroups are lumped together under the label "Latino," thereby potentially canceling out significant subgroup differences. Most of the participants in the study reported here were Puerto Rican, and it would be incorrect to assume that findings could be generalized to other Latino subgroups (in terms of their drug use patterns alone, there are significant differences generally between Puerto Rican and Cuban drug users in the United States, for example). Assessing the generalizability of the findings of this research for other Latino subgroups, or even Puerto Rican drug users in other parts of the United States or in Puerto Rico, remains an issue for future research.

REFERENCES

Aguirre-Molina, M., Molina, C. & Zambrana, R. (2001). *Health issues in the Latino community.* San Francisco: Jossey-Bass.

Alvidrez, J., & Arean, P. (2002). Psychosocial treatment research with ethnic minority populations: Ethical considerations in conducting clinical trials. *Ethics and Behavior, 12*(1), 103–116.

Anderson, E., & DuBois, J. (2007). The need for evidence-based research ethics: A review of the substance abuse literature. *Drugs and Alcohol Dependence, 86,* 95–105.

Armstrong, T., Crum, L., Rieger, R., Bennett, T., & Edwards, L. (1999). Attitudes of African Americans toward participation in medical research. *Journal of Applied Social Psychology, 29,* 552–574.

Birman, D. (2006). Ethical issues in research with immigrants and refugees. In Trimble, J., & Fisher, C. (Eds.), *The handbook of ethical research with ethnocultural populations and communities.* (pp. 155–177). Thousand Oaks, CA: Sage.

Brody, J., Gluck, J., & Aragon, A. (1997). Participants' understanding of the process of psychological research. *Ethics and Behavior, 7,* 285–298.

Buchanan, D., Koshnood, K., Stopka, T., Santelices, C., & Singer, M. (2002). Ethical dilemmas created by the criminalization of status behaviors: Case studies from ethnographic field research with injection drug users. *Health Education and Behavior, 29,* 30–42.

Calderón, J., Baker, R., Fabrega, H., Conde, J., Hays, R., Fleming, E., et al. (2006). An ethno-medical perspective on research participation: A qualitative pilot study. *Medscape General Medicine, 8*(2), 23–30.

Charland, L. (2002). Cynthia's dilemma: Consenting to heroin prescription. *American Journal of Bioethics, 2,* 37–47.

Corbie-Smith, G., Thomas, S., Williams, M., & Moody-Ayres, S. (1999). Attitudes and beliefs of African Americans toward participation in medical research. *Journal of General Internal Medicine, 14,* 537–546.

Deren, S., Shedlin, M., Decena, C., & Mino, M. (2006). Research challenges to the study of HIV/AIDS among migrant and immigrant Hispanic populations in the United States. *Journal of Urban Health, 82*(Supplement 3), iii13–iii25.

Falicov, C. (1995). Training to think culturally: A multidimensional comparative framework. *Family Process, 34,* 373–388.

Fisher, C. (2002). Participant consultation: Ethical insights into parental permission and confidentiality procedures for policy relevant research with youth. In R. M. Lerner, F. Jacobs, & D. Wertlieb (Eds.), *Handbook of applied developmental science* (Vol. 4, pp. 371–396). Thousand Oaks, CA: Sage.

Fisher, C., & Fyrberg, D. (1994). Participant partners: College students weigh the costs and benefits of deceptive research. *American Psychologist, 49*(5), 417–427.

Fisher, C., Higgins-D'Allesandro, A., Rau, J., Kuther, T., & Belanger, S. (1996). Reporting and referring research participants: The view from urban adolescents. *Child Development, 67,* 2086–2099.

Fisher, C., Hoagwood, K., Boyce, C., Duster, T., Frank, D., Grisso, T., et al. (2002). Research ethics for mental health science involving ethnic minority children and youths. *American Psychologist, 57*(12), 1024–1040.

Fisher, C. B., Oransky, M., Mahadevan, M., Singer, M., Mirhej, G., & Hodge, G. D. (2008). Marginalized populations and drug addiction research: Realism, mistrust, and misconception." *IRB: Ethics & Human Research, 30,* 1–9.

Fisher, C. B., Oransky, M., Mahadevan, M., Singer, M., Mirhej, G., & Hodge, G. D. (2009). Do drug abuse researchers have a "duty to protect" third parties from HIV transmission? Moral perspectives of street drug users. In Buchanan, D., Fisher, C. B., & Gable, L. (Eds.), *Ethical and legal issues in research with high risk populations* (pp. 189-206). Washington, DC: APA Books.

Fisher, C., & Wallace, S. (2000). Through the community looking glass: Re-evaluating the ethical and policy implications of research on adolescent risk and psychopathology. *Ethics and Behavior, 10,* 99–118.

Flores, G., Fuentes-Afflick, E., Barbot, O., Carter-Pokras, O., Claudio, L., Lara, M., et al. (2003). The health of Latino children: Urgent priorities, unanswered questions, and a research agenda. *Journal of the American Medical Association, 288*(1), 82–90.

Fontes, L. (1998). Ethics in family violence research: Cross cultural issues. *Family Relations, 47,* 53–61.

Freimuth, V., Quinn, S., Thomas, S., Cole, G., Zook, E., & Duncan, T. (2001). African Americans' views on research and the Tuskegee syphilis study. *Social Science and Medicine, 52,* 797–808.

Frias, S., & Angel, R. (2005). The risk of partner violence among low-income Hispanic subgroups. *Journal of Marriage and Family, 67,* 552–564.

Fry, C., & Dwyer, R. (2001). For love or money? An exploration of why injection drug users participate in research. *Addiction, 96,* 1319–1325.

Gold, A. G. (2003). *Ethical issues in medical anthropology: Different knowledge, same bodies.* Retrieved February 19, 2009, from http://www.researchethics.org/uploads/pdf/agg.Med_Anth_Ethic.pdf

Grunbaum, J., Kann, L., Kinchen, S., Ross, J., Hawkins, J., Lowery, R., et al. (2004). Youth risk behavior surveillance—United States, 2003. *Morbidity and Mortality Weekly Report, 53,* 2–9.

Hauser, R., Simmons, S., & Pager, D. (2000). *High school dropout, race-ethnicity, and social background.* Unpublished manuscript, University of Wisconsin.

Healthy People 2010. (2009). *Healthy People 2010* (2nd ed., Vol. 1). Office of Disease Prevention and Health Promotion, U.S. Department of Health and Human Services. Retrieved February 18, 2009, from http://www.healthypeople.gov/document/html/volume1/11healthcom.htm#_edn30

Hirschman, C. (2001). The educational enrollment of immigrant youth: A test of the segmented-assimilation hypothesis. *Demography, 38*(3), 317–336.

Hispanic Health Council. (2006). *A profile of Latino health in Connecticut.* Hartford, CT: Author.

Hoeyer, K., Dahlager, L., & Lynöe, N. (2005). Conflicting notions of research ethics: The mutually challenging traditions of social scientists and medical researchers. *Social Science and Medicine, 61*(8), 1741–1749.

Hoffman, N. (2004). Toward critical research ethics: Transforming ethical conduct in qualitative health care research. *Health Care for Women International, 25,* 647–662.

Interagency Forum on Child and Family Statistics (2008). *America's children in brief: Key national indicators of well-being, 2008.* Retrieved February 18, 2009, from http://www.childstats.gov/pdf/ac2008/ac_08.pdf

Lange, J. (2002). Methodological concerns for non-Hispanic investigators conducting research with Hispanic Americans. *Research in Nursing and Health, 25*(5), 411–419.

LaVeist, T. (2005). *Minority populations and health: An introduction to health disparities in the United States.* San Francisco: Jossey-Bass.

Leon, D., & Walt, G. (Eds.). (2001). *Poverty, inequality and health: An international perspective.* Oxford, UK: Oxford University Press.

Marín, G., & Marín, B. (1991). *Research with Hispanic populations.* Newbury Park, CA: Sage.

Marshall, P. (2005). Human rights, cultural pluralism, and international health research. *Theoretical Medicine and Bioethics, 26*(6), 529–557.

Martinez, R. (1997). *Facing violent crime among Latinos?* (JSRI Working Paper #35). East Lansing: Julian Samora Research Institute, Michigan State University.

Miskimen, T., Marín, H., & Escobar, J. (2003). Psychopharmacological research ethics: Special issues affecting U.S. ethnic minorities. *Psychopharmacology, 171,* 98–104.

Molyneux, C., Peshu, N., & Marsh, K. (2005). Trust and informed consent: Insights from community members on the Kenyan coast. *Social Science and Medicine, 61*(7), 1463–1473.

Molyneux, C., Wassenaar, D., Peshu, N., & Marsh, K. (2005). "Even if they ask you to stand by a tree all day, you will have to do it (laughter) . . . !": Community voices on the notion and practice of informed consent for biomedical research in developing countries. *Social Science and Medicine 61*(2): 443–454.

Napoles-Springer, A., Grumbach, K., Alexander, M., Moreno-John, G., Forté, D., Rangel-Lugo, M., et al. (2002). Clinical research with older African Americans and Latinos: Perspectives from the community. *Research on Aging, 22,* 668–691.

Naranjo, L., & Dirksen, S. (1998). The recruitment and participation of Hispanic women in nursing research: A learning process. *Public Health Nursing 15*(1), 25–29.

Oransky, M., Fisher, C. B., Mahadevan, M., & Singer, M. (in press). Barriers and opportunities for recruitment for non-intervention studies on HIV risk: Perspectives of street drug users. *Substance Use & Abuse.*

Pamuk, E., Makuc, D., Heck, K., Reuben, C., & Lochner, K. (1998). *Socioeconomic status and health chartbook: Health, United States, 1998.*

Hyattsville, MD: National Center for Health Statistics.

Pew Research Center (2007). *Changing faiths: Latinos and the transformation of American religion*. Washington, DC: Author.

Preble, E., & Casey, J. (1969). Taking care of business: The heroin user's life on the street. *International Journal of the Addictions, 4*, 2–26.

Rapp, R. (2000). *Testing women, testing the fetus*. London: Routledge.

Rios-Ellis, B., Fritz, N., Duran, A., & Leon, R. (2004). *Be safe: A cultural competency model for Latinos*. U. S. Department of Health and Human Services, Health Resources and Service Administration. Retrieved January 6, 2007, from http://www.hrsa.gov/

Roberts, L., Warner, T., & Brody, J. (2000). Perspectives of patients with schizophrenia and psychiatrists regarding ethically important aspects of research participation. *The American Journal of Psychiatry, 157*, 6–74.

Robinson, S., Ashley, M., & Haynes, M. (1996). Attitude of African-Americans regarding prostate cancer clinical trials. *Journal of Community Health, 21*, 77–87.

Rudd, R., Kirsch, I., & Yamamoto, K. (2004). *Literacy and health in America*. Princeton, NJ: Educational Testing Service.

Sabogal, F., Marín, G., Otero-Sabogal, R., & Marín, B. (1987). Hispanic familism and acculturation: What changes and what doesn't? *Hispanic Journal of Behavioral Sciences, 9*, 396–412.

Sengupta, S., Strauss, R., DeVellis, R., Quinn, S., DeVellis, B., & Ware, W. (2000). Factors affecting African-American participation in AIDS research. *Journal of Acquired Immune Deficiency Syndromes, 24*, 275–284.

Singer, M. (1999). The ethnography of street drug use before AIDS: A historic review. In P. Marshall, M. Singer, & M. Clatts (Eds.), *Cultural, observational, and epidemiological approaches in the prevention of drug abuse and HIV/AIDS* (pp. 228–264). Bethesda, MD: National Institute on Drug Abuse.

Singer, M. (2006). A dose of drugs, a touch of violence, a case of AIDS, part 2: Further conceptualizing the SAVA syndemic. *Free Inquiry in Creative Sociology, 34*(1), 39–51.

Singer, M., Huertas, E., & Scott, G. (2000). Am I my brother's keeper? A case study of the responsibilities of research. *Human Organization, 59*(4), 389–400.

Singer, M., Marshall, P., Trotter, R., Schensul, J., Weeks, M., Simmons, J., et al. (1999). Ethics, ethnography, drug use and AIDS: Dilemmas and standards in federally funded research. In P. Marshall, M. Singer, & M. Clatts (Eds.), *Cultural, observational, and epidemiological approaches in the prevention of drug abuse and HIV/AIDS* (pp. 198–222). Bethesda, MD: National Institute on Drug Abuse.

Smedley, B., Stith, A., & Nelson, A. (Eds.). (2002). *Unequal treatment: Confronting racial and ethnic disparities in health*. Washington, DC: National Academies Press.

Sue, D. & Sue, D. (2003). *Counseling the culturally diverse*. New York: John Wiley.

Sugarman, J., Kass, J., Goodman, S., Parentesis, P., Fernandes, P., & Faden, R. (1998). What patients say about medical research. *IRB: A Review of Human Subjects Research, 20*, 1–7.

Turner, L. (2005). From the local to the global: Bioethics and the concept of culture. *The Journal of Medicine and Philosophy, 30*(3), 305–320.

U.S. Census Bureau. (2000). *Census 2000: Summary File 4: Hispanic or Latino (of any race) median family income in 1999 (dollars) by family size*. Retrieved September 12, 2005, from http://www.census.gov/Press-Release/www/2003/SF4.html

U.S. Centers for Disease Control and Prevention. (2002). *Racial/ethnic disparities in mortality by cause: USA 2000*. Retrieved December 4, 2005, from http://www.cdc.gov/nchs/hus.htm

Vigil, D. (1999). Streets and schools: How educators can help Chicano marginalized gang youth. *Harvard Educational Review, 69*(3), 270–288.

Villa, M., Cuellar, J., Gamel, N., & Yeo, G. (1993). Cultural traditions, beliefs, values, and ethical issues. In *Aging and health: Hispanic American elders* (2nd ed., SGEC Working Paper Series, No. 5, Ethnogeriatric Reviews). Stanford, CA: Stanford Geriatric Education Center.

6

LATINO ETHNIC IDENTITY

STEPHEN M. QUINTANA AND NICHOLAS C. SCULL

The way Latinos develop their ethnic identities is remarkable for several reasons. First, Latinos must develop an identification and a sense of identity in the context of stigmatization and oppression. In an important way, their development is unlike that described by Piaget for nonminority populations. Piaget conceived of children going through a gradual process of decentering, in which they realize that they are not the center of the world (Inhelder & Piaget, 1958). Children become less egocentric as they realize their views are not more privileged than others' views. In contrast, for Latinos and other minority groups, children's decentering is accelerated. They learn that their group is not just one group among others—they also learn that their group is less privileged and is considered inferior relative to another group. Consequently, any naïve ethnocentrism necessarily dissipates for Latino children as awareness grows of their group's stigmatized social status (see Quintana, 1994). Like Piaget's, most long-standing theories of development did not consider the decentering process for children who belong to stigmatized groups.

Second, Latinos' development of ethnic identity is fascinating because it reflects the sociocultural context of Latinos, which involves rich and diverse origins and complex sociological processes (also see Padilla, 2006). Latinos'

sociocultural contexts include diverse cultural, national, linguistic, and racial origins. Historically, one defining feature of Latinos, relative to other ethnic groups in the United States, is their mixed heritage. Having mixtures of European and indigenous heritages, as well as connections to Africa, creates a complex confluence of cultural, ethnic, and racial origins. Moreover, Latinos share features of other ethnic groups who are recent immigrants to the United States, such as Asian Americans; yet, they also share some aspects of a diaspora for racial minorities in the United States, such as African Americans and American Indians. Maintaining claims to some European heritage, Latinos are sometimes reluctant to consider themselves a racial minority. Nonetheless, from a sociological perspective, there are clear indicators that the social distance between them and Anglos is often equivalent to the social distance between African and White Americans. Given these cross-currents in Latinos' sociocultural contexts, it is intriguing how Latinos make sense out of the sometimes quixotic, sometimes gritty realities that constitute the complex sociocultural contexts of Latinos. Children's ability to make sense of the social status of Latinos and the children's own connection to Latino people is further complicated by the tendency for parents to ethnically socialize their children in indirect ways. In short, Latinos, especially Latino children, develop ethnic identifications and identities under challenging circumstances.

SOCIOLOGICAL, SOCIAL, AND DEVELOPMENTAL INFLUENCES OF ETHNIC IDENTITY

To understand Latinos' ethnic identity requires an appreciation of sociological, social psychological, and developmental processes. Sociologists have described acculturation and enculturation processes that involve, respectively, (a) the transformations and adaptations that occur when two or more cultural, ethnic, or racial groups come into contact with each other and (b) the maintenance of cultural traditions and heritage, either in reaction to cross-cultural contact or independently of cross-cultural contact (for review, see Padilla & Perez, 2003). Acculturation processes involve the adoption of new cultural patterns in reaction to contact with another cultural group. Often, the contact involves a cultural minority or immigrant group's contact with a majority and/or host culture. Adaptation in response to this cultural contact can occur in both dominant and minority groups, but attention is usually focused on the acquisition of the host culture by the minority or immigrant cultural group. The indices of acculturation and enculturation processes include language usage, cultural practices (e.g., religious practices, cultural traditions), social connection to and distance from cultural groups (e.g., intermarriage, neighborhood segregation), and identification with cultural or ethnic labels. Markers of enculturation reflect the degree to which culture-of-origin practices, language, and identification are maintained or passed from one generation to another. It is worth noting that acculturation can come at the cost of enculturation practices, such as the loss of culture-of-origin language, but groups can and often do develop new cultural practices without displacing culture-of-origin practices. At a general level, stronger identification with Anglo cultural and ethnic groups is promoted through acculturation processes, usually in schools and through interactions with members of the dominant group. Conversely, identification with Latino culture is maintained through enculturation processes, usually promoted by parents and the larger Latino community. Importantly, contact between two cultural groups can result in the creation of novel cultural characteristics that do not necessarily reflect the traditions of either cultural group but result from attempts to cope with the cultural contact and conflict. Primary cultural characteristics are those patterns that reflect the culture of origin, whereas secondary cultural characteristics reflect those novel cultural characteristics that are secondary to, or occur in response to, the cultural contact (Ogbu, 1994). For example, the formation of gangs can be a secondary cultural characteristic in response to ethnic-group stigmatization, particularly when the group has not been allowed to assimilate to dominant group norms and where the group's ties to its cultural of origin have loosened over several generations (ibid.).

Analogously, social psychological theories help us understand Latino ethnic identity. Social identity theory (Tajfel, 1978) describes the psychological sequelae of identification with a social group. Even when the group membership is artificially manufactured, people have strong psychological responses to identifying with a social group (Tajfel & Turner, 1978). For example, individuals will often perceive more similarity with other members of their own social group than with members of other social groups. Characteristics of a social group, such as its standing in society, will influence the psychological sequelae of identifying with the group. When identifying with a stigmatized minority social group, individuals will adopt particular attitudes and orientations as ways of maintaining esteem in the face of stigmatization as a member of that group (Tajfel, 1978). Consequently, to understand Latino ethnic identity requires an appreciation of the psychological consequences of identifying with a stigmatized minority group. In short, Latino identity will reflect the sociological processes associated with acculturation and enculturation, as well as the psychological principles associated with social identity and other social psychological theories.

For children and youth, Latino identity develops from nascent ethnic self-labeling (Bernal, Knight, Garza, Ocampo, & Cota, 1990) into more mature forms of ethnic identity (Quintana, 1998). Consequently, there are developmental principles associated with the development of ethnic identity for Latino children and adolescents. For example, Mexican American children's cognitive or social cognitive development was believed to influence the development of their ethnic identities (Bernal et al., 1990; Quintana, 1994). Current theory on adult development has not been applied to understanding Latino ethnic identity, although this would seem to be a promising area for future theory and research. To recap, Latino ethnic identity will be influenced by acculturation and enculturation processes, psychological principles associated with social identity theory, and for Latino children and adolescents, developmental theory associated with identity development.

Essentialism and Generalizing Across Latino Subgroups

Research reviewed in this chapter spans several Latino subgroups, including Mexican Americans, Puerto Ricans, and Cuban Americans, as well as recent immigrants from Latin America. These subgroups share many features, such as connections to the Spanish language and to cultural values, but there are important demographic differences across Latino subgroups. These differences are based on regions of origin (i.e., Caribbean and North, Central, and South America), reasons for and context of immigration (e.g., political asylum, financial motivations), and sociocultural histories in the United States. The considerable heterogeneity across and within Latino subpopulations undermines attempts to identify homogenous subgroups of Latinos (Umaña-Taylor & Fine, 2001). Researchers of Latino populations identify demographic characteristics of their participants, typically including country of ancestral origin, social class, generation of immigration, and language characteristics, often implying that study results could be generalized to the subpopulation defined by these demographic characteristics. Unfortunately, because random sampling is rarely used, study results cannot be generalized based on these sample characteristics. On the other hand, study results may be applicable to some populations that were not sampled. For example, there are parallels in the effect of discrimination on youth across Black and Latino youth, and these parallels exist even though the two groups have different ethnic and racial heritages (see Quintana, 2007, for review). Consequently, it is difficult to know how widely or how narrowly results of a study can be generalized when even a conservative level of generalization based on sample demographics is not supported by statistical theory and, in other cases, more liberal generalizations of results to nonsampled populations may be justified. These dilemmas represent challenges to constructing a science of Latino psychology.

Quintana and colleagues (Quintana et al., 2000; Quintana, Troyano, & Taylor, 2001) proposed principles for cultural validity as well as heuristics for responding to these dilemmas. Generalization across demographically defined populations can be facilitated by understanding that demographic characteristics are associated with psychological processes. Quintana and colleagues' position suggests that differences between two demographic groups (e.g., Mexican American and Puerto Rican) are due to the psychological differences associated with the demographic differences rather than to some essential differences between the populations. On the other hand, an essentialist approach to cultural differences presumes that members of a cultural group share a unique essence and that differences between groups should be attributed to the essential difference between the cultural groups. We reject the essentialist view and suggest that cultural groups are made up of complex combinations of psychological characteristics and that demographic differences are associated with different combinations of psychological characteristics rather than differences in essences. A Latino psychology, therefore, could be constructed based on an understanding of the interplay among psychological processes (i.e., psychological theory) and identification of the psychological characteristics associated with various demographic characteristics (Quintana et al., 2001). Hence, our assumptions are that, all things being equal, psychological principles can be generalized across demographic groups, and differences in psychological processes across demographic groups could be accounted for by an understanding of the psychological implications of the various demographic characteristics. To illustrate, Fuligni, Kiang, Wikow, and Baldelomar (2008) found no differences in academic achievement based on ethnic self-identification (e.g., Mexican vs. Mexican American vs. Hispanic), but there were differences in academic achievement based on adolescents' psychological investment in the ethnic labels with which they identified. In this example, any demographic differences between subgroups of Latinos based on ethnic label clearly were unimportant, but the psychological investment in the various labels was important in predicting achievement. Hence, the psychological principles associated with psychological investment could be generalized across demographic groups. Similarly, differences between Puerto Rican and Mexican American children, we believe, are due not to some differences in the essence of being Puerto Rican or Mexican American but to psychological characteristics associated with demographic differences between these groups.

Consequently, our approach to reviewing the literature and proposing theoretical principles associated with Latino ethnic identity is to identify broad theoretical principles that have been found to be associated with ethnic identity development. However, before these principles are applied to a specific Latino subgroup, we encourage the reader to consider how the demographic characteristics associated with the specific group might be associated with psychological characteristics that might interact in complex ways with the psychological principles described in this chapter.

To explain, the three broad influences of ethnic identity that we identified previously—sociological processes, social psychological processes associated with social identity theory, and developmental processes—seem to be generalizable across demographic contexts, but to understand how ethnic identity might form or develop in a specific sociocultural context requires an understanding of how the contextual features might influence these psychological processes.

Dimensions of Ethnic Identification and Identity

We recognize that there are many different forms of identity throughout the life span, particularly for Latinos. Quintana (1998) argues that ethnic labels such as *Latino, Hispanic, Spanish,* and *Mexican American,* for example, have very different meanings depending on the age of the person being labeled. Some young children have no concept of what these terms mean but only a notion of being "brown skinned." As children mature, they have more adult-like understandings, but these ethnic terms have different connotations depending on age (Quintana, 1994). Consequently, we depart

somewhat from previous literature by using the term *ethnic identification,* not *ethnic identity,* to refer to the ethnic labels with which a person chooses to identify. We reserve *ethnic identity* to refer to the broader psychological processes associated with the psychological and social meaning invested in these ethnic identifications. Hence, despite both having the same ethnic identification (e.g., Mexican American), a 7-year-old will not have the same ethnic identity as a 17-year-old, because the 17-year-old will have the benefit of more complex maturational resources and a longer history of interethnic and intraethnic interactions. Quintana, Segura-Herrera, and Nelson (in press) differentiate ethnic self-concepts, such as ethnic identifications, from ethnic identity, with the latter referring to a process similar to Erikson's (1968) description of ego identity. In short, although ethnic identity is often used more colloquially to refer to a broad range of ethnic self-concepts and identifications, we restrict its use to its more Eriksonian connotations.

We also recognize that there are multiple dimensions of ethnic identity. Dimensions of ethnic identity include a sense of affirmation and belonging to an ethnic group (Phinney, 1992), which reflects an affective or attitudinal bond with the ethnic group. Alternatively, ethnic identity achievement and exploration are theoretical concepts borrowed from the Eriksonian (1968) theory of ego identity development. *Identity achievement* refers to the developmental process by which adolescents accomplish the complex integration of senses of selves into a coherent identity; *ethnic identity* represents the manner in which they integrate a sense of ethnicity into a sense of self. As a point of contrast, early in childhood, ethnic identification is similar to other ways of describing the self, including, for example, one's hair color. Later in adolescence, however, *identity exploration* represents how the adolescent explores the psychological significance of ethnic-group membership for the his or her sense of self. Ethnic identity achievement will result, for some, in the sense that the ethnic identification represents a central aspect of the self, not merely one way of describing the self. Unfortunately, researchers do not always differentiate among these dimensions or use measures that confound these dimensions. Consequently, for this review, where possible we differentiate when one of these dimensions is the focus of the measurement procedures.

Acculturation and Enculturation Influences of Ethnic Identification and Identity

Most researchers differentiate acculturation and ethnic identity. However, Keefe and Padilla (1987) and, later, Padilla and Perez (2003) defined *ethnic identification* as a marker of acculturation. Keefe and Padilla suggested that acculturation of Hispanics was associated with *cultural awareness,* reflecting the way in which culture-of-origin characteristics are maintained in the context of contact with another cultural group, and with *ethnic loyalty,* reflecting a psychological identification with an ethnic heritage. To Keefe and Padilla, parents' enculturation of their children into their ethnic culture represented a response to acculturation pressures. That there is a close connection between acculturation and ethnic identification is not surprising, therefore, given that some researchers considered ethnic identification to be a subcomponent of acculturation. Researchers have, however, adopted different measurement strategies to operationalize acculturation and ethnic identity, although some overlap remains.

Young children's exposure to acculturation and enculturation processes are primarily determined by their parents' lifestyle circumstances and generally reflect the sociological characteristics of the family, the family's neighborhood, and the social environments to which the parents expose the children. As mentioned above, children's ethnic identifications as Mexican American or other ethnic labels reflecting Latino heritage (e.g., Hispanic) are influenced by sociological processes of acculturation and enculturation (Bernal, Knight, Ocampo, Garza, & Cota, 1993). The more children are exposed to Latino culture and people, the more likely they are to identify with their ethnic heritage, and the more children are exposed to Anglo culture and people, the less likely they are to identify as Latino. The sociological markers of enculturation and acculturation include language preferences, ethnicity of peers, and personal identification (Cuéllar, Arnold, & Maldonado, 1995; Cuéllar, Siles, & Bracamontes, 2004). Research confirms that children whose parents were more closely identified with Mexico and Mexican culture were more likely to identify themselves as Mexican (Bernal et al., 1990; Bernal et al., 1993). Bernal and colleagues (1993) found that the connection between parents' level of acculturation and children's ethnic identification was mediated through parental teachings; those parents who taught their children more about their ethnic background had children who identified with their ethnicity more closely. Similarly, Quintana and Vera (1999) found that parents' levels of acculturation predicted the levels of enculturation or ethnic socialization of their children. Moreover, Quintana and Vera found that ethnic enculturation was empirically associated with dimensions of children's ethnic identifications, including their ethnic knowledge and the extent to which they manifested behaviors reflective of their ethnic culture. Research on parents suggests that those who are least acculturated to U.S. culture tend to engage in more active ethnic socialization of their children (Romero, Cuéllar, & Roberts, 2000).

Research on adolescence confirms that acculturation and enculturation factors influence ethnic labels chosen by Latino adolescents. Eschbach and Gómez (1998) investigated youths' tendency to switch from a Hispanic identification to a non-Hispanic one 2 years later. Those youth who spoke only English and those who attended school with few other Hispanic youth tended to drop their Hispanic identification over 2 years in high school. Fuligni and colleagues (2008) found that first-generation youth were more likely than second-generation youth to identify with their country of origin (e.g., Mexican) than with a pan-ethnic label (e.g., Hispanic or Latino) or with an ethnic label that is hyphenated with *American* (e.g., Mexican-American; see also Portes & Rambaut, 2001).

Further research on adolescence and adults indicates that acculturation and enculturation factors are associated with ethnic identity, which extends beyond simple ethnic labeling and includes the sense of affirmation and belonging that youth feel within their ethnic group (see Phinney, 1992). Schwartz, Zamboanga, and Jarvis (2007) found that youth's Hispanic orientation, but not their orientation toward U.S. culture, was associated with their ethnic identity. Although levels of parental acculturation predicted adolescents' ethnic identity, most research found more direct relationships between parental ethnic socialization and adolescent ethnic identity (e.g., Quintana, Castañeda-English, & Ybarra, 1999; Umaña-Taylor, Ruchi, & Nana, 2006). Therefore, as in research cited earlier, parental acculturation level appears to be an indirect influence on adolescent ethnic identity, and its influence is mediated through parental ethnic socialization. More generally, research demonstrates strong empirical connections between, for example, enculturation and either ethnic identity or ethnic identifications for adults, youth, and young children (e.g., Bernal & Knight, 1997; Marín, 1993; Umaña-Taylor & Updegraff, 2007). Indeed, a few items on Phinney's ethnic identity scale reflect indices of acculturation, such as ethnic participation (Yancey, Aneshensel, & Driscoll, 2001) or ethnic behaviors (Phinney, 1992). Umaña-Taylor, Bhanot, and Shin (2006) found strong connections between cultural enculturation into Latino culture and adolescents' ethnic identity. Generational status and time in the United States are associated with greater levels of ethnic identity achievement for young adults (Ontai-Grzebik & Raffaelli, 2004). As with acculturation, linguistic preferences and ability are strong predictors of ethnic identity scores, with those favoring Spanish having stronger attachments to and affiliations with Latinos. Weisskirch (2005) found that youth who engaged in language brokering (e.g., translating English for parents) tended to have higher ethnic identity scores— suggesting that these bilingual skills were sources of ethnic pride. More recent immigrants from Mexico, Puerto Rico, and other Caribbean and Latin American countries tend to have stronger affiliations to their ethnic groups, compared to those who have longer histories in the United States (Vaquera & Kao, 2006; see also Portes & Rambaut, 2001). Finally, Cuéllar, Nyberg, Maldonado, and Roberts (1997) found strong negative relationships between levels of acculturation and ethnic identity for Mexican American adults, with those scoring higher on acculturation scoring lowering on several dimensions of ethnic identity.

An important line of research among community-based samples has examined the relationship of ethnic identity, acculturation, and discrimination among Latino adults. Research suggests that perceived discrimination among Latino adults is generally lower than among other racial and ethnic minority groups (Pérez, Fortuna, & Alegría, 2008). In general, it appears that low acculturation levels are associated with lower levels of perceived discrimination (Finch, Kolody, & Vega, 2000; Pérez et al., 2008). It may be that as Latinos assimilate and acculturate to U.S. cultural norms, they become more sensitive to acts of discrimination as compared to their less assimilated counterparts (Pérez et al., 2008). Moreover, greater proficiency with the English language may enable Latino immigrants to understand subtler, everyday forms of discrimination. Interestingly, high levels of ethnic identity appear to be protective against discrimination by equipping the adults with ways of coping with discrimination (ibid.). These protective functions have also been found with other racial and ethnic minority samples (Mossakowski, 2003). In conclusion, research evidence strongly supports the connection between (a) acculturation and the levels of enculturation and (b) ethnic identification and ethnic identity across the life span for Latinos and many Latino subgroups.

Social Identity Influences on Ethnic Identification and Identity

For the reasons just described, Latinos' ethnic identifications and identity are influenced by acculturation and enculturation processes like those of many immigrant groups who come into contact with a dominant or host culture group. However, important social consequences are associated with identifying with Latinos, because of their status as an ethnic minority group in U.S. culture. Like other ethnic or racial minority groups, those identifying as Latino are affected by the ethnic group's stigmatized status. There are, consequently, similarities between Latino ethnic identity and racial identity for other stigmatized groups. Latino researchers and theoreticians have seemed ambivalent over whether the social status and treatment of Latinos should be considered racialized in some ways. By *racialization*, we mean that Latinos experience significant stigmatization, discrimination, and oppression that is tantamount to the experiences of racial minorities. For example, the English-Only and anti-immigration movements tend to single out, or at least focus on, Latinos and attempt to codify into law the second-class or perceived inferior social status of Latinos that derives largely from the prejudice and discrimination against Latinos of mainstream society. Researchers look for evidence of the racialization of Latinos by looking for connections associated with racial phenotype (e.g., skin color) and find that those whose phenotypes are less Caucasian in appearance tend to have less social capital, compared to those who appear more Caucasian (Espino & Franz, 2002; Montalvo, 2004). Our focus is less on equating race with racial phenotype and more on the sociological factors associated with racial minority populations, such as degree of social distance between racial groups and degree of antipathy toward putatively racial minority groups.

To date, most empirical definitions of Latino ethnic identity have focused on cultural features and have paid relatively little attention to how ethnic identity is affected by racialization processes. To illustrate, the ethnic identity measures of Phinney (1992) and Umaña-Taylor, Yazedjian, and Bàmaca-Gómez (2004) are examples, given that neither includes items specific to discrimination or racism that Latino youth experience. Qualitative research, on the other hand, has conceptualized more directly the presence of a racialized component of Latinos' ethnic identity. For example, Holleran (2003) found that Latino youth tended to use racial terms to describe their ethnic-group membership. Similarly, Niemann, Romero, Arredondo, and Rodriguez (1999) identified an important theme in Latino adults' interviews about ethnicity that reflected their minority status as well as the discrimination, stigmatization, and injustice that they and their group experience. Finally, Quintana, Segura-Herrera, and Nelson (in press) also found in interviews with Latino youth that some socialization processes, mostly from the Anglo community, reflected a racialization for Latinos. This qualitative research provides support for the notion that ethnic identity for Latinos includes some dimensions of racialization, even though extant quantitative measures do not reflect the overlap with racialization processes. Nonetheless, there is growing encouragement in conceptual frameworks to consider Latinos' ethnic identity as reflecting some dimensions of racialization (Padilla & Perez, 2003; Padilla, 2006).

Social Identity Theory and Latino Ethnic Identity. Social identity theory (SIT; Tajfel, 1978) provides a theoretical account for the noncultural aspects of Latinos' ethnic identity. SIT posits that an individual's identification with a group functions to enhance the standing or esteem of that individual. However, identification with a stigmatized ethnic group could come at a cost to the individual's social and personal standing. Members of stigmatized ethnic and racial groups undergo a remarkable psychological transformation in their views of themselves and their ethnic group in a way that enhances their esteem and standing vis-à-vis their ethnic or racial identification. This and allied transformational processes have been termed *nigrescence* (Cross, 1971) for African Americans, *ethnic identity achievement* (Phinney, 1989), *ethnic-group consciousness* (Quintana, 1994), and *political consciousness* (Arce, 1981). Similarities across groups in ethnic identity result from facing similar challenges in the context of ethnic or racial stigmatization. Investigations into social identity influences of ethnic identity often are multiple-group studies in which, for example, Asian and African American youth are included with a sample of Latinos; this reflects the sense that the relatively stigmatized status of the adolescents' social identity influences the nature of their ethnic identity.

Research has supported the application of SIT to Latinos' ethnic identity. Phinney, Chavira and Tate (1993) investigated the effect of ethnic threat on Hispanic adolescents' self and ethnic esteem. The ethnic threat, represented by exposure to stigmatizing information about their ethnic group, was associated with more negative ethnic attitudes for Latino adolescents but did not reduce their level of ethnic identification. Similarly, reading about ethnic prejudice toward Latinos in another experimental design (McCoy & Major, 2003) and experiencing discrimination in a longitudinal study (Pahl & Way, 2006) were associated with increases in Latinos' ethnic identification. Taken together, these findings suggest that experiencing threat and discrimination may positively influence the strength of ethnic identification for Latinos, but this exposure to threat also negatively influenced their attitudes toward their ethnicity. Consequently, Latinos face the dilemma of maintaining esteem in the context of discrimination and stigmatization, which increase ethnic identification with the stigmatized group but also increase the adolescents' own negative attitudes toward their ethnic group.

Additional research suggests processes by which Latinos respond to this dilemma. Those Latinos who closely identify with their ethnicity appear to immerse themselves in their ethnic group, but those who are not strongly attached to their ethnicity seem to lessen their identification with being Latino. Support for these trends results from a variety of sources and approaches. To begin, Ethier and Deaux (1994) found that in response to being exposed to a predominantly

White university, Latinos who were strongly identified with their ethnicity became more involved in Latino cultural activities, thereby increasing their social and psychological identification with Latinos. On the other hand, those who identified less strongly engaged less in Latino cultural activities or groups, thereby lessening their social and psychological identification with their ethnicity. Research on younger adolescents also supports this tendency to respond to discrimination by becoming more immersed in the ethnic group. Brown, Herman, Hamm, and Heck (2008) found that Latino youth who experienced high levels of discrimination tended to associate with an ethnically oriented clique. The social connections found within an ethnically oriented clique appear to result in more positive attitudes toward ethnicity. Similarly, Weisskirch (2005) found that those Latino youth who reported that they departed from the "typical American" stereotype and presumably experienced more stigmatization tended to identify more strongly with their ethnicity. Moreover, research on Latino youth with mixed ethnic heritage (i.e., Anglo and Hispanic) indicates that youth who are more strongly connected to Latino peers and whose physical appearance is more stereotypically Hispanic tended to identify with being Hispanic, whereas those biethnic youth who could "pass" as Anglo tended to identify more strongly with being Anglo (Herman, 2005). These patterns, taken together, support the application of social identity theory to Latinos' ethnic identity, with stigmatization of Latinos resulting in stronger identifications for those who already had strong identifications and weaker identifications for those who did not have strong identifications. These patterns parallel similar processes for other ethnic and racial groups, given the social consequences associated with identifying with a stigmatized social group.

Parents' Ethnic Socialization. Parents' ethnic socialization plays an important role in helping children prepare for the social consequences of identifying with an ethnic minority group. Hughes and colleagues' (2008) study indicated that mothers help their children prepare for the discrimination and stigmatization they will face in society. Most Latino mothers indicated that they believed that having discussions about discrimination are important because experiencing bias and discrimination are inevitable aspects of life in the United States. These mothers prepare their children for discrimination by purposely teaching specific tools (e.g., academic achievement and taking advantage of opportunity), helping them develop proactive psychological coping mechanisms (e.g., self-confidence), and facilitating mechanisms to help protect their emotional reactions to experiences of discrimination. On the other hand, those mothers who decided against speaking with their children about discrimination did so because they worried that that such discussions would cause their children to develop animosity toward other ethnic groups or because their children were not yet old enough to understand (Hughes et al., 2008). Although most mothers prepared their children for discrimination, there is some evidence that some of the same mothers also took their socialization a step further by either implicitly or explicitly communicating messages that promote mistrust toward other ethnic groups (Hughes, 2003; Hughes et al., 2008). For example, unlike messages that prepare youth for discrimination, socialization practices that promote mistrust encourage youth to be cautious of other racial/ethnic groups. These types of messages encourage youth to cultivate social relationships within their own ethnic groups and to be wary of people from other ethnic groups. Moreover, research suggests that Latina mothers who cultivated mistrust of other ethnic groups identified particularly strongly with their ethnic and cultural traditions and reported high levels of discrimination against Latinos (ibid.).

A third form of ethnic socialization that appears to respond to Latinos' stigmatized status in society is the promotion of an egalitarian view toward all racial and ethnic groups. For example, research with Latina mothers suggests that they teach their children to respect people from all racial/ethnic groups yet discourage using race as a basis for making important life decisions (Hughes, 2003; Hughes et al., 2008). Latina mothers might encourage their children to downplay the salience of race and ethnicity because it could help ease living as a minority among racial and ethnic majority groups. Moreover, promoting egalitarianism and encouraging children to develop self-respect may be another method of preparing children to combat the deleterious effects of bias and discrimination (ibid.).

Ontological Development of Ethnic Identifications and Identity

Latinos of all ages appear to be influenced by acculturation and enculturation, as well as the social consequences of identifying with a stigmatized minority group. However, children and young adolescents are also influenced by developmental processes on their way to developing a mature, adult-like ethnic identity. How do children's nascent ethnic identifications, such as "brown skinned," evolve into mature understanding of ethnicity that includes awareness of the social consequences of identifying with a stigmatized ethnic group? Two main theoretical traditions have influenced theories of ethnic and racial identity, the neo-Piagetian and the Eriksonian. Neo-Piagetian theories describe the implications of cognitive and social cognitive development for the development of ethnic identifications primarily in early to middle childhood (Bernal & Knight, 1997; Quintana, 1994). Eriksonian theory, which has articulated ego identity development (Erikson, 1968; Marcia, 1966), has been extended to account for ethnic identity development during adolescence (Phinney, 1989). These theoretical heuristics rely on the assumption that normative development associated with other developmental domains (social cognition, ego development) can be applied to understand development specific to ethnic identity. Considerable research supports the validity of this theoretical heuristic (Phinney, 1989; Quintana, 2008).

We organize this review of the ontological development of ethnic identity using Quintana's (1994, 1998) theory of the development of ethnic perspective-taking ability (EPTA) because it provides a framework that integrates the sociological and social psychological principles associated with ethnic identity described previously. EPTA theory articulates the development of social cognition applied to the ethnic domain across a wide developmental period from early childhood through early adulthood. This theory also identifies the cognitive foundation for ethnic identity achievement that is consistent with Phinney's (1989) extension of Erikson's (1968) theory of ego identity development.

To begin, Quintana (1998) has articulated the different levels of children's understanding of ethnicity and race based on their level of social cognitive development (i.e., social perspective-taking ability). At each level, children employ a particular logic associated with their reasoning about ethnicity. Each current level of development encompasses previous levels, whereas movement to a new level is marked by the integration of a new perspective of ethnicity into the previously acquired perspectives of ethnicity. Details about Quintana's model of EPTA as applied to Mexican American children can be found elsewhere (Quintana, 1994); what follows is only a brief review.

Physical Perspective of Ethnicity. In early childhood (up to 6–8 years of age), Latino children associate ethnic and racial status with physical phenotype, such as skin, hair, and eye coloration. Ethnic and racial status are conceived as being only skin deep in the sense that young children equate racial status with external appearances, especially racial phenotype, and if these appearances change, then racial status is thought to change (Aboud, 1987). Quintana (1994) has noted that some children may confuse linguistic with racial status, such that a person is Spanish when speaking Spanish and English when speaking English. These nascent confusions illustrate children's reliance on observations in forming conceptions of ethnic status. Bernal and colleagues (1993) pointed out that because the physical appearances between Latino and Anglo children were subtler than differences between races (e.g., White and Black children), Latino children's awareness of their ethnic status would develop later, as compared to awareness of race. Bernal and Knight found that Mexican American children younger than 5 years of age were unaware of their ethnic status, but between 5 and 10 years, children were accurate in their ethnic identification and could apply the correct ethnic label to themselves and their peers. Quintana's (1994) interviews further supported Bernal and colleagues' (1990) sequencing of racial and ethnic awareness: Second-grade children interviewed knew they were not Black, but a few were unaware that they were Mexican American. Interestingly, many of the children considered themselves White and identified as being White and Mexican American. Bernal and colleagues (1990) also suggested that young children would be unaware of the constancy of their ethnic status and would believe that change in ethnic status is possible concomitantly with other changes, such as growing up or changing one's physical appearance. These descriptions have been supported by Bernal and her colleagues' investigation of young Mexican American children between 4 and 8 years of age (see Bernal et al., 1990; Bernal et al., 1993; Knight, Bernal, Garza, & Cota, 1993; Ocampo, Knight, & Bernal, 1997).

Literal Perspective of Ethnicity. Early in elementary school (approximately second through fourth or fifth grades), Mexican American children show important changes in their understanding of ethnicity. Quintana (1994, 1998) describes these as changes from a physical perspective of ethnicity to a more literal one. Instead of equating ethnic status with physical or observable features, children in early elementary school understand nonobservable aspects of their ethnicity. They understand, for example, that ethnic status is determined by familial ancestry, not phenotype per se. In an important way, children demonstrate awareness of the sociological components of acculturation and enculturation in understanding their ethnicity.

Their growing social cognitive abilities allow children to enhance their understanding of ethnicity by associating ethnic status with a host of features that are labeled as ethnic (e.g., Mexican food, speaking Spanish, having Mexican heritage), instead of perceiving these cultural features as being coincidental with their skin coloration. This development toward a more literal understanding of ethnicity has been demonstrated for Latino children (Quintana et al., 1999), as has its correspondence to social cognitive development (Quintana et al., 2001). Bernal and colleagues' (1990) model identified other markers of development in Latino children's understanding of and identification with their ethnicity. These milestones include increased knowledge about their ethnic group, accuracy of ethnic identification, and development of ethnic constancy. Note that Bernal and Knight's milestones tend to focus on the more literal or objective aspects of ethnicity, or what is generally defined as being associated with Latino or Mexican American ethnic status, suggesting convergence between Quintana's theory of development and that of Bernal and colleagues. Indeed, most research and theory on Latinos' ethnic identifications during early to middle childhood are focused on assessing the accuracy of children's ethnic cognitions and identifications. At this age, children are able to correctly choose ethnic terms that apply to themselves and reject terms for other ethnic groups. By middle childhood, Mexican American and other Latino children have acquired an understanding that matches standard denotations of ethnicity (Quintana, 1998).

Social Perspective of Ethnicity. From middle to late childhood, children's awareness of ethnicity expands to understanding the social implications of ethnic-group membership (Quintana, 1994), or the components of ethnicity associated with social identity theory (Tajfel, 1978). Their understanding includes the implications of such ethnic attitudes as prejudice in their experience of ethnicity and ethnic self-concepts. During this developmental period, children are able to understand how others perceive them based on ethnic-group status. How their ethnic status is perceived by other ethnic groups becomes more central in Latino children's understanding of ethnicity and the role of ethnic status in social relationships (Brown et al., 2008; Umaña-Taylor, 2004; Vaquera & Kao, 2006). During middle to late childhood, children have many of the social cognitive abilities requisite to perceiving and detecting ethnic discrimination against them and their ethnic group (Brown & Bigler, 2005). Whereas younger children's notions of ethnicity were limited to those literal features that were obviously connected to their ethnic-group membership (e.g., Central American heritage, speaking Spanish, eating Mexican food), older children extend their notions of ethnic group to include more subtle correlates of ethnic-group status, such as the disparity in social class associated with ethnic-group membership. In a sense, at this age children act like lay sociologists, using their social observations, rather than merely what they been taught, to expand their notions of the implications for ethnic-group membership. Additionally, children at this level of development more readily associate other interpersonal implications for ethnic-group membership. They recognize, for example, that intraethnic friendships may be more easily formed than interethnic friendships, due to the presumed social similarities among members of the same ethnic group. To reiterate, the social perspective is associated with children's abilities to understand social consequences, sociological factors, and interpersonal dynamics associated with ethnic-group membership. Quintana and colleagues' (1999) research supports the description and emergence of this level of development. Moreover, basic research on children's social and ethnic cognitions supports the growing awareness of social and sociological processes in children's associations with ethnicity (Brown et al., 2008; McGlothlin, Edmonds, & Killen, 2008).

Group Perspective of Ethnicity. During late childhood and early adolescence, Latino youth develop an ethnic-group consciousness that allows them to expand further their notions of ethnic-group membership. Quintana (1994, 1998) described two main advances for adolescents. First, younger children tended to view discrimination as isolated events, whereas adolescents can generalize across discrete events and abstract patterns to discrimination and societal attitudes. Additionally, younger children tended to focus on the obvious interpersonal components of discrimination, whereas adolescents become more aware of systematic forms of racism, such as institutional and societal discrimination. In these developments, adolescents are better able to group together isolated events and to group together members of institutions and societies into coherent units that in some cases have intentionality. Using these skills, Mexican American adolescents can generalize across isolated historical events reflecting discrimination against their own ethnic group and make connections with contemporary events. Similarly, they can become aware of societal forms of discrimination that have not only influenced them directly but more often have affected their ethnic group.

The second major advance in developing a group perspective of ethnicity for adolescents is what Cross (1995) described as a merging of personal and reference group identities. Earlier in development, children's ethnic identifications were made in terms of personal characteristics, much like brown eyes or skin are personal attributes, but they lacked the esprit de corps characteristic of adolescents' conceptions of ethnic-group membership. In other words, young children may classify themselves as belonging to a particular ethnic heritage but lack the psychological connections associated with group membership. Indeed, adolescents are cognizant of the psychological and

social connection among members of ethnic groups such that the actions of one person reflect upon the larger ethnic group. Moreover, adolescents across ethnic and racial groups have the enhanced sense of group membership that is often associated with peer cliques and often involves some merging of personal identity with a group identity, sacrificing personal individuality by conforming to group norms. Latinos and other members of minority ethnic groups apply these tendencies to their ethnic-group identity and membership (Quintana, 1998).

The combination of these social cognitive, social, and peer-group dynamics, as well as the increasing importance of ethnicity in friendships and other interpersonal relationships during adolescence, coalesce to increase the psychological significance of ethnicity and ethnic-group membership during adolescence. Phinney (1989) described the sequencing of three stages of ethnic identity formation: from ethnic identity diffusion to exploration and then ethnic identity achievement. Phinney (1992) also articulated two main components of ethnic identity: (a) a sense of affirmation and belonging to an ethnic group and (b) exploration of the meaning of ethnic identity for adolescents.

Much of the empirical work on developmental processes associated with Latino adolescents' ethnic identity supports Quintana's (1994, 1998) notions of adolescent development of a group perspective of ethnicity and Phinney's (1989) notions of the identity searching and exploration that occur during adolescence. Recent longitudinal research confirms that there is an acceleration of identity exploration during early adolescence, but somewhat surprising was a deceleration of exploration during middle and late adolescence for both Latino and African Americans (e.g., Pahl & Way, 2006). Other research also suggested identity searching, as evidenced by adolescents changing the ethnic terms with which they were identifying (Fuligni et al., 2008). That is, Fuligni and colleagues found that nearly half their sample changed the ethnic labels they used to describe themselves over their high school years. Interestingly, further evidence suggests that the experience of discrimination catalyzed identity searching (Pahl & Way, 2006), which suggests that developmental and social identity theories need to be integrated if we are to more fully understand adolescent ethnic identity.

Psychological Benefits of Latinos' Ethnic Identity

Considerable support exists for the connection between strong ethnic identification and adjustment for Latino adolescents. In most cases, strong ethnic identification allows youth to draw from the social and psychological resources from their ethnic-group membership and demonstrate psychological adjustment (e.g., Altschul, Oyserman, & Bybee, 2006; Bracey, Bámaca, & Umaña-Taylor, 2004; Roberts et al., 1999). In one particularly interesting research finding, Kiang, Yip, Gonzales-Backen, Witkow, and Fuligni (2006) found that stronger regard for their ethnic group buffered youth against stress such that the connection between stress and psychological distress was neutralized in the context of Latinos' strong ethnic identifications. This last research finding goes beyond previous research in finding that strong ethnic identity commitments are associated with dealing effectively with ethnicity-related stress, but Kiang and colleagues' (2006) research suggests that strong ethnic identity commitments are also associated with managing stress that is independent of ethnic status. Umaña-Taylor and colleagues investigated connections between self concept and ethnic identity. In several cross-sectional analyses (Bracey et al., 2004; Umaña-Taylor, Vargas-Chanes, Garcia, & Gonzales-Backen, 2008; Umaña-Taylor & Updegraff, 2007), they found strong relationships between self and ethnic concept but not in longitudinal analyses (Umaña-Taylor et al., 2008). However, Umaña-Taylor and colleagues (2008) found that ethnic identity was associated with proactive coping. Taken together, this research suggests important benefits for adaptation for the ethnic identity of Latino adolescents. In a few cases, specifically those situations in which there were high levels of discrimination, strong ethnic-group connections were either not associated with psychological adjustment or at times were inversely associated with adjustment (e.g., Greene, Way, & Pahl, 2006).

EMERGING DOMAINS OF ETHNIC IDENTITY

Attitudes Toward Other Ethnic Groups

Most conceptions of ethnic identity focus on intragroup relations, but ethnic identity also involves adolescents' attitudes and orientation toward other ethnic groups, particularly the dominant group. Indeed, research suggests that frequency of interactions with members of other ethnic groups whereby Latinos are afforded opportunities to reflectively contemplate the importance of their own ethnicity and ethnic identity (i.e., exploration) is associated with ethnic identity development (Phinney, 1989, 1992).

Research also finds that Latinos' attitudes toward other groups predict their adjustment in some contexts (Gloria & Hird, 1999; Guzmán, Santiago-Rivera, & Hasse, 2005). That is, these contexts appear to be predominantly White contexts, such as predominantly White universities (PWIs) or some public schools. It makes intuitive sense that when another ethnic group controls much of the social capital in a context, adjustment is predicted by Latinos' attitudes toward the dominant social group, such that those who are more open to the dominant ethnic group tend to reflect better adjustment in the context that favors the dominant group.

Identification With Other Ethnic Groups and Culture

Interesting research has investigated the implications of Latinos incorporating identification with Whites or as Americans into their ethnic identity. Much of this research focused on the identification labels chosen and whether these labels include *American,* such as *Mexican American.* Not surprisingly, acculturation level influences the tendency to identify as American, with those more acculturated including *American* in their self-identifications. Third-generation Latinos are more like to identify with hyphenated ethnic descriptors that include *American,* such as *Dominican-American,* instead of unhyphenated ones, such as *Dominican* (Fuligni et al., 2008). Fuligni and colleagues (2008) also found that lower levels of proficiency in Spanish were associated with greater tendency to include *American* in self-identifications among Latinos. In related fashion, Phinney has investigated Latinos' willingness to identify with being American. Phinney, Cantu, and Kurtz (1997) found that the more Latinos identified as American, the higher their grade-point averages, but high levels of identification as American were not correlated with higher levels of self-esteem. (Interestingly, there were also positive relationships among ethnic identity, grade-point average, and self-esteem.) Hence, identifying at least in part as American tends to be associated with some forms of adjustment in traditionally dominant contexts such as schools and planning for college (Phinney et al., 1997; Zarate, Bhimji, & Reese, 2005), but across several studies, identification with their ethnic group and with being American were independent, as indicated by nonsignificant relationships (e.g., Phinney et al., 1997).

A second innovative line of research investigating consequences of identifications with other ethnic groups has been research with biracial youth. Herman (2008) used a large data set to examine those youth who had partial Hispanic heritage combined with either White or another minority heritage; she then compared them with youth of monoracial/monoethnic heritage. For example, she compared part-White and part-Hispanic youth with only-White and only-Hispanic youth. Not surprisingly, those who were biracial/biethnic with part-Hispanic heritage were midway on a number of characteristics, compared to those who were only White or only Hispanic. To illustrate, monoracial Whites had higher GPAs but less exposure to discrimination than biracial White/Hispanic, who in turn had higher GPAs and lower exposure to discrimination than monoracial Hispanic youth (Herman, 2008). In an interesting extension of this work, Herman examined differences when youth were forced to choose either White or Hispanic but not both, even though they were biracial. She compared those biracial youth who identified as White to those who identified as Hispanic. Compared to those White/Hispanic youth who identified as White, those who identified as Hispanic tended to have lower GPAs, greater valuing of ethnic heritage, and lower levels of conduct problems in school. Interestingly, there was a significant relationship between the number of Whites in the school and the tendency for White-Hispanic youth to identify more strongly with their Hispanic heritage rather than with their White heritage (Herman, 2005).

A challenge with this research is that it is difficult to know whether there are sequelae associated with identifying more strongly as White or Hispanic or the ethnic identification is a function of acculturation/enculturation features, and whether all the correlates associated with a particular ethnic identification are caused by acculturation/enculturation processes or some specific effects are associated with how a person identifies, independent of their acculturation level. Clearly, more research needs to be completed that examines not only intraethnic orientations but also Latinos' attitudes toward other ethnic groups as well as other mixed forms of ethnic identifications.

Adult Expression of Ethnic Identity Through Parental Socialization

Not only is ethnic socialization meaningful for children, but it is also a way for adults to express their own ethnic identity. Research suggests that ethnic minority parents in general (i.e., Black and Chinese) and Latinos in particular tend to believe that ethnic socialization is "somewhat" important. Latina/o parents in Hughes and colleagues' (2008) study reportedly placed greater importance on ethnic socialization than did their Chinese and White counterparts. In fact, ethnic minority parents in general who report greater connections to their own ethnic groups appear to engage in more cultural socialization practices (Hughes, 2003). Parents who feel connected to their own ethnic group may be more involved with particular community groups (e.g., religious organizations) and may engage in ethnic practices at home (e.g., speaking Spanish, observing ethnic celebrations and holidays, serving ethnic foods, and listening to ethnic music). In so doing, parents send both implicit and explicit messages to their children about the salience of their ethnic identity. Latina/o parents engage in ethnic socialization practices as a way of communicating self-pride, pride in their ethnic background, and pride in their ability to overcome barriers they have encountered in the United States. Ethnic minority parents in general (including Latinos) who have personally experienced discrimination more commonly report preparing their children for bias (Hughes, 2003; Hughes & Chen, 1997; Hughes et al., 2008). Ultimately, for Latino parents, ethnic socialization practices might help them feel reassured that aspects of their own ethnic identity will be passed down from generation to generation in a generative fashion.

SUMMARY AND GENERAL EVALUATION OF EXTANT RESEARCH

To understand Latinos' ethnic identity requires an appreciation of sociological, social psychological, and developmental factors. The nature of Latinos' ethnic identity represents an intersection of these factors. In some ways, ethnic identity is a reflection of and marker for acculturation processes; in other ways, ethnic identity functions as a protection against the social consequences of identifying with a stigmatized ethnic group; and in still other ways, ethnic identity represents the culmination of a remarkable developmental process. Extant quantitative measures of Latinos' ethnic identity ignore the ways in which Latinos function and are treated like a stigmatized racial groups. The heterogeneity of Latinos makes generalizations of research findings and theories challenging. Nonetheless, this chapter has identified some broad trends that appear applicable across some subgroups. However, more information is needed if we are to understand how some sociological factors influence psychological processes, which in turn influence ethnic identity for Latinos. There are some shortcomings in the extant literature. There is disproportionate research on Latino university students relative to their representation among Latinos. The research on children and youth seems more representative across social class but does seem disproportionately focused on Latinos acculturated enough to respond to English-based questionnaires. Much of the research was conducted on Mexican Americans, and representation of other Latino subgroups was small and usually combined into a more general Latino group. Nonetheless, there are intriguing parallels between Latinos and other ethnic or racial minority children. Moreover, the developmental factors associated with ethnic identity development seem to overlap with more general maturational factors associated with how children from a variety of ethnic or racial backgrounds understand their social worlds and how adolescents develop identities across domains of social category. Some interesting emerging areas of research include biracial children, which provide an interesting perspective on the process of ethnic identification and ethnic identity. More research should be devoted to conceptualizing the ways in which Latino adults' ethnic identity continues to grow and evolve. More research could also be devoted to the intersection of a variety of social identities, such as gender, social class, ethnicity, and sexual orientation, to reflect even more heterogeneity within the Latino communities.

REFERENCES

Aboud, F. E. (1987). The development of ethnic self-identification and attitudes. In J. S. Phinney & M. J. Rotheram (Eds.), *Children's ethnic socialization* (pp. 32–55). Newbury Park, CA: Sage.

Aboud, F. (2008). A social-cognitive developmental theory of prejudice. In S. Quintana & C. McKown (Eds.), *Handbook of race, racism and the developing child* (pp. 55–71). Hoboken, NJ: John Wiley.

Altschul, I., Oyserman, D., & Bybee, D. (2006). Racial-ethnic identity in mid-adolescence: Content and change as predictors of academic achievement. *Child Development, 77*, 1155–1169.

Arce, C. (1981). A reconsideration of Chicano culture and identity. *Daedalus, 110*, 177–191.

Arce, C., Murguia, E., & Frisbie, W. (1987). Phenotype and life chances among Chicanos. *Hispanic Journal of Behavioral Sciences, 9*(1), 19–32.

Bernal, M., & Knight, G. (1997). Ethnic identity of Latino children. In J. Garciá & M. Zea (Eds.), *Psychological interventions and research with Latino populations* (pp. 15–38). Needham Heights, MA: Allyn & Bacon.

Bernal, M. E., Knight, G. P., Garza, C. A., Ocampo, K. A., & Cota, M. K. (1990). The development of ethnic identity in Mexican-American children. *Hispanic Journal of Behavioral Sciences, 12*, 3–24.

Bernal, M. E., Knight, G. P., Ocampo, K., Garza, C., & Cota, M. (1993). Development of Mexican American identity. In M. E. Bernal & G. P. Knight (Eds.), *Ethnic identity: Formation and transmission among Hispanics and other minorities* (pp. 31–46). Albany: State University of New York Press.

Betancourt, H., & López, S. (1993). The study of culture, ethnicity, and race in American psychology. *American Psychologist, 48*(6), 629–637.

Bracey, J., Bámaca, M., & Umaña-Taylor, A. (2004). Examining ethnic identity and self-esteem among biracial and monoracial adolescents. *Journal of Youth and Adolescence, 33*(2), 123–132.

Brown, B., Herman, M., Hamm, J., & Heck, D. (2008). Ethnicity and image: Correlates of crowd affiliation among ethnic minority youth. *Child Development, 79*(3), 529–546.

Brown, C., & Bigler, R. (2005). Children's perceptions of discrimination: A developmental model. *Child Development, 76*(3), 533–553.

Crocker, J., & Major, B. (1989). Social stigma and self-esteem: The self-protective properties of stigma. *Psychological Review, 96,* 608–630.

Cross, W. E. (1971). The Negro to Black conversion experiences. *Black World, 20,* 13–27.

Cross, W. E., Jr. (1995). The psychology of nigrescence: Revising the Cross model. In J. G. Ponterotto, J. M. Casas, L. A. Suzuki, & C. M. Alexander (Eds.), *Handbook of multicultural counseling* (pp. 93–122). Thousand Oaks, CA: Sage.

Cuéllar, I., Arnold, B., & Maldonado, R. (1995). Acculturation rating scale for Mexican Americans-II: A revision of the original ARSMA scale. *Hispanic Journal of Behavioral Sciences, 17*(3), 275–304.

Cuéllar, I., Nyberg, B., Maldonado, R., & Roberts, R. (1997). Ethnic identity and acculturation in a young adult Mexican-origin population. *Journal of Community Psychology, 25,* 535–549.

Cuéllar, I., Siles, R., & Bracamontes, E. (2004). Acculturation: A psychological construct of continuing relevance for Chicana/o psychology. *The handbook of Chicana/o psychology and mental health* (pp. 23–42). Mahwah, NJ: Lawrence Erlbaum.

Erikson, E. H. (1968). *Identity: Youth and crisis.* New York: W. W. Norton.

Eschbach, K., & Gómez, C. (1998). Choosing Hispanic identity: Ethnic identity switching among respondents to high school and beyond. *Social Science Quarterly, 79,* 74–90.

Escobar, J. (1998). Immigration and mental health: Why are immigrants better off? *Archives of General Psychiatry, 55*(9), 781–782.

Espino, R., & Franz, M. (2002). Latino phenotypic discrimination revisited: The impact of skin color on occupational status. *Social Science Quarterly, 83*(2), 612–623.

Ethier, K., & Deaux, K. (1994). Negotiating social identity when contexts change: Maintaining identification and responding to threat. *Journal of Personality and Social Psychology, 67*(2), 243–251.

Finch, B., Hummer, R., Kolody, B., & Vega, W. (2001). The role of discrimination and acculturative stress in the physical health of Mexican-origin adults. *Hispanic Journal of Behavioral Sciences, 23*(4), 399–429.

Finch, B., Kolody, B., & Vega, W. (2000). Perceived discrimination and depression among Mexican origin adults in California. *Journal of Health and Social Behavior, 41,* 295–313.

French, S., Seidman, E., Allen, L., & Aber, J. (2000). Racial/ethnic identity, congruence with the social context, and the transition to high school. *Journal of Adolescent Research, 15*(5), 587–602.

French, S., Seidman, E., Allen, L., & Aber, J. (2006). The development of ethnic identity during adolescence. *Developmental Psychology, 42*(1), 1–10.

Fuligni, A. J., Kiang, L., Witkow, M. R., & Baldelomar, O. (2008). Stability and change in ethnic labeling among adolescents from Asian and Latin American immigrant families. *Child Development, 79,* 944–956.

Fuligni, A. J., Witkow, M., & Garcia, C. (2005). Ethnic identity and the academic adjustment of adolescents from Mexican, Chinese, and European backgrounds. *Developmental Psychology, 41,* 799–811.

Gloria, A., & Hird, J. (1999). Influences of ethnic and nonethnic variables on the career decision-making self-efficacy of college students. *Career Development Quarterly, 48*(2), 157–174.

Greene, M., Way, N., & Pahl, K. (2006). Trajectories of perceived adult and peer discrimination among Black, Latino, and Asian American adolescents: Patterns and psychological correlates. *Developmental Psychology, 42*(2), 218–238.

Guzmán, M., Santiago-Rivera, A., & Hasse, R. (2005). Understanding academic attitudes and achievement in Mexican-origin youths: Ethnic identity, other-group orientation, and fatalism. *Cultural Diversity and Ethnic Minority Psychology, 11*(1), 3–15.

Herman, M. (2005). Forced to choose: Some determinants of racial identification in multiracial adolescents. *Child Development, 75*(3), 730–748.

Herman, M. (2008). Racial identification among multiracial youth: Implications for adjustment. In S. Quintana & C. McKown (Eds.), *Handbook of race, racism and the developing child* (pp. 203–225). Hoboken, NJ: John Wiley.

Holleran, L. (2003). Mexican American youth of the Southwest borderlands: Perceptions of ethnicity, acculturation, and race. *Hispanic Journal of Behavioral Sciences, 25,* 352–369.

Hughes, D. (2003). Correlates of African American and Latino parents' messages to children about ethnicity and race: A comparative study of racial socialization. *American Journal of Community Psychology, 31*(1), 15–33.

Hughes, D., & Chen, L. (1997). When and what parents tell children about race: An examination of race-related socialization among African American families. *Applied Developmental Science, 1,* 200–214.

Hughes, D., Rivas, D., Foust, M., Hagelskamp, C., Gersick, S., & Way, N. (2008). How to catch a moonbeam: A mixed-methods approach to understanding ethnic socialization processes in ethnically diverse families. In S. Quintana & C. McKown (Eds.), *Handbook of race, racism, and the developing child* (pp. 226–277). Hoboken, NJ: John Wiley.

Inhelder, B., & J. Piaget (1958). *The growth of logical thinking from childhood to adolescence.* New York: Basic Books.

Keefe, S., & Padilla, A. (1987). *Chicano ethnicity.* Albuquerque: University of New Mexico Press.

Kiang, L., Yip, T., Gonzales-Backen, M., Witkow, M., & Fuligni, A. (2006). Ethnic identity and the daily psychological well-being of adolescents from Mexican and Chinese backgrounds. *Child Development, 77*(5), 1338–1350.

Knight, G., Bernal, M., Garza, C., & Cota, M. (1993). A social cognitive model of the development of ethnic identity and ethnically based behaviors. In M. E. Bernal & G. P. Knight (Eds.), *Ethnic identity: Formation and transmission among Hispanics and other minorities* (pp. 213–234). Albany: State University of New York Press.

Marcia, J. E. (1966). Development and validation of ego-identity status. *Journal of Personality and Social Psychology, 3,* 551–558.

Marín, G. (1993). Influence of acculturation on familialism and self-identification among Hispanics. In M. E. Bernal & G. P. Knight (Eds.), *Ethnic identity: Formation and transmission among Hispanics and other minorities* (pp. 181–196). Albany: State University of New York Press.

McCoy, S., & Major, B. (2003). Group identification moderates emotional responses to perceived prejudice. *Personality and Social Psychology Bulletin, 29*(8), 1005–1017.

McGlothlin, H., Edmonds, C., & Killen, M. (2008). Children's and adolescents' decision-making about intergroup peer relationships. In S. M. Quintana & C. McKown (Eds.), *Handbook of race, racism, and the developing child* (pp. 424–451). Hoboken, NJ: John Wiley.

Montalvo, F. (2004). Surviving race: Skin color and the socialization and acculturation of Latinas. *Journal of Ethnic & Cultural Diversity in Social Work, 13*(3), 25–43.

Mossakowski, K. (2003). Coping with perceived discrimination: Does ethnic identity protect mental health? *Journal of Health and Social Behavior, 44*(3), 318–331.

Niemann, Y., Romero, A., Arredondo, J., & Rodriguez, V. (1999). What does it mean to be "Mexican"? Social construction of an ethnic identity. *Hispanic Journal of Behavioral Sciences, 21,* 47–60.

Ocampo, K., Knight, G., & Bernal, M. (1997). The development of cognitive abilities and social identities in children: The case of ethnic identity. *International Journal of Behavioral Development, 21*(3), 479–500.

Ogbu, J. (1994). From cultural differences to differences in cultural frame of reference. In P. M. Greenfield & R. R. Cocking (Eds.), *Cross-cultural roots of minority child development* (pp. 365–391). Hillsdale, NJ: Lawrence Erlbaum.

Okagaki, L., Frensch, P., & Dodson, N. (1996). Mexican American children's perceptions of self and school achievement. *Hispanic Journal of Behavioral Sciences, 18*(4), 469–484.

Ong, A., Phinney, J., & Dennis, J. (2006). Competence under challenge: Exploring the protective influence of parental support and ethnic identity in Latino college students. *Journal of Adolescence, 29,* 961–979.

Ontai-Grzebik, L., & Raffaelli, M. (2004). Individual and social influences on ethnic identity among Latino young adults. *Journal of Adolescent Research, 19,* 559–575.

Padilla, A. (2006). Bicultural social development. *Hispanic Journal of Behavioral Sciences, 28,* 467–497.

Padilla, A., & Perez, W. (2003). Acculturation, social identity, and social cognition: A new perspective. *Hispanic Journal of Behavioral Sciences, 25*(1), 35–55.

Pahl, K., & Way, N. (2006). Longitudinal trajectories of ethnic identity among urban Black and Latino adolescents. *Child Development, 77*(5), 1403–1415.

Pérez, D., Fortuna, L., & Alegría, M. (2008). Prevalence and correlates of everyday discrimination among U.S. Latinos. *Journal of Community Psychology, 36*(4), 421–433.

Phinney, J. (1989). Stages of ethnic identity development in minority group adolescents. *Journal of Early Adolescence, 9*(1), 34–49.

Phinney, J. (1992). The multigroup ethnic identity measure: A new scale for use with diverse groups. *Journal of Adolescent Research, 7*(2), 156–176.

Phinney, J., Cantu, C., & Kurtz, D. (1997). Ethnic and American identity as predictors of self-esteem among African American, Latino, and White adolescents. *Journal of Youth and Adolescence, 26,* 165–185.

Phinney, J., & Chavira, V. (1992). Ethnic identity and self-esteem: An exploratory longitudinal study. *Journal of Adolescence, 15*(3), 271–281.

Phinney, J., Chavira, V., & Tate, J. (1993). The effect of ethnic threat on ethnic self-concept and own-group ratings. *Journal of Social Psychology, 133,* 469–478.

Phinney, J., & Rosenthal, D. (1992). Ethnic identity in adolescence: Process, context, and outcome. In G. R. Adams, T. P. Gullotta, & R. Montemayor (Eds.), *Adolescent identity formation* (pp. 145–172). Thousand Oaks, CA: Sage.

Portes, A., & Rambaut, R. G. (2001). *Legacies: The story of the immigrant second generation*. Berkeley: University of California Press and Russell Sage.

Quintana, S. M. (1994). A model of ethnic perspective-taking ability applied to Mexican-American children and youth. *International Journal of Intercultural Relations, 18*, 419–448.

Quintana, S. M. (1998). Development of children's understanding of ethnicity and race. *Applied and Preventive Psychology: Current Scientific Perspectives, 7*, 27–45.

Quintana, S. M. (2007). Racial and ethnic identity: Developmental perspectives and research. *Journal of Counseling Psychology, 54*, 259–270.

Quintana, S. M. (2008). Racial perspective taking ability: Developmental, theoretical, and empirical trends. In S. M. Quintana & C. McKown (Eds.), *Handbook of race, racism, and the developing child* (pp. 16–36). Hoboken, NJ: John Wiley.

Quintana, S. M., Castañeda-English, P., & Ybarra, V. C. (1999). Role of perspective-taking ability and ethnic socialization in the development of adolescent ethnic identity. *Journal of Research on Adolescence, 9*, 161–184.

Quintana, S. M., Segura-Herrera, T., & Nelson, M. L. (in press). Latino high school students' ethnic self-concepts and identity. *Journal of Self and Identity*.

Quintana, S. M., Troyano, N., & Taylor, G. (2001). Cultural validity and inherent challenges in quantitative methods for multicultural research. In J. G. Ponterotto, J. M. Casas, L. A. Suzuki, & C. M. Alexander (Eds.), *Handbook of multicultural counseling* (2nd ed., pp. 604–630). Thousand Oaks, CA: Sage.

Quintana, S. M., & Vera, E. M. (1999). Mexican American children's ethnic identity, understanding of ethnic prejudice, and parental ethnic socialization. *Hispanic Journal of Behavioral Sciences, 21*, 387–404.

Quintana, S. M., Ybarra, V. C., Gonzalez-Doupe, P., & de Baessa, Y. (2000). Cross-cultural evaluation of ethnic perspective-taking ability in two samples: U.S. Latino and Guatemalan Ladino children. *Cultural Diversity and Ethnic Minority Psychology, 6*, 334–351.

Roberts, R., Phinney, J., Masse, L., Chen, Y., Roberts, C., & Romero, A. (1999). The structure of ethnic identity of young adolescents from diverse ethnocultural groups. *Journal of Early Adolescence, 19*(3), 301–322.

Rogler, L., Cortes, D., & Malgady, R. (1991). Acculturation and mental health status among Hispanics: Convergence and new directions for research. *American Psychologist, 46*(6), 585–597.

Romero, A., Cuéllar, I., & Roberts, R. (2000). Ethnocultural variables and attitudes toward cultural socialization of children. *Journal of Community Psychology, 28*, 79–89.

Schwartz, S., Zamboanga, B., & Jarvis, L. (2007). Ethnic identity and acculturation in Hispanic early adolescents: Mediated relationships to academic grades, prosocial behaviors, and externalizing symptoms. *Cultural Diversity and Ethnic Minority Psychology, 13*(4), 364–373.

Syed, M., Azmitia, M., & Phinney, J. (2007). Stability and change in ethnic identity among Latino emerging adults in two contexts. *Identity, 7*, 155–178.

Tajfel, H. (1978). *Differentiation between groups: Studies in the social psychology of intergroup relations*. London: Academic Press.

Tajfel, H., & Turner, J. C. (1978). An integrative theory of intergroup conflict. In W. G. Austin & S. Worchel (Eds.), *The social psychology of intergroup relations* (pp. 33–48). Monterey, CA: Brooks/Cole.

Umaña-Taylor, A. (2004). Ethnic identity and self-esteem: Examining the role of social context. *Journal of Adolescence, 27*, 139–146.

Umaña-Taylor, A., Bhanot, R., & Shin, N. (2006). Ethnic identity formation during adolescence: The critical role of families. *Journal of Family Issues, 27*, 390–414.

Umaña-Taylor, A., & Fine, M. (2001). Methodological implications of grouping Latino adolescents into one collective ethnic group. *Hispanic Journal of Behavioral Sciences, 23*, 347–362.

Umaña-Taylor, A., & Updegraff, K. (2007). Latino adolescents' mental health: Exploring the interrelations among discrimination, ethnic identity, cultural orientation, self-esteem, and depressive symptoms. *Journal of Adolescence, 30*(4), 549–567.

Umaña-Taylor, A., Vargas-Chanes, D., Garcia, C., & Gonzales-Backen, M. (2008). A longitudinal examination of Latino adolescents' ethnic identity, coping with discrimination, and self-esteem. *The Journal of Early Adolescence, 28*,16–50.

Umaña-Taylor, A. J., Yazedjian, A., & Bámaca-Gómez, M. Y. (2004). Developing the Ethnic Identity Scale using Eriksonian and social identity perspectives. *Identity: An International Journal of Theory and Research, 4*, 9–38.

Vaquera, E., & Kao, G. (2006). The implications of choosing 'no race' on the salience of Hispanic identity: How racial and ethnic backgrounds intersect among Hispanic adolescents. *The Sociological Quarterly, 47*(3), 375–396.

Weisskirch, R. (2005). The relationship of language brokering to ethnic identity for Latino early adolescents. *Hispanic Journal of Behavioral Sciences, 27*(3), 286–299.

Yancey, A., Aneshensel, C., & Driscoll, A. (2001). The assessment of ethnic identity in a diverse urban youth population. *Journal of Black Psychology, 27*(2), 190–208.

Zarate, M., Bhimji, F., & Reese, L. (2005). Ethnic identity and academic achievement among Latino/a adolescents. *Journal of Latinos and Education, 4*(2), 95–114.

7

IMMIGRATION AND ADAPTATION

ANDREW J. FULIGNI AND KRISTA M. PERREIRA

Since the Hart-Cellar Act of 1965 liberalized immigration policy, immigration has fueled a dramatic rise in the Latino population living in the United States. The story of Latino adjustment, therefore, must encompass the process of immigrating and adapting to a new and different society. The complexity of this process is the focus of this chapter. The first three sections focus on trends in Latin American immigration and the sociopolitical contexts of immigration from Latin America to the United States, patterns of settlement in the United States, and variations among the population in status and socioeconomic resources. The last two sections review research on the psychological, behavioral, and academic adjustment of immigrants from Latin America and the key determinants of that adjustment. Finally, the chapter closes with a brief discussion of the existing gaps in our knowledge about immigrants from Latin America that need to be addressed in the future.

TRENDS IN IMMIGRATION FROM LATIN AMERICA AND SETTLEMENT PATTERNS IN THE UNITED STATES

Immigrants from Latin American countries have dominated the surge in immigration to the United States that began in the 1960s. A total of 19.1 million immigrants (53% of the foreign born) from Latin America and the Caribbean lived in the United States in 2005, more than twice as many as the total number of foreign born from South and East Asia (8.4 million), the second-largest sending region (Pew Hispanic Center, 2006). Mexico sends the largest number of immigrants, and the almost 11 million foreign born from Mexico living in the United States in 2005 easily make Mexicans the dominant immigrant Latino group in this country. Immigration from such countries as El Salvador, Guatemala, and the Dominican Republic has increased in recent years, but their combined total of only 2.3 million in 2005 means that together they still represent only a fraction of the total immigrant Latino population.

During the last 2 decades, the increase in Latin American immigration has been associated with a dispersal of immigrants from traditional settlement states (i.e., California, New York, Texas, Florida, New Jersey, and Illinois) to emerging settlement states with little history of incorporating immigrant or Latino populations (Suro & Tafoya, 2004). Between 1990 and 2000, the foreign-born population in the United States grew by 57%. In emerging settlement states in the Midwest, the Rocky Mountain region, and the Southeast, the foreign-born population grew by over 95% (Figure 7.1). During the next 5 years

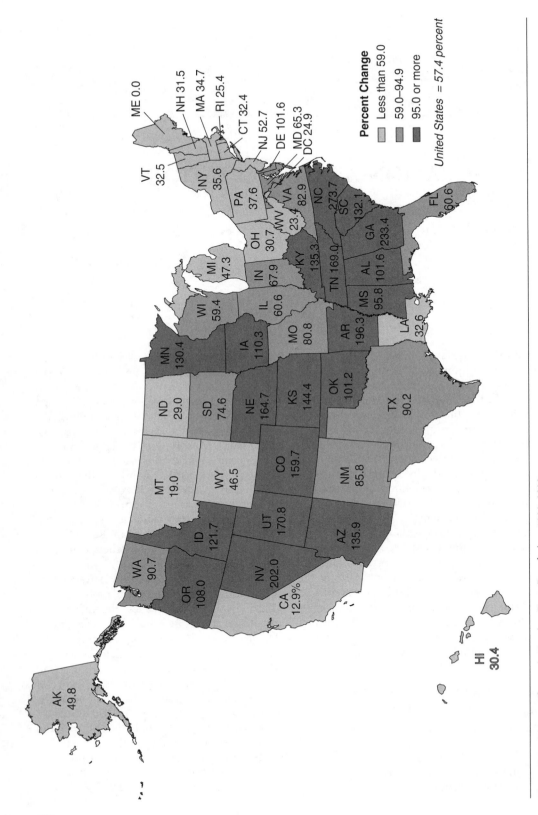

Figure 7.1 Percent Change in Foreign-Born Population, 1990–2000

Source: U. S. Census Bureau, Population Estimates Program, July 1, 2006.

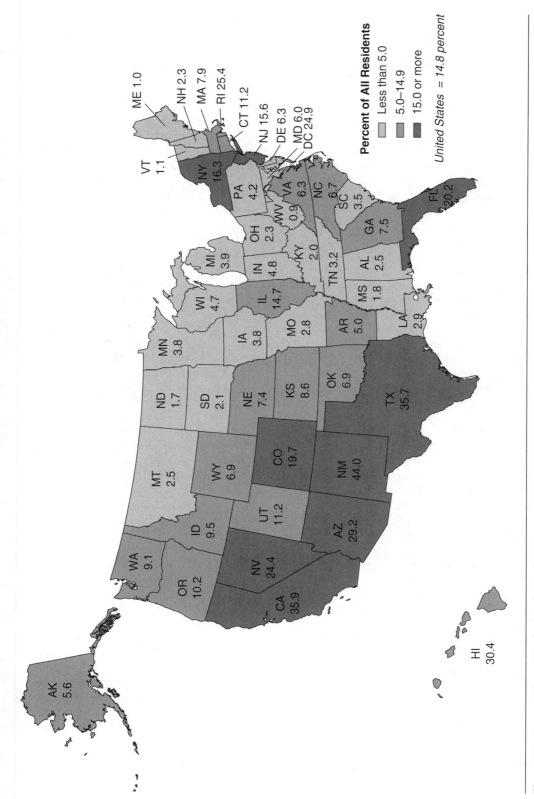

Figure 7.2 Percent Hispanic in the Population for States: 2006

Note: Hispanics may be any race.

Source: U. S. Census Bureau, Population Estimates Program, July 1, 2006.

(2000–2005), the foreign-born population in the United States increased another 16% and continued to increase by 30–50% in the Southeast and the Midwest (U.S. Census Bureau, 2005).

As the result of this dispersal of immigrants, states in the Midwest, Rocky Mountain, and Southeast regions now have sizable Latino populations (Figure 7.2), settled both by foreign-born immigrants who migrated directly to these communities from Latin America and by the secondary domestic migration of foreign-born and U.S.-born Latino residents from traditional receiving communities (Schachter, 2003). This secondary migration of U.S.-born Latinos was part of a more general population trend that included the internal migration of African America and white residents as well (Frey & Liaw, 1998, 2005; Schachter, 2003). Thus, the representation of Latinos in new settlement areas grew rapidly, but whites and African Americans still made up the largest share of total population growth in these areas (Donato, Tolbert, Nucci, & Kawano, 2007; Kochhar, Suro, & Tafoya, 2005).

The rapid increase in the size of the foreign-born Latino population since 1965 can be attributed to changes in U.S. immigration policies, the size and cohesiveness of binational migration networks, economic conditions in sending countries and the demand for capital, and the structure of postindustrial labor markets (Massey et al., 1993; Massey & Espinosa, 1997). Similarly, the dispersal of these immigrants in the late 1980s and 1990s can be attributed to immigration policies enacted under the Immigration Reform and Control Act of 1986 (IRCA 86), to labor market opportunities with higher wages in new settlement states, and to active recruitment by employers in new settlement states (Donato & Bankston, 2007; Johnson-Webb, 2003).

In 1965, federal policymakers dismantled the 1921 national-origin quota systems and established employment- and family-based visa preferences (Tichenor, 2002). Within a few years of liberalization, however, restrictive measures were put in place to limit immigration from any one country to 7% of the total employment- and family-based preference caps (i.e., 25,620 currently). Overall, caps for these visas are currently set at 140,000 and 226,000, respectively (U.S. Department of State, 2007), from all countries. In addition, policymakers instituted global and hemispheric ceilings that forced individuals from Latin America and the Caribbean to compete both worldwide and regionally for U.S. visas. These actions have led to backlogs of up to 15 years for family-based visas from Latin American countries with high demand for U.S. visas (ibid.). Although employment-based visas are currently available for Latin Americans with advanced degrees, exceptional abilities, or money to invest in U.S. industry, no employment-based visas exist for less skilled laborers. Thus, U.S. legal immigration policies strongly favor immigrants of high socioeconomic status and immigrants from countries in Europe where demand for U.S. visas is relatively low.

To control the rise in unauthorized immigration caused by these policies, Congress passed the Immigration Reform and Control Act of 1986 (IRCA 86) and granted amnesty to immigrants who had been unlawfully present in the United States since 1982. Nearly 3 million persons (including 2.3 million Mexicans) were legalized through IRCA 86 (U.S. Immigration and Naturalization Service, 1994). At the same time, Congress enacted sanctions on employers who knowingly hired undocumented workers, and increased enforcement at U.S. borders. Over the past decade, research has shown that these and other border enforcement efforts failed to reduce undocumented immigration at the U.S.-Mexico border (Massey, Durand, & Malone, 2002). Instead, migrants shifted to less well-patrolled and more isolated crossing points, and given the increased physical risks and financial costs associated with migration under the new enforcement regime, undocumented migrants chose to stay longer in the United States and to return home less frequently.

On the whole, therefore, IRCA 86 perpetuated migration from Latin America by fostering the binational social networks that facilitate migration. It increased the number of naturalized citizens eligible to apply for family-based immigration visas for their relatives, as well as the number of unauthorized immigrants who chose to permanently settle in the United States and to send for their families to join them. Among individuals considering migration, these social ties to current migrants provide a form of social capital that helps potential migrants acquire information about the migration process and its risks, identify job opportunities in the United States, and establish a new home (Munshi, 2003; Palloni, Massey, Ceballos, Espinosa, & Spittel, 2001).

Social capital refers to "the ability of actors to secure benefits by virtue of membership in social networks or other social structures" (Portes, 1998, p. 3). While the evidence suggests that access to social capital plays a leading role in fostering migration to the United States (Massey & Aysa, 2005), economic conditions in Latin America also promote migration. However, the key macroeconomic factor explaining migration from Latin America, especially Mexico, is interest rates, not wages (Massey & Espinosa, 1997). In many Latin American countries, future, capital, and insurance markets are nonexistent or poorly functioning and inaccessible to the average person. Therefore, a substantial amount of migration occurs as individuals seek to earn money in the United States to finance land and home purchases or the establishment of small businesses back in their home countries (Taylor et al., 1996).

Finally, migration occurs in response to the intense demand for immigrant workers by U.S. employers (Piore, 1979). In the postindustrial era, developed nations demand more unskilled labor than is available from their own citizens. Immigrant workers who are willing to work in labor-intensive jobs that are typically seen as low-status jobs by citizens provide a flexible source of labor that can easily be expanded and contracted in response to changes in the economy. In particular, the textile and food processing industries (e.g., meatpacking) in the U.S. South and Midwest have actively recruited workers from Central American countries and from traditional receiving communities over the last 2 decades (Fink, 2003; Griffith, 1995; Johnson-Webb, 2003; Hernández-Léon & Zúñiga, 2000). As immigrants move to the United States to take these jobs, they develop human capital (i.e., education, work experience, and job skills) that increases the economic benefit of remaining in the United States and that can lead to additional labor market opportunities in the future.

Additionally, foreign-born workers, especially those from Central America, have been recruited to work in the United States under the H-2A program. Established by IRCA 86, the H-2A program is the U.S. equivalent of a guest worker program designed to allow agricultural employers to recruit foreign workers during harvest seasons. Although these workers are required to return to their home countries after each harvest, they inevitably establish social ties, develop social networks, and gain knowledge about communities in the United States that facilitate future immigration. Moreover, social networks developed through the recently established H2-A program further facilitate the movement of Latino families from traditional to emerging settlement states, especially in the South. It is no coincidence that North Carolina, the state with the fastest-growing Latino population between 1990 and 2000, was also the state with largest H2-A worker program in the country.

VARIATIONS IN STATUS AND SOCIOECONOMIC RESOURCES

These selection processes strongly shape the characteristics of individuals who choose to migrate to the United States from Latin America (U.S. Census Bureau, 2003). Due to the strong economic demand for unskilled labor, the majority (59%) of immigrants from Latin America are between the ages of 20 and 44, and 73% have no more than a high school education. Although Latin American immigration historically was dominated by single men, immigration in the past decade has not been as gendered. Forty-eight percent of Latin American immigrants are women, and 59% of those age 15 and over are married. Rates of employment are high among both men and women, despite their low levels of education. Overall, 92% of Latin American immigrants age 16 and older are employed, especially in service (28%), construction (18%), and retail (16%) occupations. As a result, the median household income among Latin American immigrants was $36,755, and only 1 in 5 lived in poverty in 2003.

Selection processes and immigration laws also shape differences in the socioeconomic and legal status of Latin American immigrants by country of origin. Given the proximity of many Central American countries to the United States and the existence of social and employment networks across borders, substantial proportions of Central American immigrants are labor migrants. These labor migrants include both unauthorized immigrants and legal immigrants who have entered the United States through family reunification visas. The exact percentage is by nature difficult to establish, but some estimates have suggested that as many as 50% of the foreign born from Mexico currently reside in the United States without citizenship, legal permanent residence, or other authorized statuses that allow for long-term residence or work (Passel, 2005). As unskilled and semiskilled laborers, they primarily work in low-wage occupations not filled by U.S. citizens, such as those in the agricultural, meatpacking, and poultry industries (Portes & Rumbaut, 2006). Labor migrants from Mexico and other Central American countries (e.g., El Salvador, Nicaragua, and Guatemala) tend to have the lowest levels of education and income as compared to immigrants from other Latin American countries.

Latin American immigrants from South American countries are more likely to be professionals and to enter the United States legally through employment-based visa categories. These professionals have advanced training and skills deemed to be needed but lacking in the U.S. labor pool. Professional immigrants in the United States have tended to come largely from Asian countries, in part because the strict limitations on immigration from Asia prior to 1965 resulted in few opportunities for Asian immigrants to enter through family reunification visas. Nevertheless, South American immigrants from such countries as Venezuela, Argentina, and Brazil have entered the country as professional immigrants and therefore have higher levels of education than their counterparts from Central American countries (Dixon & Gelatt, 2006).

Lastly, both labor and professional migrants from Latin America have entered the United States through special provisions available for refugees and asylees fleeing political persecution in their home countries. These provisions, which allow legal entry into the country as well as access to social welfare benefits, historically have been used in accordance with the political goals of the U.S. government. Petitioners from countries with Communist or left-leaning governments were more likely to be granted refugee or asylee status than those wishing to escape rightist regimes. Therefore, refugee and asylee status was much more likely to be granted to those from Cuba and Nicaragua than to those from El Salvador and Guatemala (Portes & Rumbaut, 2006). Economically, the refugee and asylee group is highly variable, due in part to the timing of individuals' departures from their countries of origin. Due to the greater ease of the wealthy in escaping their countries, early waves of refugees and asylees may be better educated and have higher incomes than those who come later (e.g., pre-1980 waves of Cuban refugees were of higher socioeconomic status than later waves). But the drop-off can be fast for countries with lower levels of education and wealth overall, which is one reason why refugees and asylees from Central America generally have low socioeconomic profiles in the United States.

PATTERNS OF PSYCHOLOGICAL, BEHAVIORAL, AND EDUCATIONAL ADJUSTMENT

Because of the challenges that the foreign born face in their adaptation to a new and different society, many observers originally believed that immigrants would show higher levels of psychological distress and behavioral dysfunction than their U.S.-born counterparts from similar ethnic backgrounds. But as findings from systematic studies of reasonably representative samples of immigrants emerged, they painted a very different picture of the psychological and behavioral health of the population. Immigrants from Latin America generally show similar or even better psychological health than U.S.-born Latinos. Similar findings have been obtained for other immigrant groups (e.g., Asians), giving rise to idea of the *immigrant paradox,* whereby foreign-born individuals show better adjustment despite the fact that they experience higher levels of economic and social risk. The research summarized following focuses on the adjustment of Latino immigrants in a variety of domains. Studies have not always broken down the larger Latino category into distinct ethnic groups, but these within-group variations are discussed when possible.

Numerous studies have demonstrated the paradox. Burnam, Hough, Karno, Escobar, and Telles (1987) reported the lifetime prevalence of psychiatric disorder to be lower among the foreign born than the U.S. born, in a sample of adult Mexican Americans in the Los Angeles area. Vega and colleagues (1998) found similar patterns in a sample of urban and rural Mexican American adults; and Ortega, Rosenheck, Alegría, and Desai (2000) reported that that paradox was also evident in a national sample. Finally, Alegría, Mulvaney-Day, et al. (2007) reported that immigrants had lower overall rates for psychiatric disorders than second- and third-generation Latinos. This difference was most evident for substance-use disorders as compared to affective disorders. Yet, finer-grained analyses have suggested that the paradox is more evident among the Mexican population as compared to other specific Latino groups, such as Puerto Ricans (Alegría, Canino, Stinson, & Grant, 2006; Ortega et al., 2000). It is unclear why generational differences in psychological distress may be less evident among Puerto Ricans, but one possibility is that given that island-born Puerto Ricans are U.S. citizens, and given the high level of interchange between Puerto Rico and the U.S. mainland, the differences between the two settings may be less distinct than for other groups.

Similar findings have been obtained among children and adolescents. Harris (1999) reported nearly equivalent levels of psychological distress but substantial generational differences in risky behavior, such that foreign-born adolescents reported significantly lower rates of substance use, delinquency, early sexuality, and teenage pregnancy. Immigrant children also tend to perform just as well in both high school and college as compared to their coethnic peers (Fuligni, 1997; Fuligni & Witkow, 2004; Glick & White, 2004; Kao & Tienda, 1995; Perreira, Harris, & Lee, 2006).

Finally, variability exists in the adjustment of Latino immigrants according to their specific countries of origin. Generally speaking, island-born Puerto Rican adults show higher rates of psychiatric disorders, compared to immigrants from such Latin American countries as Cuba or Mexico (e.g., Alegría et al., 2006). Similar patterns have been found among adolescents, with Cubans evidencing lower levels of depressive symptoms than those from the Dominican Republic, Mexico, and Central or South America (Portes & Rumbaut, 2001). Achievement differences among Latino immigrants are less clear; some studies have observed greater academic success among Cubans, whereas others have found no difference according to specific country of origin (Portes & Rumbaut, 2001).

KEY DETERMINANTS OF ADJUSTMENT

This section focuses on key factors in the adaptation and adjustment of Latino immigrants. Some of these factors have been included in traditional measures and conceptualizations of acculturation (e.g., age of immigration, language use, cultural values), whereas others have

been considered independent (e.g., socioeconomic resources). The focus is on factors that have been shown to be most relevant for adjustment and adaptation and those that are understudied but merit closer consideration in future research.

Socioeconomic Resources

Studies of adult immigrants and their offspring have often shown that immigrants with higher levels of education, occupation, and income show lower levels of psychological distress and behavioral problems (e.g., Vega et al., 1998). Immigrant children with less educated parents who work in low-wage occupations have more academic difficulty at all educational levels and are at risk for such behavioral problems as delinquency, early pregnancy, and substance use (Glick & White, 2004; Harris, 1999; Perreira et al., 2006). The lower levels of education and greater economic distress among the Latin American immigrant population overall are two important reasons why they show poorer psychological, behavioral, and educational adjustment when compared to other immigrant groups, such as those from Asia, who tend to come to the United States with higher levels of education that enable them to obtain higher status and better-paying jobs (Fuligni, 1997; Harris, 1999). Similarly, the generally poorer outcomes among immigrants from specific Latin American countries (e.g., Mexico, the Dominican Republic) can be at least partially attributed to their lower socioeconomic standing in the United States.

Yet, socioeconomic factors do little to explain the pattern of equal or better psychological and behavioral adjustment among immigrants from Latin America as compared to Latinos born in the United States. Part of the reason for this may be that education as an indicator underestimates the human capital of many immigrants, who come from countries in which completing 9 or 12 years of education is a much more difficult achievement than it is in the United States (Fuligni & Yoshikawa, 2003). Another reason may be that although immigrants lack human and financial capital when compared to their U.S.-born peers, they sometimes demonstrate higher levels of social capital, at least as it pertains to psychological and behavioral adjustment. This seems particularly true for children from immigrant families, for whom higher levels of social cohesion and community interchange can be beneficial for development (ibid.). Studies have suggested that communities with dense coethnic networks have a similarity in values and traditions that support the efforts of parents to socialize their children (Portes & Rumbaut, 2006). In addition, these communities may have high levels of intergenerational closure, in which the parents of different children have relationships with one another that allow for group monitoring and socialization of children. Having the support of other parents who share similar goals and values can help immigrant families keep their children out of trouble and focused on working hard in school (Fuligni & Yoshikawa, 2003).

Cultural Practices, Values, and Identification

The consistent findings regarding the immigrant paradox have led numerous observers to suggest that the better adjustment of the foreign born may be due to the retention of traditional values and practices that help buffer immigrants from the stresses involved in adapting to a new society. In support of this theory, retention of the native language has often been associated with better psychological health among adult immigrants (Vega et al., 1998; Alegría, Mulvaney-Day et al., 2007). In addition, immigrant Latino families emphasize such cultural traditions as familism, family assistance, and *respeto,* which provide meaning and purpose for children and adolescents and potentially protect them from risky behavior (e.g., Gil, Wagner, & Vega, 2000; Ramirez et al., 2004). Some Latino parents send their children back to their home countries to live with relatives in order to enhance traditional values if they are "on the bad path" and getting into too much trouble (Reese, 2002).

The surprising academic success of many children from immigrant families has been partially attributed to the greater value of education among their foreign-born parents, despite the fact that the parents themselves often have lower levels of education (Fuligni & Yoshikawa, 2004; Kao & Tienda, 1995). Children from immigrant families internalize their parents' emphasis on education, endorsing the importance placed upon the utility of education for later adult success and linking their educational motivation to

their desire to repay their parents for the sacrifices they made to come to the United States (Fuligni & Fuligni, 2007). In a community sample, Fuligni (1997) observed that adolescents from immigrant families had higher levels of academic motivation across a variety of measures and that these differences partially explained the generational differences in actual achievement.

Finally, identification with one's ethnic and cultural background has been shown to be associated with a variety of positive outcomes for both immigrant and U.S.-born Latinos alike, including higher levels of self-esteem and psychological health (Kiang, Yip, Gonzales-Backen, Witkow, & Fuligni, 2006; Umaña-Taylor, Yazedjian, & Bámaca-Gómez, 2004). Ethnographic work has suggested that immigrants who retain their Mexican identity over such labels as *Chicano* or *Hispanic* show higher levels of academic motivation and achievement (Matute-Bianchi, 1991; Rumbaut, 1994). Yet Fuligni, Witkow, & Garcia (2005) did not find such an association between ethnic labels and academic achievement among immigrant children in a different sample, suggesting that the links between ethnic labeling and adjustment may be dependent upon the immediate local and ethnic context. For example, the distinction between *Chicano* and *Mexican* may be most important in a predominantly Latino community or school such as that studied by Matute-Bianchi (1991).

Age of Immigration

Numerous studies have reported an association between age of immigration and adjustment, whereby immigrants entering the United States at later ages often exhibit better psychological and behavioral adjustment (Harris, 1999; Vega, Sribney, Aguilar-Gaxiola, & Kolody, 2004). Yet, other studies that have sampled individuals from across the life span have demonstrated that the advantage of later immigration attenuates and even reverses during adulthood. Alegría et al. (2007), using the NLAAS, showed that individuals who emigrated before the age of 13 or after the age of 34 showed higher rates of psychiatric disorders than those who emigrated between these two ages. Age of immigration has been inconsistently related to academic achievement among immigrant children; Portes & Rumbaut (2001) reported higher grade-point averages among later arrivals, despite the fact that they received lower standardized test scores. Fuligni (1997), however, did not find an association between age of immigration and grade-point averages.

The reasons for variations in adjustment according to age of immigration are not clear. Some observers have suggested that immigrants with earlier ages of entry simply have lower levels of the cultural practices, values, and identification that have been associated with psychological and behavioral adjustment. Individuals who immigrate at earlier ages are less likely to retain proficiency in their native languages, and other studies have suggested that they also are less likely to identify with their cultures of origin (e.g., Finch & Vega, 2003). Alegría, Sribney, Woo, Torres, and Guarnaccia (2007) suggest an additional intriguing explanation: that the protective effect of later ages of immigration may be due largely to the protective effect of living more years in the native society, particularly during the late teens and early twenties, when many psychiatric disorders begin to emerge. There seems to be little difference according to age of immigration in the rates of the occurrence of new disorders after the foreign born have entered the United States.

Age of immigration likely has an impact on substance use and risky behavior through its channeling of individuals into different peer groups (Fuligni, 2005). Substance use and risk behavior among adolescents is higher in the United States than in many Latin American countries, and peer influence is one of the strongest predictors of risk behavior during the teenage years (Moffitt & Caspi, 2001). Yet, peer groups are highly segregated by ethnicity, and they divide even further according to birthplace and age of immigration among coethnics, such that immigrants arriving from Latin America at older ages find themselves unable to join peer groups of U.S.-born Latinos or younger arriving immigrants from Latin America because of language barriers and stereotypical attitudes (Matute-Bianchi, 1991). Ironically, social exclusion in this case may actually protect immigrants who migrate during adolescence from the peer pressure to engage in the types of risky behaviors more typical of adolescents in U.S. society.

Contexts of Reception

As argued by segmented assimilation theory, the adaptation of immigrants and their children will depend on three dimensions of the communities in which they settle: (1) the policies of the receiving government; (2) conditions in school, work, and neighborhood environments; and (3) preexisting race relations and coethnic communities (Portes & Rumbaut, 2001; Reitz, 2002; Waters & Jiménez, 2005). Additionally, research by Wilson (1987) and Massey (1990) suggests that joblessness and concentrated poverty, especially in U.S. inner cities, combined with the social isolation or the segregation of minority populations, can create a context that undermines the successful adaptation of immigrants and their children. Although theories of immigrant adaptation account for the role of context in shaping psychological and behavioral adjustments, few researchers have explicitly examined this relationship. Doing so requires substantial variation across time, school, and neighborhood contexts, and many studies of immigrants have been cross sectional, ethnographic, or geographically limited to a few communities or schools with large immigrant populations. Studies based upon large national datasets (e.g., NLASS and Add Health) often control for contextual factors in their models, but few examine differences in the effects of context by race-ethnicity and immigrant generation.

Policy Context. Set at a national level, U.S. immigration policies have varied throughout history from open-door policies that welcome immigrants and assist them with the process of settlement to regulatory and restrictive policies that exclude particular groups of immigrants based upon their literacy levels, political ideology, sexual preferences, and national origins (Tichenor, 2002). Current policies emphasize family reunification and employment-based immigration but provide no governmental support to assist families with their transitions to the United States. Active support for migration and settlement is restricted to select refugee flows (e.g., Southeast Asian and Cuban refugees). In these select cases, active support for migration and settlement has been tremendously successful in accelerating the social integration and economic mobility of refugee populations in the United States (Rumbaut, 1991). Unauthorized immigrants who face active resistance to their migration and settlement are most disadvantaged and face institutional barriers to adaptation and integration (Chavez, 1997).

Recently, researchers have begun evaluating the effects of U.S. deportation policies and practices on the health and well-being of immigrants and their children, many of whom are U.S. citizens. A study by Capps, Castañeda, Chaudry, and Santos (2007) found that children experienced feelings of abandonment and showed symptoms of psychological distress after the arrest of their parents. Moreover, immigrants (regardless of their legal status) living in communities where large deportation raids occurred reported experiencing fear, isolation, and economic hardships that induced mental health problems. However, few sought mental health care for themselves or their children.

Collectively referred to as "integration policies," government policies that facilitate (or impede) an immigrant's transition to the United States include public assistance and medical, housing, and education policies at both national and state levels (Fix, 2007). At the national level, welfare reform policies introduced in 1996 limited noncitizens' access to cash and medical assistance programs. These policies have been found to promote employment among foreign-born women (Kaushal & Kaestner, 2005) but also to reduce health insurance coverage among these women and their children and their utilization of health care (Kandula, Grogan, Rathouz, & Lauderdale, 2004; Kaushal & Kaestner, 2005; Park, Sarnoff, Bender, & Korenbrot, 2000). Thus, these policies reduce immigrants' access to medical care that may help them cope with the stresses of migration.

At the state and local levels, policies enacted as a component of No Child Left Behind (NCLB) have made the education of students with limited English proficiency a national priority and have helped spur investment in the education of children of immigrants (Louie, 2005; Murray, Batalova, & Fix, 2007). At the same time, however, laws prohibiting the college enrollment of U.S. high school graduates who are undocumented, or denying them access to financial aid or in-state tuition, marginalize these youth and reduce their incentive to graduate from high school and reach their full academic potential (Horwedel, 2006; Murray et al., 2007).

School, Work, and Neighborhood Environments. For the children of immigrants, schools are a source of many of their socialization experiences. In schools, youth become exposed to the native culture for the first time, interact with coethnic immigrant and U.S.-born children, and form beliefs about what society and people outside their families expect from them. Work environments serve the same socialization function for adults. Outside of school and work, neighborhood conditions define opportunity structures and the normative climate for immigrant children and their parents.

Latino immigrant children have been found to attend larger, more impersonal schools with fewer resources and low academic pressure (Matute-Bianchi, 1991; Valenzuela, 1999). They also tend to be in segregated schools with larger minority, coethnic, and poor students (Orofield, 1998). These school characteristics have been associated with poorer academic performance, an increased likelihood of school failure, and poorer mental health among children of immigrants (Crosnoe, 2005; Crosnoe & Lopez-Gonzalez, 2005; Perreira et al., 2006; Portes & MacLeod, 1996; Portes & Rumbaut, 2001). In contrast, interpersonal functioning (e.g., the ability to get along with others) improves in more segregated schools (Crosnoe, 2005). Along at least some dimensions of psychosocial well-being, children of color and immigrant background may benefit from a more ethnically and economically homogeneous environment, where they are buffered from the effects of prejudice, racism, and discrimination (García Coll et al., 1996). However, research on the relationships between school context and the psychosocial well-being of the children of immigrants is sparse.

We are not aware of any research on how the context of work shapes the psychosocial adaptation of adult immigrants. Employment, especially with coethnic colleagues who can provide a cultural bridge, could provide an opportunity for immigrants to learn the language and cultural expectations of their new homeland (Portes & Rumbaut, 2001). At the same time, employment in night-shift jobs, low-status occupations, and physically exhausting work with a high risk of injury can potentially increase immigrants' risks for low self-esteem and depression.

Several studies have examined the effects of neighborhood context for children from Latino immigrant families. Research focusing on the children of immigrants strongly suggests that residence in urban and disadvantaged communities with high poverty and unemployment rates hinders the academic performance and progress of Latino youth (Perreira et al., 2006; Portes & Rumbaut, 2001). In addition, residence in inner-city and disadvantaged communities places the children of immigrants at increased risk for mental health problem (Harris, 1999; Xue, Leventhal, Brooks-Gunn, & Earls, 2005) and the adoption of risky behaviors (Browning, Leventhal, & Brooks-Gunn, 2004; Frank, Cerdá, & Rendón, 2007; Harris, 1999; Sampson, Morenoff, & Raudenbush, 2005). Although gang activity is becoming an increasingly prominent feature of rural areas as well, neighborhood violence and unsafe or disruptive conditions in urban school environments can partially explain the adoption of risk behaviors and the academic challenges faced by the children of immigrants (Portes & Rumbaut, 2001). Latino youth growing up in more economically disadvantaged areas where gang activity is prevalent are at higher risk of engaging in risky behaviors and delinquent activity (Simons, Stewart, Gordon, Conger, & Elder, 2002).

Race Relations and Coethnic Communities. A community's existing ethnic stratifications and the size of its coethnic social networks structure opportunities for new immigrants (Alba & Nee, 2003; García Coll et al., 1996). Coethnic communities and communities with a history of multiculturalism and inclusion can cushion the impact of cultural change and provide resources (e.g., language services) that help newcomers learn the ropes and establish themselves (Portes & Rumbaut, 2001). Moreover, high coethnic concentrations can promote social cohesion and collective efficacy within a community. Higher levels of social cohesion and collective efficacy can counterbalance the potentially negative effects of neighborhood poverty and hostility in the broader receiving community (Frank et al., 2007; Sampson et al., 2005).

Little research exists on the role of positive race relations in promoting psychosocial health. The research on race relations and immigrant adaptation primarily emphasizes the roles of discrimination, racism, and prejudice (García Coll et al., 1996). Immigrant adults as well as their children report feeling discriminated against or being treated unfairly because they are Latino or do not have a strong command of English (Padilla, Cervantes, & Maldonado, 1988; Gil, Vega, & Dimas, 1994; Rumbaut, 1994). Among both adults and children, discriminatory experiences and the perceived likelihood of discrimination have been associated with depression, poor self-esteem, and reduced educational aspirations or expectations (Finch, Kolody, & Vega, 2000; Gil et al., 1994; Padilla et al., 1988; Rumbaut, 1994).

Because of the harmful psychosocial consequences of discrimination, racism, and prejudice, researchers have hypothesized that segregation, measured as coethnic concentration, can be protective and potentially can promote the psychosocial health of Latino and other minority immigrant populations (García Coll et al., 1996). The research is mixed. Some studies find that coethnic concentrations positively affect psychosocial health (Frank et al., 2007; Sampson et al., 2005). Others find weak or insignificant associations between immigrant concentration and educational outcomes, mental health outcomes, or risk behaviors (Alaniz, Cartmill, & Parker, 1998; Perreira et al., 2006; Xue et al., 2005).

CONCLUSION

The future of the Latino population in the United States rests largely upon the ability of immigrants from Latin America and their offspring to successfully adapt to the country. As described in this chapter, the foreign born face substantial challenges to their social and economic integration into U.S. society. Socioeconomically, many immigrants come to the United States with limited education that tracks them into low-level occupations with little economic stability. The tenuous economic standing of many families leads them to settle in lower-income and more dangerous neighborhoods that present many difficulties for their children, not the least of which are underfunded and overcrowded schools with few experienced teachers and few opportunities for advanced course work. These challenges exist within a larger context of rapidly changing and often contradictory federal, state, and municipal policies regarding the rights of immigrants and the enforcement of immigrant laws. Finally, newer immigrants settling in nontraditional areas can face the hostility and suspicion of communities that have little experience with immigrant or Latino populations.

At the same time, immigrant Latinos and their families possess a number of strengths that enable them to demonstrate better psychological, behavioral, and academic adjustment than would be predicted from their life circumstances. Immigrants come with a strong desire to succeed in U.S. society, which they attempt to instill in their children. Parents have high aspirations for their children's education, with educational goals that often surpass those of nonimmigrant parents. Students in immigrant families endorse these goals and report high levels of academic motivation and a strong belief in the utility of education. The aspirations and motivation of immigrants and their children, in turn, are fueled by a strong value placed upon family togetherness, sacrifice, and support, as well as a high level of identification with their ethnic and cultural backgrounds.

Although this chapter highlights how these challenges and strengths interact in shaping adjustment, future research needs to focus on emerging issues that are currently not well understood. Little attention has been paid to the great diversity among Latino immigrants. Although Mexicans constitute the largest group of foreign-born Latinos by far, increasing numbers of immigrants from Central and South America and the Caribbean are entering the United States with potentially quite different social, economic, and cultural backgrounds. Future studies need to go beyond the Mexican population and sample sufficient numbers of Latino immigrants from other regions. Another source of diversity about which little is known is the role of documentation among Latino immigrants. Unauthorized status is a fact of life for a substantial portion of the population, yet few studies have examined how this may impact psychological, behavioral, and educational adaptation. In addition, the increasing trend for immigrants to settle in new and different areas of the country raises questions about whether the bulk of existing research, which has been conducted largely with populations in traditional receiving locations, would apply to immigrants who are building new immigrant and ethnic communities. Finally, the coming decades will likely include an increasingly complex and changing mix of federal, state, and local policies regarding immigration and the rights of the foreign born. If the past 4 decades are any guide, these changing policy contexts will continue to shape both the nature of the foreign-born population and the challenges they face in ways that cannot be anticipated today.

REFERENCES

Alaniz, M. L., Cartmill, R. S., & Parker, R. N. (1998). Immigrants and violence: The importance of neighborhood context. *Hispanic Journal of Behavioral Sciences, 20,* 155–174.

Alba, R., & Nee, V. (2003). *Remaking the American mainstream: Assimilation and contemporary immigration.* Cambridge, MA: Harvard University Press.

Alegría, M., Canino, G., Stinson, F., & Grant, B. (2006). Nativity and DSM-IV psychiatric disorders among Puerto Ricans, Cuban Americans and non-Latino Whites in the United States: Results from the National Epidemiologic Survey on Alcohol and Related Conditions. *Journal of Clinical Psychiatry, 67,* 56–65.

Alegría, M., Mulvaney-Day, N., Torres, M., Polo, A., Cao, Z., & Canino, G. (2007). Prevalence of psychiatric disorders across Latino subgroups in the United States. *American Journal of Public Health, 97,* 68–75.

Alegría, M., Sribney, W., Woo, M., Torres, M., & Guarnaccia, P. (2007). Looking beyond nativity: The relation of age of immigration, length of residence, and birth cohorts to the risk of onset of psychiatric disorders for Latinos. *Research in Human Development, 41,* 19–47.

Browning, C. R., Leventhal, T., & Brooks-Gunn, J. (2004). Neighborhood context and racial differences in early adolescent sexual activity. *Demography, 41,* 697–720.

Burnam, M. A., Hough, R., Karno, M., Escobar, J., & Telles, C. (1987). Acculturation and lifetime prevalence of psychiatric disorders among Mexican Americans in Los Angeles. *Journal of Health and Social Behavior, 28,* 89–102.

Capps, R., Castañeda, R. M., Chaudry, A., & Santos, R. (2007). *Paying the price: The impact of immigration raids on America's children.* Washington, DC: Urban Institute.

Chavez, L. R. (1997). *Shadowed lives: Undocumented immigrants in American society.* Belmont, CA: Wadsworth.

Crosnoe, R. (2005). Double disadvantage or signs of resilience? The elementary school contexts of children from Mexican immigrant families. *American Educational Research Journal, 42,* 269–303.

Crosnoe, R., & Lopez-Gonzalez, L. (2005). Immigration from Mexico, school composition, and adolescent functioning. *Sociological Perspectives, 48,* 1–24.

Dixon, D., & Gelatt, J. (2006). *Detailed characteristics of the South American born in the United States.* Washington, DC: Migration Policy Institute.

Donato, K., & Bankston, C., III (2007). The origins of employer demand for immigrants in a new destination: The salience of soft skills in a volatile economy. In D. S. Massey & C. Hirschmann (Eds.), *New faces in new places: The changing geography of American immigration* (pp. 124–148). New York: Russell Sage.

Donato, K. M., Tolbert, C., Nucci, A., & Kawano, Y. (2007). Changing faces/changing places: The emergence of non-metropolitan immigrant gateways. *Rural Sociology, 72*(4), 537–559.

Finch, B. K., Kolody, B., & Vega, W. (2000). Perceived discrimination and depression among Mexican-origin adults in California. *Journal of Health and Social Behavior, 41,* 295–313.

Finch, B. K., & Vega, W. A. (2003). Acculturation stress, social support, and self-rated health among Latinos in California. *Journal of Immigrant Health, 5,* 109–117.

Fink, L. (2003). *The Maya of Morgantown: Work and community in the nuevo New South.* Chapel Hill: University of North Carolina Press.

Fix, M. (2007). Immigrant integration and comprehensive immigration reform: An overview. In M. Fix (Ed.), *Securing the future: U.S. immigrant integration policy, a reader.* Washington, DC: Migration Policy Institute.

Frank, R., Cerdá, M., & Rendón, M. (2007). Barrios and burbs: Residential context and health-risk behaviors among Angeleno adolescents. *Journal of Health and Social Behavior, 48,* 283–300.

Frey, W. H., & Liaw, K. L. (1998). The impact of recent immigration on population redistribution within the United States. In J. P. Smith & B. Edmonston (Eds.), *The immigration debate: Studies of the economic, demographic, and fiscal effects of immigration* (pp. 388–448). Washington, DC: National Academies Press.

Frey, W. H., & Liaw, K. L. (2005). Migration within the United States: Role of race and ethnicity. *Brookings-Wharton Papers on Urban Affairs, 6,* 207–262.

Fuligni, A. J. (1997). The academic achievement of adolescents from immigrant families: The roles of family background, attitudes, and behavior. *Child Development, 68,* 261–273.

Fuligni, A. J. (2005). Convergence and divergence in developmental contexts among immigrants to the United States. In W. Schaie & G. Elder (Eds.), *Historical influences on lives and aging* (pp. 89–98). New York: Springer.

Fuligni, A. J., & Fuligni, A. S. (2007). Immigrant families and the educational development of their children. In J. Lansford, K. Deater Deckard, & M. Bornstein (Eds.), *Immigrant families in America* (pp. 231–249). New York: Guilford Press.

Fuligni, A. J., & Witkow, M. (2004). The postsecondary educational progress of youth from immigrant families. *Journal of Research on Adolescence, 14,* 159–183.

Fuligni, A. J., Witkow, M., & Garcia, C. (2005). Ethnic identity and the academic adjustment of adolescents from Mexican, Chinese, and European backgrounds. *Developmental Psychology, 41,* 799–811.

Fuligni, A. J., & Yoshikawa, H. (2003). Socioeconomic resources, parenting, and child development among immigrant families. In M. Bornstein & R. Bradley (Eds.), *Socioeconomic status, parenting, and child development* (pp. 107–124). Mahwah, NJ: Lawrence Erlbaum.

Fuligni, A. J., & Yoshikawa, H. (2004). Investments in children among immigrant families. In A. Kalil & T. DeLiere (Eds.), *Family investments in children's potential.* Mahwah, NJ: Lawrence Erlbaum.

García Coll, C. G., Lamberty, J., McAdoo, H. P., Crnic, K., Wasik, J., & Garcia, V. H. (1996). An integrative model for the study of developmental competencies in minority children. *Child Development, 67*(5), 1891–1914.

Gil, A. G., Vega, W. A., & Dimas, J. M. (1994). Acculturative stress and personal adjustment among Hispanic adolescent boys. *Journal of Community Psychology, 22,* 43–54.

Gil, A. G., Wagner, E. F., & Vega, W. A. (2000). Acculturation, familism and alcohol use among Latino adolescent males: Longitudinal relations. *Journal of Community Psychology, 28,* 443–458.

Glick, J. E., & White, M. J. (2004). Post-secondary school participation of immigrant and native youth: The role of familial resources and educational expectations. *Social Science Research, 33,* 272–299.

Griffith, D. (1995). Hay Trabajo: Poultry processing, rural industrialization, and the emergence of a Mexican immigrant community in an industrial region of the U.S. historic South. *Social Science Quarterly, 81,* 49–66.

Harris, K. M. (1999). The health status and risk behavior of adolescents in immigrant families. In D. H. Hernandez (Ed.), *Children of immigrants: Health, adjustment, and public assistance.* Washington, DC: National Academies Press.

Hernández-Léon, R., & Zúñiga, V. (2000). Making carpet by the mile: The Latinization of low-wage labor. In D. D. Stull, M. J. Broadway, & D. Griffith (Eds.), *Any way you cut it: Meat processing and small-town America* (pp. 129–152). Lawrence: University Press of Kansas.

Horwedel, D. M. (2006). For illegal college students, an uncertain future. *Diverse: Issues in Higher Education, 23,* 22–26.

Johnson-Webb, K. (2003). *Recruiting Hispanic labor: Immigrants in non-traditional areas.* New York: LFB Scholarly.

Kandula, N. R., Grogan, C. M., Rathouz, P. J., & Lauderdale, D. S. (2004). The unintended impact of welfare reform on the Medicaid enrollment of eligible immigrants. *Health Services Research, 39,* 1509–1526.

Kao, G., & Tienda, M. (1995). Optimism and achievement: The educational performance of immigrant youth. *Social Science Quarterly, 76,* 1–19.

Kaushal, N., & Kaestner, R. (2005). Welfare reform and health insurance of immigrants. *Health Services Research, 40,* 697–721.

Kiang, L., Yip, T., Gonzales-Backen, M., Witkow, M., & Fuligni, A. J. (2006). Ethnic identity and the daily psychological well-being of adolescents with Chinese and Mexican backgrounds. *Child Development, 27,* 1338–1350.

Kochhar, R., Suro, R., & Tafoya, S. (2005). *The new Latino South: The context and consequences of rapid population growth.* Washington, DC: Pew Hispanic Center.

Louie, V. (2005). Immigrant newcomer populations, ESEA, and the pipeline to college: Current considerations and future lines of inquiry. In L. Parker (Ed.), *Review of research in education.* Washington, DC: American Educational Research Association.

Massey, D. (1990). American apartheid: Segregation and the making of the underclass. *American Journal of Sociology, 96,* 329–357.

Massey, D. S., Arango, J., Hugo, G., Kouaouci, A., Pellegrino, A., & Taylor, J. E. (1993). Theories of international migration: A review and appraisal. *Population and Development Review, 19,* 431–466.

Massey, D. S., & Aysa, M. (2005). Social capital and international migration from Latin America. Presented at the International Symposium on International Migration and Development, Turin, Italy. Retrieved November 15, 2007, from http://www.un.org/esa/population/migration/turin/Symposium_Turin_files/P04_Aysa-Lastra.pdf

Massey, D. S., Durand, J., & Malone, N. J. (2002). *Beyond smoke and mirrors: Mexican immigration in an era of economic integration.* New York: Russell Sage.

Massey, D. S., & Espinosa, K. E. (1997). What's driving Mexico-U.S. migration? A theoretical, empirical, and policy analysis. *American Journal of Sociology, 102,* 939–999.

Matute-Bianchi, M. E. (1991). Situational ethnicity and patterns of school performance among immigrant and non-immigrant Mexican-descent students. In M. A. Gibson & J. U. Ogbu (Eds.), *Minority status and schooling: A comparative study of immigrant and involuntary minorities* (pp. 205–248). New York: Garland.

Moffitt, T. E., & Caspi, A. (2001). Childhood predictors differentiate life-course persistent and adolescent-limited antisocial pathways among males and females. *Development and Psychopathology, 13,* 355–375.

Munshi, K. (2003). Networks in the modern economy: Mexican migrants in the U.S. labor market. *Quarterly Journal of Economics, 118,* 549–597.

Murray, J., Batalova, J., & Fix, M. (2007). Educating the children of immigrants. In M. Fix (Ed.), *Securing the future: US immigrant integration policy, a reader.* Washington, DC: Migration Policy Institute.

Orofield, G. (1998). Commentary on the education of Mexican immigrant children. In M. Suárez-Orozco (Ed.), *Crossings: Mexican immigration in interdisciplinary perspectives.* Cambridge, MA: Harvard University Press.

Ortega, A., Rosenheck, R., Alegría, M., & Desai, R. (2000). Acculturation and the lifetime risk of psychiatric and substance use disorders among Hispanics. *Journal of Nervous and Mental Disorders, 188,* 728–735.

Padilla, A. M., Cervantes, R. C., & Maldonado, M. (1988). Coping responses to psychosocial stressors among Mexican and Central American immigrants. *Journal of Community Psychology, 16,* 418–427.

Palloni, A., Massey, D. S., Ceballos, M., Espinosa, K., & Spittel, M. (2001). Social capital and international migration: A test using information on family networks. *American Journal of Sociology, 106,* 1262–1298.

Park, S. L., Sarnoff, R., Bender, C., & Korenbrot, C. (2000). Impact of recent welfare and immigration reforms on use of Medicaid for prenatal care by immigrants in California. *Journal of Immigrant Health, 2,* 5–22.

Passel, J. S. (2005). *Estimates of the size and characteristics of the undocumented population.* Washington, DC: Pew Hispanic Center.

Perreira, K., Harris, K. M., & Lee, D. (2006). Making it in America: High school completion among immigrant youth. *Demography, 43,* 511–536.

Pew Hispanic Center (2006). *A statistical portrait of the foreign-born population at mid-decade.* Washington, DC: Author.

Piore, M. J. (1979). *Birds of passage: Migrant labor in industrial societies.* New York: Cambridge University Press.

Portes, A. (1998). Social capital: Its origins and applications in modern sociology. *Annual Review of Sociology, 24,* 1–24.

Portes, A., & MacLeod, T. (1996) Educational progress of children of immigrants: The roles of class, ethnicity, and social context. *Sociology of Education, 69,* 255–275.

Portes, A., & Rumbaut, R. G. (2001). *Legacies: The story of the second generation.* Berkeley: University of California Press.

Portes, A., & Rumbaut, R. G. (2006). *Immigrant America: A portrait* (3rd ed.). Berkeley: University of California Press.

Ramirez, J. R., Crano, W. D., Quist, R., Burgoon, M., Alvaro, E. M., & Grandpre, J. (2004). Acculturation, familism, parental monitoring, and knowledge as predictors of marijuana and inhalant use in adolescents. *Psychology of Addictive Behaviors, 18,* 3–11.

Reese, L. (2002). Parental strategies in contrasting cultural settings: Families in México and "El Norte." *Anthropology and Education Quarterly, 33,* 30–59.

Reitz, J. G. (2002). Host societies and the reception of immigrants: Research themes, emerging theories, and methodological issues. *International Migration Review, 36,* 1005–1019.

Rumbaut, R. (1991). The agony of exile: A study of the migration and adaptation of Indochinese refugee adults and children. In F. L. Ahearn & J. L. Athey (Eds.), *Refugee children: Theory, research, and service* (pp. 59–91). Baltimore: Johns Hopkins University Press.

Rumbaut, R. G. (1994). The crucible within: Ethnic identity, self-esteem and segmented assimilation among children of immigrants. *International Migration Review, 28,* 748–794.

Sampson, R. J., Morenoff, J. D., & Raudenbush, S. (2005). Social anatomy of racial and ethnic disparities in violence. *American Journal of Public Health, 95,* 224–232.

Schachter, J. (2003). *Migration by race and Hispanic origin: 1995–2000.* Washington, DC: U.S. Government Printing Office.

Simons, R. L., Stewart, E., Gordon, L. C., Conger, R. D., & Elder, G. H., Jr. (2002). A test of life-course explanations for stability and change in antisocial behavior from adolescence to young adulthood. *Criminology, 40,* 401.

Suro, R., & Tafoya, S. (2004). *Dispersal and concentration: Patterns of Latino residential settlement.* Washington, DC: Pew Hispanic Center.

Taylor, J. E., Arango, J., Hugo, G., Kouaouci, A., Massey, D. S., & Pellegrino, A. (1996). International migration and community development. *Population Index, 62,* 181–212.

Tichenor, D. J. (2002). *Dividing lines: The politics of immigration control in America.* Princeton, NJ: Princeton University Press.

Umaña-Taylor, A. J., Yazedjian, A., & Bámaca-Gómez, M. (2004). Developing the Ethnic Identity Scale using Eriksonian and social identity perspectives. *Identity: An International Journal of Theory and Research, 3,* 9–38.

U.S. Census Bureau. (2003). *Foreign-born population of the United States: American community survey–2003, Special tabulation (ACS-T-2).* Retrieved November 15, 2007, from http://www.census.gov/population/www/socdemo/foreign/acst2.html#la

U.S. Census Bureau. (2005). *2005 American community survey data.* Retrieved December 1, 2007, from http://factfinder.census.gov/servlet/DatasetMainPageServlet?_program=ACS&_submenuId=datasets_2&_lang=en&_ts=

U.S. Department of State. (2007). *Visa bulletin 8*(113). Retrieved November 15, 2007, from http://travel.state.gov/visa/frvi/bulletin/bulletin_3841.html

U.S. Immigration and Naturalization Service (1994). *1993 yearbook of the Immigration and Naturalization Service.* Washington, DC: U.S. Government Printing Office.

Valenzuela, A. (1999). *Subtractive schooling: U.S.–Mexican youth and the politics of caring.* New York: State University of New York Press.

Vega, W. A., Kolody, B., Aguilar-Gaxiola, S., Alderte, E., Catalano, R., & Caraveo-Anduaga, H. (1998). Lifetime prevalence of DSM-III-R psychiatric disorders among urban and rural Mexican Americans in California. *Archives of General Psychiatry, 55,* 771–778.

Vega, W. A., Sribney, W., Aguilar-Gaxiola, S., & Kolody, B. (2004). 12-month prevalence of DSM-III-R psychiatric disorders among Mexican Americans: Nativity, social assimilation, and age determinants. *Journal of Nervous and Mental Disease, 192,* 532–541.

Waters, M. C., & Jiménez, T. R. (2005). Assessing immigrant assimilation: New empirical and theoretical challenges. *Annual Review of Sociology, 31,* 105–125.

Wilson, W. J. 1987. *The truly disadvantaged: The inner city, the underclass and public policy.* Chicago: University of Chicago Press.

Xue, Y., Leventhal, T., Brooks-Gunn, J., & Earls, F. J. (2005). Neighborhood residence and mental health problems of 5- to 11-year-olds. *Archives of General Psychiatry, 62,* 554–563.

8

ACCULTURATION, ENCULTURATION, AND THE PSYCHOSOCIAL ADAPTATION OF LATINO YOUTH

NANCY A. GONZALES, FAIRLEE C. FABRETT, AND GEORGE P. KNIGHT

The Latino population accounted for over 50% of the U.S. population growth between 2000 and 2005 (Pew Hispanic Center, 2006) and is expected to increase from 14.5% currently to more than 25% of the total U.S. population by 2050 (U.S. Census Bureau, 2003). A deeper examination of these numbers reveals that a quarter of this population is young, with 11.3 million under age 18, and a large proportion are immigrants or children of immigrant parents. Thus, in the next decade, a growing and substantial proportion of U.S. Latino youth will face the challenge of adapting to life as a member of a political minority group in a host culture that may have different rules, different values, and a different language from their cultures of origin. Several authors suggest that their challenges created by these experiences may increase the risk for such negative mental health outcomes as conduct problems, drug and alcohol abuse, depression, and low self-esteem, as well as such negative life outcomes as school failure and economic instability (e.g., Gonzales & Kim, 1997; Phinney, 1990; Szapocznik & Kurtines, 1980).

As one of the most important intragroup characteristics of Latinos, *acculturation* is the term originally used to describe the cultural changes that result at both the group level and the individual psychological level from sustained contact between two or more distinct cultures (Berry, Trimble, & Olmedo, 1986). At the individual level, this process may result in the gradual incorporation of cultural beliefs, values, behaviors, and language of the host culture, as well as changes in one's identification with and sense of belonging to the host culture (i.e., *acculturation*). Simultaneously, individuals also adapt to the cultural beliefs, values, behaviors and language of their heritage cultures and develop an understanding and sense of belonging to their ethnic groups (i.e., *enculturation*). Drawing on contemporary theory and research with Latinos and other cultural groups (e.g., Berry, 2003; Tsai, Chentsova-Dutton, & Wong, 2002), we use the term *cultural adaptation* to refer collectively to the dual processes of acculturation and enculturation (Gonzales, Knight, Morgan-Lopez, Saenz, & Sorolli, 2002). Understanding these interrelated processes and their roles in psychosocial adaptation has been a ubiquitous yet elusive goal in research with Latinos. While evidence links indicators of cultural adaptation to nearly every domain of psychosocial adjustment studied, findings have been inconsistent and often contradictory across studies (Gonzales et al., 2002; Lara, Gamboa, Kahramanian, Morales, & Hayes Bautista, 2005; Rogler, Cortes, & Malgady, 1991). Moreover, despite intense focus on Latino cultural adaptation over the years, the current literature offers limited evidence of the underlying mechanisms that explain why or how it relates to specific psychological variables of interest.

In this chapter, we focus on the dual processes of acculturation and enculturation and their role in the psychological adaptation of Latino children and adolescents 18 years or younger. However, we do not aim here to provide an exhaustive review of the literature or to reconcile conflicting findings reported across studies. Advances in our understanding of cultural adaptation over the past decade and failed efforts to find consistent effects in previous reviews have underscored its complex, highly contextualized nature. Portes and Zady (2002) reported significant differences in psychosocial correlates of cultural adaptation across Latino subgroups and proposed that these group differences were due to at least four interacting factors: "(a) the cultural history and traits of the immigrant group; (b) the degree to which the latter are compatible with or conducive toward adaptation into either domestic minorities' cycle of poverty and/or compatible with the mainstream; (c) the host/mainstream's reception of the immigrant group, inclusive of its reaction to ethnic markers (phenotypic and cultural) in a particular historical period; and (d) the political and social capital developed by the immigrants' ethnic group in the host culture that supports its members' agency in the community" (p. 312). Within group differences are also expected based on individual and family factors, such as income, education level, and family members' abilities to successfully navigate mainstream institutions; and on community factors, such as neighborhoods where crime, poverty, and unemployment rates are either high or low, where one's cultural traditions and values are either valued or not valued, and where discrimination is either a rare event or a recurring reality. Given such complexity,

divergent findings regarding the link between cultural adaptation and psychological outcomes should be expected in studies typically conducted with widely varying local samples. Indeed, it is surprising that some consistent patterns have nevertheless emerged in the literature.

As such, the current chapter has two goals. One is to highlight findings on the link between cultural adaptation and psychosocial adjustment that have been replicated across studies. Identification of these robust effects is important to guide targeted studies, interventions, and policies that are likely to have a broad public health impact. The second goal is to identify underlying processes or mechanisms that have been examined and supported in the literature that can explain *how* cultural adaptation operates to impact psychosocial adjustment of Latino youth. Lack of research on mediating mechanisms was highlighted as a significant gap in a review of the literature that we conducted previously (Gonzales et al., 2002), but studies published subsequent to that review have begun to address this gap. Before proceeding with our review of this research, the following section first provides a brief overview of theoretical advances that have guided the most current research on cultural adaptation.

Contemporary Theory on the Dual Processes of Acculturation and Enculturation

Until recently, acculturation was typically operationalized as a unidimensional continuum ranging from retention of heritage-culture characteristics to acquisition of receiving-culture characteristics, with simple markers such as English-language versus Spanish-language use as indicators. This practice persisted widely in the literature, despite the recommendations of contemporary scholars in cultural psychology who proposed bidimensional models in which acculturative and enculturative processes are separable, each representing distinct axes of culture change (Berry, 2003; Cuellar, Arnold, & Maldonado, 1995; Zane & Mak, 2003). The dual-axis model rejects the assumption that loss of one's ethnic culture necessarily occurs when new cultural characteristics are adopted from the host ("mainstream") culture, and asserts instead that individuals have the potential to achieve simultaneously high, simultaneously low, or quite different levels of adaptation to both mainstream and ethnic cultures.

Berry (1980) was one of the first to propose a dual-axis model and to suggest that acculturative and enculturative dimensions intersect to define different types of adaptive strategies: *Bicultural/integration* reflects active involvement in both the culture of origin and the host culture; *assimilation* occurs when an individual does not maintain connections with the culture of origin and seeks out strong connections with the host culture; *separation/withdrawal* occurs when an individual holds strongly to the culture of origin while avoiding involvement in the host culture; *alienation/marginalization* is a strategy in which there is little maintenance of the original culture and little participation in the new culture. This typology provided a useful heuristic from which to view patterns of cultural adaptation across individuals and has given rise to hypotheses and analyses to determine which typologies are associated with more deleterious or more optimal psychological outcomes (e.g., Bacallao & Smokowski, 2005; Coatsworth, Maldonado-Molina, Pantin, & Szapocznik, 2005; De la Rosa, 2002).

Current theoretical approaches also emphasize the multidimensional nature of acculturation and enculturation, although consensus regarding the relevant psychosocial dimensions has not been established. Examples of proposed dimensions include knowledge of cultural facts, communication styles, affiliation preferences, daily habits, participation in cultural activities, language use and preference, cultural beliefs, values, cognitive styles, personality, self-concept, and ethnic or cultural identity (see Knight, Jacobson, Gonzales, Roosa, & Saenz, 2009, for a review). Increasingly, studies have broadened the type and number of dimensions included, allowing for more nuanced hypothesis testing. This research has shown that the effects of acculturation and enculturation vary substantially depending on the specific dimensions studied and the outcomes targeted. For example, although linguistic acculturation has been associated with negative outcomes, ethnic identity generally has been associated with such positive outcomes as self-esteem (Phinney, Cantu, & Kurtz, 1997) and academic success (Fuligni, Witkow, & Garcia, 2005).

LATINO YOUTH ACCULTURATION AND RISK FOR PROBLEM BEHAVIOR

In a previous chapter on Latino youth cultural adaptation, we reviewed studies published between 1980 and 2000 and found that the overwhelming majority of studies focused on problem outcomes and psychopathology during adolescence; relatively few studies focused on younger children or adaptive psychological functioning (Gonzales et al., 2002). This description still applies, for the most part, although a few more studies now include indicators of adaptive functioning. While the overall number of such studies is still too sparse for a focused review, we incorporate relevant findings throughout the chapter to promote a more balanced understanding of the link between Latino youth cultural adaptation and psychosocial adjustment.

The research we summarized in our prior review relied almost exclusively on demographic proxies of acculturation, such as U.S. nativity or generation status, or on unidimensional acculturation scales predominantly based on English-language use. That review found a consistent, positive association between these indicators and externalizing problems in adolescence, including conduct problems, aggression, substance use, and early sexual activity. Studies published since then, summarized hereinafter, generally support these effects but also go beyond simple associations to better reflect the complexities of cultural adaptation described by contemporary theory. Although studies linking acculturation indicators with internalizing problems (e.g., depression and anxiety) were also identified in our prior review (Hovey & King, 1996; Katragadda & Tidwell, 1998; Rumbaut, 1995) and in a small number of subsequent studies (Glover, Pumariega, Holzer, Wise, & Rodriguez, 1999; Pina & Silverman, 2004), these findings are inconsistent and the number of studies too few to support any firm conclusions. Nevertheless, this scant body of research seems to suggest that the link between cultural adaptation and depression centers on the culture-related stressors that youth encounter as they interact within mainstream and ethnic settings and on the protective resources they have to cope with these stressors. A modest collection of studies have examined associations between acculturation and eating disorders (e.g., Chamorro & Flores-Ortiz, 1998; Joiner & Kashubeck, 1996; Lester & Petrie, 1995); however, this research has not shown a consistent link with cultural adaptation and will not be discussed in this chapter.

The acculturation-problem behavior link has been supported with a number of outcomes during adolescence, including conduct problems, juvenile arrest, peer delinquency, and gang involvement (Gonzales et al., 2002). This pattern has been shown in some longitudinal studies and in studies using nationally representative samples, although these types of designs are still rare in this field. Bui and Thongniramol (2005) used data for 18,907 Latino adolescents participating in the National Longitudinal Study of Adolescent Health. Odds ratios indicated that youth who were second- or third-generation Latinos were 60% and 88% more likely to report violent delinquency, compared to their first-generation counterparts. Studies also show a positive effect of linguistic acculturation, U.S. nativity, and years in the United States on levels of substance use, including use of illicit drugs, alcohol, and smoking (e.g., Eamon & Cray, 2005; Gfroerer & Tan, 2003; Gil, Wagner, & Vega, 2000). English-language use also predicts earlier age of sexual activity, more sexual partners, and increased partner violence during adolescence (Reynoso, Felice, & Shragg, 2002; Sabogal, Pérez-Stable, Otero-Sabogal, & Hiatt, 1995; Upchurch, Aneshensel, Mudgal, & McNeely, 2001).

Although these findings lend support to what seems a fairly robust pattern of increased involvement in problem or risky behaviors for adolescents who have a longer history of contact and a stronger orientation toward the "mainstream" U.S. culture, the bulk of this literature still remains largely focused on simplistic demographic or behavioral measures in which language plays a key role. Studies that rely on such demographic markers as nativity offer limited understanding of the risk processes involved and provide little guidance as to effective strategies to counteract these risks. Use of nativity to assess acculturation and enculturation also is problematic because a number of studies suggest that U.S.-born and foreign-born youth may be exposed to such distinct cultural experiences and challenges that their cultural adaptation processes may not be equivalent. Indeed, a number of studies have shown that the effects of acculturation are moderated by nativity (e.g., Vega, Khoury, Zimmerman, Gil, & Warheit, 1995). For example, among new immigrants, adolescents living in English-speaking homes are at lower risk for engaging in sexual activity than their counterparts in Spanish-speaking homes, while the opposite is true among U.S.-born Latino youth (Guilamo-Ramos, Jaccard, Pena, & Goldberg, 2005).

Further, it should be noted that some studies have failed to support the acculturation-problem behavior link (Bird, Davies, & Duarte, 2006; Carvajal, Hanson, Romero, & Coyle, 2002), or they have found only an indirect link when other variables related to the acculturation process are included as mediators (Gonzales et al., 2008). This is not surprising, given the wide variations across samples on factors expected to impact cultural adaptation, including differences in the Latino subpopulations targeted as well as geographic and other contextual differences. For example, in a probability sample of 2,491 Puerto Rican youth living in San Juan (Puerto Rico) and the South Bronx (New York City), Bird et al. (2006) found that youth acculturation level was not associated with disruptive behavior problems. Although mainland and island Puerto Rican youth alike are U.S. citizens, there are substantial contextual differences between these two locations that are likely confounded with acculturation level. Schwarz and colleagues also failed to find a direct link between U.S. cultural orientation and externalizing symptoms in a sample of 349 Latino middle school students (Schwarz, Zamboanga, & Jarvis, 2007). This study was notable because it targeted a midsized Midwestern community as opposed to a large gateway city (e.g., Miami, Los Angeles) or one of the more established ethnic communities in the Southwest that are typically studied. Schwarz et al. (2007) suggest that their failure to find the acculturation-externalizing effect may be due to the fact that most adolescents in their sample reported high orientation to mainstream culture and low orientation to Hispanic culture, with limited variability on these dimensions. They and others (Smokowski & Bacallao, 2006) also argue that, in contrast to ethnic enclaves where traditional cultural ties are supported and valued, acculturation may be protective in contexts in which the adoption of U.S. cultural practices is the most feasible option.

Finally, in contrast to prior findings linking acculturation and problem outcomes, a small but growing number of studies illustrate the potential advantages of greater integration with Anglo culture. For example, a number of studies have supported a direct link between acculturation to the Anglo culture and higher educational achievement (Goldenberg, Gallimore, Reese, & Garnier, 2001; Kao & Tienda, 1995), educational goals (McWhirter, Hackett, & Bandalos, 1998; Ramos & Sanchez, 1995), and college attendance (Hurtado & Gauvain, 1997), although conflicting findings have also been reported for these outcomes. As another example, Schwarz et al. (2007) used a biaxial framework to assess adolescents' Hispanic and U.S. cultural orientations and found they each had positive, unique effects on adolescents' prosocial behavior. This finding suggests, albeit indirectly, that integration within the dominant society and within one's cultural community are both important for adaptive functioning and that biculturalism may be the most adaptive strategy for many Latino youth. These studies also offer a more mixed picture of the potential risk of Latino youth integration with mainstream culture by showing that this risk may come with increased opportunities for greater success or competence in social and academic domains.

Latino Youth Enculturation: Ethnic Identity and Traditional Cultural Values

For more than 2 decades, acculturation researchers have emphasized the need to incorporate dimensions of enculturation in research with Latinos (Rogler et al., 1991). However, until recently, cultural identity (i.e., ethnic identity) was the only marker of adaptation or integration with one's ethnic culture examined with any regularity in research with Latino youth. The term *ethnic identity* refers to the psychological process by which individuals explore their ethnic background, resolve the meaning of their ethnicity, and come to feel positively about their ethnic background (Umaña-Taylor, Yazedjian, & Bámaca-Gomez, 2004). Ethnic identity is a core aspect of one's enculturation or ethnic socialization (Knight, Bernal, Garza, Cota, & Ocampo, 1993); and Phinney (1990) asserts that a strong

ethnic identity is a key factor in the way immigrants meet the challenges in their new countries.

Ethnic identity may operate to provide strong positive feelings about one's ethnicity and a cognitive framework for counteracting ethnically based stereotypes and attributions imposed by others, thus enabling one to maintain a positive self-concept when one is a member of a group that is devalued (Tajfel & Turner, 1986). Accordingly, studies consistently find a moderately strong positive relation between ethnic identity and self-esteem (Martinez & Dukes, 1997; Phinney et al., 1997; Umaña-Taylor, 2004). A growing body of evidence also supports Phinney's assertion (e.g., Phinney, 1990) that ethnic identity is a resource with which minority youth can counteract the negative effects of discrimination; this research is summarized following, in our discussion of mechanisms or mediators of the effects of cultural adaptation on youth psychological functioning.

Ethnic identity is rarely assessed in research on externalizing outcomes. However, Schwarz et al. (2007) showed that ethnic identity was indirectly related to decreased externalizing symptoms and higher grades through its association with increased self-esteem. In one of the few studies focused on younger children, Knight, Cota, and Bernal (1993) found ethnic identity to be positively associated with a preference for cooperative versus competitive social behavior in a sample of 9-to-12-year-old Mexican American children. These researchers posit that Latino children who have strong ethnic identities are predisposed to internalize traditional cultural values that promote prosocial behaviors, and this may reduce their risk for later disruptive behaviors. In a rare study focused on prosocial functioning that was also noteworthy in its longitudinal design, Armenta, Knight, Carlo, and Jacobson (2009) recently demonstrated that the ethnic affirmation dimension of ethnic identity development was associated with higher familism values and in turn with prosocial tendencies, thereby providing some support for this perspective.

A number of studies have examined the link between ethnic identity and substance use, but findings have been inconsistent. Some have found ethnic identity to be associated with decreased drug use (e.g., Burnam, Hough, Karno, Escobar, & Telles, 1987; Holley, Kulis, Marsiglia, & Keith, 2006); others have found a positive relationship (e.g., Amaro, Whitaker, Coffman, & Hereen, 1990; Markides, Krause, & Mendes de Leon, 1988); and still others find no significant effects (Szapocznik & Kurtines, 1980). A group of studies suggest that ethnic identity is best conceptualized as a risk-moderating factor in relation to substance use (Schinke, Moncher, Palleja, Zayas, & Schilling, 1988). In a study of Puerto Rican adolescents living in East Harlem, Brook and colleagues (Brook, Whiteman, Balka, Win, & Gursen, 1998) found that ethnic identity buffered the effects of risk factors for substance use and also increased the potency of other protective factors. Similar interactive effects were found by Félix-Ortiz and Newcomb (1995) in a study predicting frequency and quantity of drug and alcohol use among predominantly Mexican American adolescents in Los Angeles, and by Scheier and colleagues (Scheier, Botvin, Diaz, & Ifill-Williams, 1997) in a prospective study of risk factors predicting a 7th-to-8th-grade increase in substance use among Latino youth in New York City. These studies seem to suggest that ethnic identity is not, on its own, a robust predictor of adolescent risky behavior but that it becomes important in conditions of high risk, such as when adolescents are exposed to peers who model risky behavior or when their positive self-concepts are threatened.

Among the multiple dimensions expected to shift during the dual processes of acculturation and enculturation, cultural values are frequently cited as potentially the most important dimension for explaining variations in family and individual adaptation (Marín, 1992). Indeed, efforts to explain significant effects of cultural adaptation, when found, almost invariably invoke one or more core cultural values as the underlying dimension of change responsible. For example, a common explanation for increased problem behaviors among more acculturated youth is that core values of respect (respeto) are undermined when youth are exposed to the more individualistic and self-directed value system in the United States (Pantin, Schwartz, Sullivan, Coatsworth, & Szapocznik, 2003). Similarly, shifts in traditional gender roles are expected to increase the risk of substance use, particularly for females, and familism values have been implicated as the underlying explanation for a host of outcomes among more acculturated Latino youth, including increased family conflict, Latino youth susceptibility to deviant peers, and poor pregnancy outcomes (Cuadrado & Lieberman, 1998; Félix-Ortiz & Newcomb, 1995; Unger et al., 2002). Increasingly, cultural values are being incorporated in studies to provide more direct tests of such hypotheses. However, research on cultural values is still fairly limited to date and, with the exception of familism values, which we summarize below, it has not as yet generated any conclusive evidence.

Familism refers to a strong identification with and attachment to the family (nuclear and extended); strong feelings of loyalty, reciprocation, and solidarity among members of the same family; and the belief that individual family members should behave in ways that reflect well on the family (e.g., Sabogal, Marín, Otero-Sabogal, Marín, & Pérez-Stable, 1987). Several authors suggest that familism values are important for youth development and mental health in general because they strengthen family bonds and parental authority, which are important for optimal development (Germán, Gonzales, & Dumka, 2009), and enable Latino families to cope with the many challenges they encounter in their lives, including those associated with low-income status (Roosa, Dumka, & Tein, 1996). Familism values also can play an important role in fostering the conventional ties and behaviors of Latino youth through the desire to protect family honor and avoid bringing *vergüenza* (shame) to the family (Vega, Gil, Warheit, Zimmerman, & Apospori, 1993). A number of studies provide support for these hypothesized effects and find that adolescents with higher familism values have lower levels of externalizing behaviors, deviance, alcohol and substance use, and violence (Félix-Ortiz & Newcomb, 1995; Gil et al., 2000; Gonzales et al., 2008; Kaplan, Erickson, Stewart, & Crane, 2001; McQueen, Getz, & Bray, 2003; Sommers, Fagan, & Baskin, 1993). Familism values also predict increased self-esteem (Fuligni & Pederson, 2002), psychological well-being (Fuligni & Pederson, 2002; Gil et al., 2000), use of solution-oriented conflict strategies (Thayer, Updegraff, & Delgado, 2008), and increased engagement and motivation in school (Gonzales et al., 2008). Familism also operates as a moderator to reduce the negative impact of deviant peers on adolescent substance use (Brook et al., 1998; Kaplan et al., 2001) and externalizing behaviors (Germán et al., 2009).

BIDIMENSIONAL MODELS AND CULTURAL ADAPTATION

A group of studies published just in the past few years has assessed multiple dimensions of dual cultural adaptation and examined cultural adaptation styles or typologies to determine which are associated with adaptive and maladaptive outcomes (Carvajal et al., 2002; Coatsworth et al., 2005; Knight et al., in press; Sullivan et al., 2007). This research is important because it has advanced new methods for identifying typologies and because emerging findings suggest a more refined perspective on the link between acculturation and a range of adolescent psychological outcomes, including externalizing problem behaviors. Using the Bicultural Involvement Questionnaire (BIQ; Szapocznik, Kurtines, & Fernandez, 1980) to assess Hispanic involvement and Anglo American involvement, Coatsworth et al. (2005) used a person-centered analytic approach to identify patterns of adaptation and to examine their association with a range of outcomes, including conduct problems, anxiety and depression, substance use, and academic competence. Adolescents also reported on perceived levels of family support, family conflict, and parental monitoring. Though aiming to test the fourfold typology described by Berry (1980), the researchers found that those four categories (alienation, separation, assimilation, and bicultural) did not represent the full spectrum of acculturation styles and created a fifth category, *moderate,* that included youth who received average scores on both dimensions, indicating comfort with either culture. Two of the most important hypotheses of the study were that assimilated youth would show poor adaptation and that bicultural youth would be the best adapted. Contrary to expectations, assimilated adolescents did not show poor adaptation except on problem behaviors, where they reported higher problems than youth in other categories, and they also reported lower parental monitoring. This finding is consistent with prior studies suggesting that highly acculturated adolescents tend to have more behavior problems and lower parental monitoring. Bicultural adolescents showed the most adaptive pattern across outcomes, including more academic competence, more parental monitoring, and less problem behavior than other categories.

Sullivan et al. (2007) derived a classification system based on the scaling of the BIQ; prior studies have been criticized for using arbitrary or empirically derived cut points for acculturation categories because they are potentially inaccurate and misleading (Knight et al., 2009). Sullivan et al. also failed to identify a marginalized

group. Further, they found that integrated (bicultural) adolescents who reported involvement with mainstream and ethnic cultural practices also reported the highest levels of parental involvement, positive parenting, and family support, and that assimilated adolescents, who adopt receiving-culture practices and do not retain heritage-culture practices, reported the greatest levels of aggressive behavior.

Knight et al. (in press) examined trajectories of acculturation and enculturation among 300 Mexican-American adolescent boys who had committed serious offenses. Trajectories were identified through the use of growth-mixture modeling to examine changes over 3 years in ethnic affirmation/belonging and ethnic identity achievement (based on the Multigroup Ethnic Identity Scale, MEIM; Phinney, 1992); and in Spanish-language use, English-language use, Mexican/Mexican American affiliation/identification, and Anglo affiliation/identification (based on the Acculturation Rating Scale for Mexican Americans II, ARSMA II; Cuellar et al., 1995). The observed trajectory groups did not support the notion that marginalized and/or assimilated adolescents may be overrepresented and that bicultural adolescents may be underrepresented among Mexican American adolescent offenders. A substantial majority of these adolescents were moderately high or higher in ethnic identity, high in ethnic affiliation/identification, and either bicultural or moderately bicultural. In addition, although there were distinct trajectory groups based on substantial differences in absolute levels on language use and affiliation/identification, overall the Mexican American adolescent offenders were relatively stable over time in these dimensions. It is likely that the developmental changes in the language dimensions, and perhaps the affiliation patterns, occur at a younger age. This possibility is consistent with the suggestion of Knight et al. (2009) that the developmental state of the individual may determine to some degree the specific nature of the psychological dimensions undergoing acculturative and enculturative changes at any given time. Following up on these trajectory findings, Losoya et al. (2008) also examined the relationship of changes in these culturally related variables to patterns of heavy episodic drinking and marijuana use in this sample. They found that bicultural Mexican American adolescents (i.e., those who maintain some elements of the ethnic culture while also adapting to the mainstream culture) were less likely to be heavy users of alcohol or marijuana.

Several important consistencies have emerged from these studies that have moved the field forward methodologically and theoretically. Specifically, these findings support a refinement of the conclusion that acculturation to mainstream U.S. cultural practices places Latino youth at risk for behavior problems, in that increased mainstream integration may be problematic only when it is not coupled with retention of Latino cultural practices. The finding that integrated adolescents reported the most favorable levels of parental involvement, positive parenting, and support is consistent with the hypothesis that youth who are most comfortable with both their heritage and their receiving cultural contexts are most likely to relate well to their families. Finally, these findings emphasize the importance of dual-axis models for understanding cultural adaptation and for Berry's contention (Berry, 2003) that individuals utilize a variety of strategies to adapt within multicultural contexts. However, these studies also suggest that marginalization may not be a viable or common strategy for most Latino youth. Indeed, in one of the relatively better attempts to categorize participants, Coatsworth et al. (2005) identified only 1 marginalized participant and 13 separated participants in a sample of 315 Hispanic adolescents, using much less arbitrary criteria than most such attempts. Knight et al. (in press) also suggest that separated and marginalized individuals may be either quite rare or difficult to recruit in most studies because they are not psychologically connected to the mainstream culture from which most research efforts originate.

MEDIATING PROCESSES THAT EXPLAIN CULTURAL ADAPTATION EFFECTS

Another notable advance in the literature on Latino youth cultural adaptation is an increase in studies that aim to test putative mediators or mechanisms through which adolescents' cultural adaptation can increase or decrease their risk for poor psychological adjustment. Not surprisingly, much of this research has focused on processes by which cultural adaptation leads to externalizing behavior problems and substance use. One hypothesis is that youth become more integrated within mainstream social groups and begin to adopt behaviors and values that are tolerated by the host society (Castro, Coe, Gutierres, & Saenz, 1996). Assimilating individuals initiate alcohol and substance use, for example, to fit into American peer groups. Proponents of this behavior adaptation hypothesis might suggest that assimilating adolescents, especially those immersed in disadvantaged, high-crime communities, adopt aggressive and risky behaviors they see used in their new environments. Pantin et al. (2003) also suggest that assimilated adolescents, who adopt American cultural practices while rejecting Hispanic cultural practices, may gravitate toward Americanized peers who socialize them toward behavior problems.

Despite evidence to support this view, emerging research highlights other processes that likely contribute as well and may help to account for the effects of cultural adaptation on psychosocial adjustment more broadly. In this section, we focus on the most dominant explanations that have been examined and supported in the literature, organized according to three broad categories: (1) acculturation stress theory, (2) family as mediator, and (3) protective effects of biculturalism. Although we discuss relevant theory and findings within each of these categories as if they were distinct processes, these categories were created only to provide an organizational framework for our discussion. The explanatory processes discussed in this section are interrelated and most likely operate together to shape Latino youth adaptation, with some processes having more or less relevance, depending on the broader context in which cultural adaptation unfolds for any specific Latino youth.

Acculturation Stress Theory

The stress of integrating two sets of cultural norms and values often emerges in the form of culturally linked stressors, often called acculturation stress, which can include, for example, increased conflicts with peers, language difficulties, and discrimination experiences. The extant literature shows quite clearly that these stressors are associated with higher levels of externalizing and internalizing problems for Latino youth (Gil, Vega, & Dimas, 1994; Hovey & King, 1996; Romero & Roberts, 2003; Vega et al., 1993; Vega et al., 1995) and may help to explain why cultural adaptation can lead to such psychological problems as depression for some youth and for some samples but not for others (Hovey & King, 1996; Katragadda & Tidwell, 1998; Szalacha et al., 2003).

The nature and degree of stress vary substantially depending on the broader social context, the developmental stage of the individual, and the individual's stage of migration. For example, the process of learning English is more difficult for older immigrant youth than for younger, particularly when they attend schools that provide inadequate learning environments for students with limited English proficiency. Studies also suggest that U.S.-born and more acculturated Latino adolescents are more sensitized to the presence of, and more vulnerable to the effects of, discrimination against their group (Gil et al., 2000). Further, Vega, Gil, and Wagner (1998) found that U.S.-born Latino adolescents with low acculturation levels experienced the highest rates of acculturative stress and substance-use initiation of all the Latino adolescents in their sample. These researchers attribute their findings to the "double jeopardy" situation in which these adolescents may find themselves. They encounter language barriers and limited opportunities associated with low acculturation, and in addition they encounter discrimination experiences and acculturation conflicts that are more common for U.S.-born Latino adolescents.

Among the various domains of acculturation stress identified in the literature, the experience of discrimination is one that stands out as particularly important in the lives of Latino youth. Ethnic or racial discrimination—defined as unfair, differential treatment on the basis of race or ethnicity—is a common experience for Latinos and other minority groups in the United States (Garcia Coll et al., 1996; Greene, Way, & Pahl, 2006). Latino youth describe discrimination based on limited English fluency, immigration concerns, negative stereotypes, poverty, and skin color (Edwards & Romero, 2008). Stereotypes of Latinos often include expectations of academic incompetence and, for Latino boys, assumptions about the propensity for violence and delinquency (Gibbs, 1998) that likely lead to more explicit forms of discrimination (e.g., being stopped by policemen, being followed in stores). In addition to discrimination, minority status frequently includes real or perceived structural barriers to success in mainstream society, also a source of stress (Baca Zinn & Wells, 2000; Cooper, Denner, & Lopez, 1999; Garcia Coll & Magnuson, 2000; Vega & Gil, 1999). Structural impediments include reduced access to personal, social, and economic resources, such as advanced education.

Research on the effects of discrimination has shown that it is associated with depression, anxiety, anger, lowered self-esteem, reduced academic expectations and goals, and risky health behaviors for minority youth (Chavez, Moran, Reid, & Lopez, 1997; Cooper et al., 1999; Greene et al., 2006; Romero, Carvajal, Valle, & Orduña, 2007; Szalacha et al., 2003; Vega, 1995). These findings are consistent with social psychological research, which shows that experiences in which one's ethnic group is devalued can lead to negative self-perceptions and increased susceptibility to mental and physical illness (Tajfel, 1981). For example, Blascovich, Spencer, Quinn, and Steele (2001) have demonstrated that when students' ethnic identity is attached to a negative stereotype in a testing environment, students underperform academically and suffer from high blood pressure and increased anxiety levels. Gil et al. (1994) also suggested that perceived discrimination and perceptions of a closed society fuel the relationship between assimilation and youth violence by prompting youth to fight against societal injustices and marginalization.

The experience and impact of discrimination also vary as a function of an individual's social position. For example, Portes and Zady (2002) found that perceived discrimination positively predicted self-esteem for Cuban Americans attending private schools, but not for Cuban Americans attending public school nor for Mexican, Nicaraguan, or Colombian high school students. They explained that this group, the most advantaged and least discriminated against, may be aware of discrimination in the United States but may not feel threatened because they are protected by an empowered Cuban enclave and do not feel that it pertains directly to them.

As previously reported, a number of studies support the role of ethnic identity as a protective resource for coping with discrimination. Studies that directly test the protective effects of ethnic identity find a significantly weaker association between perceived discrimination and depression among individuals who report high levels of ethnic identity, compared to their counterparts who report lower levels of ethnic identity (Mossakowski, 2003; Romero & Roberts, 2003).

Research also suggests that mainstream integration may also play a role in adolescents' vulnerability to the psychological impact of discrimination. Specifically, Umaña-Taylor and Updegraff (2007) found that Latino youth were more vulnerable to low self-esteem and depressive symptoms as a result of discrimination if they had a strong orientation to the mainstream culture but not if they had a low mainstream orientation. It is possible that Latino youth are more susceptible to negative ethnic prejudices and stereotypes when they become more invested in the majority culture and spend significant amounts of time in mainstream social contexts.

Family as Mediator

The acculturative stress perspective also has been applied to the family; several studies have shown that increased acculturation has a deleterious impact on family functioning. This research has shown that the relationship between youth acculturation and problem behavior is mediated by a number of family disruptions, including increased family conflict (Gonzales, Deardorff, Formoso, Barr, & Barrera, 2006; Samaniego & Gonzales, 1999), parents' decreased monitoring of adolescents (Fridrich & Flannery, 1995), disruptions in parent-child bonds (McQueen et al., 2003), and decreased parental involvement (Dinh, Roosa, Tein, & Lopez, 2002). These acculturation-related family processes have also been associated with depression in some cases. For example, Gonzales et al. (2006) found that Mexican-origin adolescents' reports of general family conflict and their mothers' reports of interparental conflict both mediated the effects of linguistic acculturation on adolescents' conduct problems and depressive symptoms.

The link between acculturation, parent-child conflict, and adolescent problem behavior has been attributed most frequently to the discrepancies in parent-child acculturation levels that result when parents retain traditional values and acculturate less rapidly than adolescents (e.g., Szapocznik, Kurtines, Santisteban, & Rio, 1990). Intergenerational acculturation gaps are purported to produce a clash of values and expectations between parents and teens, leading to increased family conflict, parent-child alienation, and youth maladjustment. Furthermore, the more stressful the process of acculturation to the host culture is for parents and adolescents,

the more likely and frequently acculturation-related conflicts are to occur between parents and adolescents (Gil et al., 1994; Smokowski & Bacallao, 2006). For example, as immigrant parents experience increasing frustration in their unsuccessful efforts to reestablish authority with their more "Americanized" youth, they may begin to reduce their attempts to support, communicate with, and monitor their teens, thereby increasing the teens' susceptibility to peer influences and substance use (Kurtines & Szapocznik, 1996).

Although the theoretical underpinnings of differential acculturation have been described previously, and a number of studies have documented the presence of parent-child acculturation gaps, only a few studies have shown that these gaps lead to adjustment problems for parents and youth. Recently, Martinez (2006) operationalized differential acculturation as greater youth Americanism relative to parents and found a relation with youth substance use in a sample of Mexican American early adolescents. That relationship was fully mediated by the effects of differential acculturation on family cultural stress and effective parenting practices. Similarly, Elder and colleagues found that children who were more oriented to the Anglo culture and less oriented to the Mexican culture than their parents were more likely to develop risk factors for tobacco and alcohol use (Elder, Broyles, Brennan, Zuniga de Nuncio, & Nader, 2005). However, other studies provide disconfirmatory evidence for the acculturation gap distress hypothesis (Fuligni, 1998; Lau et al., in press). It is possible these inconsistencies are due to sample differences. For example, Martinez (2006) found evidence for the discrepancy effects with a sample of immigrant families for whom such discrepancies were likely to be most pronounced. Consensus is also lacking about the best methods to measure discrepancies. Theoretical discussions typically focus on value discrepancies between parents and adolescents, but most studies use language-based measures to form discrepancy scores. Such alternative methods as latent profile analyses or measures that better track the theoretical underpinnings might shed more light on the role of parent-child acculturation discrepancies, which are still the most widely cited explanation for the deleterious effects of acculturation on Latino youth.

A family-stress perspective also recognizes that cultural adaptation presents multiple challenges for all family members that require each of them to respond as an individual. For example, parents' experience of acculturation stressors impacts their own psychological functioning and parenting which, in turn, impact youth adjustment (White, Roosa, Weaver, & Nair, in press). Language barriers and feelings of marginalization are typically more pronounced for parents than for their children, particularly those who have limited opportunities to interact in mainstream settings (Garrison, Roy, & Azar, 1999). These parents will experience the greatest difficulty linking to their children's schools or accessing other needed services for family members, and their children may be placed in the position of being responsible for negotiating important family matters on their behalf. This phenomenon, known as *cultural brokering*, can disrupt normative parent-child roles, place a substantial burden on youth, and negatively impact children's ability to invest in their own educational and developmental needs (Cooper et al., 1999).

Some evidence exists that maternal acculturation may be associated with better psychological outcomes for Latino youth (Dumka, Roosa, & Jackson, 1997); this research is based primarily on research with mothers. There are a number of possible explanations, including reduction in the mother-child cultural gap, mothers' access to resources that promote family resilience, and changes in mothers' cultural values that alter their expectations, goals, and parenting strategies. For example, more acculturated Mexican American mothers have reported less rejection, less hostile control, less inconsistent discipline, increased parent-child interaction, and more cohesion than less acculturated Mexican American mothers (Cabrera, Shannon, West, & Brooks-Gunn, 2006; Dumka et al., 1997; Hill, Bush, & Roosa, 2003; Knight, Virdin, & Roosa, 1994). It is possible that contact with another culture provides alternative discipline strategies, such as time-out or removal of privileges, that can help decrease the use of hostile parenting and other more controlling strategies (Parke et al., 2004). Parental monitoring, which refers to parental awareness of children's behaviors and whereabouts, has shown to be a protective factor for boys whose mothers are highly acculturated by buffering the effects of risks on delinquent behavior and internalizing problems; but this was not the case

for the boys of mothers who were less acculturated (Loukas, Suizzo, & Prelow, 2007). Different factors could be playing a role in this relationship. For example, acculturated mothers who have better English skills have the opportunity to interact with their children's friends, which may enable them to monitor more effectively.

On the other hand, parents' increased acculturation also is associated with increased family conflict, including general levels of conflict among family members, parent-child conflict, and interparental conflict (Flores, Tschann, Marín, & Pantoja, 2004; Gonzales et al., 2006; Parke et al., 2004). Perhaps as Latino parents experience shifts in cultural values regarding family hierarchies and the importance of child respect and obedience, they adopt less controlling parenting strategies and greater tolerance for expressions of conflict. Shifts in parents' values and role expectations may also explain why marital conflict is positively associated with mothers' and fathers' acculturation level as well (Flores et al., 2004; Parke et al., 2004). Problems may also arise when men and women acculturate at different rates. Although this type of acculturation discrepancy has not been examined directly, Montoya (1996) found that Latinas are more likely than Latinos to favor modern roles for women and suggests that this places more acculturated Latinas at greater risk of violence if their partners maintain more traditional sex roles.

These findings illustrate that cultural adaptation can produce a variety of challenges and changes for individuals and for the family as a whole; some changes may foster family resilience, whereas others may contribute to disruptions in family processes and relationships. However, a growing body of research suggests that when traditional familism values and behaviors are maintained during the process of cultural adaptation, they function to promote healthy family interactions and decrease susceptibility to acculturative strains and other negative influences (Apospori, Vega, Zimmerman, Warheit, & Gil, 1995; Germán et al., 2009; Gil et al., 1994; Szapocznik et al., 1990; Vega et al., 1993). For example, support from strong family ties and kinship networks promotes positive adaptation during such important life transitions as pregnancy and the transition to parenthood, potentially offering some explanation for the better birth outcomes consistently reported for low-income Latino women relative to other low-income groups (Heilemann, Frutos, Lee, & Kury, 2004; Page, 2004). In a diverse sample of Mexican American families, White et al. (in press) found that familism values buffered the negative impact of neighborhood and acculturative stress on parents' depression and negative parenting behaviors. Germán et al. (2009) found that mothers,' fathers,' and adolescents' familism values each attenuated the relation between Mexican American adolescents' deviant peer association and their own deviant behavior at school. Altogether, these findings highlight the importance of a family systems perspective on cultural adaptation, as emphasized in the classic theoretical work of Szapocznik and colleagues (e.g., Szapocznik & Kurtines, 1993). The family unit, as well as each individual within the family, must adapt to the broader cultural context; in so doing, each reciprocally influences the family system and its members. For example, it is likely that acculturation pathways of older siblings influence those taken by younger siblings. However, other than studies that test the parent-child acculturation gap hypothesis, few attempts have been made to capture these dynamic cultural family systems.

Protective Effects of Biculturalism: Greater Than the Sum of Its Parts

Accumulating research also supports the view that the most resilient youth may be those who develop strong ties and the ability to interact effectively within both ethnic and mainstream contexts (e.g., LaFromboise, Coleman, & Gerton, 1993; Rogler et al., 1991; Szapocznik & Kurtines, 1980). This conclusion has now been supported by numerous studies using divergent methodologies, different indicators of biculturality, and different outcomes. In their discussion of findings, Schwartz et al. (2007) suggest that biculturalism appears to be "greater than the sum of its parts," a condition separate from endorsement of either of the component cultures.

A variety of explanations have been offered, all of which have to do with the flexibility that a bicultural framework offers for individuals for coping with multiple, competing demand and social contexts. Bicultural individuals benefit from knowledge and resources they accrue through participation in the host culture, while they also retain the positive, protective factors of their traditional cultures. Thus, bicultural youth can navigate successfully within multiple cultural contexts and thus experience less stress than could result from conflicting cultures. Bicultural individuals also appear to benefit from the ability to shift sociocognitive perceptual schemas in order to fit situational demands. This ability, called *cultural frame-switching*, is more highly developed in bicultural individuals than in their low- or high-acculturated peers, allowing them to handle a wider range of culture-laden situations (Harritatos & Benet-Martinez, 2002).

Consistent with this theorizing, biculturalism has been related to a number of indicators of positive adaptation and resilience among Latino youth, including greater self-esteem (Birman, Trickett, & Vinokurov, 2002), the ability to socialize in diverse settings (Bautista de Domanico, Crawford, & Wolfe, 1994), peer competence (Coatsworth et al., 2005; Lopez, Ehly, & Garcia-Vazquez, 2002), academic competence and motivation, and psychological well-being (Gomez & Fassinger, 1994; Lopez et al., 2002; Parke & Buriel, 1998; Phinney, 1990; Szapocznik et al., 1980). Evidence also suggests that biculturalism reduces the risk of substance abuse and problem behaviors and increases school engagement and achievement (Feliciano, 2001; Goldberg & Botvin, 1993; Gonzales et al., 2008; Schinke et al., 1988). The findings that integrated adolescents reported the most favorable levels of parental involvement, positive parenting, and support is consistent with the hypothesis that youth who are most comfortable with both their heritage and receiving cultural contexts are most likely to relate well to their families (Coatsworth et al., 2005; Sullivan et al., 2007). Finally, the limited research that has examined cultural adaptation at the family level has shown that, compared to low- and high-acculturated families, bicultural families display lower levels of conflict and demonstrate more commitment and support among family members (Miranda, Estrada, & Firpo-Jimenez, 2000).

PROGRESS AND GAPS IN RESEARCH ON LATINO YOUTH CULTURAL ADAPTATION

The past decade brought tremendous progress in efforts to characterize and measure the processes of cultural adaptation and to examine their impact on the psychosocial adjustment of

Latino youth. Studies published since our last review, completed just 8 years ago, have broadened the dimensions of cultural adaptation assessed in order to test biaxial and multidimensional models; they have advanced new strategies for testing patterns or typologies of cultural adaptation; and they have examined mediating mechanisms that better reflect the complexities that were previously found only in the theoretical literature. Although the bulk of this research continues to focus primarily on adolescents, as opposed to younger children, studies have begun to focus on indicators of adaptive functioning, in contrast with prior research that focused almost exclusively on the risky outcomes of adolescence (e.g., substance use, delinquency, teenage pregnancy).

Although there is still much progress to be made, findings from these studies better illustrate the complex nature of acculturation and enculturation and how they can lead to increased opportunities for the development of competence or to increased risk and distress. In particular, the research we reviewed clearly shows the importance of a biaxial framework and adds to growing evidence that an integrated or bicultural strategy is optimal for promoting positive psychological outcomes.

Despite this progress, gaps and unanswered questions still remain. Given such a heavy focus on adolescence, very little is known about processes of cultural adaptation at earlier stages of development or how processes of cultural adaptation unfold across stages of development. Indeed, with the exception of research on ethnic identity development, the current research on cultural adaptation lacks a developmental focus in several respects. A large majority of studies are cross sectional and, as such, include only measures of acculturation at a single point in time. Although there has been an increase in prospective studies that provide important information about how one's cultural orientation at an earlier point in time predicts subsequent changes in later psychological outcomes, we found very few studies that assess *changes* over time in dimensions of cultural adaptation (Knight et al., in press). It is possible and quite likely that individuals experience changes in cultural orientation—for example, switching from a monocultural to a bicultural strategy or vice versa. Recent research also has shown that changes happen at different rates across dimensions

and at different developmental stages in life. Whereas language acquisition typically occurs early in life or soon after migration for children who attend U.S. schools, shifts in ethnic identity and cultural values are likely to occur during adolescence (Knight et al., 2009). These developmental issues are rarely considered in the literature. Along these same lines, the extant research largely has not distinguished between cultural adaptation that is volitional or motivated by personal preference and that which is largely imposed by external forces.

Another notable gap is a limited understanding of the broader context in which cultural adaptation unfolds and how context shapes the cultural challenges, adaptive choices, and their effects for diverse Latino population in the United States. Context has gained more prominence in recent years. For example, studies are being conducted increasingly with youth in the newer receiving communities (e.g., North Carolina, Kentucky, Tennessee, Minnesota), where the Latino population has doubled or tripled since 1990 (Marotta & Garcia, 2003). This development should help to correct biases that may have resulted from decades of research focused only on the urban poor, a critically important subgroup of the Latino population but by no means representative of all. Progress also is evident in studies that recognize and test differences between the Latino subgroups rather than collapsing across groups (a practice characteristic of earlier research with Latinos) and is further evident in the increased attention to the potential confound between cultural adaptation and socioeconomic status (SES). On the other hand, the extant research on Latino youth is still primarily restricted in its focus on lower-income communities, which limits our ability to understand how SES, cultural adaptation, and community context operate together to shape cultural trajectories and adaptive outcomes.

As results continue to emerge from diverse samples and geographic regions, the role of context may become more apparent, particularly in studies that are sensitive to the contextual challenges youth experience locally and that use this information to select samples, measures, and hypotheses to be tested. However, in addition, studies that sample Latinos across diverse geographic and socioeconomic contexts and that directly assess contextual variability are also needed to model the complex interplay of factors involved in predicting psychological functioning for Latino youth (e.g., Roosa et al., 2008). A greater understanding of context is especially important to guide intervention efforts so they are directed at those subgroups and communities that are most likely to benefit.

REFERENCES

Amaro, H., Whitaker, R., Coffman, G., & Heeren, T. (1990). Acculturation and marijuana and cocaine use: Findings from HHANES 1982–84. *American Journal of Public Health, 80,* 54–60.

Apospori, E., Vega, W. A., Zimmerman, R. S., Warheit, G. J., & Gil, A. G. (1995). A longitudinal study of conditional effects of deviant behavior on drug use among three racial/ethnic groups of adolescents. In H. B. Kaplan (Ed.), *Drugs, crime, and other deviant adaptations: Longitudinal studies.* New York: Plenum Press.

Armenta, B. E., Knight, G. P., Carlo, G., & Jacobson, R. P. (2009). *The relation between ethnic group attachment and prosocial tendencies: The mediating role of cultural values.* Manuscript under review.

Bacallao, M. L., & Smokowski, P. R. (2005). "Entre dos Mundos" (between two worlds): Bicultural skills training with Latino immigrant families. *Journal of Primary Prevention, 26*(6), 485–509.

Baca Zinn, M., & Wells, B. (2000). Diversity within Latino families: New lessons for family social science. In D. H. Demo, K. R. Allen, & M. A. Fine (Eds.), *Handbook of family diversity* (pp. 252–273). New York: Oxford University Press.

Bautista de Domanico, Y., Crawford, I., & Wolfe, A. S. (1994). Ethnic identity and self-concept in Mexican-American adolescents: Is bicultural identity related to stress or better adjustment? *Child and Youth Care Forum, 23*(3), 197–206.

Berry, J. W. (1980). Acculturation as varieties of adaptation. In A. Padilla (Ed.), *Acculturation: Theory, models and some new findings* (pp. 9–26). Boulder, CO: Westview Press.

Berry, J. W. (2003). Origins of cross-cultural similarities and differences in human behavior: An ecocultural perspective. In A. Toomela (Ed.), *Cultural guidance in the development of the human mind: Advances in child development within culturally structured environments.* Westport, CT: Ablex.

Berry, J. W., Trimble, J. E., & Olmedo, E. L. (1986). Assessment of acculturation. In W. J. Lonner & J. W. Berry (Eds.), *Field methods in cross-cultural research* (pp. 291–324). Beverly Hills, CA: Sage.

Bird, H. R., Davies, M., & Duarte, C. S. (2006). A study of disruptive behavior disorders in Puerto Rican youth: II. Baseline prevalence, comorbidity, and correlates in two sites. *Journal of the American Academy of Child and Adolescent Psychiatry, 36,* 1260–1268.

Birman, D., Trickett, E. J., & Vinokurov, A. (2002). Acculturation and adaptation of Soviet Jewish refugee adolescents: Predictors of adjustment across life domains. *American Journal of Community Psychology, 30*(5), 585–607.

Blascovich, J., Spencer, S. J., Quinn, D., & Steele, C. (2001). African Americans and high blood pressure: The role of stereotype threat. *Psychological Sciences, 12*(3), 225–229.

Brook, J. S., Whiteman, M., Balka, E. B., Win, P. T., & Gursen, M. D. (1998). Drug use among Puerto Ricans: Ethnic identity as a protective factor. *Hispanic Journal of Behavioral Sciences, 20*(2), 241–254.

Bui, H. N., & Thongniramol, O. (2005). Immigration and self-reported delinquency: The interplay of immigration generations, gender, race and ethnicity. *Journal of Crime and Justice, 28*(2), 71–99.

Burnam, M. A., Hough, R. L., Karno, M., Escobar, J. T., & Telles, C. A. (1987). Acculturation and lifetime prevalence of psychiatric disorders among Mexican Americans in Los Angeles. *Journal of Health and Social Behavior, 28*(1), 89–102.

Cabassa, L. J. (2003). Measuring acculturation: Where we are and where we need to go. *Hispanic Journal of Behavioral Sciences, 25*(2), 127–146.

Cabrera, N. J., Shannon, J. D., West, J., & Brooks-Gunn, J. (2006). Parental interactions with Latino infants: Variation by country of origin and English proficiency. *Child Development, 77*(5), 1190–1207.

Carvajal, S. C., Hanson, C. E., Romero, A. J., & Coyle, K. K. (2002). Behavioral risk factors and protective factors in adolescents: A comparison of Latinos and non-Latino Whites. *Ethnicity and Health, 7*(3), 181–193.

Castro, R., Coe, K., Gutierres, S., & Saenz, D. (1996). Designing health promotion programs for Latinos. In P.M. Kato & T. Mann (Eds.), *Handbook of diversity issues in health psychology* (pp. 319–356). New York: Plenum Press.

Chamorro, R., & Flores-Ortiz, Y. (1998). Acculturation and disordered eating patterns among Mexican American women. *International Journal of Eating Disorders, 28*(1), 125–129.

Chavez, D. V., Moran, V. R., Reid, S. L., & Lopez, M. (1997). Acculturative stress in children: A modification of the SAFE scale. *Hispanic Journal of Behavioral Sciences, 19*(1), 34–44.

Coatsworth, J. D., Maldonado-Molina, M., Pantin, H., & Szapocznik, J. (2005). A person-centered and ecological investigation of acculturation strategies in Hispanic immigrant youth. *Journal of Community Psychology, 33*(2), 157–174.

Cooper, C. R., Denner, J., & Lopez, E. M. (1999). Cultural brokers: Helping Latino children on pathways toward success. *The Future of Children, 9*(2), 51–57.

Cuadrado, M., & Lieberman, L. (1998). Traditionalism in the prevention of substance misuse among Puerto Ricans. *Substance Use and Misuse, 33*(14), 2737–2755.

Cuellar, I., Arnold, B., & Maldonado, R. (1995). Acculturation rating scale for Mexican Americans-II: A revision of the original ARSMA scale. *Hispanic Journal of Behavioral Science, 17,* 275–304.

De la Rosa, M. (2002). Acculturation and Latino adolescents' substance use: A research agenda for the future. *Substance Use and Misuse, 37*(4), 429–456.

Dinh, K. T., Roosa, M. K., Tein, J. Y., & Lopez, V. A. (2002). The relationship between acculturation and problem behavior proneness in a Hispanic youth sample: A longitudinal mediation model. *Journal of Abnormal Child Psychology, 30*(3), 295–309.

Dumka, L. E., Roosa, M. W., & Jackson, K. M. (1997). Risk, conflict, mothers' parenting, and children's adjustment in low-income, Mexican immigrant, and Mexican American families. *Journal of Marriage and the Family, 59,* 309–323.

Eamon, M. K., & Cray, M. (2005). Predicting antisocial behavior among Latino young adolescents: An ecological systems analysis. *American Journal of Orthopsychiatry, 75*(1), 117–127.

Edwards, L. M., & Romero, A. J. (2008). Coping with discrimination among Mexican descent adolescents. *Hispanic Journal of Behavioral Sciences, 30*(1), 24–39.

Elder, J. P., Broyles, S. L., Brennan, J. J., Zuniga de Nuncio, M. L., & Nader, P. R. (2005). Acculturation, parent-child acculturation differential, and chronic disease risk factors in a Mexican-American population. *Journal of Immigrant Health, 7*(1), 1–9.

Feliciano, C. (2001). The benefits of biculturalism: Exposure to immigrant culture and dropping out of school among Asian and Latino youths. *Social Science Quarterly, 82*(4), 865–879.

Félix-Ortiz, M., & Newcomb, M. D. (1995). Cultural identity and drug use among Latino adolescents. In G. Botvin, S. Schinke, & M. Orlandi (Eds.), *Drug abuse prevention with multiethnic youth* (pp. 147–165). Newbury Park, CA: Sage.

Flores, E., Tschann, J. M., Marín, B. V., & Pantoja, P. (2004). Marital conflict and acculturation among Mexican American husbands and wives. *Cultural Diversity and Ethnic Minority Psychology, 10*(1), 39–52.

Fridrich, A. H., & Flannery, W. P. (1995). The effects of ethnicity and acculturation on early adolescent delinquency. *Journal of Child and Family Studies, 4*(1), 69–87.

Fuligni, A. (1998). The adjustment of children from immigrant families. *Current Directions in Psychological Science, 7,* 99–103.

Fuligni, A. J., & Pederson, S. (2002). Family obligation and the transition to young adulthood. *Developmental Psychology, 38*(5), 856–868.

Fuligni, A. J., Witkow, M., & Garcia, C. (2005). Ethnic identity and the academic adjustment of adolescents from Mexican, Chinese, and European backgrounds. *Developmental Psychology, 41*(5), 790–811.

Garcia Coll, C., Lamberty, G., Jenkins, R., McAdoo, H. P., Crnic, K., Wasik, B., et al., (1996). An integrative model for the study of developmental competencies in minority children. *Child Development, 67,* 1891–1914.

Garcia Coll, C., & Magnuson, K. (2000). Cultural differences as sources of developmental vulnerabilities and resources: A view from developmental research. In S. J. Meisels & J. P. Shonkoff (Eds.), *Handbook of early childhood intervention* (pp. 94–111). Cambridge, UK: Cambridge University Press.

Garrison, E. G., Roy, I. S., & Azar, V. (1999). Responding to the mental health needs of Latino children and families through school-based services. *Clinical Psychological Review, 19*(2), 199–219.

Germán, M., Gonzales, N. A., & Dumka, L. E. (2009). Familism values as a protective factor for Mexican-origin adolescents exposed to deviant peers. *Journal of Early Adolescence, 29,* 16–42.

Gfroerer, J. C., & Tan, L. L. (2003). Substance use among foreign-born youths in the United States: Does length of residence matter? *American Journal of Public Health, 93*(11), 1892–1895.

Gibbs, J. T. (1998). African American adolescents. In J. T. Gibbs & H. L. Nahme (Eds.), *Children of color: Psychological interventions with culturally diverse youth* (pp. 171–214). San Francisco: Jossey-Bass.

Gil, A. G., Vega, W. A., & Dimas, J. M. (1994). Acculturative stress and personal adjustment among Hispanic adolescent boys. *Journal of Community Psychology, 22,* 43–54.

Gil, A. G., Wagner, E. F., & Vega, W. A. (2000). Acculturation, familism, and alcohol use among Latino adolescent males: Longitudinal relations. *Journal of Community Psychology, 28*(4), 443–458.

Glover, S. H., Pumariega, A. J., Holzer, C. E., Wise, B. K., & Rodriguez, M. (1999). Anxiety symptomatology in Mexican American adolescents. *Journal of Child and Family Studies,* 8(1), 44–57.

Goldberg, C. J., & Botvin, G. J. (1993). Assertiveness in Hispanic adolescents: Relationship to alcohol use and abuse. *Psychological Reports 73*(1), 227–238.

Goldenberg, C., Gallimore, R., Reese, L., & Garnier, H. (2001). Cause or effect? A longitudinal study of immigrant Latino parents' aspirations and expectations and their children's school performance. *American Educational Research Journal, 38*(3), 547–582.

Gomez, M. J., & Fassinger, R. E. (1994). An initial model of Latina achievement: Acculturation, biculturalism, and achieving styles. *Journal of Counseling Psychology, 41*(2), 205–215.

Gonzales, N. A., Deardorff, J., Formoso, D., Barr, A., & Barrera, M. (2006). Family mediators of the relation between acculturation and adolescent mental health. *Family Relations, 55,* 318–330.

Gonzales, N. A., Germán, M., Kim, S. Y., George, P., Fabrett, F. C., Millsap, R., et al. (2008). Mexican American adolescents' cultural orientation, externalizing behavior and academic engagement: The role of traditional cultural values. *American Journal of Community Psychology, 41,* 151–164.

Gonzales, N. A., & Kim, L. (1997). Stress and coping in an ethnic minority context: Children's cultural ecologies. In S. A. Wolchik & I. N. Sandler (Eds.), *Children's coping with common stressors: Linking theory, research and interventions* (pp. 481–551). New York: Plenum Press.

Gonzales, N. A., Knight, G. P., Morgan-Lopez, A., Saenz, D., & Sorolli, A. (2002). Acculturation and the mental health of Latino youths: An integration and critique of the literature. In J. Contreras, A. Neal-Barnett, & K. Kerns (Eds.), *Latino children and families in the United States: Current research and future directions* (pp. 45–74). Westport, CT: Praeger.

Greene, M. L., Way, N., & Pahl, K. (2006). Trajectories of perceived adult and peer discrimination among Black, Latino and Asian American adolescents: Patterns and psychological correlates. *Developmental Psychology, 42*(2), 218–238.

Guilamo-Ramos, V., Jaccard, J., Pena, J., & Goldberg, V. (2005). Acculturation-related variables, sexual initiation, and subsequent sexual behavior among Puerto Rican, Mexican, and Cuban youth. *Health Psychology, 24*(1), 88–95.

Harritatos, J., & Benet-Martinez, V. (2002). Bicultural identities: The interface of cultural, personality, and socio-cognitive processes. *Journal of Research in Personality, 36,* 598–606.

Heilemann, M. S., Frutos, L., Lee, K. A., & Kury, F. S. (2004). Protective strength factors, resources, and risks in relation to depressive symptoms among childbearing women of Mexican descent. *Health Care for Women International, 25,* 88–106.

Hill, N. E., Bush, K. R., & Roosa, M. W. (2003). Parenting and family socialization strategies and children's mental health: Low-income Mexican-American and Euro-American mothers and children. *Child Development, 74*(1), 189–204.

Holley, L., Kulis, S., Marsiglia, F. F., & Keith, V. (2006). Ethnicity versus ethnic identity: What predicts substance use norms and behaviors? *Journal of Social Work Practice in the Addictions, 6*(3), 53–79.

Hovey, J. D., & King, C. A. (1996). Acculturative stress, depression, and suicidal ideation among immigrant and second-generation Latino adolescents. *Journal of the American Academy of Child and Adolescent Psychiatry, 35*(9), 1183–1192.

Hurtado, M. T., & Gauvain, M. (1997). Acculturation and planning for college among youth of Mexican descent. *Hispanic Journal of Behavioral Sciences, 19,* 506–516.

Joiner, G. W., & Kashubeck, S. (1996). Acculturation, body image, self-esteem, and eating-disorder symptomatology in adolescent Mexican American women. *Psychology of Women Quarterly, 20,* 419–435.

Kao, G., & Tienda, M. (1995). Optimism and achievement: The educational performance of immigrant youth. *Social Sciences Quarterly, 76*(1), 1–19.

Kaplan, C. P., Erickson, P. I., Stewart, S. L., & Crane, L. A. (2001). Young Latinas and abortion: The role of cultural factors, reproductive behavior, and alternative roles to motherhood. *Health Care for Women International, 22,* 667–689.

Katragadda, C. P., & Tidwell, R. (1998). Rural Hispanic adolescents at risk for depressive symptoms. *Journal of Applied Social Psychology, 28*(20), 1916–1930.

Knight, G. P., Bernal, M. E., Garza, C. A., Cota, M. K., & Ocampo, K. A. (1993). Family socialization and the ethnic identity of Mexican-American children. *Journal of Cross-Cultural Psychology, 24*(1), 99–114.

Knight, G. P., Cota, M. K., & Bernal., M. E. (1993). The socialization of cooperative, competitive, and individualistic preferences among Mexican American children: The mediating role of ethnic identity. *Hispanic Journal of Behavioral Sciences, 15*(3), 291–309.

Knight, G. P., Jacobson, R. P., Gonzales, N. A., Roosa, M. W., & Saenz, D. S. (2009). An evaluation of the psychological research on acculturation and enculturation processes among recently immigrating populations. In R. L. Dalla, J. DeFrain, J. Johnson, & D. Abbot (Eds.), *Strengths and challenges of new immigrant families: Implications for research, policy, education, and service* (pp. 9–51). Lanham, MD: Lexington.

Knight, G. P., Vargas-Chanes, D., Losoya, S. H., Cota-Robles, S., Chassin, L., & Lee, J. (in press). Acculturation and enculturation trajectories among Mexican American adolescent offenders. *Journal of Research on Adolescence.*

Knight, G. P., Virdin, L. M., & Roosa, M. (1994). Socialization and family correlates of mental health outcomes among Hispanic and Anglo-American children: Considerations of cross-ethnic scalar equivalence. *Child Development, 65*, 221–224.

Kulis, S., Marsiglia, F. F., & Hurdle, D. (2003). Gender identity, ethnicity, acculturation, and drug use: Exploring differences among adolescents in the southwest. *Journal of Community Psychology, 31*(2), 167–188.

Kurtines, W. M., & Szapocznik, J. (1996). Family interaction patterns: Structural family therapy within contexts of cultural diversity. In E. D. Hibbs & P. S. Jensen (Eds.), *Psychosocial treatments for child and adolescent disorders: Empirically based strategies for clinical practice* (pp. 671–697). Washington, DC: American Psychological Association.

LaFromboise, T., Coleman, H. L. K., & Gerton, J. (1993). Psychological impact on biculturalism: Evidence and theory. *Psychological Bulletin, 114*, 395–412.

Lara, M., Gamboa, C., Kahramanian, M. I., Morales, L. S., & Hayes Bautista, D. E. (2005). Acculturation and Latino health in the United States: A review of the literature and its sociopolitical context. *Annual Review of Public Health, 26*, 367–397.

Lau, A. S., McCabe, K. M., Yeh, M., Garland, A. F., Wood, P. A., & Hough, R. L. (in press). The acculturation gap-distress hypothesis among high-risk Mexican American families. *Journal of Family Psychology, 19*(3), 367–375.

Lester, R., & Petrie, T. A. (1995). Personality and physical correlates of bulimic symptomatology among Mexican American female college students. *Journal of Counseling Psychology, 42*(2), 199–203.

Lopez, E. J., Ehly, S., & Garcia-Vazquez, E. (2002). Acculturation, social support and academic achievement of Mexican and Mexican American high school students: An exploratory study. *Psychology in the Schools, 39*(3), 245–257.

Losoya, S. H., Knight, G. P., Chassin, L., Little, M., Vargas-Chanes, D., Mauricio, A., et al. (2008).

Trajectories of acculturation and enculturation in relation to heavy episodic drinking and marijuana use in a sample of Mexican American serious juvenile offenders. *Journal of Drug Issues, 38* (1), 171–198.

Loukas, A., Suizzo, M. A., & Prelow, H. M. (2007). Examining resource and protective factors in the adjustment of Latino youth in low income families: What role does maternal acculturation play? *Journal of Youth Adolescence, 36*, 489–501.

Marín, G. (1992). Issues in the measurement of acculturation among Hispanics. In Geisinger, K. F. (Ed.), *Psychological testing of Hispanics.* Washington, DC: American Psychological Association.

Markides, K. S., Krause, N., & Mendes de Leon, C. F. (1988). Acculturation and alcohol consumption among Mexican Americans: A three-generation study. *American Journal of Public Health, 78*, 1178–1181.

Marotta, S. A., & Garcia, J. G. (2003). Latinos in the United States in 2000. *Hispanic Journal of Behavioral Sciences, 25*(1), 13–34.

Marsiglia, F. F., Kulis, S., Hecht, M. L., & Sills, S. (2004). Ethnicity and ethnic identity as predictors of drug norms and drug use among preadolescents in the U.S. Southwest. *Substance Use and Misuse, 39* (7), 1061–1094.

Martinez, C. R. (2006). Effects of differential family acculturation on Latino adolescent substance use. *Family Relations, 55*, 306–317.

Martinez, R. O., & Dukes, R. L. (1997). The effects of ethnic identity, ethnicity, and gender on adolescent well-being. *Journal of Youth and Adolescence, 26*, 503–516.

McQueen, A., Getz, J. G., & Bray, J. H. (2003). Acculturation, substance use, and deviant behavior: Examining separation and family conflict as mediators. *Child Development, 74*(6), 1737–1750.

McWhirter, E. H., Hackett, G., & Bandalos, D. L. (1998). A causal model of the educational plans and career expectations of Mexican American high school girls. *Journal of Counseling Psychology, 45*, 166–181.

Miranda, A., Estrada, D., & Firpo-Jimenez (2000). Differences in family cohesion, adaptability, and environment among Latino families in dissimilar stages of acculturation. *The Family Journal: Counseling and Therapy for Couples and Families, 8*(4), 341–350.

Montoya, L. J. (1996). Latino gender differences in public opinion: Results from the Latino National Political Survey. *Hispanic Journal of Behavioral Sciences, 18*, 255–276.

Mossakowski, K. N. (2003). Coping with perceived discrimination: Does ethnic identity protect mental health? *Journal of Health and Social Behavior, 44*(3), 318–331.

Page, R. L. (2004). Positive pregnancy outcomes in Mexican immigrants: What can we learn? *Journal of Obstetric, Gynecologic, and Neonatal Nursing, 33,* 783–790.

Parke, R. D., & Buriel, R. (1998). Socialization in the family: Ecological and ethnic perspectives. In W. Damon (Ed.), *Handbook of child psychology* (Vol. 3, pp. 463–552). New York: John Wiley.

Parke, R. D., Coltrane, S., Duffy, S., Buriel, R., Dennis, J., Powers, J., et al. (2004). Economic stress, parenting, and child adjustment in Mexican American and European American families. *Child Development, 75*(6), 1632–1656.

Pantin, H., Schwartz, S. J., Sullivan, S., Coatsworth, J. D., & Szapocznik, J. (2003). Preventing substance abuse in Hispanic immigrant adolescents: An ecodevelopmental, parent-centered approach. *Hispanic Journal of Behavioral Sciences, 25,* 469–500.

Pew Hispanic Center. (2006). *Pew Hispanic Center fact sheet: Statistical portrait of Hispanics in the United States 2006: Summary and chart pack.* Los Angeles: Annenberg School for Communication, University of Southern California. Retrieved February 19, 2008, from http://pewhispanic.org/files/other/middecade/Table-3.pdf

Phinney, J. S. (1990). Ethnic identity in adolescents and adults: Review of research. *Psychological Bulletin, 108*(3), 499–514.

Phinney, J. S. (1992). The Multigroup Ethnic Identity Measure: A new scale for use with diverse groups. *Journal of Adolescent Research, 7,* 156–176.

Phinney, J. S., Cantu, C. L., & Kurtz, D. A. (1997). Ethnic and American identity as predictors of self-esteem among African American, Latino, and White adolescents. *Journal of Youth and Adolescence, 26*(2), 165–185.

Pina, A. A., & Silverman, W. K. (2004). Clinical phenomenology, somatic symptoms, and distress in Hispanic/Latino and European American youth with anxiety disorders. *Journal of Clinical Child and Adolescent Psychology, 33*(2), 227–236.

Portes, P. R., & Zady, M. F. (2002). Self-esteem in the adaptation of Spanish-speaking adolescents: The role of immigration, family conflict, and depression. *Hispanic Journal of Behavioral Sciences, 24*(3), 296–318.

Ramos, L., & Sanchez, A. R. (1995). Mexican-American high school students: Educational aspirations. *Journal of Multicultural Counseling and Development, 23,* 212–221.

Reynoso, T. C., Felice, M. E., & Shragg, G. P. (2002). Does American acculturation affect outcome of Mexican-American teenage pregnancy? *Journal of Adolescent Health, 14*(4), 257–261.

Rogler, L. H., Cortes, D. E., & Malgady, R. G. (1991). Acculturation and mental health status among Hispanics: Convergence and new directions for research. *American Psychologist, 46*(6), 585–597.

Romero, A. J., Carvajal, S. C., Valle, F., & Orduña, M. (2007). Adolescent bicultural stress and its impact on mental well-being among Latinos, Asian Americans and European Americans. *Journal of Community Psychology, 35*(4), 519–534.

Romero, A. J., & Roberts, R. E. (2003). Stress within a bicultural context for adolescents of Mexican descent. *Cultural Diversity and Ethnic Minority Psychology, 9*(2), 171–184.

Roosa, M. W., Dumka, L., & Tein, J. (1996). Family characteristics as mediators of the parent problem drinking child mental health relationship. *American Journal of Community Psychology, 24,* 607–624.

Roosa, M. W., Liu, F. F., Torres, M., Gonzales, N. A., Knight, G. P., & Saenz, D. (2008). Sampling and recruitment in studies of cultural influences on adjustment: A case study with Mexican Americans. *Journal of Family Psychology, 22,* 293–302.

Rumbaut, R. G. (1995). The new Californians: Comparative research findings on the educational progress of immigrant children. In R. G. Rumbaut & W. A. Cornelius (Eds.), *California's immigrant children: Theory, research and implications for educational policy* (pp. 17–69). San Diego, CA: Center for U.S.-Mexican Studies.

Sabogal, F., Marín, G., Otero-Sabogal, R., Marín, B. V., & Pérez-Stable, E. J. (1987). Hispanic familism and acculturation: What changes and what doesn't? *Hispanic Journal of Behavioral Sciences, 9*(4), 397–412.

Sabogal, F., Pérez-Stable, E. J., Otero-Sabogal, R., & Hiatt R. A. (1995). Gender, ethnic, and acculturation differences in sexual behaviors: Hispanic and non-Hispanic White adults. *Hispanic Journal of Behavioral Sciences, 17*(2), 139–159.

Samaniego, R. Y., & Gonzales, N. A. (1999). Multiple mediators of the effects of acculturation status on delinquency for Mexican American adolescents. *American Journal of Community Psychology, 27*(2), 189–209.

Scheier, L. M., Botvin, G. J., Diaz, T., & Ifill-Williams, M. (1997). Ethnic identity as a moderator of psychosocial risk and adolescent alcohol and marijuana use: Concurrent and longitudinal analyses. *Journal of Child and Adolescent Substance Abuse, 6*(1), 21–47.

Schinke, S. P., Moncher, M. S., Palleja, J., Zayas, L. H., & Schilling, R. F. (1988). Hispanic youth, substance abuse, and stress: Implications for prevention research. *Substance Use and Misuse, 23*(8), 809–826.

Schwartz, S. J., Zamboanga, B. L., & Jarvis, L. H. (2007). Ethnic identity and acculturation in Hispanic early adolescents: Mediated relationships to academic grades, prosocial behaviors, and externalizing symptoms. *Cultural Diversity and Ethnic Minority Psychology, 13*(4), 364–373.

Smokowski, P. R., & Bacallao, M. L. (2006). Acculturation and aggression in Latino adolescents: A structural model focusing on cultural risk factors and assets. *Journal of Abnormal Child Psychology, 34*, 659–673.

Sommers, I., Fagan, J., & Baskin, D. (1993). Sociocultural influences on the explanation of delinquency for Puerto Rican youths. *Hispanic Journal of Behavioral Sciences, 15*(1), 36–62.

Sullivan, S., Schwartz, S. J., Prado, G., Huang, S., Pantin, H., & Szapocznik, J. (2007). A bidimensional model of acculturation for examining differences in family functioning and behavior problems in Hispanic immigrant adolescents. *Journal of Early Adolescence, 27*(4), 405–430.

Szalacha, L. A., Erkut, S., Garcia Coll, C., Fields, J. P., Alarcon, O., & Ceder, I. (2003). Perceived discrimination and resilience. In S. S. Luthar (Ed.), *Resilience and vulnerability: Adaptation in the context of childhood adversities* (pp. 414–435). New York: Cambridge University Press.

Szapocznik, J., & Kurtines, W. (1980). Acculturation, biculturalism and adjustment among Cuban Americans. In A. M. Padilla (Ed.), *Acculturation: Theory, models, and some new findings* (pp. 139–159). Boulder, CO: Westview Press.

Szapocznik, J., & Kurtines, W. M. (1993). Family psychology and cultural diversity. *American Psychologist, 48*, 400–407.

Szapocznik, J., Kurtines, W., & Fernandez, T. (1980). Biculturalism and adjustment among Hispanic youths. *International Journal of Intercultural Relations, 4*, 353–375.

Szapocznik, J., Kurtines, W., Santisteban, D. A., & Rio, A. T. (1990). Interplay of advances between theory, research, and duplication in treatment interventions aimed at behavior problem children and adolescents. *Journal of Consulting and Clinical Psychology, 58*, 696–703.

Tajfel, H. (1981). *Human groups and social categories: Studies in social psychology.* Cambridge, UK: Cambridge University Press.

Tajfel, H., & Turner, J. C. (1986). The social identity theory of intergroup behavior. In S. Worchel & W. G. Austin (Eds.), *Psychology of intergroup relations* (pp. 7–24). Chicago: Nelson-Hall.

Thayer, S. M., Updegraff, K. A., & Delgado, M. Y. (2008). Conflict resolution in Mexican American adolescents' friendships: Links with culture, gender and friendship quality. *Journal of Youth and Adolescence, 37*, 783–797.

Tsai, J. L., Chentsova-Dutton, Y., & Wong, Y. (2002). Why and how researchers should study ethnic identity, acculturation, and cultural orientation. In G. C. N. Hall & S. Okazaki (Eds.), *Asian American psychology: The science of lives in context* (pp. 41–65). Washington, DC: American Psychological Association.

Umaña-Taylor, A. J. (2004). Ethnic identity and self-esteem: Examining the role of social context. *Journal of Adolescence, 27*, 139–146.

Umaña-Taylor, A. J., & Updegraff, K. A. (2007). Latino adolescents' mental health: Exploring the interrelations among discrimination, ethnic identity, cultural orientation, self-esteem, and depressive symptoms. *Journal of Adolescence, 30*, 549–567.

Umaña-Taylor, A. J., Yazedjian, A., & Bámaca-Gomez, M. Y. (2004). Developing the Ethnic Identity Scale using Eriksonian and social identity perspectives. *Identity: An International Journal of Theory and Research, 4*, 9–38.

Unger, J., Ritt-Olson, A., Teran, L., Huang, T., Hoffman, B. R., & Palmer, P. (2002). Cultural values and substance use in a multiethnic sample of California adolescents. *Addiction Research and Theory, 10*(3), 257–279.

Upchurch, D. M., Aneshensel, C. S., Mudgal, J., & McNeely, C. S. (2001). Sociocultural contexts of time to first sex among Hispanic adolescents. *Journal of Marriage and the Family, 63*(4), 1158–1169.

U.S. Census Bureau. (2003). *Facts for features: Hispanic heritage month 2003: September 15–October 15.* Retrieved March 26, 2009, from http://www.census.gov/Press-Release/www/releases/archives/facts_for_features_special_editions/005338.html

Vega, W. A. (1995). The study of Latino families: A point of departure. In R. E. Zambrana (Ed.), *Understanding Latino families: Scholarship, policy and practice* (pp. 3–17). Thousand Oaks, CA: Sage.

Vega, W. A., & Gil, A. G. (1999). A model for explaining drug use behavior among Hispanic adolescents. *Drugs and Society, 14*, 57–74.

Vega, W. A., Gil, A., & Wagner, E. (1998). Cultural adjustment and Hispanic adolescents. In W. A. Vega & A. Gil (Eds.), *Drug use and ethnicity in early adolescence* (pp. 125–148). New York: Plenum Press.

Vega, W. A., Gil, A. G., Warheit, G. J., Zimmerman, R. S., & Apospori, E. (1993). Acculturation and delinquent behavior among Cuban American adolescents: Toward an empirical model. *American Journal of Community Psychology, 21*(1), 113–125.

Vega, W. A., Khoury, E. L., Zimmerman, R. S., Gil, A. G., & Warheit, G. J. (1995). Cultural conflicts and problem behaviors of Latino adolescents in home and school environments. *Journal of Community Psychology, 23,* 167–179.

White, R. M. B., Roosa, M. W., Weaver, S. R., & Nair, R. L. (in press). Cultural and contextual influences on parenting in Mexican American families. *Journal of Marriage and the Family.*

Zane, N., & Mak, W. (2003). Major approaches to the measurement of acculturation among ethnic minority populations: A content analysis and an alternative empirical strategy. In K. M. Chun, P. Balls Organista, & G. Marín (Eds.), *Acculturation: Advances in theory, measurement, and applied research.* Washington, DC: American Psychological Association.

9

ACCULTURATIVE STRESS AND ADAPTATION

ADRIANA J. UMAÑA-TAYLOR AND EDNA C. ALFARO

Acculturative stress is generally defined as psychological stress that results from the process of acculturation (Berry & Annis, 1974). As defined previously in this book, acculturation is the term originally used to describe the cultural changes that result at both the group level and the individual psychological level from sustained contact between two or more distinct cultures (Berry, Trimble, & Olmedo, 1986). Given that Latinos often enter the United States without mastery of the English language and with values and behaviors that differ from mainstream U.S. values (Salgado de Snyder, 1987), the process of acculturation may be especially challenging for Latino immigrants. Furthermore, unlike previous cohorts of immigrants to the United States (e.g., Germans, Irish), Latinos are more likely to maintain their cultural traditions and language, which increases the likelihood that acculturative stressors will be experienced by Latinos who have been in the United States for multiple generations. Put differently, acculturative stress is not an experience unique to *recent* Latino immigrants.

Acculturative stress results from the *process* of acculturation; however, there is little consensus among scholars with respect to whether acculturative stress is a process or a discrete status.

Some discuss acculturative stress as a process that diminishes as individuals become more acculturated to the mainstream (Miranda & Matheny, 2000), but it is also possible to view certain aspects of acculturative stress (such as experiences with discrimination) as stressors that may persist throughout generations. For example, it is possible that stress resulting from limited facility with the English language follows a progression that maps closely onto the process of acculturation; however, other acculturative stressors may be more discrete and dependent on contextual characteristics that change little over the life course (e.g., indigenous features).

In addition, because many demographic and contextual factors (e.g., national origin, socioeconomic status, neighborhood characteristics) introduce variability into whether individuals will experience acculturative stress, as well as the type of acculturative stress they will experience, it is difficult to conceptualize acculturative stress as a uniform process that follows the same trajectory for all. Rather, it may be more useful to examine the conditions under which individuals will experience acculturative stress and the conditions under which these stressors will be associated with poor adaptation. Within the literature on Latinos' acculturative stress, adaptation has focused primarily on psychological adjustment (e.g., depressive symptoms), although a few studies have examined other indices of well-being, such as physical health.

Although all immigrants are expected to experience some stress associated with the process of acculturation, and this stress is expected to contribute to their ability to adapt to their environment, high levels of acculturative stress are of particular concern because they are believed to result in poor psychological functioning (Williams & Berry, 1991), which can limit individuals' ability to adapt to their environments. The process of acculturation, however, does not lead to high levels of acculturative stress for all individuals; scholars argue that individuals' levels of acculturative stress are determined by their own individual characteristics in conjunction with the characteristics of the environment (Berry & Annis, 1974). For example, those who are less psychologically differentiated (i.e., less independent of events in their social context) will be more susceptible to changes in their environment due to the process of acculturation and hence may exhibit more acculturative stress (ibid.). Furthermore, in societies where ethnic diversity is not as valued and pressures to acculturate are high (i.e., assimilationist societies), acculturative stress will be higher (ibid.). Thus, those who are less psychologically differentiated and who live in societies where acculturation pressures are high will likely experience the highest levels of acculturative stress. Although the United States is a country of immigrants, pressures to assimilate are high. This is evident in the attempts of several businesses, states (e.g., Massachusetts), and the nation as a whole to pass English-only policies. These policies are reflective of an anti-immigrant sentiment that has recently pervaded the United States and has resulted in a backlash against Latino immigrants (Claffey, 2006). Thus, acculturative stress and its potentially negative effect on individuals' psychological functioning is a significant concern for Latinos in the United States. This chapter (a) discusses methodological challenges faced in the measurement of acculturative stress among Latinos; (b) reviews the existing literature on Latinos' acculturative stress, highlighting the strengths and limitations of existing work as well as identifying the findings that are consistent across the broad literature; and (c) concludes with recommendations for future research.

MEASUREMENT CHALLENGES IN ASSESSING ACCULTURATIVE STRESS

Although there is a broad literature on Latinos' acculturative stress and psychological functioning, and existing findings point to a consistent association between high acculturative stress and poor psychological outcomes (discussed in detail following), it is a complex literature to navigate due to its somewhat fragmented nature. For instance, in our review of the literature we found 46 published empirical studies that included quantitative measures of acculturative stress. Of these 46 studies, 4 focused on children, 10 focused on adolescents, 10 focused on college student samples, and 22 focused on adults (see Table 1). Thus, there is a great deal of diversity with regard to the developmental period studied, and to our knowledge no attempt has been made to integrate these findings and to consider the process of acculturative stress across the life span. Somewhat relatedly, some literature has focused on acculturative stressors that are specific to family relationships, particularly parent-child relationships and marital relationships, but there has been little to no integration of this literature, and thus our understanding of the interactive nature of acculturative stressors within the family context is limited. Finally, within this literature there is considerable variation regarding generational status in the Latino populations examined. Some studies have focused on acculturative stressors specific to first-generation immigrants (e.g., Hovey, 2000a), others have included Latinos of varied generations and nativity (e.g., Rodriguez, Myers, Mira, Flores, & Garcia-Hernandez, 2002), and some have limited their studies to U.S.-born Latinos (e.g., Chavez, Moran, Reid, & Lopez, 1997).

Interestingly, the operationalization of acculturative stress has been consistent across studies. Of the 46 empirical studies, 33 used a variation of one of two measures: the Hispanic Stress Inventory (HSI; Cervantes, Padilla, & Salgado de Snyder, 1991) and the Societal, Attitudinal, Familial, and Environmental Acculturative Stress Scale (SAFE; Padilla, Wagatsuma, & Lindholm, 1985; Mena, Padilla, & Maldonado, 1987). The HSI assesses the psychosocial stress experiences of Hispanics who were either recent immigrants (i.e., the 73-item immigrant version) or born in the United States (i.e., the

Table 9.1 Studies Focused on Latinos' Acculturative Stress by Population Studied and Measure Utilized

Authors	Developmental Period	Authors' Description of Participants' Ethnic Background	Measure Utilized
Chavez et al. (1997)[a]	Children (8–11 yrs.)	Mixed ethnic group with some Hispanics	36-item SAFE-C
Hawley et al. (2007)[a]	Children (8–11 yrs.)	Mixed ethnic group with some Hispanics	36-item SAFE-C
Suarez-Morales et al. (2007)	Children (5th grade)	Mixed ethnic group with some Hispanics	12-item SAFE-C
Weisskirch & Alva (2002)	Children (5th grade)	Latinos, majority Mexican	36-item SAFE-C
Balcazar et al. (1997)	Adolescents	Mexican	10-item SAFE
Gil & Vega (1996)[b]	Adolescents	Cuban and Nicaraguan	English language conflicts, discrimination, acculturation conflicts in family and in general
Gil et al. (1994)[b]	Adolescents	Cuban, Nicaraguan, and other Hispanic	English language conflicts, discrimination, acculturation conflicts in family and in general
Gil et al. (2000)[b]	Adolescents	Central American, South American, and Caribbean	English language conflicts, discrimination, acculturation conflicts in family and in general
Hokoda et al. (2007)	Adolescents	Mexican	Family acculturation conflict, language-related conflict, ethnic awareness of prejudice, conflicted ethnic loyalty
Hovey (1998)	Adolescents	Mexican	SAFE; items not specified
Hovey & King (1996)	Adolescents	Mexican, Central American, South American, and Spanish	24-item SAFE
Joe et al. (1991)	Adolescents	Mexican	Language difference between the parent and youth
Romero & Roberts (2003)	Adolescents	Mexican	Bicultural Stressors Measure
Schwartz et al. (2007)	Adolescents	Mexican, Central American, South American, and Caribbean	SAFE-C (process-oriented subscale)
Chávez & French (2007)	College students	Latino, majority Mexican	Minority Stresses Measure

(Continued)

Table 9.1 (Continued)

Authors	Developmental Period	Authors' Description of Participants' Ethnic Background	Measure Utilized
Constantine et al. (2004)	College students	Mexican, Central American, South American, and Caribbean	ASSIS
Crockett et al. (2007)	College students	Mexican	24-item SAFE
Fuertes & Westbrook (1996)	College students	Mexican, Caribbean, Central American, South American, and Spanish	24-item SAFE
Mangold et al. (2007)	College students	Mexican	58-item U.S.-born HSI
Mena et al. (1987)	College students	Mixed ethnic group with some Hispanics	24-item SAFE
Perez et al. (2002)	College students	Mixed ethnic group with some Hispanics	24-item SAFE
Saldaña (1994)	College students	Mixed ethnic group with some Hispanics	Minority Status Stress
Sanchez & Fernandez (1993)	College students	Cuban, Puerto Rican, Latin, North and Central American, and other	24-item SAFE
Vazquez & Garcia-Vazquez (1995)	College students	Mexican	60-item SAFE
Alderete et al. (1999)	Adults	Mexican	13-item HSI
Allen et al. (1998)[c]	Adults	Mexican and Salvadoran	3-item SAFE
Amason et al. (1999)[c]	Adults	Mexican and Salvadoran	4-item SAFE
Arciniega et al. (1996)	Adults	Mixed ethnic group with some Hispanics	22-item HSI (cult/fam conflict)
Caetano et al. (2007)	Adults	Hispanic	Conflicts with family and friends due to values, English communication problems, ethnic culture adjustment problems
Cervantes et al. (1991)	Adults	Hispanics, Mexican, Central Americans, and other	Both versions of full HSI

Authors	Developmental Period	Authors' Description of Participants' Ethnic Background	Measure Utilized
Conway et al. (2007)	Adults	Puerto Rican	20-item HSI
Finch et al. (2001)[d]	Adults	Mexican	10-item HSI
Finch et al. (2000)[d]	Adults	Mexican	12-item HSI
Finch & Vega (2003)[d]	Adults	Mexican	12-item HSI
Hovey (2000a)[e]	Adults	Mexican	24-item SAFE
Hovey (2000b)[e]	Adults	Mexican	24-item SAFE
Hovey & Magaña (2000)	Adults	Mexican	24-item SAFE
Hovey & Magaña (2002a)[f]	Adults	Mexican	24-item SAFE + 2 items
Hovey & Magaña (2002b)[f]	Adults	Mexican	24-item SAFE + 2 items
Hovey & Magaña (2002c)[f]	Adults	Mexican	24-item SAFE + 2 items
Hovey & Magaña (2003)	Adults	Mexican	24-item SAFE + 2 items
Miranda & Matheny (2000)	Adults	Mexican, Central American, and South American	24-item SAFE
Rodriguez et al. (2002)	Adults	Mexican	MASI
Salgado de Snyder (1987)	Adults	Mexican	LASI
Thoman & Surís (2004)	Adults	Hispanic	Both versions of full HSI
Turner et al. (2006)	Adults	Cuban and other Hispanic	Life history calendar

Note: Studies with the same superscript appear to have utilized the same sample.

59-item U.S.-born version). Each version assesses marital stress (e.g., "Spouse and I disagreed on language spoken at home"), parental stress (e.g., "Difficult to decide how strict to be with children"), occupational/economic stress (e.g., "I've been forced to accept low-paying jobs"), and cultural/family conflict stress (e.g., "I had serious arguments with family members"). And the immigrant version assesses a fifth domain, immigration stress (e.g., "I feared the consequences of deportation").

The 60-item SAFE was designed to assess stressors encountered by both immigrant and nonimmigrant students in familial (e.g., "Close family members and I have conflicting expectations about my future"), attitudinal (e.g., "I often think about my cultural background"), social (e.g., "I don't feel at home"), and environmental domains (e.g., "It bothers me when people pressure me to assimilate"). A 24-item revised version of the SAFE (see Mena et al., 1987) has been the most commonly used with Latinos. It includes 17 items from the original measure and 7 additional items focused on perceived discrimination against and majority-group stereotypes of immigrants (ibid.). The SAFE does not have separate versions for U.S.-born and immigrant Latinos, but certain items seem less relevant to U.S.-born Latinos (e.g., "People think I am unsociable when in fact I have trouble communicating in English").

A significant strength of these two measures is their comprehensive nature. They each capture various domains of Latinos' lives (e.g., work, social relationships), which likely capture all possible acculturative stressors that Latinos experience. Unfortunately, researchers typically do not capitalize on this strength; shortened versions of these measures are used in almost all studies. In fact, we found that only two studies used the complete HSI (Mangold, Veraza, Kinkler, & Kinney, 2007; Thoman & Surís, 2004), and only one used the 60-item version of the SAFE (i.e., Vazquez & Garcia-Vazquez, 1995). Another related strength is the ability to capture stressors that are unique to foreign-born Latinos. This is important, given that research suggests that nativity and acculturation level are necessary to understand not only the influence of acculturative stress on psychological functioning but also the likelihood of experiencing certain stressors. For instance, U.S.-born Latinos whose families have been in the United States for

multiple generations are less likely to experience such stressors as English-language difficulties, lack of knowledge regarding mainstream cultural norms, and immigration-related stressors (e.g., "It's hard to be away from the country I used to live in"). Thus, there is a need to consider the different acculturative stress experiences of U.S.-born and foreign-born Latinos.

Although the HSI accounts for different experiences for U.S.-born and foreign-born Latinos, and the authors recommended using two separate versions of the scale, researchers have typically chosen a subset of items (taken from both versions) and have administered the items to both U.S.-born and foreign-born participants. Though the SAFE does not have unique versions for immigrants and U.S.-born Latinos, some of the items appear more relevant to immigrants and almost irrelevant to U.S.-born Latinos (e.g., "I don't feel at home"). Nevertheless, researchers have administered these items to both immigrant and U.S.-born populations. This creates a problem because the scores obtained may actually be underreporting the level of stress experienced for U.S.-born populations in particular. For instance, if items that are not applicable to a certain group are administered to that group (e.g., having a U.S.-born participant report on stress due to not speaking English), and respondents are to indicate a score of 0 for these items, which is then added into their overall score, the level of stress may be underreported.

This can be a significant problem for a number of reasons. First, the association between acculturative stress and outcome variables may be stronger than what studies have found, due to measurement error that is introduced by asking (and scoring) questions that are irrelevant for certain participants. Specifically, when an item that is not applicable to a participant is summed into participants' scores (i.e., counted as a meaningful zero), this can erroneously lower participants' acculturative stress score relative to other participants. Participants may actually be experiencing high levels of stress for the stressors that *are* applicable to them; however, because their total scores include responses to items that are not applicable, their acculturative stress scores may be lower than they should be (i.e., validity threat). Thus, it may be more accurate to calculate a mean or sum score based on the items that are applicable to participants, rather than including all items in the scoring. This strategy will capture levels of acculturative stress, which will more accurately reflect the degree of stress experienced with regard to each *applicable* item, and this may be a more valid indicator of what will affect functioning.

Inaccuracies in measurement can be problematic when researchers use findings based on this measurement strategy to make recommendations for future research and intervention efforts. For example, in a study of Latino college students that varied by immigrant status such that 52% of participants were U.S. born, it was concluded that those who had come to the United States after the age of 12 were particularly at risk for negative outcomes because they had the highest levels of acculturative stress (Fuertes & Westbrook, 1996). The authors recommended that special interventions geared specifically to late immigrants were needed; however, the measure used to assess acculturative stress included items more relevant to immigrants (e.g., problems loosening ties with their country of origin). Thus, because it is unlikely that these items would be endorsed by U.S.-born Latinos, their scores may inevitably be lower than those of immigrant Latinos. Unfortunately, this was not taken into consideration when the authors conducted their analyses or when they discussed their results.

Nevertheless, some scholars have accounted for this potential confound and score their measures in a manner that considers whether or not the stressor is applicable to the participant. For example, Romero and Roberts (2003) developed the Bicultural Stressors Measure to examine stressors that arise from the native Latino culture and from mainstream culture (e.g., family stressors, monolingual stressors). In administering the measure, participants are asked whether or not they have experienced the stressor. If they *have* experienced the stressor, they are asked to indicate the degree of stress on a scale of 1 (not stressful) to 5 (extremely stressful). Items that do not apply to participants (i.e., participants did not experience the stressor) are not included in participants' scores. Put differently, participants' responses are averaged across items, but the mean is calculated using only the number of stressors that respondents indicated having experienced. If this scoring method is not used, U.S.-born participants' scores may underrepresent the amount of stress experienced, and this error may misrepresent the strength of the association between acculturative stress and outcomes.

LATINOS' ACCULTURATIVE STRESS AND ADAPTATION

Despite the existing methodological limitations of assessing acculturative stress, a considerable body of work has emerged that examines the association between acculturative stress and Latinos' adaptation. Early work that linked acculturation, or lack thereof, to problems with psychological adjustment resulted in mixed findings (see Rogler, Cortes, & Malgady, 1991, for a review). This led scholars to suggest that perhaps it was not the acculturation process itself that resulted in psychological maladjustment but rather the stressors experienced during the process of acculturation that could impact psychological functioning. Theoretical work has often implied this association. For instance, Williams and Berry (1991) explained that acculturative stress could result in various emotions and behaviors, including depression and anxiety, feelings of marginality and alienation, heightened psychosomatic symptoms, and identity confusion. Subsequent empirical work (discussed in the following sections) has provided support for these ideas with samples of children (Suarez-Morales, Dillon, & Szapocznik, 2007), adolescents (Romero & Roberts, 2003), college students (Constantine, Okazaki, & Utsey, 2004), and adults (Thoman & Surís, 2004). Thus, the link between acculturative stress and psychological functioning has been well established in the literature. Nevertheless, support for the association between acculturative stress and psychological functioning is strong for certain developmental cohorts (e.g., adults) but more limited for other groups (e.g., children).

Children. Studies examining children's acculturative stress have been limited. In fact, of the 46 studies we identified, only 4 measured children's acculturative stress, and 2 of the 4 studies appeared to use the same sample (i.e., Chavez et al., 1997; Hawley, Chavez, & St. Romain, 2007). Findings indicated that higher acculturative stress was associated with greater manifest anxiety (Suarez-Morales et al., 2007) and social acceptance (Weisskirch & Alva, 2002), but it was unrelated to academic achievement (Hawley et al., 2007).

Two of the studies were designed to validate a modified version of the SAFE. The first study

(Chavez et al., 1997) modified the SAFE to be administered to children and tested the revised measure (SAFE-C) with a sample of U.S.-born Latino and European American children. Chavez and colleagues (1997) concluded that the significant differences found between the Latino and European American children helped establish the validity of the SAFE-C. Ten years later, Suarez-Morales and colleagues (2007) revised the SAFE-C by reducing the number of items from 20 to 12 and renaming it the Acculturative Stress Inventory for Children (ASIC). Their analyses indicated that acculturative stress was positively associated with manifest anxiety and provided preliminary support for the use of this shortened version of the SAFE-C.

Beyond these findings, we know little about acculturative stress and its significance during childhood. It is possible that the limited interest in understanding experiences with acculturative stress during childhood is due to the belief that children will not experience acculturative stressors until they have developed an ethnic identity, which allows them to categorize others and make comparisons between groups and could increase the risk for conflicts or stressors (see Chavez et al., 1997, for a discussion of this rationale). We disagree with this reasoning and argue that acculturative stressors are likely salient in the lives of children, especially children in immigrant Latino families. Although an understanding of ethnic identity may prompt new questions for children and could lead to additional acculturative stressors, it is likely that children experience acculturative stressors well before they understand the concept of ethnicity and before they are able to categorize others according to ethnic group. For instance, young children who are recent immigrants and who have not learned English will have difficulties communicating with teachers and others outside of the family context, which can be a source of stress. Furthermore, children as young as 7 years of age may serve as language brokers for their parents, and this experience can serve as a source of acculturative stress for children regardless of their understanding of ethnicity (Martinez, McClure, & Eddy, 2009). In fact, there is some evidence that language brokering can lead to feelings of discomfort for children (Tse, 1996; Weisskirch & Alva, 2002). Thus, it is possible that this process may cause stress for young children. Others, however, found that language brokering was a source of pride for children (Tse, 1996). Martinez and colleagues (2009) suggest that the inconsistent findings with respect to outcomes associated with language brokering may be a function of the broader social context, such that those in communities who have few supports available to immigrants may fare more poorly. Put differently, acculturative stress in the form of pressure to serve as a child language broker and its subsequent outcomes may be largely defined by the context in which children's lives are embedded.

In sum, the literature on children's acculturative stress is limited, and there is a need to increase the field's understanding not only of acculturative stress experiences of Latino children but also of the association of acculturative stress with psychological functioning. If acculturative stressors are associated with negative outcomes, discovering ways to reduce their negative effects early on may decrease the risks for maladjustment during adolescence and adulthood. Put differently, if factors that place Latino children at increased risk are identified during childhood, it may be possible to intervene and perhaps prevent the onset of more serious disorders later in life.

Adolescents. There is a somewhat more developed body of work with regard to Latino adolescents' acculturative stress and outcomes (i.e., 10 of the 46 studies identified in our review). Among these studies, higher levels of acculturative stress were associated with lower self-esteem (Gil & Vega, 1996; Gil, Vega, & Dimas, 1994; Schwartz, Zamboanga, & Jarvis, 2007), higher levels of depressive symptoms (Hovey, 1998; Hovey & King, 1996; Romero & Roberts, 2003), and greater suicidal ideation (Hovey, 1998; Hovey & King, 1996). Thus, a consistent association between acculturative stress and adolescents' internalizing behaviors has emerged in existing work. This is not surprising, given the salience of identity formation (Erikson, 1968) and egocentrism (Elkind, 1967) during adolescence. It is possible that the increased focus on defining the self during this time, coupled with the preoccupation with others' perceptions of oneself, may predispose adolescents who are experiencing acculturative stressors to have negative feelings about themselves and potentially to display more internalizing symptoms.

In contrast, researchers have found that acculturative stress is not directly associated with externalizing behaviors. For instance, acculturative stress was not associated with Mexican Americans' inhalant use (Joe, Barrett, & Simpson, 1991), Latinos' externalizing behaviors (e.g., fighting, rule breaking, stealing; Schwartz et al., 2007), or Latinos' alcohol use (Gil, Wagner, & Vega, 2000). There is some evidence, however, that the association between acculturative stress and Latinos' externalizing behaviors is mediated by such factors as traditional family values (ibid.) and self-esteem (Schwartz et al., 2007). This is consistent with a risk and resilience perspective, which suggests that individual (e.g., self-esteem) and environmental (e.g., familial context) characteristics have the potential to protect individuals from the negative effects of risks (Rutter, 1987). Nevertheless, further research is needed to better understand these associations.

Although the work that has been conducted with adolescents has been informative regarding the associations among adolescents' acculturative stress, internalizing behaviors, and externalizing behaviors, a significant limitation of this work is that the findings are based almost exclusively on correlational analyses from cross-sectional studies. Furthermore, these studies have been based largely on survey methods with reports from a single informant, and it is possible that the strength of this association is inflated due to shared method variance. Thus, additional research is needed in which researchers implement longitudinal designs and involve multiple methods of assessments and multiple reporters in their studies. Such research will inform regarding the strength of the association between acculturative stress and various outcome variables, as well as the direction of this association (e.g., does acculturative stress lead to internalizing behaviors, or do the two merely co-occur?).

Understanding the implications of acculturative stress among adolescents is particularly important because of the salience of identity formation during adolescence (Erikson, 1968). Latino adolescents are especially vulnerable to issues of identity formation because they are likely to be developing their identities within multiple cultural contexts, and the stress associated with defining the self, especially with respect to ethnicity, can make the normative process of identity development even more challenging than is typical for all youth (Umaña-Taylor, Diversi, & Fine, 2002). This can occur if adolescents are repeatedly faced with negative perceptions of their ethnic groups and/or overt acts of ethnic discrimination against them. It is also possible, however, that acculturative stressors could contribute in a positive manner to the process of identity formation by encouraging adolescents to explore their identity. Thus, there are multiple mechanisms by which acculturative stress may interact with normative processes occurring during adolescence, and these should be explored in future research.

College Students. Like the work with adolescents, a number of studies have examined acculturative stress among Latino college students (10 of the 46 studies identified in our review). Consistent with findings for children and adolescents, researchers have found that acculturative stress is associated with poorer psychological adjustment. For instance, among samples described as Hispanic, Mexican, and international students from multiple Latin-origin countries, higher acculturative stress has been associated with increased anxiety (Chávez & French, 2007; Crockett et al., 2007) and depressive symptoms (Constantine et al., 2004; Crockett et al., 2007). Others found higher acculturative stress to be associated with more general psychological distress among a predominantly Mexican sample of Latinos (Saldaña, 1994). Findings demonstrate a robust association between acculturative stress and psychological adjustment, as this relation remains significant after accounting for the variance explained by demographic characteristics as English-language fluency and socioeconomic status, as well as such other important predictors such as general college stressors.

In addition to examining acculturative stress and outcomes, researchers have studied how acculturative stress varies by college students' generational status. Findings are inconclusive. Among four studies that examined variation by generational status, two found no differences between groups of Mexican American college students (Mangold et al., 2007; Vazquez & Garcia-Vazquez, 1995), and two found significant differences between groups (Fuertes & Westbrook, 1996; Mena et al., 1987). Interestingly, studies that found generational differences included foreign-born participants, whereas those that did not find differences included only U.S.-born participants. Perhaps generational differences are largely due to nativity rather than generations in the United States. Because the studies that found differences in acculturative stress used the SAFE measure, it is possible that differences emerged because the measure included items not applicable to U.S.-born Latinos, which ultimately created an artificial gap between the two groups. However, further research is needed to draw more definite conclusions.

Though researchers have advanced the field with respect to college students' experiences with acculturative stress, a number of questions remain unanswered. For instance, does acculturative stress serve as a risk enhancer? In a study focused on eating disorders among ethnic minority college students, Perez, Voelz, Pettit, and Joiner (2002) found that acculturative stress moderated the association between body dissatisfaction and bulimic symptoms such that the relation between these variables was significant for women only when they reported high levels of acculturative stress. The authors concluded that acculturative stress may render women more vulnerable to bulimic symptoms. Thus, future work is needed to understand whether acculturative stress places Latino college students at increased risk for negative outcomes.

Somewhat related to the foregoing discussion is the need to understand how to minimize Latino college students' acculturative stress. Existing research demonstrates that parental support and active coping strategies can modify the negative effects of acculturative stress on Mexican Americans' psychological functioning (Crockett et al., 2007). For instance, with regard to parental support, acculturative stress was related to psychological functioning only when Mexican American college students reported low levels of parental support (ibid.). More research is necessary to understand other variables that can modify this risk and/or factors that can minimize college students' acculturative stress. Findings from these studies can inform preventive intervention programs and ultimately lead to better psychological adjustment and academic outcomes among Latino youth.

Another area that is ripe for study among Latino college students is the degree to which characteristics of their college campuses interact with their acculturative stress to impact outcomes. For instance, Latino college students are in a unique position to potentially experience conflicting pressures from within their groups as well as pressures arising from college mainstream norms (Chavez & French, 2007). Thus, being a minority on a college campus that comprises mainly other minorities could potentially minimize experiences with acculturative stress that arise from mainstream society (e.g., discrimination) but could increase experiences with acculturative stress that arise from in-group expectations (e.g., Spanish fluency). Future work should explore Latino college students' experiences with acculturative stress, with a special focus on how the university environment contributes unique variability to this experience.

Adults. Our review of the empirical work indicated that adults were the most commonly studied population for research focused on Latinos' acculturative stress (i.e., 22 of the 46 studies identified in our review). Empirical findings revealed that acculturative stress was associated with increased psychological distress. For instance, Mexican-origin adults who reported higher acculturative stress also tended to report more depressive symptoms (Alderete, Vega, Kolody, & Aguilar-Gaxiola, 1999; Finch, Kolody, & Vega, 2000; Hovey, 2000b; Hovey & Magaña, 2000), anxiety (Hovey & Magaña, 2002a), and suicidal ideation (Hovey & Magaña, 2003). In addition, increased acculturative stress was associated with poorer physical health among Mexican Americans (Finch, Hummer, Kolody, & Vega, 2001; Finch & Vega, 2003).

One notable difference between studies with adults and those with younger populations was that studies with adults explored acculturative stress in the domain of employment. Acculturative stress in the domain of work was significantly associated with poorer physical health among adults, even after controlling for the effects of depression on physical health (Finch et al., 2001). In addition, social support from Anglo coworkers was associated with lower levels of acculturative stress among Mexican and Salvadoran workers (Amason, Allen, & Holmes, 1999), and praise from others in the work environment (i.e., supervisors, Hispanic coworkers, and Anglo coworkers) was associated with lower acculturative stress among Mexican and Salvadoran men (Allen, Amason, & Holmes, 1998). Although findings are based on only two studies, they support the notion that job-related stress is an important domain when assessing acculturative stress among adults; they further suggest that understanding stress in this domain could help explain reports of poor health among some Latino groups (Zsembik & Fennell, 2005). Nevertheless, more work is needed to understand the generalizability of these results, given that these findings are based largely on immigrant Mexican-origin samples, and it is unclear whether findings would vary by national origin, geographic region, nativity, or time spent in the United States.

Among the studies conducted with Latino adults, some evidence suggests that increased exposure to U.S. culture may be associated with decreased acculturative stress. Specifically, researchers have found a negative association between length of time in the United States and acculturative stress among immigrants from Mexico, Central America, and South America (Miranda & Matheny, 2000). Furthermore, lower levels of acculturation have been associated with increased acculturative stress (Caetano, Ramisetty-Mikler, Vaeth, & Harris, 2007; Miranda & Matheny, 2000). However, the association between acculturation and acculturative stress is likely a complicated one. For example, Finch and colleagues (2000) found that Mexican immigrants who were more acculturated reported more acculturative stress with regard to discrimination than Mexican immigrants who were less acculturated, while U.S.-born Mexican Americans who were more acculturated reported *less* acculturative stress than their counterparts who were less acculturated. Thus, nativity and acculturation may interact to inform acculturative stress. Furthermore, because some studies do not report nativity (e.g., Caetano et al., 2007), it is unclear whether the findings linking acculturation and acculturative stress are specific to immigrant samples or would generalize to U.S.-born Latinos as well.

Summary. In sum, there is an established literature on Latinos' acculturative stress, but the extent of our knowledge varies considerably by the developmental period of interest. Specifically, our understanding of children's experiences with acculturative stress, and the potential risks that acculturative stressors pose for children, is limited. A considerably larger body of work focuses on adolescent and adult populations, yet this literature is also limited with regard to potential variability in acculturative stress experiences due to demographic characteristics such as nativity, time spent in the United States, and geographic region.

It will be important for future research to understand how acculturative stressors change over the course of individuals' lives, as well as the different ways individuals adapt to these stressors. Longitudinal work will be necessary, primarily because the diversity of experiences with acculturative stress limits the developmental conclusions that can be drawn from cross-sectional studies. For instance, the stressors a first-generation immigrant Latino faces as a 9-year-old will be different from the stressors this same individual will face as an 18-year-old; similarly, the stressors a second-generation 9-year-old Latino faces will be different from the stressors this person faces as an 18-year-old. Although the acculturative stress experiences for these two different individuals are both changing over the 11-year period, the types of changes occurring are likely extremely different for the two individuals. The first-generation immigrant may be dealing with learning the English language at age 9 and the pressures associated with that, but at age 18 this person may be facing the pressures of having to serve as a language broker for his or her parents. The second-generational individual may have been dealing with language-brokering stress at the age of 9, but 9 years later, when his or her parents are more familiar with the English language, this person's acculturative stress may come more from having to make decisions that conflict with his or her family values, such as choosing to live far away from family to attend college. Thus, the issues faced at each particular developmental period will depend not only on the developmentally relevant tasks (e.g., educational/career choices) but also on the demographic characteristics of the individual (e.g., generational status). As previously mentioned, given the minimal amount of research, there is a limited understanding of whether certain acculturative stressors follow a specific progression and, if so, if the progression can be mapped on to particular developmental periods and linked to outcomes across the life span.

Despite the need for more work to better understand how acculturative stress is associated with adaptation across the life span, one consistent association that has emerged across the developmental cohorts is the relationship between acculturative stress and psychological functioning. Across all developmental periods, higher acculturative stress is associated with poorer psychological functioning. Although theorists have suggested that acculturative stress is not necessarily negative and can be a positive force that enhances individuals' psychological functioning (Dona & Berry, 1994), there is no empirical work, to our knowledge, that demonstrates a positive association. However, a small but growing body of work emphasizes conditions under which individuals demonstrate successful adaptation in the face of potentially stressful experiences. Specifically, nativity, acculturation, social support, and use of active coping strategies have been identified as significant moderators of the association between acculturative stress and psychological functioning; these findings are discussed in the following sections.

Moderators of the Relation Between Acculturative Stress and Psychological Functioning

With regard to nativity and acculturation level, researchers studying Latino adolescents (described as Cuban, Nicaraguan, and Other Hispanic) have found that the negative effects of acculturative stress on psychological functioning are stronger for U.S.-born youth when they are less acculturated, and the negative effects are stronger for foreign-born youth when they are more acculturated (Gil et al., 1994). Thus, nativity and acculturation level appear to interact to inform the association between acculturative stress and psychological outcomes. Similarly, with Latino adults, researchers found that nativity and acculturation interacted to predict acculturative stress in the form of discrimination. Mexican immigrants who were more acculturated experienced more acculturative stress than their less acculturated counterparts, but their U.S.-born counterparts who were more acculturated experienced *less* acculturative stress than the U.S.-born who were less acculturated. It is possible that acculturation serves a protective function for U.S.-born Latinos because of the social contexts within which they are embedded. U.S.-born Latinos may be more likely to be navigating mainstream society (e.g., interacting more with English speakers) and thus need to be more acculturated. Conversely, acculturation may be a risk enhancer for foreign-born Latinos because it may make them less accepted within their communities, which may be predominantly immigrant, and individuals in those communities may expect behaviors and values that are consistent with the culture of origin. Thus, high levels of acculturation may be deleterious for immigrant

Latinos because it sets them apart from those in their community and thus makes adaptation to the surrounding context more difficult.

Social support has also been found to serve a protective function for Latinos. For instance, researchers found that the positive association between Mexican American college students' acculturative stress and depressive symptoms was attenuated by high levels of parental support (Crockett et al., 2007). The protective function of parental support is not surprising, given the strong emphasis on family in Latino culture (Sabogal, Marín, Otero-Sabogal, Marín, & Pérez-Stable, 1987). Furthermore, these findings are consistent with Vega, Hough, and Miranda's (1985) model of Latino mental health, which indicates that social support is an important external coping resource that can modify the association between stress and mental health outcomes. More work is needed to understand the types of support that are protective and the contexts within which these sources of support will protect individuals.

Additionally, researchers should move toward examining how family separation during immigration influences the quality of parental support in conjunction with the quality of support from other members of the family. This is especially critical given the importance of extended family in Latinos' lives. Researchers have noted that, prior to immigrating to the United States, children are surrounded by a network of extended family members who, in addition to parents, can meet their emotional needs (Suarez-Orozco, Todorova, & Louie, 2002). Thus, immigration that results in loss of ties with nuclear or extended family members may be especially detrimental, as support from multiple significant others is the norm in the country of origin (Balcazar, Peterson, & Krull, 1997; Suarez-Orozco et al., 2002). Indeed, findings indicate that a critical stressor for recent immigrants is the lack of connectivity to family members left in the country of origin (Balcazar et al., 1997). Further, researchers have linked family separation to depressive symptoms; immigrant children who were separated from their parents during immigration were more likely to report depressive symptoms as compared to children who immigrated as intact families (Suarez-Orozco et al., 2002). Thus, it is important to extend work on familial support to capture the influence of separation from nuclear and extended family members on Latinos' lives.

Another variable that will need further study with respect to its potential protective function across the life span is individuals' familistic orientation. Latinos have been characterized as espousing a strong orientation toward the family, which includes respect for and strong emotional ties to the family (Sabogal et al., 1987). Work with children and adolescents suggests that Latinos' familistic values may minimize the negative effects of risks (e.g., parent-child conflict); however, this work has yet to be extended to literature on acculturative stress. It is possible that a strong connection to family may minimize the negative effects of acculturative stress for individuals. It will be important to explore this potential protective mechanism, particularly in light of recommendations from scholars to study adaptive aspects of culture (Garcia Coll, Akerman, & Cicchetti, 2000) and to consider how culturally based strengths may serve protective functions (Case & Robinson, 2003). On the other hand, it is possible that strong familistic values could potentially increase or contribute to acculturative stress for individuals whose familistic orientation conflicts with their behavioral and attitudinal acculturation toward mainstream culture (e.g., pursuing more individualistic goals). It is unclear what role such cultural values as familism will play in Latinos' experiences with acculturative stress, and this is certainly an area ripe for future research.

In addition, the use of active coping strategies has been found to moderate the association between acculturative stress and psychological functioning as measured by depressive and anxiety symptoms (Crockett et al., 2007). Specifically, the negative effects of acculturative stress on psychological functioning were weakened among Mexican American college students who reported using more active coping strategies (ibid.). These findings are consistent with the general stress and coping literature, which suggests that active coping can diminish the negative effects of stress on psychological functioning (Seiffge-Krenke, 1995). The moderating role of active coping is important for the development of preventive intervention programs, as active coping is a modifiable moderator; put differently, programs can be developed to enhance individuals' abilities to use active coping strategies when they encounter stress.

Variables that have not been empirically examined but may play a unique role in informing the association between acculturative stress and psychological functioning include reasons for entering the United States and other contextual factors within which Latinos' lives are embedded (e.g., physical appearance, neighborhood). For example, some Latinos voluntarily immigrate in search of education and economic opportunities, others come to the United States as political refugees, and still others became part of the United States when their land was acquired by that country (Umaña-Taylor et al., 2002). Reasons for immigrating may influence the amount of acculturative stress individuals experience and the relation between acculturative stress and Latinos' psychological functioning. For instance, individuals who immigrated to the United States in search of increased opportunities may be more likely to have positive expectations about the future; these positive expectations have been found to buffer the effect of acculturative stress on Latino adolescents' psychological outcomes (Hovey & King, 1996).

Future research should also explore how reasons for immigrating interact with time spent in the United States and family separation, to predict perceptions of acculturative stress and its association with family members' adaptation. For instance, families who immigrate in search of better economic opportunities often do so in stages, in which fathers initially immigrate alone to acquire employment, provide for the family back in the country of origin, and simultaneously save money to eventually bring other family members to the United States (Suarez-Orozco et al., 2002). Although separation from family members is considered a source of acculturative stress (Balcazar et al., 1997), researchers have yet to determine whether the effect is static, dynamic, or perpetual. Suarez-Orozco and colleagues (2002) discussed a number of possible outcomes based on this scenario. First, the influence of separation from family members may be alleviated when family members reunite. Alternatively, because immigrating in stages involves children's separation from parents and then from their substitute caregivers in order to reunite with their parents, the stress involved in separation may be replaced by stress associated with reestablishing parent-child relationships and role expectations. Finally, it may be that the influence of family separation on acculturative stress is dynamic, such that the relation may be moderated by the degree to which the substitute caregivers support the parent-child relationships. These possible alternatives have yet to be fully examined; our understanding of whether these processes are static, dynamic, or perpetual is limited, and further research is necessary to better understand the implications for acculturative stress.

Finally, the stressors that individuals experience, such as ethnic discrimination, may depend on the broader community context. In fact, in a review of the literature examining the association between acculturation and mental well-being, de la Rosa (2002) concluded that it is not possible to understand the association between these two variables without accounting for the role played by such mitigating factors as individual characteristics, family characteristics, and community context in affecting Latinos' acculturative stress, which in turn is associated with Latino adolescents' well-being (ibid.). The community context may play an influential role, particularly with regard to the ethnic composition of the community in which Latino individuals are living. Residing in neighborhoods and communities with a high concentration of Latinos may lead to increased exposure to Latino culture and the retention or maintenance of Latino values and behaviors (Lutz, 2006). This may be associated with fewer experiences of acculturative stress, due to limited contact with mainstream society and fewer pressures to acculturate. It is also possible that individuals in ethnic enclaves may be less likely to experience ethnic discrimination. Thus, community context is another variable that could introduce considerable variability into individuals' experiences with acculturative stress.

CONCLUDING COMMENTS AND RECOMMENDATIONS FOR FUTURE RESEARCH

The significant association that has emerged among indices of acculturative stress and individuals' psychological functioning is critical for the development of preventive programs designed to promote positive mental health among Latinos. Although scholars have moved the field forward with this significant contribution, considerable work is needed to understand how acculturative stress is associated with other aspects of Latinos' adaptation. One key outcome that must be examined in relation to acculturative stress is academic adjustment. Since 1972,

Latinos have had the highest high school dropout rate of all ethnic groups (National Center for Education Statistics, 2007). Given that culturally related stressors, such as discriminatory experiences in school, have been linked to academic outcomes (Martinez, DeGarmo, & Eddy, 2004), it is likely that acculturative stress contributes significantly to the academic success of Latinos.

In addition to expanding the outcomes that are examined in relation to acculturative stress, longitudinal studies are needed for an understanding of the strength and direction of the association between acculturative stress and various outcome variables across the life span. To our knowledge, longitudinal designs have not been utilized within particular developmental cohorts (e.g., adolescents) or across developmental periods (e.g., from childhood through adolescence). Specific questions to be answered include these: What are the acculturative stressors that are salient during specific periods? How are these stressors associated with adjustment across the life span? Are there certain stressors that, indeed, lead to positive outcomes? Perhaps we have yet to find acculturative stress leading to positive outcomes because this association emerges over a long period of time rather than immediately. For example, individuals may experience the acculturative stress of being language brokers during childhood, but it is not until adulthood that the benefits of this experience are realized—perhaps in the form of having developed skills that facilitate their ability to navigate social relationships and, in turn, to have greater success in their careers. Similarly, are there particular acculturative stressors that lead to long-term negative outcomes? For example, will discriminatory experiences early in the life span predispose individuals to a fatalistic worldview and perhaps reduce motivation to succeed?

Somewhat related to the limitation just cited, limited research has examined acculturative stress within the family context. We found two studies that examined acculturative stress and indices of family dynamics. In one study, researchers found that Latino adolescents who perceived greater family dysfunction also tended to report higher levels of acculturative stress (Hovey & King, 1996). The second study gathered data from both adolescents and parents from Cuban and Nicaraguan backgrounds and found that higher levels of acculturative stress reported by both adolescents and parents were associated with higher levels of cultural conflicts within the family (Gil & Vega, 1996). In addition, adolescents reported more language conflicts than their parents when length of residence in the United States was shorter, but parents reported more language conflicts than adolescents when length of residence in the United States was longer. Finally, regarding adults' marital relationships, Caetano and colleagues (2007) found that higher levels of acculturative stress were associated with a greater likelihood of involvement in intimate-partner violence among Latino married couples. Other than these three studies, however, we were unable to find studies that systematically examined acculturative stressors experienced within the family context. Given the potential for acculturative stressors to arise within parent-child relationships due to differing levels and rates of acculturation between parents and children, it is necessary to examine the unique acculturative stressors that arise from within the family context and specifically how they are associated with individual outcomes (for both parents and youth). Furthermore, future research should examine the marital dyad, as we know little about the dynamics of acculturative stress within couples.

Finally, the great diversity among Latinos may impact the types of acculturative stressors experienced as well as the degree to which individuals will experience acculturative stress. For example, Hovey and King (1996) posited that individuals who emigrated in an effort to better their educational and occupational opportunities may view acculturation to U.S. customs and beliefs as a necessary step toward gaining these opportunities and thus may report less acculturative stress. In line with this notion, Ogbu (1993) argued that voluntary immigrants often compare their situations in the United States to the situations of their peers who remained in their country of origin. Such comparisons often reinforce the notion that opportunities in the United States exceed those in their country of origin. This dual frame of reference influences the voluntary immigrants' perceptions of their lives in the United States (ibid.). Furthermore, this perspective differs greatly from the perspective of those who entered the United States as political refugees, because many political refugees have a different history with the United

States (i.e., they were often supporters of U.S. causes in their countries of origin). As a result of this connection, political refugees may be disappointed when they perceive that they are not well received in the United States (ibid.). Thus, entering the United States as a political refugee versus as a voluntary immigrant may produce sharp differences in what is perceived as a stressor and what is viewed as an opportunity.

In closing, a sizable literature has examined acculturative stress among Latino populations. This work has made significant contributions to the field's understanding of the types of acculturative stressors faced by Latinos in the United States, as well as potential factors that can introduce variability into Latinos' experiences with acculturative stress. This literature has also made significant strides in establishing the robust association between acculturative stress and Latinos' psychological functioning. Nevertheless, the need exists for methodological advances as well as more complex study designs that not only follow Latino individuals and families over time but also take into account the considerable diversity among Latino populations.

REFERENCES

Alderete, E., Vega, W., Kolody, B., & Aguilar-Gaxiola, S. (1999). Depressive symptomatology: Prevalence and psychological risk factors among Mexican migrant farmworkers in California. *Journal of Community Psychology, 27,* 457–471.

Allen, M. W., Amason, P., & Holmes, S. (1998). Social support, Hispanic emotional acculturative stress and gender. *Communication Studies, 49,* 139–157.

Amason, P., Allen, M. W., & Holmes, S. A. (1999). Social support and acculturative stress in the multicultural workplace. *Journal of Applied Communication Research, 27,* 310–334.

Arciniega, L. T., Arroyo, J. A., Miller, W. R., & Tonigan, J. S. (1996) Alcohol, drug use and consequences among Hispanics seeking treatment for alcohol-related problems. *Journal of Studies on Alcohol, 57,* 613–618.

Balcazar, H., Peterson, G. W., & Krull, J. L. (1997). Acculturation and family cohesiveness in Mexican American pregnant women: Social and health implications. *Family and Community Health, 20,* 16–31.

Berry, J. W., & Annis, R. C. (1974). Acculturative stress: The role of ecology, culture and differentiation. *Journal of Cross-Cultural Psychology, 5*, 382–406.

Berry, J. W., Trimble, J. E., & Olmedo, E. L. (1986). Assessment of acculturation. In W. J. Lonner & J. W. Berry (Eds.), *Field methods in cross-cultural research* (pp. 291–324). Beverly Hills, CA: Sage.

Caetano, R., Ramisetty-Mikler, S., Vaeth, P. A. C., & Harris, T. R. (2007). Acculturation stress, drinking, and intimate partner violence among Hispanic couples in the U.S. *Journal of Interpersonal Violence, 22*, 1431–1447.

Case, M. H., & Robinson, W. L. (2003). Interventions with ethnic minority populations: The legacy and promise of community psychology. In G. Bernal, J. E. Trimble, A. K. Burlew, & F. T. L. Leong (Eds.), *Handbook of racial and ethnic minority psychology* (pp. 573–590). Thousand Oaks, CA: Sage.

Cervantes, R. C., Padilla, A. M., & Salgado de Snyder, N. (1991). The Hispanic Stress Inventory: A culturally relevant approach to psychosocial assessment. *Psychological Assessment, 3*, 438–447.

Chavez, D. V., Moran, V. R., Reid, S. L., & Lopez, M. (1997). Acculturative stress in children: A modification of the SAFE scale. *Hispanic Journal of Behavioral Sciences, 19*, 34–44.

Chávez, N. R., & French, S. E. (2007). Ethnicity-related stressors and mental health in Latino Americans: The moderating role of parental racial socialization. *Journal of Applied Social Psychology, 37*, 1974–1998.

Claffey, J. E. (2006). Anti-immigrant violence in suburbia. *Social Text, 24*, 73–80.

Constantine, M. G., Okazaki, S., & Utsey, S. O. (2004). Self-concealment, social self-efficacy, acculturative stress, and depression in African, Asian, and Latin American international college students. *American Journal of Orthopsychiatry, 74*, 230–241.

Conway, K. P., Swendsen, J. D., Dierker, L., Canino, G., & Merikangas, K. R. (2007). Psychiatric comorbidity and acculturation stress among Puerto Rican substance abusers. *American Journal of Prevention Medicine, 32*, S219–S225.

Crockett, L. J., Iturbide, M. I., Torres Stone, R. A., McGinley, M., Raffaelli, M., & Carlo, G. (2007). Acculturative stress, social support, and coping: Relations to psychological adjustment among Mexican American college students. *Cultural Diversity and Ethnic Minority Psychology, 13*, 347–355.

de la Rosa, M. (2002). Acculturation and Latino adolescents' substance use: A research agenda for the future. *Substance Use and Misuse, 37*, 429–456.

Dona, G., & Berry, J. W. (1994). Acculturation attitudes and acculturative stress of Central American refugees. *International Journal of Psychology, 29*, 57–70.

Elkind, D. (1967). Egocentrism in adolescence. *Child Development, 38*, 1025–1034.

Erikson, E. H. (1968). *Identity: Youth and crisis.* New York: W. W. Norton.

Finch, B., Hummer, R., Kolody, B., & Vega, W. (2001). The role of discrimination and acculturative stress in the physical health of Mexican-origin adults. *Hispanic Journal of Behavioral Sciences, 23*, 399–430.

Finch, B. K., Kolody, B., & Vega, W. A. (2000). Perceived discrimination and depression among Mexican-origin adults in California. *Journal of Health and Social Behavior, 41*, 295–313.

Finch, B. K., & Vega, W. A. (2003). Acculturation stress, social support, and self-related health among Latinos in California. *Journal of Immigrant Health, 5*, 109–117.

Fuertes, J. N., & Westbrook, F. D. (1996). Using the Social, Attitudinal, Familial, and Environmental (S.A.F.E.) Acculturation Stress Scale to assess the adjustment needs of Hispanic college students. *Measurement and Evaluation in Counseling and Development, 29*, 67–77.

Garcia Coll, C., Akerman, A., & Cicchetti, D. (2000). Cultural influences on developmental processes and outcomes: Implications for the study of development and psychopathology. *Development and Psychopathology, 12*(3), 333–356.

Gil, A. G., & Vega, W. A. (1996). Two different worlds: Acculturation stress and adaptation among Cuban and Nicaraguan families. *Journal of Social and Personal Relationships, 13*, 435–456.

Gil, A. G., Vega, W. A., & Dimas, J. M. (1994). Acculturative stress and personal adjustment among Hispanic adolescent boys. *Journal of Community Psychology, 22*, 43–54.

Gil, A., Wagner, E., & Vega, W. (2000). Acculturation, familism, and alcohol use among Latino adolescent males: Longitudinal relations. *Journal of Community Psychology, 28*, 443–459.

Hawley, S. R., Chavez, D. V., & St. Romain, T. (2007). Developing a bicultural model for academic achievement. *Hispanic Journal of Behavioral Sciences, 29*, 283–299.

Hokoda, A., Galván, D. B., Malcarne, V. L., Castañeda, D. M., & Ulloa, E. C. (2007). An exploratory study examining teen dating violence, acculturation, and acculturative stress in Mexican-American adolescents. *Journal of Aggression, Maltreatment and Trauma, 14*(3), 33–49.

Hovey, J. (1998). Acculturative stress, depression, and suicidal ideation among Mexican-American adolescents: Implications for the development of suicide prevention programs in schools. *Psychological Report, 83,* 249–250.

Hovey, J. D. (2000a). Psychosocial predictors of acculturative stress in Mexican immigrants. *The Journal of Psychology, 134,* 490–502.

Hovey, J. D. (2000b). Acculturative stress, depression, and suicidal ideation in Mexican immigrants. *Cultural Diversity and Ethnic Minority Psychology, 6,* 134–151.

Hovey, J. D., & King, C. (1996). Acculturative stress, depression, and suicidal ideation among immigrant and second-generation Latino adolescents. *Journal of Academy of Child and Adolescent Psychiatry, 35,* 1183–1192.

Hovey, J. D., & Magaña, C. (2000). Acculturative stress, anxiety, and depression among Mexican immigrant farmworkers in the midwest United States. *Journal of Immigrant Health, 2,* 119–131.

Hovey, J. D., & Magaña, C. G. (2002a). Cognitive, affective, and physiological expressions of anxiety symptomatology among Mexican migrant farmworkers: Predictors and generational differences. *Community Mental Health Journal, 38,* 223–237.

Hovey, J. D., & Magaña, C. (2002b). Exploring the mental health of Mexican migrant farm workers in the Midwest: Psychosocial predictors of psychological distress and suggestions for prevention and treatment. *The Journal of Psychology, 136,* 493–513.

Hovey, J. D., & Magaña, C. (2002c). Psychosocial predictors of anxiety among immigrant Mexican migrant farmworkers: Implications for prevention and treatment. *Cultural Diversity and Ethnic Minority Psychology, 8,* 274–289.

Hovey, J. D., & Magaña, C. G. (2003). Suicide risk factors among Mexican migrant farmworker women in the midwest United States. *Archives of Suicide Research, 7,* 107–121.

Joe, G. W., Barrett, M. E., & Simpson, D. D. (1991). An integrative model for drug use severity among inhalant users. *Hispanic Journal of Behavioral Sciences, 13,* 324–340.

Lutz, A. (2006). Spanish maintenance among English-speaking Latino youth: The role of individual and social characteristics. *Social Forces, 84,* 1417–1433.

Mangold, D. L., Veraza, R., Kinkler, L., & Kinney, N. A. (2007). Neuroticism predicts acculturative stress in Mexican American college students. *Hispanic Journal of Behavioral Sciences, 29,* 366–383.

Martinez, C. R., DeGarmo, D. S., & Eddy, M. J. (2004). Promoting academic success among Latino youths. *Hispanic Journal of Behavioral Sciences, 26,* 128–151.

Martinez, C. R., McClure, H., & Eddy, J. M. (2009). Language brokering contexts and behavioral and emotional adjustment among Latino parents and adolescents. *Journal of Early Adolescence, 29,* 71–98.

Mena, F. J., Padilla, A. M., & Maldonado, M. (1987). Acculturative stress and specific coping strategies among immigrant and later generation college students. *Hispanic Journal of Behavioral Sciences, 9,* 207–225.

Miranda, A., & Matheny, K. (2000). Socio-psychological predictors of acculturative stress among Latino adults. *Journal of Mental Health Counseling, 22,* 306–318.

National Center for Education Statistics. (2007). *The condition of education 2007 in brief.* Washington, DC: U.S. Department of Education, Office of Educational Research and Improvement.

Ogbu, J. U. (1993). Differences in cultural frame of reference. *International Journal of Behavioral Development, 16,* 483–506.

Padilla, A. M., Wagatsuma, Y., & Lindholm, K. J. (1985). Acculturation and personality as predictors of stress in Japanese and Japanese-Americans. *Journal of Social Psychology, 125,* 295–305.

Perez, M., Voelz, Z. R., Pettit, J. W., & Joiner, T. E., Jr. (2002). The role of acculturative stress and body dissatisfaction in predicting bulimic symptomatology across ethnic groups. *International Journal of Eating Disorders, 31,* 442–454.

Rodriguez, N., Myers, H., Mira, C., Flores, T., & Garcia-Hernandez, L. (2002). Development of the Multidimensional Acculturative Stress Inventory for adults of Mexican origin. *Psychological Assessment, 14,* 451–461.

Rogler, L. H., Cortes, D. E., & Malgady, R. G. (1991). Acculturation and mental health status among Hispanics. *American Psychologist, 46,* 585–597.

Romero, A. J., & Roberts, R. E. (2003). Stress within a bicultural context for adolescents of Mexican descent. *Cultural Diversity and Ethnic Minority Psychology, 9,* 171–184.

Rutter, M. (1987). Psychosocial resilience and protective mechanisms. *American Journal of Orthopsychiatrics, 57,* 316–331.

Sabogal, F., Marín, G., Otero-Sabogal, R., Marín, B., & Pérez-Stable, E. J. (1987). Hispanic familism and acculturation: What changes and what doesn't? *Hispanic Journal of Behavioral Sciences, 9,* 397–412.

Saldaña, D. (1994). Acculturative stress: Minority status and distress. *Hispanic Journal of Behavioral Sciences, 16,* 116–128.

Salgado de Snyder, V. N. (1987). The role of ethnic loyalty among Mexican immigrant women. *Hispanic Journal of Behavioral Sciences, 9,* 287–298.

Sanchez, J., & Fernandez, D. (1993). Acculturative stress among Hispanics: A bidimensional model of ethnic identification. *Journal of Applied Social Psychology, 23,* 654–668.

Schwartz, S. J., Zamboanga, B. L., & Jarvis, L. H. (2007). Ethnic identity and acculturation in Hispanic early adolescence: Mediated relationships to academic grades, prosocial behaviors, and externalizing symptoms. *Cultural Diversity and Ethnic Minority Psychology, 13,* 364–373.

Seiffge-Krenke, I. (1995). *Stress, coping, and relationships in adolescence.* Mahwah, NJ: Lawrence Erlbaum.

Suarez-Morales, L., Dillon, F. R., & Szapocznik, J. (2007). Validation of the acculturative stress inventory for children. *Cultural Diversity and Ethnic Minority Psychology, 13,* 6–24.

Suarez-Orozco, C., Todorova, I. L. G., & Louie, J. (2002). Making up for lost time: The experiences of separation and reunification among immigrant families. *Family Process, 41,* 625–643.

Thoman, L. V., & Surís, A. (2004). Acculturation and acculturative stress as predictors of psychological distress and quality-of-life functioning in Hispanic psychiatric patients. *Hispanic Journal of Behavioral Sciences, 26,* 293–311.

Tse, L. (1996). Language brokering in linguistic minority communities: The case of Chinese- and Vietnamese-American students. *The Bilingual Research Journal, 20,* 485–498.

Turner, R. J., Lloyd, D. A., & Taylor, J. (2006). Stress burden, drug dependence, and the immigration paradox among U.S. Hispanics. *Journal of Drug and Alcohol Dependence, 83,* 79–89.

Umaña-Taylor, A. J., Diversi, M., & Fine, M. A. (2002). Ethnic identity and self-esteem among Latino adolescents: Making distinctions among the Latino populations. *Journal of Adolescent Research, 17,* 303–327.

Vazquez, L., & Garcia-Vazquez, E. (1995). Variables of success and stress with Mexican American students. *College Student Journal, 29,* 221–226.

Vega, W. A., Hough, R., & Miranda, M. (1985). Modeling cross cultural research in Hispanic mental health. In W. Vega & M. Miranda (Eds.), *Stress and Hispanic mental health* (pp. 1–29). DHHS Pub. No. (ADM)85–1410. Rockville, MD: National Institute of Mental Health.

Weisskirch, R., & Alva, S. (2002). Language brokering and the acculturation of Latino children. *Hispanic Journal of Behavioral Sciences, 24,* 369–378.

Williams, C. L., & Berry, J. W., (1991). Primary prevention of acculturative stress among refugees: Application of psychological theory and practice. *American Psychologist, 46,* 632–641.

Zsembik, B., & Fennell, D. (2005). Ethnic variation in health and the determinants of health among Latinos. *Social Sciences Medicine, 61,* 53–63.

10

Latino Families

Parenting, Relational, and Developmental Processes

Josefina M. Grau,* Margarita Azmitia,* and Justin Quattlebaum

As the representation of Latino children and adolescents in the United States continues to increase, so does our need to understand the family processes that lead to more optimal development and functioning among this large and rapidly growing group of children and adolescents. Although recently there has been an increase in research on family processes and child outcomes among Latino families, this literature is still quite limited. In this chapter, we review the literature examining the parenting and family processes linked to the adjustment of Latino children and adolescents across the socioemotional, cognitive, educational, and peer domains. We focus on the cultural values and socialization goals that guide the child-rearing practices of Latino parents as well as on the influence of immigration and acculturation on these processes. We first provide a brief demographic profile of Latino families in the United States to describe the context in which Latino children and adolescents are embedded. We then review the literature examining parenting and its relations to child socioemotional and cognitive outcomes. In the third

section, we review work on the role of Latino families in children's and adolescents' educational outcomes. Here, we focus on the influence of family relationships beyond parenting, as the bulk of this literature has examined the role of family processes more broadly. This section is followed by a review of research examining linkages between the family and peer worlds of Latino children in the United States. Finally, we discuss implications for future research.

DEMOGRAPHIC PATTERNS

Latinos are the largest and fastest-growing minority group in the United States. Currently, at 42.5 million, Latinos constitute 14.2% of the U.S. population, according to the U.S. Census Bureau report, *The American Community—Hispanics: 2004* (Suro et al., 2007). Between 2000 and 2006, Latinos accounted for one half of the nation's growth; 22% percent of the population under 5 years of age is Latino (U.S. Census Bureau, 2006), and Latinos make up 17% of the U.S. families with children under 18 years old (Suro, 2007). The

AUTHORS' NOTE: Josephina Grau and Margarita Azmitia both share primary authorship.

153

largest percentage of the 9.5 million Latino families identify as Mexican heritage, and the next-largest groups identify as Puerto Rican and Cuban heritage. The highest concentration of Latinos is in traditional receiving states—the Southwest, Florida, New York, and Texas. However, such midwestern and southern states as Indiana, Minnesota, Georgia, and North Carolina have reported large increases in their Latino populations (Suro et al., 2007). Given the strong presence of Latinos in the United States, there is an increasing need to understand the challenges and strengths of these families and how they relate to child development.

Compared to non-Hispanic whites, Latinos have higher fertility rates, with 75 out of 1,000 women giving birth in the last 12 months, compared to 50 out of 1,000 for non-Hispanic whites. Despite the current immigration debates, most Latino children are U.S. born (U.S. Census Bureau, 2006). Fertility rates are highest for Mexican-heritage women and lowest for Cuban-heritage women (Suro et al., 2007). Consistent with their higher fertility rates, Latino families tend to be larger, with 3.86 members, compared to 3.10, 3.35, and 3.44 for European-, African-, and Asian-heritage families respectively (Bachu & O'Connell, 2001).

Relative to other ethnic groups in the United States, Latinos are more likely to raise their children in two-parent families, but the number of single Latino parents is increasing. In 2002, 33% of the children born to Latinos were born to unmarried mothers (Suro et al., 2007).[1] Although the overall teen birth rates have decreased in the United States, such is not the case for Latinos. Latina teenagers had the highest birth rates of any racial/ethnic group, with 83 per 1,000, compared to the national average of 43 per 1,000. However, young Latina mothers tend to have high levels of family support; 80% live with their families (Population Resource Center, 2004). This level of family support is also evident in the tendency of Latino families to live in extended-family households (Baca Zinn & Wells, 2000) or to reside in the same community (Cauce & Domenech-Rodriguez, 2002).

Taken together, the fertility patterns, family size, and extended-family living patterns present a profile of both challenges and strengths. For example, the higher fertility rates and larger family size can challenge low-income families to meet the needs of their children. Yet, the availability of siblings, grandparents, and other family members who can provide economic, emotional, and informational support is a source of strength for children's and adolescents' development.

An important source of challenge for Latino families in the United States is their high rates of poverty. Twenty percent of Latino families live in poverty, compared to the 9% U.S. average; this increases neighborhood, health, and educational risks for children and adolescents. Latino families are also more likely than European-heritage families to live in inner-city neighborhoods with underresourced schools (Pew Hispanic Center, 2004). The challenges of living in poverty in inner-city metropolitan areas have motivated a large body of research that has approached Latino family socialization primarily from a deficit perspective. Increasingly, however, theory and research are examining the resources Latino families bring to children's and adolescents' development. In this chapter, we highlight sources of strengths as well as challenges in Latino families' socialization processes and outcomes.

PARENTING AND LATINO CHILDREN'S SOCIOEMOTIONAL AND COGNITIVE FUNCTIONING

Research examining Latino children's socioemotional and cognitive outcomes has focused on the role of parenting, and almost exclusively on parenting provided by mothers to infants and children. This research has been largely based on indirect indices of parenting and not on behavioral observations of parenting behaviors. It has also relied primarily on cross-sectional and comparative methodology, examining mean differences between mothers of different ethnic backgrounds, rather than on within-group designs that take into account the cultural and ecological context in which these families are embedded. Studies also rarely consider the potential moderating role of acculturation, differences between Latinos of different countries of origin, the confounding effects of SES, or the parenting behaviors of fathers. Often, researchers have been forced to use measures that have not been validated for this population or were designed to assess aspects of parenting that are central to parenting in other populations but that may not adequately reflect important aspects of parenting among Latinos. Thus, although recently there has been an increase in the number of studies examining parenting among Latinos, the parenting behaviors that lead to more optimal child development in this group have not been well established to date.

Overall, although the majority of the studies appear to assume cultural invariance in the assessment of parenting behaviors and in their relations to child outcomes, researchers have increasingly called for a culture-specific approach to the study of parenting (Contreras, Narang, Ikhlas, & Teichman, 2002; García Coll et al., 1996; Halgunseth, Ispa, & Rudy, 2006), and empirical evidence of lack of measurement equivalence across groups is now beginning to accumulate. For example, in a national sample of European, African, and Latino American children, Raver, Gershoff and Aber (2007) found "substantial evidence of nonequivalence among observed measures of parenting behavior" (p. 110) across ethnic groups. Similarly, studies also point to important differences in the ways specific parenting behaviors relate to child outcomes across groups (Carlson & Harwood, 2003; Ispa et al., 2004). Thus, in understanding Latino parenting and its relations to child outcomes, it is important to focus both on parental behaviors that may be common to parents of different ethnic backgrounds and on characteristics and behavior that are unique to Latinos. Therefore, in our review of the Latino parenting literature, we distinguish between culture-general and culture-specific behaviors.

Culture-General Behaviors

Some parenting behaviors (e.g., sensitivity, responsivity) appear to be integral aspects of competence that cut across cultural boundaries and are associated with more optimal child outcomes across groups. A substantial literature, guided by attachment theory (Ainsworth, Blehar, Waters, & Wall, 1978; Bowlby, 1973, 1982) has related maternal sensitivity to infants' and children's cues and children's functioning across different cultural groups (DeWolff & van Ijzendoorn, 1997). Research with Latino families from different countries of origin and residing in different regions of the United States has corroborated this relation. For example, using a national sample of U.S.-born Latino infants living with both biological parents, Cabrera and collaborators (Cabrera, Shannon, West, & Brooks-Gunn, 2006) found that a maternal behavior composite, reflecting sensitivity to children's cues, responsivity to their distress,

and behaviors that foster cognitive and socioemotional growth, was significantly associated with infants' cognitive functioning. In a sample of young Mexican American (MA) and Puerto Rican (PR) mothers residing in the Midwest, toddlers of mothers who displayed greater sensitivity were more affectively positive and responsive in interactions with their mothers (Contreras, Mangelsdorf, Rhodes, Diener, & Brunson, 1999). Maternal sensitivity was also significantly related to security of attachment among infants of PR and Dominican mothers residing in the Bronx (Fracasso, Busch, & Fisher, 1994). Culture-general aspects of parenting are not expected to differ based on acculturation levels. Consistent with this expectation, in two samples of young Latina mothers, acculturation level, assessed through language use and preference and cultural involvement, was not associated with maternal sensitivity (Contreras, 2004; Contreras, Mangelsdorf, et al., 1999).

These culture-general parenting characteristics are likely of evolutionary significance and need to be considered when predicting Latino children's developmental outcomes. However, they do not capture unique characteristics of Latino parents. Thus, it is also necessary to consider specific characteristics and behaviors that have their roots in the cultural and sociodemographic ecologies of Latino parents in the United States in order to arrive at a more complete understanding of Latino parenting and, in turn, how it relates to children's development. We now turn to these culture-specific behaviors.

Culture-Specific Behaviors

Some parenting behaviors must be defined within specific cultural contexts and may have differential effects on children's functioning across ethnic groups (García Coll et al., 1996). To understand these behaviors, it is necessary to consider Latino cultural values; some of these are common to all Latino groups, and others vary by nationality. The literature highlights three values as especially important for understanding parenting and family relationships among Latino families: *familism,* a set of beliefs that emphasize the importance of solidarity, obligation, reciprocity, and parental authority within the family (Cauce & Domenech-Rodriguez, 2002); *respeto,* a concept that emphasizes proper demeanor and respect for authorities and elders; and *educación:* a set of beliefs and practices that emphasize moral upbringing and being a good person (Reese, Balzano, Gallimore, & Goldenberg, 1995). Together, these values form a system of cultural beliefs that is thought to influence the types of behaviors considered appropriate within the family, parenting strategies, and socialization goals for children.

As in any culture, parenting behaviors need to be in line with socialization goals for children. These parenting behaviors are thought to predict more optimal child development because they instill characteristics and skills that are valued and needed in the local context. For example, researchers (Gonzalez-Ramos, Zayas, & Cohen, 1998; Harwood, Schoelmerich, Schulze, & Gonzalez, 1999) have described a set of culturally determined, long-term socialization goals shared by PR adult mothers of various economic backgrounds that are consistent with the Latino values described above. PR mothers emphasize child qualities related to Proper Demeanor, such as appropriate interpersonal behavior, the ability to get along with others, and the fulfillment of role obligations, particularly within the family; they rate qualities related to Self-Maximization, such as fulfillment of personal potential, self-confidence, and self-reliance as relatively less important. Characteristics related to Proper Demeanor and Respeto have also been found to be highly valued by MA parents (Arcia & Johnson, 1998; Azmitia & Brown, 2002; Reese et al., 1995). In contrast, European American (EA) mothers place relatively greater emphasis on qualities related to Self-Maximization than on those related to Proper Demeanor. These child socialization goals, in turn, are in line with the parenting behaviors exhibited by mothers (Harwood et al., 1999; Harwood, Miller, Carlson, & Leyendecker, 2002).

For immigrant populations such as Latinos in the United States, however, it is also necessary to consider the fact that as children develop, they must adapt to a context that does not necessarily match the original context of their parents (Ogbu, 1981). Therefore, parenting that is in line with traditional Latino cultural values will not necessarily lead to successful child adaptation in the United States when adaptation is defined based on mainstream EA values that are different from those of the original culture. For example, child characteristics related to Respeto and Proper Demeanor, such as obedience and conformity, are valued by Latino families and presumably lead to successful adaptation in Latino countries, but may make children's adaptation to U.S. schools harder, as schools tend to value independence, self-direction, and creativity more than obedience and conformity (Laosa, 1982; Moreno, 1991). Although scholars have noted the need to consider the extent to which mainstream measures of child competence fully reflect Latino children's competencies (García Coll & Vazquez Garcia, 1996), to date this issue has received little empirical attention.

Furthermore, in understanding relations between Latino parenting and child outcomes, it is also important to consider acculturation level. Given that Latino parents vary in level of acculturation and adhere to Latino and mainstream values to different degrees, the set of cultural values that guide their parenting behaviors is likely to vary accordingly. For example, among adult PR mothers, those who were more highly acculturated rated the child-rearing values of independence and creativity higher than those who were less acculturated; these values were among the top three ranked by EA mothers (Gonzalez-Ramos et al., 1998). Thus, parents of different acculturation levels may rely on somewhat different parenting behaviors. Although culture-general aspects of parenting are not expected to differ based on acculturation levels, culture-specific aspects are likely to differ, with more highly acculturated mothers displaying parenting that coincides more with that displayed by EAs. The associations between parenting behaviors and child outcomes could also differ across acculturation levels.

A few studies have begun to provide empirical evidence of Latino-specific aspects of parenting. These studies have demonstrated differences in parenting behaviors between Latino and EA parents and between relatively unacculturated and highly acculturated Latinos, as well as differences in the constellation of behaviors displayed by Latinos and EA parents and by Latino parents of different acculturation levels. We organize our review of these studies according to the evidence they provide for each of these differences.

Differences in Parenting Behaviors Used by Latina and European American Mothers. Latina mothers of both PR and Mexican heritage have been found to be more controlling with their children. They have been described as placing more demands and restrictions on their children and have been observed to physically guide and structure their children's environment and behavior more than EA mothers (Cardona, Nicholson, & Fox, 2000; Harwood et al., 1999; Harwood et al., 2002; Ispa et al., 2004; Knight, Virdin, & Roosa, 1994). Based on self-report as well as child report, MA mothers also score higher than EA mothers on a questionnaire measure of "hostile control" (Hill, Bush, & Roosa, 2003). In addition, observational studies of maternal teaching strategies have found that Latina mothers use more directive and nonverbal teaching strategies (e.g., modeling) and fewer verbal (e.g., verbal inquiry) strategies than EA mothers (Laosa, 1978, 1980; Scholmerich, Lamb, Leyendecker, & Fracasso, 1997).

Relations Between Acculturation Level and the Use of Specific Parenting Behaviors. There is evidence that aspects of control may differ according to acculturation level: Spanish-speaking (proxy for acculturation) MA school-age children report that their mothers use more "hostile control" than English-speaking MA and EA children (Hill et al., 2003). Less acculturated parents of PR and Mexican heritage are more controlling, endorse a stricter style of parenting, and value respectfulness in their children more than highly acculturated parents (Buriel, 1993; Gonzales-Ramos et al., 1998). Similarly, among MA mothers of school-age children (primarily first-generation immigrants in two-parent families), greater acculturation level related to lower self-reported hostile parenting (although maternal hostile parenting was not related to child adjustment; Parke et al., 2004). In terms of specific teaching strategies, more highly acculturated mothers of PR, Dominican, and Mexican heritage have been found to use more verbal and less directive strategies than less acculturated mothers (Mejía-Arauz, Rogoff, Dexter, & Najafi, 2007; Planos, Zayas, & Busch-Rossnagel, 1995; Teichman & Contreras-Grau, 2006).

Differential Relations Among Specific Behaviors Between Latina and European American Mothers. There is evidence that the constellation of parenting behaviors used by Latino parents varies from that used by EA mothers: Among PR mothers, high levels of physical control were not related to high maternal insensitivity and low warmth, as commonly observed for EA mothers (Carlson & Harwood, 2003; Fracasso et al., 1994). Level of intrusiveness was not related to

maternal stress among MA mothers, as it was for EA mothers (Ispa et al., 2004). Similarly, among MA preadolescents, child-reported inconsistent discipline and hostile control were positively related to perceived maternal acceptance (Gonzales, Pitts, Hill, & Roosa, 2000).

Differential Relations Among Specific Behaviors Between High- and Low-Acculturated Latinas. Acculturation also appears to affect the patterning of behaviors. In a sample of MA mothers, the correlations between reports of maternal acceptance and hostile control differed for Spanish-speaking versus English-speaking mothers (Hill et al., 2003). Acceptance and control were also positively correlated among Spanish-speaking mothers but uncorrelated among English-speaking MA mothers; the correlation was negative among EA mothers. Thus, among Latinas, high levels of control, a variable associated with negative child outcomes in EAs, can co-occur with behaviors that are associated with more competent parenting and positive child outcomes. This association might be especially likely to occur among relatively unacculturated mothers.

Taken together, the studies just reviewed indicate two aspects of parenting that appear to be culture specific: the use of directive/controlling parenting behaviors and the use of more nonverbal and fewer verbal strategies (especially during teaching interactions). We review next the few studies that have examined relations between these behaviors and child outcomes.

Differences in the Relations Between Specific Parenting Behaviors and Child Outcomes Between Latina and European American Mothers. Importantly, the relations between control and child outcomes appear to differ between Latina and EA mothers. For example, contrary to what has been found for EAs, for PR and Dominican mothers, relatively high levels of control and physical interventions were related positively to security of attachment (Carlson & Harwood, 2003; Fracasso et al., 1994). MA mothers' physical control during teaching also predicted children's positive verbal responses and task involvement (Martinez, 1988). In a study of maternal intrusiveness and three dimensions of the mother-toddler relationship (child negativity, dyadic mutuality, child engagement), intrusiveness was not predictive of child engagement with mothers among MA mothers (of high and low acculturation levels), as it was for EAs (Ispa et al., 2004). Similarly, higher levels of hostile control were not related to children's depression or conduct problems among MA preadolescents (Gonzales et al., 2000).

Differences in the Relations Between Specific Parenting Behaviors and Child Outcomes Between Latinas of High and Low Acculturation Levels. Acculturation level also appears to affect the relations between maternal behavior and child outcomes. In the Ispa et al. (2004) study previously described, intrusiveness was related to only one of the three outcome variables among the less acculturated MA mothers; among the more acculturated mothers, intrusiveness was related to two of the three outcomes. Intrusiveness was related to all three variables among the EA mothers. Thus, intrusiveness had fewer negative consequences for MA mothers than for EA mothers, especially for less acculturated mothers. A moderating role of acculturation was also suggested in the Gonzales et al. (2000) study previously described, in that hostile control was not related to conduct problems in the complete sample, but Spanish-speaking MA preadolescents reported both higher levels of hostile control from their parents and lower levels of conduct problems.

Thus, empirical evidence is beginning to accumulate suggesting that the use of greater control by Latino parents does not relate to negative outcomes as it does among EA families. A crucial next step will be testing relations between these parenting behaviors and children's developmental outcomes across different domains in prospective designs. The evidence also suggests variability within Latino parents, both their use of control (i.e., higher control in low-acculturated vs. high-acculturated families) and the relations between control and child outcomes, with control having less negative outcomes in less acculturated than in more acculturated Latino parents. The majority of the studies have assessed acculturation level with proxy measures (e.g., language use for study participation); future studies should move beyond these crude measures and assess acculturation using the multidimensional measures that are available in order to better capture the culturally derived variability present among Latino families in the United States. Future research should also study control, as well as other culture-specific behaviors, using measures developed

specifically for this population. Given that the constellation of parenting behaviors displayed by Latinos differs from that of other parents (e.g., control does not necessarily coexist with low warmth or insensitivity), measures developed for a different population may aggregate behaviors in ways that obscure important differences among types of control behaviors (i.e., not all may be hostile or intrusive) or among the different parenting practices displayed by parents (e.g., involvement and strictness). A cleaner assessment of these behaviors would help further our understanding of factors motivating parents' use of control as well as other culture-specific behaviors. For example, it is important to differentiate when control behaviors are used to achieve culturally determined socialization goals from when they are motivated by parent characteristics, such as stress. Whereas among relatively unacculturated parents, control behaviors are more likely to be rooted in culturally determined socialization goals, among highly acculturated parents control is likely to be motivated by individual characteristics. Differentiating between these motivating factors is crucial, as they are likely to affect how control relates to children's development, with control being unrelated to negative outcomes in unacculturated families but related to negative outcomes in acculturated families. The development of indigenous measures is clearly a high priority for advancing our knowledge of culture-specific aspects of parenting.

Although we could not find research that tested how directiveness and verbal/nonverbal dimensions of teaching relate to Latino children's outcomes, the academic difficulties some Latino children exhibit in U.S. schools have been attributed to the lack of congruity between the learning experiences at home and at school (Laosa, 1982; Moreno, 1991), suggesting that greater reliance on directive and nonverbal strategies relates to more negative school readiness and cognitive outcomes. Because the extant literature has relied almost exclusively on low-income Latino families, differences that have been observed between Latinos and other ethnic groups may be driven partly by SES or education. In fact, in some studies (but not others), group differences in strategies diminish or disappear when controlling for SES or education (Laosa, 1982; Moreno, 1991). For example, in a collaborative task with their three children,

Mejía-Arauz et al. (2007) found that more acculturated MA mothers engaged in more dyadic and verbal teaching than recently immigrated MA mothers, who were more likely to use triadic, nonverbal strategies. They suggested that this difference was linked, at least in part, to differences in mothers' schooling. The more acculturated mothers had not only completed more education than the immigrant mothers but also had been educated in the United States. Thus, it would be important for future research to include Latino families from all socioeconomic and educational levels in order to better disentangle the different factors related to Latino parents' use of teaching strategies, as well as the implications for children's development, assessed both in terms of mainstream- and culture-specific measures of competence. One way to assess the implications of family for children's development is to consider their contributions to their children's educational outcomes.

Families and Children's and Adolescents' Educational Outcomes

Increasingly, research has examined the role of family processes in the academic performance and educational attainment of Latino children and adolescents. The growth of this literature is due partly to research showing that Latinos, especially those of Mexican and PR heritage, have the lowest rates of educational attainment of all ethnic groups in the United States (Bohon, Johnson, & Gorman, 2006; García & Scribner, Chapter 16, this volume). Latino students, and especially those of MA (25%) and PR (17%) heritage, have the highest high school dropout rates in the United States, compared to EA (7%) and AA (12%) students (Pew Hispanic Center, 2004). Moreover, only 6% of Latinos who enter kindergarten obtain bachelor's degrees (Williams, 2003).

Because most research has focused on low-income Latinos and recent immigrants whose children are at risk of educational failure, little is known about the educational values and practices of middle-class Latinos and about Latino children and adolescents who are succeeding in school. Increasingly, however, researchers are studying these students to understand the role of family in their educational success (Cooper, Cooper, Azmitia, Chavira, & Gullat, 2002;

Gándara, 1995; Mooney & Rivas-Drake, 2008). This more differentiated view of Latino families is reflected in research that goes beyond the view that Latino families do not value education and are not engaged in their children's schooling (for reviews of deficit perspectives, see Solórzano, 1992; Valencia & Black, 2002). Three conceptual frameworks—ecological/sociocultural, social capital, and acculturation—have provided the foundation for much of this research. We now review empirical research illustrative of these three perspectives.

Ecological/Sociocultural Perspectives on the Family and Children's and Adolescents' Education

Bronfenbrenner's (Bronfenbrenner & Morris, 1998) ecological perspective and sociocultural frameworks (e.g., Rogoff, 2003; Tharp & Gallimore, 1988) have influenced a large body of theory and research on the role of Latino families in children's schooling. Although the ecological perspective does not propose culture-specific hypotheses, because it shares some theoretical assumptions with the sociocultural perspective, it has often been used to study how different cultural groups adapt to their environments and socialize their children. Both frameworks conceptualize families as linked to other contexts of socialization, such as schools, peers, and communities, through socialization agents, values, beliefs, social interaction practices, and socialization goals. Values, beliefs, and socialization practices are dynamic and change in response to historical and proximal circumstances, such as immigration and shifts in parents' education and finances. Research that has examined continuities and discontinuities between these agents of socialization has revealed that their values, beliefs, practices, and goals are linked to developmental and academic outcomes. In a series of studies, for example, Tharp and Gallimore (1988) showed that cultural discontinuities in how ethnic minority families approached home and school tasks influenced children's classroom practices and performance and teachers' perceptions of families' involvement in their children's schooling. For example, Latino parents often defined education based on their ideas about *educación*, emphasizing appropriate behavior and respect for others more than academics, thus contributing to teachers' perceptions that these parents are not as interested in academics (Auerbach, 2007; Reese et al., 1995). Latino parents also emphasized collaboration between siblings, which contrasts with U.S. schools' emphasis on independent work (Tharp & Gallimore, 1988).

Because of their focus on children's adaptation to their ecological contexts or niches, researchers using these theoretical frameworks have also investigated family challenges *and* resources associated with children's and adolescents' school adjustment and performance (cf. Alfaro, Umaña-Taylor, & Bámaca, 2006; Auerbach, 2007; Cooper et al., 2002; González, Moll, & Amanti, 2005; Suárez-Orozco & Suárez-Orozco, 1995). These investigators often use their findings to build bridges between families, schools, and peers. In their work on Latino families' *funds of knowledge,* for example, González et al. (2005) identified information and expertise in working-class Latino families that could be incorporated in the classroom to enhance home-school connections and children's achievement. The importance of tapping family resources was also evident in Cooper et al.'s (2002) study of Latino adolescents who were participating in academic preparation programs in middle school and high school or attending a prestigious public university. Despite their parents' limited English proficiency and schooling, the students named them as their most important resource for schooling. The students reported that their parents encouraged them, communicated high educational expectations, and made sacrifices so that they could focus on their schoolwork (see also Fuligni & Perreira, Chapter 7, this volume; Suárez-Orozco & Suárez-Orozco, 2001). High educational aspirations were associated with positive educational outcomes in Catsambis's (2001) analysis of the National Educational Longitudinal Study (NELS:88), although parents also adjust their expectations as their children go through school and the parents obtain information about their children's educational performance and aspirations (Goldenberg, Gallimore, Reese, & Garnier, 2001).

Despite this more positive view of Latino families and students, however, it is still the case that low-income and immigrant Latino families are often challenged by their low levels of parental education, family practices that differ from those emphasized by schools, nonmainstream parent involvement strategies, and, for recent immigrants, low levels of English proficiency (Azmitia, Cooper, García, & Dunbar, 1996; Mehan, Villanueva, Hubbard, & Linz, 1996). For example, due to their inflexible work schedules, child-care and transportation needs, and concerns about how they will be perceived by the school, Latino parents are less likely to volunteer in the classroom and attend school meetings, a mainstream educational practice that teachers use as an index of parental involvement. These parents' nonmainstream practices, such as support and encouragement, engaging older siblings' assistance with homework, and providing advice or *consejos,* are seldom recognized as evidence of parental involvement by teachers, reinforcing the misperception that these parents do not value education (Delgado-Gaitán, 1991; Lopez, 2001).

SOCIAL CAPITAL PERSPECTIVES ON THE FAMILY AND CHILDREN'S AND ADOLESCENTS' EDUCATION

Social capital frameworks (e.g., Bourdieu, 1986; Coleman, 1988; see also Fuligni and Perreira, Chapter 7, this volume) represent another approach to examining resources and challenges in Latino families' role in their children's academic performance and educational trajectories. These frameworks focus on the reproduction of social class (and educational success or failure) across generations. The focus on social class distinguishes this research from the work on parenting and child outcomes reviewed earlier. *Social capital* refers to the resources individuals derive from their networks, such as values, information, socialization and interaction practices, and support. Bourdieu (1986), for example, discussed how the values and practices (or habitus) of the upper class bond its members together, make them recognizable to each other, and create norms of reciprocity that benefit the group and exclude nonmembers.

Coleman (1988) emphasized networks that provide educational guidance and social support to students. He proposed that by virtue of being familiar with U.S. school knowledge, middle- and upper-class parents socialize successful school practices and help their children access guidance and support from such nonfamilial social networks as teachers and community members (see also Lareau, 1989; Stanton-Salazar, 2001). Coleman underscored the importance of parents knowing and collaborating with the parents of their children's friends to supervise their children and socialize their shared values and goals. He noted that these parental networks, as well as Asian parents' initiative in obtaining academic information to guide their children's schooling, accounted for the greater educational success of Asian immigrants relative to other immigrant groups. Coleman's ideas foreshadowed recent studies that have shown that without educational knowledge, social bonds do not foster academic success (e.g., Stanton-Salazar, 2001; Valenzuela & Dornbusch, 1994; but see Azmitia, Cooper, & Brown, 2009). This research has also highlighted other forms of capital that work in concert to increase the quality of social capital. For example, financial capital can enhance families' social capital by increasing their children's educational opportunities and attainment, i.e., their human capital, and allowing parents to live in safer neighborhoods and work in jobs that allow them to spend more time with their children.

Because of their focus on observing and inventorying parents' goals and social interaction processes, ecocultural/sociocultural frameworks can be integrated with social capital frameworks to assess social class variations in parents' educational practices and educational and socialization goals. For example, Gallimore and Goldenberg (1993) observed that working-class Latino parents approached reading books with their young children differently from what has been observed for middle- and upper-class parents (e.g., van Kleeck, Gillam, Hamilton, & McGrath, 1997). In particular, they approached book reading as a context to drill vocabulary and not as a context to improve reading comprehension, the typical focus of middle- and upper-class parents and teachers. Moreno (1991) and Laosa (1982) showed that social class and ethnicity differences in parents' guidance strategies in other types of school-like tasks were linked to parents' educational attainment. Similarly, Desimone's (1999) analysis of the NELS:88 data revealed that although middle-class Latino parents' discussions with their middle-school children about school were positively associated with the children's grades, such was not the case for low-income Latinos. Desimone speculated that differences in the nature of middle-class and low-income parent-child school discussions may account for

these differences, but this speculation needs to be tested empirically. As Portes (2000) noted, it is also necessary to get a clearer shared sense of what constitutes social capital, as the concept has been used in a variety of ways that prevent an integration and strong conclusions from the findings (see also Dika & Singh, 2002).

ACCULTURATION PERSPECTIVES ON THE FAMILY AND LATINO CHILDREN'S AND ADOLESCENTS' EDUCATION

Acculturation provides another framework for examining the role of families in Latino children's and adolescents' achievement and educational trajectories. Typically, this research investigates similarities and differences in foreign-born and U.S.-born Latinos' parenting behaviors and goals as they relate to their children's academic outcomes. Studies contrasting the educational achievement of immigrant and U. S.-born students have revealed an apparent paradox, with some immigrant students outperforming their U.S.-born (and, presumably, more acculturated and English-proficient) peers (Pong, Hao, & Gardner, 2005; Suárez-Orozco & Suárez-Orozco, 2001). Research has linked the paradoxical success of these immigrant students to their parents' high educational aspirations and the students' determination to succeed on behalf of their families (Suárez-Orozco & Suárez-Orozco, 2001; Fuligni & Fuligni, 2007). Kao and Tienda (1998) have also attributed this result to immigrant parents' optimism that their children will succeed academically.

Because of familism's assumed centrality in Latino families and its association with acculturation (cf. Sabogal, Marín, Otero-Sabogal, Marín, & Pérez-Stable, 1987), a handful of studies have considered the relation between Latinos' endorsement of familism and children's and adolescents' educational outcomes. Buriel (1984), for example, theorized that familism might be especially helpful to immigrants who need a sense of identity and self-worth as they try to adapt to an unfamiliar culture. In support of Buriel's proposal, Matute-Bianchi (1991) found that adolescents who were more highly identified with their native Mexican cultural values performed better in school than less culturally identified Mexican-heritage students. When the specific dimensions of familism are considered, however, the findings are mixed. Early research suggested that familism is a liability for education because it privileges such family obligations as chores and child care over schoolwork (e.g., Chacón, Cohen, & Strover, 1986; Heller, 1966; Horowitz, 1981). Subsequently, Valenzuela and Dornbusch (1994) reported a positive link between familism and achievement for high school students, provided their parents had at least a high school education. Yet, Rodriguez (2002) did not find a significant association between familism and adolescents' achievement. The inconsistencies in the findings may reflect conceptual and methodological differences in how familism is operationalized and measured in the various studies. Like social capital, familism has a variety of meanings in the literature, which, coupled with measurement issues, have limited the predictive and explanatory value of the concept. The educational outcome under consideration may also matter—relations between familism and children's and adolescents' educational aspirations and academic motivation are often stronger than those between familism and academic performance (Esparza & Sanchez, 2008; Tseng, 2006). Taken together, the results of these studies provide much-needed information on the role of families in Latino children and adolescents' educational outcomes.

Although the increase in theory and research addressing the diversity of Latino families, their educational goals and practices, and their children's educational outcomes is a welcome addition to the literature, the results from empirical studies are far from consistent, making it very difficult to draw conclusions about the specific family values and practices linked to children's and adolescents' academic achievement. Possibly, the reliance on self-report over observational measures, as well as variations in the operational definitions of the constructs and practices of interest, contribute to the inconsistencies in the literature. In the next section, we focus on another way in which families influence their children's developmental outcomes: by providing the foundation for their peer relationships.

FAMILIES AS FOUNDATIONS FOR PEER RELATIONSHIPS

Despite a large literature on family-peer links in childhood and a growing literature on family-peer links in adolescence, research examining these links for Latinos is scarce. We begin this section by reviewing the ways in which families influence children and adolescents' peer relationships and then review research that has addressed Latino family-peer links. As will be seen, much of this small literature has drawn on the concepts of acculturation and familism to address the ways in which parental values and practices affect children's and adolescents' choices of friends and the time they spend with them. Most of these studies have also employed a between-ethnic comparative design in which the goal is to identify continuities and discontinuities in the family-peer links of different ethnic groups.

Families influence peer relationships by their choice of neighborhoods and schools, by modeling and teaching social skills and conflict resolution strategies, by providing advice about peer relationships and friendships, and by endorsing values and practices that informally or formally encourage or discourage relationships and activities with peers (Mounts & Kim, 2007; Parke, 2004). In research with ethnically diverse children and adolescents, parental behaviors—and in particular their advice, support, and monitoring—have been linked to the quality of their children's friendships as well as to their participation in deviant peer relationships (Mounts, 2004; Way, Greene, & Mukherjee, 2007). Parental monitoring of their children's peer relationships becomes more challenging as they move into adolescence, peers become more salient, and adolescents want to spend more time with their friends. Parents worry that their adolescent children will succumb to peer pressure to engage in such risky behaviors as sex, drugs, and delinquency and thus may try to enlist the support of other parents, schools, and community members to supervise their children (Azmitia & Brown, 2002). As noted by Coleman (1988), when parents know the parents of their children's friends, they are able to monitor their children more effectively. Parents' social networks in the community and school are thus a source of social capital for ensuring their children's well-being (Parke, 2004).

Research has generally revealed that across ethnic groups, children and adolescents view peers and friends as central to their lives and well-being (Levitt, Guacci-Franco, & Levitt, 1994). There are also cross-ethnic similarities in parents' beliefs and concerns about their children's friendships; all parents want their children to form high-quality, positive friendships and avoid friendships with children and adolescents who exhibit problematic behaviors (Mounts & Kim, 2007). However, there are some between- and within-ethnic variations in parents' socialization goals; EA parents are more likely than Latino and AA parents to want their children to have academically oriented friends, and Latino parents are more likely than EA and AA parents to want their children to befriend same-ethnicity peers who share their cultural values (Mounts & Kim, 2007). Also, EA and Latino adolescents are more likely than AA and Asian American (AM) adolescents to report that their parents value their friends and consider them important sources of trust and emotional support (Way et al., 2007).

The centrality of relationships with family versus peers and the degree to which parents restrict their children's activities with friends have received the greatest attention in research. These issues are related to the degree of autonomy parents grant their children, an especially important developmental task of adolescence (Grotevant & Cooper, 1998). These issues also relate to familism and familistic practices, which vary as a function of acculturation. Some studies have shown, for example, that Latino immigrant parents were more likely than Latino second- and third-generation parents to restrict their children's, especially their daughters', contact with friends and to encourage friendships with cousins and siblings (Cooper, Jackson, Azmitia, & Lopez, 1998; Reese, Kroesen, Ryan, & Gallimore, 1998). Although these findings highlight immigrants' greater adherence to familistic values and practices, they may also reflect immigrant parents' protective strategies for the low-income, dangerous neighborhoods they tend to inhabit. For example, Updegraff, Killoren, and Thayer (2007) found that well-educated, middle-class MA parents encouraged their children's peer relationships and orchestrated opportunities for them to be with their peers to a greater degree than did low-income, less educated parents. Updegraff et al. suggested that these social-class differences in MA parents' support of their children's peer relations reflected not only middle-class parents' higher levels of acculturation and endorsement of EA values that promote autonomy, but also the greater safety of their neighborhoods.

In contrast to research considering the relative importance of family and peer relationships, a few studies have examined how these two relationships work in concert to promote positive outcomes in Latino children and adolescents. For example, Cooper et al. (1998, 2002) showed how adolescents who saw their families and friends as espousing similar values and practices had higher self-esteem than adolescents who saw these two relationship worlds as discontinuous. Similarly, Levitt et al. (2005) reported that immigrant children and adolescents who were able to form new friendship networks with the support of their families were better able to weather the stresses of immigration than immigrant children and adolescents who lacked these networks. Unfortunately, this research has not revealed the specific processes through which family-peer links contribute to these positive developmental outcomes.

As can be seen from this brief review, research on Latino family-peer links is still in its infancy. We especially lack research on the specific values, practices, and processes linking these two important relational contexts. It is also important to investigate how these links change with development and the role that children and adolescents play in involving their parents in their peer relationships. Gender variations in parent-peer links also need to be examined. Although there is some suggestion that parents allow sons more contact and freedom with peers than daughters (Azmitia, Ittel, & Brenk, 2006), this restriction does not prevent girls from forming close friendships that are supported by their parents (Way et al., 2007). Research should also consider the role of siblings in Latino children's and adolescents' peer relationships, as siblings may provide an important link between the family and peer contexts. Finally, more work is needed examining between- and within-ethnic-group continuities and discontinuities in family-peer linkages and children's and adolescents' outcomes.

Conclusions and Implications for Future Research

In this chapter, we reviewed the literature examining parenting and family processes and their relations to the development of Latino children and adolescents across the socioemotional, cognitive, educational, and peer domains. Overall, in the field there has been an increased recognition of the importance of the role of culture in family and developmental processes (Quintana et al., 2006) and a corresponding increase in the number of studies focusing on Latino families. The available literature has begun to highlight such culturally invariant parenting processes as sensitivity, as well as such processes as control that appear specific to Latino families. Recognition is also increasing that the Latino subgroup as well as the level of acculturation needs to be considered. Finally, research has begun to consider the links between family processes and developmental outcomes, as well as links between the family context and other important contexts of development, such as peers and schools.

Yet, our understanding of family processes and their relations to Latino children's and adolescents' development is still somewhat limited. Although there are notable exceptions, much of the work in this area has been done from a deficit perspective and has lacked a strong theoretical framework (Rodriguez & Morrobel, 2004). The field is also lagging behind methodologically, most basically in terms of measurement, in that much of the research relies on measures developed for other populations and not validated in Latino samples.

As the field continues to move forward, it will be important to increase the conceptual and methodological sophistication of our approaches to studying Latino families. The research on family process and educational outcomes previously described stands out in its reliance on conceptual frameworks to develop and interpret research; in other areas, research has been largely atheoretical. Theoretical models and conceptual frameworks that take into account the context in which Latino families are embedded appear to be especially suited to studying Latino families in the United States (García Coll et al., 1996). Theoretically driven research is more likely to avoid a deficit perspective and stands to contribute the most to building our knowledge base and integrating the findings from different domains of Latino children's and adolescents' development.

Increased focus on the acculturation process and how it influences family and child development processes will also be important. First, future research should move beyond such widely used proxy measures as language use and should rely on available multidimensional acculturation measures that have been found to reliably assess the acculturation construct more comprehensively (see Gonzales, Fabrett, & Knight, Chapter 8, this volume). Newer acculturation measures also allow for the assessment of involvement in both the mainstream U.S. culture and the Latino culture (i.e., enculturation) independently, allowing for the examination of the role of biculturality on family and child development processes. In addition, the field should also move toward assessing more proximal cultural constructs, such as *familism* and *respeto*, to examine more directly how culture may influence family processes. Further development and refinement of these measures is critically needed. Second, in addition to these improvements in measurement, it will be important to pay closer attention to acculturation and enculturation as moderator variables, as at least some family and child development processes work differently across cultural contexts. A systemic perspective when examining influences of acculturation on the family would also be important in that acculturation may have differential effects on different family subsystems (e.g., maternal acculturation was related to lower hostile parenting but higher marital problems in MA families; Parke et al., 2004). Finally, in examining how acculturation may change parenting, the developmental nature of parenting should be considered, as parents may adapt their parenting according to changes in both their acculturation levels and their children's ages.

Content areas that may be especially important to address in future research include the parenting provided by Latino fathers. Although research in this area is emerging (Cabrera & García Coll, 2004; Cabrera et al., 2006), little is known about the unique characteristics of Latino fathers, their parenting and its influence on children's development, and the role of fathers in coparenting and other family processes. Given demographic characteristics of Latino families, it will also be helpful to study the role of siblings and members of the extended family as socializing agents, as well as triadic and family-level interactions, as the current literature focuses almost exclusively on dyadic (parent-child) interactions. Similarly, given the high birth rates observed among Latina adolescents in the United States, further research will also be needed that takes into account the developmental stage of these young mothers in understanding their parenting as well as their own and their children's developmental outcomes.

As we gain a richer understanding of Latino family processes, it will be important to move beyond descriptive studies and test, prospectively, how these processes relate to Latino children's and adolescents' developmental outcomes across different domains of functioning. In testing these longitudinal associations, it will be critical to follow comprehensive conceptual frameworks that take into account the cultural and sociodemographic ecologies of Latino families and the developmental nature of parenting and other family processes, that pay attention to the great variability observed among Latino families, and that assess outcomes in terms of both mainstream- as well as culture-specific constructs. We hope that this review will stimulate theory and research that help advance our understanding of the family processes that lead to more optimal development among the growing number of Latino children and adolescents in the United States.

NOTE

1. The report did not differentiate between unmarried mothers who were single parents and unmarried mothers who were cohabiting with a partner.

REFERENCES

Ainsworth, M. D., Blehar, M. C., Waters, E., & Wall, S. (1978). *Patterns of attachment: A psychological study of the strange situation.* Hillsdale, NJ: Lawrence Erlbaum.

Alfaro, E. C., Umaña-Taylor, A. J., & Bámaca, M. Y. (2006). The influence of academic support in Latino adolescents' academic motivation. *Family Relations, 55,* 279–291.

Arcia, E., & Johnson, A. (1998). When respect means to obey: Immigrant Mexican mothers' values for their children. *Journal of Child and Family Studies, 7*(1), 79–95.

Auerbach, S. (2007). From moral supporters to struggling advocates: Reconceptualizing parent roles in education through the experience of working-class families of color. *Urban Education, 42,* 250–283.

Azmitia, M., & Brown, J. R. (2002). Latino immigrant parents' beliefs about the "path of life" of their adolescent children. In J. M. Contreras, K. A. Kerns, & A. M. Neal-Barnett (Eds.), *Latino children and families in the United States: Current research and future directions* (pp. 77–105). Westport, CT: Praeger.

Azmitia, M., Cooper, C. R., & Brown, J. R. (2009). Support and guidance from families, friends, and teachers in Latino early adolescents' math pathways. *Journal of Early Adolescence, 29,* 142–169.

Azmitia, M., Cooper, C. R., García, E. E., & Dunbar, N. D. (1996). The ecology of family guidance in low-income Mexican-American and European-American families. *Social Development, 5,* 1–23.

Azmitia, M., Ittel, A., & Brenk, (2006). Latino-heritage adolescents' friendships. In X. Chen, D. C. French, & B. H. Schneider (Eds.), *Peer relationships in cultural context* (pp. 426–451). New York: Cambridge University Press.

Baca Zinn, M., & Wells, B. (2000). Diversity within Latino families: New lessons for family social science. In D. H. Demo, K. R. Allen, & M. A. Fine (Eds.), *Handbook of family diversity* (pp. 252–273). New York: Oxford University Press.

Bachu, A., & O'Connell, M. (2001), *Fertility of American women: June 2000* (Current Population Report No. P20–543RV). Washington, DC: U.S. Census Bureau.

Bohon, S., Jonson, M. K., & Gorman, B. K. (2006). College aspirations and expectations among Latino adolescents in the United States. *Social Problems, 53,* 207–225.

Bourdieu, P. (1986). The forms of capital. In J. G. Richardson (Ed.), *Handbook of theory and research for the sociology of education* (pp. 487–511). New York: Oxford University Press.

Bowlby, J. (1973). *Attachment and loss: Vol. 2. Separation: Anxiety and anger.* New York: Basic Books.

Bowlby, J. (1982). *Attachment and loss: Vol. 1. Attachment* (2nd ed.). New York: Basic Books.

Bronfenbrenner, U., & Morris, P. A. (1998). The ecology of developmental processes. In W. Damon & R. M. Lerner (Eds.), *Handbook of child psychology: Volume 1. Theoretical models of human development* (5th ed., pp. 993–1028). Hoboken, NJ: John Wiley.

Buriel, R. (1984). Integration with traditional Mexican-American culture and sociocultural adjustment. In J. L. Martinez & R. H. Mendoza (Eds.), *Chicano psychology* (2nd ed., pp. 95–130). New York: Academic Press.

Buriel, R. (1993). Childrearing orientations in Mexican American families: The influence of generation and sociocultural factors. *Journal of Marriage and the Family, 55*(4), 987–1000.

Cabrera, N. J., & García Coll, C. (2004). Latino father involvement: Uncharted territory in need of much exploration. In M. E. Lamb (Ed.), *The role of the father in child development* (4th ed., pp. 98–120). Hoboken, NJ: John Wiley.

Cabrera, N. J., Shannon, J. D., West, J., & Brooks-Gunn, J. (2006). Parental interactions with Latino infants: Variation by country of origin and English proficiency. *Child Development, 77*(5), 1190–1207.

Cardona, P., Nicholson, B., & Fox, R. (2000). Parenting among Hispanic and Anglo-American mothers with young children. *Journal of Social Psychology, 140,* 357–365.

Carlson, V., & Harwood, R. (2003). Attachment, culture, and the caregiving system: The cultural patterning of everyday experiences among Anglo and Puerto Rican mother-infant pairs. *Infant Mental Health Journal, 24,* 53–73.

Catsambis, S. (2001). Expanding knowledge of parental involvement in children's secondary education: Connections with high school seniors' academic success. *Social Psychology of Education, 5,* 149–177.

Cauce, A. M., & Domenech-Rodriguez, M. (2002). Latino families: Myths and realities. In J. Contreras, K. Kerns, & A. Neal-Barnett, (Eds.), *Latino children and families: Current research and future directions*. Westport, CT: Praeger.

Chacón, M. A., Cohen, E. G., & Strover, S. (1986). Chicanas and Chicanos: Barriers to progress in higher education. In M. A. Olivas (Ed.), *Latino college students* (pp. 296–324). New York: Teachers College Press.

Coleman, J. S. (1988). Social capital in the creation of human capital. *American Journal of Sociology Supplement, 94,* 95–120.

Contreras, J. (2004). Parenting behaviors among mainland Puerto Rican adolescent mothers: The role of grandmother and partner involvement. *Journal of Research on Adolescence, 14,* 341–368.

Contreras, J., López, I., Rivera, E., Raymond-Smith, L., & Rothstein, K. (1999). Social support among Puerto Rican adolescent mothers: The moderating effect of acculturation. *Journal of Family Psychology, 13,* 228–243.

Contreras, J., Mangelsdorf, S., Rhodes, J., Diener, M., & Brunson, L. (1999). Parent-child interaction among Latina adolescent mothers: The role of family and social support. *Journal of Research on Adolescence, 9,* 417–439.

Contreras, J., Narang, D., Ikhlas, M., & Teichman, J. (2002). A conceptual model of the determinants of parenting among Latina adolescent mothers. In J. Contreras, K. Kerns, & A. Neal-Barnett, (Eds.), *Latino children and families in the United States: Current research and future directions* (pp. 155–177). Westport, CT: Praeger.

Cooper, C. R., Cooper, R. G., Azmitia, M., Chavira, G., & Gullatt, Y. (2002). Bridging multiple worlds: How African American and Latino youth in academic outreach programs navigate math pathways to college. *Applied Developmental Science, 6,* 73–87.

Cooper, C. R., Jackson, J. F., Azmitia, M., & Lopez, E. M. (1998). Multiple selves, multiple worlds: Three useful strategies for research with ethnic minority youth on identity, relationships, and opportunity structures. In V. C. McLoyd & L. Steinberg (Eds.), *Studying minority adolescents: Conceptual, methodological, and theoretical issues* (pp. 111–125). Mahwah, NJ: Lawrence Erlbaum.

Delgado-Gaitán, C. (1991). Involving parents in the schools: A process of empowerment. *American Journal of Education, 100,* 20–46.

Desimone, L. (1999). Linking parent involvement with student achievement: Do race and income matter? *Journal of Educational Research, 93,* 11–30.

DeWolff, M., & van Ijzendoorn, M. (1997). Sensitivity and attachment: A meta-analysis on parental antecedents of infant attachment. *Child Development, 68,* 571–591.

Dika, S. L., & Singh, K. (2002). Applications of social capital in educational literature: A critical synthesis. *Review of Educational Research, 72,* 31–60.

Esparza, P., & Sanchez, B. (2008). The role of attitudinal familism in academic outcomes: A study of urban, Latino high school seniors. *Cultural Diversity and Ethnic Minority Psychology, 14,* 193–200.

Fracasso, M., Busch, N., & Fisher, C. (1994). The relationship of maternal behavior and acculturation to the quality of attachment in Hispanic infants living in New York City. *Hispanic Journal of Behavioral Sciences, 16,* 143–154.

Fuligni, A. J., & Fuligni, A. S. (2007). Immigrant families and the educational development of their children. In J. Lansford, K. Deater-Deckard, & M. Bornstein (Eds.), *Immigrant families in America* (pp. 231–249). New York: Guilford Press.

Gallimore, R., & Goldenberg, C. (1993). Activity settings of early literacy: Home and school factors in children's emergent literacy. In E. Forman, N. Minick, & C. A. Stone (Eds.), *Contexts for learning: Sociocultural dynamics in children's development* (pp. 315–335). Oxford, UK: Oxford University Press.

Gándara, P. (1995). *Over the ivy walls: The educational mobility of low-income Chicanos.* Albany: State University of New York Press.

García Coll, C., Lamberty, G., Jenkins, R., McAdoo, H. P., Crnic, K., Wasik, B. H., et al. (1996). An integrative model for the study of developmental competencies in minority children. *Child Development, 67,* 1891–1914.

García Coll, C., & Vazquez García, H. (1996). Definitions of competence during adolescence: Lessons from Puerto Rican adolescent mothers. In D. Cicchetti & S. Toth (Eds.), *Rochester Symposium on Developmental Psychology: Vol. 7. Adolescence: Opportunities and challenges* (pp. 283–308). New York: University of Rochester Press.

Goldenberg, C., Gallimore, R., Reese, L., & Garnier, H. (2001). Cause or effect? A longitudinal study of immigrant Latino parents' aspirations and expectations, and their children's school performance. *American Educational Research Journal, 38,* 547–582.

Gonzales, N., Pitts, S., Hill, N., & Roosa, M. (2000). A mediational model of the impact of interparental conflict on child adjustment in a multiethnic, low-income sample. *Journal of Family Psychology, 14,* 365–379.

González, N., Moll, L. C., & Amanti, C. (2005). *Funds of knowledge: Theorizing practices in households, communities, and classrooms.* Mahwah, NJ: Lawrence Erlbaum.

Gonzalez-Ramos, G., Zayas, L., & Cohen, E. (1998). Child-rearing values of low-income, urban Puerto Rican mothers of preschool children. *Professional Psychology: Research and Practice, 29,* 377–382.

Grotevant, H. D., & Cooper, C. R. (1998). Individuality and connectedness in adolescent development: Review and prospects for research on identity, relationships, and context. In E. Aspaas Skoe & A. L. von der Lippe (Eds.), *Personality development in adolescence: A cross national and life span perspective* (pp. 3–37). London: Routledge.

Halgunseth, L. C., Ispa, J. M., & Rudy, D. (2006). Parental control in Latino families: An integrated review of the literature. *Child Development, 77*(5), 1282–1297.

Harwood, R. L., Miller, A. M., Carlson, V., & Leyendecker, B. (2002). Child-rearing beliefs and practices during feeding among middle-class Puerto Rican and Anglo mother-infant pairs. In J. M. Contreras, K. A. Kerns, & A. Neal-Barnett (Eds.). *Latino children and families in the United States: Current research and future directions* (pp. 253–264). New York: Praeger.

Harwood, R. L., Schoelmerich, A., Schulze, P. A., & Gonzalez, Z. (1999). Cultural influences in maternal beliefs and behaviors: A study of middle-class Anglo and Puerto Rican mother-infant pairs in four everyday situations. *Child Development, 70,* 1005–1116.

Heller, C. (1966). *Mexican-American youth: Forgotten youth at the crossroads.* New York: Random House.

Hill, N., Bush, K., & Roosa, M. (2003). Parenting and family socialization strategies and children's

mental health: Low-income Mexican-American and Euro-American mothers and children. *Child Development, 74,* 189–204.

Horowitz, R. (1981). Passion, submission and motherhood: The negotiation of identity by unmarried innercity Chicanas. *Sociological Quarterly, 22,* 241–252.

Ispa, J., Fine, M., Halgunseth, L., Harper, S., Robinson, J., Boyce, L., et al. (2004). Maternal intrusiveness, maternal warmth, and mother-toddler relationship outcomes: Variations across low-income ethnic and acculturation groups. *Child Development, 75,* 1613–1631.

Kao, G., & Tienda, M. (1998). Educational aspirations of minority youth. *American Education Research Journal, 106,* 349–384.

Knight, G., Virdin, L., & Roosa, M. (1994). Socialization and family correlates of mental health outcomes among Hispanic and Anglo American children: Consideration of cross-ethnic scalar equivalence. *Child Development, 65,* 212–224.

Laosa, L. M. (1978). Maternal teaching strategies in Chicano families of varied educational and socioeconomic levels. *Child Development, 49,* 1129–1135.

Laosa, L. M. (1980). Maternal teaching strategies in Chicano and Anglo-American families: The influence of culture and education on maternal behavior. *Child Development, 51,* 759–765.

Laosa, L. (1982). School, occupation, culture, and family: The impact of parental schooling on the parent-child relationship. *Journal of Educational Psychology, 74,* 791–827.

Lareau, G. (1989). *Home advantage: Social class and parental intervention in elementary education.* New York: Falmer Press.

Levitt, M. J., Guacci-Franco, N., & Levitt, J. L. (1994). Social support and achievement in childhood and early adolescence: A multicultural study. *Journal of Applied Developmental Psychology, 15,* 207–222.

Levitt, M. J., Levitt, J., Hodgetts, J., Lane, J. D., Pérez, E. I., & Pierre, F. (2005, April). *Social networks of newly immigrated children and adolescents: network disruption and change over time.* Paper presented at the biennial meeting of the Society for Research in Child Development, Atlanta, GA.

López, G. R. (2001). The value of hard work: Lessons on parent involvement from an (im)migrant household. *Harvard Educational Review, 7,* 416–437.

Martinez, C. (1988). Child behavior in Mexican American/Chicano families: Maternal teaching and child-rearing practices. *Family Relations, 37,* 275–280.

Martinez, C. R., Jr., DeGarmo, D. S., & Mark, E. J. (2004). Promoting academic success among

Latino youths. *Hispanic Journal of Behavioral Sciences, 26,* 128–151.

Matute-Bianchi, M. E. (1991). Situational ethnicity and patterns of school performance among immigrant and non-immigrant Mexican-descent students. In M. A. Gibson & J. U. Ogbu (Eds.), *Minority status and schooling: A comparative study of immigrant and involuntary minorities* (pp. 205–248). New York: Garland.

Mehan, H., Villanueva, I., Hubbard, L., & Linz, A. (1996). *Constructing school success: The consequences of untracking low achieving students.* Cambridge, MA: Cambridge University Press.

Mejía-Arauz, R., Rogoff, B., Dexter, A., & Najafi, B. (2007). Cultural variation in children's social organization. *Child Development, 78*(3), 1001–1014.

Mooney, M., & Rivas-Drake, D. (2008, March 28). Colleges need to recognize, and serve, the 3 kinds of Latino students. *Chronicle of Higher Education,* p. A37.

Moreno, R. P. (1991). Maternal teaching of preschool children in minority and low-status families: A critical review. *Early Childhood Research Quarterly, 6,* 395–410.

Mounts, N. S. (2004). Adolescents' perceptions of parental management of peer relationships in an ethnically diverse sample. *Journal of Adolescent Research, 19,* 446–467.

Mounts, N. S., & Kim, H. (2007). Parental goals regarding peer relationships and management of peers in a multiethnic sample. *New Directions for Child and Adolescent Development, 116,* 17–33.

Ogbu, J. (1981). Origins of human competence: A cultural ecological perspective. *Child Development, 52,* 413–429.

Padilla, A. (1980). *Acculturation: Theory, models, and some new findings.* Boulder, CO: Westview.

Parke, R. D. (2004). Development in the family. *Annual Review of Psychology, 33,* 365–399.

Parke, R. D., Coltrane, S., Duffy, S., Buriel, R., Dennis, J., Powers, J., et al. (2004). Economic stress, parenting, and child adjustment in Mexican American and European American families. *Child Development, 75*(6), 1632–1656.

Pew Hispanic Center (2004). *Latino teens staying in high school: A challenge for all generations.* Washington, DC: Author.

Planos, R., Zayas, L., & Bush-Rossnagel, N. (1995). Acculturation and teaching behaviors of Dominican and Puerto Rican mothers. *Hispanic Journal of Behavioral Sciences, 17,* 225–236.

Pong, S., Hao, L., & Gardner, E. (2005). The roles of parenting styles and social capital in the school performance of immigrant Asian and Hispanic adolescents. *Social Science Quarterly, 86,* 928–950.

Population Resource Center (2004, March). *Latina teen pregnancy: Problems and prevention.* Retrieved February 21, 2009, from http://www.prcdc.org/files/Latina_Teen_Pregnancy.pdf

Portes, A. (2000). The two meanings of social capital. *Sociological Forum, 15,* 1–12.

Quintana, S., Aboud, F., Chao, R., Contreras-Grau, J., Cross, W., Hudley, C., et al. (2006). Race, ethnicity, and culture in child development: Contemporary research and future directions. *Child Development, 77,* 1129–1141.

Raver, C. C., Gershoff, E. T., & Aber, J. L. (2007). Testing equivalence of mediating models of income, parenting, and school readiness for White, Black, and Hispanic children in a national sample. *Child Development, 78*(1), 96–115.

Reese, L., Kroesen, K., Ryan, G., & Gallimore, R. (1998, March). *Exploring Latino adolescents' worlds through multiple methods.* Paper presented at the meeting of the Linguistic Minority Research Institute, Santa Cruz, CA.

Reese, L. S., Balzano, R., Gallimore, R., & Goldenberg, C. (1995). The concept of educación: Latino family values and American schooling. *International Journal of Educational Research, 23,* 57–81.

Rodriguez, J. L. (2002). Family environment and achievement among three generations of Mexican American high school students. *Applied Developmental Science, 6,* 88–94.

Rodriguez, M., & Morrobel, D. (2004). A review of Latino youth development research and a call for an asset orientation. *Hispanic Journal of Behavioral Sciences, 26,* 107–127.

Rogoff, B. (2003). *The cultural nature of human development.* New York: Oxford University Press.

Sabogal, F., Marín, G., Otero-Sabogal, R., Marín, B. V., & Pérez-Stable, E. J. (1987). Hispanic familism and acculturation: What changes and what doesn't? *Hispanic Journal of Behavioral Sciences, 9,* 397–412.

Scholmerich, A., Lamb, M. E., Leyendecker, B., & Fracasso, M. (1997). Mother-infant teaching interactions and attachment security in Euro-American and Central-American immigrant families. *Infant Behavior and Development, 20,* 165–174.

Solórzano, D. G. (1992). An exploratory analysis of the effects of race, class, and gender on student and parent mobility aspirations. *Journal of Negro Education, 61,* 30–44.

Stanton-Salazar, R. D. (2001). *Manufacturing hope and despair: The school and kin support networks of U.S.-Mexican youth.* New York: Teachers College Press.

Suárez-Orozco, C., & Suárez-Orozco, M. M. (1995). *Transformations: Immigration, family life, and achievement motivation among Latino adolescents.* Stanford, CA: Stanford University Press.

Suárez-Orozco, C., & Suárez-Orozco, M. M (2001). *Children of immigration.* Cambridge, MA: Harvard University Press.

Suro, R. (2007). *The Hispanic family in flux.* Center on Children and Families Working Paper. Washington, DC: Brookings Institution.

Suro, R., Kocchar, R., Passel, J., Escobar, G., Tafoya, S., Fry, R., et al. (2007). *The American Community—Hispanics: 2004.* Washington, DC: Pew Hispanic Center/U.S. Census Bureau.

Teichman, J., & Contreras-Grau, J. (2006). Acculturation and teaching styles among young mainland Puerto Rican mothers. *Hispanic Journal of Behavioral Sciences, 28,* 84–101.

Tharp, R. G., & Gallimore, R. (1988). *Rousing minds to life: Teaching, learning, and schooling in social context.* New York: Cambridge University Press.

Tseng, V. (2006). Unpacking immigration in youths' academic and occupational pathways. *Child Development, 77,* 1434–1445.

Updegraff, K. A., Killoren, S. E., & Thayer, S. M. (2007). Mexican-origin parents' involvement in adolescent peer relationships: A pattern analytic approach. *New Directions for Child and Adolescent Development, 116,* 51–65.

U.S. Census Bureau (2006, September 5). *Facts for Features: Hispanic Heritage Month.* Retrieved February 21, 2009, from http://www.census.gov/Press-Release/www/releases/archives/ facts_for_features_special_editions/007173.html

Valencia, R. R., & Black, M. S. (2002). "Mexican Americans don't value education!" On the basis of the myth, mythmaking, and debunking. *Journal of Latinos and Education, 1,* 81–103.

Valenzuela, A., & Dornbusch, S. M. (1994). Familism and social capital in the academic achievement of Mexican origin and Anglo adolescents. *Social Science Quarterly, 75,* 18–36.

Van Kleeck, A., Gillam, R. B., Hamilton, L., & McGrath, C. (1997). The relationship between middle-class parents' book-sharing discussion and their preschoolers' abstract language development. *Journal of Speech & Hearing Research, 40,* 1261–1271.

Way, N., Greene, M. L., & Mukherjee, P. P. (2007). Exploring adolescent perceptions of parental beliefs and practices related to friendships i n diverse ethnic communities. *New Directions for Child and Adolescent Development, 116,* 35–50.

Williams, B. (2003). What else do we need to know and do? In B. Williams (Ed.), *Closing the achievement gap* (pp. 13–24). Alexandria, VA: Association for Supervision and Curriculum Development.

11

A View From Within and From Without

The Development of Latina Feminist Psychology

Aída Hurtado and Karina Cervantez

The field of Latina[1] feminist psychology is relatively new, developed in the 1980s in tandem with the field of feminist psychology (Russo & Vaz, 2001). Although during the inception of the field there were not many Latina psychologists—and the number remains low—the few that were present had a significant role in developing the field of feminist psychology and were part of the broader intellectual movement to increase diversity in all academic fields. According to Russo and Vaz (2001),

> Diversity has become a concept that encompasses the complexities of dealing with effects of multiple and intersecting social categories. The term is used as shorthand to describe approaches that examine effects of different combinations of these categories. Although attempts to "understand diversity" often incorporate the categories of gender, race, and class, a whole host of social dimensions can be added to the mix. . . . One dimension of diversity of special interest to feminists reflects inequalities in power and privilege. Feminist psychologists have a basic commitment to social action. (p. 280)

Latina feminist psychology is committed to diversity as delineated by Russo and Vaz (2001), with added emphasis on Latino cultures and histories, the importance of the Spanish language, and the examination of structural variables that affect power and privilege for the Latino/a populations in the United States. For Latinas, the relevant social categories that affect access to power and privilege in U.S. society are gender, ethnicity, race, class, and sexuality (and in some cases physical ableness). Latina feminist psychology has been concerned with exploring the consequences for women's lives when these categories intersect. For purposes of this review, we cover the research areas that have received the most attention: the influence of cultural values on identity, identity's influence on therapeutic approaches with Latinas, and feminism, including feminist theory.

We begin by providing a historical overview of the assimilation/acculturation frameworks, the predominant theoretical approaches used in the 1970s through the 1990s to study Latinos/as' identities. We continue the section on identity with Tajfel's (1981) social identity theory, a more contemporary approach than the assimilation/ acculturation frameworks, to study Latinos/as' identifications. We outline the distinction, originally made by Tajfel and used by many social psychologists, between *personal* and *social identity*—a distinction that practitioners have used in developing therapeutic approaches that take into account Latinas' social identities, especially those that are a source of stigmatization, like race, class, ethnicity, gender, and sexuality.

The contributions of Latina feminist psychology to feminist theory are also discussed. In particular, the writers of Latina feminist psychology have expanded the definition of feminism. These writers place an emphasis on the history of the different Latino/a groups in the United States and advocate the inclusion of language and culture in the definition of feminism. Many of the writers of Latina feminist psychology have adopted borderland theory, as proposed by creative writer and essayist Gloria Anzaldúa, to further expand the concept of intersectionality first introduced by African American feminists. Borderland theory and intersectionality recognize that Latinas, as well as other women, suffer subordination based not only on their gender, but also on other stigmatized social categories, primarily race, class, ethnicity, sexuality, and physical ableness—the same social categories Tajfel (1981) proposes as constituting individuals' social identities. We conclude by summarizing the main concepts covered in this review of Latina feminist psychology and provide some areas for future research.

A View From Within and From Without: The Writers of Latina Feminist Psychology

The writings in these areas have been produced by Latina as well as non-Latina writers, providing a variety of perspectives from within the group as well as outside of it. The writers of Latina feminist psychology have differences in terms of race, class, ethnicity, age, and specialty within psychology. However, they also have an overarching commitment to analyzing gender as an integral part of other social categories. The approach taken by the writers of Latina feminist psychology, regardless of differences in backgrounds, is what Russo and Vaz (2001) call *diversity mindfulness,* which

. . . involves the process of perceiving and processing a multiplicity of differences among individuals, their social contexts, and their cultures. Diversity-mindfulness from a feminist perspective incorporates the feminist values of diversity, egalitarianism, and inclusiveness into critical analyses. It also recognizes the need for complex, context-based viewpoints that are incongruent with traditional intrapsychic theorizing and reductionist research methods (Comas-Díaz, 1991; Espín, 1997; 1999; Landrine, 1995a; Mays & Comas-Díaz, 1988; Reid & Comas-Díaz, 1990; Russo & Dabul, 1994; Worell & Etaugh, 1994). (p. 281)

In an effort to adhere to diversity mindfulness, most non-Latina writers have partnered with Latinas to insure that in producing Latina feminist psychology they have done justice to the complexities of Latinas' lives and experiences.

Studies do not need to adhere simultaneously to all of the principles outlined by Russo and Vaz (2001) in their concept of diversity mindfulness; rather, it is a theoretical and empirical standpoint in which self-reflexivity and inclusivity are built into the process of theorizing and conducting empirical research. The hope is that inserting diversity mindfulness into research practices will result in more egalitarian and fair-minded scholarship than has been conducted in the past. As an integral part of diversity mindfulness, the writers of Latina feminist psychology employ a variety of research methods. For example, Espín (1996) conducted life histories with lesbians who immigrated from Cuba to avoid the stigmatization and political repression in their native country because of their sexuality. She was interested in documenting the identity changes undergone by her respondents as a result of the immigration process and coming out as lesbians upon their arrival to the United States. Hurtado (2003b) conducted qualitative interviews with 101 educationally successful Chicanas (Mexican-descent Latinas) to explore their views on feminism from an intersectional perspective. Pastor and her colleagues (2007) used participant action research (PAR) to develop a collaboration between academic researchers and middle and high school students to examine the obstacles and inequalities students face in school. The academic researchers teach the students research methods, and the research team produces art pieces (spoken words and such as poetry readings), perform their work. In addition, the students collaborates on the writing of the final product for academic publication. Latina feminist psychology use of the variety of research methods is an integral part of producing a more egalitarian scholarship than is usually produced by a narrower range of research methods (Fine, 2006).

We now address identity as one of the major research areas in Latina feminist psychology.

IDENTITY

A Brief History of the Acculturation/ Assimilation Frameworks in the Study of Latino/a Identity

One of the earliest areas of focus in the study of Latinas was the issue of identity. Most researchers adhere to the classic definition of assimilation as "a process of interpenetration and fusion in which persons and groups acquire the memories, sentiments, and attitudes of other persons and groups, and, by sharing their experience and history, are incorporated with them in a common cultural life" (Park & Burgess, 1921, p. 735). The assimilation/acculturation framework was furthered developed in Milton Gordon's influential book, *Assimilation in American Life* (1964). The early research on Latino/a identity explored the process of cultural assimilation within Latino/a communities and focused on the degree to which individuals changed their personal identities to reflect the values and attitudes of the white mainstream. Early assimilation measures listed traits (e.g., work ethic, future orientation, achievement motivation) associated with white, middle-class culture and asked Latinos/as to rate themselves on these personal dimensions (Schlachet, 1975; Wallendorf & Reilly, 1983). Many studies highlighted the negative aspects and psychological difficulties encountered by individuals who did not incorporate these (considered white) cultural values quickly enough to succeed in U.S. society (Montgomery, 1992; Portes & Zhou, 1993). Later studies refined the concept of assimilation and included the process of acculturation. It was assumed that it was feasible for individuals to have more than one language and more than one set of cultural values and norms without conflict (Chun, Balls Organista, & Marín, 2003). According to this research, the most appropriate adaptation for Latinos/as was

to become bicultural in U.S. mainstream culture and in the culture of their national origin (see Hurtado, 1997, for a historical review of the concepts of assimilation and acculturation).

However, even in Gordon's elaboration, the assimilation and acculturation frameworks did not address gender, and the frameworks were "uncritically applied to all [ethnic] groups" to explain their cultural adaptations "regardless of race, history in the U.S., forms of incorporation in the U.S., or reasons for immigrating" (Hurtado, 1997, p. 301). The exclusion of gender posed a special set of questions for Latina women. The assimilation/acculturation framework conceptualizes Latino cultures, regardless of national origin, as having rigid familial roles and extreme physical and psychological restrictions based on gender (Fine, Roberts, & Weiss, 2000). Latinas were forced to negotiate archaic notions of womanhood that placed enormous psychological stress on them. Undoubtedly, the issues of acculturation stress and its mental health consequences were an important area of study. By emphasizing maladaptation as a result of not assimilating quickly enough into U.S. middle-class values and culture, the full diversity of cultural adaptations to intergroup cultural contact was weighed heavily toward a "cultural deficit" framework (Valencia, 1997). The more Latinos/as retained their culture, the less likely they were to function well and succeed in U.S. society.

Feminist Deconstructions of the Assimilation/Acculturation Frameworks

Latina feminist psychologists struggled with the limitations of the assimilation/acculturation frameworks, which examined only one social category at a time and did not take into account the complexity of Latinas' multiple social identities. During the 1980s, as Latina feminist psychologists began questioning the usefulness and completeness of the assimilation/acculturation paradigm, the feminist movement was in full swing in the United States as well as in other countries, including Latin America (Alvarez, 2000; Colón Warren, 2003). Although the feminist agendas in the United States and Latin America differed, they also had important similarities—an emphasis on "expanded schooling, housing, health, birth control, and other social services" for women (Colón Warren, 2003, p. 665). As such, patriarchal privilege, rather than culture alone, came within the scope of analysis to explain the condition of Latinas in the United States (Hurtado, 1996a).

Although both Latin American and U.S. feminist psychology moved away from purely cultural explanations for gender relations in their respective communities, they nonetheless also critiqued Latino culture regardless of national origins. Latin American and the writers of U.S. Latina feminist psychology have always stressed the fluid and changing nature of culture, placing emphasis on cultural change (not only on cultural maintenance). Their critique is especially poignant when the cultural practices and norms are sexist, homophobic, classist, or otherwise oppressive. The critique of Latino culture, however, was within the framework of cultural solidarity and maintenance (Hurtado, 2003b) rather than advocating assimilation into hegemonic, white, middle-class, U.S. cultural practices and norms. After all, U.S. culture is also based on patriarchy, a system that gave birth to the white (mostly middle-class) feminist movement (Mankiller, Mink, Navarro, Smith, & Steinem, 1998).

Many Latina and non-Latina psychologists began to address Latinas from a feminist perspective, analyzing their condition as women existing within certain cultural groups and as individuals imbedded in multiple social systems that systematically blocked their access to economic and social resources (Hurtado, 1996b). At this point, research on Latinas was moving toward a diversity of analyses and expanding the examination of identity beyond mere culture to include issues of gender, class, ethnicity, race, sexuality, and physical ableness—a paradigm that later came to be known as *intersectionality* (Collins, 2000; Crenshaw, 1989, 1995; Hurtado, 2003b).

Latina Feminist Psychology and Social Identity Theory

Besides the consideration of multiple social categories as part of Latinas' identity, another important theoretical development was the distinction made by some researchers between personal identity and social identity, both components of an integrated self (Hurtado & Gurin, 2004). Social psychologists argue that although personal and social identity are not entirely independent of each other, neither are they one and the same (Tajfel, 1981). Personality and developmental psychology do not necessarily

make the same level of distinction between personal and social identity made by Tajfel (1981) and his adherents. The writers of Latina feminist psychology, however, have found Tajfel's proposed theoretical distinction very helpful in avoiding dispositionalism—that is, the tendency in the field of psychology to overattribute all behavior to individual characteristics (mostly encased in the concept of personality or in such personality traits as self-esteem) and to underestimate the influence on behavior of social context and structural variables (Haney & Zimbardo, in press).

The distinction between personal identity and social identity stems from Henri Tajfel's (1981) social identity theory, which posits that personal identity is that aspect of self composed of psychological traits and dispositions that give rise to personal uniqueness. Personal identity is derived from intrapsychic influences, many of which are socialized within family units, however they are defined (Hurtado, 1997). From this perspective, human beings have a great deal in common, precisely because their personal identities are composed of universal processes, such as loving, mating, doing productive work—activities that are considered universal components of self. Personal identity is much more stable and coherent over time than social identity. Although social context may affect the degree to which an individual's personal identity is manifested, most individuals do not have multiple personal identities (Hurtado, 1996b); that is, a shy person may be less or more shy depending on the social context, but getting rid of shyness often takes years of professional treatment (Henderson & Zimbardo, 2001; Zimbardo, 1990).

In contrast, *social identity* is that aspect of self derived from the knowledge of being part of social categories and groups, together with the value and emotional significance attached to those group formations (Hurtado, 1997). Tajfel (1981) argues that social identities are the outcome of three social psychological processes. The first is *social categorization*. Nationality, language, race and ethnicity, skin color, or other social or physical characteristics that are meaningful in particular social contexts can be the basis for social categorization and thus the foundation for the creation of social identities. For example, Colón Warren (2003) writes about the differences in the assignment to the race category "black" of Puerto Ricans in the United States versus those in Puerto Rico:

The dichotomous racialization that is imposed in Puerto Rico by dominant (white) sectors in the United States on African Americans, as well as on colonized populations and "unassimilated" migrants (Briggs, 2002; Santiago-Valles, 1999a, 1999b), contrasts with the hierarchy of racial mixture in Puerto Rico. On the Island, race ranges along a continuum from white to Black, running through a variety of categories related to the presence of particular pherotypical traits, such as mulatto, *trigueño* (lighter skinned or as a euphemism for Black), or *grifo* (tight, curly hair) (Jorge, 1986). It is also more evidently a social definition, based on behavior as well as on physical characteristics, so that moving from a lower to a higher social status could allow for a person's whitening (Suárez Findlay, 1999). (p. 668)

As a result of these differences in race assignment, from a continuum in Puerto Rico to a dichotomous one in the United States, Puerto Ricans migrating to the U.S. mainland from the island have to readjust their self-perceptions around issues of race—from a phenotypic description (e.g., *morenito*, "a bit dark") to the racial category "black." Tajfel (1981) would call the change in "race" assignment joining a stigmatized social category tied historically to the institution of slavery and thus also tied to negative political and social connotations.

Another process underlying the construction of social identities is *social comparison*. In this process, a group's status, degree of affluence, or other characteristic achieves significance *in relation to* perceived differences and their value connotations from other social formations. For example, Hurtado (2003b) found in her qualitative study of educated Chicanas that participants considered themselves "middle class" when they lived in predominantly working-class communities. Upon entering institutions of higher education attended largely by middle- and upper-class white students, the participants shifted their comparison from neighborhood to college peers and reassessed their class identification, most often from middle class to poor or working class.

The third process involves *psychological work*, both cognitive and emotional, that is prompted by what Tajfel (1981) assumes is a universal motive—the achievement of a positive sense of self. The social groups that present the greatest obstacles to a positive sense of self are those that are disparaged, whose memberships have to be negotiated frequently because of their visibility, and that have become politicized by social movements. These group memberships are the most likely to become problematic social identities for individuals. Stigmatized social categorizations have to be negotiated every time they become socially relevant. For example, a Latina student entering an all-white university classroom headed by a white professor will more than likely immediately focus on her *latinidad*. Were she to enter a classroom either with all Latinos/as or with students of varying ethnicities, her *latinidad* might not be as socially relevant in the classroom and therefore, according to Tajfel (1981), might not require psychological work.

Moreover, stigmatized social identities become especially powerful psychologically; they are easily accessible and dwelt upon, are apt to be salient across situations, and are likely to function as schemas, frameworks, or social scripts (Gurin, Hurtado, & Peng, 1994). For example, a poor Latina with a physical disability is more likely to reflect on her social identities than is a wealthy, white, heterosexual male with no physical impediments. Unproblematic group memberships—ones that are socially valued or accorded privilege and are not obvious to others—may not even become social identities. Until very recently with the emergence of whiteness studies, being racially white was not the subject of inquiry, and it is still not widely thought of as a social identity (Fine, Weis, Powell Pruitt, & Burns, 2004; Hurtado & Stewart, 2004; Phinney, 1996). Although there may be different groups of whites, for example, varying by class—poor whites versus middle-class whites—the privileges accrued because of the racial benefits of whiteness are not easily articulated by its possessors, regardless of class, because white race privilege is considered the norm in the United States (McIntosh, 1992).

Social identities gain particular significance when they are based on what sociologists call *master statuses*. Race, social class, gender, ethnicity, physical challenges, and sexuality are the social identities assigned master statuses because individuals must psychologically negotiate their potentially stigmatizing effects. In the United States, as in many other countries, master statuses are used to make value judgments about group memberships. Tajfel's theory of social identity, which has been elaborated upon by others (Gurin et al., 1994; Hogg, 2006, 2008; Hurtado, 1997), provides a sophisticated framework for understanding how individuals make sense of their group memberships—both unproblematic and stigmatized ones.

Personal identity and social identity has been used in Latina feminist writings to understand individual outcomes (microprocesses) as a result of cultural and language practices among Latinas. Social identity has been used to understand group outcomes (macroprocesses) based on memberships in ethnic, race, class, sexuality, and physical ableness. The distinction between personal and social identity prevents the treatment of all social issues as rooted in individual psychologies correctable only by reshaping individual behaviors and leaving structural forces unexamined. In addition, this theoretical distinction validates *individual-level interventions* therapy in Spanish, such as increasing women's sense of self-efficacy and empowerment (Enns, in press) as solutions to Latinas' gender socialization when it results in negative consequences, such as remaining in a violent relationship with a partner (Flores-Ortiz, 2004). The theoretical distinction also validates *group-level interventions* such as providing workshops on the academic requirements for college admission to Latina mothers who have not had the opportunity to obtain education to help their daughters succeed educationally (Hurtado, Cervantez, & Eccleston, in press). Most recently, the writers of Latina feminist psychology have begun to explore the connections between individual and social identities, expanding the study of identity to be more inclusive and well-rounded rather than simply focusing on individual identity or on social identity (Azmitia, Syed, & Radmacher, 2008).

We turn now to the application of Latina feminist psychology by practitioners and how it addresses the obstacles encountered by Latinas in the United States.

Identity and Therapeutic Approaches With Latinas

Psychology as a discipline focuses on the understanding of individual behavior, and has developed powerful techniques of intervention to alleviate individual maladies, be it in the clinical area, in public health, or in school settings, among many other arenas. Latina feminist psychology has become very important in developing the appropriate therapeutic interventions by highlighting the importance of culturally sensitive modes of treatment, and by placing gender at the center of analyses rather than treating it as a "background" or "control variable" (Leaper, 1996). Instead, gender is conceptualized as a "relational social location rather than a fixed biological category" (Hurtado, 1997, p. 31). Stewart (1994) advocates treating "gender as defining power relations and being constructed by them" (p. 12).

In developing intervention techniques, the writers of Latina feminist psychology have also expanded the definitions of approved clinical practices. Vasquez (2007), for example, complicates the ethics code of the American Psychological Association (APA) in reference to the boundaries that are appropriate to cross between therapist and client when dealing with culturally diverse populations. Vasquez argues that a frequent challenge for psychotherapists is "whether or not to rigidly apply boundaries" or allow for more flexible ones that "one crosses from time to time" depending on the client's cultural and language background. A therapist's lack of cultural knowledge may lead to inappropriately applying boundaries that may cause clients of diverse backgrounds to feel discomfort and block the building of rapport in the therapeutic situation. Vasquez provides the example of gift giving between clients and therapists, an action that is usually discouraged because clients pay for services and because it may result in the therapist's inadvertent (or purposeful) exploitation of the client. Vasquez, however, argues that ultimately the "context of receiving gifts is crucial" (p. 407) for deciding whether it is an appropriate action or not. To illustrate this point, Vasquez provides the following example:

> . . . if a Latina client who works near a restaurant brings tacos because I squeezed her in during my lunch hour when she was in crisis, it may not be necessary to spend half an hour processing the meaning of the tacos. We know that she felt appreciative; that it was a relatively easy, warm gesture, and that food is a common gift among Latinas. Sometimes a taco is just a taco! (p. 407)

The challenge, therefore, is for therapists to know when "a taco is just a taco" and when it may have other psychological meanings that need to be explored in a therapeutic setting.

Latina feminist psychology not only emphasizes culture in considering therapeutic interventions but also is concerned about the sociopolitical experiences of clients as they enter the relationship with the therapists (Flores-Ortiz, 2004). Vasquez argues that if the therapist rejects the client's offering of the taco, the therapist's action would reinscribe the power differential between therapist and client. The potential perceived rejection of the gift may remind the client of her inferior status in society as a Latina, possibly shaming her and causing her to re-experience instances of discrimination. By accepting the taco, the therapist is acknowledging an act of kindness and thoughtfulness and creating a bridge of understanding rather than doubting the client's motives. The APA's ethical rule of not accepting gifts then becomes ambiguous because it is potentially detrimental to culturally diverse clients.

Comas-Díaz (2000) argues that given the structural discrimination that many people of Color[2] suffer in the United States (and in the world), psychologists cannot ignore the "group trauma" produced by such treatment. The experience of racism and discrimination, according to Comas-Díaz, leads to this:

> People of color are often exposed to imperialism and intellectual domination at the expense of their cultural values (Said, 1994). Furthermore, they are subjected to the cultural Stockholm syndrome, a condition in which members of an oppressed group accept the dominant cultural values, including the stereotypes of their own group (DiNicola, 1997). The cultural Stockholm syndrome involves being taken hostage by other people's cultures and perceptions of themselves, while coming to internalize and believe them. Hence, politically repressing people of color can lead to terrorism, maintaining the privileges of the dominant group, and silencing cries for racial social justice. (p. 1320)

Congruent with the writings of others in the field of Latina feminist psychology (Flores-Ortíz, 2004; Vasquez, 2006), Comas-Díaz (2000) argues for an *ethnopolitical approach* in restituting Latinas' identity after they have suffered the effects of "oppression, racism, terrorism, and political repression" (p. 1320). According to Comas-Díaz,

> By acknowledging racial, ethnic, and political realities as they interact with socioeconomic, historical, psychological, and environmental factors, this approach expands the individual focus to a collective one, one that is national as well as international. An ethnopolitical model can serve as the basis for psychologists to aid people who have suffered racism, discrimination, and repression. (p. 1320)

The ethnopolitical approach "names the terror [of oppression], developing a language that gives voice to the silenced traumatized self" (ibid.). This broader conceptualization of identity, which takes into account history as well as the sociopolitical context in which Latinas exist in the United States (and all of Latin America), leads to a diversity of therapeutic interventions, and, in fact, redefines therapy from the individual to the social and collective (Comas-Díaz, 1988, 2000; Flores-Ortiz, 2004; Vasquez, 2002). To alleviate the pervasive identity conflicts created by colonization in the forms of "identity conflicts," "shame," "rage," pressures to "assimilate" and abandon one's native culture and language, identity "ambivalence," and "alienation" (Comas-Díaz, 2000, p. 1320), the writers of Latina feminist psychology advocate using a variety of therapeutic interventions. As Comas-Díaz (2000) summarizes,

> Ethnic and indigenous psychologies provide a culturally relevant lens validating both the importance of racial and ethnic meanings and the historical and political contexts of oppression. Because working with victims of political repression forces individuals to confront questions of meaning, the spiritual beliefs of people of color are rescued and affirmed as examples of indigenous psychological approaches (Ho, 1987). Psychologists can help trauma sufferers find something of value in the traumatic experience through a renewed awareness of their strengths. (p. 1322)

Comas-Díaz, Lykes, and Alarcón (1998) propose that for some individuals indigenous approaches to psychic healing helps them remember and "retell their cultural memories," which aid in "identity construction" (Comas-Díaz, 2000, p. 1322). For other individuals who lack exposure to their indigenous origins, therapy may include the act of discovery and recuperation of culture, language, and history. Indigenous approaches may also be better suited to poor and working-class individuals whose life experiences may have been especially brutal because of poverty. For example, Comas-Díaz uses the Puerto Rican concept of *dusmic strength* with working-class clients to facilitate the "transformation of aggression and desperation into self-affirmation and hope," thus illustrating "an indigenous spiritual approach to trauma" and "making meaning out of trauma" (ibid.).

According to Comas-Díaz (2000), the goal of these diverse therapeutic interventions is for

> [i]ndividual and collective identities . . . to be reformulated in order to achieve liberation. Therapeutic decolonization entails raising consciousness of the colonized mentality, correcting cognitive distortions, recognizing the context of colonization (including post-colonization stress disorder) . . . increasing dignity and self- and social mastery, and working for personal and collective transformation. (pp. 1320–1321)

Other writers advocate the restitution of self through the use of indigenous art forms, such as dance (Roberts, 2005), visual art (Hurtado & Gurin, 2004), and spiritual practices based on wholeness and rooted in the epistemology and ontology of indigenous cultures, to foster the acquisition of both knowledge and wisdom, and the use of diverse forms of contemplative practice to elicit deep awareness, social consciousness and transformation in self and others (Rendón, 2008). As stated earlier, Latina feminist psychology does not advocate the uncritical consumption of indigenous practices and cultures but rather conceptualizes all cultural practices and norms as changing, fluid, and applicable to different individuals according to their varying social identities examined through an intersectional lens.

LATINA FEMINIST PSYCHOLOGY AND CONTRIBUTIONS TO FEMINIST THEORY

Psychology as a field developed most of its research methods and theoretical paradigms with predominantly white, middle-class populations (Guthrie, 2003). Much of the initial impetus for the development of Latina feminist psychology was to expand the topics that should be included in research by elucidating the restrictions imposed by psychology's historical tradition of ignoring diversity. The contributions of Latina feminist psychology were not independent of the contributions made by other psychologists of Color, especially African American psychologists. Writers in both fields often worked in collaboration by developing new methodologies and theoretical paradigms to fully capture the experiences of their constituencies (Mays & Comas-Díaz, 1988).

Defining Latina/Chicana Feminisms

Adhering to a diversity mindfulness paradigm also opened up the question of the potential variety in the definitions of feminism. Chicanas (Mexican-descent Latinas) in the humanities and the social sciences are the most prolific writers in this area. The project taken up by these writers is to avoid defining feminism singly and instead to examine the antecedents that led to a diversity of definitions and feminist actions. The consideration of the different historical trajectories in the United States of the various Latino/a groups is an important component in defining feminism (Hurtado & Roa, 2005). Of special significance is the history of colonization suffered by various groups of Color. As Comas-Díaz (2000) states, "As conquered enemies, Native Americans, African Americans, Latinos, and Asian Americans have been subjected to repression by the U.S. government, which has designated them as savages, slaves, and colonized entities" (pp. 1319–1320). For Chicanas, the colonization of the Southwest territories that previously belonged to Mexico at the end of the Mexican-American War in 1848 became a pivotal moment in creating the group's inferior status in the United States. Mexican nationals lost their Mexican citizenship and became culturally and linguistically conquered on their own land (Flores-Ortiz, 2004). For Puerto Rican women, the relationship between Puerto Rico as a protectorate of the United States with no official representation in the U.S. government also influenced the group's gender relations. Mostly because of economic necessity, large numbers of island residents, who are legally U.S. citizens, have historically migrated from Puerto Rico, mainly to New York City. The migration from their home country, where individuals are national citizens, to the status of "labor migrants" in the United States (regardless of their legal status as U.S. citizens) disrupts the Puerto Rican cultural patterns and social norms developed in their native country. Puerto Rican men migrating from the island to the mainland, in particular, find it difficult to enact their manhood in the United States. The lack of adjustment to their newfound situation in the United States frequently leads to family discord and even domestic abuse (Weis, Centrie, Valentin-Juarbe, & Fine, 2002).

Other groups of Latinas (e.g., Salvadorans, Guatemalans, Colombians), who immigrated from their home countries because of economic pressures or political persecution have yet another set of influences that affect their definitions of what constitutes feminism. Many are forced to leave families behind and readjust their beliefs about gender relations as they struggle economically in the United States. Latinas' varied histories, however, do not deter them from having certain concerns in common as a group when defining feminism and feminist actions. In the following sections, we summarize three major components of defining Latina feminisms: the importance of history, the importance of culture and language, and the importance of coalition building to bring about social justice.

The Importance of History for the Definition of Latina Feminisms. As with white feminisms, the recuperation of white women's history was a central component of defining first-wave feminism (Mankiller et al., 1998). History can frame the origins of gender relations and the background for normative gender practices. History can also provide examples of individuals who have questioned the restrictions imposed by gender. Historical analysis can provide a map for understanding as well as for resisting the current gender arrangements. Latina feminist psychology has highlighted the historical origins of such cultural beliefs as the value of Latinas preserving their virginity until marriage. For example, in the case of Chicanas, the historical figure of La Malinche became pivotal in understanding the logic behind women's sexual restrictions. La Malinche was an Aztec woman who "conspired" with Hernán Córtez in the conquest of Mexico by acting as his translator. Malinche's actions of betrayal of her people and her indigenous nation gave rise to the notion of *malinchismo*, women's unbridled tendency to betray unless under patriarchal control. Virginity, then,

becomes the symbol of loyalty (in body, mind, and spirit) only to the husband and to no other man (Hurtado 1996a, 2003b).

Flores-Ortiz (2004) further extends the analysis of La Malinche in the construction of Chicanas' womanhood. She draws on her work as a clinician treating Chicanas who have suffered domestic violence and highlights the importance of history in understanding why women suffering interpersonal violence are reluctant to leave the situation. From Flores-Ortiz's perspective, intimate violence for Chicanas is located in the "historical legacy of oppression and colonization" (p. 271). The historical experience of conquest by the Spaniards and the imposition of Catholicism on indigenous people produced culturally specific definitions of womanhoods—what cultural theorists have called *gendered subject positions* for Chicanas (Hurtado, 2003b). Chicana feminists propose that *marianismo* and *malinchismo* dichotomize women's womanhood into the "good woman" and the "bad woman" according to sexuality (Hurtado, 1996a). *Marianismo* is the veneration of the Virgin Mary (Nieto-Gomez, 1974). Her Mexican counterpart, La Virgen de Guadalupe, is the role model for Chicana womanhood—she is the mother, the nurturer, the one who endures pain and sorrow, the one who is willing to serve (ibid.). These values, rooted in the practice of Catholicism, become an integral part of what constitutes for Chicanos/as the most desirable womanhood (Córdova, 1994). To be a "good woman" is to remain a virgin until marriage and to invest devotion, loyalty, and nurturance in the family, specifically the definition of family adhered to in Mexican/Chicano communities, which includes extended networks of kin as well as friends (Baca Zinn, 1975). The unearthing and understanding of history becomes essential in constructing a culturally specific feminism that speaks to Latinas because it is rooted in their group's history as well as in cultural and linguistic practices.

The Importance of Culture and Language. The writings in Latina feminist psychology emphasize the importance of Latino/a cultural traditions (regardless of the national variations) in influencing perceptions and behavior (Niemann, Romero, Arredondo, & Rodríguez, 1999). Many writings have addressed the significance of cultural practices and norms, as well as the use of Spanish, on mental health (Flores-Ortiz, 2004; Russo & Tartaro, 2008), domestic violence (Flores-Ortiz, 2004; Vasquez, 1998), and gender relations in families (Hurtado, 2003b; Steinberg, True, & Russo, 2008). While recognizing that some aspects of Latino/a culture can have detrimental effects on women (as do all other patriarchal cultures), many writers have also highlighted the positive aspects of Latino/a cultures (such as the emotional and social support given in families) and have avoided simply applying a deficit framework to their analysis (Vasquez, 2002). The struggle has been to define feminism in culturally specific ways to make it applicable to the group and therefore more likely to be of use to Latinas (Hurtado, 1996a, 2003b). For example, Hurtado argues that definitions of feminism should include, or at least grapple with, the incongruence between how poor, immigrant women live their lives—often exhibiting such feminist characteristics as individual agency, fighting patriarchal control of their lives, seeking economic independence, and forming alliances with other women—and the fact that these women do not have readily available either the label *feminist* or the framework of feminism to understand their actions (Hurtado, 2003a). Perhaps by identifying as feminist, these women would benefit from joining a larger community of resisters to patriarchal norms. After analyzing the life story of Inocencia, a 68-year-old, poor, Mexican, immigrant woman, Hurtado concludes,

> It is important to recognize there are many feminisms and that their definitions are currently in flux. . . . [T]he definitions of feminism, feminist identity, and feminist consciousness should remain flexible to maximize the inclusion of a diversity of women's experiences. . . . [T]he inclusion of the cultural, artistic, and scholarly productions of Women of Color are essential to informing these evolving definitions. The story of Inocencia's life, as well as those of the lives of many other women like her who do not have access to the academy are not the usual topics of study, needs to be an integral part of the process of definition and inclusion. (p. 287)

Similarly, other writers have emphasized integrating in the definitions of feminisms the experiences of working-class Latinas (Ginorio, Lapayese, & Vásquez, 2007), young Latinas (Pastor et al., 2007; Rubin, Nemeroff, & Russo, 2004; Tolman, 2002), the incarcerated (Fine et al., 2003; Fine & Torre, 2006), political refugees (Espín, 1999), labor immigrants (Flores-Ortiz, Valdez Curiel, & Andrade Palos, 2004) and lesbians (Espín, 1997). By emphasizing the diversity of Latinas' lived experiences, and therefore variations in exposure and knowledge of Latino/a culture and language, feminism and feminist actions could be expanded and could more likely apply to, and be used by, these varied constituencies.

When the diversity of women's lived experiences are included in the definitions of feminisms, it becomes apparent that there is not just one definition of *womanhood* but rather variations determined by culture and language as well as by sexuality and social class within cultures. Thus, Latina feminist psychology's view of culture and language is multidimensional and layered. The writers of Latina feminist psychology adhere to a paradigm of culture that privileges lived experience as the basis for embodying culture and language. From this perspective, special attention must be directed, when examining Latina's culture, to regional and national origins, class background, gender, and sexuality. It is understood that, like all cultures, context is determinative in accurately assessing its impact on behavior. Furthermore, language also has variations by speech style and degrees of mastery. Not all Latinas speak Spanish, and Spanish-English bilingualism is a matter of degree as well as familiarity with different speech styles. Latina feminist psychology does not adhere to a linear acculturation model. Instead, there are many potential cultural adaptations influenced by context and exposure to the culture and language of origin (Gurin et al., 1994). For example, using a national, representative sample of Mexican descent, respondents, Gurin, Hurtado, and Peng (1994) conducted factor analyses of social identity labels between two subgroups of the Mexican-descent population. The results supported the study's prediction that the identities of English-dominant persons born in the United States (Chicanos/as) would be more differentiated than those of Spanish-dominant persons born in Mexico (Mexicanos/as). The experience of historical and structural discrimination undergone by Chicanos/as gave them a wider array of ethnic and social identity categorizations. Mexicanos/as, on the other hand, primarily had a national identity tied to their country of origin.

The Importance of Coalitions to the Definition of Feminisms. The experience of oppression based on a multiplicity of group memberships informs Latina feminist writers of the overlapping interests they may have with other subordinate groups. The definition of feminisms in Latina feminist writings is aligned with an analysis of power and privilege (Russo & Vaz, 2001) and therefore, they are committed to working in academic and political coalition with similarly situated groups. The coalition may take the form of finding similarities in the condition of Latinas with other women of Color (Comas-Díaz & Greene, 2000) and in working with white feminists to push forward a social justice agenda (Russo & Denmark, 1987).

Comas-Díaz (2000) argues that "similar to other survivors of torture, people of color need to learn to reject the feelings of inferiority instilled in them" by the historical experience of colonization and its concomitant "political repression" (p. 1322). As part of this work, oppressed people need to reject the negative attributions imputed to their identities and communities and instead "develop solidarity with other oppressed groups, thus restoring their sense of continuity with their collective identity, both local and global" (ibid.). To do coalitional work, "ethnic minorities . . . need to confront and overcome ingrained feelings of division and suspicion instilled by their ancestral history of threatened survival" (ibid.). The coalitional work is with other feminists of Color as well as with white feminists (Hurtado & Stewart, 2004).

An integral part of feminist coalition building as part of the definition of feminism is the incorporation of Latino men in feminist analyses and scholarly production. While the writers of Latina feminist psychology have written powerful critiques of the sexist elements in Latino/a culture (Fine et al., 2000; Hurtado, 2003a, b), there is an emphasis on honoring Latino/a cultures, selectively cultivating those cultural aspects that have allowed Latino/a communities to survive oppression, such as caring for family members, sharing resources with extended family, and parents' support to ensure their daughters' educational success (Cantú, 2008; Hurtado, Hurtado, & Hurtado, 2008).

Examining culture within a structure of patriarchy results in a more complicated analysis of masculinity than is ordinarily found in white feminist writings and its relationship to feminism. Instead of perceiving Latino men only as beneficiaries of patriarchy, Latino men's vulnerabilities are also taken into account in analyses of oppression. Hurtado & Sinha (2006) find that Latino families privilege sons by requiring fewer household chores and by giving them more freedom and fewer rules than they require of their daughters. These young men, however, are also more likely to be harassed by police, to be less close to their parents, and to have fewer close friends than their sisters—all of which leads to less educational success for young Latino men.

The recognition of multiple feminisms by Latina feminist psychology is necessary because the variety of womanhoods implies that there must also be multiple masculinities. To be sure, not all womanhoods are equally valued (Hurtado, 1999); this, too, is the case with non-hegemonic masculinities (Hurtado & Sinha, 2008). Of course, the systems of patriarchal privilege reward all masculinities at some level (just as all womanhoods/femininities are ultimately a source of restriction, even if it is through seduction [Hurtado, 1996a; Rubin, Nemeroff, & Russo, 2004]). Nonetheless, Latina feminist psychology embraces the deconstruction of masculinity as part of defining feminism (Hurtado & Sinha, 2008). As such, Latina feminist psychology includes men, masculinity, and gender relations within Latino/a communities as an integral part of the Latina feminist project within psychology (Weis et al., 2002).

We now turn to the contributions to feminist theory made by the writers of Latina feminist psychology.

Contributions to Feminist Theory: Borderlands Theory and Intersectionality

Latina feminist psychology has a commitment to interdisciplinarity (Azmitia, Syed, & Radmacher, 2008). The writers of Latina feminist psychology easily transcend disciplinary boundaries, venturing into other social sciences as well as the humanities (Vera & de los Santos, 2005). An important theoretical integration has been the work of Gloria Anzaldúa—writer, public intellectual, and one of the first Chicanas to publicly claim her lesbianism (1987, 2000). Anzaldúa wrote extensively on borderlands theory, as scholars in the humanities call it, before her untimely passing at the age of 61. Borderlands theory is based on the experiences of Chicanas who have grown up in South Texas on the border between the United States and Mexico (Martinez, 2005). Hurtado (2003b) summarizes Anzaldúa's geographical location as the source of her theorizing:

> The history of conquest, which basically layered another country over a preexisting nation, gave Chicana feminisms the knowledge of the temporality of nation-states (Klahn, 1994). The political line dividing the United States from Mexico did not correspond to the experiential existence on the border. Chicana feminists declare the border the geographical location (*lugar*) that created the aperture for theorizing about subordination from an ethnically specific Chicana/*mestiza* consciousness. (p. 18)

Anzaldúa (1987) argues that living in the borderlands creates a third space between cultures and social systems (Lugones, 2003) that leads to coherence by embracing ambiguity and holding contradictory perceptions without conflict. *La frontera* (the border) is also the geographical area that is most susceptible to hybridity, neither fully of Mexico nor fully of the United States. As Gloria Anzaldúa claims, *la frontera* is where you "put chile in the borscht/eat whole wheat tortillas/speak Tex-Mex with a Brooklyn accent" (Anzaldúa, 1987, p. 195). The word *borderlands* denotes that space in which antithetical elements mix, not to obliterate each other nor to be subsumed by a larger whole but rather to combine in unique and unexpected ways (Hurtado, 2003b).

Living between two countries, two social systems, two languages, two cultures, results in understanding experientially the contingent nature of social arrangements (Martinez, 2005). Anzaldúa uses the borderlands as a metaphor for all social crossings and the knowledge produced by being within a system while also retaining the knowledge of an outsider who comes from outside the system. This "outsider within" status gives Latinas' sense of self a layered complexity that is captured in Anzaldúa's concept of *mestiza consciousness*, as summarized by Hurtado (2003b):

> It was at the border that Chicanas/*mestizas* learned the socially constructed nature of all categories. By standing on the U.S. side of the river they saw Mexico and they saw home; by

standing on the Mexican side of the border they saw the United States and they saw home. Yet they were not really accepted on either side. Their ability to "see" the arbitrary nature of all categories but still take a stand challenges Chicana feminisms to exclude while including, to reject while accepting, to struggle while negotiating. Chicana feminists variously called this *facultad* (ability) a *mestiza* consciousness (Anzaldúa, 1987), differential consciousness (Sandoval, 2000), and *concientización* (Castillo, 1994, 171). The basic concept involves the ability to hold multiple social perspectives while simultaneously maintaining a center that revolves around concrete material forms of oppression. (p. 18)

Gloria Anzaldúa developed borderlands theory by examining her experiences as the daughter of farmworkers living in extreme poverty in South Texas. Other writers, however, have used borderlands theory to describe any kind of social, economic, sexual, and political dislocation. Many of Anzaldúa's insights apply to individuals who are exposed to contradictory social systems.

Borderlands theory is particularly important for social action and coalition building. There are no absolute "sides" in conflict, but rather, contingent adversaries whose perceptions can be understood by examining (and empathizing) with their subjectivities. Furthermore, no one is exempt from contributing to oppression in limited contexts (Perez, 1999). As such, self-reflexivity and seeing through the "eyes of others" becomes essential to gaining a deeper consciousness than staying within one's social milieu. As explained by Anzaldúa,

> "[I]t is not enough to stand on the opposite river bank, shouting questions, challenging patriarchal, white conventions. A counterstance locks one into a duel of oppressor and oppressed; locked in mortal combat, like the cop and the criminal, both are reduced to a common denominator of violence. The counterstance refutes the dominant culture's views and beliefs, and, for this, it is proudly defiant. . . . But it is not a way of life. At some point, on our way to a new consciousness, we will have to leave the opposite bank, the split between the two mortal combatants somehow healed so that we are on both shores at once and, at once, see through serpent and eagle eyes. . . .

The possibilities are numerous once we decide to act and not react." (1987, pp. 78–79)

Gloria Anzaldúa speaks of a mestiza consciousness that both embraces and rejects simultaneously so as not to exclude what it critically assesses. A mestiza consciousness can perceive multiple realities at once (Barvosa-Carter, 2007). Anzaldúa's work integrates indigenous Aztec beliefs and epistemologies to circumvent linear, positivist thinking that does not allow for hybridity, contradiction, and ultimately liberation from existing social arrangements (Hurtado, 2003b; Martinez, 2005). Chicanas' bodies become a *bocacalle*—crossroads (Arredondo, Hurtado, Klahn, Nájera-Ramírez, & Zavella, 2003). As Martinez (2005) analyzes,

> The "borderlands" signify Anzaldúa's family of oppression, her memory of brutal backbreaking work, and her knowledge of border history. The "borderlands" are the site of her worst struggles with racism, sexism, classism and heterosexism: "[*La] mestiza undergoes a struggle of flesh, a struggle of borders, an inner war. . . . The coming together of two self-consistent but habitually incompatible frames of reference causes un choque,* a cultural collision" (1987, p. 28). Yet, this crossroads is also the site of her greatest strength. This "floundering in uncharted seas," this "swamping of her psychological borders" (1987, p. 79) creates the other ways of coping and seeing the world. It forces the *mestiza* consciousness into existence in a psychic birthing and synthesis to become a reflection of the "borderlands" themselves—a juncture, a crossroads, and a consciousness of multiple voices and paradigms. (pp. 559–560)

Through borderlands theory, Anzaldúa (1987, 2000) provided the experiential documentation of Tajfel's (1981) social identity theory. Tajfel did not address extensively what it means to individuals, let alone women, to carry the burden of stigma when they have no control over how others categorize them into social groups. Furthermore, Tajfel did not explore how individuals cope with the incongruence between their private self-perceptions (say, as competent, intelligent, logical individuals) and others' negative perceptions shaped by the individuals' stigmatized social identities. Anzaldúa proposes that one possibility among many is to use the

contradiction to one's advantage and rise above the negative assignation to develop a complex view of self.

In many ways, Anzaldúa's work exemplifies the poetics of political resistance and rescues Chicanas' (and other Latinas') potential stigma from their derogated social identities (Bost, 2005; Tajfel, 1981). Anzaldúa presages the concept of intersectionality, discussed in the following section, by attributing Chicanas' subordination not only to patriarchy, but to the intersection of multiple systems of oppression that include gender, race, ethnicity, class, and sexuality.

Borderlands Theory and Intersectionality. Latina feminist psychology joined the increasing chorus within the academy to think in more complicated ways about gender and sexuality that go beyond the dichotomy (and tradition) of conducting research based on "sex differences" between men and women (McCall, 2005) and taking heterosexuality as the desired norm. The call for examining gender within embedded social systems of power, privilege, and complexity is embodied in the concept of intersectionality and dovetails theoretically with Tajfel's (1981) social identity theory (Hurtado, 2008a). The core of intersectionality is that women's (and most recently, men's) multiple social locations intersect, depending on context, to influence perceptions, behavior, access to resources, and in many ways, to determine life chances.

Borderlands theory has been applied to understand Latinas' multiple identities as proposed by intersectionality. Instead of expecting only conflict between social identities—say, race and gender—borderlands theory proposes that many Latinas manage the disjuncture created by their multiple identities in creative and politically progressive ways to gain a deeper understanding of social reality that may lead to a commitment to social justice (Hurtado, 2003a). For example, Hurtado (2008a) examined the impact of Chicanos' multiple identifications on their political consciousness that led to a commitment to social action, not only on behalf of their ethnic communities, but also on behalf of other oppressed groups as well. In her study, 93% of the participants were committed to working on behalf of Latino issues, and 92% were committed to working on behalf of gender issues, poverty, and social justice in general.

Intersectionality in its most direct form (and the form usually applied in psychology) takes gender, race, and ethnicity (and sometimes class) as variables to be examined and, often, controlled in quantitative analyses (McCall, 2005). In its most sophisticated forms, intersectionality advocates a definitional, context-based analysis of all phenomena that involve derogated intersecting social categories based on gender, race, class, sexuality, and physical ableness (Hurtado, 1997). Hurtado and Sinha's (2008) study illustrates the latter approach to analyzing intersectionality, focusing on a particular *identificational intersection*. In this study, the views of young, educated, working-class Latino men on manhood were examined by asking the open-ended question, "What does manhood mean to you?" They did not specify a particular context (e.g., in your family, in your culture, in your peer group) or a particular developmental stage in their life (e.g., "while you were growing up"). The question asked the Latino men about their perceptions of a particular facet of their identity. The question required the respondents to take into account how their gender, race, class, sexuality, ethnicity, and social class intersected with their concepts of manhood. The respondents spoke eloquently and freely about how their definitions of manhood were influenced by all their social identities: Of the 36 respondents, 36 mentioned their race, 32 mentioned their ethnicity, 22 mentioned their social class, and 8 mentioned their sexuality. Furthermore, rather than mentioning each social identity separately, the participants' comments on their social identities and definitions of manhood were relational and embedded in rich, textured narratives.

The theoretical framework of intersectionality facilitates an understanding of the social and economic conditions of women of Color in general and of Latinas specifically (Anzaldúa, 1987; Castillo, 1995; Collins, 2000; Pesquera & Segura, 1993; Sandoval, 2000). Sociologist Patricia Hill Collins (2000) broadly describes several components of intersectionality:

> The very notion of the intersections of race, class, and gender as an area worthy of study emerged from the recognition of practitioners of each distinctive theoretical tradition that inequality could not be explained, let alone challenged, via a race-only, or gender-only framework. No one had all the answers and no one was going to get all

of the answers without attention to two things. First, the notion of interlocking oppressions refers to the macro-level connections linking systems of oppression such as race, class, and gender. This is a model describing the social structures that create social positions. Second, the notion of intersectionality describes micro-level processes—namely, how each individual and group occupies a social position within interlocking structures of oppression described by the metaphor of intersectionality. Together they shape oppression. (p. 82)

Intersectionality theorists like Patricia Hill Collins argue that gender-only or race-only analyses lead neither to an understanding of the position of all women nor to a dismantling of the structures that oppress them. Intersectionality theorists also refuse to "rank the oppressions" (Moraga, 1981, p. 29) and instead argue that membership in oppressed groups intersect in significant ways that affect women's experiences of oppression. Theories of intersectionality have also been applied to understand categorical differences between women in different nation-states. For example, Rosa-Linda Fregoso (2003) problematizes the human rights paradigm applied by "First World Feminists" to women worldwide:

> Claiming a singular transnational identity for women ignores the profound differences among women across the globe, but especially within specific localities. . . . Although First World Feminists have contributed significantly to "the theoretical and practical revision of international rights law," especially in their redefinition of women's rights as human rights, the challenge today involves framing women's international human rights within very complex and specific cultural contexts. (p. 23)

By applying the concept of intersectionality, Fregoso avoids homogenizing all Mexican women. Thus, she can analyze more specifically why young, working-class, dark-skinned Mexican women, rather than wealthy, light-skinned Mexican women, were the victims of "feminicide" in the border city of Ciudad Juarez (across from El Paso, Texas). For Fregoso, intersectionality provides a theoretical bridge for identifying variations based on class and race among different Mexican women, giving rise to a deeper analysis of the more than 400 murders of women, as compared with the one provided by human rights discourse.

Connecting Intersectionality and Social Identity Theory. As discussed earlier, in social psychology the stigmatized social identities of sexuality, class, gender, race, ethnicity, and physical ableness are the ones that influence an individual's construction of self. The degree to which different stigmatized social identities gain significance is largely context dependent (Hurtado & Gurin, 2004). As noted, Mexican immigrants do not think frequently about being Mexican in Mexico. In fact, having a Mexican national identity does not carry negative connotations and therefore may not even be a social identity in the strictest use of the Tajfelian definition. However, upon entering the United States, the category of Mexican becomes salient and requires negotiation because of its negative implications within the U.S. context. Therefore, social identity can be conceptualized as a moving, fluid, amorphic "amoeba" that changes shape, making one (or more) social identities especially relevant depending on the context. From a social psychological point of view, intersectionality refers to the following constellation of social identities Tajfel (1981) sees as the primary basis for stigmatization: class, race, sexuality, gender, ethnicity, physical ableness.

In summary, Hurtado (1996a, b; 1997, 2003b; in press; Hurtado & Gurin, 2004) purposely links mestiza consciousness and intersectionality through Tajfel's (1981) social identity theory. By linking these three currents of intellectual production, she is able to make systematic empirical predictions about Latinas' social identifications based on Tajfel and his colleagues' exposition of the dynamics of social identities in intergroup relations and relations of domination. Many feminist scholars in various disciplines are exploring these proposed connections by taking different nodes of these linkages and exploring them in depth. McCall (2005), a sociologist, explores the nature of intersectionality in creating social inequality in different groups as categorized by social identity theory (gender, ethnicity, and race). Shields (2008), a psychologist, explores the issue of method for exploring intersectionality through social identities. Barvosa-Carter (2007), a political theorist, uses the concept of multiple social identities, borderlands theory, and its implications for "relational autonomy," a reconceptualization of autonomy

as based not only on individual will, but also on the social commitments individuals have to others. Martinez (2005), a sociologist, connects borderlands theory and intersectionality to the process of subordinate groups creating alternatives modes of cultural adaptations to circumvent stigma while creating a positive collective identity with their ethnic and racial groups. (Mitchell & Feagin, 1995). The marriage of borderlands theory, social identity theory, and intersectionality is resulting in many fruitful derivations sure to yield exciting new veins of research in psychology as well as other fields.

FUTURE DIRECTIONS IN LATINA FEMINIST PSYCHOLOGY

In many respects, Latina feminist psychology is in its infancy. As a field, it has developed an impressive volume of scholarship, much of it incorporating theoretical and empirical developments in other disciplines. The challenges that still remain are to further develop the methodological innovations used only recently to analyze research questions by applying a Latina feminist lens. For example, how might the insights gained by using PAR (participant action research) be used with predominantly Spanish-speaking women? Will the collaborative basis of defining research questions and techniques for data gathering used in PAR translate with Spanish speakers, whose cultural frameworks may be different, regardless of class, from those of English speakers? Another potential methodological application to Latina feminist questions is the field of psychology's ability to design interventions in different social spheres—say, education or health—which can be measured pre- and postintervention to assess the interventions' effectiveness. Is it possible to design feminist interventions using this paradigm to address issues in Latina communities? For example, is it possible to design a feminist curriculum that addresses the negative stereotypes of Latinas in the media to educate young Latinas in resisting dominant images and inoculating them against the detrimental effects of media (Hurtado, 2008a)?

Another area of research that merits attention from the writers of Latina feminist psychology is the high rate of intermarriage among Latinas/os. Demographers estimate that the Latino/a population currently represents 15% of the total U.S. population (45.5 million out of 301,621,157), surpassing the 40.7 million African Americans representing 13.5% of the total U.S. population (U.S. Census Bureau, 2006a, b; U.S. Census Bureau, 2008a, b). By 2050, it is estimated that Latinos/as will constitute 29% (128 million) of the U.S. population. The growing number of Latinos/as in the United States increases the importance of Latinos/as' intermarriage with other groups (Lee & Edmonston, 2006). The most recent research on intermarriage has been conducted mostly by sociologists and demographers (Jimenez, 2004; Lee & Bean, 2007; Lee & Edmonston, 2006; Qian, 2005; Qian & Cobas, 2004). Their findings indicate that Latinos/as intermarry predominantly with whites (Lee & Bean, 2004). The intermarriage rates of Latinos/as are second only to those of Asian Americans (although Asian Americans account for fewer than 4% of the U.S. population) and well below the intermarriage rates of African Americans (Lee & Bean, 2007). There are, however, several important caveats to the increase in Latino/a intermarriage rates as an indicator of the group's further integration into U.S. mainstream society. First, a substantial number of the offspring of Latino/a and white intermarriage identify as Latino/a, potentially increasing the numbers of the U.S. Latino/a population (Lee & Edmonston, 2006). Another important finding is that there is a "color line" in Latino/a and white intermarriage. Using U.S. Census data, Qian (2005) finds that for Latinos/as, "the lighter the skin color, the higher the rate of intermarriage with white Americans" (p. 35). Furthermore, "Hispanics who do not consider themselves racially white have low rates of intermarriage with whites" (p. 35). Finally, researchers on intermarriage find that the larger the ethnic and racial group, the more likely they are to find marriage partners within their own ethnic and racial group (Qian, 2005). As the Latino/a population increases faster than other ethnic and racial groups in the United States, will their intermarriage with non-Latinos/as decrease, thus slowing down their integration into the U.S. mainstream? There are many psychological questions to be addressed in research exploring these trends and their meanings for all aspects of the Latino/a population. This can be fertile ground for Latina feminist psychology to insert an analysis that addresses psychological questions using an intersectional lens that simultaneously addresses issues of gender, race, class, ethnicity, and sexuality.

CONCLUSIONS

The field of Latina feminist psychology is relatively new. Only within the last 25 years have psychologists focused on Latinas from a feminist perspective. The writings have come from both Latinas and psychologists of other ethnic and racial backgrounds. Latina feminist psychology emphasizes the areas of study, rather than the ethnicity and race, of the writers producing the scholarship. Viewing Latinas from the perspectives of writers within their own ethnic and racial group as well as from the perspectives of writers outside the group has ensured a broad and layered coverage of these areas of scholarship. Furthermore, it is also one of the areas of study within psychology that has produced significant collaborations between writers of different ethnic, class, sexuality, racial, and psychology backgrounds. As such, many of the proposals promoted in these writings are actually embodied in the scholarship produced.

Latina feminist psychology has made many contributions. The diversity of perspectives has resulted in a rich and innovative area of theorizing and research that has enriched the fields of psychology as well as ethnic studies, feminist studies, sociology, education, anthropology, and other related disciplines. The goal of this literature is to effectively capture the complexities of Latinas' lived experiences to better serve them and also to carry forward a social justice political agenda (Comas-Díaz, 2000; Russo & Vaz, 2001; Vasquez, 2002).

NOTES

1. In this chapter, the ethnic label *Latino/a* is used as an encompassing term to refer to individuals in the United States with ancestry from any Latin American country. When the literature quoted refers to specific Latin American groups (e.g., Puerto Ricans, Salvadorians, Mexicans), the specific national label will be used. In addition, there is a large amount of literature produced on Chicanas (women of Mexican ancestry either born or raised in the United States) and feminism. This literature is covered extensively in this review. It is important to note that the ethnic label *Chicana* also denotes individuals' political

consciousness about not fully being part of either Mexico or the United States, but of both countries simultaneously.

2. We use *people of Color* to refer to the following ethnic groups: Chicanos/as (and Latinos in general), Asians, Native Americans, and African Americans. Therefore, *Color* refers to the groups' ethnicities, which are conventionally capitalized (Hurtado, 1996a).

REFERENCES

Alvarez, S. E. (2000). Translating the global: Effects of transnational organizing on local feminist discourses and practices in Latin America. *Meridians: Feminism, Race, Transnationalism, 1*(1), 29–67.

Anzaldúa, G. (1987). *Borderlands—La frontera: The new mestiza.* San Francisco: Spinsters/Aunt Lute.

Anzaldúa, G. (2000). *Interviews/Entrevistas.* New York: Routledge.

Arredondo, G., Hurtado, A., Klahn, N., Nájera-Ramírez, O., & Zavella, P. (2003). *Chicana feminisms: A critical reader.* Durham, NC: Duke University Press.

Azmitia, M., Syed, M., & Radmacher, K. (Eds.). (2008). The intersections of personal and social identities. [Special issue]. *New Directions for Child and Adolescent Development, 2008*(120).

Baca Zinn, M. (1975). Political familism: Toward sex role equality in Chicano families. *Aztlán, 6*(1), 13–26.

Barvosa-Carter, E. (2007). Mestiza autonomy as relational autonomy: Ambivalence and the social character of free will. *The Journal of Political Philosophy, 15*(1), 1–21.

Bost, S. (2005). Gloria Anzaldúa's mestiza pain: Mexican sacrifice, Chicana embodiment, and feminist politics. *Aztlán: A Journal of Chicano Studies, 30*(2), 5–36.

Cantú, N. E. (Ed.). (2008). *Paths to discovery: Autobiographies from Chicanas with careers in science, mathematics, and engineering.* Los Angeles: UCLA Chicano Research Center Publications.

Castillo, A. (1995). *Massacre of the dreamers: Essays on Xicanisma.* New York: Plume Books.

Chun, K. M., Balls Organista, P., & Marín, G. (Eds.). (2003). *Acculturation: Advances in theory, measurement, and applied research.* Washington, DC: American Psychological Association.

Collins, P. H. (2000). *Black feminist thought: Knowledge, consciousness and the politics of empowerment.* New York: Routledge.

Colón Warren, A. E. (2003). Puerto Rico: Feminism and feminist studies. *Gender & Society, 17*(5), 664–690.

Comas-Díaz, L. (1988). Feminist therapy with Hispanic/Latina women: Myth or reality. *Women and Therapy, 6*(4), 39–61.

Comas-Díaz, L. (2000). An ethnopolitical approach to working with people of color. *American Psychologist, 55*(11), 1319–1325.

Comas-Díaz, L., & Greene, B. (Eds.). (2000). *Women of color: Integrating ethnic and gender identities in psychotherapy.* New York: Guilford Press.

Comas-Díaz, L., Lykes, M. B., & Alarcón, R. D. (1998). Ethnic conflict and the psychology of liberation in Guatemala, Peru, and Puerto Rico. *American Psychologist, 53*(7), 778–792.

Córdova, T. (1994). The emerging writings of twenty years of Chicana feminist struggles: Roots and resistance. In F. Padilla (Ed.), *The handbook of Hispanic cultures in the United States* (pp. 175–202). Houston, TX: University of Houston, Arte Público Press.

Crenshaw, K. W. (1989). Demarginalizing the intersection of race and sex: A Black feminist critique of antidiscrimination doctrine, feminist theory and anti-racist politics. Chicago: *University of Chicago Legal Forum, 139*–167.

Crenshaw, K. W. (1995). Mapping the margins: Intersectionality, identity politics, and violence against women of color. In K. W. Crenshaw, N. Gotanda, G. Peller, & K. Thomas (Eds.), *Critical race theory: The key writings that formed the movement* (pp. 357–383). New York: New Press.

Enns, C. (in press). Multicultural feminist therapy. In H. Landrine & N. F. Russo (Eds.), *Handbook of diversity in feminist psychology.* New York: Springer.

Espín, O. M. (1996). Leaving the nation and joining the tribe: Lesbian immigrants crossing geographical and identity borders. *Women and Therapy, 19*(4), 99–107.

Espín, O. M. (1997). *Latina realities: Essays on healing, migration, and sexuality.* Boulder, CO: Westview Press.

Espín, O. M. (1999). *Women crossing boundaries: A psychology of immigration and transformations of sexuality.* Florence, KY: Taylor & Francis/Routledge.

Fine, M. (2006). Bearing witness: Methods for researching oppression and resistance. A textbook for critical research. *Social Justice Research, 19*(1), 83–108.

Fine, M., Roberts, R., & Weiss, L. (2000). Refusing the betrayal: Latinas redefining gender, sexuality, culture and resistance. *Review of Education/Pedagogy/Cultural Studies, 22*(2), 87–119.

Fine, M., & Torre, M. E. (2006). Intimate details: Participatory action research in prison. *Action Research, 4*(3), 253–269.

Fine, M., Torre, M. E., Boudin, K., Bowen, I., Clark, J., Hylton, D., et al. (2003). Participatory action research: From within and beyond prison bars. In P. M. Camic, J. E. Rhodes, & L. Yardley (Eds.), *Qualitative research in psychology: Expanding perspectives in methodology and design* (pp. 173–198). Washington, DC: American Psychological Association.

Fine, M., Weis, L., Powell Pruitt, L., & Burns, A. (Eds.). (2004). *Off white: Readings on power, privilege, and resistance.* New York: Routledge.

Flores-Ortiz, Y. G. (2004). Domestic violence in Chicana/o families. In R. J. Velasquez, L. M. Arellano, & B. W. McNeill (Eds.), *The handbook of Chicana/o psychology and mental health* (pp. 267–284). Mahwah, NJ: Lawrence Erlbaum.

Flores-Ortíz, Y. G., Valdez Curiel, E., & Andrade Palos, P. (2004). Intimate partner violence and couple interaction among women from Mexico City and Jalisco, Mexico. *Journal of Border Health, 35*(5).

Fregoso, R. L. (2003). *MeXicana encounters: The making of social identities on the borderlands.* Berkeley and Los Angeles: University of California Press.

Ginorio, A. B., Lapayese, Y., & Vásquez, M. J. T. (2007). Gender equity for Latina/os. In S. Klein, B. Richardson, & D. A. Dwyer (Eds.), *Handbook for achieving gender equity through education* (pp. 485–499). Mahwah, NJ: Lawrence Erlbaum.

Gordon, M. M. (1964). *Assimilation in American life: The role of race, religion, and national origins.* New York: Oxford University Press.

Gurin, P., Hurtado, A., & Peng, T. (1994). Group contacts and ethnicity in the social identities of Mexicanos and Chicanos. *Personality and Social Psychology Bulletin, 20*(5), 521–532.

Guthrie, R. V. (2003). *Even the rat was white: A historical view of psychology* (2nd ed.). Boston: Allyn & Bacon.

Haney, C., & Zimbardo, P. G. (in press). Persistent dispositionalism in interactionist clothing: Fundamental attribution error in explaining prison abuse. *Personality and Social Psychology Bulletin.*

Henderson, L., & Zimbardo, P. G. (2001). Shyness as a clinical condition: The Stanford model. In W. R. Crozier & L. E. Alden (Eds.), *International handbook of social anxiety: Concepts, research and interventions relating to the self and shyness* (pp. 431–447). New York: John Wiley.

Hogg, M. A. (2006). Social identity theory. In P. J. Burke (Ed.), *Contemporary social psychological theories* (pp. 111–136). Stanford, CA: Stanford University Press.

Hogg, M. A. (2008). Personality, individuality, and social identity. In F. Rhodewalt (Ed.), *Personality and social behavior: Frontiers of social psychology* (pp. 177–196). New York: Psychology Press.

Hurtado, A. (1996a). *The color of privilege: Three blasphemies on feminism and race.* Ann Arbor: University of Michigan Press.

Hurtado, A. (1996b). Strategic suspensions: Feminists of Color theorize the production of knowledge. In N. Goldberger, J. Tarule, B. Clinchy, & M. Belenky (Eds.), *Knowledge, difference, and power: Essays inspired by women's ways of knowing* (pp. 372–392). New York: Basic Books.

Hurtado, A. (1997). Understanding multiple group identities: Inserting women into cultural transformations. *Journal of Social Issues 53*(2), 299–328.

Hurtado, A. (1999). *Disappearing dynamics of women of Color,* Working Paper No. 4. Boston: Center for Gender in Organizations, Simmons Graduate School of Management.

Hurtado, A. (2003a). Underground feminisms: Inocencia's story. In G. Arredondo, A. Hurtado, N. Klahn, O. Nájera-Ramírez, & P. Zavella (Eds.), *Chicana feminisms: A critical reader* (pp. 260–290). Durham, NC: Duke University Press.

Hurtado, A. (2003b). *Voicing Chicana feminisms: Young women speak out on sexuality and identity.* New York: New York University Press.

Hurtado, A. (2008a). "Lifting as we climb": Educated Chicanas' views on their social identities, political consciousness, and commitment to social action. In R. Gutierrez, D. Segura, & P. Zavella (Eds.), *Mexicans in California.* Chicago: University of Illinois Press.

Hurtado, A. (2008b). *Rompiendo barreras: The de(construction) of femininities and masculinities.* Manuscript in preparation.

Hurtado, A., Cervantez, K., & Eccleston, M. (in press). Infinite possibilities, many obstacles: Language, culture, identity and Latino/a educational achievement. In E. G. Murillo, Jr. & E. E. Garcia (Eds.), *Handbook of Latinos and education: Theory, research, and practice.* New York: Routledge.

Hurtado, A., & Gurin, P. (2004). *Chicana/o identity in a changing U.S. society. ¿Quién soy? ¿Quiénes somos?* Tucson: University of Arizona Press.

Hurtado, A., Hurtado, M. A., & Hurtado, A. L. (2008). Tres hermanas (three sisters): A model of relational achievement. In K. Gonzalez & R. Padilla (Eds.), *Latina/o faculty perspectives on higher education for the public good.* New York: State University of New York Press.

Hurtado, A., & Roa, J. M. (2005). Chicana feminism. In M. Cline Horowitz (Ed.), *New dictionary of the history of ideas* (pp. 815–817). New York: Charles Scribner's Sons.

Hurtado, A., & Sinha, M. (2006). Differences and similarities: Latina and Latino doctoral students navigating the gender divide. In J. Castellanos, A. M. Gloria, & M. Kamimura (Eds.), *The Latina/o pathway to the Ph.D.: Abriendo caminos* (pp. 149–168). Sterling, VA: Stylus.

Hurtado, A., & Sinha, M. (2008). More than men: Latino feminist masculinities and intersectionality. *Sex Roles, 59*(5–6), 337–349.

Hurtado, A., & Stewart, A. J. (2004). Through the looking glass: Implications of studying whiteness for feminist methods. In M. Fine, L. Weis, L. Powell Pruitt, & A. Burns (Eds.), *Off white: Readings on power, privilege, and resistance* (pp. 315–330). New York: Routledge.

Jimenez, T. R. (2004). Negotiating ethnic boundaries: Multiethnic Mexican Americans and ethnic identity in the United States. *Ethnicities, 4*(1), 75–97.

Leaper. C. (1996). Predictors of Mexican-American mother's and father's attitudes toward gender equality. *Hispanic of Behavioral Sciences, 18*(3), 343–355.

Lee, J., & Bean, F. D. (2004). America's changing color lines. *Annual Review of Sociology, 30,* 221–242.

Lee, J., & Bean, F. D. (2007). Redrawing the color line? *City and Community, 6*(1), 49–62.

Lee, S. M., & Edmonston, B. (2006). Hispanic intermarriage, identification, and U.S. Latino population change. *Social Science Quarterly, 87*(5), 1263–1279.

Lugones, M. (2003). *Pilgrimages/Peregrinajes: Theorizing coalition against multiple oppressions.* Lanham, MD: Rowman & Littlefield.

Mankiller, W., Mink, G., Navarro, M., Smith, B., & Steinem, G. (Eds.). (1998). *The reader's companion to U.S. women's history.* New York: Houghton Mifflin.

Martinez, T. A. (2005). Making oppositional culture, making standpoint: A journey into Gloria Anzaldúa's borderlands. *Sociological Spectrum, 25,* 539–570.

Mays, V., & Comas-Díaz, L. (1988). Feminist therapy with ethnic minority populations: A closer look at Blacks and Hispanics. In M. A. Dutton-Douglas & L. E. Walker (Eds.), *Feminist psychotherapies: Integration of therapeutic and feminist systems* (pp. 228–251). Norwood, NJ: Ablex.

McCall, L. (2005). The complexity of intersectionality. *Signs: Journal of Women in Culture and Society, 30*(3), 1771–1800.

McIntosh, P. (1992). White privilege and male privilege: A personal account of coming to see correspondences through work in women's studies. In M. L. Anderson & P. H. Collins (Eds.), *Race, class, and gender* (pp. 70–81). Belmont, CA: Wadsworth.

Mitchell, B. L., & Feagin, J. R. (1995). America's racial-ethnic cultures: Opposition within a mythical melting pot. In B. Browser, T. Jones, & G. A. Young (Eds.), *Toward the multicultural university* (pp. 65–86). Westport, CT: Praeger.

Montgomery, G. (1992). Comfort with acculturation status among students from South Texas. *Hispanic Journal of Behavioral Sciences, 14*(2), 201–223.

Moraga, C. (1981). La güera. In C. Moraga & G. Anzaldúa (Eds.), *This bridge called my back: Writings by radical women of color* (pp. 29–34). Watertown, MA: Persephone Press.

Niemann, Y. F., Romero, A. J., Arredondo, J., & Rodriguez, V. (1999). What does it mean to be "Mexican"? Social construction of an ethnic identity. *Hispanic Journal of Behavioral Sciences, 21*(1), 47–60.

Nieto-Gomez, A. (1974). La feminista. *Encuentro Feminil, 1*(2), 34–47.

Park, R. E., & Burgess, E. W. (1921). *Introduction to the science of sociology.* Chicago: University of Chicago Press.

Pastor, J., McCormick, J., Fine, M., Adolsen, R., Friedman, N., Richardson, N., et al. (2007). Makin' homes: An urban girl thing. In B. J. Ross Leadbeater & N. Way (Eds.), *Urban girls revisited: Building strategies* (pp. 75–96). New York: New York University Press.

Perez, E. (1999). *The decolonial imaginary: Writing Chicanas into history.* Bloomington: Indiana University Press.

Pesquera, B. M., & Segura, D. A. (1993). "There is no going back": Chicanas and feminism. In N. Alarcón, R. Castro, E. Perez, B. Pesquera, A. Sosa Riddell, & P. Zavella (Eds.), *Chicana critical issues* (pp. 95–115). Berkeley, CA: Third Woman Press.

Phinney, J. S. (1996). When we talk about American ethnic groups, what do we mean? *American Psychologist, 51*(9), 918–927.

Portes, A., & Zhou, M. (1993). The new second generation: Segmented assimilation and its variants. *The Annals of the American Academy of Political and Social Science, 530,* 74–96.

Qian, Z. (2005). Breaking the last taboo: Interracial marriage in America. *Contexts, 4*(4), 33–37.

Qian, Z., & Cobas, J. A. (2004). Latinos' mate selection: National origin, racial, and nativity differences. *Social Science Research, 33,* 225–247.

Rendón, L. I. (2008). *Sensipensante (sensing/thinking) pedagogy: Educating for wholeness, social justice and liberation.* Sterling, VA: Stylus.

Roberts, R. (2005). *Radical movements: Katherine Dunham and Ronald K. Brown teaching toward a critical consciousness.* Unpublished doctoral dissertation, City University of New York.

Rubin, L. R., Nemeroff, C. J., & Russo, N. F. (2004). Exploring feminist women's body consciousness. *Psychology of Women Quarterly, 28,* 27–37.

Russo, N. F., & Dabul, A. J. (1994). Feminism and psychology: A dynamic interaction. In E. J. Tricket, R. J. Watts, & D. Birman (Eds.), *Human diversity: Perspectives on people in context* (pp. 81–100). San Francisco: Jossey-Bass.

Russo, N. F., & Denmark, F. L. (1987). Contributions of women to psychology. *Annual Review of Psychology, 38,* 279–298.

Russo, N. F., & Tartaro, J. (2008). Women and mental health. In F. L. Denmark & M. A. Paludi (Eds.), *Psychology of women: A handbook of theories and issues* (pp. 440–483). Westport, CT: Praeger/Greenwood.

Russo, N. F., & Vaz, K. (2001). Addressing diversity in the decade of behavior: Focus on women of color. *Psychology of Women Quarterly, 25*(4), 280–294.

Sandoval, C. (2000). *Methodology of the oppressed.* Minneapolis: University of Minnesota Press.

Schlachet, P. J. (1975). Identity conflicts in minority college youth. *Journal of Contemporary Psychotherapy, 7*(2), 134–139.

Shields, S. (2008). Gender: An intersectionality perspective. *Sex Roles, 59,* 301–311.

Steinberg, J. R., True, M., & Russo, N. F. (2008). Work and family roles: Selected issues. In F. L. Denmark & M. A. Paludi (Eds.), *Psychology of women: A handbook of theories and issues* (pp. 440–483). Westport, CT: Praeger/Greenwood.

Stewart, A. J. (1994). Toward a feminist strategy for studying women's lives. In C. Frantz & A. J. Stewart (Eds.), *Women creating lives* (pp. 273–288). Boulder, CO: Westview Press.

Tajfel, H. (1981). *Human groups and social categories: Studies in social psychology.* Cambridge, UK: Cambridge University Press.

Tolman, D. L. (2002). *Dilemmas of desire: Teenage girls talk about sexuality.* Cambridge, MA: Harvard University Press.

U.S. Census Bureau. (2006a). *Louisiana loses population: Arizona edges Nevada as fastest-growing state.* Retrieved June 20, 2008, from http://www.census.gov/Press-Release/www/releases/archives/population/007910.html

U.S. Census Bureau. (2006b). *Minority population tops 100 million.* Retrieved February 23, 2009, from http://www.census.gov/Press-Release/www/releases/archives/population/010048.html

U.S. Census Bureau. (2008a). *Facts for features: Black (African-American) history month: February 2009.* Retrieved February 23, 2009, from http://www.census.gov/Press-Release/www/releases/archives/facts_for_features_special_editions/013007.html

U.S. Census Bureau. (2008b). *Facts for features: Hispanic heritage month 2008: September 15-October 16.* Retrieved July 28, 2008, from http://www.census.gov/Press-Release/www/releases/archives/facts_for_features_special_editions/012245.html

Valencia, R. (Ed.). (1997). *The evolution of deficit thinking: Educational thought and practice.* Stanford Series on Education and Public Policy. New York: Falmer Press.

Vasquez, M. J. T. (1998). Latinos and violence: Mental health implications and strategies for clinicians. *Cultural Diversity and Mental Health, 4*(4), 319–334.

Vasquez, M. J. T. (2002). Complexities of the Latina experience: A tribute to Martha Bernal. *American Psychologist, 57*(11), 880–888.

Vasquez, M. J. T. (2006). Counseling men: Perspectives and experiences of a woman of color. In M. Englar-Carlson & M. A. Stevens (Eds.), *In the room with men: A casebook of therapeutic change* (pp. 241–255). Washington, DC: American Psychological Association.

Vasquez, M. J. T. (2007). Sometimes a taco is just a taco! *Professional Psychology: Research and Practice, 38*(4), 401–410.

Vera, H., & de los Santos, E. (2005). Chicana identity construction: Pushing boundaries. *Hispanic Journal of Higher Education, 4*(2), 102–113.

Wallendorf, M., & Reilly, M. D. (1983). Ethnic migration, assimilation, and consumption. *Journal of Consumer Research, 10*(3), 292–302.

Weis, L., Centrie, C., Valentin-Juarbe, J., & Fine, M. (2002). Puerto Rican men and the struggle for place in the United States: An exploration of cultural citizenship, gender, and violence. *Men and Masculinities, 4*(3), 286–302.

Zimbardo, P. G. (1990). *Shyness: What it is, what to do about it.* New York: Perseus Books.

12

Theories and Research on Prosocial Competencies Among U.S. Latinos/as

Gustavo Carlo and Maria Rosario T. de Guzman

Only to the extent that someone is living out this self transcendence of human existence, is he truly human or does he become his true self. He becomes so, not by concerning himself with his self's actualization, but by forgetting himself and giving himself, overlooking himself and focusing outward.

—Victor Frankl, *The Unheard Cry for Meaning*, p. 35

Grant me courage to serve others; For in service there is true life.

—César E. Chávez

Social scientists and practitioners are trained to address the mental and behavioral health issues surrounding individuals in our society. The reality is that many of the efforts in research and intervention have focused on mental and behavioral illness (Seligman & Csikszentmihalyi, 2000). Indeed, this trend has existed for many years and, especially among Latinos[1] and other ethnic and racial minorities, has resulted in deficit and pathology models (García Coll et al., 1996). The overemphasis on illness and pathology has yielded a somewhat skewed and distorted understanding of human nature and behaviors and consequently has mitigated our ability to develop more effective, comprehensive intervention programs. In recent years, there have been calls for social scientists to examine normative and positive aspects of human functioning, especially among ethnic and racial minorities (McLoyd, Cauce, Takeuchi, & Wilson, 2000; Raffaelli, Carlo, Carranza, & González-Kruger, 2005). One important area of study that can help address these needs is the work on prosocial behaviors and social competence.

Dr. Carlo was supported by funding from the National Science Foundation (BNS 0132302) and a Visiting Scholar Sabbatical Fellowship from the University of Valencia, Spain.

In this chapter, we first present a conceptual framework that presents prosocial traits and behaviors as important dimensions of social competence and healthy functioning. We then briefly turn our attention to relevant theoretical frameworks that provide culturally based conceptions of prosocial development. Then, the sparse existing research on prosocial development among Latinos is reviewed. We conclude with recommendations for future research in this area. Our review of empirical studies is necessarily brief, but we hope to present theories and approaches that will spur future researchers to pursue the study of prosocial behaviors and social competencies in Latino (and other traditionally underrepresented) populations to more fully understand positive human functioning.

DEFINITIONAL ISSUES: SOCIAL COMPETENCE AND PROSOCIAL BEHAVIORS

Social Competence

In the broadest sense, social competence has been conceptualized as a tendency to get along well with others. Harter (1982) asserted that social competence reflects positive functioning across different domains, including academic, social, and personal (e.g., global self-worth). Masten and her colleagues (Burt, Obradovic, Long, & Masten, 2008; Masten et al., 1999) conceptualized and operationalized social competence as peer acceptance, popularity, friendship quality and support, and close friendships. Consistent with these conceptualizations, several studies have empirically linked social competencies to internalizing and externalizing disorders (e.g., Masten, Burt, & Coatsworth, 2006). Furthermore, a substantial body of evidence supports the contention that social competencies can act as buffers against adverse psychological and behavioral maladjustment (e.g., Lansford, Malone, Stevens, Dodge, Bates, et al., 2006; Reijntjes, Stegge, & Terwogt, 2006; Ripke, Huston, Eccles, & Templeton, 2008; for reviews, see Ladd, Herald, & Andrews, 2006; McHale, Dariotis, & Kauh, 2003). Much less studied, however, are the links between social competence and prosocial behaviors. Nonetheless, many measures of social competence include items that reflect prosocial behaviors and traits, and show that prosocial behavior items (such as kindness and generosity) load strongly on broader social competence factors (see, e.g.,

Elliott, Gresham, Freeman, & McCloskey, 1988; Gresham & Stuart, 1992; Harter, 1982).

We propose to explicitly link prosocial tendencies more directly to social competence. In our view, *social competence* refers to a set of skills, traits, and behaviors that reflect adaptive individual and interpersonal functioning (see Figure 12.1). Although beyond the scope of this chapter, social competence includes such sociocognitive and socioemotive traits and behaviors as perspective taking and theory of mind (i.e., understanding the intentions, thoughts, and emotions in others; see Carlo, Knight, McGinley, Goodvin, & Roesch, in press; Underwood & Moore, 1982), self-regulation/effortful control (i.e., processes that inhibit dominant responses and execute subdominant processes; Eisenberg et al., 2007; Rothbart, Derryberry, & Posner, 1994), empathy and sympathy (*empathy* refers to a vicarious emotional response that is consistent with the emotions of another, whereas *sympathy* is defined as feelings of sorrow or concern for another's plight or needs; Eisenberg, 1986), moral reasoning (at least two types: justice and care-based (or prosocial) moral reasoning; Carlo, 2006; Eisenberg, 1986; Narváez, 2005), and prosocial behaviors. Within this set of sociocognitive and socioemotive traits and behaviors, some traits and behaviors have been directly linked to morality, while others have not. Nonetheless, we expect these sociocognitive, sociocognitive, and behavioral dispositions to be associated with resilience, health and well-being, and positive adjustment, areas of research with Latino samples that are sorely lacking. Of particular relevance to the present chapter, we focus on prosocial behaviors as one important dimension of social competence.

Prosocial Behaviors

Prosocial behaviors can be defined as actions intended to benefit others (Eisenberg, 1986). Such actions can include sharing resources, donating goods or money, comforting and nurturing others, volunteerism, and helping or assisting needy others (including such acts under high risk to the self). The tendencies for prosocial and cooperative behaviors, as well as nurturance, empathy, and comforting behaviors directed at caregivers and siblings, are present early in life and appear to be universal across cultures (and across some animal species; DeWaal, 1996; Dunn, 1988). There is also extensive

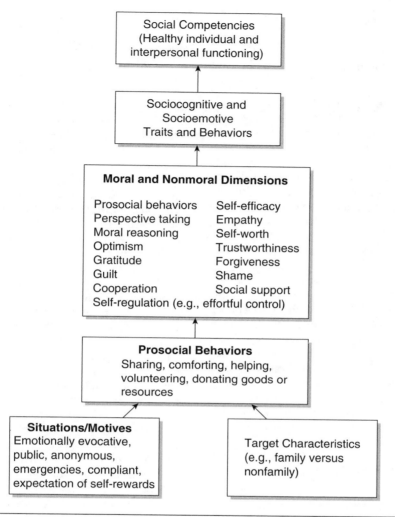

Figure 12.1   Overview of Prosocial Behaviors and Social Competence

evidence on the heritability of empathic responding, evidence of the early presence of empathy and prosocial behaviors, and evidence of stable individual differences across childhood to young adulthood (see Carlo, 2006). What is of particular interest, however, is that despite the almost universal propensity for prosocial tendencies, individual and culture group differences in prosocial behaviors are also evident.

Two aspects of the definition of prosocial behaviors merit attention. First, these actions imply beneficial consequences for others. It is not enough to suggest that there are nonharmful consequences; rather, other individuals have benefited psychologically or materially. However, positive consequences for others are not sufficient, because actions can benefit others as well as harm them. The second aspect is the underlying intention of the action. Accurately determining the underlying intent of any action is challenging, thus making this aspect of the definition the most controversial. Not surprisingly, there has been much debate and discussion surrounding the assessment of the motives underlying benevolence. Furthermore, it should be noted that not all forms of prosocial behaviors are positive—that is, sometimes individuals might engage in prosocial behaviors for egoistic or eventually harmful motives (Boxer, Tisak, & Goldstein, 2004; Carlo & Randall, 2002; Hawley, 2003). However, given space limitations and for purposes of this chapter, we assume that prosocial behaviors are generally actions deemed socially desirable (at least relative to aggressive behaviors). Now that we have defined the focus variables of this chapter, we turn our attention to the role of culture.

THEORETICAL PERSPECTIVES

The Role of Culture in Prosocial Development

Anthropologically Rooted and Cultural Psychology Perspectives. Anthropologically rooted perspectives, including cultural and sociocultural psychology, have contributed substantially to current understanding of the role of culture in human functioning and development. These approaches underscore the need to understand behavior within its cultural context and depict culture as central to and inextricable from human functioning (Markus & Hamedani, 2007).

Anthropological research has long documented the socialization of prosocial behaviors in various societies through field research and ethnographies (for review, see Eisenberg, Fabes, & Spinard, 2006). For example, John Whiting, Beatrice Whiting, and research collaborators' classic early Six Cultures Study of Socialization showed that children from subsistence-based economies who participated in wage or house labor and tended to younger children were more likely to show prosocial behaviors than those from industrialized economies (Whiting & Whiting, 1975). Subsequent analyses further showed that within cultures, opportunities and access to particular contexts partly explained those culture differences (de Guzman, Carlo, & Edwards, 2008; de Guzman, Edwards, & Carlo, 2005).

Recently, cultural psychologists and anthropologists have proposed socialization models that focus on what is referred to as the "learning environment" (Whiting, 1980), "activity settings" (Farver, 1999), "ecocultural context" (Weisner, 2002), or the "developmental niche" (Super & Harkness, 1986). These approaches emphasize children's development as competent members of their societies through their day-to-day interactions. Although this approach has not been applied extensively to understanding prosocial development in Latino cultures, the approach shows great potential, especially with regard to examining socialization processes.

Cross-Cultural Psychological Perspectives. Another approach to understanding the role of culture in human functioning is the examination of broad dimensions along which culture groups might vary. Barry, Child, and Bacon (1959) showed that agricultural societies valued interdependence and cooperation more so than societies based on hunting and fishing. Geert Hofstede's (1984) study, with more than 100,000 participants across 40 countries, revealed four dimensions along which he proposed that societies varied: power distance, uncertainty avoidance, individualism, and masculinity. Extending this work, Shalom Schwartz (1992; Schwartz & Bilsky, 1987) identified 56 values that serve as "guiding principles" for individuals and along which cultures varied (e.g., social power, obedience, equality). Those values together formed 10 broad dimensions (e.g., power, universalism, benevolence), which were further collapsed into the dimensions of individualism and collectivism, along which cultures would be mapped in their degree of adherence to such tendencies.

Those dimensions are relevant to understanding culture group differences in prosocial tendencies and have been linked to such prosocially related factors as religiosity (Cukur, de Guzman, & Carlo, 2004; Roccas & Schwartz, 1997) and other worldviews (Hunter, 2008). Often, these studies show that children from societies that foster interdependence and collectivism—for instance, Israeli kibbutz children (e.g., Madsen & Shapira, 1977), Gikuyu Kenyan children (e.g., Munroe & Munroe, 1977) and Mexican American children in the United States (e.g., Knight & Kagan, 1977)—exhibit more prosocial and/or cooperative tendencies than children from more individualistic societies like the United States. While not necessarily explaining why differences exist, cross-cultural research has nonetheless clearly illustrated that cultural groups vary in prosocial behaviors, often in ways consistent with broader cultural factors such as individualism-collectivism or values.

Traditional Models of Prosocial Behavior. Although systematic psychological studies of prosocial behaviors began earlier in the 20th century (e.g., Hartshorne, May, & Shuttleworth, 1930), research on prosocial behaviors did not become prominent until the 1970s with the pioneering work on bystander intervention studies (Latané & Darley, 1970). Based mostly on social psychological methods, this research focused on situational factors that influence people's responses to emergency situations. The research illuminated the importance of proximal contextual factors (e.g., group size, physical characteristics of the victim, mood) in helping responses. However, other scholars began investigations examining the relevance of socialization processes, sociocognitive skills, and traits such as moral reasoning, perspective taking, and empathy to helping behaviors (Batson, 1991; Eisenberg & Mussen, 1989; Hoffman, 1970; Staub, 1978). This spurt of interest and research resulted in several theoretical advances. Hoffman (1970), for example, showed substantial evidence on the central role of empathy-related processes and disciplinary practices in prosocial development. Batson (1991) developed an empathy-altruism model that asserts the role of empathy as predictive of altruistic behaviors. Both Staub (1978) and Eisenberg (1986) integrated cognitive developmental and social learning theories that resulted in comprehensive models of prosocial behaviors.

Increasing attention has been placed on understanding the developmental trajectories and correlates of specific forms of prosocial behaviors. Several scholars have developed models of prosocial behaviors that identify important distinctions between different types of prosocial behaviors (Eberly & Montemayor, 1998; Hawley, 2003; Kumru, Carlo, & Edwards, 2004). For example, some researchers have presented evidence that prosocial behaviors toward kin and in the home context are distinct from prosocial behaviors aimed at non-kin (as has been studied in much of the traditional research literature) or in nonhome contexts (Eberly & Montemayor, 1998; de Guzman et al., 2005; Kumru et al., 2004). Others have shown that prosocial behaviors have distinct underlying motives (both egoistic and selfless) that are important to discern (Batson, 1991; Hawley, 2003). Based on previous theory and research, Carlo and Randall (2002) developed a typology of prosocial behaviors based on situations and motives. Although prior research had suggested that these are important influential factors, these recent investigative approaches have attempted to systematically examine the specific correlates of these different forms of helping. The findings thus far present strong evidence for the need to examine specific forms of prosocial behaviors that differ as a function of the situational and contextual characteristics, the target of helping, and the underlying motive. Although conceptualizing prosocial behaviors as a global construct or disposition might be useful under specific circumstances, important differences among specific types of prosocial behaviors might be overlooked, or the findings might be misleading.

The accumulated work on prosocial behaviors has resulted in great advances in the conceptualization and measurement of prosocial behaviors. Furthermore, much knowledge has been gained regarding the personal, interpersonal, and contextual correlates of prosocial behaviors. However, although cultural group differences were acknowledged in some of the early work, and there were some notable examples of cross-cultural studies of prosocial development (e.g., Eisenberg, 1986; Staub, 1978), most of the early theories about and research on prosocial behavior relegated culture to be minimally relevant. Of particular relevance to the present chapter is the fact that other than a few studies on cooperative behaviors, studies of prosocial development in Latino populations are relatively few. Moreover, theories that elaborate on culture-specific processes of prosocial development in Latino populations are rare as well.

Latino-Specific Models of Prosocial Development

A Culturally Based Socialization Model of Value-Based Behaviors. One of the first models of Latino youth prosocial development was developed by Knight and his colleagues (Knight, Bernal, & Carlo 1995; Knight, Bernal, Garza, & Cota, 1993). In their model (see Figure 12.2), Knight focused on two important influences of prosocial behaviors: socialization processes (family) and ethnic identity. According to these theorists, ecological variables influence family-based and nonfamily-based socialization agents who, in turn, influence children's ethnic identity and subsequent value-based behaviors (including prosocial and cooperative behaviors). In addition, sociocognitive skills are hypothesized to moderate the paths between socialization and ethnic identity and between ethnic identity and value-based behaviors. Knight and his associates have presented some evidence in support of their model (Knight et al., 1993). This line of research supports the contention that sociocognitive skills (such as perspective taking) place an upper limit on children's abilities to develop a strong sense of ethnic identity, which in turn predicts cooperative behaviors. One might expect that as children's sociocognitive abilities mature, sociocognitive traits have more direct (mediating) effects on ethnic identity and subsequent prosocial behaviors.

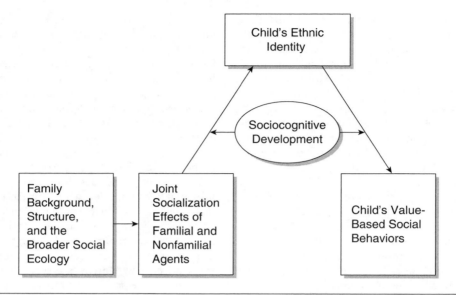

Figure 12.2   A Culturally Based Socialization Model of Value-Based Behaviors (Adapted From Knight et al., 1995)

A Model of U.S. Latino Youth Prosocial Development. Recently, we developed a model (see Raffaelli et al., 2005) that integrates knowledge regarding stress (Lazarus, 1991), acculturative stress (Berry, 2006), ethnic identity (Knight et al., 1995), sociocognitive development (Kurdek, 1981; Shantz & Shantz, 1985; Work & Olsen, 1990), and the broader influences of Latino youth development (Laosa, 1990; see also García Coll et al., 1996). This model was applied to understanding Latino prosocial development, especially among older children and adolescents (see Figure 12.3). Specifically, based on existing models of coping and stress (Compas, 1987; Lazarus & Folkman, 1984), we adopt the premise that cognitive processes, which are mediating variables of youth development in Laosa's (1990) model, are linked to youth's experience of acculturative stress. The receiving community and school context, characteristics of the family and child, and life events are posited to influence sociocognitive and socioemotive processes, which in turn influence acculturative stress, which in turn influences Latino youth's adjustment. Although not depicted in Figure 12.3 due to space limitations, it is expected that there are bidirectional effects from the acculturative stress and developmental outcomes to youth's social context and their family and personal characteristics. We now present a brief review of each component of the model.

The characteristics of the receiving community are factors over which Latino youth have no control but which may nevertheless influence the Latino child's prosocial development. For example, some communities have a substantial proportion of Latino residents, and others have a relatively small number. Prior research has shown that minority children who strongly identify with their cultures of origin tend to evidence well-being and positive adjustment, compared to minority children who reject their culture of origin (McLoyd, 1990), and that the minority status of Hispanics in the community might impact Latino youth development (Keefe & Padilla, 1987; Knight et al., 1995). One might expect that Latino children who reside in communities whose Latino population is proportionately large might be better able to retain a strong sense of ethnic identity because their peer and community institutions might foster and reward beliefs and behaviors consistent with their Latino roots (Carlo, Carranza, & Zamboanga, 2002). Thus, Latinos who reside in proportionately large Latino contexts might be better able to retain their identification with their cultures of origin, which might be associated with prosocial values and behaviors that reinforce their Latino heritage.

Because supportive parents and peers often model and promote positive social behaviors, socialization theorists (Hoffman, 1994; Staub,

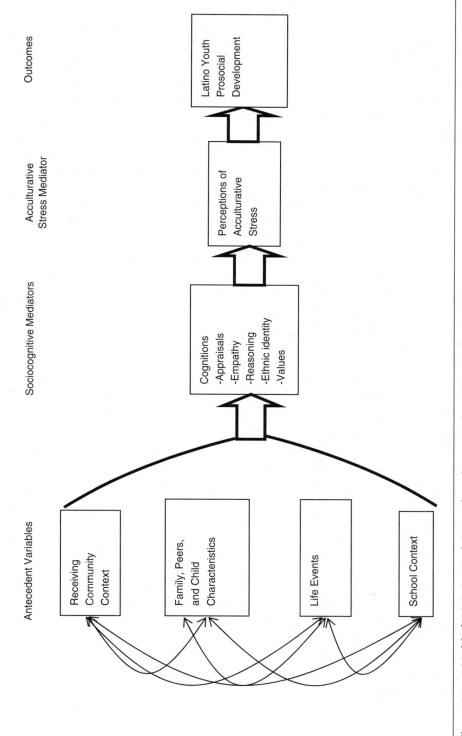

Figure 12.3 A Model of U.S. Latino Youth Prosocial Development (Adapted From Raffaelli et al., 2005)

1978) have hypothesized links between parent and peer relationships and children's moral development. Consistent with this suggestion, several researchers (see Eisenberg et al., 2006; Maccoby & Martin, 1983) have reported significant relations such that supportive parenting is generally associated with high levels of prosocial behaviors and low levels of antisocial behaviors. Furthermore, children who are raised in a warm, supportive, family environment are exposed to well-regulated emotional responding (such as sympathy responding; Eisenberg et al., 2006). These responses and skills may, in turn, lead to positive social behavioral outcomes for these children. Although supportive families may buffer children from negative symptomatology, there is substantial evidence that high levels of stress and conflict in the family may lead to negative symptomatology and low levels of well-being and social competence (Masten, Garmezy, Tellegen, & Pellegrini, 1988; Portes & Zady, 2002). Because supportive and close family relationships are considered an important source of social support, cooperative and prosocial tendencies among Latinos are deemed a strong protective factor for high-risk families. Relatedly, attachment theorists note the powerful affective, cognitive, and behavioral systems responsible for the development of secure intimate relationships (Thompson, 2006). Thus, there are conceptual reasons to believe that attachment to parents might promote prosocial competencies among Latino youth.

Closely tied to the notion of strong family characteristics is the strong value of maintaining close family relationships. Family plays a central role in shaping Latinos' experiences (Carlo et al., 2002; Fuligni, Tseng, & Lam, 1999). This value is reflected in familism—the strong identification with, and attachment and loyalty to, one's family, which has also been well documented among Latinos (e.g., Sabogal, Marín, Otero-Sabogal, Marín, & Pérez-Stable, 1987; Suárez-Orozco & Suárez-Orozco, 1995). In contrast to other societies (such as the United States), Latinos encourage close-knit families. For example, Brazilian parents guide and urge their children to stay physically and psychologically close to family, including extended family members. Furthermore, relationships with extended family members are maintained through frequent social interactions and close physical proximity. Older and extended family members maintain active roles in family activities. Young family members might be raised not only by parents but by siblings, aunts, uncles, and grandparents. Respect toward adult family members is strongly reinforced, and there are usually clear rules and consequences (e.g., social disapproval, shame) when respect is violated. Moreover, even when children enter adulthood, parents (and grandparents) are sought as sources of financial, instrumental, and emotional support. Indeed, some researchers have shown that Latinos strongly endorse connectedness with family members and respect for authority and elders—characteristics of societies that reflect a collective/interdependent orientation (see Greenfield & Cocking, 1994).

The strength of family ties in Latino families might serve as an important source of social support for Latino children who experience acculturative stress and difficulties in adjusting to the receiving community (González & Padilla, 1997). Indeed, there is evidence that Latinos strongly endorse familism and family interdependence (Raffaelli et al., 2005; Suárez-Orozco, Todorova, & Louie, 2002). Of most relevance to this chapter is that various types of prosocial behaviors are important for building and maintaining close family relationships. For example, sharing, nurturance, and comforting behaviors are types of prosocial behaviors that foster close family relationships. Frequently, prosocial behaviors trigger reciprocal prosocial behaviors and promote trust and positive affect—basic characteristics of close, intimate relationships. Furthermore, many Latino children are socialized by their families to respect authority figures (the concept of *respeto*) and to show good manners (e.g., not interrupting others while they speak, humility; concepts related to *bien educado*)—attributes that are congruent with prosocial behaviors (Knight et al., 1995).

Unfortunately, little theorizing and research have been done on the influence of peers on Latino youth's prosocial development in the United States. Theoretically, like families, peers can serve as sources of social support, which is often related negatively to stress (Barrera, 1986). However, the characteristics of peer relationships are somewhat different from those of parent-child relationships. Peers are more equal to children in social status and power than parents are; thus, peer relationships may provide opportunities for children to experiment and explore new behaviors. Furthermore, peers might expose children to values, beliefs, and behaviors alternative to those of parents and family. Prior research shows that European American children with strong attachment to and support from peers exhibit good adjustment and prosocial behaviors (e.g., Laible, Carlo, & Raffaelli, 2000). However, research on the specific relations between peer support and Latino children's prosocial development is lacking.

Laosa (1990) notes that Latinos are particularly prone to a "pile-up" of life changes and events that put them at high risk for stress and negative symptomatology (see also Olson, Lavee, & McCubbin, 1988). Evidence is growing that many Latino children and adolescents in mostly European American communities experience psychosocial difficulties, perhaps as a result of language barriers, family stress due to poverty, and cultural barriers, including discrimination and negative stereotyping. Furthermore, Werner and colleagues (e.g., Werner & Smith, 1992, 2001) identified factors that put children at risk of negative developmental outcomes; these factors include chronic poverty, low parental education, and chaotic living environments (see also García Coll et al., 1996). Research confirms that youngsters who experience negative life events are at heightened risk of negative behavioral and psychological outcomes (e.g., Compas, Malcarne, & Fondacaro, 1988; Jackson & Warren, 2000). Those risk factors are characteristic of many Latino youth; thus, one might expect adverse life events to be a predictor of stress, and in turn this might mitigate Latino youth's prosocial development.

Based on sociocultural models of development, Latino children's day-to-day social routines and interactions can impact their prosocial development. Because Latino youth spend a disproportionate amount of time at school, a number of school variables are likely relevant to Latino youth's prosocial behaviors, including structural features (e.g., school size, timing of transitions), school quality (e.g., teacher qualifications, graduation and college attendance rates), school-home connection (e.g., parental and familial involvement with school staff), and school environment (e.g., students' sense of belongingness; see Portes, 1999). Although there is ample desire for Latino families to become involved in their children's education (Bernal, Saenz, & Knight, 1995), a number of culture-specific factors (e.g., language, lack of knowledge about the school system, lack of academic self-efficacy, discrimination experiences) can mitigate strong connections to the child's school (see Delgado-Gaitán, 2004). One possible consequence is that unless parents, teachers, and staff become acquainted with each other, the Latino child's positive attitudes and beliefs regarding school involvement could be compromised. This, in turn, could result in lower levels of exhibited prosocial behaviors among Latino youth. Indeed, the existing research suggests that school connectedness is one of the most crucial factors in positive development for children and adolescents (Bernal et al., 1995; González & Padilla, 1997); in one study, students' feelings of connection to their school was the only factor that showed a consistent pattern of linkages with youth emotional well-being, risk taking, and violence (Blum & Rinehart, 1997). Given that these school-related factors are likely associated with immigration status, these processes are likely to have particular impact on Latino families who have recently immigrated.

The pattern of good adjustment exhibited by many children stems in part from the development of sociocognitive and socioemotional competencies, including stress appraisals, moral reasoning, empathy, and ethnic identity. For example, there is extensive theoretical and empirical support for the positive mediating role of challenge appraisals and the negative mediating role of threat appraisals on adjustment (see Lazarus, 1991). Individuals who use challenge appraisals tend to use approach or problem-focused coping strategies that reduce the source of the stress and minimize loss; in contrast, individuals who use threat appraisals tend to use avoidance or passive coping strategies that are linked to high stress and exacerbate loss (Folkman, Lazarus, Dunkel-Schetter, DeLongis, & Gruen, 1986; Lazarus & Folkman, 1984).

It is important to note that acculturative stress is considered a risk variable for Latino immigrants' prosocial competencies. Immigrants are particularly susceptible to stress associated with changes in adjusting to a new culture (i.e., acculturative stress). Berry (1994) suggested that a number of variables influence acculturative stress and that there is substantial evidence that acculturative stress is linked to negative adjustment and developmental outcomes among minority populations (e.g., Berry & Kim, 1988; Berry, 2005). For example, as discussed in the earlier description of the model, one would expect that the impact of acculturative stress on Latinos would depend on their appraisals of the stress in a manner analogous to the way individuals appraise and respond to other types of stress. Furthermore, the extent to which Latinos can accurately decode the situations of others (i.e., perspective taking) would likely affect their stress, and this in turn would likely impact their prosocial development. Finally, it is worth considering the possibility that moderate levels of acculturative stress might actually induce some forms of helping behaviors as a way to deal effectively with stressors.

As mentioned earlier, traditional models of prosocial development emphasize sociocognitive and socioemotive traits (e.g., moral reasoning, sympathy, perspective taking) as predictors of prosocial and moral development. Somewhat surprisingly, few studies exist with Latino samples (but see Carlo, Koller, Eisenberg, Da Silva, & Frohlich, 1996; Eisenberg, Zhou, & Koller, 2001), and to our knowledge, other than a few studies of moral reasoning, no studies exist with U.S. Latino youth. It is important to note that sociocognitive and socioemotive traits can also serve as factors that buffer or protect at-risk children from negative symptomatology (Grych & Fincham, 1992). For example, Kurdek (1981) posited that perspective taking could help children understand stressful life situations and buffer them from overexposure to those situations (see also Work & Olsen, 1990). Similarly, Spivak and Shure (1988) showed that perspective-taking skills are related to problem-solving skills and that these skills mitigate risky decision making. Wentzel and Asher (1995) found that peer-neglected and rejected-submissive children who are considerate of others were less likely to show maladjustment than rejected-aggressive children were. Given the sparse research on these processes in Latino youth samples, investigations of sociocognitive and socioemotive traits and their relations to prosocial competencies is a promising area for future studies.

Another mediating sociocognitive variable relevant to Latino youth's prosocial development is ethnic identity (Knight et al., 1995). Identity development has long been regarded as a key task for adolescents (e.g., Erikson, 1968; Marcia, 1980). In recent years, scholars have recognized that identity development is complicated for ethnically diverse adolescents because, in addition to negotiating the traditional domains of identity (e.g., love, work, ideology), they must also decide what their ethnicity means to them (Phinney, 1990). Research reveals that Latino youth who have well-developed senses of

ethnic identity also have better psychosocial outcomes (see Phinney, 1990). Others have argued that Latino youth who are capable of navigating both mainstream and ethnic conclaves might be better adjusted (Berry, 2005). However, the question of whether prosocial behaviors are linked to the development of a positive sense of ethnic identity among Latino youth remains largely unanswered. Although some research exists (reviewed directly following), much remains unknown about the links between ethnic identity and prosocial and moral behaviors, especially since few longitudinal studies are available.

In summary, available models of Latino children's prosocial development are scarce. Perhaps not surprisingly, empirical studies on this topic are rare as well. However, in the next section, we briefly summarize existing research on U.S. Latinos among a select range of positive social outcomes, including cooperative and prosocial behaviors and moral development.

EMPIRICAL RESEARCH ON PROSOCIAL COMPETENCIES AMONG LATINOS IN THE UNITED STATES

Based on the notions that a collectivist orientation and the values associated with Latino culture facilitate prosocial behaviors, researchers have conducted investigations on culture-group differences. Some studies on cooperative behaviors among Mexican Americans yield evidence that Mexican American children exhibit significantly more cooperative behaviors than European Americans (see Table 12.1; for detailed reviews, see Knight et al., 1995; McClintock, Bayard, & McClintock, 1983). Other investigators report that Mexican American children expect sharing behaviors more than African American peers do (Rotheram-Borus & Phinney, 1990), and that high-income Mexican American families valued others' help more than European American families did (Williams, 1991).

Other studies have focused on the development and correlates of prosocial behaviors among Latino families (for studies on Brazilian youth, see Carlo et al., 1996; Carlo, Roesch, Knight, & Koller, 2001; Eisenberg et al., 2001). For example, consistent with their model of value-based behaviors (discussed earlier), Knight

Table 12.1 Summary of Studies on Prosocial Behaviors and Moral Reasoning Among Latinos

Citation	Participants	Measures	Ethnic Group Main Findings
Carlo, Knight, McGinley, Zamboanga, & Jarvis (in press)	152 Mexican Americans, 290 European Americans; M age = 12.67 years	Six types of prosocial behaviors, parental monitoring, externalizing behaviors, and religiosity	European Americans reported more altruism and compliant helping than Mexican Americans. No significant differences between groups in the relations between prosocial behaviors and gender, externalizing behaviors, religiousness, and parental monitoring.
Cook-Gumperz & Szymanski (2001)	3rd-graders in a mostly bilingual (Spanish-English) classroom	One-year observations with behaviors videotaped; interaction analysis of group organization and activity. Units of observation were the small groups designated as "families" by the teacher.	Girls, more so than boys, tended to take leadership in their small groups to accomplish tasks by helping others in the group to achieve the group task. Girls also acted as brokers between their small "families" and the rest of the classroom. Some gender exclusivity emerged, with girls paying more attention to other girls' actions rather than to boys'.
Commons, Galaz-Fontes & Morse (2006)	*Study 1:* 34 adults (23–70 years, M = 49.6) with little to no education *Study 2:* 30 teens from Mexico who were in public high school	Shortened Kohlberg moral reasoning measure	*Study 1:* 75% of nonliterate respondents reached formal operations (contrary to idea of need for education to reach that stage) *Study 2:* 0% preoperational, 13% primary operations, 60% concrete operations, 23% abstract operations, 3% formal operations
Cortese (1982)	169 school children (100 Anglo Americans, 69 Chicanos) 7–15 years old	5 videotaped moral dilemmas, Defining Issue Test	Anglo Americans scored higher than Chicanos on the moral judgment measures. Results support a multidimensional nature of moral reasoning.
Cortese (1989)	70 British, Mexican American, African American, and White American male and female college students	Moral Judgment Interview	No significant differences among groups

(Continued)

Table 12.1 (Continued)

Citation	Participants	Measures	Ethnic Group Main Findings
de Guzman & Carlo (2004)	63 Latino youth from Nebraska, average age 14.52 years	Inventory of Parent and Peer Attachment, Prosocial Tendencies Measure, Family Adaptability and Cohesion Scale, Short Acculturation Scale for Hispanic Youth	Results of multiple regression analyses suggest that acculturation negatively predicted prosocial behavior tendencies (i.e., the higher the level of acculturation, the lower the tendency to perform prosocial acts). Peer but not parent attachment, and family adaptability but not cohesion, positively predicted prosocial tendencies.
Goodman, Getzel, & Ford (1996)	16-to-20-year-old African American and Latino young men on probation who were at high risk of re-arrest	Over a 4-month period, participants joined 32 sessions, which included role-playing, sharing, etc.	Group leaders served as models to young people of color. Activities served as a "catalyst" for prosocial action outside of jail.
Gump, Baker, & Roll (2000)	40 Mexican American and 40 Anglo American college students	Moral Justification Scale of care and justice, social desirability, acculturation	Mexican Americans scored higher than Anglo Americans on care orientation. Groups scored equally on justice orientation.
Hart & Fegley (1995)	15 care exemplars (2 African American males, 6 African American females, 3 Latin American males, 4 Latin American females), average age = 15.5 years; 15 matched teens	Self-descriptions, self-understanding interviews, and identity matrix	Exemplars were more likely to describe themselves in terms of moral personality traits and as having closer continuity between past and future; to think of self as incorporating their ideals and parental images; and to articulate theories of self in which personal philosophies are important.
Kagan & Knight (1979)	41 second-generation and 50 third-generation Mexican American children and 45 Caucasian American children	Self-Esteem Inventory and the Social Behavior Scale	High self-esteem was related to cooperativeness, but only among second-generation Mexican Americans who had a cultural norm of cooperativeness. High self-esteem was related to competitiveness among Anglo Americans who displayed a cultural norm of competitiveness.
Kagan & Knight (1984)	126 mothers of Anglo American children and 63 mothers of Mexican American children	Reinforcement style; Social Behavior Scale assessing prosocial and competitive motives and behaviors	Nonpunitive and rewarding parenting pattern did not predict prosocial development. Results suggest cultural variability in predictors of prosocial outcomes. Mexican American children generally showed more cooperative behaviors than Anglo American children.

Citation	Participants	Measures	Ethnic Group Main Findings
Kerr, Beck, Shattuck, Kattar, & Uriburu (2003)	446 Latino adolescents ages 14–19 years	Parental monitoring, familial connectedness, academic encouragement and support, sociocultural encouragement, problem behaviors, and prosocial behaviors	Parental monitoring was specifically associated with helping within the family and with volunteerism. Sociocultural encouragement was associated with more prosocial behavior involvement.
Knight, Cota, & Bernal (1993)	59 Mexican American children (aged 9–12 yrs) and their mothers	*Mothers:* Ethnic knowledge and preference, teaching about ethnic culture *Children:* Children's Ethnic Self-Identification Scale, Children's Ethnic Knowledge Scale, Children's Ethnic Preference Scale, and the Resource Allocation Task	Mothers' ethnic backgrounds were related to their teaching about the Mexican culture, which in turn were related to the children's ethnic identities. Furthermore, the ethnic identities of the children were related to their cooperative, competitive, and individualistic preferences.
Knight & Kagan (1977)	58 third-generation and 44 Anglo American children from 4th to 6th grades	Measure of cooperative, competitive, individualistic orientation (Social Orientation Choice Card)	Higher-generation status was associated with decreasing frequency of altruism and group enhancement and equality choices. Higher generation level associated with increasing frequency of rivalry/superiority choices.
Knight & Kagan (1977)	139 children ages 5–6 and 7–9 years from three populations: upper-middle-SES Anglo American, lower-SES Anglo American, and lower-SES Mexican American	Social Behavior Scale, which assesses altruism/group enhancement, equality, superiority, and rivalry/superiority	For the two lower-SES groups, Mexican American children tended to be more prosocial with age, while Anglo American children were increasingly competitive with age. For the two Anglo American groups, lower-SES children made more prosocial choices compared to upper-middle-SES children.
Knight & Kagan (1982)	126 Anglo American and 63 Mexican American children, ages 5–12 years	Social Behavior Scale and mothers' interviews	Mexican American children displayed more cooperative behaviors, even after controlling for number of siblings and birth order. No relations were found between cooperative-competitive behaviors and number of siblings.

(Continued)

Table 12.1 (Continued)

Citation	Participants	Measures	Ethnic Group Main Findings
Knight, Kagan, & Buriel (1982)	120 Anglo American and Mexican American 4th–6th- graders	Social Orientation Choice Card; Parent Practices Questionnaire	Mexican American children displayed more cooperative tendencies and less competitive tendencies than Anglo American children.
Knight, Nelson, Kagan, & Gumbiner (1982)	125 Mexican American and 45 Anglo American 4th–6th-graders	School achievement, responsibility, self-esteem, field independence, cooperativeness, and competitiveness	For Anglo Americans but not Mexican Americans, competitiveness was positively related to school achievement. Personality variables were moderately but not independently related to school achievement within both cultural groups, and the between-culture variance in the personality variables did not account for the between-culture variance in school achievement.
Healey & DeBlassie (1974)	425 Anglo American, 40 African American, and 142 Spanish American 9th graders	Tennessee Self Concept Scale and a demographic questionnaire on socioeconomic status	Spanish Americans had highest scores on the Moral-Ethical Self Scale, followed by the Anglo Americans and African Americans.
Longshore (1998)	90 Mexican Americans, 21% women, 13% employed, 11% married. M age=29.6	Drug-problem recognition, polydrug use, neighborhood drug problems, conventional moral beliefs	Lifetime polydrug use and conventional moral beliefs were independently related to the perception that one's own drug use is a problem (drug-problem recognition).
Samples (1997)	436 African American and 387 Latino 2nd–6th-graders, ages 5.89–13.87 years (M = 8.8 years); 52% boys, 48% girls	Normative Beliefs About Aggression, Aggressive Fantasy Scale, home interview, interpersonal negotiation strategies, negative symptoms	Latinos reported more prosocial fantasies and more normative beliefs about aggression.
Schwartz, Zamboanga, & Jarvis (2007)	347 Latinos in Michigan, 6th–8th grades	Acculturation, ethnic identity, acculturative stress, self-esteem, depression, conduct disorder, prosocial behaviors, academic grades	Participants showed greater U.S. orientation than Latino orientation, potentially because majority were U.S. born. Relations between grades and externalizing symptoms and between ethnic identity and externalizing symptoms were mediated by self-esteem. Both U.S. and Latino orientations were directly related to higher prosocial tendencies.

and colleagues (1993) found that Mexican American mothers' ethnic knowledge and culture teachings predicted the child's ethnic identity, and this in turn predicted the U.S. Latino children's cooperative behaviors. Kerr and colleagues (Kerr, Beck, Shattuck, Kattar, & Uriburu, 2003) showed that parental monitoring and sociocultural encouragement were associated with helping and prosocialness among Latino adolescents. Another small set of studies focused on closely related moral development constructs (see Table 12.1). As can be seen in the table, those studies show mixed evidence on culture-group differences in moral reasoning indices. For example, some studies showed that U.S. Latinos reported higher levels of moral reasoning than European Americans (Gump, Baker, & Roll, 2000, for care-oriented reasoning; Healey & DeBlassie, 1974); other studies reported no significant differences between groups (Cortese, 1989; Gump et al., 2000, for justice-oriented reasoning); and one reported that European Americans scored higher than U.S. Latinos (Cortese, 1982). Finally, another small set of studies examined processes associated with prosocial and moral development, such as moral identity processes (Hart & Fegley, 1995) and gender issues (Cook-Gumperz & Szymanski, 2001).

A recent study of early adolescents from the Midwest deserves special focus because the study is the largest study of prosocial behaviors among U.S. Latinos to date. Thus far, two published reports highlight findings regarding prosocial behaviors. In the first report, Schwartz, Zamboanga, and Jarvis (2007) found support that ethnic identity was related positively to prosocial behaviors (although the effects disappeared once acculturative stress and self-esteem were statistically accounted for). Interestingly, these scholars also reported positive associations between U.S. and Hispanic orientation (acculturation and enculturation) and prosocial behaviors, suggesting that both orientations might be adaptive, especially in the context of a relatively homogenous community (a community in the Midwest). Given that most prior studies of the acculturation and behavioral outcomes have been conducted in more heterogeneous communities (East, West, Southwest regions of the United States), these latter findings deserve further examination.

The second report from the study in the Midwest examined the multidimensionality of a measure of prosocial behaviors, including its correlates across Latinos and European Americans (Carlo et al., in press). In this study, researchers found evidence that both culture groups distinguished among six different types of prosocial behaviors. Moreover, functional equivalence of the measure was shown such that compliant prosocial behaviors were related negatively to externalizing behaviors; parental monitoring was positively associated with emotional, dire, and compliant prosocial behaviors; and religiosity was linked positively to compliant, anonymous, and altruistic prosocial behaviors. Finally, European Americans reported higher levels of altruistic and compliant prosocial behaviors; and Latinas reported higher levels of emotional, dire, compliant, and altruistic prosocial behaviors but lower levels of public prosocial behaviors than Latinos. The findings provide evidence that there are distinct types of prosocial behaviors, that there are culture-group differences in specific forms of prosocial behaviors, and that parenting, religiosity, and externalizing behaviors are related to specific forms of prosocial behaviors. These latter relations imply, as suggested by previous research with U.S. Latinos (see Zamboanga & Carlo, 2007), that prosocial behaviors and problem behaviors are not one continuum.

As can be seen in Table 12.1, few studies on prosocial and moral development exist. Therefore, firm conclusions regarding U.S. Latino youth prosocial and moral development are difficult to draw, and our understanding of positive social development among U.S. Latinos is quite limited. Nonetheless, some interesting methodological trends have emerged that deserve attention. We now turn briefly to some of those trends and recommend methodological directions for future research.

METHODOLOGICAL ISSUES

A glance at the studies listed in Table 12.1 also reveals general methodological and study trends that should be noted. First, there is still great need for qualitative and observational study designs to develop ecologically meaningful models of prosocial development and culturally valid measures of prosocial competencies. Second, longitudinal studies designed to focus on prosocial development in U.S. Latinos are virtually nonexistent. This hampers our ability to understand changes in prosocial competencies over time, to have adequate study controls, and to better discern direction of causality in studies. Third, there are many gaps in our knowledge regarding biological and environment influences (and their potential interactive effects) on prosocial development among U.S. Latinos. For example, studies on peer influences, media influences, temperament, self-regulation, and extended family influences are lacking. Fourth, as can be seen in the table, most researchers to date have examined either cooperative behaviors or a broad measure of prosocial behaviors or social competence. However, there is growing evidence of the need for research on different forms of prosocial behaviors (Carlo et al., in press; Eberly & Montemayor, 1998; Hawley, 2003; Kumru et al., 2004). And fifth, eventually, more sophisticated multivariate study designs will be needed to conduct more comprehensive studies that will further our understanding of the complex processes of prosocial development among U.S. Latino populations. These culturally competent and sophisticated studies will enable the development of culturally based intervention programs designed to foster prosocial development in U.S. Latino populations.

CONCLUSIONS

The calls for more normative and strength-based theories and research among ethnic minority groups in the United States coincide with the general call for more positive psychological research (see Seligman & Csikszentmihalyi, 2000). In light of the sparse research on prosocial and social competencies and the high-risk status of many Latinos in the United States, the need for research on these competencies is great. The effort will require multidisciplinary perspectives and methodologies to tackle the complexities and challenges of conducting research on Latinos. These approaches are critical for presenting a more balanced perspective on humans of all backgrounds. Furthermore, they have important implications for intervention and policy programs. Evidence is accumulating that the lack of pathology is not equal to the presence of health and well-being (Consortium on the School-Based Promotion of Social Competence, 1994). As noted earlier, with regard to prosocial behaviors, research with Latinos has yielded evidence that prosocial behaviors are not on a continuum with aggressive and problem behaviors. The implications are that intervention and policy programs must specifically address the reduction of problem behaviors *and* the promotion of positive health and well-being behaviors. As Latinos become greater in number in the United States and embed themselves deeper in the fabric of our society, we can ill afford to not heed this call. We hope the present chapter serves to inspire these efforts.

NOTE

1. There is no simple solution to the use of various terms used to describe individuals who have origins in Spanish- and Portuguese-influenced countries from North, Central, and South America and from the Caribbean. While we acknowledge that there are differences and commonalities within groups, the term *Latino* is used in the broadest sense of the word, as applicable to all people with origins in those countries.

REFERENCES

Barrera, M. (1986). Distinctions between social support concepts, measures, and models. *American Journal of Community Psychology, 14,* 413–445.

Barry, H., Child, I. L., & Bacon, M. K. (1959). Relation of child training to subsistence economy. *American Anthropologist, 61,* 51–63.

Batson, C. D. (1991). *The altruism question: Toward a social–psychological answer.* Hillsdale, NJ: Lawrence Erlbaum.

Bernal, M. E., Saenz, D. S., & Knight, G. P. (1995). Ethnic identity and adaptation of Mexican American youths in school settings. In A. M. Padilla (Ed.), *Hispanic psychology: Critical issues in theory and research* (pp. 71–88). Thousand Oaks, CA: Sage.

Berry, J. W. (1994). Acculturation and psychological adaptation: An overview. In A. Bouvy, F. J. R. van de Vijver, P. Boski, & P. G. L. Schmitz (Eds.), *Journeys into cross-cultural psychology* (pp. 129–141). Lisse, the Netherlands: Swets & Zeitlinger.

Berry, J. W. (2005). Acculturation: Living successfully in two cultures. *International Journal of Intercultural Relations, 29,* 697–712.

Berry, J. W. (2006). Acculturative stress. In P. T. P. Wong & L. C. J. Wong (Eds.), *Handbook of multicultural perspectives on stress and coping* (pp. 287–298). Dallas, TX: Spring Publications.

Berry, J. W., & Kim, U. (1988). Acculturation and mental health. In P. R. Dasen, J. W. Berry, & N. Sartorius (Eds.), *Health and cross-cultural psychology: Toward applications* (pp. 207–236). Thousand Oaks, CA: Sage.

Blum, R., & Rinehart, P. M. (1997). Reducing the risk: Connections that make a difference in the lives of youth. *Youth Studies Australia, 16,* 37–50.

Boxer, P., Tisak, M. S., & Goldstein, S. E. (2004). Is it bad to be good? An exploration of aggressive and prosocial behavior subtypes in adolescence. *Journal of Youth and Adolescence, 33,* 91–100.

Burt, K. B., Obradovic, J., Long, J. D., & Masten, A. S. (2008). The interplay of social competence and psychopathology over 20 years: Testing transactional and cascade models. *Child Development, 79,* 359–374.

Carlo, G. (2006). Care-based and altruistically based morality. In M. Killen & J. Smetana (Eds.), *Handbook of moral development* (pp. 551–579). Mahwah, NJ: Lawrence Erlbaum.

Carlo, G., Carranza, M. A., & Zamboanga, B. L. (2002). Culture and ecology of Latinos on the Great Plains: An introduction. *Great Plains Research, 12,* 3–12.

Carlo, G., Knight, G. P., McGinley, M., Goodvin, R., & Roesch, S. C. (in press). Understanding the developmental relations between perspective taking and prosocial behaviors: A meta-analytic review. In J. Carpendale, G. Iarocci, U. Muller, B. Sokol, & A. Young (Eds.), *Self- and social-regulation: Exploring the relations between social interaction, social cognition, and the development of executive functions.* Oxford, UK: Oxford University Press.

Carlo, G., Knight, G. P., McGinley, M., Zamboanga, B. L., & Jarvis, L. (in press). The multidimensionality of prosocial behaviors: Evidence of measurement invariance in early Mexican American and European American adolescents. *Journal of Research on Adolescence.*

Carlo, G., Koller, S. H., Eisenberg, N., Da Silva, M. S., & Frohlich, C. B. (1996). A cross-national study on the relations among prosocial moral reasoning, gender role orientations, and prosocial behaviors. *Developmental Psychology, 32,* 231–240.

Carlo, G., & Randall, B. A. (2002). The development of a measure of prosocial behaviors for late adolescents. *Journal of Youth and Adolescence, 31,* 31–44.

Carlo, G., Roesch, S. C., Knight, G. P., & Koller, S. H. (2001). Between or within-culture variation? Culture group as a moderator of the relations between individual differences and resource allocation preferences. *Journal of Applied Developmental Psychology, 22,* 559–579.

Commons, M. L., Galaz-Fontes, J. F., & Morse, S. J. (2006). Leadership, cross-cultural contact, socio-economic status, and formal operational reasoning about moral dilemmas among Mexican non-literate adults and high school students. *Journal of Moral Education, 35,* 247–267.

Compas, B. E. (1987). Assessment of major and daily stressful events during adolescence: The Adolescent Perceived Events Scale. *Journal of Consulting and Clinical Psychology, 55,* 534–541.

Compas, B. E., Malcarne, V. L., & Fondacaro, K. M. (1988). Coping with stressful events in older children and young adolescents. *Journal of Consulting and Clinical Psychology, 56,* 405–411.

Consortium on the School-Based Promotion of Social Competence. (1994). The School-based Promotion of Social Competence: Theory, Research, Practice and Policy. In R. J. Haggerty, L. Sherrod, N. Garmezy, & M. Rutter (Eds.), *Stress risk and resilience in children and adolescents: Processes, mechanisms, and interaction.* New York: Cambridge University Press.

Cook-Gumperz, J., & Szymanski, M. (2001). Classroom "families": Cooperating or competing—Girls' and boys' interactional styles in a bilingual classroom. *Research on Language & Social Interaction, 34,* 107–130.

Cortese, A. (1982). Moral development in Chicano and Anglo children. *Hispanic Journal of Behavioral Sciences, 4,* 353–366.

Cortese, A. J. (1989). The interpersonal approach to morality: A gender and culture analysis. *Journal of Social Psychology, 129,* 429–442.

Cukur, C. S., de Guzman, M. R. T., & Carlo, G. (2004). Religiosity, values, and horizontal and vertical individualism-collectivism: A study on Turkey, the USA, and the Philippines. *Journal of Social Psychology, 144,* 613–634.

de Guzman, M. R. T., & Carlo, G. (2004). Family, peer, and acculturative correlates of prosocial development among Latino youth in Nebraska. *Great Plains Research, 14,* 185–202.

de Guzman, M. R. T., Carlo, G., & Edwards, C. P. (2008). Prosocial behaviors in context: Examining the role of children's social companions. *International Journal of Behavioral Development, 36,* 538–546.

de Guzman, M. R. T., Edwards, C. P., & Carlo, G. (2005). Prosocial behaviors in context: A study of the Gikuyu children of Ngecha, Kenya. *Journal of Applied Developmental Psychology, 26,* 542–558.

Delgado-Gaitán, C. (2004). *Involving Latino families in schools: Raising student achievement through home-school partnerships.* Thousand Oaks, CA: Corwin Press.

DeWaal, F. (1996). *Good natured: The origins of right and wrong in humans and other animals.* Cambridge, MA: Harvard University Press.

Dunn, J. (1988). *The beginnings of social understanding.* Cambridge, MA: Harvard University Press.

Eberly, M. B., & Montemayor, R. (1998). Doing good deeds: An examination of adolescent prosocial behavior in the context of parent-adolescent relationships. *Journal of Adolescent Research, 13,* 403–432.

Eisenberg, N. (1986). *Altruistic emotion, cognition and behavior.* Hillsdale, NJ: Lawrence Erlbaum.

Eisenberg, N., Fabes, R. A., & Spinard, T. L. (2006). Prosocial development. In N. Eisenberg, W. Damon, & R. M. Lerner (Eds.), *Handbook of child psychology, Vol. 3: Social, emotional and personality development* (6th ed., pp. 646–718). New York: John Wiley.

Eisenberg, N., Michalik, N., Spinrad, T. L., Hofer, C., Kupfer, A., Valiente, C., et al. (2007). The relations of effortful control and impulsivity to children's sympathy: A longitudinal study. *Cognitive Development, 22,* 544–567.

Eisenberg, N., & Mussen, P. H. (1989). *The roots of prosocial behavior in children.* New York: Cambridge University Press.

Eisenberg, N., Zhou, Q., & Koller, S. (2001). Brazilian adolescents' prosocial moral judgment and behavior: Relations to sympathy, perspective taking, gender-role orientation, and demographic characteristics. *Child Development, 72,* 518–534.

Elliott, S. N., Gresham, F. M., Freeman, T., & McCloskey, G. (1988). Teacher and observer ratings of children's social skills: Validation of the Social Skills Rating Scales. *Journal of Psychoeducational Assessment, 6,* 152–161.

Erikson, E. (1968). *Identity: Youth and crisis.* New York: W. W. Norton.

Farver, J. A. (1999). Activity settings analysis: A model for examining the role of culture in development. In A. Goncu (Ed.), *Children's engagement in the world: Sociocultural perspectives* (pp. 99–127). Cambridge, UK: Cambridge University Press.

Folkman, S., Lazarus, R. S., Dunkel-Schetter, C., DeLongis, A., & Gruen, R. J. (1986). Dynamics of a stressful encounter: Cognitive appraisal, coping, and encounter outcomes. *Journal of Personality and Social Psychology, 50,* 992–1003.

Frankl, V. E. (1979). *The unheard cry for meaning: Psychotherapy and humanism.* New York: Touchstone Books.

Fuligni, A. J., Tseng, V., & Lam, M. (1999). Attitudes toward family obligations among American adolescents with Asian, Latin American, and European backgrounds. *Child Development, 70,* 1030–1044.

García Coll, C., Crnic, K., Lamberty, G., Wasik, B. H., Jenkins, R., García, H. V., et al. (1996). An integrative model for the study of developmental competencies in minority children. *Child Development, 67,* 1891–1914.

González, R., & Padilla, A. M. (1997). The academic resilience of Mexican American high school students. *Hispanic Journal of Behavioral Sciences, 19,* 301–317.

Goodman, H., Getzel, G. S., & Ford, W. (1996). Group work with high-risk urban youths on probation. *Social Work, 41,* 375–381.

Greenfield, P. M., & Cocking, R. R. (1994). *Cross-cultural roots of minority child development.* Hillsdale, NJ: Lawrence Erlbaum.

Gresham, F. M., & Stuart, D. (1992). Stability of sociometric assessment: Implications for uses as selection and outcome measures in social skills training. *Journal of School Psychology, 30,* 223–231.

Grych, J. H., & Fincham, F. D. (1992). Interventions for children of divorce: Toward greater integration of research and action. *Psychological Bulletin, 111,* 434–454.

Gump, L. S., Baker, R. C., & Roll, S. (2000). Cultural and gender differences in moral judgments: A study of Mexican Americans and Anglo-Americans. *Hispanic Journal of Behavioral Sciences, 22,* 78–93.

Hart, D., & Fegley, S. (1995). Prosocial behavior and caring in adolescence: Relation to self-understanding and social judgment. *Child Development, 66,* 1346–1359.

Harter, S. (1982). The Perceived Competence Scale for Children. *Child Development, 53,* 87–97.

Hartshorne, H., May, M. A., & Shuttleworth, F. K. (1930). *Studies in the nature of character.* New York: Macmillan.

Hawley, P. H. (2003). Prosocial and coercive configurations of resource control in early adolescence: A case for the well-adapted Machiavellian. *Merrill-Palmer Quarterly, 49,* 279–309.

Healey, G., & DeBlassie, R. (1974). A comparison of Negro, Anglo, and Spanish-American adolescents' self concepts. *Adolescence, 9,* 15–24.

Hoffman, M. L. (1970). Conscience, personality, and socialization techniques. *Human Development, 13,* 90–126.

Hoffman, M. L. (1994). Discipline and internalization. *Developmental Psychology, 30,* 26–28.

Hofstede, G. (1984). *Culture's consequences: International differences in work-related values* (Abridged ed.). Beverly Hills, CA: Sage.

Hunter, C. D. (2008). Individualistic and collectivistic worldviews: Implications for understanding perceptions of racial discrimination in African Americans and

British Caribbean Americans. *Journal of Counseling Psychology, 55*, 321–332.

Jackson, Y., & Warren, J. S. (2000). Appraisal, social support, and life events: Predicting outcome behavior in school-age children. *Child Development, 71*, 1441–1457.

Kagan, S., & Knight, G. P. (1979). Cooperation-competition and self-esteem: A case of cultural relativism. *Journal of Cross-Cultural Psychology, 10*, 457–467.

Kagan, S., & Knight, G. P. (1984). Maternal reinforcement style and cooperation-competition among Anglo-American and Mexican-American children. *Journal of Genetic Psychology, 145*, 37–47.

Keefe, S. E., & Padilla, A. M. (1987). *Chicano ethnicity*. Albuquerque: University of New Mexico Press.

Kerr, M. H., Beck, K., Shattuck, T. D., Kattar, C., & Uriburu, D. (2003). Family involvement, problem and prosocial behavior outcomes of Latino youth. *American Journal of Health Behavior, 27*(Supplement 1), S55-S65.

Knight, G. P., Bernal, M. E., & Carlo, G. (1995). Socialization and the development of cooperative, competitive, and individualistic behaviors among Mexican American children. In E. E. García & B. McLaughlin (Eds.), *Meeting the challenge of linguistic and cultural diversity in early childhood education* (pp. 85–102). New York: Teachers College Press.

Knight, G. P., Bernal, M. E., Garza, C. A., & Cota, M. K. (1993). A social cognitive model of the development of ethnic identity and ethnically based behaviors. In M. E. Bernal & G. P. Knight (Eds.), *Ethnic identity: Formation and transmission among Hispanics and other minorities* (pp. 213–234). Albany: State University of New York Press.

Knight, G. P., Cota, M. K., & Bernal, M. E. (1993). The socialization of cooperative, competitive, and individualistic preferences among Mexican American children: The mediating role of ethnic identity. *Hispanic Journal of Behavioral Sciences, 15*, 291–309.

Knight, G. P., & Kagan, S. (1977). Acculturation of prosocial and competitive behaviors among second- and third-generation Mexican-American children. *Journal of Cross-Cultural Psychology, 8*, 273–284.

Knight, G. P., & Kagan, S. (1982). Siblings, birth order, and cooperative-competitive social behavior: A comparison of Anglo-American and Mexican-American children. *Journal of Cross-Cultural Psychology, 13*, 239–249.

Knight, G. P., Kagan, S., & Buriel, R. (1982). Perceived parental practices and prosocial development. *Journal of Genetic Psychology, 141*, 57–65.

Knight, G. P., Nelson, W., Kagan, S., & Gumbiner, J. (1982). Cooperative-competitive social orientation and school achievement among Anglo-American and Mexican-American children. *Contemporary Educational Psychology, 7*, 97–106.

Kumru, A., Carlo, G., & Edwards, C. P. (2004). Relational, cultural, cognitive, and affective predictors of prosocial behaviors. *Turkish Journal of Psychology (Türk Psikoloji Dergisi), 19*, 109–128.

Kurdek, L. A. (1981). Correlates of children's long-term adjustment to their parents' divorce. *Developmental Psychology, 17*, 565–579.

Ladd, G. W., Herald, S., & Andrews, K. (2006). Young children's peer relations and social competence. In B. Spodek & O. N. Saracho (Eds.), *Handbook of research on the education of young children* (pp. 23–54). Mahwah, NJ: Lawrence Erlbaum.

Laible, D., Carlo, G., & Raffaelli, M. (2000). The differential relations of parent and peer attachment to adolescent adjustment. *Journal of Youth and Adolescence, 29*(1), 45–59.

Lansford, J. E., Malone, P. S., Stevens, K. I., Dodge, K. A., Bates, J. E., & Pettit, G. S. (2006). Developmental trajectories of externalizing and internalizing behaviors: Factors underlying resilience in physically abused children. *Development and Psychopathology, 18*, 35–55.

Laosa, L. M. (1990). Psychosocial stress, coping, and development of Hispanic immigrant children. In F. C. Serafica, A. I. Schwebel, R. K. Russell, P. D. Isaac, & L. B. Myers (Eds.), *Mental health of ethnic minorities* (pp. 38–65). New York: Praeger.

Latané, B., & Darley, J. M. (1970). *The unresponsive bystander: Why doesn't he help?* New York: Appleton-Crofts.

Lazarus, R. S. (1991). *Emotion and adaptation*. New York: Oxford University Press.

Lazarus, R. S., & Folkman, S. (1984). *Stress, appraisal, and coping*. New York: Springer.

Longshore, D. (1998). Drug problem recognition among Mexican American drug-using arrestees. *Hispanic Journal of Behavioral Sciences, 20*, 270–275.

Maccoby, E. E., & Martin, J. A. (1983). Socialization in the context of the family: Parent–child interaction. In P. H. Mussen (Ed.) & E. M. Hetherington (Vol. Ed.), *Handbook of child psychology: Vol. 4. Socialization, personality, and social development* (4th ed., pp. 1–101). New York: John Wiley.

Madsen, M. C., & Shapira, A. (1977). Cooperation and challenge in four cultures. *Journal of Social Psychology, 102*, 189–195.

Marcia, J. E. (1980). Identity in adolescence. In J. Adelson (Ed.), *Handbook of adolescent psychology* (pp. 159–187). New York: John Wiley.

Markus, H. R., & Hamedani, M. (2007). Sociocultural psychology: The dynamic interdependence among self systems and social systems. In S. Kitayama & D. Cohen (Eds.), *Handbook of cultural psychology* (pp. 3–39). New York: Guilford Press.

Masten, A. S., Burt, K. B., & Coatsworth, J. D. (2006). Competence and psychopathology in development. In D. Cicchetti & D. J. Cohen (Eds.), *Developmental psychopathology, Vol. 3: Risk, disorder, and adaptation* (2nd ed., pp. 696–738). Hoboken, NJ: John Wiley.

Masten, A. S., Garmezy, N., Tellegen, A., & Pellegrini, D. S. (1988). Competence and stress in school children: The moderating effects of individual and family qualities. *Journal of Child Psychology and Psychiatry, 29,* 745–764.

Masten, A. S., Hubbard, J. J., Gest, S. D., Tellegen, A., Garmezy, N., & Ramirez, M. (1999). Competence in the context of adversity: Pathways to resilience and maladaptation from childhood to late adolescence. *Development and Psychopathology, 11,* 143–169.

McClintock, E., Bayard, M. P., & McClintock, C. G. (1983). The socialization of social motivation in Mexican American families. In E. García (Ed.), *The Mexican American child: Language, cognition, and social development* (pp. 143–161). Tempe, AZ: Center for Bilingual Education.

McHale, S. M., Dariotis, J. K., & Kauh, T. J. (2003). Social development and social relationships in middle childhood. In T. B. Weiner (Series Ed.), R. M. Lerner, M. Ann Easterbrooks, & J. Mistry (Vol. Eds.), *Comprehensive handbook of psychology: Vol. 6, Developmental psychology* (pp. 241–266). New York: John Wiley.

McLoyd, V. C. (1990). The impact of economic hardship on Black families and children: Psychological distress, parenting, and socioemotional development. *Child Development, 61,* 311–346.

McLoyd, V. C., Cauce, A. M., Takeuchi, D., & Wilson, L. (2000). Marital processes and parental socialization in families of color: A decade review of research. *Journal of Marriage & the Family, 62,* 1070–1093.

Munroe, R. L., & Munroe, R. H. (1977). Cooperation and competition among East African and American children. *Journal of Social Psychology, 101,* 145–146.

Narváez, D. (2005). The neo-Kohlbergian tradition and beyond: Schemas, expertise, and character. In G. Carlo & C. P. Edwards (Eds.), *Moral motivation through the lifespan* (pp. 119–163). Lincoln: University of Nebraska Press.

Olson, D. H., Lavee, Y., & McCubbin, H. I. (1988). Types of families and family response to stress across the family life cycle. In D. M. Klein & J. Aldous (Eds.), *Social stress and family development* (pp. 16–43). New York: Guilford Press.

Phinney, J. S. (1990). Stages of ethnic identity development in minority group adolescents. *Journal of Early Adolescence, 9,* 34–49.

Portes, P. R. (1999). Social and psychological factors in the academic achievement of children of immigrants: A cultural history puzzle. *American Educational Research Journal, 36,* 489–507.

Portes, P. R., & Zady, M. F. (2002). Self-esteem in the adaptation of Spanish-speaking adolescents: The role of immigration, family conflict and depression. *Hispanic Journal of Behavioral Sciences, 24,* 296–318.

Raffaelli, M., Carlo, G., Carranza, M. A., & González-Kruger, G. E. (2005). Understanding Latino children and adolescents in the mainstream: Placing culture at the center of developmental models. *New Directions for Child and Adolescent Development, 109,* 23–32.

Reijntjes, A., Stegge, H., & Terwogt, M. M. (2006). Children's coping with peer rejection: The role of depressive symptoms, social competence, and gender. *Infant and Child Development, 15,* 89–107.

Ripke, M., Huston, A. C., Eccles, J., & Templeton, J. (2008). The assessment of psychological, emotional, and social development indicators in middle childhood. In B. V. Brown (Ed.), *Key indicators of child and youth well-being: Completing the picture* (pp. 131–165). Mahwah, NJ: Lawrence Erlbaum.

Roccas, S., & Schwartz, S. H. (1997). Church-state relations and the association of religiosity with values. *Cross-Cultural Research, 31,* 356–375.

Rothbart, M. K., & Ahadi, S. A. (1994). Temperament and the development of personality. *Journal of Abnormal Psychology, 103,* 55–66.

Rothbart, M. K., Derryberry, D., & Posner, M. I. (1994). A psychobiological approach to the development of temperament. In J. E. Bates & T. D. Wachs (Eds.), *Temperament: Individual differences at the interface of biology and behavior* (pp. 83–116). Washington, DC: American Psychological Association.

Rotheram-Borus, M. J., & Phinney, J. S. (1990). Patterns of social expectations among Black and Mexican-American children. *Child Development, 61,* 542–556.

Sabogal, F., Marín, G., Otero-Sabogal, R., Marín, B. V., & Pérez-Stable, E. J. (1987). Hispanic familism and acculturation: What changes and what doesn't? *Hispanic Journal of Behavioral Sciences, 9,* 397–412.

Samples, F. (1997). Cognitions, behaviors and psychological symptomatology: Relationships and pathways among African American and Latino children. *Journal of Negro Education, 66,* 172–188.

Schwartz, S. H. (1992). Universals in the content and structure of values: Theoretical advances and empirical tests in 20 countries. In M. P. Zanna (Ed.), *Advances in experimental social psychology* (Vol. 25, pp. 1–65). San Diego, CA: Academic Press.

Schwartz, S. H., & Bilsky, W. (1987). Toward a universal psychological structure of human values. *Journal of Personality and Social Psychology, 53,* 550–562.

Schwartz, S. J., Zamboanga, B. L., & Jarvis, L. H. (2007). Ethnic identity and acculturation in Hispanic early adolescents: Mediated relationships to academic grades, prosocial behaviors, and externalizing symptoms. *Cultural Diversity and Ethnic Minority Psychology, 13,* 364–373.

Seligman, M. E. P., & Csikszentmihalyi, M. (2000). Positive psychology: An introduction. *American Psychologist, 55,* 5–14.

Shantz, C. U., & Shantz, D. W. (1985). Conflict between children: Social-cognitive and sociometric correlates. *New Directions for Child Development, 29,* 3–21.

Spivak, G., & Shure, M. (1988). Interpersonal cognitive problem-solving. In R. Price, E., Cohen, R. Lorion, & J. Ramos-McKay (Eds.), *14 Ounces of Prevention: A Casebook for Practitioners* (pp. 69–82). Washington, DC: American Psychological Association.

Staub, E. (1978). *Positive social behavior and morality: I. Social and personal influences.* Oxford, UK: Academic Press.

Suárez-Orozco, C., & Suárez-Orozco, M. M. (1995). *Transformations: Immigration, family life, and achievement motivation among Latino adolescents.* Stanford, CA: Stanford University Press.

Suárez-Orozco, C., Todorova, I. L. G., & Louie, J. (2002). Making up for lost time: The experience of separation and reunification among immigrant families. *Family Process, 41,* 625–643.

Super, C. M., & Harkness, S. (1986). The developmental niche: A conceptualization at the interface of child and culture. *International Journal of Behavioral Development, 9,* 545–569.

Thompson, R. A. (2006). The development of the person: Social understanding, relationships, conscience, self. In N. Eisenberg, W. Damon, & R. M. Lerner (Eds.), *Handbook of child psychology: Vol. 3, Social, emotional, and personality development* (6th ed., pp. 24–98). Hoboken, NJ: John Wiley.

Underwood, B., & Moore, B. (1982). Perspective-taking and altruism. *Psychological Bulletin, 91,* 143–173.

Weisner, T. S. (2002). Ecocultural understanding of children's developmental pathways. *Human Development, 45,* 275–281.

Wentzel, K. R., & Asher, S. R. (1995). The academic lives of neglected, rejected, popular, and controversial children. *Child Development, 66,* 754–763.

Werner, E. E., & Smith, R. S. (1992). *Overcoming the odds: High risk children from birth to adulthood.* Ithaca, NY: Cornell University Press.

Werner, E. E., & Smith, R. S. (2001). *Journeys from childhood to midlife: Risk, resilience, and recovery.* Ithaca, NY: Cornell University Press.

Whiting, B. B. (1980). Culture and social behavior: A model for the development of social behavior. *Ethos, 8,* 95–115.

Whiting, B. B., & Whiting, J. W. M. (1975). *Children of six cultures: A psycho-cultural analysis.* Cambridge, MA: Harvard University Press.

Williams, F. L. (1991). Interfamily economic exchange: A function of culture and economics. *Lifestyles: Family and Economic Issues, 12,* 235–252.

Work, W. C., & Olsen, K. H. (1990). Evaluation of a revised fourth grade social problem solving curriculum: Empathy as a moderator of adjustive gain. *Journal of Primary Prevention, 11,* 143–157.

Zamboanga, B. L., & Carlo, G. (2007). Applying problem behavior theory to Latinos: Theoretical and methodological issues. *Free Inquiry in Creative Sociology, 34,* 55–68.

13

RISK, RESILIENCE, AND POSITIVE DEVELOPMENT AMONG LATINO YOUTH

GABRIEL P. KUPERMINC, NATALIE J. WILKINS, CATHY ROCHE, AND ANABEL ALVAREZ-JIMENEZ

National data indicate that Latino youth engage in high rates of many health risk behaviors, including attempted suicide (10%, a rate 32% to 86% higher than that of Black or White youth), unprotected sex (42%, a rate 12% to 26% higher than that of Black or White youth), lifetime cocaine use (11%, a rate 47% to 600% higher than that of Black or White youth; Centers for Disease Control and Prevention [CDC], 2007). Latino youth also have the highest rates of school dropout among major ethnic groups in the U.S. (26% compared to 11% of all people in the United States in the 16- to 24-year age group; National Center for Education Statistics, 2003). Youth violence, including both perpetration and victimization, are major concerns, with estimates that 9% of Latino males between the ages of 12 and 17 are victims of violence (National Center for Mental Health Promotion and Youth Violence Prevention, 2004), and that Latino gangs constitute 46% of all gangs in the United States (National Youth Gang Center, 2006).

These sobering statistics offer just a sampling of comparative national statistics on youth risk behaviors; a more complete examination would reveal varied patterns of risk by ethnicity depending on the particular behaviors being examined. The statistics showing Latino youth to be at high risk for many risk behaviors point to grave concerns for the development of a large and rapidly growing segment of the U.S. population. Attending to these statistics alone, however, does little to inform programs and policies that might improve the health, well-being, and achievement of Latinos, nor does it acknowledge that many Latino youth are developing quite well despite exposure to conditions in their social environments that reduce their chances for positive development (Ceballo, 2004; Suárez-Orozco & Suárez-Orozco, 2001). In this chapter, we argue that a broader perspective is needed, one that accounts for the full range of adaptive and maladaptive behavior and attends to risk factors in the social environment that increase the likelihood of maladaptation as well as factors that mitigate risk among Latino youth. After describing the population of Latino youth in the United States, we outline theoretical perspectives on resilience, particularly as they relate to Latino children and youth. We review literature that informs current understanding of resilience across domains of education and career development, psychosocial functioning, and health behaviors. We pay particular attention to how societal expectations and cultural beliefs and values directly influence Latino youth development. We conclude by delineating future directions to expand the horizons of research on positive development among Latino youth in the United States.

LATINOS AND RESILIENCE— SETTING THE STAGE

The U.S. Office of Management and Budget (OMB) defines Hispanics or Latinos as "person[s] of Cuban, Mexican, Puerto Rican, South or Central American, or other Spanish culture or origin regardless of race" (OMB, 1997). Latinos constitute the largest and one of the fastest-growing ethnic groups in the United States (Pew Hispanic Center, 2006). Latinos are a diverse group, varying in national origin and in immigration and migration histories; moreover, Latinos have settled in rural, suburban, and urban communities across many regions of the United States (Chun, 2007; Urban Institute, 2002). It is important that within-group studies of Latinos and race/ethnic-group comparative studies take such variation into account. These differences carry important implications for understanding the extent and nature of risk exposure, the availability of protective processes, differences in rates of engagement in problem behaviors, and opportunities for successful developmental outcomes (Cauce, 2002; Umaña-Taylor & Fine, 2001). For example, it makes little sense to compare the relative academic success of Cuban Americans in well-established Cuban communities in Miami to the relatively poorer academic performance of predominantly Mexican-origin youth in Atlanta without at least accounting for cultural and sociopolitical factors that contribute to those differences (e.g., level of education/socioeconomic status [SES] before immigrating, availability of culturally relevant services in host community).

WHAT IS RESILIENCE?

Resilience is best viewed as a dynamic and multidimensional process through which individuals experience positive outcomes despite exposure to significant adversity (Luthar, Ciccheti, & Becker, 2000; Masten, 2001, 2007). Early descriptive writings focused on individuals who appeared to "make it" despite growing up under adverse circumstances and implied that those individuals were somehow invulnerable. Recent research, however, has shown that resilience is the result of "ordinary" human adaptive processes (Masten, 2001, 2007); that is, positive adaptation occurs when young people are able to benefit from protective processes that offset the effects of risk exposure. Resilient youth are active participants in this process in that they appear to generate health-promoting opportunities for themselves, for example, by forging connections to competent and caring adults in their families and communities (e.g., Lopez & Lechuga, 2007). Resilience is increasingly viewed as a multilevel systems concept spanning biological, social, and cognitive processes in transaction with factors in the family, neighborhood, school, societal, and cultural levels of analysis (Kuperminc & Brookmeyer, 2006; Masten, 2007).

Identifying resilience involves two inferences: first, that the individual has been exposed to significant adversity and, second, that the person is functioning adequately (Luthar et al., 2000; Masten, 2001, 2007). The former is captured by assessments of an individual's exposure to conditions of risk that are known to affect development. With regard to the latter, there is some debate about what constitutes adequate functioning (e.g., absence of psychopathology, better than average academic performance, etc.); yet, there is growing consensus that the concept of resilience has utility for increasing understanding of both adaptive and maladaptive functioning (Luthar et al., 2000).

THE CULTURAL-ECOLOGICAL-TRANSACTIONAL PERSPECTIVE

The ecological-transactional perspective provides a fundamental and overarching framework for resilience research. After presenting key features of this perspective, we argue that it underestimates the ways that cultural factors contribute to development, and we offer a *cultural*-ecological-transactional perspective of resilience.

The ecological-transactional perspective identifies multiple levels of influence on the developing child, ranging from individual characteristics to broad cultural beliefs and values (Bronfenbrenner, 1979; Cicchetti & Toth, 1997), and organizes environmental characteristics hierarchically, from proximal features (e.g., family interactions) that exert direct influences on children's psychological development and behavioral adaptation to distal features that exert indirect influences (e.g., mass media). Cicchetti and Toth (1997) propose that the environment provides opportunities and constraints on development; the child's task, in turn, is to organize, coordinate, and integrate information from the environment to negotiate the tasks of each developmental phase.

Ontogenetic development lies at the center of the ecological-transactional model and refers to factors within the person that contribute to development and adaptation (Cicchetti & Toth, 1997). Foci of ontogenetic development include aspects of personality that contribute to vulnerability for maladjustment (e.g., Blatt's notion of self-critical and dependent depressive vulnerabilities; see Leadbeater, Kuperminc, Blatt, & Hertzog, 1999) or neurobiological processes (e.g., brain structures involved in emotion regulation; see Steinberg & Avenevoli, 2000). The term *microsystem* refers to the immediate settings in which the individual lives, usually including the family, school, neighborhood, and peer group. More distal levels include the *mesosystem*, which includes interactions between two or more microsystems, the *exosystem*, which includes policies, practices, and norms of the communities in which children and their families live, and the *macrosystem*, which includes underlying cultural values and beliefs (Bronfenbrenner, 1988; Cicchetti & Toth, 1997).

One limitation of the ecological-transactional model for studying resilience among Latinos and other cultural minority groups in the United States is the implication that sociocultural factors play only a distal and indirect role (García Coll et al., 1996). For example, cultural beliefs and values about child rearing and the instrumental competencies needed for successful development set the stage for variations in parenting practices (Cauce, 2002; Jurkovic et al., 2004; Ogbu, 1981). Whereas

parenting and socialization processes have been viewed as the primary conduits for the transmission of cultural beliefs and practices (Hughes et al., 2006), it is also important to recognize more proximal influences of sociocultural factors (García Coll et al., 1996). For example, Latino youth have been shown to construe the self as interdependent with important others, and the challenge of reconciling this sense of interdependence with dominant expectations for independence shapes the ways youth approach developmental tasks of relationship formation, achievement and autonomy (Greenfield, Keller, Fuligni, & Maynard, 2003). Moreover, issues of race and ethnicity, minority status, economic stratification, immigration history, and current immigration status are determinants of the neighborhoods Latino youth live in, the adult role models they are exposed to, the schools they attend, the classrooms they are placed in, and the expectations their teachers have for their educational attainment. Cultural beliefs and values form the "lens" through which Latino youth experience and organize the information they receive from their environment and delineate the strategies they undertake to meet the challenges and opportunities of their development. Thus, within-group cultural beliefs, values, and practices can help explain between-group variations in risk and protective processes (Kuperminc, Blatt, Shahar, Henrich, & Leadbeater, 2004; Smith & Guerra, 2006).

A second limitation lies in common uses of the ecological transactional model rather than in shortcomings of the model itself. Specifically, researchers drawing on this model have tended to emphasize ecological *structures,* or levels of analysis, rather than ecological *processes* (Bronfenbrenner, 1988). Relatedly, while emphasizing ecological influences on ontogenetic development, most research has failed to recognize the interdependence of development and well-being occurring at individual, relational, and collective levels (Evans & Prilleltensky, 2007). In this view, well-being occurs when individual, relational, and collective needs of individuals and communities are fulfilled. It is likely that the "proper" balance of these dimensions varies as a function of cultural beliefs and values (Birman, Weinstein, Chan, & Beehler, 2007). For example, achievement of psychological autonomy has long been considered a central developmental task of adolescence (Allen, Hauser, O'Connor, & Bell, 2002). Research over the past two decades has recognized that autonomy in the family develops optimally in the context of strong relationships with parents (e.g., Allen et al., 2002) and that there are cultural variations in how youth and their families negotiate the balance of "autonomous-related" self-development (Kagitcibasi, 2005). Kwak (2003) notes that for immigrant and nonimmigrant families from collectivist cultures who have settled in Western societies, exposure to economic hardship necessitates that youth delay establishing their autonomy. However, the youths' "self-less" contributions to the family are unlikely to lead to negative developmental consequences, because such contribution is consistent with their cultural beliefs and practices.

When seeking to understand resilience among Latino youth, it is necessary to incorporate a *cultural*-ecological-transactional perspective that holds young people's culture of origin and its interaction with mainstream cultures as central foci (García Coll et al., 1996; Ogbu, 1981; Perreira & Smith, 2007). As shown in Figure 13.1, we argue that development is influenced by individual and microsystem transactions with community and sociocultural (i.e., exosystem and macrosystem) processes. These include transactions of individuals with proximal settings of family, peers, school, and neighborhood (individual-microsystem transactions, path A-B), community norms and policies (individual-exosystem transactions, path A-C), and cultural beliefs and values (individual-macrosystem transactions, path A-D). We also consider processes involving the transactions of the family microsystem with other settings, such as school and neighborhood (mesosystem transactions, path B-B), community norms and policies

(Pathways between the letters represent transactions across ecological levels.)

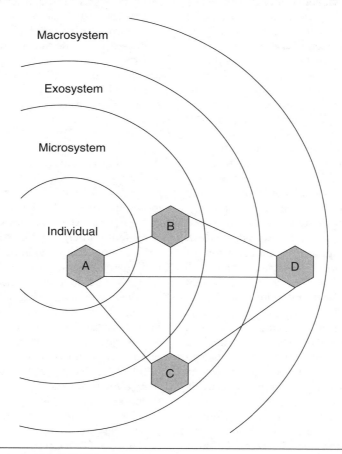

Figure 13.1   An Ecological Model of Development

(microsystem-exosystem transactions, path B-C), and cultural beliefs and values (microsystem-macrosystem transactions, path B-D).

Toward a Model of Latino Resilience

The preceding overview of the cultural-ecological-transactional perspective provides a framework for constructing a model of Latino resilience. Models of resilience must incorporate the following elements: (a) identification of risk and protective processes at each ecological level; (b) inclusion of indices of both adaptive and maladaptive development; and (c) specification of the mechanisms (i.e., direct or "main" effects, moderation, mediation) through which risk and protective processes operate. In the sections that follow, we consider each of these elements.

It is important to note that there are many methodological challenges in the existing literature on Latino youth, including the need for: (a) valid and reliable measurement instruments with established cross-ethnic equivalence (Knight & Hill, 1998) that can capture "universal" developmental processes, (b) group-specific instruments that can capture the unique experiences of diverse subgroups, (c) rigorous experimental evaluations and observational and quasi-experimental studies of programs designed to increase protective factors while limiting youths' exposure to conditions of risk (Borden et al., 2006), and (d) studies that attend to within-group differences among Latinos, such as national origin, and avoid the use of pan-ethnic labels and analyses (Umaña-Taylor & Fine, 2001). Research is beginning to attend to these challenges, and we include relevant methodological information when available in the literature review that follows, particularly as it relates to Latino youths' national origin.

Identifying Risk and Protective Processes

Risk and protective processes include characteristics of individuals, families, communities, sociocultural forces, and the interconnections among them. Risk processes are related to increased likelihood of onset, greater severity, and longer duration of mental health problems (Coie et al., 1993). Risk factors include enduring conditions that persist over time, and transient events, whose influence is likely to vary with the developmental period in which they occur

(Cicchetti & Toth, 1997). Protective factors mitigate the effects of risk exposure through direct (counteracting) effects, interactive (buffering) effects, or effects that disrupt the causal link between risk and dysfunction (Coie et al., 1993). In many cases, risk and protective factors are continuous variables (e.g., poor to adequate parenting) that can be conceptualized as two sides of a coin (Masten, 2001).

Identifying the extent to which young people are exposed to significant risks that compromise development is one of the fundamental judgments necessary to the study of resilience. Given the diversity of the Latino population, it is important to consider adversities experienced by immigrant youth, children of immigrants, and U.S.-born youth whose families have been in the United States for two or more generations. Although an exhaustive treatment of risk processes is beyond the scope of this chapter, we describe conditions of risk commonly experienced by U.S.-born and immigrant youth, including exposure to poverty, discrimination, acculturative stress, and traumatic events. We recognize likely variations in the nature and extent of risk exposures for subgroups of Latino youth.

Poverty. Past work has noted that poverty typically co-occurs with single parenthood and unemployment (Lichter, Qian, & Crowley, 2005; McLoyd, 1998). In contrast, poverty among children of immigrants (who are predominantly Latino) often occurs despite parental work and the presence of two parents in the home (Capps & Fortuny, 2006). Compared to children in native U.S. families, children of immigrants are substantially more likely to live in crowded households and to experience food scarcity and health problems, but they are much less likely to receive public benefits and social services (ibid.). Overall rates of child poverty among Hispanics stood at 27% in the 2000 census and ranged from as low as 15% among Cubans to more than 42% among Island born Puerto Ricans (Lichter et al., 2005).

Discrimination. Several observers have noted the relative lack of research on experiences of discrimination (Araujo & Borrell, 2006; García Coll et al., 1996). Most research has focused on the actions of a dominant racial or ethnic group (usually White Americans) directed at one or more marginalized groups, and research is beginning also to consider in-group discrimination or discrimination between marginalized groups (e.g., between ethnic groups or between subgroups of coethnics; Araujo & Borrell, 2006). Although varying in the operational definitions, studies conducted with samples of Mexican American, Puerto Rican, and Latinos of mixed national origins have found that discrimination is a relatively common experience among youth in the middle and high school years (Edwards & Romero, 2008; Kuperminc, Henrich, Meyers, House, & Sayfi, 2007; Szalacha et al., 2003; Umaña-Taylor & Updegraff, 2007). In our study of 176 Latino middle school students of varied national origins (predominantly Mexican), for example, substantial numbers reported experiences of being disliked (29%), being treated unfairly (23%), and seeing friends treated unfairly (43%) because of their ethnic group or race (Kuperminc et al., 2007).

Acculturative Stress. Immigrants typically experience a significant amount of stress resulting from individual, social, and cultural changes (Hovey, 2000). Whereas acculturative stress has been studied primarily among immigrants, research indicates that it also plays a significant role in the adjustment of U.S.-born Latinos (Fuertes & Westbrook, 1996). Acculturative stress involves feelings of confusion, anxiety, depression, marginality, alienation, psychosomatic symptoms, and identity confusion associated with attempts to resolve cultural differences (Hovey, 2000; Mena, Padilla, & Maldonado, 1987). Using an ecological framework, Seidman et al. (1995) conceptualized everyday stressful events as individual transactions within the family, peer, and school microsystems. The concept of acculturative stress goes beyond individual-microsystem transactions to describe transactions of individuals with broader ecological structures, including institutional barriers (exosystem processes) and cultural beliefs and values (macrosystem processes). For example, Stanton-Salazar (1997) described the process of institutionalized exclusion that many minority youth encounter at school and argued that linguistic barriers, economic constraints, inadequate support systems, and stigmatization prevent many ethnic minority youth from participating fully in school activities.

Negative and Traumatic Migration Experiences. The role of traumatic experience in the lives of refugee children and families has been well documented (Fong, 2007). In contrast to refugees, immigrants and migrants exercise some degree of choice in their decisions to resettle; perhaps because of this distinction, less attention has been given to the role of negative and potentially traumatic experiences prior to, during, and after migration. Migration stress has been defined in terms of "difficulties resulting from disruptions in children's everyday lives when removed from a familiar environment" (Birman et al., 2007, p. 14). Such stressors include feelings of loss resulting from disruptions in family relationships, social networks, and cultural context. Family separations and reunions that occur often over the course of several years can be bittersweet, as when reuniting with parents means having to say goodbye to grandparents (Gaytan, Carhill, & Suárez-Orozco, 2007). The journey from home country to a new home can be as uneventful as boarding a plane and arriving a few hours later or as traumatic as losing a limb as a result jumping from a moving train (Kovic, 2008).

Protective Processes. Research has been consistent in identifying a "short list" of protective factors that contribute to resilience (Masten, 2007), and spanning ontogenetic (e.g., positive coping strategies, self-concept, and effective self-regulation), microsystem (e.g., positive relationships in family, school, and peer systems), and exosystem/macrosystem processes (e.g., collective efficacy, bonding to prosocial institutions). Race-ethnic comparative studies have demonstrated that these processes contribute to positive development in ways that are more similar than they are different (Rowe, Vaszonyi, & Flannery, 1994). Acknowledging cross-ethnic similarities in developmental processes is critical for informing universal prevention and wellness promotion interventions, but it may overlook subtle cultural variations and adaptations that are unique in the experiences of Latino or other cultural groups (Cauce, 2002; Greenfield et al., 2003; Ibañez, Kuperminc, Jurkovic, & Perilla, 2004; Kuperminc et al., 2004). As will be discussed, salient protective processes in the lives of ethnic minority youth, particularly Latino youth, are found in the domains of religious involvement, culturally rooted family values, attitudes, and behaviors, as well as in the processes of acculturation and negotiating a bicultural identity (Padilla, 2006; Perez & Padilla, 2000).

Accounting for Adaptive and Maladaptive Functioning

The health and risk behavior profile of Latino youth in the United States seems in many ways not to follow conventional wisdom. Despite the fact that Latino youth are faced with many of the risk factors linked to, for example, substance abuse, they show lower rates of illicit drug use and smoking than their White and African American peers (U.S. Department of Health and Human Services, 2002). In contrast, Latino youth rank higher than other ethnic groups on most indicators of risky sexual behavior. Between 1991 and 2000, Latina adolescents had the smallest decrease in teen birth rates compared to other ethnic groups (Ventura, Matthews, & Hamilton, 2001). Latino youth are also at a disproportionate risk for contracting AIDS and sexually transmitted diseases (CDC, 2007).

The educational profile of Latinos is equally complex. For example, Lowell and Suro (2002) report a narrowing gap in high school completion between foreign-born Latino adults and native-born Americans. Their analysis of data from the 2000 census also shows that foreign-born Latinos who came to the United States at an early age have higher educational attainment than those who were educated abroad. Despite these trends, however, academic performance of Latinos, both immigrant and U.S. born, continues to lag behind other groups (Lowell & Suro, 2002; President's Advisory Commission on Educational Excellence for Hispanics, 2000). Research consistently points to such factors as low rates of participation in early childhood education, overrepresentation of Latino students in resource-poor schools, and instruction that is unresponsive to language differences as reasons for poor performance (President's Advisory Commission, 2000; Suárez-Orozco & Suárez-Orozco, 2001). It must be noted that there is wide variation in academic performance across subgroups of Latinos linked to national origin, immigration and generation status, and documentation status (Suárez-Orozco & Suárez-Orozco, 2001). For example, Mexican and Central American Latino immigrants are less likely to have completed either secondary or postsecondary education than are Latino immigrants from the Caribbean and South America (Lowell & Suro, 2002). Factors such as "immigrant optimism" (Kao & Tienda, 1998) may contribute to American-educated Latino immigrants completing high school and entering college at rates that are beginning to approach those of non-Latino White Americans (Lowell & Suro, 2002).

These mixed findings across domains of psychosocial, behavioral, and educational functioning point to the limits of explanatory models that focus only on conditions of risk and on maladaptive outcomes. Understanding this mixed health and risk behavior profile requires examining a complex web of factors across the social ecology that both promote and inhibit healthy behavior. The success that many Latino youth are experiencing across many domains of functioning suggests that a more productive approach to studying their development would incorporate a focus on the strengths and abilities that individuals, families, and communities draw upon to foster positive youth development (Rodriguez & Morrobel, 2004).

TRACING CULTURAL-ECOLOGICAL-TRANSACTIONAL MECHANISMS IN THE DEVELOPMENT OF RESILIENCE

Our study of racial/ethnic-group differences in developmental processes highlighted for us the need to consider how culture shapes young people's development (Kuperminc et al., 2004). Although measures of such cultural concepts as acculturation were not included in the database used for the study, we were alerted to the importance of examining direct influences of culture on individual development and family functioning. This study of 460 White, Black, and Latino young adolescents (primarily from Central and South America and the Caribbean) examined longitudinal changes in indices of *interpersonal relatedness* (quality of relationships with parents and peers) and *self-definition* (perceived self-efficacy and self-esteem). Consistent with past research, processes of relatedness and self-definition contributed to positive school adjustment and low levels of psychosocial maladjustment, but *negative changes* in relationship quality over time increased vulnerability to maladjustment for Black and Latino youth to a greater extent than for White youth. In contrast, *negative changes* in self-esteem increased vulnerability to maladjustment for White youth in comparison to Latino youth. We reasoned that a culturally rooted emphasis on interdependence and relational well-being in the African American and Latino groups (Greenfield et al., 2003) might underlie the cultural variations discovered in this research.

In the paragraphs that follow, we examine societal and institutional risk processes that affect Latino youths' development, and we illustrate cultural-ecological-transactional mechanisms by which individuals and families marshal their resources to confront those risks. These mechanisms correspond to pathways in Figure 13.1 linking youth and their families to macrosystemic (paths A-D and B-D) and exosystemic (paths A-C and B-C) mechanisms of risk and resilience. We also review microsystemic and mesosystemic mechanisms, corresponding to pathways linking individuals to the proximal settings of development (family, peers, school, neighborhood) and the interrelations among those settings (paths A-B and B-B, respectively). In Table 13.1, we provide examples drawn from the literature review to illustrate these pathways.

Macrosystemic Processes

Globalization, immigration, and the shifting ethnocultural composition of the U.S. population represent perhaps the most important macrosystemic processes affecting the development of Latino youth (Capps & Fortuny, 2006; Suárez-Orozco & Suárez-Orozco, 2001). The impact of these social changes can be seen in political struggles over immigration reform and related policymaking in such areas as criminal justice, health care, and education (Anrig & Wang, 2006). Protective processes to offset the risks associated with these macrosocial changes include the internalization of cultural and religious values and beliefs.

Lack of access to education, prevention, and health-care programs place Latino youth at risk for health problems and school failure. For example, it is estimated that up to 20% of Latino youth in middle and high school do not feel they have anywhere to go to seek medical attention (Rew, Resnick, & Beuhring, 1999). Furthermore, despite their risk for unprotected sexual activity, Latino youth receive less information about contraception and family planning than any other ethnic group (Rew, 1998). Language barriers and a lack of cultural sensitivity among many health-care providers provide additional challenges in accessing necessary sexual health services (Rew et al., 1999). With regard to substance abuse, studies have shown that Latino youth are exposed to more alcohol advertisements than non-Latino youth (Center on Alcohol Marketing and Youth, 2005), and some have suggested that heavy exposure to alcohol may lead to higher risk for illicit drug use (Warheit et al., 1996). Policies surrounding immigration reform affect Latinos regardless of their legal documentation status. Fears of deportation have been associated with concerns about seeking health services and with heightened stress, anger, and emotional and physical health problems (Cavazos-Rehg, Zayas, & Spitznagel, 2007). These risks are compounded by high rates of concentrated poverty, which itself is a risk factor linked to increased risk behavior, school failure, and compromised development (Fishbein et al., 2006; McLoyd, 1998; President's Advisory Commission, 2000).

Research is beginning to document how Latino adolescents and their families make use of cultural beliefs to resist societal pressures to engage in various forms of risk behavior. We highlight the interplay of religion, familism, and other cultural beliefs, factors that contribute to shaping the context in which young people experience, interpret, and act on societal pressures.

Religion. Religion plays a central but complex role in Latino adolescents' decisions to engage in health risk behaviors. For example, research with Mexican American and Puerto Rican adolescent girls suggests that the anticontraception beliefs of the Catholic Church often result in Latina adolescents' reluctance to use condoms and other safe-sex practices (Villarruel, 1998). This study also found that although religious beliefs were not linked to higher rates of abstinence among Latino youth, religious Latina girls were more likely to place a high value on delaying sexual intercourse as a sign of self-respect (ibid.). Religion may also influence the decisions Latina girls make when faced with pregnancy. For example, Latina teenagers have lower pregnancy rates but higher birth rates than their African American peers (Frost, Jones, Woog, Singh, & Darrocj, 2001), reflecting high rates of adherence to values of the Catholic Church that prohibit abortion (Pew Hispanic Center, 2002). Research has also shown that religion may serve as a protective factor for Mexican American youth against substance abuse, suicide ideation,

Table 13.1   Examples of Cultural-Ecological-Transactional Processes in the Development of Resilience Among Latino Youth

Ecological Processes	Pathways	Examples
Individual in Transaction With. . .		
Microsystem	A–B	*Risk Processes:* Low rates of participation in early childhood education, instructional practices that are unresponsive to language differences, and attendance at resource-poor schools contribute to poor academic performance (President's Advisory Commission, 2000). *Protective Processes:* Family support in the form of parental monitoring and family connectedness are associated with decreased risk of substance use, violence, and risky sexual behavior (Kerr et al., 2003); school support in the form of early intervention and intensive supplemental programming in schools promotes school achievement among poor Latinos (Gandara, 2006).
Exosystem	A–C	*Risk Processes:* Acculturative stress and discrimination contribute to increased substance use and other problem behaviors (Gil et al., 2000; Hovey, 2000). *Protective Processes:* Openness to interacting with members of other ethnic groups contributes to improved academic achievement (Guzman et al., 2005).
Macrosystem	A–D	*Risk Processes:* Lack of access to educational support and health care leaves youth at risk for school failure and risk behavior (e.g., Rew, 1999); Latino youth are exposed to more alcohol advertising than non-Latinos (Center on Alcohol Marketing and Youth, 2005). *Protective Processes:* Internalization of religious beliefs protects against multiple problem behaviors (Marsiglia et al., 2005; Villarruel, 1998).
Family in Transaction With. . .		
School and Neighborhood Microsystems (Mesosystem Transactions)	B–B	*Risk Processes:* Low levels of Latino parents' involvement may contribute to perceptions by their children and their children's teachers that education is not valued (Kuperminc et al., 2008). *Protective Processes:* Parental involvement in education builds social capital that supports school achievement (Kao & Rutherford, 2007; Kuperminc et al., 2008); family ethnic socialization contributes to ethnic identity development for youth in low-risk neighborhoods but not high-risk neighborhoods.
Exosystem	B–C	*Risk Processes:* Language barriers, work demands contribute to acculturative stress for parents and children, which may lead to overreliance on children (Arfaniarromo, 2001). *Protective Processes:* Family responsibilities, including language brokering, chores, and sibling caretaking, are associated with better social skills and higher levels of maturity; positive perceptions of the usefulness and fairness of responsibilities are linked to lower psychological distress and acting-out problems (Kuperminc et al., in press; Weisskirch, 2005).
Macrosystem	B-D	*Protective Processes:* Cultural values, such as familism, place parents in a culturally consonant position to provide guidance and emotional support for youths' decisions to avoid substance use and other problem behaviors (O'Sullivan et al., 2000; Sommers et al., 1993).

and other risks (Hovey, 2000; Marsiglia, Kulis, Nieri, & Parsai, 2005). In immigrant Latino communities, affiliation with the Catholic Church may help Latino youth and their families create social ties, establish a social support network, and facilitate a strong sense of community. All of these factors may then help by providing Latino youth with the support they need to resist engaging in risk behaviors.

Familism and Other Cultural Values. There are also indications that various aspects of *familism* (a strong connection with and responsibility to the family) and other culturally rooted beliefs and attitudes can serve as either risk or protective functions, depending on the particular behavior that is being examined. Familism has been credited with contributing to Puerto Rican youths' resilience in avoiding substance abuse (Sommers, Fagan, & Baskin, 1993), and research suggests that most Latino youth consider upsetting their parents to be a substantial risk involved in smoking marijuana (Office of National Drug Control Policy, 2005). This strong belief in the importance of family may help Latino youth base their decisions around the values of their families and combat peer pressure to engage in substance use.

Similarly, familism attitudes place parents and other family members in a central position to provide positive guidance and emotional support for positive sexual decision making (O'Sullivan, Meyer-Balhburg, & Watkins, 2000). In one study, Mexican and Puerto Rican mothers reported that they and other members of the family make special efforts to monitor their daughters' behavior to protect them from unintended pregnancy. Daughters, in turn, usually interpreted this supervision positively as a gesture of caring and concern (Villarruel, 1998). Research has also shown that in a sample of Latino adolescents predominantly of Mexican descent, those adolescents whose mothers engaged in open communication about sex with them were more likely to abstain from sex or delay initiation of sexual behavior (Romo, Lefkowitz, Sigman, & Au, 2002). On the other hand, traditional gender roles, in which males are expected to make decisions surrounding sex and contraception, have been linked to higher rates of unprotected sex and higher frequency of sexual behavior among Latino boys (Locke, Newcomb, & Goodyear, 2005). Research has also shown that Latina girls are more likely than their non-Latina peers to date men who are 10 or more years older (Vanoss, Coyle, Gomez, Carvajal, & Kirby, 2000). These dating practices may put Latina girls at higher risk for hazardous sexual behavior, as such an age difference may further limit their power to negotiate abstinence and safe sex practices with their partners (Villarruel, 1998).

Exosystemic Processes

We conceptualize acculturative stress and perceived discrimination as indicators of Latino youths' transactions with the social institutions and practices they and their parents encounter in their everyday lives. Latino youth and their families address institutional barriers through strategies of acculturation-enculturation and ethnic identity (path A-C) and through strategies involving the assistance of family members in maintaining family well-being via language brokering, sibling caregiving, and other family responsibilities (path B-C; Jurkovic et al., 2004).

Acculturation-Enculturation and Ethnic Identity. The so-called immigrant paradox has captured the attention of numerous scholars, lending substantial attention to understanding counterintuitive findings that immigrants often tend to show better adaptation than their national peers despite poorer socioeconomic status (Sam, Vedder, Liebkind, Neto, & Virta, 2008). Studies have shown, for example, that immigrant Latino youth are less likely to engage in risky sexual behavior and substance use than their U.S.-born Latino peers (Minnis & Padian, 2001). These findings suggest that closer ties to traditional Latino cultural values may protect Latino youth from engaging in sexual risk taking. Some researchers suggest that U.S.-born Latinos are at higher risk for hazardous behavior and psychological maladjustment due to the stress involved in negotiating a "bicultural identity" that involves the traditional Latino culture of their families and the dominant U.S. culture in which they were born (Castro, Boyer, & Balcazar, 2000; Umaña-Taylor & Updegraff, 2007).

Acculturative stressors are transactions of individuals with both the dominant culture and their culture of origin (Fuertes & Westbrook, 1996); these include perceived discrimination and discomfort with adapting to expectations of the dominant culture, as well as feelings of disconnection from the culture of origin and conflicts between personal and parental values and attitudes. Acculturative stress may have differing effects on Latino youth's adaptation, depending on where they are in the acculturation process. For example, Cabrera-Strait (2001) found that Latino youth who reported high rates of *acculturative stress* reported drinking more than their less stressed peers, while Guilamo-Ramos and colleagues (2004) found a more complex, curvilinear relationship such that alcohol abuse was most prevalent among youth who were either high or low on indicators of acculturation.

Gil, Wagner, and Vega's (2000) study of acculturative stress, family processes, and alcohol use among immigrant and U.S.-born Latino young adolescents in South Florida (whose countries of origin were in Central and South American and the Caribbean) further illustrates this complexity, in that English-language preference contributed to higher acculturative stress among immigrants but lower acculturative stress among U.S.-born youth. For both groups, acculturative stress predicted lower parental respect and familism attitudes, which in turn contributed to greater disposition to deviance and greater alcohol involvement. These findings suggest that acculturative stress can operate differently at various stages of the acculturation process.

Acculturation and identity development processes may put stress on the relationships between adolescents and their parents, which may in turn lead to a breakdown in the familial support systems linked to preventing risk behavior and psychosocial difficulties among Latino youth (Gil et al., 2000). Yet the weight of evidence in U.S. samples suggests that many youth are able to develop positive American and ethnic identities regardless of their immigration status (Phinney & Ong, 2007). A positive ethnic identity has been shown to offset the negative associations of perceived discrimination with self-esteem and depressive symptoms among immigrant and U.S.-born Latino youth of primarily Mexican origin (Umaña-Taylor & Updegraff, 2007). The use of active coping strategies, such as finding someone to talk to about feelings, has also been shown to reduce the negative association of perceived discrimination with self-esteem among Mexican-American adolescents (Edwards & Romero, 2008).

A study by Guzman, Santiago-Rivera, and Haase (2005) illustrates the interplay of cultural beliefs and identity processes in the educational resilience of Latino youth. Those authors studied 222 youth in Austin, Texas, with at least one parent of Mexican ancestry and an average age of 16 years. Participants completed measures of ethnic identity and such Mexican cultural constructs as fatalism, familism, folk beliefs, *machismo,* and *personalismo.* One of the strongest predictors of academic achievement and positive school attitudes was the extent to which youth reported a willingness to interact with members of other ethnic groups (i.e., an other-group orientation). The authors were careful to note that a positive other-group orientation did not mean that one has to be assimilated into dominant American culture or have a low ethnic identity in order to perform well in school. Instead, the study suggested that interventions with non-Mexican school personnel and students to help them become more welcoming to Mexican students might facilitate a positive other-group orientation, and that this, in turn, might contribute indirectly to improved academic achievement, perhaps via reductions in acculturative stress. This study indicates that cultural values and experiences with mainstream Anglo-Whites may all play a role in academic attitudes and achievement.

Family Responsibilities. Scholars from multiple perspectives (e.g., cultural, clinical, sociological, anthropological) have raised concerns about potential deleterious consequences of family responsibilities on children's development (Jurkovic et al., 2004). Family obligations may limit Latino youth's access to programs and services. For example, many Latino adolescents drop out of school in order to work and help support their families financially. Youth who drop out or do poorly in school, especially those who live in poor neighborhoods, are often at high risk for joining gangs and/or becoming involved in violence (Arfaniarromo, 2001).

While acknowledging those concerns, recent research with Latino youth predominantly of Mexican descent indicates that Latino children's contributions to the maintenance and well-being of their families may promote competence and maturity, particularly when they feel their efforts are valued, acknowledged, and reciprocated by parents or other family members (Kuperminc, Jurkovic, & Casey, in press; Weisskirch, 2005). For example, Weisskirch's (2005) study of 55 sixth graders (primarily U.S.-born children of Mexican immigrant parents) found that most children engaged in *language brokering* for their parents. Language brokering and positive feelings about language brokering both had significant correlations with ethnic identity, but when entered in a multiple regression equation, only positive feelings contributed to higher levels of ethnic identity. In our research focused on the broader construct of *filial responsibility* among 129 Latino, predominantly Mexican, high school youth from immigrant families (Kuperminc et al., in press), we found that engaging in *caregiving activities* (including sibling caregiving, chores, and assisting family members in negotiating cultural expectations) was associated cross-sectionally with high levels of self- and teacher-reported social competence. Perceptions of the *fairness* of caregiving activities were associated with low levels of psychological distress and low levels of teacher-reported acting-out behavior. Longitudinal analyses with 199 middle school Latino, predominantly Mexican, students from the same community have largely replicated those results, indicating that increases in perceived fairness contribute to declines over time in aggressive behavior and psychological distress, while increases in caregiving activities contribute to increases in cooperative behavior and interpersonal skills (Kuperminc, 2007). In all, these findings suggest that family responsibilities carry some risk for the educational and psychosocial development of Latino youth but may also protect against maladjustment and promote positive psychosocial outcomes when those activities are valued and acknowledged by important others.

Microsystemic and Mesosystemic Processes

Individual-microsystem transactions are often operationalized in terms of youth's perceptions of stress and support related to the important settings in their lives. In this section, we examine individual transactions with family, school, peer, and neighborhood settings (path A-B) and also explore mesosystemic transactions, the linkages between these microsystems (path B-B).

Family Support. Experiencing support from parents and other family members has been associated with positive psychosocial functioning and health behavior (Kuperminc et al., 2004). Kerr, Beck, Shattuck, Kattar, & Uriburu (2003) found in a sample of 446 Latino adolescents that perceived parental monitoring and family connectedness were associated with less engagement in problem behavior (substance use, violence, and risky sexual behavior), and parental encouragement to explore non-Latino social and cultural experiences was associated with high levels of prosocial behavior (e.g., volunteering in the community, extracurricular activity involvement).

The role of family support in promoting academic achievement is less clear. Whereas research in ethnically diverse samples has documented a link between affective quality of relationships with parents and school grades (e.g., Kenny, Gallagher, Alvarez-Salvat, & Silsby, 2002), within-group analyses of Latino youth have not consistently replicated those findings (Kuperminc et al., 2004). For example, using data from the National Longitudinal Study of Youth on more than 1,000 Mexican, Mexican American, and Puerto Rican adolescents, Schmitz (2006) found that quality of the home environment, assessed in terms of cognitive stimulation and emotional support from parents, was unrelated to scholastic self-perceptions. Overall, these findings indicate that whereas parental support clearly plays a role in the psychosocial development and health behavior of Latino youth, more work is needed to understand how parents can facilitate those youth's academic development.

Peer Relationships. An extensive body of research has established that adolescent friendships contribute to development of interpersonal and relational skills, to cognitive and social development, and to psychological adjustment (Way & Pahl, 2001). Scholars (Azmitia, Ittel, & Brenk, 2006; Stanton-Salazar & Spina, 2005) have suggested that a preference for interdependence equips Latino youth with relational styles that are conducive to sharing and exchange of social support. Consistent with this expectation, Way, Cowal, Gingold, Pahl, and Bissessar (2001) used cluster analysis on data from 213 Black (predominantly African American), Latino (predominantly Puerto Rican and Dominican), and Asian (predominantly Chinese) high school students to identify friendship typologies and found that Latinos, particularly Latina girls, were more often represented than other ethnic groups in an "ideal" cluster characterized by high levels of positive friendship characteristics (e.g., intimacy, companionship, alliance, affection, and satisfaction) and low levels of negative characteristics (conflict and antagonism). Qualitative analysis of in-depth interviews revealed that ideal friendships were characterized by mutual affection and trust, long duration, and an ability to resolve conflicts.

Friendships may be particularly important in the lives of recent immigrants. Friends, particularly those who are more acculturated, can compensate for the inability of parents to provide needed supports due to work demands and lack of experience with the school setting (Azmitia et al., 2006). However, immigrant parents may be more likely than others to restrict interaction with peers as a result of an emphasis on family cohesion and familism and fears that their children will be exposed to negative influences (ibid.). Moreover, poverty can adversely affect the quality of peer relationships and friendships. For example, Stanton-Salazar & Spina (2005) describe the peer networks of low-income, Mexican-origin adolescents as often characterized by alienation and social isolation despite being embedded in relatively large amounts of peer interaction. The lack of ability of many youth to form friendships characterized by mutual trust and support reflects the broader context of poverty, including lack of resources and harsh conditions in which they were living. The importance of institutional contexts, such as community and afterschool programs offering safety, mentoring, enrichment activities, and educational outreach is underscored in the work of both Azmitia and colleagues (2006) and Stanton-Salazar & Spina (2005), as a means of facilitating positive peer relationships.

School Support. School support can come in the form of policies and programs designed to increase academic achievement among Latino youth, as well as general perceptions of support and belongingness at school that can contribute both to academic achievement and to psychosocial adjustment. Gandara (2006) has argued that many Latino children of immigrant parents are at particular risk for school problems because the combination of poverty and low English skills puts them at a double disadvantage compared to middle-class, monolingual peers. She notes that early intervention (i.e., pre-K) and intensive supplemental programming have been shown to promote school achievement for Latinos in the face of poverty. In the face of these challenges, it may be that increasing the number of Hispanic or Latino teachers (Crosnoe, 2005) or undertaking strategies to increase Latino

students' sense of belonging in school (Ibañez et al., 2004; Kuperminc, Darnell, & Alvarez-Jimenez, 2008) can contribute to improvements in academic motivation and achievement.

Interventions to make school environments more welcoming and supportive have demonstrated that culturally relevant interventions can have a positive impact on education and career development (Conchas & Clark, 2002; Denner, Cooper, Dunbar, & Lopez, 2005; Rodriguez & Blocher, 1988). For example, Rodriguez & Blocher (1988) studied 75 Puerto Rican women in their first year at an urban college. They found that a culture-specific, 10-week career development program led by Puerto Rican counselors increased participants' career maturity and internal loci of control.

Neighborhood. Recent research indicates that structural qualities of neighborhood resources (e.g., poverty levels, employment, education levels, proportion of English-speaking neighbors) and perceptions of the availability of those resources in the neighborhood are related to psychosocial development, health behavior, and educational outcomes. Plunkett, Abarca-Mortensen, Behnke, and Sands's (2007) study of 534 Latinos in one Los Angeles high school found that students' neighborhood perceptions contributed positively to self-esteem, perceived self-efficacy, school grades, and academic aspirations. Structural qualities, assessed via neighborhood-level census data, had indirect associations with each of these outcomes mediated through student perceptions, and a direct effect only on self-esteem. Similarly, Eamon and Mulder (2005) found that poor neighborhood quality (measured in terms of mothers' ratings of such items as lack of respect for rules and laws, abandoned or run-down buildings, and parents not supervising their children) was associated with lower levels of reading achievement among 388 Mexican American youth (ages 10 to 14) sampled from the National Longitudinal Study of Youth. Using the same data set, Eamon and Mulder (2005) also found that poor neighborhood quality predicted increased risk of antisocial behavior.

This brief review of microsystem processes occurring as the transactions of Latino youth with their families, peer groups, schools, and neighborhoods demonstrates the importance of experiences in everyday settings for promoting or constraining resilient outcomes among Latino youth. These processes in many ways have effects for Latino youth that are similar to those for youth from other ethnic/cultural groups. The cultural-ecological-transactional framework, however, directs us to look beyond risk and protective factors in these settings that are common across ethnic-cultural groups to also consider processes that are linked to the minority experience broadly (e.g., experiences of discrimination at school) or unique to the experience of Latino youth (e.g., language barriers; Smith & Guerra, 2006). We next turn to an examination of mesosystem processes involving connections between the family, school, and neighborhood settings.

Parent-School Connections. A promising approach to furthering knowledge of how parents and schools can promote academic attainment is to consider connections between these two important settings in the lives of Latino youth. Research has shown that whereas many Latino families place strong emphasis on the importance of education, Latino parents often avoid visiting their children's schools because of fear of formal institutions (especially for parents lacking legal papers; Bacallao & Smokowski, 2007), time constraints due to long work hours, and cultural barriers (i.e., language, different ideas about respect for schools' authority, etc.; Delgado-Gaitan, 1990).

The mesosystemic transactions between parents and schools can also be viewed as building social capital that can contribute to Latino youth's academic achievement (Kao & Rutherford, 2007; Kuperminc, Darnell, & Alvarez-Jimenez, 2008). Using parental involvement as an example, McNeal (1999) defined social capital as including three elements: (1) social ties between various members of a network (parents, teachers, students), (2) norms of obligation and reciprocity, and (3) investment of resources.

Kao & Rutherford (2007) examined parent involvement and another measure of social capital, which they labeled *intergenerational closure* (i.e., the extent to which youth know the parents of their friends), as longitudinal predictors of academic achievement in a large ethnically diverse sample of Latino, Asian, Black, and White adolescents who were first surveyed in 8th grade. High levels of both forms of social capital were associated cross-sectionally with higher 8th-grade academic performance and longitudinally with increases in academic performance by 12th grade. Kuperminc et al. (2008) examined

cross-sectional samples of Latino middle ($N = 195$) and high school students ($N = 129$) of predominantly Mexican descent to test a path model in which contributions of parental involvement to academic self-concept and school grades were mediated by student perceptions of school belonging and teacher expectations of students' academic attainment. The hypothesized model fit the data well, suggesting that parental involvement functions to increase Latino youth's social capital in the educational arena and pointing to ways that parents and school officials can work together to make school environments more welcoming and increase expectations for young people's achievement.

Family and Neighborhood Connections. Mesosystem transactions between the family and neighborhood microsystems are also important to the Latino youth's development. Using data on 800 African American and Latino 10- to 14-year-olds from the Three Cities Study, Roche, Ensminger, and Cherlin (2007) found that protective associations of uninvolved and permissive parenting with delinquency, depressive symptoms, and school problem behavior were strongest among youth living in high-risk neighborhoods. A study of family ethnic socialization and ethnic identity among 187 Latino young adolescents of Mexican, Guatemalan, and Salvadorian decent (Supple, Ghazarian, Frabutt, Plunkett, & Sands, 2006) found that family ethnic socialization was associated positively with youth's perceived ethnic affirmation when youth lived in low-risk neighborhoods (perceived as having low levels of drug use, illegal activity, etc.) but negatively associated with ethnic affirmation when neighborhood risk was high. Furthermore, ethnic affirmation mediated both the negative association of neighborhood risk with school performance and the positive association of having a high percentage of Latino neighbors with school performance.

Taken together, research on family, school, peer, and neighborhood (microsystem) processes in the development of Latino youth points to the importance not only of ensuring that youth experience support in each of these settings but also of building social capital across those settings (mesosystem processes). Parents' efforts to encourage their children's academic achievement and to protect them from involvement in problem behaviors may be most effective when reinforced by supportive processes in their neighborhoods and at school. The cultural-ecological-transactional framework highlights specific processes occurring in each setting (e.g., areas of agreement or disagreement in parents' and teachers' conceptions of a good education) and points to strategies for bridging cultural gaps between them.

Conclusions and Future Directions

In this chapter, we have presented a model of resilience framed within a cultural-ecological-transactional model that accounts for proximal influences of cultural processes in the everyday lives of Latino youth, and views their individual well-being as interdependent with the relational and collective well-being of their families, schools, and neighborhoods. This model directs us toward research that can illuminate how youth reconcile the seemingly conflicting goals of developing both an independent and an interdependent sense of self through transactions with their social environment. Important protective processes are found at each level of the social ecology and include the internalization of cultural and religious values and beliefs, involvement in maintaining the well-being of the family, and development of a bicultural identity. Supportive relationships in the family, peer group, school, and neighborhood, reinforced by relationships that bridge those important settings of development, are also critical. As active agents in their own development, youth can make use of their experiences with each of these processes to forge a sense of self as both autonomous and connected to others (Kagitcibasi, 2005).

Tracing the history of research on resilience, Masten and her colleagues (Masten, 2007; Masten & Obradović, 2006) have noted that technological and conceptual-theoretical advances have led to a new wave of understanding resilience as a multilevel process. This new perspective defines *resilience* as the interplay between neurobiological, psychosocial, societal, and global influences on development. We believe that the study of resilience and positive development among Latino youth in the United States offers a window of opportunity to advance the broader field of resilience research beyond its potential contributions to a particular ethnocultural group. We make this claim because Latino youth growing up in the United States are situated in a social context punctuated by the effects of rapid social change that can be observed daily in debates over globalization, immigration reform, accountability-based educational practices, and so forth, issues that in some way affect all youth in the United States.

Studying the varied contexts in which Latino youth are developing throughout the United States offers opportunities for natural experiments that can inform understanding of how exosocial and macrosocial processes affect developmental pathways. For example, the "new growth" states of the southeastern and midwestern United States have drawn large numbers of immigrant and migrant Latino families with the promise of economic advancement (Anrig & Wang, 2006), but the relative recency of the phenomenon often leaves families to build their own support networks in the absence of adequate formal support systems. Future research is needed to study how families and communities in these newly established migration destinations develop functioning social networks to fill the void. Existing rules of thumb about Latino communities in the more established destinations (e.g., Mexicans in California, Illinois, and Texas; Cubans and Central Americans in Florida; Dominicans and Puerto Ricans in New York) may become less useful as new patterns of immigration and migration bring together Latinos with multiple ethnic, racial, and national identifications. Future research should investigate how these varied contexts influence the development of ethnic identities rooted in national origin, race, or increasingly pan-ethnic communities of residence (Masuoka, 2008).

Although sociocultural processes offer a unique opportunity to expand understanding of cultural-ecological-transactional processes, it is important that research also work to better articulate the meaning of adaptive and maladaptive functioning in this population. Rodriguez and Morrobel's (2004) comprehensive review of more than 1,000 published articles found that Latino youth were underrepresented in leading developmental journals and that studies including Latino youth tended to be deficit oriented and to lack a specific theoretical framework. Building a science of resilience among Latino youth is fraught with challenges that include developing a greater understanding of variations in how Latino youth experience mental health and illness (Gorman, Brough, & Ramirez, 2003) and how stereotyped perceptions of Latino youth's risk behavior (Erkut,

Szalacha, Alarcon, & García Coll, 1999) serve to maintain a persistent deficit orientation in developmental studies. Current research is also limited by a lack of longitudinal studies on the interplay of acculturation and trajectories of development over time (Fuligni, 2001). In the spirit of a resilience perspective, we view these limitations not as deficits but as rich opportunities to advance the field and contribute to improving the life chances of Latino youth in the United States.

REFERENCES

Allen, J. P., Hauser, S. T., O'Connor, T. G., & Bell, K. L. (2002). Prediction of peer-rated adult hostility from autonomy struggles in adolescent-family interactions. *Development and Psychopathology, 14,* 123–137.

Anrig, G., & Wang, T. A. (2006). *Immigration's new frontiers: Experiences from the emerging gateway states.* New York: Century Foundation Press.

Araujo, B. Y., & Borrell, L. N. (2006). Understanding the link between discrimination, mental health outcomes, and life chances among Latinos. *Hispanic Journal of Behavioral Sciences, 28,* 245–266.

Arfaniarromo, A. (2001). Toward a psychosocial and sociocultural understanding of achievement motivation among Latino gang members in U.S. schools. *Journal of Instructional Psychology, 28,* 123–136.

Azmitia, M., Ittel, A., & Brenk, C. (2006). *Latino-heritage adolescents' friendships.* In X. Chen, D. C. French, & B. H. Schneider (Eds.), *Peer relationships in cultural context* (pp. 426–451). New York: Cambridge University Press.

Bacallao, M., & Smokowski, P. (2007). The costs of getting ahead: Mexican family system changes after immigration. *Family Relations, 56,* 52–67.

Birman, D., Weinstein, T., Chan, W. Y., & Beehler, S. (2007). Immigrant youth in U.S. schools: Opportunities for prevention. *The Prevention Researcher, 14,* 14–17.

Bloomberg, L., Ganey, A., Alba, V., Quintero, G., & Alvarez Alcantara, L. (2003). Chicano-Latino youth leadership institute: An asset-based program for youth. *American Journal of Health Behavior, 27*(Supplement 1), S45–S54.

Borden, L. M., Perkins, D. F., Villarruel, F. A., Carleton-Hug, A., Stone, M. R., & Keith, J. G. (2006). Challenges and opportunities to Latino youth development: Increasing meaningful participation in youth development programs. *Hispanic Journal of Behavioral Sciences, 28,* 187–208.

Bronfenbrenner, U. (1979). *The ecology of human development.* Cambridge, MA: Harvard University Press.

Bronfenbrenner, U. (1988). Interacting systems in human development. Research paradigms: Present and future. In N. Bolger, A. Caspi, G. Downey, & M. Moorehouse (Eds.), *Persons in context: Developmental perspectives* (pp. 25–49). New York: Cambridge University Press.

Cabrera-Strait, S. (2001). An examination of the influence of acculturative stress on substance use and related maladaptive behavior among Latino youth. *Dissertation Abstracts International: Section B: The Sciences and Engineering, 62,* 2532.

Capps, R., & Fortuny, K. (2006, January). *Immigration and child and family policy.* Washington: The Urban Institute and Child Trends.

Castro, F. G, Boyer, G. R., & Balcazar, H. G. (2000). Healthy adjustment in Mexican American and other Hispanic adolescents. In R. Montemayor, G. R. Adams, & T.P. Gullotta (Eds.), *Adolescent diversity in ethnic, economic, and cultural contexts.* Thousand Oaks, CA: Sage.

Cauce, A. M. (2002). Examining culture within a quantitative empirical framework. *Human Development, 45,* 294–298.

Cavazos-Rehg, P. A., Zayas, L. H., & Spitznagel, E. L. (2007). Legal status, emotional well-being and subjective health status of Latino immigrants. *Journal of the National Medical Association, 99,* 1126–1131.

Ceballo, R. (2004). From barrios to Yale: The role of parenting strategies in Latino families. *Hispanic Journal of Behavioral Sciences, 26,* 171–186.

Center on Alcohol Marketing and Youth. (2005). *Exposure of Hispanic youth to alcohol advertising, 2003–2004.* Retrieved April 15, 2007, from http://www.rwjf.org/files/research/AlcoholAdsHispanicYouth.pdf

Centers for Disease Control and Prevention (CDC). (2007). National Youth Risk Behavior Survey: Health risk behaviors by race/ethnicity. MMWR, 55 (No. SS-5). Retrieved May 17, 2008, from http://www.cdc.gov/HealthyYouth/yrbs/pdf/yrbs07_us_disparity_race.pdf

Chun, S. (2007). The "other Hispanics"—What are their national origins? Estimating the Latino-origin populations in the United States. *Hispanic Journal of Behavioral Sciences, 29,* 133–155.

Cicchetti, D., & Toth, S. L. (1997). *Transactional ecological systems in developmental psychopathology.* In S. S. Luthar, J. A. Burack, D. Cicchetti, & J. R. Weisz (Eds.), *Developmental psychopathology: Perspectives on adjustment, risk, and disorder* (pp. 317–349). New York: Cambridge University Press.

Coie, J. D., Watt, N. F., West, S. G., Hawkins, J. D., Asarnow, J. R., Markman, H. J., et al. (1993).

The science of prevention: A conceptual framework and some directions for a national research program. *American Psychologist, 48,* 1013–1022.

Conchas, G., & Clark, P. (2002). Career academies and urban minority schooling: Forging optimism despite limited opportunity. *Journal of Education for Students Placed at Risk, 7,* 287–311.

Crosnoe, R. (2005). The diverse experiences of Hispanic students in the American educational system. *Sociological Forum, 20,* 561–588.

Delgado-Gaitan, C. (1990). Involving parents in the schools: A process of empowerment. *American Journal of Education, 100,* 20–46.

Denner, J., Cooper, C., Dunbar, N., & Lopez, E. (2005). Latinos in a college outreach program: Application, selection and participation. *Journal of Latinos and Education, 4,* 21–41.

Eamon, M. (2005). Social-demographic, school, neighborhood, and parenting influences on the academic achievement of Latino young adolescents. *Journal of Youth and Adolescence, 34,* 163–174.

Eamon, M. K., & Mulder, C. (2005). Predicting antisocial behavior among Latino young adolescents: An ecological systems analysis. *American Journal of Orthopsychiatry, 75,* 117–127.

Edwards, L. M., & Romero, A. J. (2008). Coping with discrimination among Mexican descent adolescents. *Hispanic Journal of Behavioral Sciences, 30,* 24–39.

Erkut, S., Szalacha, L. A., Alarcon, O., & García Coll, C. (1999). Stereotyped perceptions of adolescents' health risk behaviors. *Cultural Diversity and Ethnic Minority Psychology, 5,* 340–349.

Evans, S. D., & Prilleltensky, I. (2007). Youth and democracy: Participation for personal, relational, and collective well-being. *Journal of Community Psychology, 35,* 681–692.

Fishbein, D. H., Herman-Stahl, M., Eldreth, D., Paschall, M. J., Hyde, C., Huban, R., et al. (2006). Mediators of the stress–substance-use relationship in urban male adolescents. *Prevention Science, 7,* 113–126.

Fong, R. (2007). Immigrant and refugee youth: Migration journeys and cultural values. *The Prevention Researcher, 14,* 3–5.

Frost, J. J., Jones, R. K., Woog, V., Singh, S., & Darrocj, J. E. (2001). *Teenage sexual and reproductive behavior in development countries: Country report for the United States.* New York: Alan Guttmacher Institute.

Fuertes, J. N., & Westbrook, F. D. (1996). Using the Social, Attitudinal, Familial, and Environmental (S.A.F.E.) Acculturation Stress Scale to assess the adjustment needs of Hispanic college students. *Measurement and Evaluation in Counseling and Development, 29.*

Fuligni, A. J. (2001). A comparative longitudinal approach to acculturation among children from immigrant families. *Harvard Educational Review, 71,* 566–578.

Gandara, P. (2006). Strengthening the academic pipeline leading to careers in math, science, and technology for Latino students. *Journal of Hispanic Higher Education, 5,* 222–237.

García Coll, C., Crnic, K., Lamberty, G., Wasik, B. H., Jenkins, R., Vazquez Garcia, H., et al. (1996). An integrative model for the study of developmental competencies in minority children. *Child Development, 67,* 1891–1914.

Gaytan, F. X., Carhill, A., & Suárez-Orozco, C. (2007). Understanding and responding to the needs of newcomer immigrant youth and families. *The Prevention Researcher, 14,* 10–13.

Gil, A. G., Wagner, E. F., & Vega, W. A. (2000). Acculturation, familism, and alcohol use among Latino adolescent males: Longitudinal relations. *Journal of Community Psychology, 28,* 443–458.

Gorman, D., Brough, M., & Ramirez, E. (2003). How young people from culturally and linguistically diverse backgrounds experience mental health: Some insights for mental health nurses. *International Journal of Mental Health Nursing, 12,* 194–202.

Greenfield, P. M., Keller, H., Fuligni, A., & Maynard, A. (2003). Cultural pathways through universal development. *Annual Review of Psychology, 54,* 461–490.

Guilamo-Ramos, V., Jaccard, J., Johansson, M., & Turrisi, R. (2004). Binge drinking among Latino youth: Role of acculturation-related variables. *Psychology of Addictive Behaviors, 18,* 135–142.

Guzman, M., Santiago-Rivera, A., & Haase, R. (2005). Understanding academic attitudes and achievement in Mexican-origin youth: Ethnic identity, other-group orientation, and fatalism. *Cultural Diversity and Ethnic Minority Psychology, 11,* 3–15.

Hernandez, M., & McGoldrick, M. (1999). Migration and the family life cycle. In B. Carter & M. McGoldrick (Eds.), *The expanded family life cycle: Individual, family, and social perspectives* (3rd ed., pp. 169–184). Needham Heights, MA: Allyn & Bacon.

Hovey, J. D. (1998). Acculturative stress, depression, and suicidal ideation among Mexican American adolescents: Implications for the development of suicide prevention programs in school. *Psychological Reports, 83,* 249–250.

Hovey, J. D. (2000). Psychosocial predictors of acculturative stress in Mexican immigrants. *Journal of Psychology, 134,* 490–502.

Hughes, D., Rodriguez, J., Smith, E., Johnson, D. J., Stevenson, H.C., & Spicer, P. (2006). Parents' ethnic-racial socialization practices: A review of research and future directions. *Developmental Psychology, 42,* 747–770.

Ibañez, G. E., Kuperminc, G. P., Jurkovic, G., & Perilla, J. (2004). Cultural attributes and adaptations linked to achievement motivation among Latino adolescents. *Journal of Youth and Adolescence, 33,* 559–568.

Jurkovic, G. J., Kuperminc, G., Perilla, J., Murphy, A. D., Ibañez, G., & Casey, S. (2004). Ecological and ethical perspectives on filial responsibility: Implications for primary prevention with immigrant Latino adolescents. *Journal of Primary Prevention, 25,* 81–104.

Kagitcibasi, C. (2005). Autonomy and relatedness in cultural context: Implications for self and family. *Journal of Cross-Cultural Psychology, 36,* 403–422.

Kao, G., & Rutherford, L. T. (2007). Does social capital still matter? Immigrant minority disadvantage in school-specific social capital and its effects on academic achievement. *Sociological Perspectives, 50,* 27–52.

Kao, G., & Tienda, M. (1998). Educational aspirations of minority youth. *American Journal of Education, 106,* 349–384.

Kenny, M., Gallagher, L., Alvarez-Salvat, R., & Silsby, J. (2002). Sources of support and psychological distress among academically successful inner-city youth. *Adolescence, 37,* 161–182.

Kerr, M. H., Beck, K., Shattuck, T. D., Kattar, C., & Uriburu, D. (2003). Family involvement, problem and prosocial behavior outcomes of Latino youth. *American Journal of Health Behavior, 27*(Supplement 1), S55–S65.

Knight, G. P., & Hill, N. E. (1998). Measurement equivalence in the study of race, class, and ethnicity. In V. C. McLoyd & L. Steinberg (Eds.), *Studying minority adolescents: Conceptual, methodological, and theoretical issues* (pp. 183–210). Mahwah, NJ: Lawrence Erlbaum.

Kovic, C. (2008). Jumping from a moving train: Risk, migration, and rights at NAFTA's southern border. *Practicing Anthropology, 30,* 32–36.

Kuperminc, G. P. (2007, March). *Changing Family Roles and Psychosocial Functioning of Latino Adolescents from Immigrant Families.* Presented at the Risk and Prevention in Education Sciences Speaker Series, Curry Graduate School of Education, University of Virginia, Charlottesville. Retrieved May 17, 2008, from http://www.teach.virginia.edu/files/pdf/RPES/k uperminc.pdf

Kuperminc, G. P., Blatt, S. J., Shahar, G., Henrich, C., & Leadbeater, B. J. (2004). Cultural equivalence and cultural variance in longitudinal associations of young adolescent self-definition, interpersonal relatedness to psychological and school adjustment. *Journal of Youth and Adolescence, 33,* 13–31.

Kuperminc, G. P., & Brookmeyer, K. A. (2006). Developmental psychopathology. In R. Ammerman (Ed.), *Comprehensive handbook of personality and psychopathology* (Vol. 3, pp. 100–113). New York: John Wiley.

Kuperminc, G. P., Darnell, A. J., & Alvarez-Jimenez, A. (2008). Parent involvement in the academic adjustment of Latino middle and high school youth: Teacher expectations and school belonging as mediators. *Journal of Adolescence, 31,* 461–483.

Kuperminc, G., Henrich, C., Meyers, J., House, D., & Sayfi, S. (2007, June). The role of perceived discrimination in the academic adjustment of Latino youth from immigrant families. In N. Wilkins (Chair), *Academic attainment among Latino youth: A social justice issue.* Symposium conducted at the 11th biennial meeting of the Society for Community Research and Action, Pasadena, CA.

Kuperminc, G. P., Jurkovic, G. J., & Casey, S. (in press). Relation of filial responsibility to the personal and social adjustment of Latino adolescents from immigrant families. *Journal of Family Psychology.*

Kwak, K. (2003). Adolescents and their parents: A review of intergenerational family relations for immigrant and non-immigrant families. *Human Development, 46,* 115–136.

Leadbeater, B. J., Kuperminc, G. P., Blatt, S. J., & Hertzog, C. (1999). A multivariate model of gender differences in adolescents' internalizing and externalizing problems. *Developmental Psychology, 35,* 1268–1282.

Lichter, D. T., Qian, Z., & Crowley, M. L. (2005). Child poverty among racial minorities and immigrants: Explaining trends and differentials. *Social Science Quarterly, 86*(Supplement), 1037–1059.

Locke, T. F., Newcomb, M. D., & Goodyear, R. K. (2005). Childhood experiences and psychosocial influences on risky sexual behavior, condom use, and HIV attitudes-behaviors among Latino males. *Psychology of Men & Masculinity, 6,* 25–38.

Lopez, N., & Lechuga, C. E. (2007). They are like a friend: Othermothers creating empowering, school-based community living rooms in Latina and Latino middle schools. In B. J. R. Leadbeater & N. Way (Eds.), *Urban Girls Revisited: Building Strengths.* New York: New York University Press.

Lowell, B. L., & Suro, R. (2002, December). *The improving educational profile of Latino immigrants.* Washington, DC: Pew Hispanic Center.

Luthar, S. S., Cicchetti, D., & Becker, B. (2000). The construct of resilience: A critical evaluation and guidelines for future work. *Child Development, 71,* 543–562.

Marsiglia, F. F., Kulis, S., Nieri, T., & Parsai, M. (2005). God forbid! Substance use among religious and nonreligious youth. *American Journal of Orthopsychiatry, 75*, 585–598.

Masten, A. S. (2001). Ordinary magic: Resilience processes in development. *American Psychologist, 56*, 227–238.

Masten, A. (2007). Resilience in developing systems: Progress and promise as the fourth wave rises. *Development and Psychopathology, 19*, 921–930.

Masten, A. S., & Obradović, J. (2006). Competence and resilience in development. *Annals of the New York Academy of Sciences, 1094*, 13–27.

Masuoka, N. (2008). Defining the group: Latino identity and political participation. *American Politics Research 2008, 36*, 33–61.

McLoyd, V. C. (1998). Socioeconomic disadvantage and child development. *American Psychologist, 53*, 185–204.

McNeal, R. B. (1999). Parental involvements as social capital: Differential effectiveness on science achievement, truancy, and dropping out. *Social Forces, 78*, 117–144.

Mena, F. J., Padilla, A. M., & Maldonado, M. (1987). Acculturative stress and specific coping strategies among immigrant and later generation college students. *Hispanic Journal of Behavioral Sciences, 9*, 207–225.

Minnis, A. M., & Padian, N. S. (2001). Reproductive health differences among Latin American- and U.S.-born young women. *Journal of Urban Health, 78*, 627–637.

National Center for Education Statistics. (2003). *Status and trends in the education of Hispanics* (NCES 2003–008). Washington, DC: U.S. Department of Education.

National Center for Mental Health Promotion and Youth Violence Prevention. (2004, April). *Meeting the needs of Latino youth*. Retrieved April 22, 2007, from http://www.promote prevent.org/documents/prevention_brief_latino _youth.pdf

National Youth Gang Center. (2006). *National youth gang survey analysis*. Retrieved April 22, 2007, from http://www.iir.com/nygc/nygsa/

Office of Management and Budget (OMB). (1997, October). *Federal register notice: Revisions to the standards for the classification of federal data on race and ethnicity*. Retrieved March 17, 2008, from http://www.whitehouse.gov/omb/ fedreg/1997standards.html.

Office of National Drug Control Policy. (2005). *Substance use among Hispanic youth in the U.S.* Retrieved April 15, 2007, from http://www.mediacampaign.org/hispnc_yth/ substance_use.html

Ogbu, J. U. (1981). Origins of human competence: A cultural ecological perspective. *Child Development, 52*, 413–429.

O'Sullivan, L. F., Meyer-Balhburg, H. F., & Watkins, B. X. (2000). Social cognitions associated with pubertal development in a sample of urban, low-income African American and Latina girls and mothers. *Journal of Adolescent Health, 27*, 227–235.

Padilla, A. M. (2006). Bicultural social development. *Hispanic Journal of Behavioral Sciences, 28*, 467–497.

Perez, W., & Padilla, A. M. (2000). Cultural orientation across three generations of Hispanic adolescents. *Hispanic Journal of Behavioral Sciences, 22*, 390–398.

Perreira, K. M., & Smith, L. (2007). A cultural-ecological model of migration and development: Focusing on Latino immigrant youth. *The Prevention Researcher, 14*, 6–9.

Pew Hispanic Center (2002, December). *2002 National survey of Latinos*. Retrieved February 25, 2009, from http://pewhispanic.org/files/ reports/15.pdf

Pew Hispanic Center. (2006). *Pew Hispanic Center tabulations of 2000 census and 2006 American community: Statistical portrait of Hispanics in the United States*. Retrieved March 25, 2008, from http://pewhispanic.org/files/fact sheets/hispanics2006/hispanics.pdf

Phinney, J. S., & Ong, A. D. (2007). Conceptualization and measurement of ethnic identity: Current status and future directions. *Journal of Counseling Psychology, 54*, 271–281.

Plunkett, S. W., Abarca-Mortensen, S., Behnke, A. O., & Sands, T. (2007). Neighborhood structural qualities, adolescents' perceptions of neighborhoods and Latino youth development. *Hispanic Journal of Behavioral Sciences, 29*, 19–34.

President's Advisory Commission on Educational Excellence for Hispanics (2000). *Creating the will: Hispanics achieving educational excellence*. Washington, DC: White House Initiative on Educational Excellence for Hispanic Americans. Retrieved May 6, 2008, from http://eric.ed.gov/ ERICWebPortal/custom/portlets/recordDetails/ detailmini.jsp?_nfpb=true&_&ERICExtSearch_ SearchValue_0=ED446195&ERICExtSearch_Sea rchType_0=no&accno=ED446195

Rew, L. (1998). Access to health care for Latina adolescents: A critical review. *Journal of Adolescent Health, 23*, 194–204.

Rew, L., Resnick, M., & Beuhring, T. (1999). Usual sources, patterns of utilization, and foregone health care among Hispanic adolescents. *Journal of Adolescent Health, 25*, 407–413.

Riggs, N. R. (2006). After-school program attendance and the social development of rural Latino children of immigrant families. *Journal of Community Psychology, 34*, 75–87.

Roche, K. M., Ensminger, M. E., & Cherlin, A. J. (2007). Variations in parenting and adolescent outcomes among African American and Latino families living in low-income urban areas. *Journal of Family Issues, 28,* 882–909.

Rodriguez, M., & Blocher, D. (1988). A comparison of two approaches to enhancing career maturity in Puerto Rican college women. *Journal of Counseling Psychology, 35,* 275–280.

Rodriguez, M. C., & Morrobel, D. (2004). A review of Latino youth development research and a call for an asset orientation. *Hispanic Journal of Behavioral Sciences, 26,* 107–127.

Romo, L. F., Lefkowitz, E. S., Sigman, M., & Au, T. K. (2002). A longitudinal study of maternal messages about dating and sexuality and their influence on Latino adolescents. *Journal of Adolescent Health, 31,* 59–69.

Rowe, D. C., Vazsonyi, A. T., & Flannery, D. J. (1994). No more than skin deep: Racial and ethnic similarity in developmental process. *Psychological Review, 101,* 396–413.

Sam, D. L., Vedder, P., Liebkind, K., Neto, F., & Virta, E. (2008). Immigration, acculturation, and the paradox of adaptation in Europe. *European Journal of Developmental Psychology, 5,* 138–158.

Schmitz, M. F. (2006). Influence of social and family contexts on self-esteem of Latino youth. *Hispanic Journal of Behavioral Sciences, 28,* 516–530.

Seidman, E., Allen, L., Aber, J. L., Mitchell, C., Feinman, J., Yoshikawa, J., et al. (1995). Development and validation of adolescent-perceived microsystem scales: Social support, daily hassles, and involvement. *American Journal of Community Psychology, 23,* 355–388.

Smith, E. P., & Guerra, N. G. (2006). Introduction. In. N. G. Guerra & E. P. Smith (Eds.), *Preventing youth violence in a multicultural society.* Washington, DC: American Psychological Association.

Smokowski, P., & Bacallao, M. (2006). Acculturation and aggression in Latino adolescents: A structural model focusing on cultural risk factors and assets. *Journal of Abnormal Child Psychology, 34,* 659–673.

Smokowski, P., & Bacallao, M. (2007). Acculturation internalizing mental health symptoms, and self-esteem: Cultural experiences of Latino adolescents in North Carolina. *Child Psychiatry and Human Development, 37,* 273–292.

Sommers, I., Fagan, J., & Baskin. D. (1993). Sociocultural influences on the explanation of delinquency for Puerto Rican youths. *Hispanic Journal of Behavioral Sciences, 15,* 36–62.

Stanton-Salazar, R. (1997). A social capital framework for understanding the socialization of racial minority children and youths. *Harvard Educational Review, 67,* 1–40.

Stanton-Salazar, R. D., & Spina, S. U. (2005). Adolescent peer networks as a context for social and emotional support. *Youth and Society, 36,* 379–417.

Steinberg, L., & Avenevoli, S. (2000). The role of context in the development of psychopathology: A conceptual framework and some speculative propositions. *Child Development, 71,* 66–74.

Suárez-Orozco, C., & Suárez -Orozco, M. (2001*). Children of immigration.* Cambridge, MA: Harvard University Press.

Supple, A. J., Ghazarian, S. R., Frabutt, J. M., Plunkett, S. W., & Sands, T. (2006). Contextual influences on Latino adolescent ethnic identity and academic outcomes. *Child Development, 77,* 1427–1433.

Szalacha, L. A., Erkut, S., García Coll, C., Alarcon, O., Fields, J. P., & Ceder, I. (2003). Discrimination and Puerto Rican children's and adolescents' mental health. *Cultural Diversity and Ethnic Minority Psychology, 9,* 141–155.

Szapocznik, J., & Kurtines, W. M. (1980). Acculturation, biculturalism and adjustment among Cuban Americans. In A. Padilla (Ed.), *Acculturation: Theory, models, and some new findings* (pp. 139–159). Boulder, CO: Praeger.

Umaña-Taylor, A. J., & Fine, M. A. (2001). Methodological implications of grouping Latino adolescents into one collective ethnic group. *Hispanic Journal of Behavioral Sciences, 23,* 347–361.

Umaña-Taylor, A. J., & Updegraff, K. A. (2007). Latino adolescents' mental health: Exploring the interrelations among discrimination, ethnic identity, cultural orientation, self-esteem, and depressive symptoms. *Journal of Adolescence, 30,* 549–567.

Urban Institute. (2002, November). *The dispersal of immigrants in the 1990s* (Brief No. 2). Washington, DC: Author.

U.S. Census Bureau (2007, April). *Cumulative estimates of the components of population change for the United States, regions, and states: April 1, 2000, to July 1, 2007* (NST-EST2007–04). Washington, DC: Author. Retrieved March 17, 2008, from http://www.census.gov/popest/states/NST-comp-chg.html

U.S. Department of Health and Human Services. (2002). *Overview of findings from the 2002 National Survey on Drug Use and Health.* Retrieved April 15, 2007, from http://www.oas.samhsa.gov/NHSDA/2k2NSDUH/2k2SoFOverviewW.pdf

Vanoss, M. B., Coyle, K. K., Gomez, C. A., Carvajal, S. C., & Kirby, D. B. (2000). Older boyfriends and girlfriends increase risk of sexual initiation in young adolescents. *Journal of Adolescent Health, 27,* 409–418.

Ventura, S. J., Matthews, T. J., & Hamilton, B. E. (2001). Births to teenagers in the United States, 1940–2000. *National Vital Statistics Reports, 49,* 1–23.

Villarruel, A. M. (1998). Cultural influences on the sexual attitudes, beliefs and norms of young Latina adolescents. *Journal of the Society of Pediatric Nurses, 3*, 69–81.

Warheit, G. J., Vega, W. A., Khoury, E. L., & Gil, A. A. (1996). A comparative analysis of cigarette, alcohol, and illicit drug use among an ethnically diverse sample of Hispanic, African American, and non-Hispanic White adolescents. *Journal of Drug Issues, 126*, 901–922.

Way, N., Cowal, K., Gingold, R., Pahl, K., & Bissessar, N. (2001). Friendship patterns among African American, Asian American, and Latino adolescents from low-income families. *Journal of Social and Personal Relationships, 18*, 29–53.

Way, N., & Pahl, K. (2001). Individual and contextual predictors of perceived friendship quality among ethnic minority, low-income adolescents. *Journal of Research on Adolescence, 11*, 325–349.

Weisskirch, R. S. (2005). The relationship of language brokering to ethnic identity for Latino early adolescents. *Hispanic Journal of Behavioral Sciences, 27*, 286–299.

14

Health and Mental Health Perspectives on Elderly Latinos in the United States

Steven R. Applewhite, Mary Jo Garcia Biggs, and Angelica P. Herrera

The influence of culture and ethnicity on the aging process receives considerable attention in the field of gerontology and related disciplines. From this perspective, Latino aging can be viewed as a phenomenological experience, best understood as a complex interplay of biological, psychosocial, cultural, and spiritual constructs. It involves the interaction of the individual, the family, and the social environment, which includes finding a personal balance between the host culture and the culture of origin. For older Latinos, successful aging and quality of life are largely described by intraethnic and interethnic differences and similarities based on cultural beliefs, traditions, behavioral patterns, life perspectives, socioeconomic status, and health inequities.

This chapter defines "Latino aged" chronologically as persons 55 years and older but also considers physiological differences moderated by functional impairment, culturally rooted views toward physical and mental health, socially prescribed roles, availability of social and instrumental support, economic resources,

and ability to navigate health and social services. The following literature, however, is synthesized with the knowledge that some variation and inconsistency in the definition of "older adult" exists. Lamentably, legions of elderly Latinos/as face severe economic hardships and problems of both health and mental health, as well as a history of social neglect, discrimination, and oppression. Existing conditions place them in multiple types of jeopardy—old, poor, minority, disabled, economically disenfranchised, and chronically ill, with limited resources and weak family and community support systems. Despite these problems, elderly Latinos will enter *la tercera edad* (old age) as lifelong contributors and *sobrevivientes* (survivors) of this nation's growth and social revolution.

This chapter examines the essence of old age in the U.S. Latino community. It provides an overview of the demographic profile of elderly Latinos/as, health and mental health disparities, barriers to good-quality care and family caregiving, and the significance of culture in understanding ethnocultural patterns and behaviors necessary for culturally competent practice with elderly Latinos/as.

DEMOGRAPHICS OF OLDER LATINOS

Population demographics provide an overview of the changes in societal structures. Older Latinos/as represent the fastest-growing segments of the 65-and-older age group, and roughly 50% are of Mexican origin (U.S. Department of Health and Human Services [HHS], 2008a). Projections indicate that between 2005 and 2050, the older Latino/a population will increase from 2.4 million to more than 15 million, accounting for 17.5% of the older adult population (Federal Interagency Forum on Aging-Related Statistics [FIFARS], 2008). It is estimated that by 2008, Latinos/as will be the largest racial/ethnic minority group in the 65-and-older age category (HHS, 2008a).

In terms of geographic distribution, the greatest concentrations of older Latinos/as reside in California (27%), Texas (19%), Florida (15%), and New York (9%; HHS, 2008a). In the Midwest, many Latinos/as live in Michigan, Illinois, Wisconsin, and Ohio, owing to early-life migration to agriculture states as farmworkers. Ultimately, many stayed on to work in the iron, steel, and the auto industries throughout the Midwest. Latin American communities, particularly of older Puerto Ricans, live in such metropolitan centers as New York and Boston, as well as other cities along the Eastern seaboard. Mexican Americans tend to live in the rural Southwest and in such metro centers as Los Angeles, Phoenix, Houston, Dallas, and San Antonio. Elderly Cuban populations are concentrated in Florida.

Gender Differences

Gender patterns of older Latinos/as emulate trends observed in older people in the general population; women live longer and outnumber men, with some intergroup variation (Hooyman & Kiyak, 2008). Among Puerto Ricans aged 65–74, the ratio is 76 men per 100 women; for Cuban Americans, the ratio is 78 men per 100 women; and among Mexican Americans, the ratio is highest, with 83 men per 100 women (Hooyman & Kiyak, 2008; Angel & Hogan, 2004). Women in the general population more often remain widowed and live alone than do men, whereas Latina women are more likely than non-Latina women to live with relatives other than a spouse—34% versus 14%, respectively (Hooyman & Kiyak, 2008; FIFARS, 2008). Over 80% of older Latino males marry or remarry—more often than men in other ethnic groups (Hooyman & Kiyak, 2008). As of 2006, 69% of older Latino men reported living with their spouses, 12% lived with other relatives, 3% lived with nonrelatives, and 17% lived alone (HHS, 2008a).

Poverty and Education

Not discounting the complexities of the health-care system and the prevalence of racial discrimination, race and ethnicity continue to have a relationship with poverty, particularly among the elderly. The poverty rate among Latinos/as aged 65 and older is 19.4%, more than twice that of non-Latino/a whites 7% (HHS, 2008a). Median income in 2006 for families headed by Latinos/as 65 and older was only $29,868, compared with $41,220 for non-Latino/a whites (ibid.). Among those households, 19% had an income of less than $15,000, compared to 5.9% for non-Latino/a white households (ibid.). Gender also figures into the equation: Households headed by Latina women generally have the highest poverty rate among all ethnic and age categories (Hooyman & Kiyak, 2008).

Overall, educational attainment has increased in older adults over the years, but substantial educational differences persist among racial and ethnic groups. Educational levels are strongly associated with increased poverty and lower health literacy. About 70% of older Latinos/as never completed high school, compared to 30% of the overall population. In 2007, 42% of Latinos/as older than 65 had completed high school, compared to 81% of non-Latino/a whites aged 65 and over (FIFARS, 2008).

HEALTH STATUS AND CHRONIC ILLNESSES

Ethnicity is factor in the incidence of chronic illness. After adjusting for age and gender, Latinos/as are twice as likely to have diabetes as non-Latino/a whites (Centers for Disease Control and Prevention [CDC], 2004b). Complications from diabetes may include heart disease and stroke, high blood pressure, blindness, kidney disease, nervous system disease, amputations, and dental disease. Although Latinos/as have shown lower rates for cancer overall, they have a higher rate of cancer associated with infections (e.g., liver cancer, stomach cancer, and uterine cancer; American Cancer Society [ACS], 2007). Ethnicity does not seem to be a factor with hypertension or arthritis: Older Latinos/as report similar levels of hypertension when compared with non-Latino/a whites, and lower levels of arthritis (FIFARS, 2008).

Schneider (2004) adds that mortality risks from both cancer and coronary vascular disease are intermediate mechanisms associated with depression, psychological stress, low socio-economic status, and behavioral and lifestyle variables. Likewise, hypertension, known to accompany diabetes, is highly associated with cognitive decline and is correlated with lack of formal education, age, stroke, and depression in elderly Mexican Americans (Insel, Palmer, Stroup-Benham, Markides, & Espino, 2005).

Although older Latinos/as have lower mortality rates for heart disease, cancer, and stroke than non-Latino/a whites do, these diseases remain the leading causes of death for the Latino/a population (FIFARS, 2008). It is estimated that 85% of older Latinos/as have at least one chronic condition that significantly impairs their quality of life. As with other ethnic minority elders, the cumulative effects of poverty and cultural affronts begin to take their toll later in life and influence Latinos/as' ability to access good-quality, affordable health care that might prevent or delay the onset of disabling conditions (Wykle & Ford, 1999). Moreover, older women suffer an undue burden in older age as well. Elderly Mexican American immigrant women consistently report higher rates of disability than native-born women and non-Latino/a whites (Markides, Eschbach, Ray, & Peek, 2007).

LONGEVITY VERSUS QUALITY OF LIFE

Regardless of the high incidence of chronic conditions, national trends indicate that the Latino/a population is living longer. Older Latinos/as have a higher life expectancy compared to other racial and ethnic groups but do not enjoy a comparable quality of life in their golden years. Life expectancy for the year 2010 ranges from 76.2 years for males to 82.2 years for females (U.S. Census Bureau, 2008). However,

ethnic minorities may have different expectations about growing old in the United States. In a study conducted at 14 community-based senior centers in Los Angeles, researchers concluded that Latinos/as had significantly lower age-expectations than non-Latino/a whites and African Americans, even after adjusting for health characteristics and age (Sarkisian, Shunkwiler, Aguilar, & Moore, 2006). When asked to rate their health, older Latinos/as are more likely to report a lower health status than non-Latino/a whites; Latino men aged 85 and older report the lowest health ratings (FIFARS, 2008). More Latinos/as also report needing help from other persons for personal care, 11.1% compared with 5.3% for non-Latino/a whites (5.3%; HHS, 2008a).

A closely related area that has received considerable attention in the last decade is the "Latino/a epidemiological paradox," which states that despite worse socioeconomic indicators, Latinos/as live longer than non-Latino/a whites (Abraido-Lanza, Dohrenwend, Ng-Mak, & Turner, 1999). A review of the evidence from studies on the Latino/a paradox concluded that a mortality advantage among older Mexican American males is conceivable. This implies support for the "salmon bias" effect (Markides & Eschbach, 2005), which posits that Latinos engage in selective return migration to their country of origin and are typically in poorer health than migrants who stay behind in the United States, which results in the biased appearance that Latinos are healthier.

BARRIERS TO AFFORDABLE AND GOOD-QUALITY CARE

Older Latinos/as face numerous obstacles in health-care services (Zunker & Cummins, 2004). Disparities in health-care access may be attributed to age; lower income; inadequate health insurance; geographic, cultural, and language barriers; severity of conditions; and racial/ethnic biases (HHS, 2008b; American Cancer Society, 2007) In 2001, 20.7% of older Latinos/as reported dissatisfaction with the quality of the health care they received; few had a usual source of medical care (HHS, 2008a). There is a need for mental health services, particularly for those suffering from depression, among Latino/a older adults. Latinos/as have long been underserved in the mental and behavioral health services arena, due in part to the lack of bilingual counseling psychologists (Mallen, Vogel, Rochlen, & Day, 2005). Latinos/as' negative perception of mental illness and psychological services increases their resistance to seeking assistance (Gary, 2005). Moreover, Spanish-speaking Latinos are more likely to enter the mental health system through outpatient clinics, compared to emergency-room care, as reported in a large-scale study in San Diego County (Folsom et al., 2007).

Health Literacy

Health literacy—the ability to read and comprehend basic health-related materials, such as prescription bottles and hospital forms—presents both individual and system-level barriers to health care and mental health service utilization (Kutner, Greenberg, Jin, & Paulsen, 2006). Disadvantages and challenges in acquiring affordable and good-quality care are more prominent among elderly Latinos/as (Baker, Gazmararian, Sudano, & Patterson, 2000; Gazmararian et al., 1999; Lee, Gazmararian, & Arozullah, 2006), and the low health-literacy rates observed in this population contribute to inequities in mental health by exacerbating problems in comprehending and interpreting mental health or health-care information. Low health-literacy in older Latinos/as is problematic for a host of reasons. The National Assessment of Adult Literacy reports that 29% to 52% of people with low health-literacy have higher hospitalization rates than more health-literate persons (Kutner et al., 2006). Furthermore, persons with chronic diseases with low health-literacy may have less knowledge of their disease and plausible treatment methods, worse self-management of their disease, and inferior overall health (ibid.). This is troubling because health materials are often written at levels that exceed the reading skills of such populations.

Health-Care Costs

Health-care costs and medical insurance constitute another barrier for older Latinos/as. In 2004, the average Medicare health-care costs among Latino/a enrollees aged 65 and older averaged $11,962. They have the highest uninsured rates of any racial or ethnic group within the United States (CDC, 2004a). Among the Latino/a subgroups, 39.1% of Mexicans, 47.3% of Puerto Ricans, 57.9% of Cubans, and 45.1% of other Latino/a groups have private insurance coverage (CDC, 2004a). Older Latinos/as are less likely to receive pension benefits, interest on investments, or supplemental "Medigap" health insurance. They may have not been able to accumulate sufficient financial resources to sustain themselves during retirement (Villa & Aranda, 2000). Enough money to meet needs, affordable housing, and safe neighborhoods were higher priorities than health concerns for older Latinos/as (Napoles-Springer et al., 2000).

A large segment of Latino/a domestic workers are ineligible for social benefits because they or their employers do not pay taxes (Cruz, 2005). Considering that the family unit and cohabitation are cultural attributes of the Latino/a community, the National Hispanic Council on Aging noted that sometimes there are disincentives for cohabitation in terms of Supplemental Security Income (SSI) benefits that can result in reduction of benefits.

CULTURAL CONSIDERATIONS IN MENTAL HEALTH

In the last decade, ethnic and cultural considerations have received growing attention in the fields of health and mental health. The U.S. Department of Health and Human Services (HHS, 2001) and the Kaiser Family Foundation (2007) concluded that such factors as race and ethnicity are directly correlated with health and mental health disparities. The most critical of these reports to date was issued by the HHS (2001) and which noted that racial and ethnic minorities have less access to care, are less likely to receive needed care, and are more likely to receive poor quality of care. The report noted that "minorities bear a greater burden from unmet mental health needs and thus suffer a greater loss to their overall health and productivity" (HHS, 2001, p. 3). Thus, a compelling argument is made that the intersection of race, ethnicity, and culture provides insight into the nature and etiology of mental health problems and the urgency of developing culturally competent systems of care, including clinical assessment, diagnosis, and therapeutic and community-based interventions.

The cultural influences on mental health perceptions play a considerable role in the manifestation of symptoms, support system, coping style, diagnosis, willingness to seek treatment, and the treatment itself (Versola-Russo, 2006). The need to address mental health issues facing elderly Latinos/as in a holistic fashion is significant for several reasons. According to Beyene, Becker, and Mayen (2002), "the integrations of physical, emotional and spiritual, family and good interpersonal relationships are often mentioned by older Latino/a participants as factors that contribute to well-being" (p. 167). Moreover, elderly Latinos/as report a high incidence of coexisting illnesses or comorbidity (e.g., diabetes, cardiovascular disease, hypertension, stroke, and cancer [Black & Markides, 1999]) that affect their emotional or mental well-being. These chronic conditions are predictive of high levels of depression. For example, elderly Latinos/as have a higher incidence of depression and diabetes than their non-Latino/a white counterparts (Dunlop, Song, Manheim, Lyons, & Chang, 2003). And like African Americans, they tend to receive less psychotherapy or medication treatment even after they have been diagnosed (Crystal, Sambamoorthi, Walkup, & Akincigil, 2003; Strothers et al., 2005). The major factors associated with depression and, arguably, other health and mental health problems, tend to be less education, lower income, lack of health insurance, physical limitations and chronic conditions, lack of acculturation, and being monolingual in Spanish (Dunlop et al., 2003; Gonzalez, Haan, & Hinton, 2001).

There is also a widespread cognitive deficit in this population (Royal, Espino, Polk, Palmer, & Markides, 2004), greater functional and cognitive impairment than is found among whites (Carrasquillo, Lantigua, & Shea, 2000; Tomaszewski Farias, Mungas, Hann, & Jagust, 2004) and a higher prevalence of dementia (Gurland et al., 1999). Thus, it is urgent that effective, culturally validated, and relevant diagnostic measures be established in order to provide quality health and mental health care to elderly Latinos/as.

With respect to cognitive disabilities, older Latinos/as are disproportionately affected by mental illness and Alzheimer's disease (CDC, 2004a; Haan et al., 2003; Hayward & Heron, 1999; Wallace & Villa, 2003). It is estimated that about 5% of the U.S. population aged 55 and older suffer from mild to moderate clinical depression (Choi & Kim, 2007). The incidence of depression is especially high among Latino/a elderly and it is compounded among those with disabilities and chronic illnesses (Bullard, 2008; Raji, Reyes-Ortiz, Kuo, Markides, & Ottenbacher, 2007). Compounding this problem, older Latinos/as face critical challenges in accessing mental health services and tend to grapple with an unfriendly social environment and the stigma associated with mental health disorders. Barrio et al. (2008) found that systematic barriers to mental health services, particularly for depression, included cultural and linguistic barriers and unmet needs in social integration and support. Ostensibly, the lack of culturally competent providers may be the most significant barrier yet to providing effective and responsive mental health services to elderly Latinos.

Mental Health Stigma

One area that demands greater attention is the role of stigmas and stigmatization in hindering access to mental health services. Research indicates that negative perceptions of mental illness and psychological services among Latinos/as have been linked to increased resistance in seeking medical assistance (Gary, 2005; Ojeda & McGuire, 2006). Moreover, this stigma is more prevalent in immigrant-born populations, compared to U.S.-born populations (Nadeem et al., 2007). Depression, for example, may be viewed as a personal issue unrelated to health, and women prefer to turn to family or friends for help in resolving it (Van Hook, 1999). Dementia and Alzheimer's disease, however, may be viewed slightly differently. Latinos/as' lack of knowledge of dementia-related disorders, their symptoms and behavioral changes, may determine how caregivers perceive those symptoms and behaviors and how they respond to their need for care, as well as contribute to delays in seeking care for older relatives (Novak & Riggs, 2004). In the early stages of dementia, Latinos/as tended to stigmatize older relatives suffering from dementia and label them "crazy" (Gallagher-Thompson et al., 1997). Other research shows that Latinos/as have a high acceptance of cognitive impairment and view dementia as a normal part of aging, to be managed by the family (Novak & Riggs, 2004). The failure of relatives to recognize the symptoms of dementia and acknowledge the condition may lead them to pass up opportunities to participate in long-term care services suitable for persons with dementia-related disorders. In fact, Kosloski, Montgomery, and Karner (1999) contend that these differences in attitudes toward illnesses may contribute to the underutilization of formal health services by Latinos/as. Although some of the literature categorizes these misplaced perceptions toward dementia as having a cultural basis, they may be attributed to older Latinos' and their caregivers' lack of knowledge about the disease, resulting from lower educational attainment and limited access to health education.

The Confluence of Culture With Diagnostic Assessment

Culture is perhaps the most difficult concept to operationally define in clinical practice. Culture is best understood as a worldview and a way of life. It is a blueprint for understanding, without predicting, human behavior in the social environment. Culture is the context within which people interact with each other, bound by a set of shared values, beliefs, norms, lifestyles, identity, and developmental patterns.

In mental health practice, culture is an essential construct that influences Latinos/as' perceptions of mental health, the severity of a mental illness, and their decision to access mental health services. The *Diagnostic and Statistical Manual of Mental Disorders* (*DSM-IV-TR;* American Psychiatric Association, 2000) recognizes the importance of culture in diagnosis and includes the sections "Outline for Cultural Formulation" and "Glossary of Culture-Bound Syndromes." The *DSM-IV-TR* provides five categories for clinicians to consider when formulating clinical diagnoses with diverse clients, which take into account an individual's cultural and social reference group and the cultural context necessary for relevant clinical practice. The five categories described in the *DSM* include cultural identity, cultural explanations, cultural factors, cultural elements, and culture-bound syndromes (APA, 2000, pp. 897–898).

The first category, "cultural identity of the individual," refers to a client's ethnic or cultural reference groups, culture of origin, and involvement with a host culture, including language abilities, use, and preferences. "Cultural explanations of the individual's illness" refers to the idioms of distress by which a client communicates the meaning, severity, and perceived causes of illness, as well as preference for and past experiences with professional care. "Cultural factors related to psychosocial environment and levels of functioning" refers to the interpretation of social stressors, available social supports, levels of functioning, and the client's level of disability. Included in this category are myriad stressors in the local environment, and such structures as religion and kin networks that help mediate emotional, instrumental, and informational support. "Cultural elements of the relationship between the individual and clinician" refers to level of cultural congruence and social status between the clinician and client, and problems that can emanate from these differences in diagnosis and treatment. The last category, "overall cultural assessment for diagnosis and care," refers to cultural considerations that can influence comprehensive diagnosis and care. "Culture-bound syndromes" refers to aberrant behavior not attributed to a *DSM* diagnostic category but commonly attributed to specific cultures and indigenous folk illnesses. Based on these formulations and the glossary of culture-bound syndromes from the *DSM*, the following examples are representative of mental health problems exacerbated by the lack of cultural knowledge and skills on the part of practitioners and services unfamiliar with cultural phenomena.

Susto ("fright" or "soul loss") is a fright-induced illness exacerbated by witnessing an accident or other unexpected occurrence (Glazer, Baer, Weller, Garcia de Alba, & Liebowitz, 2004). *Susto* has also been attributed to the "loss of a vital substance or force" (p. 273). The soul (*espiritu*) is believed by some to exit the body, creating a destabilization that results in feelings of unhappiness and sickness. It is also an ethnomedical term used to explain the onset of an illness, such as diabetes (Rhoades, 2005). An elderly person experiencing a diabetic complication may be said to have witnessed a frightening or stressful event. *Susto* becomes the culprit for the acuity of an illness. Furthermore, in a study by Weller et al. (2002), *susto* was described as an outcome of personal or social stress. In Latino/a cultures, the elderly may manifest trauma and dissociation deriving from *susto,* describing their condition by saying "*está fuera de si*" ("out of character," "out of touch with reality," "not themselves"). That is, the person's outward behavior after the *susto* is contrary to his or her prior behavior. The person may exhibit active symptoms, such as hallucinations, responses to internal stimuli (e.g., voices in the head), crying and hysterical crying, and heightened physical or verbal aggression. The person is no longer in touch with reality; he or she experiences deep depression, loss of interest in daily activity, sleep disturbances, and appetite disturbance. Somatic symptoms may be encountered in the form of gastrointestinal disturbances with nausea and vomiting (p. 464). Hedonic and depressive symptoms may also indicate the presence of dementia or a cognitive disorder.

Ataque de nervios ("panic attack" or "anxiety attack") is a term used among Latinos/as to cover a wide range of psychological distress and mental illnesses. It may include a dissociative episode, such as a seizure-like or fainting episode, and suicidal gestures. Individuals report a sense of being out of control, including uncontrollable shouting, attacks of crying, verbal or physical aggression, and trembling (APA, 2000). Individuals may seem to act out of character, and *ataque de nervios* may range from cases free of mental disorders to presentations resembling anxiety, mood, depressive, dissociative, and somatoform disorders. According to Somers (1998), "[s]ymptoms include palpitations, tight chest, trembling, shortness of breath, problems with memory and striking out at people—which frequently gets the attention of police or forensics, falling down and convulsing often follow, which can create difficulty in learning whether epilepsy or a psychiatric condition is involved." In older adults, the news of the death of a spouse may trigger such an event, followed by amnesia regarding what occurred, and then a rapid return to their usual level of functioning. U.S. and Latin American Latinos/as may refer to *locura* ("chronic psychosis") to describe a severe form of chronic psychosis that includes a variety of symptoms, among them incoherence, agitation, auditory and visual hallucinations, inability to follow rules of social interaction, unpredictability, and possible violence (APA, 2000).

Locura ("severe chronic psychosis") in older adults is similar to schizophrenic symptoms and carries a strong stigma, so family members may minimize *locura* by referring to it as *locura de nervios* ("panic attack"; Jenkins, 1988). *Nervios* is a lesser form of *locura*. In Latino/a cultures, *nervios* manifests itself through a variety of symptoms, including chronic somatic emotional and behavior symptoms (e.g., headaches, nausea, fatigue, dizziness, anxiety, emotional distress, concentration difficulties, and reduced appetite; APA, 2000). Nervios is most often referred to as a chronic state of vulnerability, such as the way an older Latino/a copes with the death of a spouse or problems with their adult children or grandchildren. The stigma of *nervios* is not as negative as *locura*, because *nervios* is said to occur as a reaction to stressful life experiences and events.

The last mental health issue examined, *mal de ojo,* or simply *ojo* ("evil eye") is used to describe a variety of problems, including misfortunes or social disruption, vomiting, fever, and crying, and is believed to cause emotional, physical, and mental symptoms (APA, 2000). *Ojo* may be used to describe symptoms of a family member who is experiencing dementia or psychotic symptoms. It is believed that *mal de ojo* can occur as a result of an "incomplete" compliment. Complimenting someone, when not followed by a simple touch of the item or person, is said to bring on *ojo* and may cause sickness or poor health. *Mal de ojo* is thought to also cause fever, relationship problems, and bad luck. Should an older Latino/a share a picture of a grandchild with a practitioner, and should the practitioner respond with admonishment for the child, it is believed that *mal de ojo* could result if the picture is not touched.

Relevant Cultural Concepts and Perceptions of Illness and Disability

Machismo has mostly been studied from historical, anthropological, and psychosocial perspectives. The study of *machismo* has generally focused on how this system negatively affects women with regard to domestic violence, infidelity (including fathering children in multiple households), alcohol abuse, sexual dominance practices, and male abandonment of family. Machismo has been studied as a "psychocultural phenomenon" originating in child-rearing practices in Latino families that encourages the suppression of emotions (Torres, Solberg, & Carlstrom, 2002) and emerges as a defense mechanism later in life.

Limited research exists on how *machismo* is related to illness or depression; however, a few studies with mixed views conclude that *machismo* is not necessarily an unconstructive attitude; it may push men to improve their health because illness impairs their ability to perform their daily activities and work responsibilities. Sobralske (2004) states that most men are not fatalistic by nature; in addition, Talavera, Elder, and Velasquez (1997) note that most men feel they have control over their lives. Meanwhile, a dichotomy exists within these studies, for they suggest that once control is lost, fatalism becomes a strong influence on how health and illness are perceived. Sobralske (2004) notes that men perceive illness as fatal or detrimental when they can no longer provide resources for their families. These studies demonstrate that health is culturally defined and valued, and that it reflects on the ability of individuals to perform their daily activities in a culturally meaningful way. In many cases, men will delay seeking medical care until they are unable to work (Zoucha & Purnell, 2003). Villarruel (1995) noted that traditional Mexican American men's identities are deeply embedded within the values of *machismo*. In this sense, it appears that Latino males with *machismo* attitudes have a harder time coping with illness and disability. They have a harder time coping because they tend to feel worthless due to their view of manliness, which is based on being strong, dominant, independent, and indebted to no one (Urrabazo, 1985). The study of gender roles in older age deserves greater attention, given the increasing pressure on females to take on emotionally stressful caregiving roles and the pressure on males to cope with the mental health impact of chronic illnesses, which become more common as they age.

Family Caregiving and Its Emotional Toll

Cultural norms in Latino/a families call for the intimate involvement of family in caring for aging or infirm relatives (Crist, Woo, & Choi, 2007; Herrera, Lee, Palos, & Torres-Vigil, 2008). Family caregivers are central components of the long-term care system, and older Latinos/as are especially inclined to turn to family when making important health decisions and managing chronic diseases. Devoted family caregivers, however, are predisposed to deteriorating emotional and physical health over the course of their tenure. Latino/a caregivers report poor emotional and physical health, higher mortality, and lower immune function associated with the burden of caregiving (Schulz & Beach, 1999; Schulz, O'Brien, Bookwala, & Fleissner, 1995). Depression is particularly high among caregivers, estimated at 30%–59% (Mittelman et al., 1995; Ory, Hoffman,

Yee, Tennstedt, & Schultz, 1999), but it is higher in Latino/a caregivers (Herrera et al., 2008; Weiss, Gonzalez, Kabeto, & Langa, 2005). Because older Latinos/as experience higher rates of morbidity (Hayward & Heron, 1999; Wallace & Villa, 2003) and disproportionately higher rates of chronic illness and morbidity (Markides et al., 2007; Moritz et al., 1994; Tienda & Mitchell, 2006), their family caregivers can expect to care for more frail and morbid elders. Financial hardships are more common among older foreign-born Mexican Americans (Angel, Angel, Lee, & Markides, 1999), which may promote a cycle of poverty in the caregiving dyad. With fewer economic resources than the general population (Cox & Monk, 1993; HHS, 2008a), financial hardships are aggravated as Latino/a family caregivers frequently forgo work outside the home to care for older relatives (Guarnaccia, Parra, Deschams, Milstein, & Argiles, 1992).

The Role of Social Support in Elders' Well-Being

Culturally rooted values of the Latino/a population greatly emphasize the family rather than the individual, with strong reciprocity between generations (Martinez, 1999), and this allocentrism may have a positive and supportive influence on Latinos/as as they age. Research supports the positive influence of social support on the well-being of the elderly and their family caregivers. A few studies recognized that family is integral to chronic disease management of older adults. For example, perceived family support has been shown to be a critical component in the diabetes self-care management of Mexican Americans aged 55 and older (Wen, Shepherd, & Parchman, 2004). The mechanism by which social support functions is less well understood, although differences by gender and age have been noted. Mulvaney-Day, Alegría, and Sribney (2007) found that although support from family and friends was positively related to self-rated physical and mental health, family cultural conflict was negatively related when controlling for gender and age. Kawachi and Berkman (2000) have also noted how gender differences may affect the Latino/a social network in subtle ways, possibly due to women's greater proclivity for social interactions, which may lead to stress. Finch and Vega (2003) discovered that stressful acculturation experiences, such as discrimination and U.S. citizenship status, had a gross effect on self-rated fair/poor health among

Mexican-origin adults aged 18–59, but having a greater number of peers and family members residing in the United States often mitigated this effect. Older Latinos/as were shown to receive significantly more hours of informal care on average than other ethnic groups in a large national sample of Latinos/as (Weiss et al., 2005). However, in more recent research, Phillips and Crist (in press) point to the limited informal social support network of Mexican American families compared to non-Latino/a whites. These findings raise the question of the foreseeable impact of a dwindling support network on Latino/a elders' mental health.

That some caregivers are able to mitigate inevitable emotional and physical deterioration, whereas others succumb to caregiving-induced stressors, is a misunderstood phenomenon. Variations in social support may partly explain these apparent differences. Social support has been associated with less acculturative stress (Finch & Vega, 2003), better caregiver adjustment (Grant et al., 2006), less caregiver depression in Mexican-origin adults (MaloneBeach & Zarit, 1995), and positive health behaviors in Latino/a study populations (Ingram et al., 2007). More research in this area is warranted, and we need to clarify how to design interventions to benefit both elders and their caregivers.

Filial Piety and Gender Roles in Late Life

Bullard (2008) posited that cultural norms, family support, and gender roles contribute to individuals' experience in coping with the diminished functional capacity associated with the onset of disease or chronic illnesses. Older Mexican Americans' limited financial resources can lead to a dependence on family for care. Women are submissive and live in the shadows of the men in their lives (e.g., fathers, brothers, and husbands; Gil & Vazquez, 1996). Because Latino/a caregivers are most likely to be daughters or daughters-in-law (Cox & Monk, 1993; Harwood, Barker, Ownby, Mullan, & Duara, 1999), the expectation to provide care for aging relatives and parents, which originates in familism, may also surface in the form of *marianismo* (the traditional gender role of women). In a study of Mexican American female caregivers, for example, Jolicoeur and Madden (2002) found the "good daughter" role (i.e., accommodating, obedient, and strongly tied to family) to be more prevalent among non-English-speaking participants.

The Healing Touch of Faith

Religiosity and spirituality may have profound effects on physical and mental health outcomes (Juarez, Ferrell, & Borneman, 1998; Levin, 1997; Matthews et al., 1998; Powell, Shahabi, & Thoreson, 2003). Research provides strong support that Judeo-Christian religious practices can be linked to lower blood pressure and improved immune function (Seeman, Dubin, & Seeman, 2003). Higgins and Learn (1999) also demonstrated significant positive correlations between social support, religious well-being, and hope.

Family caregivers of disabled elderly persons, in particular, are known to utilize religious and spiritual beliefs as coping mechanisms in the face of worsening circumstances (Chang, Noonan, & Tennstedt, 1998; Pearce, 2005). Mausbach, Coon, Cardenas, and Thompson (2003) discovered that Latino/a caregivers may benefit from seeking solace in religious faith and are more likely than their white counterparts to view religion as a crucial component of their lives. The impact of religiosity can be so profound that it influences the emotional health of caregivers. This impact was shown in a study of Mexican American family caregivers, where Herrera, Lee, Nanyonjo, Laufman, and Torres Vigil (in press) concluded that certain types of religiosity had unique and significant influence on well-being. Intrinsic (i.e., internalized faith) and organizational (i.e., publicly practiced faith) religiosity were associated with lower perceived burden, whereas nonorganizational (i.e., privately practiced) religiosity was associated with poorer mental health. Negative religious coping (e.g., feelings that the caregiver burden is a punishment) was correlated with higher levels of depressive symptomatology.

HOME- AND COMMUNITY-BASED SERVICES

Older adults who utilize home- and community-based services reported better health outcomes, compared with nonusers (Fortinsky, Madigan, Sheehan, Tullai-McGuinness, & Fenster, 2006). Compared with other ethnic groups, however, aging Latinos/as consistently report lower rates of long-term care use, opting instead to remain at home and rely on relatives to care for them as they become less self-sufficient (Cox & Monk, 1993; Crist, 2002; Johnson, Schweibert, Albarado-Rosenmann,

Pecka, & Shirk, 1997; Lim et al., 1996). Particularly in the case of dementia patients, caregivers reportedly delay seeking respite until the care recipients' behavior has severely worsened (Thomas et al., 2004). Unfortunately, in doing so, Latinos/as and their caregivers underutilize needed long-term care services that may actually protect their health and reduce caregiver-related stress and burden (National Alliance for Caregiving, 2004). The elder care recipients' health may also worsen as caregivers' mental and physical health deteriorates and their capacity to fulfill the daunting role of caregiving diminishes. The under-utilization of formal care services and dependency on familial support reportedly decrease the inde-pendence of the care recipient, a factor associated with depression (Purdy & Arguello, 1992). The use of home- and community-based long-term care also delays institutionalization of the relative care recipient, which aligns with cultural preferences in Latino/a communities. Thus, increasing aware-ness and participation of elders in home- and community-based long-term care services may benefit the dyad's health on multiple levels.

As we look toward the future of long-term care arrangements both formal and informal, we can expect that social forces and changing family networks will be severely strained and will impair a family's capacity to care for elders in the home in alignment with their cultural preferences. Foreign-born Latinos/as may have a greater num-ber of kin available to provide care for aging par-ents (Torres-Gil & Villa, 1993). However, as more females work outside the home or become geo-graphically separated, there will be a clear impact on the social network that was once available to care for aging relatives (Angel & Angel, 2006). We already see conflicts between working outside the home (in order to bring in substantial income) and staying at home to care for an ill relative (Cox & Monk, 1990; Guarnaccia et al., 1992). Older Latinos/as and their families may face dwindling networks of informal social support (Phillips & Crist, in press).

FUTURE DIRECTIONS AND PRACTICAL IMPLICATIONS

In this chapter, we highlight the growing mental and physical health disparities among older Latinos/as, and their social and cultural deter-minants. The cumulative effects of poverty, discrimination, and neglecting to seek out

affordable and good-quality care take their toll in late life. Concomitant chronic illness and mental instability are becoming more common-place. However, there are insufficient explana-tory and etiological models to describe this delicate relationship, which are needed to inform a holistic approach to screening, preven-tion, and treatment in a culturally competent manner, particularly among ethnic minority elders. The lack of research with Latino/a elders continues, despite the increased attention on the fastest-growing segment of the population. Greater efforts must also center on developing data-driven, evidence-based practices based on longitudinal intervention-based studies, which may be relevant to the diseases, illnesses, etiolo-gies, and cultural perceptions of this population. Elderly Latinos/as would benefit from improve-ments in conventional therapy and the develop-ment of ethnomedical and mental health explanatory models for distinct subpopulations, cohorts, genders, and nativity groups, particu-larly in light of the disproportionately high rate of mental illness, Alzheimer's disease, and dia-betes among older Latinos/as.

One of the biggest challenges is the training of a racially and ethnically diverse cadre of men-tal health professionals who are linguistically and culturally competent. Under ideal circum-stances, practitioners would understand that the Latino/a culture views health in a holistic man-ner, particularly concerning mental and physical health, unlike the conceptual view among non-Latino individuals in the United States. A practi-tioner would look at an illness/event in a way that fit the individual's understanding, as well as from the practitioner's perspective. This is par-ticularly important in the area of mental health, where stigma tends to override access to needed mental health services.

Perhaps the most important part of working with Latino/a elders is to understand the culture of the Latino/a family. Culture is multidimen-sional, however, so there is no single approach to successfully working with Latino/a elders. Instead, a professional must use a multifaceted, multidimensional approach, taking into account the various factors that surround the individual, his or her family, and the larger community and culture. To guide professionals in this complex endeavor, we must build a stronger research and knowledge base that is empirically and cultur-ally validated. As we build on existing research, public policy must also move toward establishing equity in all aspects of health and mental health programs, services, and research by providing the appropriate resources. To be truly successful in creating effective services for the Latino/a elderly, we must forge a national strategic plan, using contemporary research and practice strategies that are culturally grounded and that will eliminate disparities in our health and mental health systems. In this way, we will develop a culturally competent system of care with programmatic benchmarks that help ensure that elderly Latinos/as receive the quality of care they so richly deserve.

References

Abraido-Lanza, A. F., Dohrenwend, B. P., Ng-Mak, D. S., & Turner, J. B. (1999). The Latino morality paradox: A test of the "salmon bias" and healthy migrant hypotheses. *American Journal of Public Health, 89*, 1543–1548.

American Cancer Society (ACS). (2007). *Cancer facts and figures 2007*. Atlanta, GA: Author. Retrieved May 8, 2008, from http://www.cancer.org/downloads/STT/CAFF2007PWSecured.pdf

American Psychiatric Association (APA). (2000). *Diagnostic and statistical manual of mental disorders: DSM-IV-TR*. Washington, DC: Author.

Angel, J., & Hogan, D. (2004). Population aging and diversity in a new era. In K. E. Whitfield (Ed.), *Closing the gap: Improving the health of minority elders in the new millennium*. Washington, DC: Gerontological Society of America.

Angel, J. L., & Angel, R. J. (2006). Minority group status and healthful aging: Social structure still matters. *American Journal of Public Health, 96*, 1152–1159.

Angel, R. J., Angel, J. L., Lee, G. Y., & Markides, K. S. (1999). Age at migration and family dependency among older Mexican immigrants: Recent evidence from the Mexican American HEPESE. *Gerontologist, 39*, 59–65.

Baker, D. W., Gazmararian, J. A., Sudano, J., & Patterson, M. (2000). The association between age and health literacy among elderly persons. *The Journals of Gerontology Series B: Psychological Sciences and Social Sciences, 55*, S368–S374.

Barrio, C., Palinkas, L. A., Yamada, A. M., Fuentes, D., Criado, V., Garcia, P., et al. (2008). Unmet needs for mental health services for Latino older adults: Perspective from consumers, family members, advocates, and service providers. *Community Mental Health Journal, 44*, 57–74.

Beyene, Y., Becker, G., & Mayen, N. (2002). Perception of aging and sense of well-being among Latino elderly. *Journal of Cross-Cultural Gerontology, 17*, 155–172.

Black, S. A., & Markides, K. S. (1999). Depressive symptoms and morality in Mexican Americans. *Annals of Epidemiology, 9*, 45–52.

Bullard, K. M. (2008). Biological and cultural influences in the relationship between depressive symptoms, type 2 diabetes risk, and all-cause mortality in older Mexican Americans. *Journal of Dissertation Abstracts International: Section B: The Sciences & Engineering, 68*, 5167.

Carrasquillo, O., Lantigua, R. A., & Shea, S. (2000). Differences in functional status of Hispanic versus non-Hispanic White elders: Data from the Medical Expenditure Panel Survey. *Journal of Aging and Health, 12*, 342–361.

Centers for Disease Control & Prevention (CDC). (2004a). Health disparities experienced by Hispanics—United States. *Morbidity & Mortality Weekly Report, 40*, 935–937.

Centers for Disease Control & Prevention (CDC). (2004b). Prevalence of diabetes among Hispanics: Selected areas, 1998–2002. *Morbidity & Mortality Weekly Report, 53*, 941–944.

Chang, B. H., Noonan, A. E., & Tennstedt, S. L. (1998). The role of religion/spirituality in coping with caregiving for disabled elders. *Gerontologist, 38*, 463–470.

Choi, N. G., & Kim, J. S. (2007). Age group differences in depressive symptoms among older adults with functional impairments. *Health & Social Work, 3*, 177–188.

Cox, C., & Monk, A. (1990). Minority caregivers of dementia victims: A comparison of Black and Hispanic families. *Journal of Applied Gerontology, 9*, 341–351.

Cox, C., & Monk, A. (1993). Hispanic culture and family care of Alzheimer's patients. *Health & Social Work, 18*, 92–99.

Crist, J. D. (2002). Mexican American elders' use of skilled home care nursing services. *Public Health Nursing, 19*, 366–376.

Crist, J. D., Woo, C., & Choi, M. (2007). Mexican American and Anglo elders' use of home care services. *Journal of Transcultural Nursing, 18*, 339–348.

Cruz, Y. (2005). Improving the well-being of Latino older adults: Recommendations and solutions. Deliberations from the 2005 National Hispanic Council Leadership Roundtable. National Hispanic Council on Aging. Retrieved August 4, 2008, from http://www.whcoa.gov/about/des_events_reports/PER_DC_09_30_05.pdf

Crystal, S., Sambamoorthi, U., Walkup, J., & Akincigil, A. (2003). Diagnosis and treatment of depression in the elderly Medicare population:

Predictors, disparities, and trends. *Journal of the American Geriatrics Society, 51,* 1718–1728.

Dunlop, D., Song, J., Manheim, L., Lyons, J., & Chang, R. (2003). Racial/ethnic differences in rates of depression among pre-retirement adults. *American Journal of Public Health, 93,* 1945–1952.

Federal Interagency Forum on Aging-Related Statistics (FIFARS). (2008). *Older Americans 2008: Key indicators of well-being.* Federal Interagency Forum on Aging-Related Statistics. Washington, DC: U.S. Government Printing Office. Retrieved June 30, 2008, from http://www.agingstats.gov/agingstatsdotnet/Main_Site/Data/2006_Documents/OA_2006.pdf

Finch, B. K., & Vega, W. A. (2003). Acculturation stress, social support, and self-rated health among Latinos in California. *Journal of Immigrant Health, 5,* 109–117.

Folsom, D. P., Gilmer, T., Barrio, C., Moore, D. J., Bucardo, J., Lindamer, L. A., et al. (2007). A longitudinal study of the use of mental health services by persons with serious mental illness: Do Spanish-speaking Latinos differ from English-speaking Latinos and Caucasians? *American Journal of Psychiatry, 164,* 1173–1180.

Fortinsky, R. H., Madigan, E. A., Sheehan, T. J., Tullai-McGuinness, S., & Fenster, J. R. (2006). Risk factors for hospitalization among Medicare home care patients. Western *Journal of Nursing Research, 28,* 902–917.

Gallagher-Thompson, D., Leary, M. C., Ossinalde, C., Romero, J. J., Wald, M. J., & Fernandez-Gamarra, E. (1997). Hispanic caregivers of older adults with dementia: Cultural issues in outreach and intervention. *Group, 21,* 211–232.

Gary, F. A. (2005). Stigma: Barrier to mental health care among ethnic minorities. *Issues in Mental Health Nursing, 26,* 979–999.

Gazmararian, J. A., Baker, D. W., Williams, M. V., Parker, R. M., Scott, T. L., Green, D. C. et al. (1999). Health literacy among Medicare enrollees in a managed care organization. *Journal of the American Medical Association, 281*(6), 545–551.

Gil, R., & Vazquez, C. I. (1996). *The Maria paradox: How Latinas can merge old world traditions with new world self-esteem.* New York: G.P. Putnam.

Glazer, M., Baer, R. D., Weller, S. C., Garcia de Alba, J. E., & Liebowitz, S. W. (2004). Susto and soul loss in Mexicans and Mexican Americans. *Cross-Cultural Research, 38,* 270–288.

Gonzalez, H. M., Haan, M. N., & Hinton, L. (2001). Acculturation and the prevalence of depression in older Mexican Americans: Baseline results of the Sacramento area Latino study on aging. *Journal of American Geriatrics, 49,* 948–953.

Grant, J. S., Elliott, T. R., Weaver, M., Glandon, G. L., Raper, J. L., & Giger, J. N. (2006). Social support, social problem-solving abilities, and adjustment of family caregivers of stroke survivors. *Archives of Physical Medicine & Rehabilitation, 87,* 343–350.

Guarnaccia, P. J., Parra, P., Deschams, A., Milstein, G., & Argiles, N. (1992). Si dios quiere: Hispanic families' experiences of caring for a seriously mentally ill family member. *Culture, Medicine and Psychiatry, 16,* 187–217.

Gurland, B. J., Wilder, D. E., Lantigua, R., Stern, Y., Chen, J., Killeffer, E. H., et al. (1999). Rates of dementia in three ethnoracial groups. *International Journal of Geriatric Psychiatry, 14,* 481–493.

Haan, M. N., Mungas, D. M., González, H. M., Ortiz, T. A., Acharya, A., & Jagust, W. J. (2003). Prevalence of dementia in older Mexican Americans: The influence of type 2 diabetes, stroke and genetic factors. *Journal of the American Geriatrics Society, 51,* 169–177.

Harwood, D., Barker, W., Ownby, R., Mullan, M., & Duara, R. (1999). Factors associated with depressive symptoms in non-demented community-dwelling elderly. *International Journal of Geriatric Psychiatry, 14,* 331–337.

Hayward, M. D., & Heron, M. (1999). Racial inequality in active life among adult Americans. *Demography, 36,* 77–92.

Herrera, A. P., Lee, J. W., Nanyonjo, R., Laufman, L., & Torres Vigil, I. (in press). Religious coping and caregiver well-being in Mexican American families. *Aging and Mental Health, 13*(1), 84–91.

Herrera, A. P., Lee, J. W., Palos, G., & Torres-Vigil, I. (2008). Cultural influences in the patterns of long-term care use among Mexican American family caregivers. *Journal of Applied Gerontology, 27,* 141–165.

Higgins, P. G., & Learn, C. D. (1999). Health practices of adult Hispanic women. *Journal of Advanced Nursing, 29,* 1105–1112.

Hooyman, N. R., & Kiyak, H. A. (2008). *Social gerontology: A multidisciplinary perspective* (8th ed.). Boston: Pearson Education.

Ingram, M. I., Torres, E., Redondo, F., Bradford, G., Wang, C., & O'Toole, M. L. (2007). The impact of promotoras on social support and glycemic control among members of a farmworker community on the U.S.-Mexico border. *Diabetes Educator, 33,* 172S–178S.

Insel, K., Palmer, R., Stroup-Benham, C., Markides, K., & Espino, D. (2005). Association between change in systolic blood pressure and cognitive decline among elderly Mexican Americans. *Experimental Aging Research, 31,* 35–54.

Jenkins, J. H. (1988). Conceptions of schizophrenia as a problem of nerves: A cross-cultural comparison of Mexican-Americans and Anglo-Americans. *Social Science & Medicine, 26,* 1233–1244.

Johnson, R. A., Schweibert, V. L., Albarado-Rosenmann, P., Pecka, G., & Shirk, N. (1997). Residential preferences and eldercare views of Hispanic elders. *Journal of Cross-Cultural Gerontology, 12,* 91–107.

Jolicoeur, P. M., & Madden, T. (2002). The good daughters: Acculturation and caregiving among Mexican American women. *Journal of Aging Studies, 16,* 107–120.

Juarez, G., Ferrell, B., & Borneman, T. (1998). Perceptions of quality of life in Hispanic patients with cancer. *Cancer Practice, 6,* 318–324.

Kaiser Family Foundation. (2007). Key fact: Race, ethnicity, and medical care. Retrieved May 1, 2008, from http://www.kff.org/minorityhealth/upload/6069–02.pdf

Kawachi, I., & Berkman, L. (2000). Social cohesion, social capital, and health. In L. F. Berkman & I. Kawachi (Eds.), *Social epidemiology* (pp. 174–190). Oxford, UK: Oxford University Press.

Kosloski, K., Montgomery, R., & Karner, T. X. (1999). Differences in the perceived need for assistive services by culturally diverse caregivers of persons with dementia. *Journal of Applied Gerontology, 18,* 239–256.

Kutner, M., Greenberg, E., Jin, Y., & Paulsen, C. (2006). *The health literacy of America's adults: Results from the 2003 National Assessment of Adult Literacy.* (NCES 2006–483). U.S. Department of Education. Washington, DC: National Center for Education Statistics.

Lee, S. D., Gazmararian, J. A., & Arozullah, A. M. (2006). Health literacy and social support among elderly Medicare enrollees in a managed care plan. *Journal of Applied Gerontology, 25,* 324–337.

Levin, J. (1997). Religion and spirituality in medicine: Research and education. *Journal of the American Medical Association, 278,* 792–793.

Levin, J., & Chatters, L. (1998). Religion, health, and psychological well-being in older adults: Findings from three national surveys. *Journal of Aging & Health, 10,* 504–531.

Lim, Y. M, Luna, I., Cromwell, S. L., Phillips, L. R., Russell, C. K., & Torres de Ardon, E. (1996). Toward a cross-cultural understanding of family caregiving burden. *Western Journal of Nursing Research, 18,* 252–266.

Mallen, M. J., Vogel, D. L., Rochlen, A. B., & Day, S. X. (2005). Online counseling: Reviewing the literature from a counseling psychology framework. *Counseling Psychologist, 33,* 819–871.

Malone-Beach, E. E., & Zarit, S. H. (1995). Dimensions of social support and social conflict as predictors of caregiver depression. *International Psychogeriatrics, 7,* 25–38.

Markides, K. S., & Eschbach, K. (2005). Aging, migration, and mortality: Current status of research on the Hispanic paradox. *Journals of Gerontology Series B: Psychological Sciences & Social Sciences, 60,* S68–S75.

Markides, K. S., Eschbach, K., Ray, L., & Peek, K. (2007). Census disability rates among older people by race/ethnicity and type of Hispanic origin. In J. L. Angel & K. E. Whitfield (Eds.), *The health of aging Hispanics: The Mexican-Origin population* (pp. 26–39). New York: Springer.

Martinez, R. J. (1999). Close friends of God: An ethnographic study of health of older Hispanic adults. *Journal of Multicultural Nursing & Health, 5,* 40–45.

Matthews, D., McCullough, M., Larson, D., Koenig, H., Swyers, J., & Milano, M. (1998). Religious commitment and health status. *Archives of Family Medicine, 7,* 118–124.

Mausbach, B. T., Coon, D. W., Cardenas, V., & Thompson, L. W. (2003). Religious coping among Caucasian and Latina dementia caregivers. *Journal of Mental Health & Aging, 9,* 97–110.

Mittelman, M. S., Ferris, S. H., Shulman, E., Steinberg, G., Ambinder, A., Mackell, J. A., et al. (1995). A comprehensive support program: Effect on depression in spouse-caregivers of Alzheimer's disease patients. *Gerontologist, 35,* 792–802.

Moritz, D. J., Ostfeld, A. M., Blazer, D., II, Curb, D., Taylor, J. O., & Wallace, R. B. (1994). The health burden of diabetes for the elderly in four communities. *Public Health Reports, 109,* 782–790.

Mulvaney-Day, N., Alegría, M., & Sribney, W. (2007). Social cohesion, social support and health among Latinos in the United States. *Social Science & Medicine, 64,* 477–495.

Nadeem, E., Lange, J. M., Edge, D., Fongwa, M., Belin, T., & Miranda, J. (2007). Does stigma keep poor young immigrant and U.S.-born Black and Latina women from seeking mental health care? *Psychiatric Services, 58,* 1547–1549.

Napoles-Springer, A. M., Grumbach, K., Alexander, M., Moreno-John, G., Forte, D., Rangel-Lugo, M., et al. (2000). Clinical research with older African Americans and Latinos: Perspectives from the community. *Research on Aging, 24,* 668–691.

National Alliance for Caregiving and American Association of Retired Persons. (2004). *Caregiving in the U.S.* Retrieved May 3, 2008, from http://research.aarp.org/il/us_caregiving.pdf.

Novak, K., & Riggs, J. (2004). *Hispanic/Latinos and Alzheimer's disease.* Retrieved May 25, 2008, from http://www.alz.org/Downloads/Hispanic ReportEnglish.pdf

Ojeda, V. D., & McGuire, T. (2006). Gender and racial/ethnic differences in use of outpatient mental health and substance use services by depressed adults. *Psychiatric Quarterly, 77,* 211–222.

Ory, M., Hoffman, R., Yee, J., Tennstedt, S., & Schultz, R. (1999). Prevalence and impact of caregiving: A detailed comparison between dementia and nondementia caregivers. *Gerontologist, 39,* 177–185.

Pearce, M. (2005). A critical review of the forms and value of religious coping among informal caregivers. *Journal of Religion & Health, 44,* 81–119.

Phillips, L. R., & Crist, J. D. (in press). Social relationships among Mexican American caregivers: A cross-cultural comparison. *Journal of Transcultural Nursing.*

Powell, L. H., Shahabi, L., & Thoresen, C. E. (2003). Religion and spirituality: Linkages to physical health. *American Psychologist, 58,* 36–52.

Purdy, J. K., & Arguello, D. (1992). Hispanic familism in caretaking of older adults: Is it functional? *Journal of Gerontological Social Work, 19,* 29–43.

Raji, M., Reyes-Ortiz, C. A, Kuo, Y-F., Markides, K., & Ottenbacher, K. J. (2007). Depressive symptoms and cognitive change in older Mexican Americans. *Journal of Geriatric Psychiatry & Neurology, 20,* 145–152.

Rhoades, Jr., G. F. (2005). Cross-cultural aspects of trauma and dissociation. *Journal of Trauma Practice, 4,* 21–33.

Royal, D., Espino, D., Polk, M., Palmer, R., & Markides, K. (2004). Prevalence and patterns of executive impairment in community dwelling Mexican Americans: Results from the Hispanic EPESE study. *International Journal of Geriatric Psychiatry, 19,* 926–934.

Sarkisian, C. A., Shunkwiler, S. M., Aguilar, I., & Moore, A. A. (2006). Ethnic differences in expectations for aging among older adults. *Journal of American Geriatric Social Work, 54,* 1277–1282.

Schneider, M. (2004). The intersection of mental and physical health in older Mexican Americans. *Hispanic Journal of Behavioral Sciences, 26,* 333–355.

Schulz, R., & Beach, S. R. (1999). Caregiving as a risk factor for mortality: The Caregiver Health Effects Study. *Journal of the American Medical Association, 282,* 2215–2219.

Schulz, R., O'Brien, A.T., Bookwala, J., & Fleissner, K. (1995). Psychiatric and physical morbidity effects of dementia caregiving: Prevalence, correlates, and causes. *Gerontologist, 35,* 771–791.

Seeman, T. E., Dubin, L. F., & Seeman, M. (2003). Religiosity/spirituality and health: A critical review of the evidence for biological pathways. *American Psychologist, 58,* 53–63.

Sobralske, M. C. (2004). Health care seeking beliefs and behaviors of Mexican American men living in south central Washington (Doctoral dissertation, Gonzaga University, 1990). *Dissertation Abstracts International, 65,* 2346.

Somers, S. L. (1998). Examining anger in culture-bound syndromes. *Psychiatric Times, 15,* 1–7.

Strothers, H. S., III, Rust, G., Minor, P., Fresh, E., Druss, B., & Satcher, D. (2005). Disparities in antidepressant treatment in Medicaid elderly diagnosed with depression. *Journal of the American Geriatrics Society, 53,* 456–461.

Talavera, G. A., Elder, J. P., & Velasquez, R. J. (1997). Latino health beliefs and locus of control: Implication for primary care and public health practitioners. *American Journal of Preventive Medicine, 13,* 408–410.

Thomas, P., Ingrand, P., Lalloue, F., Hazif-Thomas, C., Billon, R., Vieban, F., et al. (2004). Reasons of informal caregivers for institutionalizing dementia patients previously living at home: The Pixel study. *International Journal of Geriatric Psychiatry, 19,* 127–135.

Tienda, M., & Mitchell, F. (2006). *Hispanics and the future of America.* New York: National Academy Press.

Tomaszewski Farias, S., Mungas, R. B., Haan, M., & Jagust, W. (2004). Everyday functioning in relation to cognitive functioning and neuroimaging in community-dwelling Hispanic and non-Hispanic older adults. *Journal of the International Neuropsychological Society, 10,* 342–354.

Torres, J. B., Solberg, V. S., & Carlstrom, A. H. (2002). The myth of sameness among Latino men and their machismo. *American Journal of Orthopsychiatry, 72,* 163–181.

Torres-Gil, F., & Villa, V. (1993). Health and long-term care: Family policy for Hispanic aging. In M. Sotomayor & A. Garcia (Eds.), *Elderly Latinos: Issues and solutions for the 21st century* (pp. 45–58). Westport, CT: Greenwood Press.

Urrabazo, R. (1985). Machismo: Mexican American male self-concept. (Doctoral dissertation, Graduate Theological Union, Berkeley, CA).

U.S. Census Bureau. (2008). *Statistical abstract of the United States.* Washington, DC: U.S. Government Printing Office.

U.S. Department of Health and Human Services (HHS). (2001). *Mental health: Culture, race, and ethnicity—A supplement to Mental Health: A Report of the Surgeon General.* Rockville, MD: Author.

U.S. Department of Health & Human Services (HHS). (2008a). *Administration on Aging: A statistical profile of Hispanic older Americans aged 65+.* Retrieved May 7, 2007, from http://www.aoa.gov

U.S. Department of Health and Human Services (HHS). (2008b). *2007 National healthcare disparities report* (AHRQ Publication No. 08–0041). Rockville, MD: Author.

Van Hook, M. P. (1999). Women's help-seeking patterns for depression. *Social Work in Health Care. 29*, 15–34.

Versola-Russo, J. (2006). Cultural and demographic factors of schizophrenia. *International Journal of Psychosocial Rehabilitation, 10*, 89–103.

Villa, V. M., & Aranda, M. P. (2000). The demographic, economic, and health profile of older Latinos: Implications for health and long-term care policy and the Latino family. *Journal of Health and Human Services Administration, 23*, 161–180.

Villarruel, A. M. (1995). Mexican American cultural meanings, expression, self-care and dependent-care actions associated with experiences of pain. *Research in Nursing and Health, 18*, 427–436.

Wallace, S. P., & Villa, V. M. (2003). Equitable health systems: Cultural and structural issues for Latino elders. *American Journal of Law and Medicine, 29*, 247–267.

Weiss, C. O., Gonzalez, H. M., Kabeto, M. U., & Langa, K. M. (2005). Difference in amount of informal care received by non-Hispanic Whites and Latinos in a nationally representative sample of older Americans. *Journal of the American Geriatric Society, 53*, 146–151.

Weller, S. C., Baer, R. D., Garcia De Alba, J., Glazer, M., Trotter, R. et al. (2002). Regional variation in Latino descriptions of susto. *Culture, Medicine and Psychiatry, 26*, 449–472.

Wen, L. K., Shepherd, M. D., & Parchman, M. L. (2004). Family support, diet, and exercise among older Mexican Americans with type 2 diabetes. *Diabetes Educator, 30*, 980–993.

Wykle, M., & Ford, A. (Eds.). (1999). *Serving minority elders in the 21st century.* New York: Springer.

Zoucha, R., & Purnell, L. D. (2003). People of Mexican heritage. In L. D. Purnell & B. J. Paulanka (Eds.), *Transcultural health care: A culturally competent approach* (2nd ed., pp. 264–278). Philadelphia: F. A. Davis.

Zunker, C. L., & Cummins, J. J. (2004). Elderly health disparities on the U.S.-Mexico border. *Journal of Cross-Cultural Gerontology, 19*, 13–25.

15

EARLY INTERVENTION PROGRAMS

The Case of Head Start for Latino Children

NATASHA J. CABRERA, JACQUELINE D. SHANNON,
VANESSA RODRIGUEZ, AND ALEXIS LUBAR

The United States has the second-highest rate of child poverty among developed countries (Mexico has the highest; Federal Interagency Forum on Child and Family Statistics, 2002). In 2000, approximately 2.8 million or 16% of children in the United States were classified as poor. In the same year, 27% of Latino children under age 18 lived in poverty, compared to 30% of Black children and 9% of non-Latino White children (ibid.). Although there is significant variation, overall, children growing up in poverty are more likely than other children to live in communities characterized by high levels of unemployment and crime; single-parent households; poor-quality housing, schooling, and health care; and lack of resources (Duncan & Brooks-Gunn, 1997; Huston, 1994). Poverty places children at risk for a host of negative developmental and academic outcomes (Huston, 1994). The consequences of poverty are compounded for Latino children, the largest ethnic group in the United States, who experience additional hardship as a result of the stresses related to immigration, acculturation, language differences, and social marginalization (Ramirez & De la Cruz, 2003).

To alleviate the effects of poverty on families' well-being, several intervention programs (e.g., Head Start, Medicaid, food stamps) and policies (e.g., antipoverty policies) at the federal and state levels have targeted low-income families. Of these, Head Start, a federally funded program for impoverished children, is one of the longest-running intervention programs in the country, and it has received much policy and research attention. The federal Head Start program was created in 1965 to provide low-income children a "head start" by offering two-generational services to mitigate the effects of poverty and prepare children to succeed in school (Zigler & Valentine, 1979). In this chapter, we focus on Latino children served by Head Start. To this end, we first describe Head Start and how it has been used as a tool to combat poverty. We then examine the prevalence of Head Start use among Latino families and follow it with a discussion of the cultural challenges that Head Start must meet to achieve its goals of giving a head start to economically disadvantaged children. Next, we review the evidence on whether Head Start enhances the academic and social skills of low-income Latino children. We conclude with a discussion of future directions for research and policies that would help early childhood programs, such as how Head Start can close the achievement gap between Latino children and other children.

HEAD START: A TOOL TO COMBAT POVERTY

During the mid-1960s, numerous federal policies and programs were created to wage the War on Poverty (Zigler, Styfco, & Gilman, 1993). This loosely related set of policies included such programs as Head Start, which seeks to improve the outcomes of low-income and minority children. Policymakers and researchers believed that poverty and its consequences posed a major threat to the economic and social well-being of the United States. High levels of poverty are linked to increased crime rates and decrease the pool of educated workers. One way to address this issue was through compensatory programs that provided employment, community empowerment, and education as means to reduce poverty (ibid.).

In 1965, the first 300 Head Start centers opened their doors to 561,000 children across the country (National Head Start Association, 2005).The project was quickly transformed from a summer program to a 9-month, half-day program and eventually to a full-year program. In 1980, it became integrated into the Administration on Children, Youth and Families in the Department of Health and Human Services (DHHS). During fiscal year 2005, there were more than 19,000 Head Start centers (49,000 classrooms) serving more than 906,000 children (ibid.). Head Start has enrolled more than 22 million children since 1965 (ibid.).

Although the success of Head Start in combating poverty has been mixed (Aughinbaugh, 1999; Currie & Thomas, 1994), it continues to receive federal bipartisan support as well as research and public attention. This bipartisan support is partly based on the symbolic nature of Head Start, which provides hope to thousands of poor children and their families and offers to break the cycle of poverty (Phillips & Cabrera, 1996). Some of this public attention has been beneficial because it has helped to improve both the quality and scope of programs

for children and their families. For example, the 1990s research on early brain development paved the way for the idea that educational programs that start when children are 4 years old may be 4 years too late (Shonkoff & Phillips, 2002). Given that rapid brain growth during the first 5 years of life offers a critical period for intervening with young children, interventions need to start during pregnancy or at infants' birth. In 1994, Congress reauthorized the Head Start Act and implemented Early Head Start, which serves pregnant mothers and children from birth to 3 years of age. This act stipulates that Early Head Start should receive a set portion of the annual appropriation for Head Start. The Early Head Start program has grown rapidly, in successive cohorts or "waves," from 68 programs in 1995 to 635 programs in 2001 serving 45,000 children. In 2005, there were more than 62,000 children enrolled in Early Head Start nationwide (National Head Start Association, 2005).

The Improving Head Start for School Readiness Act of 2007, which reauthorized Head Start and Early Head Start, was passed by both the House and the Senate and signed into law by President George W. Bush in December 2007 (Library of Congress, n.d.). This reauthorization bill included, but was not limited to, the following changes: (1) increased funding for Migrant and Seasonal Head Start programs (serving mainly Latino; only 6% of children are English speaking), (2) increased flexibility for Head Start programs that are part-day to provide full-day, year-round services or to convert programs serving preschoolers to programs serving infants and toddlers, (3) set new standards for Early Head Start home visitors and required early childhood teachers and assistant teachers to have training in early childhood education, and (4) improved coordination of early childhood services at the state and local level.

Head Start and Early Head Start primarily serve children whose family incomes are at or below the poverty line or who are eligible for public assistance. However, regulations also permit up to 10% of the Head Start population in local programs to come from families whose combined incomes are above the eligibility criteria. In addition, a minimum of 10% of children with disabilities are required to participate. The children enrolled in Head Start and Early Head Start are racially, ethnically, and linguistically diverse; these children and their families, collectively, speak more than 140 languages (Joseph & Cohen, 2000). A study of 30 Head Start programs across the nation revealed that the majority of children enrolled in Head Start are members of minority groups; the largest minorities represented are Blacks (36%) and Latinos (23%; ibid.). Similarly, in Early Head Start 25% of enrolled children are Latino, and 20% speak a language other than English at home. Spanish is spoken by 81% of children in Early Head Start (Vogel et al., 2006).

In addition to serving underserved children in urban and rural settings, Head Start also serves children whose parents are migrant workers in the United States. During 2005, the Migrant and Seasonal Head Start (Migrant Head Start) programs assisted 30,568 migrant children and 3,052 children whose parents were seasonal workers in the United States in 450 Migrant Head Start centers across the nation (Vogel et al., 2006).

Overall, Head Start provides comprehensive services for children from birth to 5 years of age and their families. Services include comprehensive early education, medical, dental, mental health care, and nutrition. Parent services emphasize parental involvement activities, mental health, and referrals to social service providers. Head Start and Early Head Start programs are community based, an approach best suited to meeting the needs of the children in the geographic areas they serve (Phillips & Cabrera, 1996). Head Start programs may provide center-based services or home-based services or may use a combined approach (i.e., center- and home-based services) as well as family child care.

Although Head Start centers are community-based, allowing their directors to implement programs best suited to the needs of the families they serve, all federally funded Head Start centers must adhere to the Head Start Program Performance Standards. These standards provide a framework for agencies to follow when designing programs but also allow some flexibility to fit the needs and resources of the families in each community. For home-based services, each family receives one home visit per week for a minimum of 90 minutes duration and must attend two developmentally appropriate group socialization experiences per month. Center-based programs provide traditional child services either 4 or 5 days a week for full day (6 or more hours) or part day (less than 6 hours per day; National Head Start Association, 2005). In terms of curricula, Head Start and Early Head Start centers maintain local autonomous authority (although there are some recommended curricula) with the overall goal of fostering cognitive and social competence skills in the lives of low-income children through four component areas: educational services, health services, social services, and parent development (Washington & Bailey, 1995). Head Start sets goals and measures program outcomes for children in emergent literacy, numeracy, and vocabulary.

Head Start services are delivered by a diverse staff who, for the most part, represent the families they serve. Head Start's staff includes racially and ethnically diverse individuals and parents from the neighborhood. The diversity of Head Start is an important component of service delivery. Minority parents feel more at ease and more connected to the center when they can communicate with staff in their own languages (Joseph & Cohen, 2000). For example, staff who share a similar cultural background with the parents in Head Start understand the basic needs and services they may require as new residents of the United States and can help them locate basic resources in their new communities, provide translation services, and accompany families on visits to social service agencies or healthcare appointments (Joseph & Cohen, 2000).

In summary, approximately 16% of U.S. children live below the poverty line and are at great risk for developmental delays. Latinos are the largest ethnic group in the United States; most Latino children live in economically disadvantaged families and are at risk for school failure. Head Start was created in 1965 to bridge the achievement gap between minorities and other children in the United States. Almost 30 years after the inception of Head Start, Early Head Start was developed in 1994 to serve pregnant women and children from birth to 3 years of age. Both home-based and center-based programs are offered through Head Start and Early Head Start, which mostly serves Black and Latino children, with the majority of English Language Learners speaking Spanish. Despite Head Start's mixed effect on participating children's developmental outcomes, it continues to receive bipartisan support and is regarded as the best hope for families and children to break the cycle of poverty.

PREVALENCE OF HEAD START AND EARLY HEAD START USE AMONG LATINO FAMILIES

Latinos are the largest and fastest-growing minority group in the United States, accounting for more than one out of eight of the 288.4 million people in the country. Latino children under the age of 18 constitute 17.7% of all children in the nation and 22% of all children under the age of 5; 30.4% of Latino children live in poverty (U.S. Census Bureau, 2002). It is estimated that Latino (8.6 million) and Black (4 million) children under the age of 5 will outnumber non-Latino, White children under 5 (12.3 million) by the year 2050 (U.S. Department of Health and Human Services [USDHHS], 2004). Between 2005 and 2050, this represents an increase of 146%, in comparison to expected growth of Black and Asian children (131% and 54%; Calderon, 2005). These statistics suggest that the demand for Head Start services is increasing over time; the question is, How many Latino children will have access to these services? In this section, we briefly describe the supply and demand for Head Start services among Latino families and the structural and personal barriers that might prevent Latino families from enrolling their children into Head Start programs.

The Supply and Demand for Head Start Services for Latino Families

Paralleling the increase of Latinos in the United States, the number of Latino families enrolled in Head Start and Early Head Start has steadily increased over time. The Head Start program's informal policy of "don't ask, don't tell" allowed Latino parents, many of whom reside in the United States illegally, to enroll their children in Head Start programs. Latino children attending Head Start also include children born to undocumented (i.e., illegal) workers in the United States; as American citizens, these children are legally entitled to federally supported educational and health services. The increased demand for Head Start services for Latino children is fueled in part by the demographic shift in the population of the United States but also by parents' beliefs about the importance of early education for their children. A survey of 1,000 working-class Latino parents from 10 states found that the majority of parents believed that it is very important or somewhat important for children to attend prekindergarten (Perez & Zarate, 2006). Almost all parents who responded to the questionnaire said that they would send their children to publicly funded, voluntary prekindergarten if it were available in their communities, and almost three quarters believed that availability of prekindergarten for their children was an important priority for the government to address now (ibid.). The majority of parents believed that their children's participation in prekindergarten could help children learn literacy and social skills as well as help them learn English and become prepared for kindergarten (ibid.).

An analysis of the Head Start Family and Child Experiences Survey (FACES) found that between 1994 and 1999, Latino enrollment increased almost 20%, compared with 3% for non-Latino Whites and 8% for Black children (Garcia & Levin, 2001). From 2000 to 2001, of the 950,000 children served at any time of the year by Head Start, 22% spoke Spanish as their dominant language (Schumacher & Rakpraja, 2003). During the period between 2002 and 2005, Latinos in Head Start constituted approximately a third of total enrollment. Spanish was the dominant language for almost 20% of Latino children (USDHHS, 2004).

However, this increase in enrollment has not been enough to meet the increasing demand for Head Start services (Garcia & Gonzales, 2006). This is also true for all children living in poverty. Despite the overall increased enrollment of low-income children in Head Start programs since its inception in 1964, Head Start programs enroll only about 35% of eligible children (ibid.). Although Migrant and Seasonal Head Start programs have enrolled 19% (31,400 out of 161,400) of migrant farmworker children, the majority of states fail to reach one third of eligible farmworker children (National Head Start Association, 2005). Nevertheless, compared to other minority groups, enrollment of Latino children in Head Start is lower. Black and Latino children are more likely to be economically disadvantaged than White children and thus should be more likely to participate in publicly funded preschool programs. However, although 36% of Latino children lived under the federal poverty level in 2000, only one quarter attended Head Start programs (Zambrana, 2003; Zambrana & Zoppi, 2002). Rates of preschool enrollment for Latino children have remained consistently below those of other children. In 2000, only 23% of Latino 3-year-olds were in preschool, compared with 49% of Black children and 43% of White children (Magnuson & Waldfogel, 2005). Although reasons vary, other studies showed that only 20% of Latino children younger than 5 were in early education programs, compared to 42% of Whites and 44% of Blacks (Reardon-Anderson, Capps, & Fix, 2002). In 2005, a national survey found that 30.5% of Latino 3-year-olds attended center-based preschool education programs, as opposed to 45.8% of non-Latino 3-year-old children who attended Head Start (Magnuson & Waldfogel, 2005).

Barriers to Latino Children's Participation in Head Start

What might explain the gap between demand for and supply of Head Start services for Latino families? Both structural and personal barriers can explain this discrepancy. In terms of structural barriers, an important obstacle to Latino enrollment is lack of funding to increase the supply of Head Start services to keep up with the demand. Although the federal government spends over $10 billion per year on child-care programs, including Head Start, it is too little to serve all or most disadvantaged children (Garcia, Jensen, Miller, & Huerta, 2005). In particular, funding for Migrant Head Start programs is lacking. More than 80% of farmworker families do not have access to Migrant Head Start programs due to a lack of federal funding (ibid.). The result is that early childhood programs, including Head Start, are largely unavailable, unaffordable, and inaccessible to parents in Latino communities.

In addition to structural barriers, Latino families report several barriers that prevent them from accessing early-childhood education programs, including Head Start. Overall, Latino parents report more personal barriers to involvement in early childhood programs than other parents (USDHHS, 2004). Frequently cited personal obstacles include low levels of family income; lack of information about the availability and affordability of state and federally funded early-childhood education programs, including Head Start; fear of enrollment because of their illegal status; and language/culture differences, beliefs, and values regarding the use of early childhood education (Garcia et al.,

2005; Garcia & Levin, 2001; USDHHS, 2004). Preschool attendance has been shown to be closely linked to family income; even though Head Start and other local- and state-funded prekindergarten school programs are available to some children in low-income families, they are not available or accessible to all children who need it (Garcia et al., 2005). When prekindergarten programs are offered in public schools, Latino children are more likely to participate (Takanishi, 2004). Low-income families may have low education and literacy levels, which may prevent them from accessing information about available programs in the community. In one survey, one third of participating Latino parents believed that not knowing what services are available to them was the primary reason they did not enroll their children in prekindergarten programs (Perez & Zarate, 2006).

Other studies have cited parents' fears of current immigration policies as an important factor that keeps parents from enrolling their children in preschool and other center-based programs (Matthews & Jang, 2007). Intertwined with uncertainties about their immigration status are deeply held cultural and personal beliefs regarding the type of child care parents believe is best for their children. Findings from a national survey from 1989–1998 showed that immigrant families are less likely than nonimmigrant families to use center-based care (Reardon-Anderson et al., 2002). Among Latino parents, almost 40% used relative care, a quarter used nonrelative care, and approximately 20% used parent and center-based care. Among native-born families, Mexican American families are less likely than other ethnic groups to use center-based care (ibid.). Similarly, a recent study of a national sample of Latino babies born in the United States showed that many Latino families prefer family members and babysitters to schooling or center-based care (Lopez, Barrueco, & Miles, 2006).

Even when Latino parents want to enroll their children into prekindergarten programs, concerns about the nature of the programs may keep them away from center-based programs. A study of Latino families that included interviews with parents showed that issues of language, personal connection with child-care staff, and shared values were important components of Latina mothers' decisions to send their children to prekindergarten programs (Fuller, Eggers-Pierola, Holloway, & Liang, 1997; Perez &

Zarate, 2006). Another study found that the majority of parents wanted their children to be educated by bilingual teachers who would be able to communicate with them in Spanish. These parents wanted instruction and activities with children to be conducted in both English and Spanish (Perez & Zarate, 2006). These parental views support current research findings suggesting that high-quality early childhood programs for young English Language Learners must emphasize the bilingual nature of these children's lives in order for these programs to be an option for parents (see Takanishi, 2004).

However, there is also evidence that Latino mothers' preference for type of child care may also be related to other pragmatic concerns, such as who will take care of the children when they are at work. An early study found that Latino families are likely to enroll their children in preschools when the mother is employed and more educated, when family income is higher, and when the father resides with the family (Fuller et al., 1997). However, even among employed Latina mothers, level of participation in Head Start and other similar programs is lower than for other groups. A national study found that for only 15.5% of children of employed Latina mothers was organized care utilized (i.e., centers, preschools, Head Start, or pre-K/kindergarten), in comparison to 34.4% of Black children and 26.7% of non-Latino White children (Currie & Thomson, 1999). These researchers found that this difference remained even with higher levels of participation in early-childhood education programs. Other recent evidence refutes this finding and suggests that with increased acculturation, parents' preferences for child care gravitated toward center-based care. A study found that English-speaking Latinos were 26% as likely and Spanish speakers only 17% as likely to select a center-based program, compared with White parents (Hirshberg, Huang, & Fuller, 2005). Collectively, these findings suggest that when researchers account for acculturation variables, Latino parents' use of center-based child care is higher.

In summary, despite the number of Latino children who are enrolled in Head Start and Early Head Start, many more children are not able to attend high-quality early childhood programs, either because such programs are inaccessible to parents or because parents are unaware of the programs (Perez & Zarate, 2006).

Findings suggest that, relative to White children, gaps in enrollment might be as large as 9 percentage points for Black children and 31 percentage points for Latino children (Magnuson & Waldfogel, 2005). If Latino children are less likely to enter preschool than children from other racial and ethnic groups (ibid.), then they are more likely to have delayed entry into formal schooling, to have limited exposure to enriching home learning and literacy environments, and consequently to be at greater risk for delays in prereading, prewriting, and premath skills when entering kindergarten than children who have had a preschool experience. A recent analysis suggests that Latino children, both immigrant and nonimmigrant, enter kindergarten with lower skills than other groups (Reardon-Anderson et al., 2002). These disparities can contribute to the widening of the academic gap between White and minority children, especially Latino children.

How Does Head Start Meet the Linguistic and Cultural Challenge?

The success of Head Start programs to meet the contextual and developmental needs of children who live in disadvantaged homes and who are at risk for host of negative outcomes depends on a multitude of factors. First, people in poverty are a heterogeneous group, and poverty's negative consequences for children and families depend on a multitude of factors, some of which may not be easily addressed by Head Start programs. Second, parents' characteristics (e.g., motivation, mental health, level of education), contextual characteristics (e.g., neighborhood and communities), quality of the Head Start program, and macro factors, including the state of the economy and welfare policies, can result in wide variation in who benefits from Head Start services. Third, families enrolled in Early and Head Start programs differ in their levels of need and consequently have different trajectories and outcomes. For families experiencing mental health issues, substance abuse, and chronic poverty, the intervention services provided by Head Start might not be enough to help the family and the children in a short period of time. Fourth, given the diversity of the families Head Start serves, a formidable challenge is to provide culturally sensitive and appropriate services for all the families it serves. The focus of this section is on strategies used by Head Start programs to provide culturally sensitive services and the specific cultural challenges faced by programs that serve Latino children and their families.

Strategies for Providing Culturally Sensitive Head Start Services to Latino Children

The Head Start Bureau in the Administration on Children, Youth and Families (ACYF), the agency that administers Head Start programs, has acknowledged in its policies and programs that Early Head Start and Head Start must meet the cultural and linguistic needs of Latino children and has implemented several initiatives to meet the cultural challenges facing Head Start. In 1992, the ACYF established 10 principles that form the framework for multicultural programming as stated in the federal Head Start Program Performance Standards (Section 1304):

1. Every individual is rooted in culture.

2. The cultural groups represented in the communities and families of each Head Start program are the primary source of culturally relevant programming.

3. Culturally relevant and diverse programming requires learning accurate information about the culture of different groups and discarding stereotypes.

4. Addressing cultural relevance in making curriculum choices is a necessary, developmentally appropriate practice.

5. Every individual has the right to maintain his or her own identity while acquiring the skills required to function in our diverse society.

6. Effective programs for children with limited English-speaking ability require continued development of the primary language while the acquisition of English is facilitated.

7. Culturally relevant programming requires staff who reflect the community and families served.

8. Multicultural programming for children enables children to develop an awareness of, respect for, and appreciation of individual cultural differences. It is beneficial to all children.

9. Culturally relevant and diverse programming examines and challenges institutional and personal biases.

10. Culturally relevant and diverse programming and practices are incorporated in all components and services. (USDHHS, n.d.)

Another example of the Head Start Bureau's efforts to provide a culturally sensitive education is the Head Start Higher Education Latino/Latino Service Partnerships program, which was created in Portland in 1999 to help Latino teachers obtain associate's degrees in the field of early childhood education. Participants were given Spanish classes, bilingual classes, English-language support for advanced classes, mentoring, tutoring, and tuition assistance (Calderon, 2005). Whether or not these strategies have succeeded in providing culturally sensitive services to Latino families remains to be answered.

Challenges to Providing Culturally Sensitive Head Start Services

Despite policies in place to provide culturally sensitive programs to families at the federal and local levels, challenges to institute best practices for Latino children and their families persist. Given that one in four low-income children are immigrants and disadvantaged in terms of family economic security, access to health care, and access to sound early education (Takanishi, 2004), the challenge to meet the needs of the parents and children is Herculean. For low-income Latino children who live with parents with limited human capital (i.e., education, income), Head Start programs must provide services for parents to become English proficient and must increase parental education while focusing on improving children's cognitive, social-emotional, and physical health outcomes. In this section, we highlight the following significant challenges faced by Head Start and Early Head Start programs as they try to meet the developmental needs of Latino children: (1) recruitment of bilingual staff, (2) use of appropriate curriculum, (3) lack of culturally appropriate assessment tools, (4) provision of comprehensive health services, and (5) need for increased parent involvement in Head Start programs and governance.

Recruiting Bilingual Staff. Recruiting teachers who meet the reauthorization mandate requiring a bachelor's degree is a major barrier to providing culturally appropriate services to Latino children enrolled in Head Start (Calderon, 2005; Joseph & Cohen, 2000). Although survey data showed that nationwide Head Start staff generally reflected the ethnicity of the children and families they served, it also showed that there were more White staff (44% of all staff) than White children (35% of all children). Blacks, Latinos, and Asian American/Pacific Islander staff were slightly underrepresented, compared to children from these backgrounds. Most lead teachers spoke primarily English, while the assistant teachers or aides spoke a second language (Joseph & Cohen, 2000). In Early Head Start programs, 20% of all staff were Latino and spoke a language other than English (USDHHS, 2004). Thus, one of the most salient challenges in serving Latino families is the discrepancy between the language spoken by the staff and the language spoken by the children and families enrolled in Head Start. This issue was cited as a source of major communication problems between staff and parents (Joseph & Cohen, 2000). Because many Latino parents want their children to learn English so that they will succeed in school, this is not a problem for children. Teachers report that although many children enter Head Start speaking little or no English, nearly all children are fluent in conversational English by the time they graduate from Head Start (ibid.). The lack of linguistic match between parents and teachers is a major obstacle for parent involvement because it is considered to be an important mechanism in the influence of Head Start on children's development.

Using a Culturally Sensitive Curriculum. Another important challenge is the choice of curriculum used to teach Latino children in Head Start. Education coordinators reported that their greatest challenge was to find, adapt, and/or develop multicultural/bilingual curricula appropriate to the populations they serve (Joseph & Cohen, 2000). More than three fourths of the 3-year-old group enrolled in Early Head Start and approximately 80% of children in the 4-year-old group were in classrooms that used either High Scope or The Creative Curriculum (Zill, Sorogon, & Kim, 2003), which was not developed for a minority language population.

There is some debate in the field over the best method (e.g., English immersion, bilingual education, and dual-language/two-way) to teach Latino children (Gersten & Jiménez, 1994). Some research suggests that two-way immersion bilingual (dual-language) programs are best for Latino children. In this approach, children gain proficiency in English while maintaining their first language (e.g., Spanish; Cardena-Hagan & Carlson, 2007; Cummins, 1979; Laosa & Ainsworth, 2007). Building on this research, the ACYF has initiated the Cultural Responsiveness and Dual Education (CRADLE) project in an effort to better meet the needs of families whose home language is not English. This project selected 20 Early Head Start and Migrant Head Start centers in 2006 and 24 in 2007 to receive training aimed an increasing understanding of linguistic and cultural features of children under 3 years of age, the linguistic and cultural issues and concerns affecting families and expectant parents, and approaches for implementing promising practices in dual-language acquisition for infants and toddlers. In dual-language programs, all children, including English-proficient children, receive an education in two languages—classrooms alternate between Spanish-only and English-only classes. This new approach is based on research findings suggesting that first-language proficiency strengthens second-language acquisition and that bilingualism has cognitive benefits for children (Barnett, Yarosz, Thomas, Jung, & Blanco, 2006; Laosa & Ainsworth, 2007).

In practice, Head Start programs that serve mainly Latino children base their programming on multicultural classroom practices. Multiculturalism is loosely defined as an approach to education based on the premise that all children in the United States should receive proportional attention in the curriculum. This broad goal is believed to be achieved through multicultural infusion, which expects teachers to make multiculturalism an explicit part of their curricula and programs (Langer de Ramirez, 2007). In this sense, promoting multiculturalism in early-childhood education programs means that teachers should design curricula and instructional processes taking into account the ways that culture can influence work habits, interpersonal relations, and children's general outlook on life (Morrison, 2009). However, there is no consensus on a definition of multiculturalism and how it should be integrated into the curriculum. According to Joseph and Cohen (2000), most of the 30 Head Start programs they visited described their multicultural programming efforts almost solely in terms of holidays, cooking, and materials, mainly posters, books, and pictures that represent both mainstream and ethnic or racial minority communities. Although multicultural materials were plentiful in classrooms, teachers did not often use them in their daily activities (Joseph & Cohen, 2000). Consequently, it is difficult to discern the impact of multiculturalism on children's learning.

Assessing Latino Children's Academic Progress. Another challenge is the lack of culturally appropriate measures to assess children's academic and social progress. In 2003, the Head Start Bureau developed the Head Start National Reporting System (NRS) to systematically assess early literacy, language, and numeracy skills of all 4- and 5-year-olds enrolled in Head Start. It did not incorporate research-based recommendations for Latino children, such as required use of bilingual assessors and valid and reliable Spanish-language measures (Calderon, 2005). Although the NRS is no longer required under the 2007 reauthorization bill, availability of appropriate instruments continues to be a major problem. For example, there are few developmental and health screening and assessment instruments that can be administered to non-English-speaking children, and most of the available tools have not been normed with minority or non-English-speaking populations (Joseph & Cohen, 2000). Thus, data resulting from the use of these instruments are likely to underrepresent the capabilities of Latino children or misinterpret their difficulties.

Providing Comprehensive Health Services. Another challenge that has cultural implications is providing health services to ensure the healthy development of children. Head Start emphasizes the importance of early identification of health and developmental problems and provides health services either directly or through community referrals and partnerships. However, in a study of select programs across the country that included interviews conducted with administrators and staff, many programs reported difficulty coordinating with low-cost health-care providers who speak Head Start families' home languages and who understand issues relevant to serving these multicultural families (Joseph & Cohen, 2000). Other studies find that compliance with medication to take care of such common children's ailments as ear infections is difficult for some Latino parents. Some Latino mothers stop administering antibiotics to their children when they do not observe any symptoms, which is contrary to doctors' instructions to administer the medicine for a specified period of time. Other parents may decide to treat common illness with home remedies, which in some cases may exacerbate the original problem.

Increasing Parent Involvement. Part of the success of the Head Start program is its emphasis on services provided to parents; however, engaging Latino parents in the program and in a variety of other services offered to families is an ongoing challenge to providers. A fundamental principle of Head Start is the belief that to provide a more stimulating home environment for their children, parents need to have opportunities to participate in the program and to make personal progress in terms of education and employment. Hence, increasing parenting involvement in Head Start is an important goal of the program. Some Head Start programs have experimented with numerous strategies to increase parent involvement, including parent appreciation activities and production and circulation of newsletters and flyers, translated into several languages (Joseph & Cohen, 2000). There are no evaluation data on these strategies, and hence their effectiveness is unknown.

Another way to increase parent involvement is to assess parents' needs and provide services that help them meet those needs. Several Head Start programs offer English as a second language (ESL) and literacy training for parents. In some Head Start programs, staff reported that ESL classes were the most important service offered to parents (Joseph & Cohen, 2000). Parents reported, in focus group interviews conducted during site visits, that they were pleased with program attempts to respond to the linguistic and cultural uniqueness of their children and families (ibid.). However, transportation issues and staff who did not speak the parents' language were often cited as important barriers that prevented parents from participating in Head Start meetings and other events (ibid). Translators are not often consistently available at every site or at every meeting, and parents feel helpless when they are unable to communicate in these settings, which may result in diminished participation in Head Start parent meetings and events.

A study of Latino parents' involvement in Head Start showed that parents can play a valuable role in multicultural classroom programming by bringing items from home that represent their culture, giving presentations on cultural traditions, cooking ethnic foods, and teaching ethnic songs and dances to teachers and children (Joseph & Cohen, 2000). Participating in these activities can empower parents and increase their sense of efficacy in the role they play in their children's education, while also sending the message to their children that their culture is important (ibid.). However, some Head Start programs report that celebrating one's culture in a multicultural context poses unanticipated challenges. Some parents and educators support the idea of celebrating holidays from different cultures in the classrooms; others oppose this idea in favor or a more insular approach because a multicultural approach is inadequate (ibid.).

In summary, although a framework for multicultural programming was established by the ACYF in 1992, challenges to institute best practices for Latino children and their families persist. One of the greatest challenges lies in hiring ethnically and racially diverse, bilingual teachers with appropriate early-childhood education training and obtaining access to culturally appropriate curriculum and assessment measures. Head Start recently began a pilot project to examine the effectiveness of teaching Latino children with a dual-language program in which all children receive education in two languages. This approach holds great promise for Latino children maintaining their language and culture while also acquiring a second language (English).

IS HEAD START EFFECTIVE IN PROVIDING A HEAD START TO LATINO CHILDREN?

Research findings on whether Head Start is effective in giving children a head start that can help them succeed in school have been mixed. In 1969 and the late 1970s, the Westinghouse Learning Corporation and the Consortium for Longitudinal Studies found that although Head Start children's initial increase in IQ scores faded over time, they were less likely to be assigned to special education classrooms and to be held back a school year than children who did not attend Head Start (Vinovskis, 2008; Zigler et al., 1993). Since that time, researchers have continued to examine whether Head Start is effective, for whom, and under what conditions. In this section, we review the literature on the effects of Head Start on Latino children's academic achievement. Given the limited number of studies specifically on Latino children and Head Start, we also draw from research on the effects of other early childhood programs to highlight the importance of high-quality early childhood education for Latino children.

Research has shown that high-quality early childhood education can have a positive effect on low-income minority children's academic and social development (Laosa & Ainsworth, 2007). Specifically, Head Start and other similar early-childhood education programs are believed to be able to close the achievement gap between minority and non-Latino White children. The evidence to support this belief is mixed. Some researchers have argued that although Latino children are able to learn and make gains once they enter formal schooling, they are not able to catch up to their peers because of the initial disadvantages that Latino families and children face (Laosa & Ainsworth, 2007). In a study based on the Early Childhood Longitudinal Study Kindergarten cohort (ECLS-K) data, approximately 75% of White children could recognize letters by the beginning of kindergarten, whereas only half of Latino children could do so (Rathbun & West, 2002). The inconsistency of findings might also reflect the fact that Latinos are heterogeneous groups. Children's academic gains may vary by immigration status, levels of acculturation, and country of origin (Cabrera, Shannon, West, & Brooks-Gunn, 2006). When studies account for these factors, the findings are most consistent with research on the positive effects of early childhood education on children's academic outcomes. In the next paragraph, we highlight several studies that have found that early childhood education programs, including Head Start, have a positive effect on Latino children's achievement.

While many researchers and educators would argue that a great disparity still remains between Latino children and non-Latino, White children, an emerging body of research suggests that Latino children enrolled in high-quality programs can catch up to their peers and that there has been a slight closing of the gap in recent years. For example, a study found that children of immigrants enrolled in early childhood education programs fared as well or better than native children on measures of school engagement, including doing homework, caring about school, and frequency of suspension or expulsion from school (Reardon-Anderson et al., 2002). However, children in immigrant families were also generally poorer, in worse health, and more likely to experience food insecurity and crowded housing conditions, which can have a negative effect on their long-term academic success (ibid.). Another study reported increases in language and literacy test scores for Latino children attending Head Start programs (Currie & Thomson, 1999). A study of a nationally representative sample of approximately 2,400 racially and ethnically diverse 3- and 4-year-old children and their families from 63 Head Start programs who participated in the Head Start FACES in 2003 found significant gains in children's vocabulary, early math, and early writing skills, as well as small gains in other literacy-related areas, such as phonemic awareness and print concepts, during the Head Start program year. Latino children, who were the largest group of English-language learning children in this study, showed significant gains in vocabulary—gains larger than White children's and Black children's.

Similarly, Magnuson and her colleagues found that Head Start participation for 6-year-old children increased scores on a vocabulary test by close to 7 points higher than their siblings' scores. These effects persisted in elementary school for White and Latino children but not for Black children (Magnuson & Waldfogel, 2005). Research on Oklahoma's universal prekindergarten program (Oklahoma is the only state that provides a high-quality, universal prekindergarten program for all children) showed that Latino students experienced greater test-score improvements in prereading skills, prewriting skills, and premath skills than any other racial or ethnic group (Gormley & Gayer, 2005; Gormley, Gayer, Phillips, & Dawson, 2005).

Consistent with the above findings, the National Head Start Impact Study, a $23 million longitudinal study mandated by Congress in 1998, examined the effectiveness impact of Head Start on approximately 5,000 children randomized to Head Start or non-Head Start programs (Puma et al., 2005). While results were mixed, for Latino 3-year-olds positive gains were found in prereading, vocabulary, and prewriting. These effects, however, were not found with Latino 4-year-olds. Similarly, the National Early Head Start Research and Evaluation project, a congressionally mandated study of the effects of Early Head Start on children's development, found positive effects. This project evaluated the effectiveness of Early Head Start through a randomized trial of 3,001 families in 17 programs when children were 14, 24, 36, and 60 months of age and then again when children were in grade 5. Families in this study were low income, racially and ethnically diverse (23% of program and control families were Latino; Love et al., 2005). At 36 months of age, children who attended Early Head Start performed better on measures in cognitive and language development, displayed higher emotional engagement of the parent and sustained attention with play objects, and were lower in aggressive behavior than peers who did not participate in Early Head Start (Love et al., 2005). The strongest impacts were found for programs that offered a mix of home visiting and center-based services and that fully implemented the performance standards early.

These positive effects have also been reported by researchers using a national data set on the trajectories of kindergarten children. Based on analyses of the ECLS-K Class of 1998–99, researchers found that Latino children benefited more in terms of cognitive development from center-based attendance than White or Black children with similar characteristics (Loeb, Fuller, & Kagan, 2004). Test score gains were dramatically larger for Latino students than for the other groups. For instance, center-based attendance was associated with an increase in the reading scores among Latino children—about three times that reported for White children and about double that seen for Black children. Latino children who attended Head Start were found to perform better in reading than those who received maternal care (ibid.). These studies offer strong evidence that Latino children can make significant academic gains in high-quality early childhood education. The question is whether these gains are enough to close the achievement gap. There is some evidence that Head Start can close at least one fourth of the gap between

Latino and non-Latino White children, with Mexican American children having the largest gains (Laosa & Ainsworth, 2007).

How does Head Start work? Research focusing on the mechanism by which Head Start works is just beginning to emerge. The theoretical assumption on which Head Start programs were based is that parents are central to children's success. Thus, one mechanism by which Head Start might have an effect on children's development is through improved parenting. Consequently, an important goal of Head Start is to increase positive parent involvement. To this end, Head Start provides parenting programs, includes parents in its governance, and offers them social support, all of which are designed to improve parent's mental health as well as their parenting skills (e.g., more responsive to children's developmental needs, less use of harsh punishment). The National Early Head Start Research and Evaluation study revealed that program parents were more emotionally supportive, provided more language and learning stimulation, read to their children more, and spanked less often than parents in the control group (Love et al., 2005). These effects were strongest for programs with mixed approaches—home based and center based—and when families participated in Early Head Start for at least 1 year. The Early Head Start study also reported that English- and Spanish-speaking Latino mothers read significantly less frequently to their 14-month-olds than did White or Black mothers. Spanish-speaking Latino families also had far fewer children's books than did other families in the sample, suggesting that other non-English-speaking families may also have limited access to children's books in their home languages. However, Spanish-speaking mothers who read daily for at least some period during the first 3 years of their children's lives had children with higher scores on receptive vocabulary (e.g., understanding of spoken words, such as asking a child to point to a picture that represents a word spoken in the child's language) and cognitive tests (Raikes et al., 2006).

In summary, the studies reviewed here make a strong case for the effectiveness of Head Start and Early Head Start and for the benefits that Latino children can reap from such programs. Latino children enrolled in Head Start showed significant gains in vocabulary, early math skills, early writing skills, phonemic awareness, and print concepts; further, greater gains were made by Latino children who attended Head Start than were made by children who did not attend Head Start. based and center-based services resulted in the most gains in children's and parents' outcomes. These academic gains can close the gap between Latino and non-Latino White children, which can ensure that Latino children have as many opportunities as any other children in the United States to succeed academically, socially, and economically and to become productive citizens.

Closing the Gap: Policy and Research Directions

Researchers, policymakers, and others concerned with narrowing the gap in academic achievement between low-income children and other children argue that there is enough empirical evidence to do so, but that other factors, including political will, may prevent us from accomplishing this goal. We end this chapter with a brief exploration of the research and policies that support educational policies central to the national debate on closing the achievement gap between Latino and White children: (1) providing universal high-quality early childhood education; (2) addressing the linguistic and cultural needs of children; (3) training a cadre of professionals who can provide top-quality education, and (4) connecting Latino families to schools and communities.

Providing Universal High-Quality Early Childhood Education

There is a growing body of evidence that high-quality early-childhood education programs—Early Head Start, Head Start, and Universal Pre-kindergarten—can have a positive impact on young children's school readiness, particularly children from low socioeconomic status (SES) and Latino backgrounds, with long-lasting effects (e.g., Gormley & Gayer, 2005; Gormley et al., 2005; Love et al., 2005). For example, educational improvements can substantially narrow the Black-White reading gap at school entry as much as 24% and the Latino-White reading gap as much as 36% (Magnuson & Waldfogel, 2005). However, high-quality early childhood education is not universally available to all children who need it. Head Start serves only 35% of eligible low-income children and

20% of eligible Migrant and Seasonal Head Start children. In addition to increased funding to serve all eligible low-income children, there is consensus regarding the urgent need to create partnerships (e.g., to pull together multiple funding sources) at the state and local levels among child-care, Early Head Start, Head Start, and prekindergarten programs to improve services to underserved children and their families (Calderon, 2005; USDHHS, 2004). Such coordination can increase the supply of Head Start programs and move toward meeting the increased demand for such services.

Addressing the Linguistic and Cultural Needs of Children

For high-quality early-childhood education programs to be effective in closing the achievement gap, they need to address the linguistic needs of low-income Latino children. A substantial body of evidence suggests that the dual-language (two-way immersion) program, which integrates both Spanish and English into the curriculum and instruction, is the best method for Spanish-speaking Latinos (Cardena-Hagan & Carlson, 2007; Cummins, 1979; Gormley & Gayer, 2005; Gormley et al., 2005; Laosa & Ainsworth, 2007; Takanishi, 2004). In dual-language programs, all children receive an education in two languages; classrooms alternate between Spanish-only and English-only classes. Research shows that children's first-language proficiency strengthens their second-language acquisition and that bilingualism improves cognition (Barnett et al., 2006; Laosa & Ainsworth, 2007). Overall, this method fosters Latino children's bilateral/bilingual cultural identities, helps them to maintain their Spanish language and culture, and influences how they approach learning and become socialized as language users (Espinosa, 2005). It is not clear from the available evidence whether Head Start programs have the necessary supports to develop more dual-language programs; this would be a critical area for intervention.

Training a Cadre of Professionals Who Can Provide Top-Quality Education

An integral component of providing high-quality early childhood education is high-quality teachers, who must be properly trained in early childhood development (e.g., bachelor's or master's degrees in early childhood education or in infancy and child development), must be proficient in both English and Spanish, and must be knowledgeable about Latino culture (Matthews & Jang, 2007). Because there is a shortage of Latino and Spanish-speaking teachers in Head Start, it is recommended that Head Start programs recruit and train teachers and other paraprofessionals within Latino communities (ibid.). There is some evidence that the federal government is working toward this end. In 2006 and 2007, Head Start began the CRADLE project with 44 Early Head Start and Migrant Head Start centers. Teachers received training in the linguistic and cultural features of Latino children under 3 years of age and their families, and in approaches for implementing dual-language acquisition for infants and toddlers.

Connecting Latino Families to Schools and Communities

Latino parents' involvement in Head Start, as well as in children's literacy activities at home, have been associated with children's language and literacy skills in English and Spanish as well as their cognition (Haneda, 2007; Raikes et al., 2006; Takanishi, 2004). One way to ensure that Latino children receive the language stimulation they need for optimal language development and to increase parent involvement in their children's schooling is for Head Start programs to establish two-generational early-education and family literacy programs. For example, intervention programs may need to provide additional supports in the home (e.g., children's books, educational videos, educational games) to Latino parents, particularly those with low verbal/literacy skills and lower levels of education (Marsh & Thompson, 2001; Raikes et al., 2006). Head Start staff's efforts to engage the child's parents should be extended to other family members, including grandparents, who are often actively engaged in the children's lives (Cuellar, Arnold, & Gonzales, 1995). It is also important to acknowledge real barriers (e.g., fear of deportation) that may prevent immigrant families from participating in Head Start programs (Matthews & Jang, 2007). Moreover, the use of paraprofessionals and other community leaders can be enlisted as a bridge between government services and parents.

Head Start and Early Head Start represent a tangible hope that Latino children in this country can indeed get a head start that can ensure their success later in life. However, many economic, social, and programmatic issues must be addressed before this hope becomes a reality for all minority children. If all these issues are addressed in a timely and effective manner, Head Start can provide a high-quality early childhood education for Latino children, which can greatly reduce the gap between low-income minority children and White children and thus address one of the most salient sources of inequality in the United States, namely the lack of affordable, accessible, and high-quality education for all children.

REFERENCES

Aughinbaugh, A. (1999, April). *Does Head Start yield long-term benefits?* Paper presented at the National Head Start Research Meeting, Washington, DC.

Barnett, W. S., & Yarosz, D. J. (2004).Who goes to preschool and why does it matter? *Preschool Policy Matters, 8,* 2–16.

Barnett, W. S., Yarosz, D. J., Thomas, J., Jung, K., & Blanco, D. (2007). Two-way and monolingual English immersion in preschool education: An experimental comparison. *Early Childhood Research Quarterly, 22,* 277–293.

Cabrera, N., Shannon, J., West, J., & Brooks-Gunn, J. (2006). Parental interactions with Latino infants: Variation by country of origin and English proficiency. *Child Development, 74,* 1190–1207.

Calderon, M. E. (2005). *Head Start reauthorization: Enhancing school readiness for Latino children.* Washington, DC: National Council of La Raza.

Cardena-Hagan, E., & Carlson, C. D. (2007). The cross-linguistic transfer of early literacy skills: The role of initial L1 and L2 skills and language of instruction. *Language, Speech, and Hearing Services in Schools, 38*(3), 249–259.

Cuellar, I., Arnold, B., & Gonzales, G. (1995). Cognitive referents of acculturation: Assessment of cultural constructs in Mexican Americans. *Journal of Community Psychology, 23*(4), 339–356.

Cummins, J. (1979). Linguistic interdependence and the educational development of bilingual children. *Review of Educational Research, 49*(2), 222–251.

Currie, J., & Thomas, D. (1999). Does Head Start help Latino children? *Journal of Public Economics, 74*(2), 235–262.

Duncan, G. J., & Brooks-Gunn, J. (1997). *Consequences of growing up poor.* New York: Russell Sage.

Espinosa, L. M. (2005). Curriculum and assessment considerations for young children from culturally, linguistically, and economically diverse backgrounds. *Psychology in the Schools, 42*(8), 837–853.

Federal Interagency Forum on Child and Family Statistics (2002). *America's children: Key national indicators of well-being, 2002.* Washington, DC: Government Printing Office.

Fenichel, E., & Mann, T. L. (2001). Caring for infants and toddlers. *The Future of Children, 11*(1), 134–141.

Fuller, B., Eggers-Pierola, C., Holloway, S. D., & Liang, X, (1997). Rich culture, poor markets: Why do Latino parents forgo preschooling? *Teachers College Record, 97,* 400–418.

Garcia, E., & Gonzales, D. M. (2006). *Pre-K and Latinos: The foundation for America's future.* Washington, DC: Pre-K Now.

Garcia, E. E., Jensen, B., Miller, L. S., & Huerta, T. (2005). *Early childhood education of Hispanics in the United States.* Tempe, AZ: The National Task Force on Early Childhood Education for Hispanics. Retrieved June 2008, from http://www.ecehispanic.org/work/

Garcia, G., & Levin, M. (2001). *Latino children in Head Start: Family characteristics, parent involvement and satisfaction with the Head Start program.* Retrieved April 3, 2008, from http://www.acf.hHead Start.gov/programs/core/ongoing_research/faces/2001_latino_poster_ppt/2001_latino_poster.htm ht

Gersten, R. M., & Jiménez, R. T. (1994). A delicate balance: Enhancing literacy instruction for students of English as a second language. *The Reading Teacher, 476,* 438–449.

Gormley, W., & Gayer, T. (2005). Promoting school readiness in Oklahoma: An evaluation of Tulsa's pre-K program. *Journal of Human Resources, 40,* 533–558.

Gormley, W., Gayer, T., Phillips, D., & Dawson, B. (2005). The effects of Universal Pre-K on cognitive development. *Developmental Psychology, 41,* 872–884.

Haneda, M. (2007). Becoming literate in a second language: Connecting home, community, and school literacy practices. *Theory into Practice, 45*(4), 337–345.

Hirshberg, D., Huang, D., & Fuller, B. (2005). Which low-income parents select child-care? Family demand and neighborhood organizations. *Children and Youth Services Review, 27*(10), 1119–1148.

Huston, A. (1994). Children in poverty: Designing research to affect policy. *Social Policy Report, 8,* 1–12.

Joseph, G. E., & Cohen, R. C. (2000). *Celebrating cultural and linguistic diversity in Head Start.* Washington, DC: U.S. Department of Health and Human Services.

Langer de Ramirez, L. (2007). *Take action! Lesson plans for the multicultural classroom.* Upper Saddle River, NJ: Merrill/Prentice Hall.

Laosa, L. M., & Ainsworth, P. (2007). *Is public pre-K preparing Latino children to succeed in school?* New Brunswick, NJ: National Institute for Early Education Research.

Library of Congress. (n.d.) *H.R. 1429.* THOMAS [online database]. Retrieved March 30, 2009, from http://thomas.loc.gov/cgi-bin/bdquery/z?d110:h.r.01429

Loeb, S., Fuller, B., Kagan, S. L., & Abioseh Carrol, B. (2004). Child care in poor communities: Early learning effects of type, quality and stability. *Child Development, 75*(1), 47–65.

Lopez, M., Barrueco, S., & Miles, J. (2006). *Latino infants and families: A national perspective of protective and risk factors for development.* Tempe: National Task Force on Early Childhood Education for Hispanics, Arizona State University.

Love, J. M., Kisker, E. E., Ross, C., Constantine, J., Boller, K., Chazan-Cohen, R., et al. (2005). The effectiveness of Early Head Start for 3-year-old children and their parents: Lessons for policy and programs. *Developmental Psychology, 41*(6), 885–901.

Magnuson, K. A., & Waldfogel, J. (2005). Early childhood care and education: Effects on ethnic and racial gaps. *The Future of Children, 15*(1), 169–196.

Marsh, J., & Thompson, P. (2001). Parental involvement in literacy development: Using media texts. *Journal of Research in Reading, 24*(3), 266–278.

Matthews, H., & Jang, D. (2007). *The challenges of change: Learning from the child care and early education experiences of immigrant families.* Washington, DC: Center for Law and Social Policy.

Morrison, G. S. (2009). *Early childhood education today* (11th ed.). Upper Saddle River, NJ: Merrill/Prentice-Hall.

National Head Start Association. (2005). *Head Start: The nation's pride . . . Celebrating 40 years of success.* Alexandria, VA: Author.

Perez, P., & Zarate, M. E. (2006). *Latino public opinion survey of prekindergarten programs: Knowledge, preferences, and public support.* Los Angeles: Tomás Rivera Policy Institute.

Phillips, D., & Cabrera, N. (1996). *Beyond the blueprint: Directions for research on Head Start families.* Washington, DC: National Academy Press.

Puma, M., Bell, S., Cook, R., Heid, C., Lopez, M., Zill, N., et al. (2005). *Head Start impact study: First year findings.* Washington, DC: U.S. Department of Health and Human Services.

Raikes, H., Luze, G., Brooks-Gunn, J., Raikes, H. A., Pan, B. A., Tamis-LeMonda, C. S., et al. (2006). Mother-child book reading in low-income families: Correlates and outcomes during the first three years of life. *Child Development 77*(4), 924–953.

Ramirez, R. R., & De la Cruz, G. P. (2003). The Hispanic population in the United States: March 2002. *Current Population Reports, P20–545.* Washington, DC: U.S. Census Bureau.

Reardon-Anderson, J., Capps, R., & Fix, M. (2002). *The health and well-being of children in immigrant families.* Washington DC: Urban Institute.

Rathbun, A., & West, J. (2004). *From kindergarten through third grade: Children's beginning school experiences* (NCES 2004–007). Washington, DC: U.S. Department of Education. Retrieved March 30, 2009, from http://nces.ed.gov/pubs2004/2004007.pdf

Schumacher, R., & Rakpraja, T. (2003, March). *A snapshot of Head Start children, families, teachers, and programs: 1997 and 2001* (Brief No. 1, Head Start Series). Center for Law and Social Policy (CLASP). Retrieved March 4, 2009, from http://www.clasp.org/publications/Head_Start_brief1.pdf

Shonkoff, J., & Phillips, D. (Eds.). (2000). *From neurons to neighborhoods: The science of early childhood development.* Washington, DC: National Academy Press.

Takanishi, R. (2004). Leveling the playing field: Supporting immigrant children from birth to eight. *The Future of Children, 14*(2), 61–79.

U.S. Census Bureau (2002). *Current Population Survey (March 2002).* Retrieved March 30, 2009, from http://www.census.gov/popest/archives/2000s/vintage_2002/NA-EST2002–06.html

U.S. Department of Health and Human Services (USDHHS). (n.d.) Head Start Program Performance Standards and Other Regulations. Retrieved March 30, 2009, from http://eclkc.ohs.acf.hhs.gov/hslc/Program%20Design%20and%20Management/Head%20Start%20Requirements/Head%20Start%20Requirements

U.S. Department of Health and Human Services (USDHHS). (2004). *Latinos and child care: The changing landscape.* Washington, DC: Author.

U.S. Department of Health and Human Services (USDHHS). (2005). *Head Start impact study: First year findings.* Washington, DC: Author.

Vogel, C., Aikens, N., Burwick, A., Hawkinson, L., Richardson, A., Mendenko, L., et al. (2006). *Findings from the survey of Early Head Start programs: Communities, programs, and families.* Washington, DC: U.S. Department of Health and Human Services.

Washington, V., & Bailey, U. J. (1995). *Project Head Start: Models and strategies for the twenty-first century.* New York: Garland.

Vinovskis, M. (2008). *From a nation at risk to No Child Left Behind: National education goals and the creation of federal education policy.* New York: Teachers College Press.

Zambrana, R. (2003). Promoting Latino child and family welfare: Strategies for strengthening the child welfare system. *Children and Youth Services Review, 25*(10), 755–780.

Zambrana, R. E., & Zoppi, I. M. (2002). Latino students: Translating cultural wealth into social capital to improve academic success. *Journal of Ethnic and Cultural Diversity in Social Work, 11,* 33–53.

Zigler, E., Styfco, S. J., & Gilman, E. (1993). The national Head Start Program for disadvantaged preschoolers. In E. Zigler & S. J. Styfco (Eds.), *Head Start and beyond* (pp. 1–41). New York: Yale University Press.

Zigler, E., & Valentine, A. (Eds.). (1979). *Project Head Start: A legacy of the War on Poverty.* New York: The Free Press.

Zill, N., Sorogon, A., & Kim, K. (2003). *FACES 2003 Research Brief, Children's Outcomes and Program Quality.* Washington, DC: U.S. Department of Health and Human Services.

16

LATINO PRE-K-3 EDUCATION

A Critical Foundation

EUGENE E. GARCÍA AND KENT P. SCRIBNER

The educational well-being of young children from racial and ethnic minority backgrounds has received significant attention over the past few decades. Despite this attention, disparities persist in key domains of development between Whites and some racial/ethnic groups. These disparities demonstrate the relative strengths and weaknesses of certain groups and imply the need for further research and action by educational policymakers and practitioners. We must think critically about group differences—including within-group variation as a unit of analysis—and what they mean to the well-being of children and their families. Moreover, our conception of "development" should be holistic and should comprise numerous social and individual dimensions, such as physical health, mental health, language, culture, family, and cognitive and socioemotional factors. In many cases, groups we tend to label "at risk" in terms of educational outcomes actually present a number of favorable outcomes, compared to Whites and the majority population. Empirical studies have shown, for example, that compared to children from U.S.-born families, children from immigrant families in low socioeconomic circumstances have lower

infant mortality rates, have fewer physical and mental health problems, and are less likely to engage in such risky behaviors as substance abuse, early sexual intercourse, and delinquent or violent activity (Shields & Behrman, 2004). These strengths, however, are not always sufficient to keep children on pathways to educational success over time.

In this chapter, we focus on the educational and linguistic experiences of young children from homes in which English is not the primary language, with an emphasis on young Latino students. This group makes up some 80% of the English Language Learner (ELL) population. We discuss the demographic profile of these children across the United States, their language environments, and their patterns of early academic achievement. Data presented here must be conceptualized by the reader within a larger framework, one that conceives of child development as an amalgamation of individual, family, school, and community factors. Research presented here suggests a number of actions to be taken by educational policymakers and practitioners in order to improve the early educational trajectory of young children from Latino origins. We conclude the chapter by offering recommendations not only to researchers but to parties involved with the provision of educational services and programs to young Latino children ages 3–8 years.

DEMOGRAPHIC AND LINGUISTIC PROFILE

Latinos are the largest and youngest ethnic minority in the United States (Hernandez, 2006; Montemayor & Mendoza, 2004; Ramirez & de la Cruz, 2003). Children of Latino (or Hispanic) heritage in the United States are not a homogenous group. These children and students come from diverse social, cultural, and linguistic backgrounds. Latino children represent, for example, long-term populations native to the United States and to various other countries of origin, each of which is associated with a unique combination of histories, cultural practices, perspectives, and traditions. Recent growth in the young Latino population in the United States has been driven, to a high degree, by immigration patterns from Latin America (Ramirez & de la Cruz, 2003). In 2000, one in five children ages 0–8 in the United States was Latino (Hernandez, 2006). Of these children, more than 64% were born into immigrant families in which at least one parent was born outside the United States. Table 16.1 shows the percent and number of Latino children ages 0–8 by parent immigrant status and native country. As shown, a large majority of young Latino children are of Mexican origin (68%), but substantial proportions have origins in Puerto Rico (9%), Central America (7%), South America (6%), Cuba (3%), or the Dominican Republic (3%). Two thirds of Mexican-origin and Cuban-origin young children live in immigrant families, and this rises to about 9 in 10 for those with origins in the Dominican Republic and Central or South America. Especially important is that the vast majority of young Latino children are themselves U.S. citizens: 85% for those of South American origin, 88% for those of Mexican origin, and 91–92% for those of Dominican and Central or South American origin (Capps, Fix, Ost, Reardon-Anderson, & Passel, 2004; Hernandez, 2006).

Compared to Whites and other racial/ethnic groups, Latino children and families demonstrate a number of favorable attributes. In an analysis of census data, Hernandez (2006) found that a large proportion of Latino children live in two-parent households. Indeed, 77% of young Latino children (ages 0–8) lived with two parents in 2000. The proportion rises to 81–86% for young children in immigrant families from Mexico, Central and South America, and Cuba. These proportions decrease, however, in native families from these regions as well as those from the Dominican Republic and Puerto Rico.

Young Latino children, on average, live in families with a strong work ethic and desire to succeed (Hernandez, 2006). Ninety-three percent of these children have fathers who worked during the year prior to the Census 2000 survey. The proportion is the same in both native-born and immigrant families. Moreover, Latino children are approximately three times more likely to have a third adult or more (in addition to father and mother) in the home who is in the workforce.

Despite low socioeconomic circumstances, Latino families demonstrate various positive physical health outcomes. Studies have consistently found that Latinos have lower infant mortality rates, better birth outcomes, healthier diets, and lower rates of obesity, compared to Whites (Escarce, Morales, & Rumbaut, 2006). Variations on these domains have been found to vary between national-origin groups and by immigrant generation status. Latinos of Puerto Rican descent, for example, tend to have worse health status indicators than other national-origin groups, while Latinos of Mexican and Central American origin often exhibit the most favorable health outcomes despite their poverty.

Survey data have also highlighted that Latino parents demonstrate a positive attitude toward education and the schooling of their children. Although parents of young Latinos, on average, do not have high levels of formal education, they express interest in enrolling their children in early education programs and supporting them through postsecondary schooling. They have high educational aspirations for their children (Nuñez, Cuccaro-Alamin, & Carroll, 1998). A survey conducted by the Tomás Rivera Policy Institute found that more than 90% of Latino parents felt that it was very important or somewhat important for children to attend preschool (Perez & Zarate, 2006).

Young Latino children live in a variety of home language environments. In general, Spanish dominates such environments, with

Table 16.1   Percent and Number of Children Ages 0–8 by Immigrant Country

Latino Country of Origin	Percent	Number
Latino Groups	**100.0**	6,797,303
Puerto Rican	9.3	629,881
Mexican	65.2	4,432,161
Central American	7.2	489,884
Cuban	2.3	158,035
Dominican	2.5	172,466
South American	5.5	372,046
Other Latino/Latino	8.0	542,830
Latinos in Native or Immigrant Groups	**100.0**	**6,797,303**
Latino Native, Total	35.6	*2,421,900*
Latino Immigrant, Total	64.4	*4,375,403*
Puerto Rican, Mainland Origin[a]	4.6	312,396
Puerto Rican, Island Origin[a]	4.7	317,485
Mexican, Native	21.9	1,489,518
Mexican, Immigrant	43.3	2,942,643
Central American, Native	0.4	26,404
Central American, Immigrant	6.8	463,480
Cuban, Native	0.8	53,496
Cuban, Immigrant	1.5	104,539
Dominican, Native	0.3	21,499
Dominican, Immigrant	2.2	150,967
South American, Native	0.5	32,547
South American, Immigrant	5.0	339,499
Latinos 1st and 2nd Generation	**100.0**	**4,375,403**
Latino Immigrant, 1st Generation, Total	11.9	*522,141*
Latino Immigrant, 2nd Generation, Total	88.1	*3,853,262*

(Continued)

Table 16.1 (Continued)

Latino Country of Origin	Percent	Number
Puerto Rican, 1st [a]	1.3	55,341
Puerto Rican, 2nd [a]	6.0	262,144
Mexican, 1st	7.9	345,822
Mexican, 2nd	59.4	2,596,821
Central American, 1st	0.9	39,317
Central American, 2nd	9.7	424,163
Cuban, 1st	0.2	10,112
Cuban, 2nd	2.2	94,427
Dominican, 1st	0.3	14,977
Dominican, 2nd	3.1	135,990
South American, 1st	1.2	52,029
South American, 2nd	6.6	287,470

Calculated from Census 2000 5% microdata (IPUMS) by Donald J. Hernandez. In Hernandez, D. (2006). *Young Hispanic children in the U.S.: A demographic portrait based on Census 2000*. A report to the National Task Force on Early Childhood Education for Hispanics. Albany: State University of New York.

access to English as a significant factor. Because early language development is strongly associated with cognitive development and academic success (Risley & Hart, 2006), it is important to understand the intersection of Spanish and English for these children and how the native language can be leveraged to increase school success. Some young Latinos acquire English as their first language and maintain only monolingual proficiency throughout their lives. Others speak Spanish as their first language and learn English as they enter public schooling. The proportional size of this particular subpopulation has been growing rapidly over the past few decades. Indeed, the percentage of the overall child population in the United States who spoke a non-English native language rose from 6% in 1979 to 14% in 1999. The National Clearinghouse for English Language Acquisition (NCELA) reported that from the 1993–1994 to the 2003–2004

school year, K–12 enrollment of ELL grew over 65%, while the total K–12 population grew less than 7%. The majority of this growth is attributable to increases in populations of Latin American origin. In 2000, Spanish accounted for 76% of all ELL students in preschool to 5th grade (NCELA, 2006).

Using data from a national sample of children born between December 2001 and January 2002, López, Barrueco, and Miles (2006) described the home language environments of Latino infants. The largest group (34%) of Latino infants lived in homes in which Spanish was the primary language, with some English. Twenty-two percent lived in a home in which English was primarily spoken, with some Spanish; 21% in English-only homes; and 19% in Spanish-only homes. In sum, it was found that approximately three in four Latino infants were exposed to Spanish in the home.

LANGUAGE AND SCHOOLING

The knowledge base reviewed is directly related to understanding instructional programs, teaching strategies, and educational policies that seek to provide optimal literacy and academic outcomes for young Latino children. The demographic data, for example, demonstrate that most young Latino children in the United States are exposed, at some level, to Spanish in the home—approximately three in four (López et al., 2006) and that the home environment is likely to be characterized by aspects of the immigrant experience. This set of circumstances is very important given that home language practices—different from "language use"—are highly relevant to early literacy outcomes (Goldenberg, Rueda, & August, 2006; Nord, Lennon, Liu, & Chandler, 1999; Tabors, 1997; Tabors & Snow, 2002). Moreover, given that higher-order cognitive and literacy skills tend to transfer from the native language to the second language (August, Calderón, & Carlo, 2002; Genesee, 2003; Genesee, Geva, Dressler, & Kamil, 2006; Goldenberg, Rezaei, & Fletcher, 2005), it is critical that educators adequately assess, develop, and leverage the child's non-English native language skills. This means tailoring instruction, curricular content, and schooling practices in general to meet the child's particular language development circumstances—based on individual, school, and family factors—as well as the social and cultural contexts to take full advantage of the child's home resources and parental support (Genesee et al., 2006; Goldenberg, Gallimore, Reese, & Garnier, 2001; Goldenberg et al., 2006; Reese, Garnier, Gallimore, & Goldenberg, 2000; Scheffner Hammer & Miccio, 2004; Shannon, 1995). In this section, we discuss the present status of young Latinos' academic achievement levels—including early literacy skills—and discuss how policies and practices play a part in these outcomes. We comb the literature to highlight which programs are used to leverage young Latino children's strengths to produce the most favorable outcomes—and, more specifically, the features and strategies of the most effective programs—with a particular exploration of preschool participation.

Present Circumstances

Currently, Latinos lag behind their White and Asian American peers at all proficiency levels of reading and mathematics (at least a half of a standard deviation) at the beginning and throughout K-12 schooling (Braswell, Daane, & Grigg, 2003; García, Jensen, Miller, & Huerta, 2005; National Center for Education Statistics [NCES], 2003; Reardon & Galindo, 2006). Educational achievement patterns of virtually all racial/ethnic groups are established during the early years of school and change little thereafter. Although some of the difference between racial/ethnic groups is accounted for by socioeconomic differences between groups (on average, Latinos have lower socioeconomic status [SES] than Whites and Asian Americans), much of it is not (Reardon & Galindo, 2006). Using data from the Early Childhood Longitudinal Study, Kindergarten Cohort (ECLS-K; NCES, 2001), Reardon and Galindo (2006) found that Latino children scored .3 to .5 standard deviation lower in mathematics and reading than their White peers within all five SES quintiles (SES in ECLS-K is a composite of household income and parents' level of education and occupation). Hence, race/ethnicity had a substantial effect on early achievement over and above SES. In a separate analysis of ECLS-K data, Reardon (2003) noted that achievement differences by SES and race/ethnicity from kindergarten through 1st grade were attributable to processes within, between, and out of schools. That is, practices in the home and school have meaningful influences on racial/ethnic and SES achievement gaps in early education (García, Jensen, & Cuéllar, 2006).

Reardon and Galindo (2006) also found that reading and mathematics achievement patterns from kindergarten through 3rd grade varied by home language environments. Latino children living in homes in which primarily Spanish or only Spanish was spoken lagged further behind White children than did Latinos who lived in homes in which primarily English or only English was spoken Rosenthal, Baker, and Ginsburg (1983) documented the low literacy levels of children from Spanish-speaking homes over 2 decades ago. The impact of language background on achievement outcomes should not necessarily be surprising, given the relationship of SES with achievement and the positive correlation between low SES and non-English-language use in homes of young Spanish-speaking children in the United States (Collier, 1987;

Jensen, 2007). Nonetheless, it does bring to light the academic risk faced by young Latinos who come from homes in which little or no English is spoken. The academic risk of children from non-English-speaking homes has been documented as early as the preschool years (NCES, 1995).

Not all young ELLs are equally at risk for academic underachievement and reading difficulties. In their analyses of group differences on mathematics and reading outcomes from kindergarten through 3rd grade, Reardon and Galindo (2006) found that Latino children from Mexican, Central American, and Puerto Rican ethnic backgrounds scored lower than those from South American and Cuban backgrounds; and first- and second-generation children from Mexican backgrounds scored lower than those of the third generation or more. Moreover, achievement differences between Whites and Latinos were found within SES quintiles, suggesting that the difference is attributable to factors beyond socioeconomic conditions. Indeed, early risk is attributable by a combination of factors, rather than just one or two features. A report on the prevalence of selected accomplishments and difficulties in a national sample of children ages 3 to 5 years by the NCES (1995) found that small motor skills and signs of emerging literacy skills varied by a number of family characteristics. Authors specifically identified five family risk factors to be associated with fewer accomplishments and more difficulties: (1) maternal education levels, (2) family income, (3) maternal English-language proficiency, (4) mother's marital status at the time of birth, and (5) single- versus dual-parent homes.

Because Latino children, on average, exhibit more risk factors that White children, in general they are at greater risk for academic underachievement (Hernandez, Denton, & Macartney, 2007). It is important to note that risk is due not solely to non-English proficiency but to a number of sociodemographic conditions that correlate with Spanish use in the home. Therefore, the low scores of young Latino children, compared to Whites and Asians, during the early years of schooling (Reardon & Galindo, 2006) are associated with a combination of family risk factors, including Spanish home-language use, low income, and low educational attainment of parents.

HOME LANGUAGE PRACTICES

In a recent analysis of developmental protective and risk factors in a nationally representative sample of children born in 2001 (i.e., ECLS-B data), López, Barrueco, and Miles (2006) found differences in parenting practices between SES and racial/ethnic groups. Among other important findings relative to the early health and development of Latino infants and the homes in which they are reared, López et al. (2006) found important differences in parent-child interactions. Namely, differences were found in parent-child linguistic engagement—assessing how often parents engaged with their infants (at 9 months) by reading, telling stories, or singing songs—and parenting practices, as measured by the Nursing Child Assessment Teaching Scale (NCATS), used to assess parent-child teaching interactions for early precursors of cognitive and social skills. For the linguistic engagement construct, means of self-reported ratings were compared across racial/ethnic groups; it was found that Latino parents read, told stories, and sang songs to their infants less frequently than White and multiracial families (all comparisons were statistically significant). In addition, Latino mothers scored statistically lower than White, multiracial, and Asian mothers on the NCATS, suggesting that Latino mothers in general were less responsive to their infants' distress and less likely to foster socioemotional and cognitive growth. Controlling for SES, group differences remained—Latino mothers scored significantly lower than White and Asian mothers. It should be noted that some concern has arisen as to the cultural sensitivity of the NCATS (Gross, Conrad, Fogg, Willis, & Garvey, 1993).

The National Task Force on Early Childhood Education for Hispanics (2007) provides an overview of cultural and linguistic contrasts that relate to discontinuities between parental/family interaction and schooling expectations in both the quantity and quality of social interaction. This report provides research related to ways in which linguistic and educational practices in the home influence early literacy outcomes and ways in which cultural practices of meaning making interact with this development. In general, Latino social interactions in the home that are similar to school-like tasks are absent in Latino homes. This is not a new finding. Various disparities exist in the ways Latino parents engage their young children and the ways early childhood educators engage those same children, including the framing of questions, the generation of discourse patterns, and expectations of language development.

Cuéllar (2008) specifically investigated the conceptualizations of emergent literacy held by teachers and Mexican American mothers at a Head Start program serving second-generation Mexican American children and the culturally responsive teaching practices occurring in that setting. The center's lead and assistant teachers and the first-generation Mexican American mothers of five of the center's students were interviewed using both ethnographic techniques and case study methodologies to better understand their cultural models for emergent literacy. The teachers' and mothers' cultural models for emergent literacy development proved to be almost completely discontinuous. The mothers' cultural models were found to emphasize the clarity of language output, the importance of Spanish development as a means of cultural and ethnic identity development, and the concept of *educación,* which in their view is the foundation for all learning in the early years (Goldenberg et al., 2001). On the other hand, the teachers emphasized the complexity of language output, the importance of English-language development in preparation for English-only kindergarten, and the appropriateness of phonics-based instruction to further the children's preliteracy skills.

The intersection of language, culture, and schooling is highly significant for Latino children and families. Familial and cultural attributes that are highly adaptive in home situations in some cases (but not all) intersect in significant ways when children engage in today's "schooling." Given this knowledge, the goal is not to make "home" more like "school" or "school" more like "home" but to more fully understand this dimension of the development/education continuum.

Duration of English Acquisition

In order for young Latinos to succeed in academic contexts and perform well in comparison to their peers, they need strong English skills. For a majority of Latino children, this means acquiring strong skills in a second language. An important aspect for the second-language development of young children is the time required to attain proficiency—how long does it take to attain English proficiency? Second-language proficiency refers generally to two types, oral and academic. Oral proficiency generally precedes academic proficiency and refers to the development of conversational vocabulary, grammar, and listening comprehension. Academic proficiency refers to various skills, including word reading, spelling, reading fluency, reading comprehension, and writing. Under the U.S. Supreme Court's interpretation of the Civil Rights Act in *Lau v. Nichols* (1974), local school districts and states have an obligation to provide linguistically appropriate services to students of limited English profiency, yet policymakers often debate how much time students need to attain English proficiency and therefore how long they should receive services. Indeed, estimates suggest that academic English proficiency takes ELL students anywhere from 3 to 10 years to develop (Collier, 1989, 1995; Cummins, 1981; Mitchell, Destino, & Karam, 1997).

Reporting on data from 5,585 ELLs from four different school districts (two from the San Francisco Bay Area and two from Canada) to address the question of duration, Hakuta, Goto Butler, and Witt (2000) analyzed various forms of English proficiency as a function of length of exposure to English. Using standardized tests to determine both oral (i.e., Idea Proficiency Test [IPT], Language Assessment Scales [LAS], Bilingual Syntax Measure [BSM]) and academic proficiency (i.e., SAT-9, CTBS), this study plotted English proficiency as a function of length of residence, which was calculated by subtracting age of immigration from present age. Hakuta and colleagues (2000) found that "even in districts that are considered the most successful in teaching English to ELL students, oral proficiency takes 3 to 5 years to develop, and academic English proficiency can take 4 to 7 years" (p. 13). It is important to note that the authors found socioeconomic factors to be related to the rate of English acquisition. Moreover, studies on the duration of English acquisition have been mostly conducted with school-age children. Comparable evidence for preschool-age children, to our knowledge, does not exist. Yet, it has been posited that the duration of second-language acquisition is shorter for ELLs exposed to English at any earlier age.

Rather than stipulating time limits for ELLs to attain English skills, education policy and practices should continue to identify and leverage children's abilities and provide empirically sound instructional and curricular practices to help children succeed academically, understanding that the development of satisfactory English skills requires a number of years. Historically, school districts and states have approached the language development and education of ELLs in very different ways; these approaches are typically influenced not by rigorous research but by politics and ideology (Jensen, 2008).

Enhancing Reading/Literacy Development

The development of reading in all its complex forms for young children has become a key ingredient of U.S. education goals (August & Shanahan, 2006). The issue of primary language instruction has been an important focus of literacy/reading research, especially for those studying Latino children. Instead of assessing the influence of language use (i.e., whether Spanish or English is primarily spoken in the home) on literacy outcomes, linguistics research has evaluated ways in which literacy outcomes for English and Spanish are related. They have considered the extent to which oral, word-level, text-level, and comprehension skills in both languages correlate, assessing cross-linguistic literacy skills.

August and colleagues (2002), for example, followed a cohort of 287 Spanish-speaking students in Boston, El Paso, and Chicago from the end of 2nd grade through the end of 4th grade. Researchers examined how performance on indicators of Spanish reading at the end of 2nd grade predicted parallel indicators of English reading at the end of 3rd and 4th grades. More specifically, transfer from Spanish to English was examined in the areas of phonological awareness, letter identification, word reading, word knowledge, and comprehension over a 3-year period. In each analysis, authors controlled for general ability, oral English proficiency, performance in English on the reading measure of interest at the beginning of the study, and number of years of formal instruction in English reading.

In the context of this review, three findings from this longitudinal study are worth noting. First, it was found that Spanish phonemic awareness, Spanish letter identification, and Spanish word reading were all reliable predictors of performance on parallel tasks in English at the end of 3rd and 4th grades. Second, with regard to passage comprehension, a positive relationship was found between Spanish passage comprehension at the end of 2nd grade and English passage comprehension at the end of 4th grade. In other words, those who had the highest Spanish passage comprehension at the end of 2nd grade had the highest English passage comprehension scores at the end of 4th grade. Third, it was found that the effect of Spanish letter identification and Spanish word reading on English letter identification and English word reading emerged only for students who had received formal instruction in Spanish reading. That is, successful transfer was at least partially due to whether Spanish was integrated in classroom instruction. In short, findings from this study indicate that an effect of transfer from Spanish to English exists for phonemic segmentation skills for all Spanish-speaking students and for letter identification and word reading skills for those Spanish-speaking students who received initial instruction in their native language.

Another study, by Goldenberg et al. (2005), supported the idea that knowledge and skills developed in one language are transferable to another. Authors of this study conducted a year-long analysis of oral language literacy development among Spanish-speaking children during the 2001–2002 school year. It involved 14 schools and their surrounding communities in Texas and California and included 904 students in grades K–2 in different types of instructional programs for English learners. The sample comprised children from urban, suburban, and rural communities in Southern California, central Texas, and along the Texas/Mexico border. Analyses were conducted to determine the relationship between home language use, grade (K–2), and the program language. Among other findings, analyses supported the transfer hypothesis—i.e., common underlying proficiency—on measures of basic reading and passage comprehension. They found, however, that oral language skills did not correlate (or transfer) across languages. Authors show that variation in oral language skills was more strongly accounted for by home experiences. Family members in this sample conversed predominantly in Spanish in the home.

A cross-sectional study evaluated developmental changes in lexical comprehension and cognitive processing in early sequential bilinguals for whom Spanish was the native language and English was the second language (Kohnert & Bates, 2002). A total of 100 participants—20 in each of the five age groups (ages 5–7, 8–10, 11–13, 14–16, and adults)—were evaluated in both Spanish and English in order to explore the effects of age, years of experience, and basic-level cognitive processing on lexical comprehension. Gains in lexical comprehension were found in all age groups in both languages. These gains, however, were greater in English. Participants in the youngest age group were relatively balanced in their cross-linguistic performance. By middle childhood, however, performance was better in English. These findings show a clear shift from Spanish to English.

Lesaux and Geva (2006) provide a comprehensive literature review focused on the literacy development of language-minority students in the United States. They note that literacy skills for language-minority children and youth, on average, take longer to develop and lag behind those of their English monolingual peers. Children learning English as a second language, therefore, often find themselves more likely to be categorized as having a specific learning disability in reading (Artiles, Rueda, Salazar, & Higareda, 2002). Moreover, the process underlying literacy skills in a second language follows the same general pattern for monolinguals. In a loosely linear fashion, oral and phonological processing skills (including phonemic awareness and rapid naming skills) precede word-level skills and text-level skills, such as reading comprehension and writing abilities. As expected, variations in student characteristics (e.g., working memory, attention), student background (e.g., parent education, socioeconomic status), and the quality of language and literacy development in Spanish (i.e., native language) influence the rate and quality of literacy acquisition (Lesaux & Geva, 2006; Lesaux, Koda, Siegel, Shanahan, 2006).

Several studies have incorporated correlation-based models to understand how aspects of linguistic development (i.e., oral proficiency and phonological processing) relate to and predict literacy outcomes (i.e., word-level skills, text-level skills, reading comprehension) for young Latinos learning English as a second language. Two major findings have emerged from this research. First, aspects of native-language oral proficiency (i.e., Spanish phonological awareness skills) predict word-level skills in English (Durgunoglu, Nagy, & Hancin-Bhatt, 1993; Geva & Genesee, 2006; Quiroga, Lemos-Britton, Mostafapour, Abbott, & Berninger, 2002). To date,

two studies have shown that the Spanish phonological awareness skills of native Spanish-speaking children accounted significantly for variations in word reading and pseudo word decoding in English (Durgunoglu et al., 1993; Quiroga et al., 2002). This might not be surprising, given the strong correlation between phonological awareness skills across languages, which suggests that that phonological awareness is a common underlying proficiency (Geva & Genesee, 2006, p. 186). Atwill, Blanchard, Gorin, and Burnstein (2006) recently provided evidence that phonological awareness skills of Spanish-speaking kindergartners indeed correlate with the same skills in English but only for those who attain oral proficiency (measured in this study by receptive vocabulary scores) in Spanish, their native language. As mentioned earlier, other aspects of Spanish oral proficiency (i.e., morphology, syntax, and semantics) have not generally been found to predict word-level English skills.

Second, in terms of bilingual (Spanish/English) literacy outcomes, data support the notion of linguistic transfer. Dressler and Kamil (2006) conducted a thorough research review of the intersection between first- and second-language literacy of ELL children and youth—a synthesis of the cross-linguistic influences of literacy knowledge, processes, and strategies. While more research is needed in this area, extant data suggest that word reading skills (Durgunoglu et al., 1993), vocabulary (García, 1991; Jiménez, García, & Pearson, 1996; Nagy, García, Durgunoglu, & Hancin-Bhatt, 1993), and reading comprehension (Goldman, Reyes, & Varnhagen, 1984; Nagy, McClure, & Mir, 1997; Reese et al., 2000; Royer & Carlo, 1991) transfer between languages. For transfer of vocabulary skills, it should be noted that cognate rather than complex vocabulary skills transfer between Spanish and English. Moreover, Nagy et al. (1997) observe that this transfer can be negative, as when meaning is erroneously assigned to words based on the first language's syntax or when meanings between languages are not differentiated.

Learning English as part of an academic task has continued to confront many Latino students in U.S. schools. Utilizing Spanish to achieve this academic goal is supported by theoretical and empirical contributions related to research in this area. Transfer opportunities and mechanisms from Spanish to English have been identified and transformed into educational practices.

Available Programs

There are many possible program options for bilingual students and children learning English as a second language. These carry various titles: transitional bilingual education, maintenance bilingual education, 90–10 bilingual education, 50–50 bilingual education, developmental bilingual education, dual-language, two-way immersion, English-as-a-second-language, English immersion, sheltered English, structured English, submersion, and so forth. These programs differ in the way they use the native language and English during instruction (Ovando, Collier, & Combs, 2006). They also differ in terms of theoretical rationale, language goals, cultural goals, academic goals, student characteristics, ages served, entry grades, length of student participation, participation of mainstream teachers, teacher qualifications, and instructional materials (Genesee, 1999). The extent to which a program is successful depends on local conditions, choices, and innovations.

The effectiveness of programs targeted at young ELLs is a widely contested issue. Debates regarding program types that best develop the academic skills of children whose native language is not English continue to cause tumult among practitioners, academics, and policymakers. The fundamental issue underlying this argument has been whether bilingual or English-only approaches are more effective in boosting and sustaining the academic achievement of ELLs. Early research surrounding this issue was inconclusive. Some, such as Baker and de Kanter (1981) and Baker and Pelavin (1984), asserted that the research evidence did not support the effectiveness of bilingual instruction and that bilingual education simply does not work. Others, such as Willig (1985), refuted this argument and provided evidence to support the efficacy of bilingual programs. Here, we present the most recent empirical evidence—including original studies, syntheses, and meta-analyses—that assess this question at the national level. Greene (1998) was one of the first to conduct a systematic meta-analysis of the effectiveness of bilingual education. He included 11 of 75 original studies in the study; each of the 11 met minimal standards for the quality (i.e., randomization) of their research design. They included standardized test scores from 2,719 students, 1,562 of whom were enrolled in bilingual programs, in 13 states. The average student in bilingual programs was tested in 3rd grade after 2 years of bilingual instruction. Greene found, overall, that bilingual programs produced .21 of a standard deviation improvement on reading tests and .12 of a standard deviation improvement on math tests measured in English. The gain in all test scores measured in Spanish was .74 of a standard deviation. The author noted that although these data show the general academic benefits of bilingual programs, a few critical programmatic concerns were left unclear. Namely, this study did not ascertain the ideal length of time students should be in bilingual programs, the ideal amount of native language used for instruction, and the age groups for which these techniques are most appropriate. These concerns are especially important for young Latino children.

More recently, Slavin and Cheung (2005) published a "best evidence synthesis" (Slavin, 1986) reviewing experimental studies that compared bilingual and English-only reading programs for ELLs. In this review, authors employed a systematic literature search, quantification of outcomes as effect sizes, and extensive discussion of individual studies ($N = 17$) that met inclusion criteria. Thirteen of the 17 studies focused on elementary school reading for Spanish-dominant students. Of these, 9 favored bilingual approaches on English reading measures, and 4 found no significant difference, producing a median effect size of .45 in favor of bilingual approaches. Weighted by sample size, an effect size of .33 was calculated, in favor of programs with bilingual approaches. Authors conclude that the available body of empirical research is limited; to ensure effectiveness of reading programs for ELLs, more high-quality studies should be conducted. They recommend that such studies should incorporate longitudinal, randomized designs to produce satisfying answers to questions surrounding program effectiveness for ELLs.

Rolstad, Mahoney, and Glass (2005) present another meta-analysis. In this piece, authors included 17 studies conducted since 1985 on the effectiveness of bilingual approaches, compared to English-only approaches. Unlike the studies mentioned above, authors in this review decided to include as many studies as possible in their analysis instead of excluding on the basis of a priori criteria. Effect size of program effectiveness was computed by calculating mean outcome differences between new treatment and traditional treatment groups and subsequently dividing by the standard deviation of the traditional treatment group (Glass, McGaw, & Smith, 1981). Using this method, authors found that bilingual approaches were consistently better than English-only approaches. Controlling for ELL status, analysis yielded a positive effect for bilingual programs at .23 of a standard deviation.

Unlike the aforementioned reviews, August, Calderón, Carlo, and Nuttall (2006) focused their follow-up study of program effectiveness on a particular linguistic group: 5th-grade Spanish-speaking students ($N = 113$). Moreover, authors evaluated the effectiveness of language of instruction on broad reading outcomes (combining word reading and passage comprehension) for three groups: (1) Spanish-speaking students instructed in Spanish only, (2) Spanish-speaking students instructed in English, and (3) Spanish-speaking students instructed first in Spanish and then transitioned into English-only instruction in 3rd or 4th grade. All students included in the study were in one of the three programs from the time they began school and were exposed to the same intervention, with parallel versions in English and Spanish. Implementation data were collected across classrooms and sites to ensure integrity of implementation.

All assessments were conducted in Spanish and English. Using an ANCOVA and controlling for mother's level of education and initial performance (during 2nd grade), meaningful between-group differences were found on students' broad reading scores in English and Spanish. In terms of English reading scores, those in the Spanish-only group scored significantly lower than those in the bilingual and English-only groups. No significant difference was found between the bilingual and English-only group. In terms of the Spanish reading scores, significant differences were found between all three groups. Moreover, the bilingual group scored significantly higher than the English-only group, and the Spanish-only group scored significantly higher than the bilingual group. These findings suggest that sound instruction in Spanish followed by sound instruction in English benefits Spanish-speaking children. These data support the notion that bilingual instruction is beneficial in that students acquire bilingual literacy skills and are not disadvantaged with regard to the acquisition of literacy in English.

Finally, Borman, Hewes, Reilly, and Alvarado (2006) did not assess program differences directly but conducted a meta-analysis on the achievement effects of the nationally disseminated and externally developed school improvement programs known as "whole-school" or "comprehensive" reforms implemented in schools that predominantly served Latino students. They also compared the specific achievement effects of the 12 most widely implemented models of comprehensive school reform (CSR) for Latinos. They found that the effects of CSR for schools serving mostly Latino students was somewhat limited but that the current body of evidence suggests that CSR programs that show particular promise for Latino students "are built around valuing and teaching relevant culture and traditions, and address language directly."

Meta-analyses and best-evidence studies conclude that the academic benefits of bilingual over English-only programs demonstrate, on average, an academic performance benefit of .2 to .3 standard deviations for young Latino ELLs over and above English-only programs. This is enough to close about one fifth to one third of the overall Latino-White achievement gap in reading in the early elementary school years.

Dual-Language Programs

Dual-language (DL) programs—also known as two-way immersion (TWI)—are relatively new in the United States. Unique among program alternatives, the goals of DL programs are to provide high-quality instruction for students who come to school speaking primarily a language other than English, and simultaneously to provide instruction in a second language for English-speaking students. Schools offering DL programs thus teach children language through content; teachers adapt their instruction to ensure children's comprehension and use content lessons to convey vocabulary and language structure. Striving for half language-minority students and half native English-speaking students in each classroom, DL programs also aim to teach cross-cultural awareness. Programs vary in terms of the amount of time they devote to each language, the grade levels they serve, the degree of structure they impose for the division of language and curriculum, and the populations they serve. The Center for Applied Linguistics (CAL, 2005) has compiled research-based strategies and practices associated with DL program development and implementation. Titled *Guiding Principles for Dual-Language Education,* seven dimensions to help with planning and ongoing implementation of DL programs are discussed: (1) assessment and accountability, (2) curriculum, (3) instruction, (4) staff quality and professional development, (5) program structure, (6) family and community, and (7) support and resources.

The installation of DL programs is based on a strong theoretical rationale and supported by empirical research findings concerning both first- and second-language acquisition (Genesee, 1999). This rationale grows out of sociocultural theory, which maintains that learning occurs through naturalistic social interaction (Vygotsky, 1978); that is, the integration of native English speakers and speakers of other languages facilitates second-language acquisition because it promotes natural, substantive interaction among speakers of different languages.

Currently, there are more than 600 DL programs in the United States, and the number is growing rapidly. While the vast majority offers instruction in Spanish and English, there are also DL programs that target Korean, Cantonese, Arabic, French, Japanese, Navajo, Portuguese, and Russian (Howard, Sugarman, & Christian, 2003; García, 2005).

These programs typically aim to achieve three major goals for their students:

1. To help children to learn English and find success in U.S. schools

2. To help these children become competent in their own languages without sacrificing their own success in school

3. To promote linguistic and ethnic equity among the children, encouraging children to bridge the gaps between cultures and languages

These goals are naturally interdependent and relate to the individual student at differing levels, depending on his or her particular sociolinguistic and sociocultural background. For example, a native English-speaking child benefits by coming to understand that another language and culture hold equal importance to their own. A Spanish-speaking Latino child who is enrolled in a DL program is given equal school status due to knowledge of his or her home language rather than being penalized and segregated because of it.

Research evidence suggests that DL programs can be an excellent model for academic achievement for both language-minority and -majority children. Studies have shown DL programs to promote English-language learning as well as or better than other special programs designed for language-minority children. For example, 100% of Spanish-dominant children in the Key School, a 50/50 DL school in Arlington County, Virginia, demonstrated oral English fluency by 3rd grade, as shown by the LAS-O Oral English Proficiency measure and classroom observations (Center for Applied Linguistics, 2002). In a separate study of four DL schools following the 90:10 program model in California, it was found that by 5th grade most students were clearly fluent in English and made gains in English reading at most school sites (although they did not attain grade-level performance in reading; Lindholm, 1999).

Dual-language immersion programs appear to encourage achievement in academic subjects in both English and the minority languages. In an early study comparing DL students to a control population, Christian (1994) found that 3rd-graders from the Amigos Dual Immersion Program in Cambridge, Massachusetts, outperformed a Spanish-speaking cohort in a more conventional bilingual education program in reading and mathematics in both Spanish and English—using English-plus-Spanish (EPS) approaches. In fact, students in this program performed consistently at grade-level norms for children their age, which included children who spoke only English. This finding was replicated in another study conducted several years later at the Amigos school. Here, children from 4th through 8th grades performed consistently as well as, and often significantly better than control populations on standardized tests in both English and Spanish (Cazabon, Lambert, & Hall, 1999).

In another longitudinal study, Cobb, Vega, and Kronauge (2005) analyzed the effects of a DL elementary school program on academic achievement at the end of elementary school and at the end of the first year of junior high school. Achievements scores were obtained from standardized measures in reading, writing, and mathematics from native English speakers ($n = 83$) and native Spanish speakers ($n = 83$) from DL programs and matched controls, using an ex post facto quasi-experimental design. All students were continuously enrolled in their schools (experimental or control) for a minimum of 4 years before initial data collection. Participants were tracked from 3rd grade through middle school and were measured on their reading, writing, and mathematics achievement in 6th and 7th grades. Mean differences between groups were analyzed using a series of ANOVA. English and Spanish native speakers in DL programs scored as well or better than their peers in control groups. The greatest effect for native English speakers was in reading, while native Spanish speakers appeared to benefit more in writing and mathematics. Due to the small sample size in this study, however, it is difficult to assess the generalizability of their results.

As a follow-up to the longitudinal study by Sugarman and Howard (2001) study, Howard et al. (2003) summarized the research literature on DL programs, synthesizing key findings across studies and highlighting areas in need of further research. Specifically, they looked at studies analyzing achievement patterns of DL participants, language and literacy outcomes, the cultural context and social impact of DL programs, the integration of language-minority and language-majority students, language status issues, students' attitudes, teacher experiences, and parent attitudes and involvement. In terms of academic achievement and language and literacy development, they found that both native Spanish speakers and native English speakers in DL programs performed as well as or better than their peers educated in other types of programs, both on English standardized achievement tests and Spanish standardized achievement tests. Within DL programs, they found that native speakers tended to perform better than second-language learners, such that native English speakers scored higher on English achievement tests and native Spanish speakers scored higher on Spanish achievement tests. Moreover, balanced bilingual children, on average, outperformed other students. The authors mentioned, however, that many of the studies reviewed did not control sufficiently for student background, general quality of the school environment, and fidelity of program implementation. Nevertheless, the consistency of the findings across studies (of varying degrees in methodological rigor) suggests credibility.

Positive effects of DL programs have also been found for Latinos during the earliest years of schooling. Figueroa (2005) conducted a study with 24 Spanish-speaking kindergarteners (10 girls, 14 boys) in a DL program, looking at associations between the development of prereading knowledge in the child's native language and the development of English skills. The researcher examined means and standard deviations from tests of phonological reasoning and oral fluency during the fall of kindergarten, the winter of kindergarten, and the spring of kindergarten. She found that participants made significant gains in Spanish and English for every subtest of phonological awareness, in both languages, and at each of the three waves of data collection. Moreover, all participants met or exceeded district requirements. Though the sampling methods in this study don't allow for robust generalizations to the larger population of young Latino ELLs, the results support what we know regarding the relationships between first- and second-language acquisition: Meaningful use and development of the primary language in the early years facilitate prereading skills in a second language.

In an experimental study, Barnett, Yarosz, Thomas, and Blanco (2006) compared the effects of a DL and a monolingual English immersion (EI) preschool program on children's learning. Children in the study ($N = 150$) were from both English and Spanish home language backgrounds. Eighty-five were randomly assigned to the DL program, and 65 were randomly assigned to the EI program in the same school district. The two programs were compared on measures of children's growth in language, emergent literacy, and mathematics. Compared to those in the EI group, children in the DL program produced large and significant gains in Spanish vocabulary. In addition, all children (including native Spanish- and native English-speakers) in the DL program made greater phonological awareness gains in English, yet no group differences were found on measures of English-language and literacy development. This study, therefore, suggests that early DL programs can provide support for native-language development without sacrificing gains in English-language development. Moreover, English-native children in the DL program also made gains in Spanish language and literacy without hindering native-language development. Additional analyses would be needed to determine the longitudinal impact of preschool DL programs on literacy development and academic outcomes throughout the elementary years.

Thus, the present knowledge base demonstrates that DL programs bear positive achievement outcomes for both language-minority and language-majority students, especially for young children developing fundamental language and literacy skills. Research supports the notion that higher-order cognitive and literacy skills transfer between languages, that developing native language skills can improve second-language skills, and that the DL program model corresponds well with these findings.

Prekindergarten

Across the United States, policymakers at all levels of government are making substantial investments and commitments to prekindergarten programs (for children ages 3 and 4). The provision of high-quality educational access for young children in the country is motivated by research in child development and economics. In terms of development, neuropsychological research shows that the brains of very young children are extremely malleable during the early years of life (Ramey & Ramey, 1998; Shonkoff & Phillips, 2000). Indeed, a key characteristic of early childhood (0–3 years old) is the remarkably rapid brain development that occurs during this period. In many ways, these early years provide the foundation for the brain's lifelong capacity for growth and change. A strong neurological groundwork is established in early childhood through rich experiences that allow the brain to develop to the point of being able to process, encode, and interact with the environment (Goncz & Kodzepeljic, 1991). High-quality early education programs are able to provide the necessary scaffolding and facilitate this development.

With regard to the financial investment in early education programs, economists Heckman and Masterov (2004) found that "enriched prekindergarten programs available to disadvantaged children on a voluntary basis . . . have [a] strong track record of promoting achievement for disadvantaged children, improving their labor market outcomes and reducing involvement in crime" (p. 68). Moreover, educational policies that stress financial investment in early educational development are much cheaper than those that seek to remedy early educational deficits at the middle school and high school levels. Simply stated, the later in life attempts are made to repair early deficits, the costlier remediation becomes (Ramey & Ramey, 1998; Reynolds, 2003; Reynolds & Temple, 2005).

Given their size, rapid growth, and comparatively low achievement levels, young Latino children are situated particularly well to benefit from high-quality prekindergarten programs (García & González, 2006). However, although enrollments among Latinos are increasing, they are less likely than their White, Asian, and African American peers to attend any sort of preschool program (García et al., 2005). Given the potential benefits of prekindergarten programs, efforts are currently being made to increase enrollments of Latino children in high-quality programs.

Current empirical evidence suggests that young Latino children benefit cognitively from such programs. An evaluation of the public prekindergarten program in Tulsa, Oklahoma, found benefits for all racial/ethnic and SES groups (Gormley, Gayer, & Dawson, 2004). Gains for Latino students in this program were especially impressive. Latinos experienced a 79% gain in letter-word identification, a 39% gain in spelling, and a 54% gain in applied problem solving. These gains outpaced those that naturally would have occurred during 1 year of children's development (ibid.).

High-Quality, Effective Teachers. The provision of rich language environments and high-quality dual-language programs across the pre-K-3 spectrum necessitates high-quality, effective teachers. This means teachers who are bilingual, proficient in both English and Spanish, and knowledgeable regarding the cultural and linguistic circumstances of Latino families, particularly the educational strengths and needs of their children. Indeed, research shows that the transfer of academic skills between languages is heightened and early achievement outcomes increased for young bilingual and emergent bilingual students when teachers use Spanish in the classroom (García, 2005). The most successful teachers are fluent in both languages, understand learning patterns associated with second-language acquisition, have a mastery of appropriate instructional strategies (i.e., cooperative learning, sheltered instruction, differentiated instruction, and strategic teaching), and have strong organizational and communication skills (García et al., 2006). With these skills, teachers will be able to interact with Latino parents appropriately, encouraging them to engage in literacy activities with their children at home; they will be able to find out as much detail as possible about the linguistic backgrounds of their students; and they will be able to develop creative and accurate assessments of the each child's linguistic ability and development.

Relevant to high-quality, effective teaching for young Latinos, Vaughn, Linan-Thompson, Pollard-Durodola, Mathes, & Hagan (2006) offer a few research-based principles to guide reading instruction for ELL Latino children. These highlight the need to use many commonalities between reading instruction in English and Spanish to design reading programs; to recognize the complexity of English reading—i.e., phonics and word reading—compared to Spanish and that English literacy will require more explicit instruction; to make connections between students' knowledge in Spanish and its application to English; to offer as many opportunities as possible for students to use oral language (in Spanish or English) to address higher-order questions; to capitalize on all opportunities to teach and engage in vocabulary and concept building; and to organize effective use of peer and cooperative group work to enhance learning.

The optimal situation is for lead teachers and school staff in general to be proficient in both languages and familiar with students' cultures. However, when this is not possible, it is recommended that a "language specialist" be provided. Language specialists are bilingual professionals who serve as consultants to teachers and aides in the classroom to help ELL Latino students learn and achieve, recognizing and leveraging existent strengths. A language specialist in the classroom would also help monolingual teachers make essential links with Spanish-speaking parents (National Task Force on Early Childhood Education for Hispanics, 2007).

School-Level Leadership. Latino parents and families continue to rely on effective leaders to provide educational opportunity for their children. Scholars of educational leadership have convincingly argued that effective school and district leadership is far more than the acquisition of technical management skills. Leadership in successful schools and districts where achievement gaps are being closed require leaders who can build community in and around schools. These leaders exhibit a social and political consciousness that informs organizational visions and drive leaders' actions and decisions. They have an ability to create and foster connections among stakeholders within and around schools and districts. In fact, characteristic of educational leaders who successfully advocate for Latino school communities are their capacity as hybrid border-crossers (Lopez, Gonzalez, & Fierro, 2006), as "bridge people" with personal and professional commitments to school communities (Merchant & Shoho, 2006), and as caring advocates of social justice (Scheurich, 1998; Scheurich & Skrla, 2003). Such conceptions of leadership challenge historic administrative practices that have marginalized communities of color by silencing their voices in school and district decision making or through culturally irrelevant pedagogy, and by reproducing deficit perspectives (Valencia, 1997) or "subtractive" schooling (Valenzuela, 1999) evidenced in policies, practices and organizational structures.

The influence of effective leaders of Latino-serving schools and districts reaches beyond organizational boundaries—spanning linguistic, cultural, and social borders. Such leaders use their influence to proactively engage communities, mobilizing organizational, political, and cultural resources to meet the needs of students and families (Reyes, Scribner, & Paredes Scribner, 1999). In their study of educational leadership along the U.S.-Mexico border, Lopez and colleagues (2006) trace how a successful school leader "took his blinders off" and took political risks to mobilize parent political involvement in district politics in the interest of dual-language programming. The authors argue that leaders like this understand (many due to their own personal experiences) that schools can be catalysts for democratic communities (Lopez et al., 2006). Thus, school leaders make connections between school, district, and community resources in order to develop and connect school programming to student and family needs. They also tap into community services and family assets (such as home language, cultural knowledge, or political support) in order to build the necessary capacity to effectively serve Latino school communities (ibid.). As a result, these kinds of leaders exemplify a "hybrid" style of leading "that blurs the rigidity between the school and the community, the professional and the political, the personal and the social, the leaders and the supporter and the self and other" (ibid., p. 77). Lopez and his colleagues (2006) describe this dimension of leadership this way:

> It is a way of thinking and working with others, a motivation to challenge oppressive systems, a desire to work toward social justice ends, and a willingness to take personal as well as professional risks to ensure that justice is being served. This mind-set requires leaders to step outside their proverbial comfort zones and examine the possibilities that become available when one crosses cultural and social borders and engages the community in such a critical fashion. (p. 77)

Merchant and Shoho (2006) describe leaders who made a difference in Latino school communities as "bridge people" who create "bridges between themselves and others for the purposes of improving the lives of all those with whom they work" (p. 86). Again, these leaders believe in the notion that educational attainment and social justice are inextricably linked and that being bridge people is inherently a political endeavor. This leadership perspective assumes that leaders know and understand both the community served by the school—its social, cultural and political histories—as well as how policy and practices can impact—and have impacted—such communities. This requires that leaders at both the district and the building levels, question traditional measures of success and support multiple methods and authentic measures of teaching and learning.

Leading and cultivating successful school communities in the interest of social justice also require that leaders not only take their own blinders off but that they also make visible damaging disparities in educational programming and student achievement (Scheurich & Skrla, 2003; Skrla, Scheurich, García, & Nolly, 2004). Such disparities include teacher quality, curricular programming, or students' opportunities to learn, as well as student achievement. Skrla and her colleagues (2004) suggest that leaders conduct "equity audits" to uncover concrete examples of inequitable practices and engage stakeholders in difficult conversations necessary to address the disparities.

Leadership is inherently a moral endeavor. The moral dimensions of educational leadership must embody an ethic of community (Furman, 2004) that "shifts the locus of moral agency to the community as a whole." This means that leadership is distributed across the school community and rests on such skills as "listening with respect; striving for knowing and understanding others; communicating effectively; working in teams; engaging in ongoing dialogue; and creating forums that allow all voices to be heard" (p. 222). Leaders in multicultural, traditionally underserved school communities may do well to shed corporate, individualistic models of leadership and adopt community-oriented models (Larson & Murtadha, 2002). Scheurich (1998) identified core beliefs that reflect a communal and caring leadership ethic in highly successful Latino-serving schools, including a strong, shared vision; loving, caring environments for children and adults; collaborative culture; innovation and openness to new ideas; and collective responsibility for the success of all students.

These and other characteristics support the tenet that successful school leaders are more than technocrats. While facility with and an understanding of data are crucial in today's accountability environment, leaders must also be skilled in relationship building (bridge people), must have and be able to mobilize a diverse body of cultural knowledge in order to cross organizational, community and personal borders, and must be committed to the belief that schools can be catalysts for democratic communities. At the district level, this requires leaders to build a professional community among staff and building leaders that supports creative and responsive programming and advocacy.

Summary

The United States has long been a nation of incredible cultural and linguistic diversity. The trend toward ethnic and racial population diversification continues most rapidly among young and school-age children. In 2005, 25% of the birth cohort in the United States, some 1 million newborns, was Latino, with more than 70% born to mothers whose primary language was Spanish. Nationwide, White, non-Latino student enrollment has decreased since 1976 by 13%, or a total of 5 million students.

Therefore, as U.S. educators welcome students to their classrooms, they frequently see a picture much different from the images of their own childhoods. Academic achievement gaps for this diverse population, especially those who come to school speaking no English, are present at the beginning of kindergarten, become more solidified at grades 3 through 8, and are realized dramatically by significantly lower high school completion and college attendance rates. Moreover, today's population continues to have deep concerns about the quality of education; the public has acted at the federal level and state levels to mount educational policies directed at these achievement gaps.

These children bring a set of welcomed assets to the education process. They are more likely to live in two-parent families, to have strong family support systems that utilize extended members of the family, to demonstrate better early health practices and outcomes than their socioeconomic peers, to hold as most positive the role of education in advancing their lives as a whole, and, most significantly, to be willing to work hard in and out of educational environments to advance their learning opportunities (National Task Force on Early Childhood Education for Hispanics, 2007).

Education Practices That Count

Many of these specific reform initiatives have been aimed at linguistically and culturally diverse students for several decades. These reforms have generated some movement at the policy, practice, and achievement levels. Unfortunately, "reform" as it has been implemented to date has not produced the needed robust changes in academic performance. These reforms have ignored what counts for the academic success of these students:

- They speak a language other than English, and that cannot be ignored in the construction of core academic curriculum and related instruction.

- They must acquire high levels of academic vocabulary, discourse, and inquiry in English associated with all academic content areas.

- They come from immigrant backgrounds and tend to reside in families in which success in formal education in the United States or the sending countries is not an attribute.

- Their own cultural and linguistic contexts are critical ingredients in forming a bridge to developed understandings of academic concepts.

New educational practices that have the following characteristics are beginning to demonstrate significant promise for young Latino students:

- Strategies that begin with the linguistic and cultural attributes of the students and build from there; they respect and engage previous knowledge bases regarding the student and cultural conceptualizations of academic content areas.

- Strategies directly responsive to the utilization of the linguistic background of the student, which forms a bridge to high levels of vocabulary, concept, and repertoires in English.

- Strategies that assess development and learning in various ways and that are utilized for changes in instructional architectures and delivery.

- Strategies that utilize multiple resources—human, fiscal, physical, temporal, and technological—to address instruction.

- Strategies that reflect a collaborative culture and encourage a communal, caring leadership ethic throughout Latino-serving school districts/schools.

- Strategies that empower all members of Latino-serving school districts/schools to succeed at what they do well.

- Strategies that uncover concrete examples of inequitable practices and encourage all stakeholders to engage in conversations necessary to address these practices.

- Strategies that promote community-oriented models in which leaders are skilled in relationship building, shared decision making, and mobilizing the diverse body of cultural knowledge that exists within Latino-serving school districts/schools.

Conducting New Research to Inform Educational Strategy Development Efforts

Currently available information on achievement patterns of Latino children, as well as on factors that influence those patterns, can contribute a great deal to long-term-oriented strategy design, testing, and evaluation efforts. (See Miller & García [2008] for a more extensive review.) This is the case not only for efforts concerned with improving literacy achievement among low SES and ELL children but also for those directed to high-SES & middle-class youngsters (García & Miller, 2008). There are important gaps in the research base that carefully designed studies should be able to help close and, in the process, inform the strategy development work. For example, one area of need is for extensive research on language development opportunities available in low-SES, middle-class, and high-SES Latino homes. As was discussed earlier, there is evidence that low-SES, middle-class, and high-SES Latino parents are somewhat less likely than their White counterparts to read frequently to their children. There also is some evidence that low-SES, middle-class, and high-SES Latino children lag behind their White counterparts on some measures of reading readiness, and that there may be substantial differences in the vocabularies of middle-class and high-SES Latino and White children as early as age 3. However, actual in-home observational data on oral language and emergent literacy environments in low-SES, middle-class, and high-SES homes is limited. Indeed, such information is really not available for any racial/ethnic group for each of these social class levels for a relatively large, nationally representative sample of children and parents. Furthermore, as also was discussed earlier, there is conflicting evidence on the sizes of the readiness differences at the start of kindergarten and on how those differences evolve from a reading skills and achievement standpoint in the primary grades.

Some evidence was presented earlier in this report that there are differences in emergent-literacy-oriented parenting practices between Spanish-speaking and English-speaking Hispanic parents, and that these differences cut across social class lines to some extent. However, observational data are not available for representative samples of Latinos, including for different national-origin segments, such as Mexican Americans and Cuban Americans. In a related vein, there is little information on why such differences exist.

In addition, little information is available regarding the extent to which reading readiness and reading achievement patterns may vary according to whether children are from first, second, third, or later generations of low-SES, middle-class, or high-SES families—and whether there also are significant generational differences in parenting practices. For example, it is unclear how parenting practices and other education-related family resources may vary among Mexican American families in which the parents are the first, second, or third generations to have a bachelor's degree or higher. (That is the case for other racial/ethnic groups as well, including Whites.) If there are large generational differences, and high percentages of Mexican American parents with college degrees are the first generation in their families to hold a bachelor's degree, current research may be underestimating the amount of intergenerational progress taking place among college-educated parents from these groups.

In a related vein, are the language development opportunities in preschools that serve mostly low-SES Latino children geared mainly to youngsters who are behind in vocabulary development and in other areas of emergent literacy? If so, are the vocabulary development and emergent-literacy opportunities often too limited for children who are average or above average in these areas? Social class and cultural differences may also negatively influence interactions between children and educators as early as the preschool years. For instance, this could be a problem for ELL Latino children. Consequently, observational information is needed on interactions between the educators and the children over a period of several years—from the start of preschool through 4th grade. It may be necessary to examine experiences in infant/toddler programs in this area as well.

CONCLUSION

There are many central themes to this chapter, all of which are framed in the educational and linguistic experiences of young children from homes in which English is not the primary language, with an emphasis on young Latino students. Again, the report concludes with recommendations for programmatic design features, which are proffered based on our comprehensive assessment of the various programs available for bilingual students and children learning English as a second language. These recommendations range from strategies that begin with the linguistic and cultural attributes of the students and build from there—they respect and engage previous knowledge bases regarding the student and cultural conceptualizations of academic content areas—to strategies that promote community-oriented models in which leaders are skilled in relationship building, shared decision making, and mobilizing the diverse body of cultural knowledge that exists within Latino-serving school districts/schools. A final recommendation argues for the heuristic value of educational strategy development.

The United States has long been a nation of incredible cultural and linguistic diversity. The trend toward ethnic and racial population diversification continues most rapidly among its young and school-age children. In 2005, 25% of the birth cohort in the United States, some 1 million newborns, was Latino, with more than 70% born to mothers whose primary language was Spanish. Nationwide, White, non-Latino student enrollment has decreased since 1976 by 13%, or a total of 5 million students.

Therefore, as U.S. educators welcome students to their classrooms, they frequently see a picture much different from the images of their own childhoods. Academic achievement gaps for this diverse population, especially those who come to school speaking no English, are present at the beginning of kindergarten, become more solidified at grades 3 through 8, and are realized dramatically by significantly lower high school completion and college attendance rates. Moreover, today's population continues to have deep concerns about the quality of education; the public has acted at the federal and state levels to mount educational policies directed at these achievement gaps.

These children bring a set of welcomed assets to the education process. They are more likely to live in two-parent families, to have strong family support systems that utilize extended members of the family, to demonstrate better early health practices and outcomes than their socioeconomic peers, to hold as most positive the role of education in advancing their lives as a whole; and, most significantly, to be willing to work hard in and out of educational environments to advance their learning opportunities (National Task Force on Early Childhood Education for Hispanics, 2007).

References

Artiles, A. J., Rueda, R., Salazar, J. J., & Higareda, I. (2002). English-language learner representation in special education in California urban school districts. In D. J. Losen & G. Orfield (Eds.), *Race inequity in special education* (pp. 117–136). Cambridge, MA: Harvard Education Press.

Atwill, K., Blanchard, J., Gorin, J., & Burnstein, K. (2006). *The influence of language proficiency on cross-language transfer of phonemic awareness in kindergarten Spanish-speaking children.* Paper presented at the annual conference for the American Education Research Association, San Francisco, CA.

August, D., Calderón, M., & Carlo, M. (2002). *Transfer of skills from Spanish to English: A study of young learners.* Washington, DC: Center for Applied Linguistics.

August, D., Calderón, M., Carlo, M., & Nuttall, M. (2006). Developing literacy in English-language learners: An examination of the impact of English-only versus bilingual instruction. In P. D. McCardle & E. Hoff (Eds.), *Childhood bilingualism: Research on infancy through school age.* Clevedon, UK: Multilingual Matters Limited.

August, D., & Shanahan, T. (Eds.). (2006). *Developing literacy in second language learners: Report of the national literacy panel on language minority youth and children.* Mahwah, NJ: Lawrence Erlbaum.

Baker, K. A., & de Kanter, A. A. (1981). *Effectiveness of bilingual education: A review of the literature.* Washington, DC: U.S. Department of Education.

Baker, K. A., & Pelavin, S. (1984). *Problems in bilingual education.* Paper presented at the annual meeting of the American Education Research Association, New Orleans, LA.

Barnett, W. S., Yarosz, D. J., Thomas, J., & Blanco, D. (2006). *Two-way and monolingual English immersion in preschool education: An experimental comparison.* New Brunswick, NJ: National Institute for Early Education Research.

Borman, G. D., Hewes, G. H., Reilly, M., & Alvarado, S. (2006). *Comprehensive school reform for Latino elementary-school students: A meta-analysis.* Commissioned by the National Task Force on Early Childhood Education for Hispanics. Madison: University of Wisconsin.

Braswell, J., Daane, M., & Grigg, W. (2003). *The nation's report card: Mathematics highlights 2003* (NCES 2004451).Washington, DC: U.S. Department of Education.

Capps, R., Fix, M., Ost, J., Reardon-Anderson, J., & Passel, J. (2004). *The health and well-being of young children of immigrants.* Washington, DC: The Urban Institute.

Cazabon, M., Lambert, W., & Hall, G. (1999). *Two-way bilingual education: A report on the Amigos Program.* Washington, DC: Center for Applied Linguistics.

Center for Applied Linguistics (CAL). (2002). *Directory of two-way bilingual immersion programs in the U.S.* Retrieved March 26, 2009, from http://www.cal.org/twi/directory

Center for Applied Linguistics (CAL). (2005, March). *Guiding principles for dual- language education.* Washington, DC: Author.

Christian, D. (1994). *Two-way bilingual education: Students learning through two languages.* Washington, DC: Center for Applied Linguistics.

Cobb, B., Vega, D., & Kronauge, C. (2005). *Effects of an elementary dual language immersion school program on junior high school achievement of native Spanish speaking and native English speaking students.* Paper presented at the American Education Research Association annual conference in Montreal, Canada.

Collier, V. (1989). How long? A synthesis of research on academic achievement in a second language. *TESOL Quarterly, 23,* 509–531.

Collier, V. P. (1987). Age and rate of acquisition of second language for academic purposes. *TESOL Quarterly, 21*(4), 617–641.

Collier, V. P. (1995). Acquiring a second language for school. *Directions in Language and Education, 1*(4), 1–12.

Cuéllar, D. (2008). *There will only be English in kindergarten: The emergent literacy cultural models that Mexican-American Spanish-dominant Head Start preschoolers encounter at home and school.* Unpublished doctoral dissertation, Arizona State University, Tempe.

Cummins, J. (1981). The role of primary language development in promoting educational success for language minority students. In California State Department of Education (Ed.), *Schooling and language minority students: A theoretical framework.* Los Angeles: National Dissemination and Assessment Center.

Dressler, C., & Kamil, M. (2006). First- and second-language literacy. In D. August & T. Shanahan (Eds.), *Report of the national literacy panel on language minority youth and children.* Mahwah, NJ: Lawrence Erlbaum.

Durgunoglu, A. Y., Nagy, W. E., & Hancin-Bhatt, B. J. (1993). Cross-language transfer of phonological awareness. *Journal of Educational Psychology, 85*(3), 453–465.

Escarce, J., Morales, L., & Rumbaut, R. (2006). Health status and health behaviors of Latinos. In M. Tienda & F. Mitchell (Eds.), *Multiple origins, common destinies: Latinos and the American future.* Washington, DC: National Research Council.

Figueroa, L. (2005). *The development of pre-reading knowledge in English and Spanish: Latino English language learners in a dual-language education context.* Paper presented at the American Education Research Association annual conference in Montreal, Canada.

Furman, G. (2004). The ethic of community. *Journal of Educational Administration, 42*(2), 215–235.

García, G. E., (1991). Factors influencing the English reading test performance of Spanish-speaking Hispanic children. *Reading Research Quarterly, 26*(4), 371–392.

García, E. E. (2005). *Teaching and learning in two languages: Bilingualism and schooling in the United States.* New York: Teachers College Press.

García, E. E., & González, D. (2006). *Pre-K and Latinos: The foundation for America's future.* Washington, DC: Pre-K Now.

García, E. E., Jensen, B. T., & Cuéllar, D. (2006). Early academic achievement of Hispanics in the United States: Implications for teacher preparation. *The New Educator, 2,* 123–147.

García, E. E., Jensen, B. T., Miller, L. S., & Huerta, T. (2005). *Early childhood education of Hispanics in the United States.* Tempe, AZ: The National Task Force on Early Childhood Education for Hispanics. Available online at http://www.ecehispanic.org/work/white_paper_Oct2005.pdf

García, E. E., & Miller, L. S. (2008). Findings and recommendations of the National Task Force on Early Childhood Education for Hispanics. *Child Development Perspectives, 2*(2), 53–58.

Genesee, F. (Ed.). (1999). *Program alternatives for linguistically diverse students.* Santa Cruz: Center for Research on Education, Diversity & Excellence (CREDE), University of California.

Genesee, F. (2003). *The capacity of language faculty: Contributions from studies of simultaneous bilingual acquisition.* Paper presented at the 4th International Symposium on Bilingualism, Tempe, AZ.

Genesee, F., Geva, E., Dressler, C., & Kamil, M. (2006). Synthesis: Cross-linguistic relationships. In D. August & T. Shanahan (Eds.), *Report of the national literacy panel on language minority youth and children.* Mahwah, NJ: Lawrence Erlbaum.

Geva, E., & Genesee, F. (2006). First-language oral proficiency and second-language literacy. In D. August & T. Shanahan (Eds.), *Report of the national literacy panel on language minority youth and children.* Mahwah, NJ: Lawrence Erlbaum.

Glass, G. V., McGaw, B., & Smith, M. L. (1981). *Meta-analysis in social research.* Beverly Hills, CA: Sage.

Goldenberg, C., Gallimore, R., Reese, L., & Garnier, H. (2001). Cause or effect? A longitudinal study of immigrant Latino parents' aspirations and expectations and their children's' school performance. *American Educational Research Journal, 38,* 547–582.

Goldenberg, C., Rezaei, A., & Fletcher, J. (2005). *Home use of English and Spanish and Spanish-speaking children's oral language and literacy achievement*. Paper presented at the annual meeting of the American Educational Research Association, Montreal, Canada.

Goldenberg, C., Rueda, R., & August, D. (2006). Synthesis: Sociocultural contexts and literacy development. In D. August & T. Shanahan (Eds.), *Report of the national literacy panel on language minority youth and children*. Mahwah, NJ: Lawrence Erlbaum.

Goldman, S. R., Reyes, M., & Varnhagen, C. K. (1984). Understanding fables in first and second languages. *Journal of the National Association for Bilingual Education, 8*, 835–866.

Goncz, B., & Kodzepeljic, D. (1991). Cognition and bilingualism revisited. *Journal of Multicultural Development, 12*, 137–163.

Gormley, W., Gayer, T., & Dawson, B. (2004). *The effects of universal pre-K on cognitive development*. Washington, DC: Public Policy Institute, Georgetown University.

Greene, J. P. (1998). *A meta-analysis of the effectiveness of bilingual education*. Claremont, CA: Tomás Rivera Policy Institute.

Gross, D., Conrad, B., Fogg, L., Willis, L., & Garvey, C. (1993). What does the NCATS (Nursing Child Assessment Teaching Scale) measure? *Nursing Research, 42*(5), 260–265.

Hakuta, K., Goto Butler, Y., & Witt, D. (2000). *How long does it take English learners to attain proficiency?* University of California Linguistic Minority Research Institute Policy Report 2000–1. Santa Barbara: University of California Linguistic Minority Research Institute.

Heckman, J., & Masterov, D. (2004). *The productivity argument for investing in young children*. Chicago: Committee for Economic Development.

Hernandez, D. (2006). *Young Hispanic children in the U.S.: A demographic portrait based on Census 2000*. A report to the National Task Force on Early Childhood Education for Hispanics. Albany: State University of New York.

Hernandez, D. J., Denton, N. A., & Macartney, S. E. (2007). Young Hispanic children in the 21st century. *Journal of Latinos and Education, 6*(3), 209–228.

Howard, E. R., Sugarman, J., & Christian, D. (2003). *Trends in two-way immersion education: A review of the research*. Washington, DC: Center for Applied Linguistics.

Huerta-Macías, A., & Quintero, E. (1992). Code-switching, bilingualism, and biliteracy: A case study. *Bilingual Research Journal, 16*(3–4), 69–90.

Jensen, B. T. (2007). The relationship between Spanish use in the classroom and the mathematics achievement of Spanish-speaking kindergartners. *Journal of Latinos and Education, 6*(3), 267–280.

Jensen, B. T. (2008). Immigration and language policy. In J. González (Ed.), *Encyclopedia of bilingual education* (pp. 372–377). Thousand Oaks, CA: Sage.

Jiménez, R. T., García, G. E., & Pearson, D. P. (1996). The reading strategies of bilingual Latina/o students who are successful English readers: Opportunities and obstacles. *Reading Research Quarterly, 31*(1), 90–112.

Kohnert, K., & Bates, E. (2002). Balancing bilinguals II: Lexical comprehension and cognitive processing in children learning Spanish and English. *Journal of Speech, Language, and Hearing Research, 45*, 347–359.

Larson, C. & Murtadha, K. (2002). Leadership for social justice. In J. Murphy (Ed.), *The educational leadership challenge: Redefining leadership for the 21st century* (pp. 134–151). Chicago: National Society for the Study of Education.

Lau v. Nichols, 414 U.S. 563 (1974).

Lesaux, N., & Geva, E. (2006). Synthesis: Development of literacy in language minority students. In D. August & T. Shanahan (Eds.), *Report of the national literacy panel on language minority youth and children*. Mahwah, NJ: Lawrence Erlbaum.

Lesaux, N., Koda, K., Siegel, L., & Shanahan, T. (2006). Development of literacy. In D. August & T. Shanahan (Eds.), *Report of the national literacy panel on language minority youth and children*. Mahwah, NJ: Lawrence Erlbaum.

Lindholm, K. J. (1999). *Two-way bilingual education: Past and future*. Paper presented at the meeting of the American Education Research Association, Toronto, Canada.

Lopez, G. R., Gonzalez, M. L., & Fierro, E. (2006). Educational leadership along the U.S.-Mexico border: Crossing borders/embracing hybridity/building bridges. In C. Marshall & M. Oliva (Eds.), *Leadership for social justice: Making revolutions in education* (pp. 64–84). Boston: Pearson.

López, M., Barrueco, S., & Miles, J. (2006). *Latino infants and families: A national perspective of protective and risk factors for development*. A report to the National Task Force on Early Childhood Education for Hispanics. Tempe: Arizona State University.

Merchant, B. M., & Shoho, A. R. (2006). Bridge people: Civic and educational leadership for social justice. In C. Marshall & M. Oliva (Eds.), *Leadership for social justice: Making revolutions in education* (pp. 85–109). Boston: Pearson.

Miller, L. S., & García, E. E. (2008). *Report of a reading-focused early childhood education research and strategy development agenda for African Americans and Hispanics at all social class levels who are English speakers or English language learners.* Tempe: Arizona State University.

Mitchell, D., Destino, T., & Karam, R. (1997). *Evaluation and English language development programs in Santa Ana Unified School District: A report on data system reliability and statistical modeling of program impacts.* Riverside: University of California, California Educational Research Cooperative.

Montemayor, R., & Mendoza, H. (2004). *Right before our eyes: Latinos past, present, and future.* Tempe, AZ: Scholarly Publishing.

Nagy, W. E., García, G. E., Durgunoglu, A. Y., & Hancin-Bhatt, B. (1993). Spanish-English bilingual students' use of cognates in English reading. *Journal of Reading Behavior, 25*(3), 165–190.

Nagy, W. E., McClure, E. F., & Mir, M. (1997). Linguistic transfer and the use of context by Spanish-English bilinguals. *Applied Psycholinguistics, 18*(4), 431–452.

National Center for Education Statistics (NCES). (1995). *Approaching kindergarten: A look at preschoolers in the United States.* National household survey. Washington, DC: U.S. Department of Education.

National Center for Education Statistics (NCES). (2001). *User's manual for the ECLS-K base year public-use data files and electronic codebook* (NCES 2001–029 [revised]). Washington, DC: Author.

National Center for Education Statistics (NCES). (2003). *Status and trends in the education of Hispanics* (NCES 2003–007). Washington, DC: U.S. Government Printing Office.

National Clearinghouse for English Language Acquisition (NCELA). (2006). *The growing numbers of limited English proficient students: 1993–94–2003/04.* Washington, DC: U.S. Department of Education.

National Task Force on Early Childhood Education for Hispanics. (2007). *Report of expanding and improving education for Hispanics.* Tempe: Arizona State University.

Nord, C. W., Lennon, J., Liu, B., & Chandler, K. (1999). *Home literacy activities and signs of children's emerging literacy, 1993 and 1999* (NCES 20000–026). Washington, DC: US Department of Education. Retrieved July 13, 2006, from http://nces.ed.gov/pubs2000/2000026.pdf

Nuñez, A., Cuccaro-Alamin, S., & Carroll, C. D. (1998). *First-generation students: Undergraduates whose parents never enrolled in postsecondary education.* Washington, DC: U.S. Department of Education.

Ovando, C., Collier, V., & Combs, V. (2006). *Bilingual and ESL classrooms: Teaching in multicultural contexts* (4th ed.). New York: McGraw-Hill.

Perez, P., & Zarate, M. E. (2006). *Latino public opinion survey of pre-kindergarten programs: Knowledge, preferences, and public support.* Los Angeles: Tomás Rivera Policy Institute.

Quiroga, T., Lemos-Britton, Z., Mostafapour, E., Abbott, R. D., & Berninger, V. W. (2002). Phonological awareness and beginning reading in Spanish-speaking ESL first graders: Research into practice. *Journal of School Psychology, 40*(1), 85–111.

Ramey, C., & Ramey, S. (1998). Early intervention and early experience. *American Psychologist, 53*(2), 109–120.

Ramirez, R. R., & de la Cruz, G. P. (2003). *The Hispanic population in the United States: March 2002.* Current Population Reports, P20–539. Washington, DC: U.S. Census Bureau.

Reardon, S. (2003). *Sources of educational inequality: The growth of racial/ethnic and socioeconomic test score gaps in kindergarten and first grade.* State College: Pennsylvania State University Population Research Institute.

Reardon, S., & Galindo, C. (2006). *K-3 academic achievement patterns and trajectories of Hispanics and other racial/ethnic groups.* Paper presented at the Annual AERA Conference, San Francisco.

Reese, L., Garnier, H., Gallimore, R., & Goldenberg, C. (2000). Longitudinal analysis of the antecedents of emergent Spanish literacy and middle-school English reading achievement of Spanish-speaking students. *American Educational Research Journal, 37*(3), 633–662.

Reyes, P., Scribner, J. D., & Paredes Scribner, A. (1999). *Lessons from high-performing Latino schools: Creating learning communities.* New York: Teachers College Press.

Reynolds, A. (2003). The added value of continuing early intervention into the primary grades. In A. Reynolds, M. Wang, & H. Walberg (Eds.), *Early childhood programs for a new century.* Washington, DC: CWLA Press.

Reynolds, A., & Temple, J. (2005). Priorities for a new century of early childhood programs. *Infants & Young Children, 18*(2), 104–118.

Risley, T. R., & Hart, B. (2006). Promoting early language development. In N. F. Watt, C. Ayoub, R. H. Bradley, J. E. Puma, & W. A. Lebeouf (Eds.), *The crisis in young mental health: Early intervention programs and policies.* Westport, CT: Praeger.

Rolstad, K., Mahoney, K., & Glass, G. V. (2005). The big picture: A meta-analysis of program effectiveness research on English language learners. *Educational Policy, 19*(4), 572–594.

Rosenthal, A. S., Baker, K., & Ginsburg, A. (1983). The effect of language background on achievement level and learning among elementary school students. *Sociology in Education, 56*(4), 157–169.

Royer, J. M., & Carlo, M. S. (1991). Transfer of comprehension skills from native to second language. *Journal of Reading, 34*(6), 450–455.

Scheffner Hammer, C., & Miccio, A. (2004). Home literacy experiences of Latino families. In B. H. Wasik (Ed.), *Handbook of Family Literacy*. Mahwah, NJ: Lawrence Erlbaum.

Scheurich, J. J. (1998). Highly successful and loving, public elementary schools populated mainly by low-SES children of color: Core beliefs and cultural characteristics. *Urban Education, 33*(4), 451–491.

Scheurich, J. J., & Skrla, L. (2003). *Leadership for equity and excellence: Creating high achievement classes, schools and districts*. Thousand Oaks, CA: Corwin Press.

Shannon, S. M. (1995). The hegemony of English: A case study of one bilingual classroom as a site of resistance. *Linguistics and Education, 7*(3), 175–200.

Shields, M., & Behrman, R. (2004). Children of immigrant families: Analysis and recommendations. *The Future of Children, 14*(2), 4–15.

Shonkoff, J. P., & Phillips, D. A. (2000). *From neurons to neighborhoods: The science of early childhood development*. Washington, DC: National Academy Press.

Skrla, L., Scheurich, J., García, J., & Nolly, G. (2004). Equity audits: A practical tool for developing equitable and excellent schools. *Educational Administration Quarterly, 40*(1), 133–161.

Slavin, R. E. (1986). Best-evidence synthesis: An alternative to meta-analysis and traditional reviews. *Educational Researcher, 15*(9), 5–11.

Slavin, R. E., & Cheung, A. (2005). A synthesis of research on language of reading instruction for English language learners. *Review of Education Research, 75*(2), 247–284.

Sugarman, J., & Howard, L. (2001, September). Two-way immersion shows promising results: Findings from a new study. *Language Links* [online newsletter of the Center for Applied Linguistics]. Retrieved March 8, 2009, from http://www.cal.org/resources/archive/langlink/0901.html

Tabors, P. O. (1997). *One child, two languages: A guide for preschool educators of children learning English as a second language*. Baltimore: Brookes.

Tabors, P. O., & Snow, C. E. (2002). Young bilingual children and early literacy development. In S. B. Neuman & D. K. Dickinson (Eds.), *Handbook of early literacy research*. New York: Guilford Press.

Valencia, R. R. (Ed.). (1997). *The evolution of deficit thinking*. London: Falmer Press.

Valenzuela, A. (1999). *Subtractive Schooling: U.S. Mexican Youth and the Politics of Caring*. Albany: State University of New York Press.

Vaughn, S., Linan-Thompson, S., Pollard-Durodola, S., Mathes, P., & Hagan, E. C. (2006). Effective interventions for English language learners (Spanish-English) at risk for difficulties. In D. K. Dickinson & S. B. Neuman (Eds.), *Handbook of early literacy research* (Vol. 2). New York: Guilford Press.

Vygotsky, L. S. (1978). *Mind in society: The development of higher psychological processes*. Cambridge, MA: President and Fellows of Harvard College.

Willig, A. C. (1985). A meta-analysis of selected studies on the effectiveness of bilingual education. *Review of Educational Research, 55*(3), 269–317.

17

PARENTING INTERVENTIONS AND LATINO FAMILIES

Research Findings, Cultural Adaptations, and Future Directions

LUIS H. ZAYAS, JOAQUIN BORREGO, JR., AND MELANIE M. DOMENECH RODRÍGUEZ

The development of parenting and behavioral family interventions, and the documenting of their effectiveness in eliminating or decreasing the risk of conduct problems in children, has grown into a substantial literature (Brestan & Eyberg, 1998; Farmer, Compton, Burns, & Robertson, 2002; Kazdin & Weisz, 1998; Taylor & Biglan, 1998). Not surprisingly, the literature is much more advanced in knowledge about mainstream families. Some advances have been made in recent years pertaining to ethnic minority families. Three interventions, with robust findings and with samples of Latino families and children, are discussed in this chapter: The Incredible Years, developed by Carolyn Webster-Stratton; Parent Child Interaction Therapy, developed by Sheila Eyberg; and Parent Management Training, which represents the category of behaviorally based interventions directed at parents only and is most often associated with Marion Forgatch

and her colleagues in Oregon and with Alan Kazdin and his colleagues.

This chapter reviews these three interventions and their effectiveness with Latino children and families. To frame the discussion, we begin by discussing concepts and models for cultural adaptations to make interventions more accessible and acceptable to Latino parents. We then review the interventions and outcomes with Latino parents.[1] We close with recommendations for future research and clinical practice.

CONCEPTUAL MODELS FOR ADAPTING PARENTING INTERVENTIONS

Like many other behavioral, psychosocial, psychoeducational, and mental health interventions, parenting interventions were developed with samples comprising mostly White, middle-class American families, and findings about the

291

interventions' effectiveness with underrepresented ethnocultural populations, such as Latinos, are relatively few and inconsistent (Hall, 2001; Herschell, McNeil, & McNeil, 2004; Miranda, et al., 2005; Webster-Stratton, 2007; Weisz, Jensen-Doss, & Hawley, 2005). When viewed through the prism of another culture, some questions emerge. What constitutes a child problem in a particular cultural context? What are appropriate ways to handle these child problems? The underlying assumptions and values of existing parenting interventions may seem odd, unappealing, or even unacceptable to parents of different cultural or ethnic groups. For example, Borrego, Ibañez, Spendlove, and Pemberton (2007) suggest that *differential attention* (i.e., actively ignoring the child when he or she misbehaves and giving positive attention when the child shows prosocial behaviors) is not rated acceptable by Latino parents as are other techniques, such as *response cost* (e.g., restriction of privileges) and *time out*. Consequently, parents may not adhere to the behaviors promoted by interventions because of their own worldviews about parenting, children, family, child–adult relations, and child-rearing, or they may simply drop out of treatment.

To prevent ineffective or iatrogenic interventions, researchers and practitioners have advocated for adapting and tailoring empirically supported interventions to meet the needs, characteristics, and cultural beliefs and practices of Latinos (Kotchick & Grover, 2008). Arguably, we can make traditional treatments more accessible to ethnocultural minorities by extracting elements from their cultures to modify the empirically supported treatments and select therapies by their cultural proximity to the target groups (Rogler, Malgady, Costantino, & Blumenthal, 1987). While the support for cultural adaptation is strong, the conceptualization of cultural adaptation is its infancy. Also limited is empirical knowledge about the cultural features that are relevant to parenting interventions and that might be integrated into treatments. For example, Dumka, Lopez, and Carter's (2002) review of 21 parenting interventions targeting Latino families shows that most studies identified one or more pan-Latino values, but no citations were presented "to substantiate the validity of these values" (p. 215). Conceptually coherent and methodologically sound approaches to intervention adaptation have appeared. Different models

and equally diverse approaches to adaptation have been advanced, but there is no agreed-upon conceptual or methodological gold standard for cultural adaptation.

Bernal's Ecological Validity Model

Bernal and his colleagues (Bernal, Bonilla, & Bellido, 1995; Bernal & Sáez-Santiago, 2006) offer an eight-dimensional framework for adaptation and tailoring that strengthens the ecological validity of interventions. The dimension of *language* ensures that the intervention matches cultural-linguistic aspects of the target group. The dimension of *persons* considers ethnoracial similarities and differences between clients and therapists in shaping the treatment relationship. Other dimensions include *metaphors* (i.e., concepts and symbols relevant to specific Latino groups), *content* (i.e., cultural knowledge such as values, history, and traditions), and *concepts* (i.e., making terms and concepts culturally sensitive). Finally, the *goals, methods,* and *context* of the intervention should fit the group's cultural values and beliefs. Consideration is given to the family's changing contexts, how therapists interact with parents, and how children and parents interact at the beginning and during the intervention, including acculturative stress and immigration of new family members.

Data-Driven Adaptation

Lau (2006) posits that scientific evidence helps in *selectively* identifying the specific problems of given communities that *direct* the cultural adaptation of treatments. Cultural adaptations cannot be decided on characteristics such as ethnicity (i.e., making one cultural adaptation for all Latino subgroups) but rather must be determined using contextual data (e.g., populations and communities with identifiable problems where an intervention has not been favorable). One set of empirical evidence takes into account the variability in risk and resilience across groups, based on translational research of communities at risk for specific psychosocial problems. Another set of data looks at social validity (i.e., understanding the preferences of target groups, determining how clients perceive the treatment and its procedures). Social validity also gauges the significance of treatment goals and client satisfaction with treatment and outcomes.

The Cultural Adaptation Process Model

Domenech Rodríguez and Wieling (2004) developed a model complementary to Bernal et al.'s to specify the broader processes involved in culturally adapting an intervention. Whereas the model by Bernal et al. focuses on the interventions, the Domenech Rodríguez and Wieling model makes recommendations for the context in which the adaptation is taking place. The process model is built on Rogers' (2000) notion of diffusion of innovations and has three main stages: preparation, active adaptation, and test of adaptation and review of adaptation procedures. Domenech Rodriguez and Wieling advocate for a balance between community needs and scientific integrity through the participation of key stakeholders: researchers, community opinion leaders, and community members likely to receive the intervention. Each brings a particular perspective that permits a common understanding about community needs and what can be reasonably accepted and integrated. The richness of these observations is integrated into enhanced interventions that are decentered (i.e., incorporating new knowledge from ethnic minority research into extant frameworks) for use across cultural groups.

Psychotherapy Adaptation and Modification Framework

Hwang (2006) identifies domains similar to those proposed in other models. Considering the *orientation of clients to therapy and its process* (e.g., conceptions of mental health treatments and therapists' roles, expectations of clients, the therapy process) is one part. *Client-therapist relationship* (i.e., understanding the rules that govern interpersonal relations and clients' expectations in therapy), *cultural differences in expression and communication* (e.g., how individuals express themselves and communicate with others), and *cultural issues of salience* (e.g., social class, social networks, stigma, generational differences, acculturation disparities) are other parts to consider. Treatment fidelity (i.e., implementing interventions as intended) can sometimes be at odds with adaptations to fit special populations (Castro, Barrera, & Martinez, 2004). Yet, adaptation can occur in the content and delivery of interventions to reduce the fidelity-fit tension. To reduce this tension and enhance effectiveness, the who,

how, and where of intervention delivery need consideration.

INTERVENTIONS FOR PARENTS OF YOUNG CHILDREN

The three parenting interventions we discuss here were developed to target socially disruptive behaviors; they are especially relevant for scholars and practitioners working with Latino families because the research that supports their efficacy and effectiveness has included culturally diverse samples. Also, some work is available documenting attempts to adapt these interventions for use with Latino families. It should be noted that not all adaptations have followed a conceptual model like those described previously. The degree of adaptation varies widely across studies, from no adaptations to the introduction of, for example, program materials in Spanish. While some adaptations include the addition of modules to core treatment protocols (Martinez & Eddy, 2005; Matos, Torres, Santiago, Jurado, & Rodríguez, 2006; McCabe, Yeh, Garland, Lau, & Chavez, 2005), examples of these are few. In fact, most reports do not specify the components or the process through which the conceptual models were integrated.

The Incredible Years

The Incredible Years (IY) is a prevention intervention program aimed at low-income families with young children (usually 3 to 8 years old) who may be at risk for developing disruptive behavior problems or who already have externalizing behavior problems (Webster-Stratton & Reid, 2008). IY is carried out in a group format in which parents watch video vignettes, which are followed by group discussions moderated by trained leaders. Each group session lasts approximately 2 hours. Over the 12- to 14-week program, parents watch approximately 250 vignettes, each lasting about two minutes (McMahon & Kotler, 2008).

The IY program has been used primarily as a selective prevention intervention program with preschool families (Webster-Stratton, 1998). Due to its focus on selective prevention in community settings, several IY studies include large and ethnically diverse samples. IY has been efficacious in different randomized clinical trials

Table 17.1 Evidence-Based Parenting Interventions With Latinos

The Incredible Years

Study & Location	Sample Size (% Latinos)	Hispanic Subgroups	Research Design	Adaptations	Findings
Barrera, Biglan, Taylor, Gunn, Smolkowski, Black, et al. (2002)[1] Three communities in Northwest	N = 284 families (n = 168 Hispanic, 59%; n = 116 European American, 41%)	94% Mexican; 5% Central American, 1% other Latin American	Random assignment 1. Intervention 2. No-intervention control group	–Translated measures –Interventions offered in both Spanish and English –Bilingual staff	–Significant intervention x ethnicity interaction for teacher-rated internalizing symptoms; no intervention effects for Hispanic children –Intervention decreased conduct problems in European Americans and Hispanic Americans –Postintervention, children in intervention showed less negative behavior than controls –At follow-up, children in intervention had less teacher-rated internalizing and less parent-rated coercive and antisocial behavior than controls
Gross, Fogg, Webster-Stratton, Garvey, Julion, & Grady (2003)[1] Chicago, IL	N = 208 parents (n = 61 Latino, 29%; n = 119 African American, 57%; n = 7 White, 3.4%; n = 9 Multiethnic, 4%; n = 12 Other 6%)	Not Specified n = 55 immigrated to the United States (26%)	The Incredible Years BASIC Centers randomly assigned to 1. Parent training only (PT) 2. Teacher training using PT program (TT) 3. PT + TT 4. Waitlist control	–At least one group leader per group ethnically matched to most parents –Spanish measures used –Bilingual interviewers assigned to Head Start centers with high proportion of Spanish-speaking parents	–PT and PT + TT parents had higher self-efficacy, less coercive discipline, and used more positive behaviors than control and TT parents –High-risk toddlers in experimental groups improved more than controls –Latino parents used less coercive discipline and more positive parenting than non-Latino parents –Latino parents reported less parenting self-efficacy –Latinos had higher retention than non-Latinos

Study & Location	Sample Size (% Latinos)	Hispanic Subgroups	Research Design	Adaptations	Findings
Linares, Montalto, Li, & Oza (2006)[1] New York, NY	N = 128 parents (n = 64 biological/foster pairs; Latino, 57%; African American, 33%; approx. 50% were foreign born)	Not specified	Random assignment: 1. Intervention 2. Usual-care condition	–Adapted for foster care setting needs –Offered interventions in both Spanish and English –Bilingual staff	–16% of families participated in six or more sessions of adapted treatment (coparenting) –Coparenting gains lost at follow-up –African American parents improved more than Latino parents in harsh discipline –Postintervention, all parents improved in positive parenting and collaborative coparenting –At follow-up, intervention parents kept improved positive parenting and clear expectations –At follow-up, intervention parents reported fewer child externalizing problems –Findings support feasibility of joint parent training for biological and foster parents –Coparenting applied to foster care families
Reid, Webster-Stratton, & Beachaine (2001)[1] Puget Sound Seattle area, WA	N = 634 families, 42% ethnic minority (n = 71 Hispanic, 11%; African American, 19%; Asian American, 12%)	Not specified	Centers randomly assigned to 1. Intervention 2. No intervention (Head Start services only)	–Video vignettes featured ethnically diverse families –Child-directed play tied to parents' upbringing, benefits to child, and parents' goals for their children –Spanish translation by trained native speaker	–Mothers were observed to be more positive, less critical, more consistent, and more competent in parenting than control group –Children of intervention parents exhibited fewer behavior problems than control group –Differences in treatment response across ethnic groups were few and did not exceed the number expected by chance –Parents from all groups reported high satisfaction levels following parenting program
Parent-Child Interaction Therapy					
Borrego, Anhalt, Terao, Vargas, & Urquiza (2006)[2] Northern CA	N = 1 foster mother (mono-lingual Spanish)	Mexican American	Single-subject design	–Verbal instruction and measures provided in Spanish –Mexican American bilingual, bicultural therapist	–Significant improvements in reported and observed increased positive and decreased negative verbalizations by mothers and decreased frequency and intensity of externalizing, aggressive, and destructive behaviors by children at posttreatment and 1-year follow-up –Decreased parenting stress at posttreatment and 1-year follow-up

(Continued)

Table 17.1 *(Continued)*

Study & Location	Sample Size (% Latinos)	Hispanic Subgroups	Research Design	Adaptations	Findings
Matos, Torres, Santiago, Jurado, & Rodriguez (2006)[2] Puerto Rico	N = 9 families (100% Puerto Rican)	Puerto Rican	No control group	–Adapted for families living in Puerto Rico –Native Puerto Rican staff –Focus on cultural values	–Improved parenting practices (e.g., more effective discipline) and satisfaction with program –Decreased parenting stress and child behavior problems
Parent Management Training					
Martinez & Eddy (2005)[2] Eugene, OR	N = 73 families (# of children per family not specified) 100% Latino; 50% foreign born	90% Mexican; 10% Peruvian and Central American	Parent Management Training: *Nuestras Familias: Andando Entre Culturas* (Our Families: Moving Between Cultures) Families randomly assigned to 1. Intervention 2. No-intervention control group	–Targeted Spanish-speaking Latino families –Latino staff –Culturally relevant topics (e.g., strong Latino roots, our many roles in the family, bridging cultures)	–Parents improved in overall effective parenting (e.g., praising, more time together, communicating clearly) –Youth decreased in likelihood of using substances, aggression, and other externalizing behaviors –Mothers and fathers participated at equal rates –High levels of satisfaction with adapted intervention

[1] Not specifically adapted for Latino families.

[2] Specifically adapted for Latino families.

(Webster-Stratton & Reid, 2008). The intervention seems to prevent child behavior problems from developing and changes parent behaviors, such as increasing their positive parenting practices (e.g., praising their children) and decreasing coercive parenting practices, such as yelling at their children (Baydar, Reid, & Webster-Stratton, 2003; Webster-Stratton, 1998).

Applications With Culturally Diverse Samples. Reid, Webster-Stratton, and Beauchaine (2001) combined data from 23 IY randomized controlled trials in Head Start centers in Seattle, Washington. They conducted ethnic-group comparisons of low-income Hispanic, Asian American, African American, and Caucasian parents. Of the 634 children participating in the IY parenting program, 11% of the sample was Hispanic (71 families). Adaptations included having the program translated into Spanish and delivered by a native Spanish-speaker. Additionally, videotapes used in treatment depicted families from culturally diverse backgrounds, and parents were asked to discuss whether parent-child play was important to the parents' own upbringing, an example of a cultural value on parent-child interaction.

Across randomized controlled trials, mothers who received IY were observed to be less critical and gave fewer commands and were more positive toward their children than mothers in the control group. In addition, children whose parents participated in parent training were observed to have fewer behavior problems when compared to children in the control condition. Parents who participated in the IY condition reported high levels of satisfaction with the program. Group analyses revealed no treatment outcome differences based on ethnicity.

Linares, Montalto, Li, and Oza (2006) applied IY in New York City with foster parents. The sample consisted of 128 parents (64 foster–biological parent pairs). Fifty-seven percent of the mothers were Latina, of whom 50% were foreign born. The children in the study ranged in age from 3 to 10 years with a mean age of 6.2 years. Since the groups were ethnically diverse, Linares and colleagues used a team of bicultural and bilingual parent leaders and provided simultaneous translation of the program for Spanish-speaking parents. Parents in the study were assigned to either IY intervention or a usual-care condition. There was a statistically significant group difference in positive parenting practices (e.g., praise, hugs) after the intervention and at follow-up for parents in the IY treatment condition in that parents in this condition reported an increase in positive parenting practices. Parents in IY also reported having clearer expectations for their children regarding chores and conduct than did parents in the usual-care condition at follow-up. Parents in IY reported being more flexible and engaging in more problem solving than parents in the usual-care condition. Although not statically significant, intervention parents reported a decrease in their children's behavior problems at 3-month follow-up.

Gross et al. (2003) tested the effectiveness of the IY program with a low-income, ethnically diverse sample of families with 2- and 3-year-old children in day care in Chicago. The sample consisted of 208 families and 77 teachers with four study conditions: (1) parent training, (2) teacher training, (3) parent + teacher training, and (4) a control condition. Of the 208 families participating in the study, 29% (N = 61) were identified as Latino, as were 22% of the teachers. In addition, 55 (26%) of the participants were immigrants. Parents gathered at their children's day care center and met in groups over a 12-week period. Adaptations for Latinos included a group leader of the same background, materials available in Spanish, and bilingual family interviewers. The overall findings suggest that parents receiving IY (i.e., those assigned to parenting training or to parent and teacher training) reported positive outcomes, such as higher self-efficacy in parenting, and lower coercive parenting practices than parents in the teacher training and the no-intervention control condition. Behavioral observations of parent-child interactions showed that parents in the two conditions displayed more positive behaviors (e.g., praising their children) than parents in the teacher training and no-intervention conditions. Latinos, specifically, reported using fewer coercive parenting practices (e.g., yelling) and more positive parenting behaviors (e.g., praising) than non-Latino parents (Gross et al., 2003). Although Latino parents had a higher retention rate than other parents in the study, they also self-reported lower parenting self-efficacy compared to non-Latino parents. Further, parents who reported lower parent self-efficacy also reported greater depression and everyday stress. The researchers speculate that the anxiety that Latino parents experience about parenting may have kept them in the study; however, this conjecture requires more empirical scrutiny. It should be noted that once ethnicity, anxiety, and depression were controlled, parents who received parent training reported greater self-efficacy than parents who did not receive parenting training.

Other prevention studies using IY have included samples of disadvantaged ethnically diverse families (e.g., Brotman et al., 2005; Reid, Webster-Stratton, & Baydar, 2004; Webster-Stratton, Reid, & Hammond, 2001), but they lack ethnic-group comparisons. The adaptations or adjustments made to the IY program reviewed include such things as translating the program and measures, using native speakers as group leaders, and presenting ethnically diverse families in vignettes.

Implementation With Latinos Only. Although the foregoing studies of the IY program included Latinos in a broader sample, one known study has focused on Latino families specifically. Barrera et al. (2002) implemented a comprehensive prevention program targeting behavior problems and reading difficulties in three different Oregon communities. The intervention, Schools and Homes in Partnership (SHIP), included 168 Hispanic and 116 non-Hispanic children and used the Incredible Years as the parent training component. Families were randomly assigned to either the intervention or a no-intervention control group. Of the Hispanic families participating, 94% were of Mexican heritage, 85% were born in Mexico, and 84% of the parents spoke only or mainly Spanish. The program and the corresponding assessment materials were available in Spanish, and program staff spoke Spanish. Results suggest that families in the intervention group benefited from being in the program, and attrition rates were similar across ethnic groups. Children in the intervention group displayed a decrease in conduct problems and were observed to engage in fewer negative social behaviors with peers than were controls.

In summary, the IY has been primarily used with the parents of preschool-age and elementary school-age children in a few regions in the country that may contain different populations of Latinos (e.g., national origin, cultural heritage, foreign and U.S. born). Since the majority of prevention studies were conducted with Head Start samples, we can surmise that most of the families were from disadvantaged backgrounds, thus providing valuable information about generalizability to other low-income Latino groups. It is also heartening that the application of the IY program resulted in moderate to high positive outcomes for Latinos, whether in retention, parent satisfaction, better parenting skills, or greater parenting self-efficacy, in comparison to other ethnic and racial groups.

Our review, however, reveals the limited manner in which the IY program has been adapted to match more of the characteristics and needs of Latino parents. Most of the published reports indicate that changes were typically in preparing and delivering the intervention in Spanish, hiring Spanish-speaking staff who may have been Latino also, using videotaped vignettes depicting ethnically diverse families, and offering discussion opportunities that may have focused on cultural values in parent-child relationships.

Parent-Child Interaction Therapy

Parent-Child Interaction Therapy (PCIT) is an empirically supported treatment originally developed for families of young children with socially disruptive behavior problems (Brestan & Eyberg, 1998; Schoenfield & Eyberg, 2005). Both parent and child are present during PCIT sessions, and therapists work directly with the parents to gradually change the child's behavior. A primary goal of PCIT is to change how the parent and child interact, by enhancing parents' acquisition of skills that improve the parent-child relationship. PCIT has two distinct treatment phases: the child-directed interaction (CDI) phase and the parent-directed interaction (PDI) phase. The focus of CDI, also known as the relationship enhancement phase, is building a positive parent-child relationship. In turn, the focus of the PDI phase, also known as the discipline phase, is to teach the parent effective child management skills. PCIT has been shown to be effective in reducing socially disruptive behavior problems (Capage, Bennett, & McNeil, 2001) and parental stress (Borrego, Urquiza, Rasmussen, & Zebell, 1999). PCIT has been applied with different diagnostic populations (e.g., separation anxiety disorder; Choate, Pincus, Eyberg, & Barlow, 2005) and clinical populations (e.g., children with chronic illness; Bagner, Fernandez, & Eyberg, 2004).

Applications With Culturally Diverse Samples. Although the majority of PCIT treatment efficacy studies have comprised mainly non-Hispanic White samples (Butler & Eyberg, 2006), recent work has begun to focus on the applicability and efficacy of PCIT with African Americans (e.g., Capage et al., 2001) and Latinos (e.g., Borrego, Anhalt, Terao, Vargas, & Urquiza, 2006; Matos et al., 2006). Other PCIT treatment outcome studies (e.g., Chaffin et al., 2004; Timmer, Sedlar, & Urquiza, 2004; Timmer, Urquiza, Zebell, & McGrath, 2005) have included Latinos, but either cultural adaptations were not made, or ethnic-group comparisons were not reported. In one study (Chaffin et al. 2004), Latino parents were combined with other ethnic-minority parents to form a non-Hispanic, Caucasian, and other-group comparison, apparently due to small sample sizes.

Implementation With Latinos Specifically. Using a single-case design, Borrego et al. (2006) showed the effectiveness of PCIT with minimal adaptations beyond conducting the therapy in Spanish with a bilingual, bicultural therapist. Data from standard self-report questionnaires and parent-child observations were collected. PCIT has built-in components that may be culturally appropriate for Latino populations. As examples, PCIT is directive, focuses on the parent-child relationship, and has a discipline component. Data were collected from a Mexican, monolingual, Spanish-speaking foster mother and her 3-year-old, bilingual foster child. The foster mother reported statistically and clinically significant decreases in the child's socially disruptive behavior problems at the end of treatment. The mother also reported a decreased stress level surrounding the parent-child relationship. Observational data showed that the mother was using more positive verbalizations (e.g., praising the child) and specific directives (e.g., giving direct, specific commands). Although such cultural values as showing *respeto* (respect) and referring to *cariño* (affection) in the context of the parent-child dyad were discussed, they were not formally evaluated.

In a slightly larger study, Matos et al. (2006) made cultural adaptations to PCIT for Puerto Rican families with young children with behavior problems, including hyperactivity. Matos and her colleagues went through four steps in culturally adapting PCIT. The first step involved translation of the PCIT treatment manual into Spanish and conducting a preliminary adaptation. The second step involved conducting a preliminary exploratory study with nine families seeking services. The third step included making further refinements to the culturally adapted treatment version. The final step involved interviewing parents and therapists to obtain their feedback about the process and outcome of PCIT.

Matos's adaptation work was guided by the framework proposed by Bernal and colleagues (Bernal et al., 1995; Bernal & Sáez-Santiago, 2005) for adapting culturally sensitive treatments. In line with these dimensions, Matos et al.'s first step in adapting PCIT was to work on a translation into the Spanish of Puerto Rico. The goal was to create a manual that was similar to the English version but also included the "sociocultural context" of Puerto Rico (Matos et al., 2006, p. 209). The translation research team was composed predominantly of staff and professionals born and raised in Puerto Rico. With respect to the dimension of *persons,* the focus on the therapeutic relationship highlighted the Latino cultural value of *personalismo* (Matos et al., 2006). Mothers in this treatment outcome study reported being supported and understood by their therapists. In addressing the *metaphors* dimension, culturally specific idioms were used with families to explain concepts. Regarding *context,* the therapists also spent time discussing issues that were not necessarily in the treatment manual but were important for the family. One of these issues was how to incorporate extended family members into PCIT treatment, which reflects the Latino cultural value of *familismo.* The research team found that the dimensions related to *concepts* and *goals* (e.g., family relationships and discipline) matched the PCIT component of family experiences. With regard to *methods,* families found the CDI component of PCIT (where the child leads and the parents follow) less favorable, as parents felt that it allowed children too much control, and they found the time-out procedure in the discipline phase of PCIT, the PDI, too demanding (Matos et al., 2006). Other modifications to PCIT were made that included extending the therapy session to 1.5 hours and making the handouts more attractive for families.

Once the translation and adaptations were made, the culturally adapted version of PCIT was implemented with nine Puerto Rican families. Matos and colleagues (2006) reported decreases in children's behavior problems and parents' level of stress from baseline to post-intervention. In addition, parents reported improvement in their parenting practices, such as using more effective discipline strategies. Treatment gains were maintained over 3 months. These positive outcomes were reported by the parents via paper-and-pencil measures. In addition to standard treatment outcome data, the research team also gathered qualitative feedback from parents who participated in the treatment and from therapists who delivered the intervention (Matos et al., 2006). As an example, parents perceived the child-directed component of PCIT less favorably, as they felt that it allowed children too much control; and they felt the time-out procedure in the parent-directed discipline phase of PCIT was too demanding. In addition to having PCIT delivered in Spanish, words were used that captured the daily experiences of Puerto Rican children, and simple words were used in place of more technical psychological terms (ibid.). The culturally adapted version of PCIT included a psychoeducational component at the beginning of treatment. This treatment component introduced parents to behavior problems and expectations.

Feedback from parents and professional staff suggested that both groups found PCIT acceptable and were satisfied with the treatment (Matos et al., 2006). In addition, parents reported that PCIT concepts were not in conflict with their cultural values. Unlike clinical research with Latinos in the United States, the culturally adapted version of PCIT with Puerto Rican families living on the island did not have to address such stressors as acculturation and immigration. Overall, the data reported by Matos and her colleagues suggest that a culturally adapted version of PCIT with Puerto Rican families is effective and acceptable. Limitations of this treatment outcome study are that a control group was not used, data were only collected from nine families, and fathers did not provide any data for analysis.

McCabe and colleagues (2005) describe their culturally adapted version of PCIT, called *Guiando a Niños Activos* (GANA, Guiding Active Children), for use with Mexican-origin families who had young children with externalizing behavior problems. While there are no published outcome data yet, the authors detail the adaptation procedures, which were guided by literature reviews, interviews, and focus groups with parents and therapists. Modifications ranged from rather modest ones, such as increasing the number of fathers recruited by using testimonials from fathers who had participated in the training, to bolder ones, such as "making ignoring procedure as active as possible so that parents feel they are disciplining, and to frame time out as a more severe punishment" (p. 119). These adaptations were made in response to Mexican American parents' preference for more active disciplining (rather than ignoring behaviors) and their emphasis on stricter forms of teaching children. A specific adaptation, in the case of time out, was to reframe the time-out chair as the "punishment chair." For parents who preferred lighter forms of punishment, the term *time-out chair* was retained. This clearly responds to parental preferences based on their belief systems. McCabe et al. also considered the importance of extended family, who might be concerned that the methods proposed in the parenting intervention were too lenient, and helped parents present it to relatives as punishment; or that the intervention was a skills-building, educational program rather than a more stigmatizing "mental health" or "parent improvement" program. In summary, the core elements of the intervention were not adapted, but rather the appeal, accessibility and acceptability were enhanced by tailoring.

Parent Management Training (PMT)

PMT is arguably one of the most researched treatment interventions to address externalizing behavior problems, and it offers promising evidence of its effectiveness (Kazdin & Weisz, 1998). Conceptually, PMT is based on the premise that parents play a key role in the development and maintenance of child behavior problems, such as tantrums and noncompliance (Patterson, 1982).[2] According to Patterson, maladaptive (i.e., coercive) parent-child interactions develop over time. In PMT, parents are taught skills to change the negative parent-child interactions and acquire effective parenting practices based on behavioral principles. Gradually, the parent-child relationship goes from one characterized as coercive to a relationship that is reinforcing to the parent and the child. This objective is accomplished through the therapist's working closely with the parent to change the maladaptive behaviors that occur at home and in public settings (e.g., store, church).

PMT can be delivered in group, couple, or individual format and can be adjusted to parents with children from preschool to high school. Initial sessions focus on improving the parent-child relationship and, after those skills have been presented and rehearsed, the treatment moves to effective discipline. Modeling and role playing are critical to PMT (Kazdin, 2005). Therapists have parents practice in the therapy room, and the therapist provides feedback about what is observed. Therapists rely on such behavioral principles as shaping, reinforcement, and prompts to bring about behavior change in the parent. Unlike PCIT, in which the therapist works with the parent and child present at the same time, therapists using PMT usually work solely with the parent. After the session, parents are encouraged to implement at home what was learned during the week and to document what worked and what did not. In turn, parents attend the following session and either fine-tune skills that may not have worked as intended and/or learn a new set of skills.

Applications With Culturally Diverse Samples. Although PMT has been studied extensively in multiple outcome studies (e.g., DeGarmo, Patterson, & Forgatch, 2004; Forgatch & DeGarmo, 1999; Kazdin, Holland, & Crowley, 1997; Kazdin & Whitley, 2003, 2006; Nock & Kazdin, 2005), the studies have not included sufficient Latino parent and child samples to conduct analyses and draw valid conclusions. To date, only one PMT treatment outcome study (Myers et al., 1992) has examined its effectiveness with an ethnic minority population (viz., African American).

Implementation With Latinos Specifically. Martinez and Eddy (2005) developed a culturally adapted version of PMT-O for Latinos in Oregon. The researchers went through several steps to adapt PMT-O for use with Latinos. The program, *Nuestras Familias: Andando Entre Culturas* (Our Families: Moving between Cultures), was adapted to predominantly Mexican-origin, monolingual, Spanish-speaking immigrants residing in the Northwest (ibid.). Conceptually, *Nuestras Familias* is based on social learning theory and ecodevelopmental theory. In addition, Martinez and Eddy relied on studies of the acculturative process in Latino families to guide the treatment adaptation. The acculturation process, along with social support and social context, influences families' environment.

Martinez and Eddy (2005) retained the core components of PMT-O (i.e., skills building, monitoring, problem solving, effective family communication, giving good directions, positive involvement, and limit setting) in the culturally adapted version. Adaptations included adding modules focusing on Latino roots, bridging two cultures, the roles of Latinos in their families, and dealing with obstacles. The authors added these treatment components as they addressed culturally relevant experiences for Latino parents and their families. The program was delivered in Spanish. Another cultural adaptation made to *Nuestras Familias* was the label that therapists used. Instead of being seen as experts in parenting, therapists assumed the role of *entrenadores* (coaches). The cultural adaptation occurred over a 2-year period and was based on the fidelity-fit considerations advanced by Castro et al. (2004), in which treatment fidelity is balanced with fit in the community. The outcome of this approach was incorporating the core prevention intervention components of PMT-O while "simultaneously adapting those intervention components and developing new intervention elements that more specifically addressed culturally relevant experiences of Latino parents and families" (Martinez & Eddy, 2005, p. 844).

Seventy-three Latino families with middle school–age children were randomized to either the culturally adapted version of PMT-O ($N = 37$) or a control group ($N = 36$). Families received the *Nuestras Familias* program at the Oregon Social Learning Center (OSLC), a community-based research agency in Eugene, Oregon. Treatment consisted of parent group sessions over a 12-week period. When compared to the control group, families participating in *Nuestras Familias* had positive outcomes in parenting practices and youth adjustment. More specifically, parents reported an increase in general parenting and overall parenting effectiveness. Parents also reported a decrease in child aggression, externalizing problems, substance abuse, and smoking.

With regard to social validity (feasibility and acceptability), all parents in *Nuestras Familias* reported that the program was somewhat or very helpful. Of the 37 families assigned to the intervention, 34 participated, and 70% completed 10 or more sessions (Martinez & Eddy, 2005). Parents also reported high levels of support from the group. In summary, Martinez and Eddy found similar treatment outcome results to other treatment outcome studies using PMT. The promises of adapting PMT to Latino families are just beginning to emerge as evident in Martinez and Eddy's work. Their outcome data are similar to other PMT studies. However, more attention will be needed to consider further the adaptations that might be necessary across Latino groups, for Latino parents of children across the age range, especially among the younger age groups that are the focus of this review, and to further examine what parenting behaviors Latino parents endorse or accept based on the age and gender of the focal or index child. In addition, it is not clear what the specific culturally relevant treatment modules (e.g., focusing on Latino roots and bridging cultures) added to the overall effectiveness and satisfaction. This question can only be answered by comparing standard PMT to a culturally adapted version.

In addition to the work in Oregon, an independently developed, culturally adapted PMT-O manual, *Criando con Amor: Promoviendo Armonía y Superación,* is being tried in a rural community in Utah with Spanish-speaking Latino families (Domenech Rodríguez & Oldham, 2008). The intervention was adapted using the Bernal et al. (1995) ecological validity model, as well as the Domenech Rodríguez and Wieling (2004) cultural adaptation process model, which include extensive pilot work. The team demonstrated the importance of word-of-mouth for recruitment efforts to secure a prevention sample (Domenech Rodríguez, Rodríguez, & Davis, 2006) and the feasibility of using a behavioral observation methodology with immigrant families (Domenech Rodríguez, Davis, Rodríguez, & Bates, 2006). Domenech Rodríguez, Davis, et al. also documented the importance of securing immigrant fathers' participation in the assessment phase of the intervention trial to better understand children's outcomes. Changes were informed by theory as well as focus group data. Focus group data led to uncovering the important parenting goals of *superación* (getting ahead) and *educación* (good behavior), which were used to frame the intervention goals (Domenech Rodríguez & Oldham, 2008). Domenech Rodríguez and her research team also found that parents were not familiar with, and thus did not use, time out as a discipline strategy (Donovick & Domenech Rodríguez, 2008). Parents felt urgency about attaining effective discipline skills because of their children's threats to call 911 as a response to parental physical discipline (Domenech Rodríguez & Oldham, 2008). A total of 85 families participated in the randomized controlled trial with wait-list control. Of the 45 families who participated in the intervention condition, 84% of families attended at least 6 of 8 groups, showing good retention rates. Longitudinal data are being collected, and outcomes will be published soon.

FUTURE DIRECTIONS FOR PRACTICE AND RESEARCH

The IY, PCIT, and PMT interventions all have as their core goals to increase positive parenting practices while decreasing negative parenting practices to improve child outcomes. Techniques vary across treatments, but the core concepts (e.g., reinforcement) are the same. That the three treatments discussed show promising results with different Latino samples is exciting. It is particularly inspiring to consider the consistency in results, given the varied methodologies used to examine the utility of these programs, as well as the differential emphases on cultural adaptation. At a methodological level, most of the data available are from self-report. Observational data are used in some studies (e.g., Borrego, et al., 2006; Reid et al., 2001), but these are few. More studies are needed on specific Latino parent-child interactions that change due to a parenting intervention.

An important area for future research concerns the impact of cultural adaptation. From a methodological perspective, none of the culturally adapted interventions discussed have been compared to the original treatment. Further, each intervention reviewed in this chapter underwent some adaptation for application with Latino parents, usually adjustments to linguistic, cultural, and community dimensions; however, no consistent—and thus replicable—model was used to help inform the future practice of cultural adaptation. Ultimately, the findings suggest that these parenting interventions work with Latino families and may be enhanced through thoughtful adaptations. However, many of the conceptual models are not tested, and models that recommend approaches are varied and not always planted in theoretical frameworks.

There is reason to develop adaptation models, as some have done already. However, our review of the literature has led us to conclude that it is not enough to develop the models and follow their recommendations. Rather, we need to test how model-based adaptations enhance the interventions. More research on the process of adaptation is needed. We agree that most interventions are tailored "on the ground" by practitioners in their agency contexts, but these are seldom reported. Indeed, we find that researchers do not always report the adaptations they have made to interventions tested with Latinos. We call for more systematic and accurate reporting of the adaptations that were made and how they were made. After all, replicability is a hallmark of scientific progression.

Despite advances, much work also remains to be done to increase the representation of Latinos in research on parenting interventions. Often, investigators do not systematically include adequate proportions of Latino parents in research samples or make sufficient cross-ethnic comparisons. This is problematic, given that a critical question in the field is to constantly determine whether the behaviors, beliefs, values, and norms that underlie a parenting intervention are considered acceptable to Latino parents. While some parenting interventions are based on egalitarian beliefs about parent-child relations, the expression of this belief in the form of parental behaviors and children's behaviors must be carefully considered in the development and adaptation of interventions. As McCabe et al. (2005) found, Mexican American parents prefer a more assertive form of parenting than some interventions recommend. The Matos et al. (2006) project identified an exemplary cultural issue: Puerto Rican parents did not like the child-directed component of the PCIT because it was perceived as giving too much authority to children, a reflection of culturally related child-rearing beliefs that parents hold the authority and the child must comply. Greater representation of Latinos in broader

research samples, as well as research conducted specifically with Latino parents, will help bridge these gaps in knowledge.

Another area for future research and clinical attention is the tension between fidelity and adaptation. In adapting, interventionists must be mindful not to alter core components. What seems to cut across reports on tested adaptations and proposed models and approaches for tailoring is that they do not change the intervention itself so much as require change in the interventionists' behaviors. Indeed, some terminology is changed to suit the preferences of the target group, and vignettes may be created to reflect the cultural practices and familiar persons, symbols, and concepts of the local culture. How the therapists engages, instructs, and supports parents and children in the parenting programs enhances the *therapeutic alliance,* a factor recognized as enormously powerful in most psychosocial interventions (Bickman et al., 2004).

With an understanding that the parenting interventions reviewed here are effective and have some history of testing with and adaptation for Latino parents, we can propose some implications for therapists and program directors implementing these or other parenting programs. Cultural adaptations can help recruitment and improve engagement and retention of ethnic minority families (Dumka, Garza, Roosa, & Stoerzinger, 1997; Kumpfer, Alvarado, Smith, & Bellamy, 2002). Dumka et al. recommend *early recruitment procedures* that start before the program is implemented. This is followed by *immediate preprogram recruitment,* which might include home visits to inform parents and engage them. McKay, McCadam, and Gonzales (1996) report success in their test of a recruitment intervention that made telephone calls a few days and the night before the beginning of therapy to engage participants through asking questions, collecting information that would be of use in the therapy, and reminding participants of time and place. Dumka et al. (1997) also recommend *monitoring and referrals* that remind parents of the weekly sessions and assess potential barriers to adherence.

In tailoring interventions for Latino parents, researchers and clinicians must identify the predominant Latino groups served. Pan-ethnic labels, such as the term *Latino,* may be useful to describe large segments of a population that has some demographic commonalities. However, because Latinos are a very diverse group with different histories, legacies, cultures, sociopolitical statuses, and generations in the United States, it is important that the specific group be identified for which the adaptation of intervention is taking place. Our interventions might be adapted differently for a third-generation Puerto Rican family and for a recently immigrated Salvadoran couple with a young child. Immigration, acculturation stress, parenting beliefs, and other cultural values will differ and inform the adaptation in distinct ways.

Staff characteristics are an important consideration, too, such as the number of paraprofessionals and professionals, how they reflect the community, their understanding of the issues faced by Latino parents, and their cultural values and typical parenting beliefs. In short, mindfulness of the match or fit between staff and clients and between the agency and the community are essential for success. We believe that in the adaptation process it is often the interventionist who changes her or his behavior with Latino parents. Therefore, it is necessary to increase the knowledge and abilities of therapists to work with Latinos, sensitizing staff's responsiveness to Latino parents while maintaining the integrity of the intervention.

Clearly, we need continued testing of parenting interventions. However, such testing and adaptations that precede or occur concurrently with testing are best done with theoretical and conceptual frameworks, allowing for future adaptations. Presently, the conceptual models and methodologies lack coherence or common logic other than emphasizing culture. Better distinctions are needed between adapting and tailoring, and regarding how much is needed without affecting the therapeutic effects of the intervention (Zayas, Bellamy, & Proctor, 2008).

Research can be further strengthened by offering greater detail on variables of interest. Unfortunately, most of the studies reviewed used broad umbrella terms such as *Hispanic* and *Latino*. The use of pan-ethnic terms offers little usefulness to clinicians who are interested in knowing more about the sample. Additionally, investigating and reporting such variables as nativity, generation status, and acculturation level can help determine whether these factors impact recruitment, retention, and outcome. The setting in which the prevention program or intervention was implanted should be described.

Finally, our review has focused on evidence-based practices. While these are, after all, usually supported by rigorous research, they often have more of an *etic* origin than an *emic* one. More attention needs to be paid to *practice-based evidence,* which encourages investigators to learn from providers and creative clinicians whose unsung, unpublished work can yield valuable interventions for parents of all ethnic, racial, and cultural groups.

NOTES

1. Treatments originally developed for older adolescents or children without a parent training component are not included in this review.

2. We use two abbreviations for parent management training. PMT refers to the general category of parenting management interventions, and PMT-O refers to the Oregon Social Learning Center model.

REFERENCES

Bagner, D. M., Fernandez, M. A., & Eyberg, S. M. (2004). Parent-child interaction therapy and chronic illness: A case study. *Journal of Clinical Psychology in Medical Settings, 11,* 1–6.

Barrera, M., Jr., Biglan, A., Taylor, T. K., Gunn, B. K., Smolkowski, K., Black, C., et al. (2002). Early elementary school intervention to reduce conduct problems: A randomized trial with Hispanic and non-Hispanic children. *Prevention Science, 3,* 83–94.

Baydar, N., Reid, M., & Webster-Stratton, C. (2003). The role of mental health factors and program engagement in the effectiveness of a preventive parenting program for Head Start mothers. *Child Development, 74,* 1433–1453.

Bernal, G., Bonillo, J., & Bellido, C. (1995). Ecological validity and cultural sensitivity for outcome research: Issues for the cultural adaptation and development of psychosocial treatments with Hispanics. *Journal of Abnormal Child Psychology, 23,* 67–82.

Bernal, G., & Sáez-Santiago, E. (2006). Culturally centered psychosocial interventions. *Journal of Community Psychology, 34,* 121–132.

Bickman, L., Andrade, A. R., Lambert, E. W., Doucette, A., Sapyta, J., Boyd, A. S., et al. (2004). Youth therapeutic alliance in intensive treatment settings. *Journal of Behavioral Health Services & Research, 31,* 134–148.

Borrego, J., Jr., Anhalt, K., Terao, S. Y., Vargas, E., & Urquiza, A. J. (2006). Parent-child interaction therapy with a Spanish-speaking family. *Cognitive and Behavioral Practice, 13,* 121–133.

Borrego, J., Jr., Ibanez, E. S., Spendlove, S. J., & Pemberton, J. R. (2007). Treatment acceptability among Mexican American parents. *Behavior Therapy, 38,* 218–227.

Borrego, J., Jr., Urquiza, A. J., Rasmussen, R. A., & Zebell, N. (1999). Parent-child interaction therapy with a family at high risk for physical abuse. *Child Maltreatment, 4,* 331–342.

Brestan, E. V., & Eyberg, S. M. (1998). Effective psychosocial treatments of conduct-disordered children and adolescents: 29 years, 82 studies, and 5,272 kids. *Journal of Clinical Child Psychology, 27,* 180–189.

Brotman, L. M., Gouley, K. K., Chesir-Teran, D., Dennis, T., Klein, R. G., & Shrout, P. (2005). Prevention for preschoolers at high risk for conduct problems: Immediate outcomes on parenting practices and child social competence. *Journal of Clinical Child and Adolescent Psychology, 34,* 724–734.

Butler, A. M., & Eyberg, S. M. (2006). Parent-child interaction therapy and ethnic minority children. *Vulnerable Children and Youth Studies, 1,* 246–255.

Capage, L. C., Bennett, G. M., & McNeil, C. B. (2001). A comparison between African American and Caucasian children referred for treatment of disruptive behavior disorders. *Child and Family Behavior Therapy, 23,* 1–14.

Castro, F., Barrera, M., Jr., & Martinez, C. R., Jr. (2004). The cultural adaptation of prevention interventions: Resolving tensions between fidelity and fit. *Prevention Science, 5,* 41–45.

Chaffin, M., Silovsky, J. F., Funderburk, B., Valle, L., Brestan, E. V., Valachova, T., et al. (2004). Parent-child interaction therapy with physically abusive parents: Efficacy for reducing future abuse reports. *Journal of Consulting and Clinical Psychology, 72,* 500–510.

Choate, M. L., Pincus, D. B., Eyberg, S. M., & Barlow, D. H. (2005). Parent-Child Interaction Therapy for treatment of separation anxiety disorder in young children: A pilot study. *Cognitive and Behavioral Practice, 12,* 126–135.

DeGarmo, D. S., Patterson, G. R., & Forgatch, M. S. (2004). How do outcomes in a specified parent training intervention maintain or wane over time? *Prevention Science, 5,* 73–89.

Domenech Rodríguez, M., Davis, M. R., Rodríguez, J., & Bates, S. C. (2006). Observed parenting practices of first-generation Latino families. *Journal of Community Psychology, 34,* 133–148.

Domenech Rodríguez, M., & Oldham, A. (2008, April). *Cultural adaptation of a PMTO intervention: Criando con Amor: Promoviendo Armonía y Superación.* Invited presentation at the Developing Interventions for Latino Children, Youth, and Families conference, Center for Latino Family Research, Washington University, St. Louis, MO.

Domenech Rodríguez, M., Rodríguez, J., & Davis, M. R. (2006). Recruitment of first-generation Latinos in a rural community: The essential nature of personal contact. *Family Process, 45,* 87–100.

Domenech Rodríguez, M., & Wieling, E. (2004). Developing culturally appropriate evidence-based treatments for interventions with ethnic minority populations. In M. Rastogi & E. Wieling (Eds.), *Voices of color: First-person accounts of ethnic minority therapists* (pp. 313–333). Thousand Oaks, CA: Sage.

Donovick, M. R., & Domenech Rodríguez, M. (2008). An examination of self-reported parenting practices among first-generation Spanish-speaking Latino families: A Spanish version of the Alabama Parenting Questionnaire. *Graduate Student Journal of Psychology, 10,* 52–63.

Dumka, L. E., Garza, C. A., Roosa, M. W., & Stoerzinger, H. D. (1997). Recruitment and retention of high-risk families into a preventive parent training intervention. *The Journal of Primary Prevention, 18,* 25–39.

Dumka, L. E., Lopez, V. A., & Carter, S. J. (2002). Parenting interventions adapted for Latino families: Progress and prospects. In J. M. Contreras, K. A. Kerns, & A. M. Neal-Barnett (Eds.), *Latino children and families in the United States: Current research and future directions* (pp. 203–231). Westport, CT: Praeger.

Farmer, E. M. Z., Compton, S. N., Burns, B. J., & Robertson, E. (2002). Review of the evidence base for treatment of childhood psychopathology: Externalizing disorders. *Journal of Consulting and Clinical Psychology, 70,* 1267–1302.

Forgatch, M. S., & DeGarmo, D. S. (1999). Parenting through change: An effective prevention program for single mothers. *Journal of Consulting and Clinical Psychology, 67,* 711–724.

Gross, D., Fogg, L., Webster-Stratton, C., Garvey, C., Julion, W., & Grady, J. (2003). Parent training of toddlers in day care in low-income urban communities. *Journal of Consulting and Clinical Psychology, 71,* 261–278.

Hall, G. C. N. (2001). Psychotherapy research with ethnic minorities: Empirical, ethical, and conceptual issues. *Journal of Consulting and Clinical Psychology, 69,* 502–510.

Herschell, A. D., McNeil, C. B., & McNeil, D. W. (2004). Clinical child psychology's progress in disseminating empirically supported treatments. *Clinical Psychology: Science and Practice, 11,* 267–288.

Hwang, W. C. (2006). The psychotherapy adaptation and modification framework. *American Psychologist, 61,* 702–715.

Kazdin, A. E. (2005). *Parent management training: Treatment for oppositional, aggressive, and antisocial behavior in children and adolescents.* New York: Oxford University Press.

Kazdin, A. E., Holland, L., & Crowley, M. (1997). Family experience of barriers to treatment and premature termination from child therapy. *Journal of Consulting and Clinical Psychology, 65,* 453–463.

Kazdin, A. E., & Weisz, J. R. (1998). Identifying and developing empirically supported child and adolescent treatments. *Journal of Consulting and Clinical Psychology, 66,* 19–36.

Kazdin, A. E., & Whitley, M. K. (2003). Treatment of parental stress to enhance therapeutic change among children referred for aggressive and antisocial behavior. *Journal of Consulting and Clinical Psychology, 71,* 504–515.

Kazdin, A. E., & Whitley, M. K. (2006). Comorbidity, case complexity, and effects of evidence-based treatment for children referred for disruptive behavior. *Journal of Consulting and Clinical Psychology, 74*(3), 455–467.

Kotchick, B. A., & Grover, R. L. (2008). Implementing evidence-based treatments with ethnically diverse clients. In R. G. Steele, T. D. Elkin, & M. C. Roberts (Eds.), *Handbook of evidence-based therapies for children and adolescents: Bridging science and practice* (pp. 487–504). New York: Springer.

Kumpfer, K. L., Alvarado, R., Smith, P., & Bellamy, N. (2002). Cultural sensitivity and adaptation in family-based prevention interventions. *Prevention Science, 3,* 241–246.

Lau, A. S. (2006). Making the case for selective and directed cultural adaptations of evidence-based treatments: Examples from parent training. *Clinical Psychology: Science and Practice, 13,* 295–310.

Linares, L. O., Montalto, D., Li, M., & Oza, V. S. (2006). A promising parenting intervention in foster care. *Journal of Consulting and Clinical Psychology, 74,* 32–41.

Martinez, C. R., & Eddy, J. (2005). Effects of culturally adapted parent management training on Latino youth behavioral health outcomes. *Journal of Consulting and Clinical Psychology, 73,* 841–851.

Matos, M., Torres, R., Santiago, R., Jurado, M., & Rodríguez, I. (2006). Adaptation of parent-child interaction therapy for Puerto Rican families: A preliminary study. *Family Process, 45,* 205–222.

McCabe, K. M., Yeh, M., Garland, A. F., Lau, A. S., & Chavez, G. (2005). The GANA program: A tailoring approach to adapting parent-child interaction therapy for Mexican Americans. *Education and Treatment of Children, 28,* 111–129.

McKay, M. M., McCadam, K., & Gonzales, J. J. (1996). Addressing the barriers to mental health services for inner city children and their caretakers. *Community Mental Health Journal, 32,* 353–361.

McMahon, R. J., & Kotler, J. S. (2008). Evidence-based therapies for oppositional behavior in young children. In R. G. Steele, T. D. Elkin, & M. C. Roberts (Eds.), *Handbook of evidence-based therapies for children and adolescents: Bridging science and practice* (pp. 221–240). New York: Springer.

Miranda, J., Bernal, G., Lau, A., Kohn, L., Hwang, W., & LaFromboise, T. (2005). State of the science on psychosocial interventions for ethnic minorities. *Annual Review of Clinical Psychology, 1,* 113–142.

Myers, H. F., Alvy, K. T., Arrington, A., Richardson, M. A., Marigna, M., Huff, R., et al. (1992). The impact of a parent training program on inner-city African-American families. *Journal of Community Psychology, 20,* 132–147.

Nock, M. K., & Kazdin, A. E. (2005). Randomized controlled trial of a brief intervention for increasing participation in parent management training. *Journal of Consulting and Clinical Psychology, 73,* 872–879.

Patterson, G. R. (1982). *Coercive family process.* Eugene, OR: Castalia.

Reid, M., Webster-Stratton, C., & Baydar, N. (2004). Halting the development of conduct problems in Head Start children: The effects of parent training. *Journal of Clinical Child and Adolescent Psychology, 33,* 279–291.

Reid, M. J., Webster-Stratton, C., & Beachaine, T. P. (2001). Parent training in Head Start: A comparison of program response among African American, Asian American, Caucasian, and Hispanic mothers. *Prevention Science, 2,* 209–227.

Rogers, E. M. (2000). Diffusion theory: A theoretical approach to promote community-level change. In J. L. Peterson & R. J. DiClemente (Eds.), *Handbook of HIV prevention* (pp. 57–65). Dordrecht, the Netherlands: Kluwer.

Rogler, L. H., Malgady, R. G., Costantino, G., & Blumenthal, R. (1987). What do culturally sensitive mental health services mean? *American Psychologist, 42,* 565–570.

Schoenfield, L., & Eyberg, S. M. (2005). Parent management training. In G. P. Koocher, J. C. Norcross, & S. S. Hill (Eds.), *Psychologist's Desk Reference* (2nd ed.). New York: Oxford University Press.

Taylor, T. K., & Biglan, A. (1998). Behavioral family interventions for improving child-rearing: A review of the literature for clinicians and policy makers. *Clinical Child and Family Psychology Review, 1,* 41–60.

Timmer, S. G., Sedlar, G., & Urquiza, A. J. (2004). Challenging children in kin versus nonkin foster care: Perceived costs and benefits to caregivers. *Child Maltreatment, 9,* 251–262.

Timmer, S. G., Urquiza, A. J., Zebell, N. M., & McGrath, J. M. (2005). Parent-child interaction therapy: Application to maltreating parent-child dyads. *Child Abuse and Neglect, 29,* 825–842.

Webster-Stratton, C. (1998). Preventing conduct problems in Head Start children: Strengthening parenting competencies. *Journal of Consulting and Clinical Psychology, 66,* 715–730.

Webster-Stratton, C. (2007). *Affirming diversity: Multi-cultural collaboration to deliver the Incredible Years parent programs.* Unpublished manuscript, University of Washington, Seattle.

Webster-Stratton, C., & Reid, M. J. (2008). Strengthening social and emotional competence in socioeconomically disadvantaged young children: Preschool and kindergarten school-based curricula. In W. H. Brown, S. L. Odom, & S. R. McConnell (Eds.), *Social competence of young children: Risk, disability, and intervention* (pp. 185–203). Baltimore: Paul H. Brookes.

Webster-Stratton, C., Reid, M., & Hammond, M. (2001). Preventing conduct problems, promoting social competence: A parent and teacher training partnership in Head Start. *Journal of Clinical Child Psychology, 30,* 283–302.

Weisz, J. B., Jensen-Doss, A., & Hawley, K. M. (2005). Evidence-based youth psychotherapies versus usual clinical care: A meta-analysis of direct comparisons. *American Psychologist, 61,* 671–689.

Zayas, L. H., Bellamy, J., & Proctor, E. K. (2008). Multiple service contexts and adaptation levels in intervention implementation. Manuscript submitted for publication.

18

EVIDENCE-BASED APPROACHES TO WORKING WITH LATINO YOUTH AND FAMILIES

GUILLERMO BERNAL, EMILY SÁEZ-SANTIAGO,
AND AMARILYS GALLOZA-CARRERO

Yo soy yo y mi circunstancia, y si no la salvo a ella no me salvo yo.

—José Ortega y Gasset

The interaction between a person and his or her context must be a central consideration in the clinical approach when working with Latino/a children and families. The opening quotation from the Spanish philosopher, "I am myself and my circumstance, and if I do not save it, I do not save myself" (Ortega y Gasset, 1914/1970, p. 30; translation ours) reflects the dialectic between person and situation or context. In today's world, we would refer to "changing" rather than "saving" one's situation. The importance of context is that provides clues to the meaning of that which surrounds us. In Gasset's own words, "*buscar el sentido de lo que nos rodea*" (ibid.). More than 26 years ago, Bernal and Flores-Ortiz (1982) offered clinical guidelines for engaging and evaluating Latino families in therapy and called attention to social conditions that undergird a cycle of poverty too often connected to a legacy of subordination and oppression. In the spirit of Ortega y Gasset's notion of "saving one's situation," a number of other authors have called attention to the importance of both context and culture when working with Latino families (Alegría et al., 2004; Betancourt & López, 1993; Cauce et al., 2002; Lewis-Fernández & Kleinman, 1994; Roosa, Morgan-Lopez, Cree, & Specter, 2002; Vega et al., 2007), and some have proposed frameworks for considering both culture and context (Falicov, 1998; Lewis-Fernández & Díaz, 2002; Rogler, 1989; Szapocznik & Kurtines,

Work on this article was supported by the NIH Research Grant R01-MH67893 funded by the National Institute on Mental Health (NIMH) and by the Division of Services and Intervention Research to Guillermo Bernal, and by K23-MH081135 to Emily Sáez-Santiago.

1993) as a fundamental aspect of working with Latino children, adolescents, and families. Indeed, a recent report on evidence-based practice with children, youth, and families (APA Task Force on Evidence-Based Practice With Children and Adolescents, 2008) is framed within a contextual-developmental-systems framework. Yet, as we enter the era of evidence-based treatments, and despite the fact that Latinos have become the largest ethnocultural group in the United States, there are few efficacious treatments available for a predominantly youthful population.

In this chapter, we review the state of the science in psychological evidence-based treatments (EBT) for Latino children, adolescents, and families. Our interest is in identifying specific treatments and "[for] whom and under what circumstances and why these treatments work to help in the improvement of mental health care" (National Institute of Mental Health, 2000, p. 46). To this end, we briefly examine the context of Latinos and Latinas living in the United States and then review developments in the literature on effective psychological treatments for children, adolescents, and families. We discuss the state of the science in the treatment of this population, focusing on issues of cultural adaptation, the role of the family, language, acculturation, and access to care. We conclude with the implications for future research and practice.

The Situation and Context of Latinos and Latinas in the United States

Latinos/as continue to be the fastest-growing population in the United States. In 2006, of the nearly 300 million residents in the United States, 44 million or 14% were Latinos/as. Of these 44 million, 15 million were children under the age of 18, meaning that 34% of the Latino/a population living in the United States is young (U.S. Census Bureau, 2006). The Latino/a population increased more than 2% after the 2000 census (U.S. Census Bureau, 2006). The present demographic profile shows that Latinos/as are already the largest ethnic minority in the United States (ibid.). By the year 2015, the Latino population is expected to be more than 50 million, representing 16.6% of the entire U.S. population (ibid.). The current demographic profile and these projections must bring attention to the Latino's living conditions and needs. Certainly,

mental health care should be a priority for this population because Latinos/as are confronting serious problems in receiving the appropriate services. The surgeon general's supplement, *Mental Health: Culture, Race and Ethnicity* (U.S. Department of Health and Human Services, 2000) pointed out that minorities, including Latinos/as, have less access to mental health services, are less likely to receive mental health services, receive poorer-quality mental health services, and are underrepresented in the treatment research.

The surgeon general's report highlights the importance of developing and evaluating effective mental health services for Latinos/as. Effective mental health for this population requires special attention to particular cultural considerations. The concept of culture can be understood as the learned and shared meanings and behaviors that are transmitted into the context of a social activity with the purpose of promoting individual and social adjustments such as growth and development (Marsella, 2003).

Latinos/as cannot be considered as a homogeneous group with a particular identity (Calderon, 1992). The U.S. Latino/a population comprises people from 20 countries in Central and South America, Spain, and the Caribbean (Añez, Silva, Paris, & Bedregal, 2008). In the 2006 U.S. census, the Latino/a population was composed of 65.6% Mexicans, 8.6% Puerto Ricans, 17.2% Central and South Americans, and 3.8% Cubans (U.S. Census Bureau, 2006). Thus, the Latino/a population is a multicultural group with diverse Spanish-language expressions, terminologies, and migration conditions that responds to the particular educational, political, and economic circumstances (Padilla, 1995). The diverse Latino communities in the United States differ in social economic status, insertion into the labor market, employment mobility, and fertility (Calderon, 1992).

Despite the aforementioned differences, many Latinos/as in the United States share a common legacy of language and cultural values, such as *personalismo, espiritualidad,* and *familismo.* These cultural values refer to the importance of social support, trust in spiritual support systems, and the extended family, respectively. Latinos/as also share the value of interdependence, in which the family and interpersonal needs are favored over the individual (Bernal, Cumba-Avilés, & Sáez-Santiago, 2006). Añez et al. (2008) point out other constructs that are particular to the Latino community, such as *respeto* (respect), *confianza* (trust), *fatalismo* (fatalism), *controlarse* (self-control), and *aguantarse* (putting up with). In addition, many Latinos/as share common life conditions and challenges, such as poverty, inadequate housing, and a high rate of single-parent households (Bernal & Sáez-Santiago, 2006). It is important to note that although several cultural values shared by Latino groups can be identified, culture is a dynamic process. Thus, Sue (1998) has proposed the notion of dynamic sizing to describe the challenge of working with cultural values without stereotyping; it is therefore critical to know when to focus on the individual and when to generalize across cultural groups.

Latino children and adolescents are considered a high-risk population for mental health problems, and so availability of effective psychological treatments is imperative for this population. This is particularly relevant because studies have shown that there are ethnic differences in the use of pharmacological treatments in high-risk U.S. children. In a study with a sample of 1,342 children, 19.4% of whom were Latinos/as, it was reported that African American and Latino youth had a reduced likelihood of using psychotropic medications, compared to non-Latino children (Weckerly, Landsverk, & Hough, 2003). Weckerly et al. point out that cultural differences may explain their findings, such as differing beliefs about the causes of an illness and the acceptability of an expectation for treatment. They also indicate that the parents' and/or caregivers' beliefs may have an impact on the efforts to seek and accept certain treatment plans. However, the latter has not been fully studied, and there may be important differences in the preferences of mental health services.

For the other hand, in a large-scale sample of 26,708 individuals, 14% of whom were Latinos/as (3,825), Latinos/as were more likely to use case management and outpatient care and less likely to use emergency care services, in comparison with Whites (Hu, Snowden, Jerrell, & Nguyen, 1991). Yet, there were no significant difference in the use of inpatient services. It is possible that the greater use of case management by Latinos may be related to a more constant interpersonal contact that is inherent in this treatment modality. These investigators add that even though Latinos/as were more likely than the Whites to use outpatient services, Latinos/as in psychotherapy attended fewer sessions than Whites. Although the authors did not consider the ethnicity of the care provider in their analysis, it is possible that the ethnicity of the therapist may explain the results. Several studies have indicated the importance of an ethnic match between patient and therapist as a means of achieving culturally sensitive treatments (Burchinal & Cryer, 2003; Flicker, Waldron, Turner, Brody, & Hops, 2008). Studies conducted with youth revealed that ethnic match could affect discharge success, length of treatment (Halliday-Boykins, Shoenwald, & Letourneau, 2005) and treatment retention (Wintersteen, Mensinger, & Diamond, 2005). Ethnic matching contributes to greater decreases in symptoms, longer times in treatment, and greater retention. Others advocate for mental health care models tailored to the context and particular needs of Latinos (Alegría et al., 2006; Bernal, Bonilla, & Bellido, 1995; López et al., 1989; Miranda et al., 2005). Herein rests the importance of adapting psychological treatments and interventions for Latino youth and families that consider culture, situation, special needs, preferences, characteristics, and context.

Recently, interest has emerged in developing approaches to adapt psychological treatments that take into consideration culture, language, and the social status of ethnocultural groups (Barrera & Castro, 2006; Bernal et al., 1995; Bernal & Sáez-Santiago, 2006; Domenech-Rodríguez, & Wieling, 2005; Hwang, 2006; Lau, 2006; Matos, Torres, Santiago, Jurado, & Rodríguez, 2006; Rosselló & Bernal, 1996). The cultural adaptation of a psychological intervention is defined by Bernal and Jimenez-Chafey (2008) as "the systematic modification of an evidence-based treatment or intervention protocol to consider language, culture, and context in such a way that it is compatible with the client's cultural patterns, meanings, and values" (p. 6). Despite the recent efforts in developing culturally informed interventions, much remains to be done to develop and implement psychosocial treatments. Mental health providers and researchers need to be aware of the barriers that Latinos/as confront in receiving mental health services. Two principal barriers are the lack of interventions delivered in Spanish and the inaccessibility of mental health services (Hough et al., 2002). In fact, Latino children are less likely to receive care for mental health problems, in comparison to children and adolescents of other ethnicities, and as many as 88% of Latino children who are in need of mental health services do not receive those services (National Center for Children in Poverty, 2006).

Other relevant cultural issues must be considered when providing a psychosocial treatment for Latinos/as, including consideration of the individual's cultural background as well as that person's exposure to U.S. culture (acculturation). The challenge here, given that culture is a dynamic process, is to adopt a nonstatic view of culture (Lewis-Fernández & Díaz, 2002; López et al., 1989). Acculturation has been described as an individual's process of learning and adoption of the European American cultural norms, and the degree to which the person maintains the group norms of his or her heritage culture (Berry, 1998, cited in Le & Stockdale, 2008). Some researchers explain that migration and acculturation processes can cause different changes in certain beliefs, values, and attitudes among family members. Because of these differences, adolescents' and parents' interactions resulted in great intergenerational and intercultural conflict (Castillo, Cano, Chen, Blucker, & Olds, 2008; Le & Stockdale, 2008; Szapocznik & Kurtines, 1993). In general, acculturation occurs faster in children and adolescents than in their parents because children are more exposed to the U.S. mainstream (through schools, television, music, peers, etc.) This difference in the levels of acculturation between parents and children can result in tensions and conflicts at home (Szapocznik & Kurtines, 1993). Children and adolescents may be affected behaviorally and emotionally by social conflicts that might arise because of their integration into the U.S. mainstream and by subsequent family conflicts.

The Evidence on Psychological Treatments with Latino Youth and Families

Several reviews of the literature on the effects of psychological treatments for youth and families point to the effectiveness of EBTs (Weisz, Jensen-Doss, & Hawley, 2006; Weisz, McCarty, & Valeri, 2006; Weisz, Weiss, Han, Granger, & Morton, 1995). Weisz and colleagues conducted a meta-analysis of evidence-based youth psychotherapies compared with usual clinical care (Weisz,

Jensen-Doss, et al., 2006). This meta-analysis examined a total of 32 studies. The effect sizes (ES) in the 32 studies ranged from small to medium at posttreatment. Analysis of the ES in the 20 studies that reported information on race and ethnicity revealed that there were no significant differences in the ES by ethnocultural groups. However, the reviewed studies include small samples of Latinos/as; only one of the studies of this meta-analysis included a large proportion of Latinos/as. More recently, Huey and Polo (2008) conducted a meta-analysis of evidenced-based psychosocial treatments for ethnic minority youth. A total of 30 studies were included (8 studies reported a considerably large Latino sample). The treatment effects reported in these studies were moderate. The results also showed that youth ethnicity did not moderate outcome, and there were no differences between studies that included cultural responsive considerations and those that did not. However, such variables as acculturation, language, and ethnic identity were not part of the meta-analysis; the definition of culturally responsive features was too broad, and some studies that were defined as not including a cultural component may have had one. In a narrative review of psychological treatment for ethnic minorities, Miranda and colleagues concluded that although the available data are limited, some culturally adapted interventions (described later in this section) are efficacious (Miranda et al., 2005). Also, there are some data on the extent to which cultural adaptations improve the intervention outcomes in ethnocultural groups (Griner & Smith, 2006). For example, the best available evidence suggests that studies that are culturally informed are effective in recruiting and engaging Latinos/as. Finally, Navarro (1993) conducted a meta-analysis on the effectiveness of psychotherapy with Latinos/as in the United States. Of 15 studies included in the meta-analysis, 11 involved children, adolescents, or families, and the majority of the interventions (57%) were conducted in Spanish. The effect sizes ranged from 0 to 2.75.

From the literature with the general population, a number of reviews synthesize the evidence on the effects of psychological treatment in youth (David-Ferdon & Kaslow, 2008; Weisz, Jensen-Doss, et al., 2006; Weisz et al., 1995). A substantial body of evidence points toward the benefit of EBTs for depression, anxiety, conduct problems, and attention deficit hyperactivity disorder (ADHD) (Kazdin & Kendall, 1998;

Weisz, Jensen-Doss, et al., 2006). Yet, little information is available on the transportability of these treatments to real-world settings, their impact on functional status at outcome, and the longer-term effects (APA Task Force on Evidence-Based Practice With Children and Adolescents, 2008; Miranda et al., 2005). And certainly, few Latinos/as are involved in large-scale clinical trials (Miranda, Nakamura, & Bernal, 2003).

The aforementioned meta-analyses showed that little information is available on the efficacy and effectiveness of psychological treatments for Latino/a children and adolescents. Moreover, the existing data come from studies with methodological limitations, small samples, and no consideration of important moderators for Latinos/as living in the United States (e.g., acculturation, language, and ethnic identity). Despite this situation, we have identified several evidenced-based psychological treatments for Latino/a children and adolescents. In this section, we review the available evidence-based psychological treatments with Latino children, adolescents, and families. This review includes only those studies that reported the inclusion of at least 40% Latinos/as in their sample. The criterion of 40% Latinos/as in the sample was used to assure that the studies included a sufficient number of Latino/a participants to sustain their findings and power analyses. Additionally, 40% represent close to the proportion of Latino/a youth living in the United States. A total of 18 treatment studies were identified. Twelve of them included a predominantly Latino sample (mostly Puerto Ricans and Cuban Americans); and only 6 studies included children from diverse ethnic backgrounds, such as Caucasians, African Americans, Haitians, and Jamaicans. Of the 18 studies, 12 targeted an internalizing disorder (depression, anxiety, phobia, posttraumatic stress disorder); 2 focused in an externalizing disorder (conduct disorder and oppositional defiant disorder); 2 were conducted on substance use; and 1 was conducted on mother-child attachment.

In the following sections, we present a brief description of each study. (See also a summary of studies in Table 18.1.) The studies are classified according to internalizing or externalizing disorders; however, this classification is to some extent arbitrary because some studies measured not a disorder per se but problems related to a condition (e.g., personality problems, inadequacy-immaturity, and socialized delinquency in Szapocznik et al., 1989), or measured both internalizing and

externalizing condition (e.g., anxiety symptoms, depression, and conduct problems (Costantino et al., 1988). Also, as another chapter in this volume is dedicated to parent training interventions, they are excluded from this review.

Internalizing Disorders

Depression. Currently, there are four published clinical trials evaluating the efficacy of cognitive-behavioral therapy (CBT) and/or interpersonal therapy (IPT) in Latino adolescents. These studies have been conducted by two independent research teams located in San Juan, Puerto Rico, and in New York City. Two clinical trials have been conducted to treat depression symptoms in Latino adolescents living in Puerto Rico. The first study included 71 adolescents from 13 to 17 years old (Rosselló & Bernal, 1999). Fifty-four percent of the participants were females, while 46% were males. Adolescents participating in the study were diagnosed with major depression and dysthymia. Each adolescent was randomly assigned to one of three conditions: (1) individual cognitive-behavioral therapy (CBT), (2) individual interpersonal psychotherapy (IPT), or (3) the waitlist control. The manuals used in CBT and IPT were culturally adapted before their use in this study. Assessments of depression were conducted using the Children's Depression Inventory (CDI) and *Diagnostic and Statistical Manual of Mental Disorders, 3rd revised edition (DSM-III-R)* diagnosis at pretreatment, posttreatment, and 3-month follow-up. Results indicated that adolescents in the CBT and IPT conditions manifested lower depressive symptoms at posttreatment than those adolescents in the waitlist control group. The adolescents who received CBT and IPT did not differ in symptoms of depression at posttreatment and follow-up evaluations.

A second study was recently published on the efficacy of individual versus group IPT and CBT (Rosselló, Bernal, & Rivera, 2008) for the treatment of Puerto Rican adolescents with symptoms of depression. The sample consisted of 112 adolescents from 12 to 18 years of age; 54% were females. In this study, participants were randomly assigned to one of the following four conditions: (1) individual CBT, (2) group CBT, (3) individual IPT, and (4) group IPT. Findings revealed that both CBT and IPT were effective interventions, but CBT produced greater reduction in depressive symptoms than IPT. There were no differences between the individual and group formats.

Table 18.1   Characteristics of Treatment Studies for Internalizing and Externalizing Disorders With Latino Youth and Families

Study and Focus of Intervention	Sample Size (% Latinos/as and Age)	Latino Subgroup	Research Design	Cultural Considerations	Relevant Findings
Rosselló & Bernal, 1999 Depression	N = 71 100% Ages 13–17	Puerto Ricans	Random assignment: 1. Individual cognitive-behavioral therapy (CBT) 2. Individual interpersonal psychotherapy (IPT) 3. Waitlist control	–CBT and IPT were culturally and developmentally adapted to Puerto Rican adolescents. –Spanish measures –Delivered in Spanish	–Adolescents in CBT and IPT manifested lower depressive symptoms than those in the waitlist control group. –The CBT and IPT did not differ in symptoms of depression at post and follow-up evaluation.
Rosselló, Bernal, & Rivera-Medina, 2008 Depression	N = 112 100% Ages 12–18	Puerto Ricans	Random assignment: 1. Individual CBT 2. Group CBT 3. Individual IPT 4. Group IPT	–Culturally adapted manuals (CBT and IPT) –Conducted in Spanish	–CBT and IPT were effective, but CBT produced greater reduction in depressive symptoms than IPT. –There were no differences between individual and group formats.
Bernal et al., 2008 Depression	N = 121 100% Ages 13–17	Puerto Ricans	Random assignment: 1. CBT 2. CBT + parent psychoeducational intervention (PPI)	–CBT and PPI were culturally informed. –Delivered in Spanish –Parental intervention	–CBT was highly effective. –72% no longer had MDD, and it appears that comorbidity and symptom severity may be important treatment moderators.
Mufson, Weissman, Moreau, & Garfinkel, 1999 Depression	N = 48 Not specified Ages 12–18	Latinos/as	Random assignment: 1. IPT 2. Clinical monitoring	–Not reported –Intervention delivered in English.	–Adolescents in IPT condition had fewer depressive symptoms that those in the control group.

Study and Focus of Intervention	Sample Size (% Latinos/as and Age)	Latinos/as Subgroup	Research Design	Cultural Considerations	Relevant Findings
Mufson, Dorta, Wickramaratne, et. al., 2004 Depression	N = 63 71% Ages 12–18	Latinos	Random assignment: 1. IPT 2. Treatment as usual (TAU)	–Some monolingual Spanish-speaking adolescents were included.	–Adolescents in IPT reported greater reduction in depressive symptoms and improvement in social and general functioning.
Costantino, Malgady, & Rogler, 1986 Anxiety symptoms	N = 210 100% Kindergarten to 3rd grade	Primarily Puerto Rican	Random assignment: 1. Original folktales 2. Integrating original folktales adapted to reflect adjustment in the United States (cuento therapy) 3. Art/play therapy 4. No-intervention control group	Use of folktales of Latino culture	–Improvement in anxiety was obtained in all intervention conditions. –Cuento therapy was shown to be the most effective condition, followed by original folktales.
Costantino, Malgady, & Rogler, 1988 Anxiety, phobic concerns, depression, and conduct problems	N = 30 100% Children	Mostly Puerto Ricans and Dominicans	Random assignment: 1. Intervention 2. Control Group	Integrated Hispanic thematic pictures	–Intervention and control groups did not differ on depressive symptoms. –Lower anxiety, phobic concerns, and conduct problems in the intervention group
Malgady, Rogler, & Costantino, 1990 Anxiety	N = 90 100% 8th- and 9th-graders	Puerto Ricans	Random assignment: 1. Cuento therapy 2. Control group	Use of Latino folktales particular to Puerto Rican culture	–No differences in symptoms of psychological distress –Intervention students in 8th grade reported lower anxiety symptoms.

(Continued)

Table 18.1 (Continued)

Study and Focus of Intervention	Sample Size (% Latinos/ as and Age)	Latino Subgroup	Research Design	Cultural Considerations	Relevant Findings
Costantino et al., 2007 Posttraumatic stress disorder	N = 229 Not specified 4th- and 5th-graders	Not specified	Random assignment: 1. Child and parent trauma-focused cognitive behavioral therapy 2. Temas narrative therapy	Use of culturally sensitive pictures	–Both treatment modalities were effective in reducing symptoms of posttraumatic stress disorder.
Silverman et al., 1999 Anxiety	N = 56 46% Ages 6–16	Not specified	Random assignment: 1. GCBT 2. Waitlist control group	Considered important aspects in Latino culture, such as peer modeling and social comparison.	–GCBT reduced anxiety symptoms. –Ethnicity did not moderate outcomes.
Pina, Silverman, Fuentes, Kurtines, & Weems, 2003 Anxiety	N = 131 40% Ages 6–16	45% Cubans; 18% Central and South Americans; others of mixed Hispanic origin	Random assignment: 1. Individual 2. Group format	Treatment was culturally competent and sensitively delivered.	–There were no differences between the Latinos and the Caucasians. –84% of Latinos and Caucasians had recovered at posttreatment.
Kataoka et al., 2003 Posttraumatic stress disorder or trauma related to depression	N = 198 100% 3rd-to-8th-graders	57% from Mexico; 18% from El Salvador; 11% from Guatemala; others from other Latin American countries	Random assignment: 1. Group cognitive behavioral intervention for trauma in schools (CBITS) 2. Waitlist control group	Treatment was delivered in Spanish by bilingual and bicultural social workers.	–CBITS produced significantly greater improvement in symptoms.

Study and Focus of Intervention	Sample Size (% Latinos/ as and Age)	Latino Subgroup	Research Design	Cultural Considerations	Relevant Findings
Stein et al, 2003 Posttraumatic stress disorder	N = 80% 6th-graders	Mexican Americans	Random assignment: 1. CBITS 2. Waitlist control group	Not reported. Intervention delivered in English.	CBITS decreased posttraumatic stress disorder symptoms.
Szapocznik et al., 1989 Conduct problems	N = 79 100% Ages 6–12	Mostly Cuban Americans	Random assignment: 1. Family effectiveness therapy (FET) 2. Minimal-contact control group	–Culturally sensitive –Family intervention –Treatment emphasized intergenerational conflicts generated by migration experiences.	FET led to greater reduction in personality problems and inadequacy-immaturity and improvement of family function than the control group.
Szapocznik, Rio, et al., 1989 Behavioral problems	N = 102 Children	Cuban Americans	Random assignment: 1. Structure family therapy 2. Individual psychodynamic therapy 3. Recreational control group	–Culturally adapted –Family intervention	–Structural family therapy was as effective as individual psychodynamic therapy. –Structural family therapy seemed to be more effective in maintaining improvement in family functioning than psychodynamic therapy.
Garza & Bratton, 2005 Externalizing problem	N = 29 100% Ages 5–11	Mexican Americans	Random assignment: 1. Child-centered play therapy (CCPT) 2. Small group counseling (SGC)	–Culturally responsive –Bilingual Hispanic counselors –Intervention in both Spanish and English –Use of multicultural toys	No treatment effect was found for the teacher's rating on externalizing problems.

(Continued)

Table 18.1 (Continued)

Study and Focus of Intervention	Sample Size (% Latinos/as and Age)	Latino Subgroup	Research Design	Cultural Considerations	Relevant Findings
Liddle, Rowe, Dakof, Ungaro, & Henderson, 2004 Substance abuse	N = 80 42% Ages 11–15	Latinos	Random assignment: 1. Multidimensional family therapy (MDFT) 2. Peer group therapy (PGT)	–Family intervention	MDFT led to grater reduction in the use of marijuana.
Santisteban et al., 2003 Substance abuse	N = 126 100% Ages 12–18	51% Cubans; 14% Nicaraguans; 10% Colombians; 6% Puerto Ricans; 3% Peruvians; 2% Mexicans; 14% other Latinos/as	Random assignment: 1. Brief Strategic Family Therapy (BSFT) 2. Counseling control group	–Family intervention –Culturally adapted	BSFT generated a decrease in marijuana use and problems associated with antisocial peers.
Lieberman, Weston, & Pawl, 1991 Infant-mother attachment bond	N = 100 100% Mothers and their 11-14-month-old children	Mexicans and Central Americans	Random assignment: For Strange Situation task: 1. Intervention 2. Control group For attached dyads: 3. Control group	–Bilingual and bicultural facilitators –Intervention in Spanish	–Children in the intervention group showed higher partnership with their mothers. –Mothers were more empathetic and engaged with their children than the control groups.

This team of investigators is currently conducting another clinical trial on the treatment of depression with CBT in Puerto Rican adolescents (Bernal et al., 2008). The study evaluates the degree to which CBT can be optimized by means of a Parent Psychoeducational Intervention (PPI). Both the CBT and the PPI interventions were culturally adapted. A total of 121 adolescents meeting criteria for major depressive disorder (MDD) were randomized to individual CBT plus PPI or to individual CBT alone. Approximately 62% of the sample had at least one comorbid disorder, and patients with high suicide risk were entered in the protocol. The preliminary results suggest that both CBT alone and CBT with PPI were highly effective. At posttreatment, 72% of the adolescents no longer had MDD, and it appears that comorbidity and symptom severity may be important treatment moderators.

Mufson and collaborators carried two randomized clinical trials evaluating the efficacy of IPT in depressed children living in impoverished areas of New York City, the majority of them Latinos/as (Mufson, Dorta, Wickramaratne, et al., 2004; Mufson, Weissman, Moreau, & Garfinkel, 1999). In a first study (Mufson et al., 1999), a total of 48 adolescents from 12 to 18 years old (predominantly females) were randomly assigned to IPT or clinical monitoring conditions. Seventy-nine percent of the adolescents in the IPT condition and 62.5% of those in the clinical monitoring condition were English-speaking Latinos/as. The IPT participants received 12 weekly sessions focusing on such adolescent interpersonal issues as separation from parents, parent authority, peer pressure, or death. Adolescents in the clinical monitoring condition received 30-minute sessions once a month (or twice a month in some cases) to discuss their symptoms and functioning. Results showed that adolescents in the IPT condition had fewer depressive symptoms than those in the control group. In a second study, Mufson and collaborators (2004) conducted an effectiveness trial at school-based health clinics. Adolescents were randomly assigned to IPT or TAU (treatment as usual). A total of 63 adolescents ages 12 to 18 from five schools in New York City participated in this study. This sample was also predominantly Latinos/as (71%), female (84%), and of low socioeconomic status. Many of the adolescents were English speaking; monolingual Spanish-speaking adolescents were accepted at only two schools. At posttreatment (after 12 months), the adolescents who received IPT reported greater reduction in depressive symptoms, improvement in general and social functioning than those in TAU.

Of the four published outcome treatment studies for Latino/a adolescents, two have clearly informed the use of culturally adapted interventions (Rosselló & Bernal, 1999; Rosselló, Bernal, & Rivera-Medina, 2008). Both IPT and CBT evaluated in the studies were translated to Spanish and were fully conducted in Spanish by Puerto Ricans therapists. The other two studies (Mufson et al., 1999, 2004) on depression did not reported cultural considerations, with the exception of the last study (Mufson et al., 2004) in which monolingual Spanish-speaking participants were included at two schools. Although the information was not explicitly stated, we can assume that the intervention was delivered in Spanish, but no information was provided about the translation process or any other cultural consideration in the study.

Anxiety Disorders. Eight treatment studies have been identified for anxiety disorders and symptoms in Latino children and adolescents. Four of these studies have been conducted with Latino children (primarily Puerto Ricans) in New York City, evaluating *cuento* therapy (Costantino et al., 2007; Costantino, Malgady, & Rogler, 1986, 1988; Malgady, Rogler, & Costantino, 1990). *Cuento* therapy integrates Puerto Rican *cuentos*, or folk stories, focusing on biographies as models of adaptive emotional and behavioral functioning. In a first study, 210 children attending kindergarten to 3rd grade were identified by teachers' reports as being in the bottom half of the class in terms of adaptive behavior (Costantino et al., 1986). Forty-eight percent of the students identified participated in a randomized clinical trial. Children were assigned to one of four treatment conditions: (1) original folktales, (2) integrating original folktales adapted to reflect adjustment in the United States (*cuento* therapy), (3) art/play therapy, or (4) a no-intervention control group. Interventions were conducted after hours at schools. Improvement in anxiety symptoms were obtained at posttreatment in all intervention conditions. *Cuento* therapy was shown to be the most effective condition, followed by the original folktales.

These results were maintained after 1-year follow-up, which may be due to the cultural meaning embedded in the intervention.

A second study included 30 Puerto Rican and Dominican children with anxiety symptoms, phobic concerns, depressive symptoms, and conduct problems (Costantino et al., 1988). These 30 children were randomly assigned to the intervention group or control group. The intervention consisted of the examination of Hispanic thematic pictures, a group discussion of the situation presented in the pictures, encouraging the children to discuss personal feelings, and acting out the picture story. After 8 weeks, the intervention and control groups did not differ on depressive symptoms, but the children in the intervention group manifested lower anxiety symptoms, phobic concerns, and conduct problems. A third study was conducted with 8th- and 9th-grade Puerto Rican adolescents (Malgady et al., 1990). A total of 90 adolescents were randomly assigned to *cuento* therapy or a control group. The intervention group consisted of 18 sessions. The control group had 8 sessions, in which current events were discussed. There were no differences in symptoms of psychological distress at posttreatment; only the intervention students in 8th grade reported lower anxiety symptoms. A more recent study focused on symptoms of posttraumatic stress disorder (Costantino et al., 2007). The sample for this study included 229 4th- and 5th-graders in two public schools in Brooklyn, New York, who had been affected by the events of September 11, 2001. Children were randomly assigned to the child and parent trauma-focused cognitive-behavioral therapy or to the *temas* narrative therapy. The first treatment modality integrated a psychoeducational component about normal reactions to trauma, stress inoculation techniques, cognitive processing, and creating and processing the trauma narratives. The *temas* narrative therapy used 18 culturally sensitive pictures. Both treatment modalities were effective in reducing symptoms of posttraumatic stress disorder at posttreatment. No significant differences were found between groups.

Two other anxiety treatment studies have been conducted by another research team. The first of these studies included 56 children and adolescents ranging from 6 to 16 years of age, of whom 46% were Latinos/as and another 46% were Caucasians (Silverman et al., 1999). Participants were included if they had any anxiety *DSM-III-R* diagnosis (social phobia, general anxiety, or overanxious disorder) as measured by a structured interview (the Anxiety Disorders Interview Schedule for Children). They were randomly assigned to a group cognitive-behavioral treatment (GCBT) or a waitlist control group. The GCTB condition integrated the parents' participation. Children and parents met in separate groups for 40 minutes, and then a conjoint meeting was conducted for the last 15 minutes of the sessions. GCBT included such strategies as peer modeling, feedback, support, reinforcement, and social comparison. In general, results showed that group GCBT led to greater reduction of the anxiety symptoms. Ethnicity did not moderate outcomes. These findings were also found in another study that also focused on phobic and anxiety disorders. The study's sample consisted of 131 youth between 6 and 16 years of age (Pina, Silverman, Fuentes, Kurtines, & Weems, 2003). Forty percent of the participants were Latinos/as, and the other 60% were Caucasians. In the case of the Latinos/as, 45% reported Cuba as their country of origin, 18% reported a Central or South American country, and the remaining reported mixed Hispanic origin. Assessment and therapies were administered primarily in English; only 4% of the Latinos/as needed the assessment and treatment in Spanish. This study examined the treatment response to and maintenance of exposure-based cognitive-behavioral therapy, which was delivered in both individual and group formats. Researchers reported that treatment was culturally competent and sensitively delivered. Cultural differences in coping strategies and definitions of anxiety-provoking objects or events were considered. Assessments were conducted at pretreatment, posttreatment, and 3, 6, and 12 months of follow-up. Results showed no differences between the Latinos/as and Caucasians. In general, about 84% of Latinos/as (84.2%) and Caucasians (83.9%) recovered at posttreatment. The positive treatment gains were maintained at follow-up.

Another study tested a school-based CBT for Latino immigrant students who had been exposed to community violence (Kataoka et al., 2003). The study included 198 children from 3rd to 8th grades who had symptoms of posttraumatic stress disorder and/or trauma-related depression. More than half of participants

(57%) were born in Mexico, 18% were from El Salvador, and 11% were from Guatemala, while the remaining migrated from other Latin American countries. The children had been living in the United States less than 3 years and were Spanish speaking. The intervention was delivered in Spanish by bilingual and bicultural school social workers. The students were randomly assigned either to a group cognitive-behavioral intervention for trauma in schools (CBITS; n = 152) or to a waitlist control (n = 46). The CBITS intervention integrated the following techniques: relaxation training, combating erroneous negative thoughts, construction to fear hierarchy, imaginary exposure, social problem solving, and exposure to trauma memory through drawing and writing. An optional psychoeducational intervention, intended to discuss the effects of trauma on children and the techniques that their children would be learning, was offered to the parents in the intervention group. Only 37% of parents attended at least one group session (of 2 hours). Results demonstrated that students in the CBITS group had significantly greater improvements in symptoms at 3-month follow-up than those in the waitlist group. Parent psychoeducation did not appear to impact the treatment.

An additional study identified on anxiety disorders also focused on posttraumatic stress disorder and evaluated the CBITS as well (Stein et al., 2003). The majority of the sample (80%) consisted of Mexican American children. As in the previous studies, children were randomized to CBITS or a waitlist control. Again, the CBIT group demonstrated a greater decrease in posttraumatic stress disorder symptoms than the waitlist group.

It is important to note that the described treatments for anxiety disorders in Latino/a children and adolescents have been culturally responsive. Half of the eight treatment studies (Costantino et al., 2007; Costantino, Malgady, & Rogler, 1986; Costantino, Malgady, & Rogler, 1988; Malgady, Rogler, & Costantino, 1990) evaluated an intervention that was actually developed taking into consideration cultural aspects. Specifically, *cuento* therapy and temas narrative therapy integrate folktales or pictures that are culturally sensitive to Latino/a children and adolescents. It is also important to mention that the names of both treatment modalities are in Spanish, which highlight the strong cultural load of the interventions. In general, the other

studies on anxiety disorders also incorporated cultural elements by conducting some assessment and treatment in Spanish (Pina et al., 2003) or entirely in Spanish with bilingual and bicultural facilitators (Kataoka et al., 2003).

Externalizing Disorders

Conduct Problems. Szapocznik and collaborators (Szapocznik, Rio, et al., 1989; Szapocznik, Santisteban, et al., 1989) have developed and evaluated a family intervention for the treatment of conduct problems and intergenerational conflicts generated by migration experiences. This intervention was tested in a randomized clinical trial, where 79 6- to 12-year-old children and adolescents were assigned to Family Effectiveness Therapy (FET) or to a minimal contact control group (Szapocznik, Santisteban, et al., 1989). Conduct problems were measured as personality problems, inadequacy-immaturity, and socialized delinquency. At posttreatment, FET led to greater reduction in personality problems and inadequacy-immaturity and improvement of family functioning than the control group. No treatment effect was found on socialized delinquency. In another study, 102 Latino children (mostly Cuban Americans) with behavioral problems and their families were randomized to one of three conditions: structural family therapy, individual psychodynamic therapy, or recreational control group (Szapocznik, Rio, et al., 1989). The structural family therapy was as effective as individual psychodynamic therapy at posttreatment, but structural family therapy seemed to be more effective than psychodynamic therapy in maintaining improvement in family functioning.

A pilot study evaluating the effects of child-centered play therapy (CCPT) on externalizing problems was conducted by Garza and Bratton (2005). A total of 29 Mexican American children between the ages of 5 and 11 constituted the sample for this study. Children who scored as at risk or in the clinically significant range for externalizing behavior problems on the Behavior Assessment Scale and in parents' and teachers' reports were randomly assigned to CCPT or to a small group counseling (SGC). The intervention was carried out at schools by professional therapists. Results revealed that parents in CCPT reported greater reduction in externalizing problems than those in SGC. No treatment effect was found for the teachers' ratings of externalizing problems.

Substance Use. A randomized clinical trial was conducted including a multiethnic sample of youth who reported the use of marijuana (Liddle, Rowe, Dakof, Ungaro, & Henderson, 2004). In this study, a total of 80 children and adolescents ages 11 to 15 were recruited. Of these 80, 73% were male, and 42% were Latinos/as. The sample also included African Americans (38%), Haitians and Jamaicans (11%), and Caucasians (4%). Participants were randomly assigned to one of two conditions: (1) multidimensional family therapy (MDFT), or (2) peer group therapy (PGT). Results at posttreatment showed that MDFT led to greater reduction in the use of marijuana, in comparison to PGT.

A variation of the FET described earlier (Szapocznik, Santisteban, et al., 1989)—Brief Strategic Family Therapy (BSFT)—was evaluated for the treatment of Latino adolescents with substance abuse problems. The BSFT is based on a structural family systems approach (Minuchin, 1974) and integrates such strategies as joining, reframing, and boundary shifting to restructure the inadequate family interactions. Santisteban and colleagues reported the results of a clinical trial with adolescents between the ages of 12 and 18 with substance abuse problems (Santisteban, Muir, Mena, & Mitrani, 2003). Participants were predominantly males (75%); 51% identified as Cuban, 14% as Nicaraguan, 10% as Colombian, 6% as Puerto Rican, 3% as Peruvian, 2% as Mexican, and 14% as other Hispanic. In this study, participants were randomly assigned to BSFT or to a counseling control group. As compared to the control group, participation in the BSFT generated a decrease in problems, association with antisocial peers, and marijuana use. Family functioning showed greater improvement in the BSFT group.

Currently, the effectiveness of the BSFT for adolescents with drug use problems has been evaluated in a multisite research study (Santisteban, Suarez-Morales, Robbins, & Szapocznik, 2006). This ongoing study is part of the NIDA Clinical Trial Network, which includes eight different sites in the United States and Puerto Rico. A total of 480 drug-using adolescents and their families will be recruited from community treatment agencies and will be randomly assigned to BSFT or to treatment as usual.

The results from this large trial are not yet available, but they will likely move the field forward in terms of dissemination of an effective EBT.

Other Conditions

Other psychological therapies have been evaluated that focus on nondiagnosable conditions in Latino children and their families. One such intervention has been conducted to improve the infant-mother attachment bond as well as the social-emotional functioning of the children (Lieberman, Weston, & Pawl, 1991). This study included a sample of 100 Mexican and Central American mothers and their 12-month-old children who had been residents of the United States for less than 5 years and were of low socioeconomic status. Participant dyads with anxious attachment, as assessed in the Strange Situation task, were randomly assigned to an intervention or to a control group. A second control group was composed of securely attached dyads. The intervention was conducted for 1 year. At posttreatment, children in the intervention group showed higher partnership with their mothers, and the mothers were more empathetic and engaging with their children, than the dyads in the control groups. There was no difference between the intervention group and the securely attached control group on any outcome measures.

STATUS OF THE BEST AVAILABLE EVIDENCE

We have come a long way since the early clinical papers of the 1970s and the 1980s. An impressive number of psychological treatments have been tested, and research teams have emerged that focus on treatment development, adaptation, efficacy, effectiveness, and dissemination. There is also a growing literature on methodological issues as these pertain to the technology of developing and testing interventions oriented toward ethnocultural groups. Nevertheless, despite these developments, the number of studies with substantial samples of Latino youth and families remains relatively few and is certainly not commensurate with population rates. While we now have 18 excellent studies, it is not clear from the available evidence that we can generalize these results to the estimated 15 million Latinos/as youth and their families living in the

United States. In fact, samples included in the studies reviewed in this chapter are not proportional to the Latino/a population rates. Also, although Mexican Americans are the largest group among Latinos, very few clinical trials have targeted this population.

According to our review, there is now a growing body of information on EBTs for depression, anxiety, and conduct disorders for Latino youth and families. The EBTs for internalizing conditions—all of which are guided by a manual—include CBT (Rosselló & Bernal, 1999; Rosselló et al., 2008) and IPT for depression (Mufson, Dorta, Wickramaratne, et al., 2004; Mufson et al., 1999; Rosselló & Bernal, 1999; Rosselló et al., 2008), group CBT for anxiety disorders (Silverman et al., 1999; Silverman et al., 2008), *cuento* therapy for anxiety conditions (Costantino et al., 1986; Malgady et al., 1990), CBT for trauma exposure and PTSD (Kataoka et al., 2003), and a CBT intervention for trauma in schools (Stein et al., 2003). For the externalizing conditions, the EBTs available include brief systems family therapy for conduct disorders (Santisteban, Coatsworth, et al., 2003; Szapocznik, Rio, et al., 1989; Szapocznik, Santisteban, et al., 1989) and substance abuse problems (Santisteban et al., 1997), child-centered play therapy for externalizing problems (Garza & Bratton, 2005), and family systems therapies, such as multidimensional family therapy (Liddle et al., 2004) for substance abuse. Finally, in the target condition of attachment bonds, infant-parent psychotherapy showed promise (Lieberman et al., 1991). Thus, there are now EBTs with demonstrated benefits for Latino youth and families for depression, anxiety, behavior problems, and substance abuse conditions.

Nearly all of these treatments conducted with Latino youth include some kind of a family component, whereas others have structured the participation of parents. The incorporation of some level of parental participation in treatment seems to be one clear aspect of how such cultural values as *familismo* are considered in treatment. Also, most treatments focused on the situation, context, and specific needs of Latino families, and in some cases the interventions were specifically adapted or tailored to the family. Interventions that are culturally informed or culturally adapted clearly show that Latinos and Latinas can be effectively engaged in treatment designed specifically for Latino families. Also, as

can be appreciated, when Latinos/as are effectively engaged, they tend to remain in treatment, and the outcomes for these interventions are quite similar to those found in the mainstream literature with comparable effect sizes.

As is evident from our review, it is certainly possible to engage and maintain Latinos/as in treatment studies when culturally informed procedures are employed. Latino youth and families participate in treatment studies when basic situational factors are considered, not the least of which is settings that are welcoming and sensitive to cultural issues. For example, bilingual staff, materials in both Spanish and English, and interventions that take into consideration the role of the family, spirituality, language, and acculturation are likely to augment engagement and retention and to produce positive outcomes.

IMPLICATIONS FOR FUTURE RESEARCH AND PRACTICE

We return to the issue of changing one's circumstances. There are now 18 studies on the psychological treatment of Latino/a youth and families, which represents a remarkable achievement from only 20 years ago. Today, there is an emerging body of EBTs, but these studies are certainly not enough, and more rigorous research is needed, not only on the outcome but also on the mediators of change. The challenge for the field will be to first develop additional research with larger sample sizes that can explore why change occurs, how it happens, and under what sets of conditions. In fact, just over 40 years ago, Paul (1967) challenged the field to reframe the research question to examining "*[w]hat* treatment, by *whom*, is most effective for *this* individual, with *that* specific problem, and under *which* set of circumstances" (p. 111). Practitioners generally know that the best treatment is one that is tailored to the needs, situation, and context of the person. Thus, the consideration of culture, language, and socioeconomic context constitute an essential lens for both research and practice with Latino youth and families.

But how do treatments work, and what is the role of such variables as ethnic identity, acculturation, acculturative stress, spirituality, gender roles, discrimination, cultural beliefs about treatment, and *familismo*? What evidence do we have of the role of these constructs in the treatment process or in treatment outcome? Do cultural values change as a result of treatment, or are they moderators of treatment? An important future direction for the field is the clear definition of these constructs, along with measures that can tap into these processes and that can be of use in treatment studies.

Increasing the number of minorities in clinical trials is now a policy of the National Institutes of Health (NIH, 2002). The policy aims to increase the participation of women and minorities in NIH-supported clinical trials in sufficient numbers to enable potential differential treatment responses to either gender or race/ethnicity to be examined. Yet, this policy is not accompanied by any consideration of the real implications of including cultural, ethnic and language minorities in large-scale clinical trials. For example, an investigator in a large metropolitan area in the United States would have to design a study such that minorities who prefer to respond in their native languages could participate. To achieve this, usually an extraordinary amount of preliminary work is required of investigators, which begins with either obtaining translations of all instruments, or, if these are unavailable, then having to perform the translations—which is a complicated process—test for equivalence (content, semantic, metric, etc.), and then test the instruments to ensure that they are working properly. When families are involved at different rates of acculturation, some fill out the questionnaire in one language, and other members in another. Logistics also becomes an issue. Thus, the more "practical" approach for some investigators is to bypass this process and simply exclude participants who are not proficient in English. But even if investigators manage to include language minorities and other ethnic minorities based on the population rates of a particular community, the results are unlikely to be helpful, since the numbers will be too small for meaningful interpretation (Miranda et al., 2003). What is needed is theory-driven studies based in communities where a substantial number of specific ethnocultural groups reside and can be entered into the trials.

In our review of the limited literature on the efficacy of psychological treatments for Latino youth and families, the available studies of treatment effects suggest that some EBTs for depression, anxiety, and conduct disorders are as effective for Latino youth as for European American youth. We encourage practitioners to consider these, as well as other EBTs not tested with Latinos/a youth and families, but to complement these treatments by tailoring them so that culture, language, and context are considered and beneficial outcomes achieved.

Important resources are available to practitioners, such as the APA report on multicultural guidelines for education, training, research, practice, and organizational change (APA, 2003). Recently, an invaluable document was published on disseminating evidence-based practice for children and adolescents (APA Task Force on Evidence-Based Practice With Children and Adolescents, 2008), which assumes a developmental-systems-contextual approach for enhancing care. In addition, guidelines for cultural adaptations of EBTs are emerging as a key methodological resource for working with culturally diverse populations in both research and clinical settings (Barrera & Castro, 2006; Bernal & Sáez-Santiago, 2006; Domenech-Rodríguez et al., 2005; La Roche, D'Angelo, Gualdron, & Leavell, 2006; Lewis-Fernández & Díaz, 2002; López et al., 1989; Rogler, Malgady, Costantino, & Blumenthal, 1987; Rosselló & Bernal, 1996; Szapocznik & Kurtines, 1993). While EBTs represent an important development in the knowledge base as evidence accumulates on the efficacy of particular treatments for specific disorders, to date we know relatively little about the generalizability of EBTs for Latino/a youth. Cultural adaptations of EBTs offer valuable tools to modify EBTs in a systematic manner so that the culture and context are considered to optimize outcomes.

References

Alegría, M., Page, J. B., Hansen, H., Cauce, A. M., Robles, R., Blanco, C., et al. (2006). Improving drug treatment services for Hispanics: Research gaps and scientific opportunities. *Drug and Alcohol Dependence, 84,* S76–S84.

Alegría, M., Takeuchi, D., Canino, G., Duan, N., Shrout, P., Meng, X.-L., et al. (2004). Considering context, place and culture: The National Latino and Asian American Study. *International Journal of Methods in Psychiatric Research, 13,* 208–220.

American Psychological Association (APA). (2003). Guidelines on multicultural education, training, research, practice, and organizational change for psychologists. *American Psychologist, 58,* 377–402.

Añez, L. M., Silva, M. A., Paris, M., Jr., & Bedregal, L. E. (2008). Engaging Latinos through the integration of cultural values and motivational interviewing principles. *Professional Psychology: Research and Practice, 39,* 153–159.

APA Task Force on Evidence-Based Practice With Children and Adolescents. (2008). *Disseminating evidence-based practice for children and adolescents: A systems approach to enhancing care.* Washington, DC: American Psychological Association.

Barrera, M., & Castro, F. G. (2006). A heuristic framework for the cultural adaptation of interventions. *Clinical Psychology: Science and Practice, 13,* 311–316.

Bernal, G., Bonilla, J., & Bellido, C. (1995). Ecological validity and cultural sensitivity for outcome research: Issues for the cultural adaptation and development of psychosocial treatments with Hispanics. *Journal of Abnormal Child Psychology, 23,* 67–82.

Bernal, G., Cumba-Avilés, E., & Sáez-Santiago, E. (2006). Cultural and relational processes in depressed Latino adolescents. In S. R. H. Beach, M. Z. Wamboldt, N. J. Kaslow, R. E. Heyman, & M. B. First (Eds.), *Relational processes and DSM-V: Neuroscience, assessment, prevention, and treatment.* (pp. 211–224). Washington, DC: American Psychiatric Association.

Bernal, G., & Flores-Ortiz, Y. (1982). Latino families in therapy: Engagement and evaluation. *Journal of Marital and Family Therapy, 8,* 357–365.

Bernal, G., & Jimenez-Chafey, M. (2008). *Beyond one size fits all: Advances in the cultural adaptation of evidence-based treatments for ethno-cultural youth.* Unpublished manuscript.

Bernal, G., Rosselló, J., Rivera-Medina, C., Nazario, L., Cumba, E., Sáez-Santiago, E., et al. (2008). *Optimizing CBT with a family psychoeducation intervention for Puerto Rican adolescents with major depression.* Paper presented at the American Psychological Association Annual Convention, Boston.

Bernal, G., & Sáez-Santiago, E. (2006). Culturally centered psychosocial interventions. *Journal of Community Psychology, 34,* 121–132.

Betancourt, H., & López, S. R. (1993). The study of culture, ethnicity, and race in American psychology. *American Psychologist, 48,* 629–637.

Burchinal, M. R., & Cryer, D. (2003). Diversity, child care quality, and developmental outcomes. *Early Childhood Research Quarterly, 18,* 401–426.

Calderon, J. (1992). "Hispanic" and "Latino": The viability of categories for panethnic unity. *Latin American perspectives, 75,* 37–44.

Castillo, L. G., Cano, M. A., Chen, S. W., Blucker, R. T., & Olds, T. S. (2008). Family conflict and intragroup marginalization as predictors of acculturative stress in Latino college students. *International Journal of Stress Management, 15,* 43–52.

Cauce, A. M., Domenech-Rodríguez, M., Paradise, M., Cochran, B. N., Shea, J. M., Srebnik, D., et al. (2002). Cultural and contextual influences in mental health help seeking: A focus on ethnic minority youth. *Journal of Consulting and Clinical Psychology, 70,* 44–55.

Costantino, G., Kalogiros, I. D., Perez, M., Borges, M., Lardiere, M., Malgady, R., et al. (2007, August). *Evidence-based treatments for postdisaster trauma symptoms in Latino children.* Paper presented at the American Psychological Association Annual convention. San Francisco.

Costantino, G., Malgady, R. G., & Rogler, L. H. (1986). Cuento therapy: A culturally sensitive modality for Puerto Rican children. *Journal of Consulting and Clinical Psychology, 54,* 639–645.

Costantino, G., Malgady, R. G., & Rogler, L. H. (1988). Folk hero modeling therapy for Puerto Rican adolescents. *Journal of Adolescence, 11,* 155–165.

David-Ferdon, C., & Kaslow, N. J. (2008). Evidence-based psychosocial treatments for child and adolescent depression. *Journal of Clinical Child and Adolescent Psychology, 37,* 62–104.

Domenech-Rodríguez, M., & Wieling, E., (2005). Developing culturally appropriate, evidence-based treatments for interventions with ethnic minority populations. In M. Rastogi & E. Wieling (Eds.), *Voices of color: First-person accounts of ethnic minority therapists* (pp. 313–333). Thousand Oaks, CA: Sage.

Falicov, C. J. (1998). *Latino families in therapy: A guide to multicultural practice.* New York: Guilford Press.

Flicker, S. M., Waldron, H. B., Turner, C. W., Brody, J. L., & Hops, H. (2008). Ethnic matching and treatment outcome with Hispanic and Anglo substance-abusing adolescents in family therapy. *Journal of Family Psychology, 22,* 439–447.

Garza, Y., & Bratton, S. C. (2005). School-based child-centered play therapy with Hispanic children: Outcomes and cultural consideration. *International Journal of Play Therapy, 14,* 51–80.

Griner, D., & Smith, T. B. (2006). Culturally adapted mental health intervention: A meta-analytic review. *Psychotherapy: Theory, Research, Practice, Training, 43,* 531–548.

Halliday-Boykins, C. A., Shoenwald, S. K., & Letourneau, E. J. (2005). Caregiver-therapist similarity predicts youth outcome from an empirically based treatment. *Journal of*

Consulting and Clinical Psychology, 73, 808–818.

Hough, R. L., Hazen, A. L., Soriano, F. I., Wood, P., McCabe, K., & Yeh, M. (2002). Mental health care for Latinos: Mental health services for Latino adolescents with psychiatric disorders. *Psychiatric Services, 53,* 1556–1562.

Hu, T. W., Snowden, L. R., Jerrell, J. M., & Nguyen, T. D. (1991). Ethnic populations in public mental health: Services choice and level of use. *American Journal of Public Health, 81,* 1429–1434.

Huey, S. J., Jr., & Polo, A. J. (2008). Evidence-based psychosocial treatments for ethnic minority youth. *Journal of Clinical Child and Adolescent Psychology, 37,* 262–301.

Hwang, W. C. (2006). The psychotherapy adaptation and modification framework: Application to Asian Americans. *American Psychologist, 61,* 702–715.

Kataoka, S. H., Stein, B. D., Jaycox, L. H., Wong, M., Escudero, P., Tu, W., et al. (2003). A school-based mental health program for traumatized Latino immigrant children. *Journal of the American Academy of Child and Adolescent Psychiatry, 42,* 311–318.

Kazdin, A., & Kendall, P. C. (1998). Current progress and future plans for developing effective treatments: Comments and perspectives. *Journal of Clinical Child Psychology, 27,* 217–226.

La Roche, M. J., D'Angelo, E., Gualdron, L., & Leavell, J. (2006). Culturally sensitive guided imagery for allocentric Latinos: A pilot study. *Psychotherapy: Theory, Research, Practice, Training, 43,* 555–560.

Lau, A. S. (2006). Making the case for selective and directed cultural adaptations of evidence-based treatments: Examples from parent training. *Clinical Psychology: Science and Practice, 13,* 295–310.

Le, T. N., & Stockdale, G. (2008). Acculturative dissonance, ethnic identity, and youth violence. *Cultural Diversity and Ethnic Minority Psychology, 14,* 1–9.

Lewis-Fernández, R., & Díaz, N. (2002). The cultural formulation: A method for assessing cultural factors affecting the clinical encounter. *Psychiatric Quarterly, 73,* 271–295.

Lewis-Fernández, R., & Kleinman, A. (1994). Culture, personality, and psychopathology. *Journal of Abnormal Psychology, 103,* 67–71.

Liddle, H. A., Rowe, C. L., Dakof, G. A., Ungaro, R. A., & Henderson, C. E. (2004). Early intervention for adolescent substance abuse: Pretreatment to posttreatment outcomes of a randomized clinical trial comparing multidimensional family therapy and peer group treatment. *Journal of Psychoactive Drugs, 36,* 49–63.

Lieberman, A. F., Weston, D. R., & Pawl, J. H. (1991). Preventive intervention and outcome with anxiously attached dyads. *Child Development, 62,* 199–209.

López, S. R., Grover, P., Holland, D., Johnson, M. J., Kain, C. D., Kanel, K., et al. (1989). Development of culturally sensitive psychology. *Professional Psychology: Research and Practice, 20,* 369–376.

Malgady, R. G., Rogler, L. H., & Costantino, G. (1990). Culturally sensitive psychotherapy for Puerto Rican children and adolescents: A program of treatment outcome research. *Journal of Consulting and Clinical Psychology, 58,* 704–712.

Marsella, A. J. (2003). Cultural aspects of depressive experience and disorders. In W. J. Lonner, D. L. Dinnel, S. A. Hayes, & D. N. Sattler (Eds.), *Online reading in psychology and culture* (United 9, Chapter 4) http:www.ac.wwu.edu/~culture/Marsella.htm

Matos, M., Torres, R., Santiago, R., Jurado, M., & Rodríguez, I. (2006). Adaptation of parent-child interaction therapy for Puerto Rican families: A preliminary study. *Family Process, 45,* 205–222.

Minuchin, S. (1974). *Families and family therapy.* Cambridge, MA: Harvard University Press.

Miranda, J., Bernal, G., Lau, A., Kohn, L., Hwang, W. C., & LaFromboise, T. (2005). State of the science on psychosocial interventions for ethnic minorities. *Annual Review of Clinical Psychology, 1,* 113–142.

Miranda, J., Nakamura, R., & Bernal, G. (2003). Including ethnic minorities in mental health intervention research: A practical approach to a long-standing problem. *Culture, Medicine and Psychiatry, 27,* 467–486.

Mufson, L., Dorta, K. P., Wickramaratne, P., Nomura, Y., Olfson, M., & Myrna, M. W. (2004). A randomized effectiveness trial of interpersonal psychotherapy for depressed adolescents. *Archives of General Psychiatry, 61,* 577–584.

Mufson, L., Weissman, M. M., Moreau, D., & Garfinkel, R. (1999). Efficacy of interpersonal psychotherapy for depressed adolescents. *Archives of General Psychiatry, 57,* 573–579.

National Center for Children in Poverty. (2006). *Children's mental health: Facts for policymakers.* Retrieved September 23, 2008, from http://nccp.org/publications/pub_687.html

National Institutes of Health (NIH). (2002). *NIH Policy and Guidelines on The Inclusion of Women and Minorities as Subjects in Clinical Research—Amended, October, 2001.* Retrieved March 10, 2008, from http://grants.nih.gov/grants/

funding/women_min/guidelines_amended_10_2001.htm

National Institute of Mental Health. (2000). *Translating behavioral science into action: Report of the National Advisory Mental Health Council's Behavioral Science Workgroup* (NIMH Publication No. 00–4699). Washington, DC: U.S. Government Printing Office.

Navarro, A. (1993). The effectiveness of psychotherapy with Latinos in the United States: A meta-analytic review. *Interamerican Journal of Psychology, 27,* 131–146.

Ortega y Gasset, J. (1914/1970). *Meditaciones del quijote.* Madrid: El arquero.

Padilla, A. M. (Ed.). (1995). *Hispanic psychology: Critical issues in theory and research.* Thousand Oaks, CA: Sage.

Paul, G. (1967). Strategy of outcome research in psychotherapy. *Journal of Consulting Psychology, 31,* 109–118.

Pina, A. A., Silverman, W. K., Fuentes, R. M., Kurtines, W. M., & Weems, C. F. (2003). Exposure-based cognitive-behavioral treatment for phobic and anxiety disorders: Treatment effects and maintenance for Hispanic/Latino relative to European-American youths. *Journal of the American Academy of Child and Adolescent Psychiatry, 42,* 1179–1187.

Rogler, L. H. (1989). The meaning of culturally sensitive research in mental health. *American Journal of Psychiatry, 149,* 296–303.

Rogler, L. H., Malgady, R. G., Costantino, G., & Blumenthal, R. (1987). What do culturally sensitive mental health services mean? The case of Hispanics. *American Psychologist, 42,* 595–570.

Roosa, M. W., Morgan-Lopez, A. A., Cree, W. K., & Specter, M. M. (2002). Ethnic culture, poverty, and context: Sources of influence on Latino families and children. In J. M. Contreras, K. A. Kerns, & A. M. Neal-Barnett (Eds.), *Latino children and families in the United States: Current research and future directions* (pp. 27–44). Westport, CT: Praeger/Greenwood.

Rosselló, J., & Bernal, G. (1996). Adapting cognitive-behavioral and interpersonal treatments for depressed Puerto Rican adolescents. In E. D. Hibbs & P. S. Jensen (Eds.), *Psychological treatments for child and adolescent disorders: Empirically based strategies for clinical practice* (pp. 157–185). Washington, DC: American Psychological Association Press.

Rosselló, J., & Bernal, G. (1999). The efficacy of cognitive-behavioral and interpersonal treatments for depression in Puerto Rican adolescents. *Journal of Consulting and Clinical Psychology, 67,* 734–745.

Rosselló, J., Bernal, G., & Rivera-Medina, C. (2008). Individual and group CBT and IPT for Puerto Rican adolescents with depressive symptoms. *Cultural Diversity and Ethnic Minority Psychology, 14,* 234–245.

Santisteban, D. A., Coatsworth, J. D., Perez-Vidal, A., Kurtines, W. M., Schwartz, S. J., LaPerriere, A., et al. (2003). Efficacy of brief strategic family therapy in modifying Hispanic adolescent behavior problems and substance use. *Journal of Family Psychology, 17,* 121–133.

Santisteban, D. A., Coatsworth, J. D., Perez-Vidal, A., Mitrani, V., Jean-Gilles, M., & Szapocznik, J. (1997). Brief structural/strategic family therapy with African American and Hispanic high-risk youth. *Journal of Community Psychology, 25,* 453–471.

Santisteban, D. A., Muir, J. A., Mena, M. P., & Mitrani, V. B. (2003). Integrative borderline adolescent family therapy: Meeting the challenges of treating adolescents with borderline personality disorder. *Psychotherapy: Theory, Research, Practice, Training, 40,* 251–264.

Santisteban, D. A., Suarez-Morales, L., Robbins, M. S., & Szapocznik, J. (2006). Brief strategic family therapy: Lessons learned in efficacy research and challenges to blending research and practice. *Family Process, 45,* 259–271.

Silverman, W. K., Kurtines, W. M., Ginsburg, G. S., Weems, C. F., Lumpkin, P. W., & Carmichael, D. H. (1999). Treating anxiety disorders in children with group cognitive-behavioral therapy: A randomized clinical trial. *Journal of Consulting and Clinical Psychology, 67,* 995–1003.

Silverman, W. K., Ortiz, C. D., Viswesvaran, C., Burns, B. J., Kolko, D. J., Putnam, F. W., et al. (2008). Evidence-based psychosocial treatments for children and adolescents exposed to traumatic events. *Journal of Clinical Child and Adolescent Psychology, 37,* 156–183.

Stein, B. D., Jaycox, L. H., Kataoka, S. H., Wong, M., Tu, W., Elliott, M. N., et al. (2003). A mental health intervention for schoolchildren exposed to violence: A randomized controlled trial. *Journal of the American Medical Association, 290,* 603–611.

Sue, S. (1998). In search of cultural competence in psychotherapy and counseling. *American Psychologist, 53,* 440–448.

Szapocznik, J., & Kurtines, W. M. (1993). Family psychology and cultural diversity: Opportunities for theory, research, and application. *American Psychologist, 48,* 400–407.

Szapocznik, J., Rio, A., Murray, E., Cohen, R., Escopetta, M., Rivas-Vazquez, A., et al. (1989). Structural family versus psychodynamic child therapy for problematic Hispanic boys. *Journal of Consulting and Clinical Psychology, 57,* 571–578.

Szapocznik, J., Santisteban, D., Rio, A., Perez-Vidal, A., Santisteban, D., & Kurtines, W. (1989). Family effectiveness training: An intervention to prevent drug abuse and problem behaviors in Hispanic adolescents. *Hispanic Journal of Behavioral Sciences, 11,* 4–27.

U.S. Census Bureau. (2006). 2006 American community survey. Retrieved April 24, 2008, from http://factfinder.census.gov

U.S. Department of Health and Human Services (USDHHS). (2000). *Mental health: Culture, race and ethnicity—Supplement to Mental Health: A Report of the Surgeon General.* Rockville, MD: Author.

Vega, W. A., Karno, M., Alegría, M., Alvidrez, J., Bernal, G., Escamilla, M., et al. (2007). Research issues for improving treatment of U.S. Hispanics with persistent mental disorders. *Psychiatric Services, 58,* 385–394.

Weckerly, L., Landsverk, L., & Hough, R. (2003). Racial/ethnic differences in the use of psychotropic medication in high-risk children and adolescents. *Journal of the American Academy of Child and Adolescent Psychiatry, 42,* 1433–1442.

Weisz, J. R., Jensen-Doss, A., & Hawley, K. M. (2006). Evidence-based youth psychotherapies versus usual clinical care: A meta-analysis of direct comparisons. *American Psychologist, 61,* 671–689.

Weisz, J. R., McCarty, C. A., & Valeri, S. M. (2006). Effects of psychotherapy for depression in children and adolescents: A meta-analysis. *Psychological Bulletin, 132,* 132–149.

Weisz, J. R., Weiss, B., Han, S. S., Granger, D. A., & Morton, T. (1995). Effects of psychotherapy with children and adolescents revisited: A meta-analysis of treatment outcome studies. *Psychological Bulletin, 117,* 450–468.

Wintersteen, M. B., Mensinger, J. L., & Diamond, G. (2005). Do gender and racial differences between patient and therapist affect therapeutic alliance and treatment retention in adolescents? *Professional Psychology: Research and Practice, 36,* 400–408.

19

CLINICAL APPROACHES TO WORKING WITH LATINO ADULTS

ESTEBAN V. CARDEMIL AND INGRID A. SARMIENTO

As others in this handbook have noted, there exist several compelling reasons to identify and disseminate effective clinical approaches to working with Latinos. In particular, the Latino population in the United States has grown tremendously over the past 10 years, and census data predict that by 2050 the number of Latinos will exceed 125 million and represent more than one fourth of the U.S. population (Passel & Cohn, 2008). In addition, a large body of literature has documented pervasive health-care disparities affecting Latinos (U.S. Department of Health and Human Services [USDHHS], 2001), suggesting that existing clinical interventions may inadequately address the needs of Latinos.

However, despite the increased attention to the development and provision of culturally appropriate clinical services for Latinos, there remain significant disparities in the mental health care received by Latinos (Blanco et al., 2007; Vega et al., 2007). We suggest that one explanation for these continuing health-care disparities may be found in the difficulty the mental health field has had in conceptualizing how best to integrate cultural considerations into clinical work (Cardemil, 2008). In particular, while there exist many different perspectives in the literature on what constitutes acceptable integration of culture into

psychotherapy (e.g., Atkinson, Bui, & Mori, 2001; Bernal & Sáez-Santiago, 2006; Hall, 2001; La Roche, 2002; Whaley & Davis, 2007), there is no overarching framework into which to organize these different perspectives. For example, the American Psychological Association has published a set of guidelines for clinicians who work with individuals from ethnic, linguistic, and culturally diverse backgrounds (American Psychological Association [APA], 1993). These guidelines focus exclusively on therapist attitudes toward issues of diversity, knowledge about particular ethnic and cultural groups, and behaviors when working with individuals from different backgrounds. No mention is made, however, about the ways in which particular interventions may or may not need to be adapted for work with particular groups of individuals. As a result, many interested clinicians and scholars may remain unsure about how to proceed with efforts to consider cultural issues in their treatment approaches with Latinos.

In this chapter, we concretize a framework proposed by Cardemil (2008) in which different perspectives on how to incorporate conceptions of culture are organized according to a variety of assumptions regarding the active therapeutic ingredients and their relation to culture. We begin by first briefly reviewing the mental health-care disparities that disproportionately affect Latino adults, in order to highlight the point that cultural considerations must begin at the systems level. Next, we describe three different perspectives on the integration of cultural considerations into clinical work with Latinos. We conclude with recommendations for clinical work and future research directions.

MENTAL HEALTH-CARE DISPARITIES AFFECTING LATINOS

Efforts to identify effective clinical approaches to working with Latinos must begin by understanding the mental health-care disparities that disproportionately affect Latinos. Considerable research has found that Latinos are less likely to receive formal mental health services (Alegría et al., 2002; Vega, Kolody, Aguilar-Gaxiola, & Catalano, 1999), especially if they are less acculturated or recent immigrants (Alegría et al., 2007; Cabassa, Zayas, & Hansen, 2006; Vega et al., 1999). Moreover, when low-income Latinos do seek services, they are more likely to prematurely terminate them (e.g., Organista, Muñoz, & González, 1994). With regard to pharmacotherapy, researchers have found that Latinos are less likely to use medication (Miranda & Cooper, 2004), as well as more likely to demonstrate worse treatment adherence to the medication regimen in disorders like depression (Sánchez-Lacay et al., 2001) and schizophrenia (Opolka, Rascati, Brown, & Gibson, 2003). Some research has even found poorer response to antidepressant medication among Latinos (Lesser et al., 2007). These disparities in use of formal mental health services have been found even when controlling for sociodemographic and clinical characteristics (Lagomasino et al., 2005; Padgett, Patrick, Burns, & Schlesinger, 1994), suggesting that mental health-care disparities are not simply the result of economic factors like poverty. Particularly troubling is that despite the increased recognition of these disparities, some recent research has found that mental health-care disparities for Latinos increased between the years 1993 and 2002 (Blanco et al., 2007).

Researchers have identified many reasons for these disparities in use of mental health services by Latinos (e.g., Alegría et al., 2002; Cabassa et al., 2006; Dwight-Johnson, Lagomasino, Aisenberg, & Hay, 2004). Some of the explanations have focused on systems-level barriers (e.g., dearth of Spanish-speaking service providers, lack of insurance), while others have focused on patient-level barriers (e.g., cultural differences in conceptions of mental health, concern regarding stigma; Harman, Edlund, & Fortney, 2004; López, 2002; USDHHS, 2001, 2005).

These mental health-care disparities are troubling and highlight the point that issues of culture are not limited to clinical work. That is, efforts to make clinical work culturally relevant to Latinos should begin at the level of the system and the organization, not merely at the level of the individual clinician. Some of these efforts could include innovative approaches to recruiting and retaining bilingual and bicultural providers, searching for funding sources to complement the insurance limitations that may exist in particular communities, and identifying mechanisms to overcome such common logistical obstacles as lack of transportation or child care. A more detailed examination of systems-level changes that could address the systems and organizational barriers that hinder the delivery of services to Latinos is beyond the scope of this chapter. Nevertheless, they warrant mention, given the research documenting the effect of such barriers on Latinos' access to mental health services.

INTEGRATION OF CULTURAL CONSIDERATIONS INTO CLINICAL WORK WITH LATINOS

In addition to creating systemic changes to make treatment more accessible to Latinos, many scholars have argued that effective clinical work with Latinos is best accomplished through the consideration of culture in a variety of explicit ways (e.g., Arredondo & Perez, 2003; Bernal & Scharrón-del Río, 2001; Miranda et al., 2005). Given the surge in attention to these issues, it should not be surprising that there exists considerable variability in how scholars conceptualize the best way to integrate culture considerations into therapy. To date, this heterogeneity has gone relatively unexamined, leading to somewhat confusing and contradictory messages regarding what constitutes culturally sensitive treatment.

Our review of the literature has led us to identify at least three different emphases posited by scholars who support the explicit consideration of culture in psychotherapy. The first focuses on the behavior of the therapist, with explicit recommendations on how to develop cultural competence. The second approach focuses on the treatment itself rather than the therapist and explores how to adapt specific treatments for particular racial, ethnic, and cultural groups. And the third perspective argues that the best way to integrate culture into psychotherapy is by developing novel therapeutic approaches that centralize culture. Each of these perspectives has intuitive appeal and some empirical support, and each has its strengths and limitations. In the following sections, we briefly describe these perspectives and review the literature as it relates specifically to Latinos.

Perspective 1: Culturally Competent Therapists

The first perspective on integrating culture into clinical work focuses primarily on the cultural sensitivity of the therapist and posits that therapists who are *culturally competent* will produce superior outcomes in therapy. Cultural competence has been defined in a variety of ways, but in general it is understood to be a therapist skill that consists of a variety of therapist attitudes, knowledge, and behaviors that allow for effective clinical work when working with culturally diverse populations (e.g., Sue, 1998; Helms & Cook, 1999; Whaley & Davis, 2007). This perspective is most consistent with those published by the APA (1993), which enumerate nine general guidelines related to conducting work with individuals from diverse ethnic, linguistic and cultural groups. In addition to highlighting the importance of self-awareness of how one's own cultural background, experiences, attitudes, values, and biases can influence clinical work, the guidelines also emphasize how critical it is to familiarize oneself with, and acquire relevant knowledge about, particular ethnic groups.

With regard to Latinos, then, cultural competence would include familiarity with and knowledge of the historical, cultural, and political experiences of the various Latino ethnic groups (e.g., Arredondo & Perez, 2003; Gloria, Ruiz, & Castillo, 2004; Mezzich, Ruiz, & Muñoz, 1999). Moreover, it is critical to understand that variability exists across Latinos in conceptions and experiences of mental health and illness, as well

as to be aware that some clients' expressions of emotion and idioms of distress may not match the European American conceptions of mental disorders (e.g., Guarnaccia & Rogler, 1999; Kleinman, 1982; Lewis-Fernández & Diaz, 2002; Rogler, Cortés, & Malgady, 1994). For instance, researchers have found strong evidence for the existence of a culture-specific syndrome, *ataques de nervios,* that is prevalent among Puerto Ricans and not adequately captured by the *Diagnostic and Statistical Manual of Mental Disorders* (DSM) nosological system (e.g., Guarnaccia, Lewis-Fernández, & Marano, 2003). Other idioms of distress among Latinos that have some empirical support include nostalgia, anger, and disillusionment among Puerto Ricans (Cortés, 2003), and the tendency to express somatically symptoms of mental illness in general and depression in particular (Snowden & Yamada, 2005).

Related to variability in conceptions of mental health and illness is the fact that scholars have noted that some Latinos attempt to make sense of illnesses through the use of nonmedical explanations, such as dream interpretation, spiritual and religious exploration, and supernatural perspectives (La Roche, 2002; Velásquez & Burton, 2004). Some Latinos may seek help from their own cultural healing traditions (e.g., priests, folk healers) in addition to connecting with standard medical-model forms (Delgado & Humm-Delgado, 1984; Rogler & Cortes, 1993; Mezzich et al., 1999). Although belief in these non-DSM and supernatural conceptions of mental health and illness is not uniform across all Latinos, an awareness of their existence can assist clinicians when working with Latinos who may not meet criteria for particular DSM disorders. Moreover, awareness of these perspectives can make it easier for clinicians to consider not adhering so rigidly to the medical model of mental health and illness, a perspective that some authors have suggested is not received well by many Latinos (Arredondo & Perez, 2003).

Many scholars have also noted the importance of understanding the role of Latino cultural values. Others in this book have described these values more fully; we mention them here to highlight their possible role in helping or hindering the treatment process. For example, some have suggested that adherence to the value of *fatalismo* (fatalism) may encourage passivity about overcoming mental health problems. This passivity may make some Latinos less likely to seek treatment (Schraufnagel, Wagner, Miranda, & Roy-Byrne, 2006) and, among those who do seek treatment, may make them more likely to prefer directive forms of treatment. Others have discussed how the Latino cultural value of *familismo* (familism) might affect treatment seeking. Some have suggested that Latinos with a strong sense of *familismo* might be less likely to seek formal mental health services due to a desire to keep problems within the family (e.g., Vega & Alegría, 2001), while others have noted that Latinos might be particularly responsive to treatment approaches that incorporate family members (Cardemil, Kim, Pinedo, & Miller, 2005; Delgado & Humm-Delgado, 1984). Similarly, the gender roles of *machismo*, which encourages men to project images of strength and self-reliance (Torres, Solberg, & Carlstrom, 2002), and *marianismo*, which encourages women to assume the burden of suffering in the family (Chiriboga, Black, Aranda, & Markides, 2002; Gloria et al., 2004), may be at odds with some of the central goals of treatment, including seeking help, relying on others, and recognizing difficulties in one's life. Interian, Martinez, Guarnaccia, Vega, and Escobar (2007) found evidence that some cultural values (working hard, fighting against problems, *familismo*) contributed to negative attributions about antidepressant medication in a qualitative study of 30 Latino outpatients receiving antidepressant treatment. Again, as with the conceptions of health and sickness, it is important to note that variability exists in adherence to these values both across Latinos and within Latino families. Thus, a comprehensive cultural conceptualization of clients is important in order to understand each particular client's understanding of mental health and illness, the treatment process, and relevant values and worldviews.

This cultural sensitivity or cultural competence must also take into consideration the socioeconomic difficulties that disproportionately affect Latinos. The life stressors that too often accompany financial difficulties (e.g., housing difficulties, exposure to violence, substandard medical care) are not characteristic of Latino culture per se, but they are common experiences of many Latinos living in the United States. Similarly, in order to be culturally competent with Latinos, clinicians must also understand the everyday experiences of prejudice, discrimination, and sense of disenfranchisement

that many Latinos report living as a racial/ethnic minority in the United States. Because these experiences are neither limited to Latinos nor directly connected to Latino culture, they may be neglected in clinical work, since their consideration requires a broader conceptualization of the aspects of culture that should be included when attempting to be culturally competent.

Strengths of the Cultural Competence Perspective. The primary strength of this perspective on cultural competence is that it can be taught to and learned by a wide range of therapists from different theoretical orientations. It is true that some multicultural scholars have lamented the slow rate at which considerations of diversity and culture have been integrated into the overall training curricula of clinical psychology programs (e.g., Abreu, Chung, & Atkinson, 2000). Nevertheless, a perspective that limits the definition of cultural competence to the therapist is more readily disseminated than are perspectives of cultural competence that focus on adaptations to existing interventions or the development of novel interventions (see the following sections). Adherents of this perspective can reasonably expect that the numbers of culturally competent therapists will increase through the dissemination of information and opportunities in which to practice particular clinical skills in working with Latinos.

Limitations of the Cultural Competence Perspective. An important limitation of this perspective, however, is the dearth of attention to the relationship between cultural competence and active therapeutic ingredients that presumably differ by theoretical orientation. Although most scholars would likely suggest that cultural competence is necessary but not sufficient to produce positive results in therapy, very little attention has been given to how cultural competence might interact with (or in some cases, interfere with) the therapeutic approaches encouraged by traditional orientations. That is, because most of the major theoretical orientations were developed without consideration of culture, it may be simplistic to assume that they can easily accommodate changes in therapist attitudes and behaviors designed to reflect cultural competence. These incompatibilities can be seen in how therapists conceptualize client distress, as well as in therapist behaviors that emerge from that conceptualization. For example, most traditional therapy orientations conceptualize distress intrapsychically (e.g., dysfunctional thoughts, unconscious conflicts), whereas models of cultural competence encourage therapists to acknowledge how societal structures can oppress individuals from particular sociodemographic groups. Thus, more reflection is needed regarding how to integrate these different worldviews. Similarly, most traditional therapy orientations have clearly prescribed and proscribed therapy behaviors that may be at odds with particular behaviors recommended by advocates of cultural competency (e.g., informality between therapist and patient, increased self-disclosure on the part of the therapist). The absence of a clear theory that provides a rationale for when to engage in particular behaviors is problematic, since therapists are left without a road map for choosing particular techniques and behaviors when conducting clinical work.

This lack of explicit attention to these issues is of concern on many levels, and it may be reflected in the lack of empirical support for the relationship between cultural competence and treatment outcome. That is, although it seems intuitive that greater cultural competence would be associated with improved treatment outcome, we are unaware of any published studies that have documented this association. We suggest that more attention to the congruence, or theoretical fit, between cultural competence and traditional therapy orientations will lead to thoughtfully designed research studies that can examine the relationships among the various therapy ingredients theorized to be related to treatment outcome.

Perspective 2: Cultural Adaptations

The second perspective on culture and therapy argues that the best way to integrate culture into treatment is to adapt existing treatments that have empirical support in ways that make them more culturally relevant and attractive to individuals from different cultures (e.g., Castro, Barrera, & Martinez, 2004; Lau, 2006; Miranda et al., 2005; Muñoz & Mendelsohn, 2005). Contained under the broad category of *cultural adaptations,* these generally include efforts to take established manual-based treatments and adapt them for Latinos. However, we also include in this category those efforts to develop novel treatments specifically for Latinos that are based on traditional psychotherapeutic theories (e.g., cognitive-behavioral therapy).

Recently, scholars have begun to distinguish between two types of cultural adaptations that lie at the ends of a continuum (Castro et al., 2004; Resnicow, Soler, Braithwaite, Ahluwalia, & Butler, 2000). Superficial, or surface, modifications are those that consist of small changes to the intervention so as to match the delivery of the intervention to observable characteristics of the target population but that leave the vast majority of the original intervention intact. Castro and colleagues (2004) give the example of changing the ethnicity of role models or characters in an intervention so that they resemble more closely the ethnicity of the participants in the program. Another example of a surface-level modification might be the decision to deliver an intervention in a community church rather than in a mental health clinic. Conversely, core, or deep, modifications consist of changes to the intervention that result in more carefully taking into consideration central cultural aspects of the relevant ethnic group. Thus, core modifications might include finding ways to incorporate into program delivery many of the salient cultural values discussed earlier in the first perspective, using relevant cultural expressions, metaphors, and proverbs to convey important themes, and changing program content to be more relevant to the lives of the participants.

Despite the differences between surface and deep cultural adaptations, they are similar in that the cultural adaptations are not typically viewed as active ingredients that will directly contribute to improvement in the functioning of the client (Lau, 2006; Miranda et al., 2006; Muñoz & Mendelson, 2005). Indeed, Castro and colleagues (2004) point out the tension between fidelity and fit, making the case that cultural adaptations that deviate from the core ingredients of the original intervention run the risk of proving ineffective when implemented. As such, then, the cultural adaptations are conceptualized more as the means by which to make existing interventions more attractive and relevant to the participants. The assumption has been that making the interventions more attractive and relevant to participants will make it more likely that participants will stay engaged with the active ingredients of the intervention and thus have improved outcome.

In order to investigate the extent to which researchers have developed and evaluated cultural adaptations of existing interventions for Latino adults, we conducted a wide review of the empirical treatment literature. We included in our review those studies that focused specifically on Latinos, as well as studies that did not focus specifically on Latinos but included significant numbers of Latinos in the sample. Because of the limited attention clinical psychology has generally given to culture (e.g., La Roche & Christopher, 2008), research that has examined cultural adaptations of interventions with Latino adults is limited. Nevertheless, this limited research investigating the effectiveness of clinical interventions in Latinos has produced promising findings, particularly in the areas of depression and schizophrenia.

Depression. With regard to depression, the majority of interventions for Latino adults have been rooted in cognitive-behavioral approaches to the treatment of depression and demonstrate considerable overlap in the types of cultural adaptations made (e.g., Comas-Díaz, 1981; Miranda et al., 2003a; Miranda, Azocar, Organista, Dwyer, & Areán, 2003b; Muñoz et al., 1995). For example, Miranda and colleagues (2003a, 2003b, 2006) have conducted a variety of randomized, controlled trials to investigate the effectiveness of cognitive-behavioral treatment with low-income racial and ethnic minority women. Across the studies, the authors made similar cultural adaptations to the treatment, including the use of bilingual and bicultural providers, translation of all materials into Spanish, reduction in the number of therapy sessions, and the use of interaction styles that incorporate the Latino values of *respeto, simpatía,* and *personalismo.* In addition, the authors made considerable effort to assist the women in attending their treatment sessions, including intensive outreach, provision of transportation and child care, and encouragement to comply with treatment recommendations. In one study (Miranda et al., 2003a, 2006), the authors provided up to four sessions of an educational meeting in which the women met with their provider to discuss depression and its treatment. In another study (Miranda et al., 2003b), the authors explicitly incorporated case management into the treatment process. Results indicated that the cultural adaptations generally resulted in positive outcomes, particularly as compared with standard community care. Of note, adding the clinical case management appeared to enhance the effect of the cognitive-behavioral

treatment, as well as make it less likely for patients to drop out of therapy. A few other studies that have included Latinos have found similarly positive results with cognitive-behavioral therapy for depression (Areán & Miranda, 1996; Comas-Díaz, 1981, 1986; Organista et al., 1994).

In addition to depression treatment, there exists an emerging literature examining the efficacy of interventions in the prevention of depression. Muñoz and colleagues (Muñoz et al., 1995) conducted an eight-session cognitive-behavioral depression prevention program with a sample of low-income primary care patients, of whom approximately 24% were Latinos. Modifications to delivery (as compared to standard interventions) included the provision of both English- and Spanish-language manuals, as well as modification of vocabulary so as to reach individuals from different education levels. Modifications to content included the use of culturally relevant metaphors and stories as a means to convey key cognitive-behavioral principles, the identification and incorporation of cultural values into relevant intervention strategies (e.g., recognizing that the cultural value of *familismo* may make immigration especially difficult for those who have left family members in their country of origin), and explicit discussion of relevant issues like spirituality and religion, acculturation, and experiences with racism, discrimination, and prejudice (Muñoz & Mendelsohn, 2005). Results from this preventive intervention were generally positive: Participants randomized to the eight-session intervention reported significantly fewer depressive symptoms than those randomized to the control conditions through 1 year of follow-up assessments.

In a similar program, Vega, Valle, Kolody, & Hough (1987) developed a cognitive-behavioral intervention for Latina women defined as at risk by virtue of their status as low income, recently immigrated, and middle aged. The authors incorporated cultural considerations into the intervention in two primary ways. First, the authors identified specific cultural reasons to explain this at-risk status. For example, their research noted that many of these women were experiencing changing role expectations whereby they needed to assume greater responsibility for income, despite having minimal English-speaking ability. Similarly, many of these women had small social support networks due to their status as recent immigrants. In addition, due to the cultural expectations for women's caregiving duties, many of these women were beginning to experience familial pressure to assist in the rearing and care of newly arriving grandchildren (Vega & Murphy, 1990). Second, the authors used *servidoras*, or indigenous Latina community helpers, to deliver the intervention to participants. In addition to having a no-intervention control condition, the research design had two active conditions: In one condition, the intervention was delivered on a one-to-one basis in the participant's home; in the second condition, the intervention was delivered in a group format in community locations, including churches, schools, and community centers. Both active interventions lasted approximately 12 weeks. Results from this intervention were also positive: Although conservative intent-to-treat analyses produced no significant effects of either intervention condition (as compared to the control conditions), subgroup analyses indicated that both active interventions produced a significant 6-month prevention effect in depressive symptoms among those participants who were initially low symptom at the start of the program (Vega & Murphy, 1990).

In a recently completed uncontrolled trial, Cardemil and colleagues (2005) reported preliminary findings from a six-session, group, cognitive-behavioral depression prevention program developed specifically for low-income Latina mothers. In addition to making many of the same cultural adaptations described earlier, this program was unique in that it explicitly recognized the importance of the family to Latinos by integrating two sessions of a brief family-based intervention with the larger group intervention. Results were promising, as participants in the program reported a significant reduction in symptoms over the course of the program. In addition, the researchers found that those participants who attended at least one family session reported significantly greater improvement in depressive symptoms than did those participants who did not attend any family sessions.

Although the overwhelming majority of cultural adaptations for Latinos have been rooted in cognitive-behavioral theory, our review of the literature identified three additional studies. Two investigated the efficacy of interpersonal psychotherapy (IPT) in samples of low-income, minority women (Spinelli & Endicott, 2003; Zlotnick, Miller, Pearlstein, Howard, & Sweeney, 2006), and one examined the adaptation of a supportive and psychodynamic group therapy for socioeconomically disadvantaged Latino outpatients with a variety of diagnoses, including mood disorders (Olarte & Masnik, 1985). The two IPT studies both focused on depression during the perinatal period, with Spinelli and Endicott focusing on treating antepartum depression, while Zlotnick and colleagues attempted to prevent postpartum depression. Both studies reported generally favorable results; however, neither provided much information regarding the cultural adaptations.

In contrast, Olarte and Masnik (1985) described in considerable detail how they incorporated cultural elements into the group process in order to enhance cohesion among group members. Participants were welcome to bring traditional dishes or musical instruments to group meetings during relevant holidays, encouraged to bring gifts for other group members and the therapists, and provided with an opportunity to consider the congruence of the group goals with their own cultural values. Although not empirically evaluated, Olarte and Masnik (1985) note that the group therapy was well received by participants and suggest that it is a cost-effective approach that can lead to improvements in functioning among the participants, healthier family environments, and decreased use of emergency rooms for treatment.

Schizophrenia. In addition to cultural adaptations of interventions for depression, a few other adaptations have begun to emerge in the area of schizophrenia. In general, the early psychosocial interventions for schizophrenia were rooted in the research demonstrating that particular forms of family communication around emotion are related to relapse rates (Butzlaff & Hooley, 1998). This research led to a variety of interventions that were highly effective at reducing family conflict through communication training and psychoeducation and subsequently reducing risk for relapse (Mari & Streiner, 1994).

Given the promising nature of these family-based psychosocial interventions for schizophrenia, researchers began to explore their utility with Latinos. Telles and colleagues (1995) conducted one of the first efforts to adapt a standard family-based intervention for Latinos. The authors modified Behavioral Family Management (BFM), a family-based intervention that focuses on psychoeducation, communication training, and problem solving (Falloon,

Boyd, & McGill, 1984). This adaptation could be conceptualized as surface level, since the modifications consisted primarily of "socioculturally appropriate translations and adaptations of the educational and instructional materials" (Telles et al., 1995, p. 474). Results indicated an interesting moderation effect of acculturation. There was no significant effect of the treatment for those Latino participants who were highly acculturated; instead, the best predictor of outcome was medication compliance. Conversely, for the less acculturated Latinos, participation in the BFM was associated with greater likelihood of relapse. The authors suggested that BFM may include activities and exercises that are incongruent with some aspects of Latino culture. They highlight in particular the communication exercises that consisted of speaking directly and assertively with parental figures as at odds with the hierarchical nature of Latino families.

The generally negative findings of BFM with Latinos is consistent with emerging research suggesting that family processes may be differentially related to the course of schizophrenia for Mexican American and Anglo American families (López et al., 2004). In particular, López and colleagues found that for Mexican American families, expressions of familial warmth were a protective factor against relapse, while for Anglo Americans, expressed criticism was a risk factor. Thus, it is plausible that adaptations of standard family-focused interventions for Latinos should pay as much attention to strengthening familial relationships and creating more positive relations as to reducing expressed criticism.

At least partly in response to these ideas, Weisman and colleagues (Weisman, 2005; Weisman, Duarte, Koneru, & Wasserman, 2006) have developed and are beginning the evaluation process of a novel, family-focused, culturally informed therapy for schizophrenia (CIT-S). This approach explicitly integrates three modules of standard family-focused techniques (i.e., psychoeducation, communication training, and problem solving) with two more culturally congruent components (family cohesion and spirituality). CIT-S aims to increase familial empathy, to lower levels of critical and hostile attitudes from family members toward the patient with schizophrenia, and to provide a more realistic set of expectations for the course of the disorder. Results from a randomized controlled trial are still pending.

One research group has taken a different approach to reducing relapse rates with schizophrenia. Kopelowicz, Zarate, Smith, Mintz, and Liberman (2003) used a social-skills training program that has been shown to be effective in schizophrenia and adapted it for Latinos. These adaptations were primarily surface-level ones, including careful translations of the material that considered relevant dialects and colloquialisms, the use of bilingual and bicultural staff, and the emphasis on an informal, friendly interaction style between therapists and patients. One deeper-level adaptation was the inclusion of family members rather than clinicians as aides to help in the generalization of skills. Results indicated that Latinos who were randomly assigned to the cultural adaptation of the social skills training had more improved outcomes than those assigned to a customary outpatient control condition. This advantage for the social skills intervention was found on symptoms, skill acquisition, level of functioning, and rates of rehospitalization.

Strengths of the Cultural Adaptation Perspective. In summary, there is increasing support for the cultural adaptation perspective, particularly in the areas of depression and schizophrenia. Among the studies that provided descriptions, the adaptations generally included both surface and deep structural adaptations in that they modified both the delivery and the content of the program (see Castro et al., 2004). Most of the studies readily identified efforts made regarding the intervention delivery, including having bilingual and bicultural therapists, attending to such cultural values as *familismo* and *personalismo*, and integrating outreach and support programs that facilitate participation in treatment (e.g., child care and transportation). Many of the studies also explicitly noted how they modified the content, or focus, of the intervention by applying the therapeutic techniques to culturally relevant life experiences, such as immigration and acculturative stress, financial stress, and racism and discrimination. Importantly, though, none of the interventions described ways in which fundamental changes were made to the underlying cognitive-behavioral or interpersonal approaches to treating or preventing depression.

A strength of this perspective is that there exists an emerging empirical base supporting the notion that culturally adapted interventions can produce effective outcome. In fact, Griner and Smith's (2006) meta-analysis of 76 studies found a generally positive effect of participating in a culturally adapted intervention ($d = 0.45$). Although the studies in this meta-analysis included participants from a variety of racial/ethnic backgrounds, findings indicated that those studies with high numbers of Latino participants had particularly stronger effects. Moreover, among studies that focused on Latinos only, those that were focused on less acculturated participants did better than those that were focused on more acculturated participants. Thus, increasing empirical support is emerging for the notion that culturally adapted interventions can be efficacious with Latinos. As a result, these interventions may be particularly well suited to address the health-care disparities discussed earlier, since they may have more legitimacy in the eyes of health-care providers, given the evidence of their efficacy.

Limitations of the Cultural Adaptation Perspective. This perspective has important limitations, however. One primary limitation is the general absence of empirical evidence demonstrating that the provision of adapted treatments produce better outcomes than the standard versions of the treatments with individuals from the targeted cultural groups in general and, in this case, with Latinos in particular (Lakes, López, & Garro, 2006). Thus, although evidence exists that these adapted interventions may be efficacious, it is not clear that they produce better outcomes than standard interventions. For example, the Griner and Smith (2006) meta-analysis did not examine the sizes of the differences in effects between adapted interventions and standard interventions but focused instead on the effect sizes of the adapted interventions only. Comparing the effectiveness of adapted interventions with standard interventions will likely be an important comparison to make, since the implementation of different versions of a treatment is costly for health-care providers. It is plausible that the adapted treatments will demonstrate superior symptom reduction compared to standard interventions; however, it is much more likely that the advantage of the adapted interventions will be found in the domains of treatment acceptability, retention, and adherence. Such an outcome would be important,

as it could make significant inroads into the mental health-care disparities described earlier.

A second important limitation is the fact that very few culturally adapted interventions are based on empirical research (Lau, 2006). That is, there has been little consideration of how basic research on risk and resiliency factors in Latinos might directly inform the adaptation of existing treatments or development of novel treatments. Instead, most adaptations have focused on enhancing the attractiveness of the intervention for potential participants (surface-structure adaptations). Even those that have incorporated deep-structure adaptations (e.g., incorporation of culturally relevant metaphors, idioms, and interaction styles) have generally not connected these adaptations to considerations of risk and resilience. The one notable exception is the Weisman (Weisman, 2005; Weisman et al., 2006) work with CIT-S. In this approach, the incorporation of the cultural components of family cohesion and spirituality were made in response to the literature documenting some differences in the risk and protective factors between schizophrenia in Latinos and in Caucasians. Weisman's work can serve as a model for a theoretically and empirically guided approach to the development of cultural adaptations of treatments. Given the recent attention to this limitation (e.g., Castro et al., 2004; Lau, 2006), we are looking forward to the next generation of cultural adaptations.

Perspective 3: Culturally Centered Therapies

The third perspective on the integration of cultural considerations into therapy is by far the most comprehensive and has been termed *culturally centered therapies* by some scholars (Bernal & Sáez-Santiago, 2006; Pedersen, 1997). From this perspective, attempts to impose traditional forms of psychotherapy upon individuals from non-European cultures are built upon faulty assumptions of universality and essentialism (Atkinson, et al., 2001; Bernal & Scharrón-del Río, 2001). Concretely, this perspective argues that it would be theoretically incongruent to provide a traditional form of psychotherapy for culturally specific expressions of distress (e.g., *ataques de nervios,* somatic symptoms). Even adaptations of traditional forms of psychotherapy would be unlikely to be effective, as they are ultimately rooted in universal conceptions of health and illness.

Further, even when programs that have been adapted for particular cultural groups have been found to be efficacious, they are inherently limited in their abilities to empower individuals to overcome societal structural obstacles. That is, because adapted interventions are rooted in traditional models of psychotherapy, they can only conceptualize health and illness from within that framework. Thus, they are less able to recognize how societal structures, like the therapeutic endeavor itself, can promote the status quo in the service of distress management. For these reasons, adherents of this perspective suggest that there is more to gain by developing novel therapeutic approaches that centralize culture in the treatment process, by working from particular cultural conceptions and idioms of distress, utilizing culture-specific traditions of pathways to health and sickness, and explicitly addressing societal structure issues in treatment (e.g., race, gender, class, sexual orientation). A culturally centered therapy need not address all of the aforementioned issues, but it must at least conceptualize distress and treatment from culturally relevant perspectives.

The most commonly cited example of a culturally centered therapy is *cuento therapy,* an approach that uses cultural folktales to increase children's connections both with their parents and with their Puerto Rican culture and heritage (Costantino, Malgady, & Rogler, 1986). Another excellent example of a culturally centered therapy is *bicultural effectiveness training* (BET; Szapocznik et al., 1986). BET was developed to improve family functioning through the explicit consideration and working through of cultural conflict that arises between family members as a result of differences in acculturation level. Both of these examples make central the culturally salient goal of developing increased connection to family and culture, and both use culturally relevant treatment approaches (family connections) to reach the goal. Thus, the entire therapy endeavor remains culturally congruent from the outset.

With regard to Latino adults, we identified several studies that could be considered culturally centered therapies. Szapocznik and colleagues (1981, 1982) described their development of life enhancement counseling for elderly Latinos, a therapeutic approach designed to address the loss of meaning and purpose in life that occurs to many individuals as they age. In both its development and implementation, life enhancement counseling is both developmentally and culturally centered, as both its goal and its methods of achieving them are relevant to elderly Latinos. The model's two primary techniques are (1) the life review and (2) ecological assessment and intervention. The life review consists of having participants describe important life events and experiences, with a particular focus on enhancing the meaning of positive memories, facilitating acceptance of unresolved events, and the rediscovery of past strengths. The ecological assessment and intervention consist of identifying current environmental sources of stress for participants and then identifying ways to change the participant-environment transactions that are causing stress. Results from an open pilot trial were positive, as significant improvements occurred over the course of the intervention on a range of outcome measures, including depression and anxious symptoms, social isolation, and general functioning (Szapocznik et al., 1981). Unfortunately, more rigorous analyses of life enhancement counseling with Latino elders have not been published.

Aviera (1996) described the development of a *dichos therapy* group for hospitalized Spanish-speaking psychiatric patients. Building on the work of others who have used *dichos* (proverbs, idioms, or metaphors) to help facilitate the therapy process with Latinos (e.g., Zuñiga, 1991, 1992), Aviera developed a group in which the consideration and discussion of dichos was the explicit focus of the group and the conceptualized active ingredient. The dichos group was part of a multimodal treatment approach that included a variety of other disciplines (e.g., psychiatric, social work, rehabilitation therapy). Participants in the dichos group were patients in a state psychiatric hospital with a variety of psychotic disorders. Aviera noted that most of the participants had limited coping skills, strained or limited family relationships, and were struggling to adapt to life in the United States. Published data supporting the efficacy of the dichos group were limited to clinical observation, but Aviera suggested that the dichos group had a variety of positive effects on both attitudes toward therapy (e.g., decreased defensiveness, increased motivation for therapy), and individual functioning (e.g., improved self-esteem, enhanced attention and emotional exploration).

More recently, Guinn and Vincent (2002) described the development and preliminary evaluation of a novel educational intervention to enhance Latina spiritual well-being. Building on the work of an already established educational health promotion program, the authors described a participatory action approach in which the community participated in the initiation, development, implementation, and evaluation of a holistic approach to enhancing Latinas' spiritual well-being. The intervention is described as consisting of two sets of educational sessions: personal growth and entrepreneurial intervention. Personal growth sessions included sessions on a range of psychological, health, and social topics, including spiritual issues, parenting and child development, safety, hygiene, and domestic violence. Entrepreneurial interventions included sessions on elder care, general equivalency diploma (GED) attainment, citizenship procedures, and other vocational skill development. One-time comparisons between participants in the intervention and community controls revealed higher religious and existential well-being scores among those Latina women who had participated in the intervention.

Some other examples of this perspective with adults, although not Latinos in particular, can be found in the counseling psychology tradition, which has historically focused less on resolving pathology and more on promoting developmental well-being. The scholars who have developed therapies that centralize multiculturalism in both mental health and treatment have tended to give attention to the relationship between the client and therapist, as well as a variety of sociocultural developmental issues, including racial and ethnic identity, spirituality and religion, and social class struggles (e.g., Atkinson, Morten, & Sue, 1998; Sue, Ivey, & Pedersen, 1996).

Strengths of the Culturally Centered Perspective. Although less attention has been given to treatment approaches that fall into this perspective, the examples we found have considerable appeal. Unlike the examples from the other two perspectives, all of the treatment approaches provided compelling descriptions of the culturally specific problems they were attempting to help (e.g., parent-child problems, loss of meaning and purpose with advancing age, difficulty adjusting to U.S. culture). Because there was very little mention of diagnostic categories, the treatments were free to address psychosocial stressors that were relevant to the lives of the participants in that particular cultural moment. Moreover, these approaches generally tended to be less pathology focused, and more focused on enhancing the well-being of their participants.

Another important strength of this perspective is the coherence between the cultural conceptualization of the problem and the resultant approach to treating the problem. Treatment approaches varied and included the use of culturally salient cuentos, dichos, life reviews, and psychoeducational workshops. Because these treatment approaches were conceptualized as the active ingredient or mechanism of change, the concern about potential incongruities between cultural elements and theoretically active elements is not relevant.

LIMITATIONS OF THE CULTURALLY CENTERED PERSPECTIVE

Despite the obvious strength of centralization of culture within the treatment paradigm, this perspective has several notable weaknesses. Primarily, the dearth of examples of this approach speaks to the difficulty of developing a treatment that stands outside of Western conceptions of health and sickness. Because these treatments were developed for highly specific situations, they are less easily transported and disseminated to other locations. As a result, it is unlikely that these approaches will be on the front line of reducing the mental health-care disparities described earlier.

Further, although it centralizes culture in both the conception of illness and in the route to wellness, this perspective offers little guidance on working with individuals who may prefer a standard treatment approach or who may not be presenting with culturally influenced distress. For instance, it is plausible that culturally centered therapies would work less well with more assimilated individuals, who may not resonate with approaches that utilize traditional healing pathways. Very little guidance is given to help with these determinations.

SUMMARY AND RECOMMENDATIONS

In sum, our review of the literature on clinical work with Latino adults suggests that there are important differences in the centrality with which scholars believe that attention should be given to culture. The first perspective views the integration of culture as a process that happens through the attitudes, knowledge, and behavior of the therapist; the second sees the integration of culture as best occurring through the adaptation of existing therapies for particular cultural groups; and the third conceptualizes the integration of culture as a process that is central to the entire therapeutic endeavor.

As we have noted throughout, each of these perspectives has important strengths and limitations, and the body of research is still in its relatively early stages. Thus, we remain uncommitted regarding which perspective might ultimately prove most useful in reducing health-care disparities and increasing treatment opportunities for Latinos. Of course, our own experiences lie in the area of cultural adaptations because we believe that the strengths of this perspective are considerable. However, we also recognize that the overwhelming majority of therapists do not work with culturally adapted interventions, and so training in the development of cultural competence with Latinos would likely produce considerable benefit. Similarly, we see that culturally centered interventions offer the most promise for the long term in helping develop novel theoretical approaches to conceptualizing and treating distress that explicitly incorporate culture.

Importantly, despite distinct differences across these perspectives, several commonalities warrant mention because they lead directly to concrete clinical and research recommendations.

1. Acquire the relevant cultural knowledge, and modify therapist behavior accordingly.

There was broad consistency across studies regarding the importance of the incorporation of Latino cultural values into the treatment process. Moreover, many authors noted that clinicians should also be familiar with the specific cultural conceptualizations of mental health and illness of the Latino ethnic groups with whom they are working. Importantly, several authors also described concrete changes to traditional therapist behavior in response to this knowledge. For example, a few studies suggested that they attempted to create an informal approach to therapy, in recognition of the cultural value *personalismo*. Others described how they encourage more self-disclosure from therapists than is typically sanctioned by traditional therapy approaches. In our prevention work with Latina mothers, we have found that our groups work well when we balance a less formal

approach to therapy that includes more self-disclosure with the formality in how we address our participants (e.g., use of the formal second person, *Ud,* rather than the informal second person, *Tu*). These concrete modifications were described more fully with regard to the cultural values, but it is not difficult to imagine therapists explicitly discussing traditional views of mental health and illness as a way to increase rapport and trust in the treatment process. Thus, cultural sensitivity requires more than just an awareness of the values and culturally specific conceptions of mental health; it requires that the therapist's behavior be congruent with those values and conceptions.

2. Attempt to understand culturally relevant life stressors.

We found that the majority of examples in the literature conceptualized Latino culture very complexly in that they recognized the importance of attending to life events that are commonly reported by Latinos living in the United States. Some of these life events include the stressors associated with the immigration and acculturation process, issues related to socioeconomic status, and issues related to minority status. These life events and experiences are not specific to Latino culture, as many individuals from other low-income and racial/ethnic minority backgrounds have similar experiences. Moreover, some of these life events are not likely to be found among Latinos living in Latin America (e.g., immigration stress, minority status). However, because they are so commonly experienced by Latinos living in the United States, it is important that clinicians understand both the general sociocultural contexts, as well as the particular life experiences, of their Latino clients.

3. Acknowledge the importance of religion and spirituality.

Several authors discussed the centrality of religion and spirituality in the lives of Latinos and suggested that clinicians make efforts to acknowledge this fact. One culturally adapted intervention went so far as to specifically create a module that focused on spirituality, and one of the culturally centered interventions specifically targeted spirituality. However, unlike the other Latino cultural values, considerably less attention has been given to the integration of religion and spirituality into the treatment process, most likely due to the traditionally secular stance of psychotherapy. The consistently positive experiences reported by the authors who have attempted to integrate religion and spirituality suggest that some minimum acknowledgment of this aspect of Latinos' lives could increase rapport with clients.

4. Conceptualize clinical work more broadly than is traditionally done.

We also found considerable agreement across studies in their recognition of the serious mental health-care disparities affecting Latinos. Thus, many researchers explicitly documented ways in which their approaches to treatment included elements not traditionally thought of as therapy. For example, several authors noted that they provided transportation and child-care accommodations for their participants in recognition of the financial stressors many faced. Some of the authors described providing more psychoeducation regarding mental health and psychotherapy for their Latino clients, many of whom may not have had prior experience with therapy. Miranda and colleagues (2003a, 2003b, 2006) formalized the provision of this information, allowing as many as to four sessions of psychoeducation prior to starting treatment. Finally, a few authors described the utility of formal case management that was useful in supplementing the therapy itself. Taken as a whole, it seems that the successful treatment approaches were those that sought out creative ways to help their Latino clients overcome common instrumental barriers to treatment.

5. Consider integrating family members into the treatment process.

Interestingly, few of the studies we reviewed explicitly incorporated family members into the treatment process, despite the general recognition that many Latinos consider the family very important. The few that did reported considerable success regarding both participation from family and acceptance of the familial treatment approach (e.g., Cardemil et al., 2005). We suspect the reason so few treatments explicitly incorporate family members is that there is a general lack of familiarity with family-based treatment approaches. Some support for this explanation can be seen in the fact that the overwhelming

majority of treatments in the cultural adaptation perspective were individually focused (either cognitive-behavioral or interpersonal). We believe that there are many potential benefits from the integration of family members into treatment, including reduction of family resistance to treatment, increasing familial emotional support for the client, and modifying familial problem-solving and communication patterns. In our prevention work with Latina mothers, we have consistently found increased attendance and participation when we have met other family members (e.g., husband, mother, siblings). Thus, we recommend that clinicians and researchers consider the formal inclusion of family members in some portion of the treatment process.

6. Recognize that many Latinos use alternate sources of health care.

Several scholars noted that many Latinos seek out help for mental health problems from traditional sources rather than from formal mental health services. These traditional providers can include religious leaders and traditional cultural healers as well as family members. In much the same way that clinicians should be aware that some of their clients may be receiving several different treatments from different providers (e.g., pharmacotherapy, psychotherapy, family therapy), clinicians working with Latinos should be cognizant of the fact that some may be seeking help from informal and traditional sources. Validation of these help-seeking behaviors, rather than dismissal of them as ineffective, could lead to a strengthening of the rapport between clinicians and their clients.

7. Whenever possible, use bilingual and bicultural clinicians.

Finally, the overwhelming majority of the studies we reviewed had bicultural and bilingual clinicians deliver the treatment, highlighting the importance of depth of familiarity with Latino culture. Given the wide variability among Latinos in Spanish- and English-speaking ability, it is important that health centers have the versatility to provide services in either Spanish or English, and ideally have bilingual and bicultural clinical health providers. Relatedly, Latino scholars were involved in the development and conceptualization of the treatments in many of the studies we reviewed. This speaks to the importance of continuing to support Latino students and early career professionals who are entering the field. It is unlikely that we would have had so much literature to review without the impressive work of those Latino scholars who began to question the general absence of attention to Latino populations and issues.

Concluding Thoughts

In this chapter, we have reviewed the literature on clinical approaches to working with Latinos. We have placed our review in the context of the troubling mental health-care disparities that currently exist in the United States and that in some cases appear to be increasing (Blanco et al., 2007). Of course, there exist many economic, political, and social structural reasons for the continuing disparities. However, we believe that more explicit attention to the heterogeneity in the literature regarding clinical work with Latinos can provide some clarity to the occasionally contradictory recommendations that currently exist. Our hope has been to increase the awareness of the heterogeneity in approaches that currently exist in the literature. A better understanding of this variability, along with careful consideration of the strengths and weaknesses of each perspective, can serve only to advance the literature on clinical work with Latinos.

References

Abreu, J. M., Chung, R. H. G., & Atkinson, D. R. (2000). Multicultural counseling training: Past, present, and future directions. *The Counseling Psychologist, 28,* 641–656.

Alegría, M. A., Canino, G., Ríos, R., Vera, M., Calderón, J., Rusch, D., et al. (2002). Inequalities in use of specialty mental health services among Latinos, African Americans, and non-Latino Whites. *Psychiatric Services, 52,* 1547–1555.

Alegría, M. A., Mulvaney-Day, N., Woo, M., Torres, M., Gao, S., & Oddo, V. (2007). Correlates of past-year mental health service use among Latinos: Results from the National Latino and Asian American Study. *American Journal of Public Health, 97,* 76–83.

American Psychological Association (APA). (1993). Guidelines for the provision of psychological services to ethnic, linguistic, and culturally diverse populations. *American Psychologist, 48,* 45–48.

Areán, P. A., & Miranda, J. (1996). The treatment of depression in elderly primary care patients. *Journal of Clinical Geropsychology, 2,* 241–259.

Arredondo, P., & Perez, P. (2003). Counseling paradigms and Latina/o Americans: Contemporary considerations. In F. D. Harper & J. McFadden (Eds.), *Culture and counseling: New approaches* (pp. 115–132). Boston: Allyn & Bacon.

Atkinson, D. R., Bui, Y., & Mori, S. (2001). Multiculturally sensitive empirically supported treatments—An oxymoron? In J. G. Ponterotto, J. M. Casas, L. A. Suzuki, & C. M. Alexander (Eds.), *Handbook of multicultural counseling* (2nd ed., pp. 542–574). Thousand Oaks, CA: Sage.

Atkinson, D. R., Morten, G., & Sue, D. W. (1998). *Counseling American minorities.* (5th ed.). Boston: McGraw-Hill.

Aviera, A. (1996). "Dichos" therapy group: A therapeutic use of Spanish language proverbs with hospitalized Spanish-speaking psychiatric patients. *Cultural Diversity and Mental Health, 2,* 73–87.

Bernal, G., & Sáez-Santiago, E. (2006). Culturally centered psychosocial interventions. *Journal of Community Psychology, 34,* 121–132.

Bernal, G., & Scharrón-del Río, M. R. (2001). Are empirically supported treatments valid for ethnic minorities? Toward an alternative approach for treatment research. *Cultural Diversity and Ethnic Minority Psychology, 7,* 328–342.

Blanco, C., Patel, S. R., Liu, L., Jiang, H., Lewis-Fernandez, R., Schmidt, A. B., et al. (2007). National trends in ethnic disparities in mental health care. *Medical Care, 45,* 1012–1019.

Butzlaff, R. L., & Hooley, J. M. (1998). Expressed emotion and psychiatric relapse: A meta analysis. *Archives of General Psychiatry, 55,* 547–552.

Cabassa, L. J., Zayas, L. H., & Hansen, M. C. (2006). Latino adults' access to mental health care: A review of epidemiological studies. *Administration and Policy in Mental Health and Mental Health Services Research, 33,* 316–330.

Cardemil, E. V. (2008). Culturally sensitive treatments: Need for an organizing framework. *Culture and Psychology, 14,* 357–367.

Cardemil, E. V., Kim, S., Pinedo, T. M., & Miller, I. W. (2005). Developing a culturally appropriate depression prevention program: The Family Coping Skills Program. *Cultural Diversity and Ethnic Minority Psychology, 11,* 99–112.

Castro, F. G., Barrera, M., & Martinez, C. R. (2004). The cultural adaptation of prevention interventions: Resolving tensions between fidelity and fit. *Prevention Science, 5,* 41–45.

Chiriboga, D., Black, S., Aranda, M., & Markides, K. (2002). Stress and depressive symptoms among Mexican American elders. *Journals of Gerontology: Series B: Psychological Sciences and Social Sciences, 57B*(6), P559–P568.

Comas-Díaz, L. (1981). Effects of cognitive and behavioral group treatment on the depressive symptomatology of Puerto Rican women. *Journal of Consulting and Clinical Psychology, 49,* 627–632.

Comas-Díaz, L. (1986). Cognitive and behavioral group therapy with Puerto Rican women: A comparison of content themes. *Hispanic Journal of Behavioral Sciences, 7,* 273–283.

Cortés, D. E. (2003). Idioms of distress, acculturation, and depression: The Puerto Rican experience. In K. M. Chun, P. B. Organista, & G. Marín (Eds.), *Acculturation: Advances in theory, measurement, and applied research* (pp. 207–222). Washington, DC: American Psychological Association.

Costantino, G., Malgady, R. G., & Rogler, L. H. (1986). Cuento therapy: A culturally sensitive modality for Puerto Rican children. *Journal of Consulting and Clinical Psychology, 54,* 639–645.

Delgado, M., & Humm-Delgado, D. (1984). Hispanics and group work: A review of the literature. In L. Davis (Ed.), *Ethnicity in social group work practice* (pp. 85–96). New York: Haworth Press.

Dwight-Johnson, M., Lagomasino, I. T., Aisenberg, E., & Hay, J. (2004). Using conjoint analysis to assess depression treatment preferences among low-income Latinos. *Psychiatric Services, 55,* 934–936.

Falloon, I. R., Boyd, J. L., & McGill, C. W. (1984) *Family care of schizophrenia.* New York: Guilford Press.

Gloria, A. M., Ruiz, E. L., & Castillo, E. M. (2004). Counseling and psychotherapy with Latino and Latina clients. In T. B. Smith (Ed.), *Practicing multiculturalism: Affirming diversity in counseling and psychology* (pp. 167–189). Boston: Allyn & Bacon.

Griner, D., & Smith, T. B. (2006). Culturally adapted mental health interventions: A meta-analytic review. *Psychotherapy: Theory, Research, Practice, Training, 43,* 531–548.

Guarnaccia, P. J., Lewis-Fernández, R., & Marano, M. R. (2003). Toward a Puerto Rican popular nosology: *Nervios* and *ataque de nervios. Culture, Medicine, and Psychiatry, 27,* 339–366.

Guarnaccia, P. J., & Rogler, L. H. (1999). Research on culture-bound syndromes: New directions. *American Journal of Psychiatry, 156,* 1322–1327.

Guinn, B., & Vincent, V. (2002). A health intervention on Latina spiritual well-being constructs: An evaluation. *Hispanic Journal of Behavioral Sciences, 24,* 379–391.

Hall, G. C. N. (2001). Psychotherapy research with ethnic minorities: Empirical, ethical, and conceptual issues. *Journal of Consulting and Clinical Psychology, 69,* 502–510.

Harman, J. S., Edlund, M. J., & Fortney, J. C. (2004). Disparities in the adequacy of depression treatment in the United States. *Psychiatric Services, 55,* 1379–1385.

Helms, J. E., & Cook, D. A. (1999). *Using race and culture in counseling and psychotherapy.* Boston: Allyn & Bacon.

Interian, A., Martinez, I. E., Guarnaccia, P. J., Vega, W., & Escobar, J. I. (2007). A qualitative analysis of the perception of stigma among Latinos receiving antidepressants. *Psychiatric Services, 58,* 1591–1594.

Kleinman, A. (1982). Neurasthenia and depression: A study of somatization and culture in China. *Culture, Medicine, and Psychiatry, 6,* 117–190.

Kopelowicz, A., Zarate, R., Smith, V. G., Mintz, J., & Liberman, R. P. (2003). Disease management in Latinos with schizophrenia: A family-assisted, skills training approach. *Schizophrenia Bulletin, 29*(2), 211–228.

Lagomasino, I. T., Dwight-Johnson, M., Miranda, J., Zhang, L., Liao, D., Duan, N., et al. (2005). Disparities in depression treatment for Latinos and site of care. *Psychiatric Services, 56,* 1517–1523.

Lakes, K., López, S. R., & Garro, L. C. (2006). Cultural competence and psychotherapy: Applying anthropologically informed conceptions of culture. *Psychotherapy: Theory, Research, and Practice, 43,* 380–396.

La Roche, M. (2002). Psychotherapeutic considerations in treating Latinos. *Harvard Review of Psychiatry, 10,* 115–122.

La Roche, M. J., & Christopher, M. S. (2008). Culture and empirically supported treatments: On the road to a collision? *Culture and Psychology, 14,* 333–356.

Lau, A. S. (2006). Making the case for selective and directed cultural adaptations of evidence-based treatments: Examples from parent training. *Clinical Psychology: Science and Practice, 13,* 295–310.

Lesser, I. M., Castro, D. B., Gaynes, B. N., Gonzalez, J., Rush, A. J., Alpert, J. E., et al. (2007). Ethnicity/race and outcome in the treatment of depression: Results from STAR*D. *Medical Care, 45,* 1043–1051.

Lewis-Fernández, R., & Diaz, N. (2002). The cultural formulation: A method for assessing cultural factors affecting the clinical encounter. *Psychiatric Quarterly, 73,* 271–295.

López, S. R. (2002). A research agenda to improve the accessibility and quality of mental health care for Latinos. *Psychiatric Services, 53,* 1569–1573.

López, S. R., Hipke, K. N., Polo, A. J., Jenkins, J. H., Karno, M., Vaughn, C., et al. (2004). Ethnicity, expressed emotion, attributions, and course of schizophrenia: Family warmth matters. *Journal of Abnormal Psychology, 113,* 428–439.

Mari, D. J. D., & Streiner, D. L. (1994). An overview of family interventions and relapse on schizophrenia: Meta-analysis of research findings. *Psychological Medicine, 24,* 565–578.

Mezzich, J. E., Ruiz, P., & Muñoz, R. A. (1999). Mental health care for Hispanic Americans: A current perspective. *Cultural Diversity and Ethnic Minority Psychology, 5,* 91–102.

Miranda, J., Azocar, F., Organista, K. C., Dwyer, E., & Areán, P. (2003b). Treatment of depression among impoverished primary care patients from ethnic minority groups. *Psychiatric Services, 54,* 219–225.

Miranda, J., Bernal, G., Lau, A., Kohn, L., Hwang, W., & LaFramboise, T. (2005). State of the science on psychosocial interventions for ethnic minorities. *Annual Review of Clinical Psychology, 1,* 113–142.

Miranda, J., Chung, J. Y., Green, B. L., Krupnick, J., Siddique, J., Revicki, D. A., et al. (2003a). Treating depression in predominantly low-income young minority women: A randomized controlled trial. *Journal of the American Medical Association, 290,* 57–65.

Miranda, J., & Cooper, L. A. (2004). Disparities in care for depression among primary care patients. *Journal of General Internal Medicine, 19,* 120–126.

Miranda, J., Green, B. J., Krupnick, J. L., Chung, J., Siddique, J., Belin, T., et al. (2006). One-year outcomes of a randomized clinical trial treating depression in low-income minority women. *Journal of Consulting and Clinical Psychology, 74,* 99–111.

Muñoz, R. F., & Mendelsohn, T. (2005). Toward evidence-based interventions for diverse populations: The San Francisco General Hospital Prevention and Treatment Manuals. *Journal of Consulting and Clinical Psychology, 73,* 790–799.

Muñoz, R. F., Ying, Y., Bernal, G., Pérez-Stable, E. J., Sorensen, J. L., Hargreaves, W. A., et al. (1995). Prevention of depression with primary care patients: A randomized control trial. *American Journal of Community Psychology, 23,* 199–222.

Olarte, S. W., & Masnik, R. (1985). Benefits of long-term group therapy for disadvantaged Hispanic outpatients. *Hospital and Community Psychiatry, 36,* 1093–1097.

Opolka, J. L., Rascati, K. L., Brown, C. M., & Gibson, P. J. (2003). Role of ethnicity in predicting antipsychotic medication adherence. *Annals of Pharmacotherapy, 37,* 525–630.

Organista, K. C., Muñoz, R. F., & González, G. (1994). Cognitive-behavioral therapy for depression in low-income and minority medical outpatients: Description of a program and exploratory analyses. *Cognitive Therapy and Research, 18,* 241–259.

Padgett, D. K., Patrick, C., Burns, B. J., & Schlesinger, H. (1994). Ethnicity and the use of outpatient mental health services in a national insured population. *American Journal of Public Health, 84,* 222–226.

Passel, J. S., & Cohn, D. (2008). *U.S. population predictions: 2005–2050.* Washington, DC: Pew Research Center.

Pedersen, P. D. (1997). *Culture-centered counseling interventions: Striving for accuracy.* Thousand Oaks, CA: Sage.

Resnicow, K., Soler, R., Braithwaite, R. L., Ahluwalia, J. S., & Butler, J. (2000). Cultural sensitivity in substance use prevention. *Journal of Community Psychology, 28,* 271–290.

Rogler, L. H., & Cortes, D. E. (1993). Help-seeking pathways: A unifying concept in mental health care. *American Journal of Psychiatry, 150,* 554–561.

Rogler, L. H., Cortés, D. E., & Malgady, R. G. (1994). The mental health relevance of idioms of distress: Anger and perceptions of injustice among New York Puerto Ricans. *Journal of Nervous and Mental Disease, 182,* 327–330.

Sánchez-Lacay, J. A., Lewis-Fernández, R., Goetz, D., Blanco, C., Salmán, E., Davies, S., et al. (2001). Open trial of nefazodone among Hispanics with major depression: Efficacy, tolerability, and adherence issues. *Depression and Anxiety, 13,* 118–124.

Schraufnagel, T. J., Wagner, A. W., Miranda, J., & Roy-Byrne, P. P. (2006). Treating minority patients with depression and anxiety: What does the evidence tell us? *General Hospital Psychiatry, 28,* 27–36.

Snowden, L., & Yamada, A. M. (2005). Cultural differences in access to care. *Annual Review of Clinical Psychology, 1,* 143–166.

Spinelli, M. G., & Endicott, J. (2003). Controlled clinical trial of interpersonal psychotherapy versus parenting education program for depressed pregnant women. *American Journal of Psychiatry, 160,* 555–562.

Sue, D. W., Ivey, A. E., & Pedersen, P. B. (1996). *A multicultural theory of counseling and psychotherapy.* Pacific Grove, CA: Brooks/Cole.

Sue, S. (1998). In search of cultural competence in psychotherapy and counseling. *American Psychologist, 53,* 440–448.

Szapocznik, J., Rio, A., Perez-Vidal, A., Kurtines, W., Hervis, O., & Santisteban, D. (1986). Bicultural effectiveness training (BET): An experimental test of an intervention modality for families experiencing intergenerational/intercultural conflict. *Hispanic Journal of Behavioral Sciences, 8*, 303–330.

Szapocznik, J., Santisteban, D., Hervis, O., Spencer, F., & Kurtines, W. M. (1981). The treatment of depression among Cuban American elders: Some validational evidence for a life enhancement approach. *Journal of Consulting and Clinical Psychology, 49*, 752–755.

Szapocznik, J., Santisteban, D., Kurtines, W. M., Hervis, O., & Spencer, F. (1982). Life enhancement counseling and the treatment of depressed Cuban American elders. *Hispanic Journal of Behavioral Sciences, 4*, 487–502.

Telles, C., Karno, M., Mintz, J., Paz, G., Arias, M., Tucker, D., et al. (1995). Immigrant families coping with schizophrenia: Behavioral family intervention vs. case management with a low-income Spanish-speaking population. *British Journal of Psychiatry, 167*, 473–479.

Torres, J. B., Solberg, S. H., & Carlstrom, A. H. (2002). The myth of sameness among Latino men and their machismo. *American Journal of Orthopsychiatry, 72*, 162–181.

U.S. Department of Health and Human Services (USDHHS). (2001). *Mental health: Culture, race, and ethnicity—A supplement to Mental Health: A Report of the Surgeon General.* Rockville, MD: Author. Retrieved September 26, 2004, from http://media.shs.net/ken/pdf/SMA-01-3613/sma-01-3613

U.S. Department of Health and Human Services (USDHHS). (2005). *National healthcare disparities report.* Rockville, MD: Agency for Healthcare Research and Quality.

Vega, W. A., & Alegría, M. (2001). Latino mental health and treatment in the United States. In M. Aguirre-Molina, C. W. Molina, & R. E. Zambrana (Eds.), *Health issues in the Latino community* (pp. 179–208). San Francisco: Jossey-Bass.

Vega, W. A., Karno, M., Alegría, M., Alvidrez, J., Bernal, G., Escamilla, M., et al. (2007). Research issues for improving treatment for U.S. Hispanics with persistent mental disorders. *Psychiatric Services, 58*, 385–394.

Vega, W. A., Kolody, B., Aguilar-Gaxiola, S., & Catalano, R. (1999). Gaps in service utilization by Mexican Americans with mental health problems. *American Journal of Psychiatry, 156*, 928–934.

Vega, W. A., & Murphy, J. (1990). *Culture and the restructuring of community mental health.* Westport, CT: Greenwood Press.

Vega, W. A., Valle, R., Kolody, B., & Hough, R. (1987). The Hispanic Network Preventive Intervention Study. In R. F. Muñoz (Ed.), *The prevention of depression: Research foundations* (pp. 217–234). Washington, DC: Hemisphere.

Velásquez, R. J., & Burton, M. P. (2004). *Psychotherapy of Chicano men.* In R. J. Velásquez, L. M. Arellano, & B. W. McNeill (Eds.), *The handbook of Chicana/o psychology and mental health* (pp. 177–192). Mahwah, NJ: Lawrence Erlbaum.

Weisman, A. (2005). Integrating culturally based approaches with existing interventions for Hispanic/Latino families coping with schizophrenia. *Psychotherapy: Theory, Research, Practice, Training, 42*, 178–197.

Weisman, A., Duarte, E., Koneru, V., & Wasserman, S. (2006). The development of a culturally informed, family-focused treatment for schizophrenia. *Family Process, 45*, 171–186.

Whaley, A. L., & Davis, K. E. (2007). Cultural competence and evidence-based practice in mental health services. *American Psychologist, 62*, 563–574.

Zlotnick, C., Miller, I. W., Pearlstein, T., Howard, M., & Sweeney, P. (2006). A preventive intervention for pregnant women on public assistance at risk for postpartum depression. *American Journal of Psychiatry, 163*, 1443–1445.

Zuñiga, M. E. (1991). "Dichos" as metaphorical tools for resistant clients. *Psychotherapy, 28*, 480–483.

Zuñiga, M. E. (1992). Using metaphors in therapy: *Dichos* and Latino clients. *Social Work, 37*, 55–60.

20

THE PSYCHOLOGY OF HEALTH

*Physical Health and the Role of
Culture and Behavior*

HECTOR BETANCOURT AND PATRICIA M. FLYNN

In 2000, the U.S. Department of Health and Human Services set two overarching goals to achieve within the decade: to improve the quality and longevity of healthy life and to eliminate health disparities (U.S. Department of Health and Human Services [USDHHS], 2000). In fact, health disparities among ethnic groups in the United States have been recognized as one of the most important obstacles to better health in general and among ethnic minority and economically disadvantaged groups in particular (Smedley, Stith, & Nelson, 2003). Latino Americans (Latinos)[1] are the fastest-growing ethnic group in the United States (U.S. Census Bureau, 2006). They are overrepresented at low socioeconomic status (SES) levels, have less access to health care, and encounter linguistic and culturally based barriers within the health-care system (Reimann, Talavera, Salmon, Nunez, & Velasquez, 2004). In order to advance Latino health psychology, a number of issues relevant to this population must be addressed. In particular, issues pertaining to health disparities must be considered, including risk factors that may contribute to

health inequities, and protective factors that may result in health advantages.

Psychological research on Latino health in general and health disparities in particular is rather complex. For instance, to understand the health status of the Latino and Anglo American (Anglo)[2] populations, one must consider such factors as the role of culture and related psychological processes as they may impact health behavior. In addition, intragroup diversity associated with national origin, immigration status, and acculturation are also important to consider. Moreover, the U.S. health-care system is generally based on Anglo American cultural assumptions (Roosa, Dumka, Gonzales, & Knight, 2002), and programs directed at Latino communities are often guided by stereotypical views of Latinos. Hence, addressing the role of culture in Latino health behavior as well as in the delivery of health services may significantly enhance the effectiveness of health care and interventions with this population.

Consistent with this view, this chapter begins with a discussion of issues relevant to the study of health among Latino Americans in the United States, highlighting the intragroup diversity of this and other U.S. ethnic groups. Then, a comparative analysis of disparities in various health outcomes among Latinos and Anglos is undertaken. The following section describes some of the culture-based protective factors and risk factors that may contribute to the noted health disparities among Latinos. To this end, research is reviewed that moves beyond the comparative analysis of ethnic-group differences and aims to investigate plausible explanations for the noted health disparities. Last, the study of culture and related psychological factors is highlighted in order to further understanding of health behavior and the delivery of health-care services in a culturally diverse society. A conceptual model explaining the structure of relations among culture, health behavior, and related psychological factors is presented, and methodological approaches consistent with this model are discussed. Health research and intervention approaches are discussed from a cultural and psychological perspective aimed at reducing health disparities and promoting Latino health and well-being.

ISSUES IN THE STUDY OF LATINO HEALTH PSYCHOLOGY

Intragroup Diversity of the Latino Population

According to the 2007 U.S. Census Bureau population estimate, there are approximately 45.5 million Latinos living in the United States, representing 15% of the total population. Based on data from 2004, Mexican Americans represented the largest Latino subpopulation (66%), followed by Central and South Americans (13%), Puerto Ricans (9.4%), and Cubans (3.9%); the remaining 7.5% included individuals of other Latino origin (U.S. Census Bureau, 2007). Moreover, 34.3% of Latinos in 2004 were under the age of 18, as compared with only 22.3% of non-Latino Whites.

Until recently, the complexity of phenomena relevant to the study of Latino health has been overlooked. For instance, investigators have typically classified Latinos from various backgrounds as one group (e.g., Latinos or Hispanics) and compared outcomes to Anglo Americans. However, this ignores the diversity of the Latino population and the influence of such factors as

country of origin and immigration status on health behavior and outcome (see Betancourt & Fuentes, 2001). The Latino population comprises many diverse groups in terms of their national origin, region of the United States, education, and income, all of which may cause variations in culture (see Betancourt & Lopez, 1993). Such cultural variations are often ignored in health psychology research and intervention. In fact, demographic information can be misleading when within-group diversity is not considered.

Such realities as the regional migration patterns of Latinos in the United States have resulted in the formation of communities in which one dominant group is overrepresented. For instance, Mexican American immigrants have a strong presence in Southern California and Texas, Cuban American immigrants represent the dominant Latino group in the Miami area, New Jersey and New York have strong contingents of Dominican and Puerto Rican immigrants, and so on. The concentration of a Latino group within a region creates the impression of homogeneity, which often leads one to incorrectly attribute to all Latinos the cultural and behavioral characteristics of the "average" individual from the corresponding dominant Latino group. For instance, cultural aspects characteristic of Mexican Americans in Texas may be perceived as common to all Latinos in that region or in the country. This perspective does not take into consideration the differences observed among individuals from Puerto Rico, Cuba, and Central and South America.

Recent data highlight the diversity of Latinos in the United States and the nature of culture-based protective factors and risk factors associated with one or another Latino subgroup. For instance, Zsembik and Fennell (2005) reported variations in health outcomes among various Latino populations using data from the 1997–2001 National Health Interview Survey (NHIS). Their research revealed that Mexican Americans had health advantages, Puerto Ricans experienced health disadvantages, and Cubans and Dominicans experienced a mix of both health advantages and disadvantages. Moreover, the social determinants of health were also found to vary with country of origin. For instance, among Mexican Americans, higher SES and greater acculturation were associated with poorer health, whereas among Latinos from the

Caribbean, lower SES and lower acculturation were associated with worse health outcomes. Similar subgroup trends emerged based on mortality rates, using data from the NHIS 1986 through 1995, indicating that Mexican Americans had the lowest mortality rates and Puerto Ricans the highest (Hummer, Rogers, Amir, Forbes, & Frisbie, 2000).

Immigration Status, Acculturation, and Culture

The Latino population of the United States is different from other nondominant ethnic groups in that the influx of new immigrants is greater and steadier, resulting in a population with various levels of acculturation. Consequently, while new Latino American immigrants settle in various regions of the country, those already established in the United States acculturate to the mainstream Anglo culture. With this acculturative change, their beliefs, values, norms, expectations, and practices relative to health also change, along with their views of the health-care system and health professionals. In addition, the variety of experiences and forms of acculturation associated with different regional and socioeconomic realities within which they are hosted significantly enhances the intragroup diversity of Latinos.

The intragroup diversity associated with the continuous influx of immigrants, their countries of origin, and the localities that host them is extremely important for an understanding of the complexities faced in health research and the development of interventions with Latinos in the United States. For instance, recent Latino American immigrants show better health outcomes than those who have lived in the country for an extended period of time. Based on NHIS data from 1979 to 2003, Latino immigrants were found to have longer life expectancy and lower mortality for a number of diseases, including cancer, cardiovascular disease, unintentional injuries, and suicide (Singh & Hiatt, 2006). These findings highlight the importance of considering immigration status and the cultural reality of Latino individuals and communities.

The issues just described highlight the need for health psychologists working with Latino Americans to identify the background and cultural reality of the individuals and communities participating in their research or interventions.

The complexity of such cultural realities suggest that even traditional measures of acculturation may not be appropriate to a full understanding of the role of "Latino culture" in the health behavior and outcome of individuals from that population. In fact, the study of acculturation has been criticized for using indirect measures of acculturation instead of directly measuring change in the corresponding cultural variables of interest (Betancourt & Fuentes, 2001; Koneru, Weisman de Mamani, Flynn, & Betancourt, 2007). To understand the health behavior and outcomes of Latinos, research must identify changes in health-related cultural variables that are likely to be associated with variations in acculturation, such as value orientations, beliefs, norms, and practices. The direct study of cultural factors that influence psychological functioning and behavior can be more informative to health psychologists working with Latinos than mere assessment of acculturation level.

Socioeconomic Status

Another issue adding complexity to Latino health psychology has to do with the overrepresentation of this population at lower levels of income and education. According to data from the 2007 Current Population Survey, approximately 21.5% of Latinos were living in poverty, compared to 8.2% of non-Latino Whites (U.S. Census Bureau, 2008). In fact, the median household income for Latinos was less than three quarters of the median household income for Anglos. Levels of education are also quite low for Latinos. Based on data from 2006, only 55% of Latinos have a high school degree, compared to 85% of Anglos (U.S. Census Bureau, 2007). Moreover, a greater number of Latinos are represented in service industries, compared to Anglos.

The overrepresentation of Latinos at lower levels of income and education is particularly important for the study of Latino health, for a growing body of evidence demonstrates important disparities in health care and outcome associated with SES (Smedley et al., 2003). For instance, it has been reported that lower levels of socioeconomic status are associated with poorer health outcomes and higher mortality rates (Adler et al., 1994).

The noted research findings highlight the importance of acknowledging the diversity and distinctiveness of the Latino population in the

United States, which may contribute to a better understanding of ethnic and SES health disparities. Since research on health disparities has become a national concern, inequities associated with ethnicity as well as those associated with SES should also be a focus of Latino health psychology. In fact, understanding the cultural and socioeconomic reality of Latinos, including their own intragroup diversity, is important not only for an understanding of the health behavior and outcome of this population but also for an understanding of health disparities in the United States in general.

THE STUDY OF LATINO HEALTH

As indicated in the previous section, the study of Latino health behavior and outcome is quite complex. In this section, national data regarding Latino health outcomes are compared to those of Anglos in order to identify some of the predominant health disparities among these two broad cultural groups. Of course, the comparative study of health in general and health disparities in particular implies not only inequities (Hebert, Sisk, & Howell, 2008). In fact, some disparities among Latinos and other ethnic minority and majority groups reflect health advantages for Latinos. Efforts have been made to report research findings that take into consideration the diversity of the Latino population in the United States when available (e.g., immigration/generation status, Latino subpopulation, SES). However, research that recognizes the complexity of the Latino population is more recent, and much of the national data therefore focus on Latinos as a broad group. Such research can also be useful in terms of understanding the existence of broad disparities among all Latino groups in comparison to Anglos.

In this section, research studies are reviewed that investigate the underlying factors responsible for the noted disparities in health outcomes. To this end, research findings are discussed regarding culturally based protective factors as well as culturally based risk factors. These studies move beyond the comparative analysis of ethnic-group differences based on a particular health behavior or outcome and examine variations in the culturally based protective and risk factors. Such a perspective reflects the importance of diversity factors associated with cultural

variation and psychological processes relevant to Latino health behavior and outcome.

Disparities: Health Risks and Positive Health Outcomes Among Latinos

One health issue that remains at the forefront of national concern for Latinos is the incidence of diabetes. According to data from 2006, Latinos were over one and a half times as likely to be diagnosed with diabetes, compared to Anglos (Centers for Disease Control and Prevention [CDC], 2007). In fact, data from 2005 indicate that Mexican Americans were almost twice as likely as Anglos to be diagnosed with diabetes. Moreover, the prevalence of diabetes among male Latinos was higher than among female Latinos. Mexican Americans also had higher rates of end-stage renal disease as a result of their diabetes and were 50% more likely than Anglos to die from diabetes. Using data from the National Vital Statistics Systems and the 1990 and 2000 censuses, findings reveal that within-group diabetes mortality rates were twice as high among Mexican Americans and Puerto Ricans, compared to Cuban Americans (Smith & Barnett, 2005).

According to the Healthy People 2010 Midcourse Review (USDHHS, 2006) the number of new AIDS cases and HIV infection deaths remains quite high among Latinos in the United States. In fact, data from 2006 indicate that Latino men were 2.8 times as likely to be diagnosed with HIV/AIDS than were non-Latino Whites, whereas Latino women were 5 times as likely. Moreover, mortality data from 2004 indicate that Latino men were 2.6 times as likely to die from HIV/AIDS, and Latino women were 4 times as likely to die from HIV/AIDS, than were non-Latino Whites (CDC, 2007). In an analysis of within-group differences based on place of birth, CDC data from 2003 to 2006 revealed that HIV infection is more prevalent among Latinos born outside the United States (61%; Espinoza, Hall, Selik, & Hu, 2008). Moreover, a short HIV-to-AIDS interval was more common among Latinos born in Mexico and Central America than among those born in the United States.

Findings regarding disparities among Latino and non-Latino Whites in relation to cancer are mixed. For instance, Latino men and women reported higher incidence and mortality rates for stomach and liver cancer, according to data from 2004 (CDC, 2007). In addition, Latino women were twice as likely as non-Latino Whites to be diagnosed with cervical cancer and 1.5 times as likely to die from the disease.

Despite the prevalence of disadvantages such as these, Latinos have better health outcomes for a number of conditions, compared to other ethnic minority groups and Anglos. For instance, based on 2004 data, Latino men were 13% less likely to be diagnosed with prostate cancer than were non-Latino White men (SEER, 2007). Furthermore, in 2004 Latino women were 33% less likely to be diagnosed with breast cancer than were non-Latino White women.

Research also indicates that Latinos have lower rates of adult-mortality stroke and cardiovascular disease (CVD) than Anglo Americans (CDC, 2007; Hummer et al., 2000). In fact, based on data from 2005, Latino men were 15% less likely and Latino women 25% less likely to die from stroke than were non-Latino Whites. Regarding cardiovascular health, Latinos were 10% less likely than non-Latino Whites to have heart disease. In fact, Latino men were 30% less likely to die from CVD complications, compared to non-Latino White men, and Latino women were 20% less likely to die from complications, compared to non-Latino White women. Within-group analyses reveals that Mexican Americans have lower total CVD than non-Latino Whites, African Americans, and Puerto Ricans but higher rates than Cuban Americans (Durazo-Arvizu, Barquera, Lazo-Elizondo, Franco, & Cooper, 2008).

Regarding the developmental health of the Latino population, data from 2005 demonstrate that infant mortality rates are lower for all Latino subpopulations, compared to Anglos, with the exception of Puerto Rican infants (CDC, 2008). In fact, Puerto Rican infants had 1.4 times the infant mortality rate, compared to non-Latino White infants, and were nearly twice as likely to die from causes associated with low birth weight. Cuban American infants had the lowest mortality rates. Despite these favorable rates, data reveal that all Latino subpopulations were more likely to receive late or no prenatal care. In fact, Mexican Americans were 2.5 times more likely than non-Latino White mothers to receive late or no prenatal care.

A number of culturally based protective factors may contribute to the noted health advantages for Latinos. The study and understanding of such factors is not only likely to benefit research and intervention with Latinos but also may be helpful in the development and implementation of interventions with mainstream groups as well as other minority groups. Such research recognizes culture as an integral part of health, not a barrier to it (Hayes-Bautista, 2003).

Latino Protective Factors

Although Latinos report higher rates of poverty and lower levels of education and health insurance, there are still many health benefits associated with Latinos—which leads to what some researchers have called the *Latino mortality paradox* (Abraido-Lanza, Dohrenwend, Ng-Mak, & Turner, 1999). Some plausible explanations for the Latino mortality paradox include migratory patterns, proposing that healthy Latinos migrate to the United States, and unhealthy Latino Americans return to their places of origin to die; however, this was proven untrue, according to one study (Abraido-Lanza et al., 1999). These authors concluded that healthy behaviors associated with cultural values and such practices as dietary intake and smoking behaviors are possible explanations for the Latino mortality paradox.

Nutrition. The Mediterranean diet is comprised of foods low in saturated fat and high in polyunsaturated fat, such as olive oil, nuts, and fish. High consumption of fruits, vegetables, legumes, nuts, cereals, olive oil, and fish, along with lower consumption of animal and dairy fats, is typical of the Mediterranean diet (Schröder, 2007). The beneficial effects of the Mediterranean diet are well documented, including a reduced rate of coronary heart disease (Keys, 1980; Salas-Salvado et al., 2008) and reduced rates of obesity and diabetes (Mendez et al., 2006; Panagiotakos, Pitsavos, Arvaniti, & Stefanadis, 2007).

Similarities between the agricultural and fishing environments of Mediterranean countries and several Latin American countries are evident. In fact, Rozowski and Castillo (2004) compared the traditional Chilean diet to that of the Mediterranean. However, these investigators raise concerns about a recent shift in the Chilean diet toward a more Western (U.S.-like) diet due to economic and media-based cultural change. A similar pattern of increased energy-dense food consumption has been observed in several other Latin American countries (Bermudez & Tucker, 2003; Rivera, Barquera, Gonzalez-Cossio, Olaiz, & Sepulveda, 2004). Despite the benefits of the Mediterranean diet, these recent trends in food consumption in Latin America are resulting in the consumption of food rich in saturated fats, sugar, and refined foods (Vio & Albala, 2000), which has been associated with an increased risk for diabetes and obesity (Schulze et al., 2005). Still, studies examining the dietary patterns of recent immigrants in the United States confirm the healthier dietary intake of Latinos from Latin American countries.

For instance, first-generation Latino adolescents reported more servings of fruit and vegetables and less soda consumption, compared to Anglos (Allen et al., 2007). Other investigators (Dixon, Sundquist, & Winkleby, 2000) found that Mexican American women born in Mexico consumed significantly less fat and more fiber, vitamins, and minerals than Mexican Americans born in the United States. It appears that as Latinos spend more time in the United States, they adopt more of the behaviors and habits of mainstream Anglos, including a less healthy diet (Dixon et al., 2000). The role of acculturation is discussed in greater detail in the following section on risk factors.

Drinking, Smoking, and Substance Abuse. Latino lifestyles may also serve as protective mechanisms for addictions, which impact health outcomes in such areas as cancer and cardiovascular disease. According to data from the National Health Interview Survey, Latinos report lower rates of smoking and alcohol consumption than Anglo Americans (Adams & Schoenborn, 2006). Specifically, Latinos are less likely to be current smokers (15.2%), compared to both Anglos (23%) and non-Latino African Americans (20.9%). Latinos are also less likely to be current alcohol drinkers (50%), compared to Anglos (63%), with larger differences among women. In fact, Anglo women are more than twice as likely to be heavy drinkers than Latino women.

Differences in tobacco-smoking rates are also found, based on immigration status and Latino subpopulations. For instance, based on a national data set, the odds of being a daily smoker were highest among individuals born in the United States to U.S.-born parents and lowest among foreign-born individuals, even after controlling for age, gender, race/ethnicity, SES,

and central-city residency (Acevedo-Garcia, Pan, Jun, Osypuk, & Emmons, 2005). According to data from the National Household Survey on Drug Abuse (National Institute on Drug Abuse, 2003), Central/South Americans and Cubans were the least likely to have recently smoked, whereas Puerto Ricans were the most likely to have done so. Other studies have found no significant differences among men in smoking rates based on national origin. However, Puerto Rican women had the highest rates of smoking compared to other Latino women (Pérez-Stable et al., 2001).

Similar trends for illicit drug use emerged across ethnic and racial categories. According to data from the National Household Drug Survey 1999–2000 (National Institute on Drug Abuse, 2003), aside from Puerto Ricans, all other Latino subgroups in the United States report lower prevalence rates of illegal drug use than Anglo Americans, African Americans, and American Indian/Alaska Natives.

Social Support. One explanation for the lower rates of substance abuse and other health advantages observed among certain Latino American populations is social support, which is conceived as a culturally based protective factor. Generally speaking, Latino families are likely to be larger, with greater generational variability, and to include extended and non-kin family members (Knight et al., 2002). These social support systems have been associated with better physical health outcomes (Berkman & Glass, 2000), such as improvements in cardiovascular, neuroendocrine, and immune function (Uchino, 2006).

Although little research has been conducted on the biological implications of social support among Latino Americans, there is evidence of its influence on physical health outcomes. For instance, in a study with Mexican American adults, greater numbers of peers and family members in the United States were associated with better health (Finch & Vega, 2003). Moreover, family emotional support has been found to influence self-rated physical health among Latinos, even after controlling for several demographic factors, such as income and education (Mulvaney-Day, Alegría, & Sribney, 2007).

According to Uchino (2006) and other social support theorists (Berkman & Glass, 2000; Cohen, 1988), there are two major pathways by which social support influences morbidity and mortality: behavioral processes and psychological processes. For example, social support has been found to influence health behaviors, such as greater leisure-time physical activity (Marquez & McAuley, 2006) and cancer-screening behaviors (Katapodi, Facione, Miaskowski, Dodd, & Waters, 2002), among Latinos in the United States. Social support has also been found to influence psychological processes, such as levels of distress among Latino women treated for early stage breast cancer (Alferi, Carver, Antoni, Weiss, & Duran, 2001).

Another study, which investigated alcohol use among adolescent Latinos, found that the cultural value of *familism* was associated with a lower disposition to deviance, which in turn predicted lower levels of alcohol use (Gil, Wagner, & Vega, 2000). However, more research is needed, specifically examining the mediating role of behavioral and psychological processes on health outcomes (House, Landis, & Umberson, 2003), particularly among Latino populations.

The protective factors associated with some of the Latino American groups, such as eating a nutritious diet, less smoking, lower use of alcohol and drugs, and the existence of social support networks, can be conceived as culturally based. Socially shared values, beliefs, norms, and practices associated with a particular view of the world are important aspects of culture (Betancourt & Lopez, 1993) that influence motivation and behavior, including health behavior. Therefore, to better understand the protective and risk factors associated with health outcomes among Latinos in the United States, it is necessary also to examine the effects of cultural factors and related psychological processes on health behavior and practices. The role of culture in health behavior and outcome is examined later in this chapter.

Latino Risk Factors

Access to Care. As indicated earlier, Latinos in the United States are overrepresented at lower levels of income, which has implications for access to health care. For instance, compared to any other ethnic or racial group in the United States, Latinos have the highest rate of uninsured individuals. Based on data from 2007, 32.1% of Latinos are uninsured, compared to 19.5% of African Americans, 16.8% of Asian Americans, and 10.4% of Anglo Americans. Insurance status

also varies among Latinos of different background. For instance, Mexican Americans are the least likely to report having private health insurance (39%), compared to Puerto Ricans (47%), Cubans (58%), and other Latinos (45%).

Disparities in access to care based on immigration status also exist. Data from 2007 indicate that only 12.7% of U.S.-born Latinos are uninsured, whereas 33.2% of foreign-born Latinos are uninsured. Furthermore, among the foreign born, 17.6% of naturalized citizens are uninsured, whereas 43.8% of noncitizens are uninsured (DeNavas-Walt, Proctor, & Smith, 2007). A study conducted in California found that according to the 2003 California Health Interview Survey, 52.8% of undocumented Mexicans in the United States reported having no health insurance, compared to 32.5% of Mexicans with green cards, 20.5% of naturalized Mexican American citizens, and 14.8% of U.S.-born Mexican Americans (Ortega et al., 2007). Similar results were found for other Latino populations, with 56.8% of undocumented Latinos uninsured, compared to 30.9% of Latinos with green cards, 15.6% of naturalized Latinos, and 15.6% of U.S.-born Latinos.

Despite these barriers to health care access, research findings demonstrate health advantages for recent immigrants (Singh & Hiatt, 2006). In fact, Singh and Hiatt (2006) suggest that if immigrants and natives had similar health-care access, the mortality of U.S.-born Latinos might be even higher than that of Latino Americans born outside the United States. These investigators point to the culturally based protective health behaviors among recent immigrants that are likely to lead to better health outcomes among some Latino groups. Still, numerous studies report that such health behaviors decline with acculturation (Nieri, Kulis, Keith, & Hurdle, 2005; Perez-Escamilla & Putnik, 2007).

Acculturation. As discussed earlier, aspects of culture can have positive as well as negative effects on health behavior and outcome. From an acculturation perspective, it is possible that as Latinos adapt to the cultural views, values, and beliefs of the host society, they may in fact adopt unhealthy behaviors and practices (Koneru et al., 2007). Although this is not always the case, according to Berry's (2005) multidimensional conceptualization of acculturation, it is possible that some individuals could be slowly losing their own cultural values, beliefs, norms, and practices that are protective in terms of influence on health behavior and outcome.

Acculturation appears to have varying effects based on the behavior or outcome of interest and the way in which acculturation is assessed (Koneru et al., 2007). For instance, it has been found that acculturation has a positive effect on health-care use and self-perceptions of health, whereas it has a negative effect on substance abuse, dietary practices, and birth outcomes (Lara, Gamboa, Kahramanian, Morales, & Hayes Bautista, 2005). Depending on the health behavior under consideration, acculturated Latinos reported poorer health behaviors and outcomes than Anglos (Lara et al., 2005).

A recent study (Burns, Levinson, Lezotte, & Prochazka, 2007) found that highly acculturated Latinos smoke for longer periods of time than Anglos. However, this relationship was not observed after accounting for socioeconomic status. These findings suggest that highly acculturated Latinos may be at even greater risk for lung cancer and other chronic diseases associated with socioeconomic status.

Another study, which examined adolescent participation in preventive health behaviors, found that compared to Anglos, third-generation Latinos were less likely to consume fruits and vegetables and were more likely to drink soda, watch television, and play video games (Allen et al., 2007). These findings emerged based on generation status, as first-generation Latino adolescents had healthier nutritious intake than Anglo adolescents.

The aforementioned studies examined acculturation using such proxy measures as generation status and language preference. These types of measures have some methodological limitations. Specifically, these measures do not account for the multidimensional nature of the acculturation construct, in which culture-of-origin and host cultural identities can vary independently. Cultural change implies changes in the components of culture, such as values, beliefs, expectations, norms, and roles, as well as changes in cultural practices and related psychological functioning (Koneru et al., 2007). Research examining the role of acculturation in relation to health behaviors and outcomes might elicit more systematic results when such aspects are considered.

Acculturative Stress. A growing body of literature has examined stress typically associated with the Latino acculturation process and its influence on health behaviors and outcomes. Acculturative stress has been described as including the incidence of family conflict between less and more acculturated individuals, as well as experiences of discrimination (Gil et al., 2000). Although not a great deal of research has been done in this area, preliminary findings suggest that greater acculturative stress is associated with poorer health behaviors and outcomes. For instance, among a group of adolescent Latinos, those who experienced greater acculturative stress reported more smoking, drinking, drug use, violence, and depressive symptoms (Romero, Martinez, & Carvajal, 2007). Gil and colleagues (2000) examined acculturative stress factors, including perceived discrimination, language conflicts, and acculturation conflicts, in relation to alcohol use among adolescent Latino boys. These researchers found that acculturation stress influenced alcohol use primarily through the deterioration of family values, attitudes, and behaviors.

Perceived Discrimination. Another area of research relevant to Latino health that is receiving significant attention as a health risk factor is the impact of perceived discrimination. The implications of health-care discrimination can be quite deleterious for individuals from minority groups. For instance, perceptions of health-care discrimination have been associated with such health behaviors as delay in seeking health care (Hobson, 2001) and adherence to cancer screening guidelines (Moy, Par, Feibelmann, Chiang, & Weissman, 2006). In fact, perceptions of discrimination also have a direct influence on an individual's psychological health and physiological reactivity. In a review of the literature, Krieger (1999) found that perceived discrimination was associated with poorer mental health and, more often than not, that discrimination had a negative effect on reported blood pressure and hypertension. Clark and Gochett (2006) also found that blood pressure reactivity among African American youth was influenced by perceived racism.

Perceptions of discrimination are likely to be associated with higher stress, which may be responsible for the poorer health outcomes of certain groups. More recently, allostatic load (a construct used to quantify stress-induced biological risk based on a number of physiological measures) has been associated with accelerated disease processes (McEwen, 2000). Differences in allostatic load have been associated with differences in stress exposure and tend to be more prevalent among individuals from lower socioeconomic groups (Szanton, Gill, & Allen, 2005).

Although the majority of research examining perceived discrimination has focused on the African American population (Smedley et al., 2003), preliminary evidence suggests that Latinos also experience the deleterious effects of discrimination. Finch, Hummer, Kolody, and Vega (2001) found that in California, Mexican Americans who reported greater perceptions of discrimination also reported poorer physical health, even after factors such as socioeconomic status, country of origin, level of acculturation stress, and social support were controlled for.

Perceptions of discrimination also appear to be influenced by generation/immigration status. In fact, immigrants report greater instances of "othering" (Viruell-Fuentes, 2007), perceptions of everyday discrimination (Perez, Fortuna, & Alegría, 2008), and perceptions of health-care discrimination (Gee, Ryan, Laflamme, & Holt, 2006) with increasing time spent in the United States. Viruell-Fuentes (2007) argued that the longer immigrants are in the United States, the more adept they become at learning and interpreting the racial/ethnic dynamics of the United States and the implication of their minority status.

The literature examining risk factors associated with health behaviors and outcomes among Latinos is quite diverse. Despite the health advantages relevant to the Latino mortality paradox, research reveals that as Latinos spend more time in the United States and acculturate to mainstream cultural practices, their health outcomes tend to suffer. Because most research in this area examines either protective factors or risk factors associated with Latinos in the United States, research examining both protective and risk factors under a single research paradigm appears necessary to advance knowledge in this area.

Can Protective Health Factors Outweigh the Risk Factors for Latinos in the United States?

Despite the influence of the noted risk factors (e.g., income, education, access to care, acculturation, and discrimination), which results in poorer health outcomes among Latinos, when protective factors are also evident, the gravity of their effect on health outcomes can be ameliorated. For instance, among a group of Latino adolescent males born in the United States and Latin America, higher levels of acculturation were found to increase the use of alcohol (Gil et al., 2000). However, familism values and parental respect mediated the influence on alcohol use. These researchers found that greater familism values and parental respect predicted a lower disposition to deviance, which in turn predicted less alcohol use. Another study found that bicultural Latino adolescents who adopted aspects of the mainstream culture while holding onto their own cultural ways had better mental health outcomes than the marginalized students with fewer attachments and adaptations to Latino culture (Carvajal, Hanson, Romero, & Coyle, 2002).

The discrimination literature also highlights various protective mechanisms that can ameliorate the negative effects of perceived discrimination on health outcomes among diverse groups. For instance, Clark and Gochett's (2006) study, discussed earlier, tested the mediating effect of coping mechanisms on blood pressure and vascular reactivity among African Americans. Results indicated that some coping strategies were protective, whereas others influenced blood pressure reactivity negatively. Similarly, Finch and Vega (2003) found that both instrumental and religious social support moderated the effects of discrimination on reported physical health among Latinos in California. Findings revealed that discrimination was associated with poorer health only among the Latinos who lacked social support.

Taken together, these findings demonstrate two important aspects relevant to the study of culture in relation to health behavior and outcome, which are discussed in greater detail in the next section. First, when investigating the protective and risk factors associated with culture among diverse ethnic and socioeconomic groups, it is important to examine cultural influences on psychological factors relevant to the health behavior of patients. Second, when research is conducted in such a manner, findings may reveal that such protective factors as social support may ameliorate the negative effects of the risk factors. For instance, acculturation or perceived discrimination may not have such a negative impact on health outcomes when individuals maintain some of the protective cultural values, beliefs, and practices of their native Latino cultures.

INVESTIGATING THE ROLE OF CULTURE IN HEALTH BEHAVIOR AND HEALTH-CARE DELIVERY

Because Latinos are the fastest-growing ethnic group and are currently the largest minority group in the United States, it is important to recognize how culture may influence the health behaviors of patients as well as the way they are treated by health-care professionals. In a culturally diverse society, health disparities among individuals from different ethnic, racial, and economic groups may be in part a function of cultural differences between a health-care system primarily based on Anglo cultural assumptions and the populations it serves (Roosa et al., 2002). This incongruence between culturally diverse patients and the delivery of health-care services based on mainstream cultural assumptions may lead to negative interactions, unequal quality of care, and perceptions of discrimination on the part of ethnic minority and low-SES individuals (Smedley et al., 2003). For instance, research indicates that Latino Americans are 20% more likely to report poorer-quality health care, compared to mainstream Americans (Agency for Healthcare Research and Quality, 2006). Latinos are also significantly more likely to report that they personally have been treated unfairly by doctors and health-care professionals based on their ability to pay for care (20%), ethnic background (15%), insurance status (21%), and ability to speak English (14%; Lillie-Blanton, Brodie, Rowland, Altman, & McIntosh, 2000).

Theory-Based Research on Culture and Disparities in Health Behavior and Outcome

It is apparent that understanding and reducing health disparities is a major challenge to health care. In order to advance the study of culture-based health risk and protective factors associated with Latino culture in the United States, research and intervention strategies must be guided by theoretical models and appropriate methodology. Consistent with this view, this section introduces a conceptual and methodological approach for the study of culture and behavior that has been applied to the study of health disparities among Anglo and Latino Americans. Research guided by the corresponding model and methodological approach is used to illustrate the kind of research thought to more effectively contribute to the understanding of health issues relevant to Latinos and other underserved groups.

The model represented in Figure 20.1 is based on the postulates for the study of culture in psychology developed by Betancourt and collaborators (Betancourt & Fuentes, 2001; Betancourt, Hardin, & Manzi, 1992; Betancourt & Lopez, 1993). This model, adapted for the study of health behavior, has guided research in such areas as adherence to diabetes treatment and cancer screening among Latino and Anglo Americans in the United States (Flynn, 2005; McMillin-Williams, 2004).

As observed in Figure 20.1, the model articulates (a) how culture relates to population categories that serve as sources of cultural variation and (b) how culture influences the behavior of health personnel (e.g., interactions with patients) and the health behaviors of patients (e.g., screening, treatment adherence), both directly and through psychological processes and dispositions. An important underlying principle of the model is that relations among the variables conceived as determinants of health behavior are structured from most distal to more proximal (moving from A to D), with proximity to behavior determining a greater impact. According to the model, health behavior (D) is a function of psychological processes (C), which are the most proximal determinants and therefore have the greatest influence on behavior. Health behavior (D) is also associated with such aspects of culture as value orientation, beliefs, and expectations (B). These aspects of culture may be directly or indirectly associated with behavior through mediating psychological processes (C). Moving farther away from behavior are social or population categories, such as race, ethnicity, and SES (A), which may represent sources of cultural variation. However, these categories are more distal determinants (and not necessarily directly associated with a particular health behavior). Therefore, the model highlights that it is culture, not just race, ethnicity, or membership in any other category of people, that influences health behaviors and potentially mediating psychological processes.

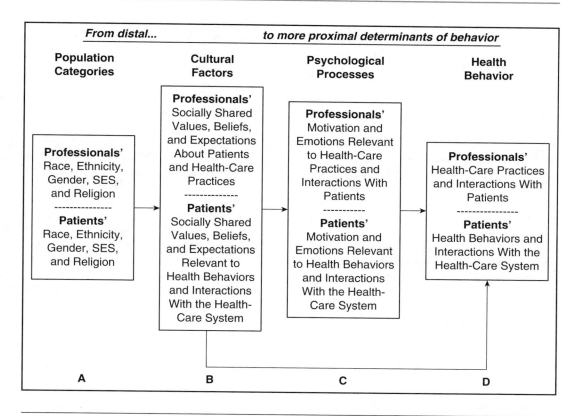

From distal...   **to more proximal determinants of behavior**

| Population Categories | Cultural Factors | Psychological Processes | Health Behavior |

Professionals'
Race, Ethnicity, Gender, SES, and Religion

Patients'
Race, Ethnicity, Gender, SES, and Religion

Professionals'
Socially Shared Values, Beliefs, and Expectations About Patients and Health-Care Practices
----
Patients'
Socially Shared Values, Beliefs, and Expectations Relevant to Health Behaviors and Interactions With the Health-Care System

Professionals'
Motivation and Emotions Relevant to Health-Care Practices and Interactions With Patients
----
Patients'
Motivation and Emotions Relevant to Health Behaviors and Interactions With the Health-Care System

Professionals'
Health-Care Practices and Interactions With Patients

Patients'
Health Behaviors and Interactions With the Health-Care System

A   B   C   D

Figure 20.1   Betancourt's Model of Culture and Behavior Adapted for the Study of Health Behavior

Two different but complementary methodological approaches consistent with the theoretical model described above have recently been applied to the comparative study of Anglo and Latino American health behavior and outcome (e.g., Flynn, 2005; McMillin-Williams, 2004). For instance, the bottom-up approach can be used to identify specific aspects of culture that may be relevant to health behavior or outcome. Then, instruments can be developed to measure these cultural elements. The resulting cultural instruments can be used to assess the degree to which individuals and groups endorse certain cultural factors relevant to a particular health behavior. Another methodological approach is the top-down approach. With this approach, one begins with a theory of health behavior, and then cultural elements thought to be relevant are incorporated to broaden the theory's conceptualization. The ultimate and common goal in both approaches is hypotheses testing concerning the role of culture, psychological processes, and health behavior or outcome.

CULTURE-BASED HEALTH RESEARCH AND INTERVENTION

The model and methodological approaches described can contribute to the advancement of research on aspects of culture that may influence the behaviors of health-care personnel as well as those affecting the health behaviors and outcomes of patients from various cultural and economic backgrounds. For instance, based on the definition of culture highlighted in the model and the corresponding bottom-up methodological approach, researchers can gain a better understanding of the cultural beliefs, values, expectations, and norms of patients as well as health care providers. This can be accomplished by conducting interviews and focus groups with diverse patients as well as their health-care providers, that is, physicians, surgeons, nurses, medical technicians, and receptionists. A cultural instrument can then be developed and used to assess these cultural elements. Once these aspects of culture have been assessed, one can test their relations with mediating psychological processes such as cognitions and emotions and subsequent health behaviors and outcomes.

The resulting information obtained through research employing the model and methodological approaches to the study of culture can then be used to develop culturally appropriate interventions. Interventions can be developed for culturally diverse patients as well as their health-care providers. It is particularly important that information gained from culturally diverse patients be used not only to develop interventions with this population but also to educate and inform health-care providers about their patients' cultural values, beliefs, expectations, and norms, which may in turn influence their health behaviors and outcomes. Therefore, from the perspective of health-care professionals, interventions should include two components. First, professionals should be made aware of their own cultural values, beliefs, expectations, and stereotypes that may influence the way they provide and deliver health-care services. Second, they should be educated about the cultural values, beliefs, expectations, and norms of their culturally diverse patients so that they are better prepared to deliver effective and appropriate health-care services.

Finally, as discussed in the corresponding section of this chapter, it is particularly important for health psychologists working with Latinos in the United States to recognize that there is as much within-group as between-group variation in cultural factors relevant to psychological functioning and health behavior. Latinos from Cuba may not hold the same cultural values, beliefs, norms, and health practices as Latinos from Mexico. At the same time, depending on such factors as generation, immigration status, acculturation, and education, some Latino patients may share health-related cultural beliefs and practices with mainstream Anglo Americans more than with the average Latino. Hence, it is important for research and intervention to assess how individuals or communities score on cultural factors relevant to the corresponding health concern rather than assuming that because of their ethnic backgrounds, individuals will engage in certain health behaviors or practices. In fact, based on evidence included in this chapter, such an approach may in fact be responsible, at least in part, for health inequities by perpetuating stereotypical views of culturally diverse groups.

It is expected that a better understanding of the role of culture in health behavior and care, within the context of relevant social-structural factors, may significantly contribute to improving the health outcomes and quality of life of Latinos and other nondominant ethnic groups in the United States. This implies, among other things, advancing the study of culture in health psychology. Such research should include the role of culture in the health behavior of Latinos and their interactions with the health-care system, as well as the role of mainstream cultural factors in the behavior of health-care personnel and policy decisions. By such inclusion, the study of culture-based protective and risk factors influencing Latino health and well-being might contribute to advancing not only the health outcomes of Latinos but also those of Anglos & other ethnic groups.

NOTES

1. The term *Latino* refers to the individuals or populations of the United States who came originally from Latin America or from a region of the United States that was once part of Latin America. This population is sometimes referred to as *Hispanic*, although this term is often rejected by Latinos because it excludes important segments of the Latino population who do not share the Spanish language or cultural heritage—for example, a significant portion of the indigenous people of Latin America and those whose ancestors came from other countries in Southern Europe (e.g., Brazilians), Africa, or Asia (see Betancourt & Fuentes, 2001).

2. *Anglo American* (shortened herein to *Anglo*) refers to the mainstream non-Latino White individuals or populations of the United States who came originally from the United Kingdom or other European backgrounds, who share the English language and Anglo American cultural heritage (see Betancourt & Fuentes, 2001).

REFERENCES

Abraido-Lanza, A. F., Dohrenwend, B. P., Ng-Mak, D. S., & Turner, J. B. (1999). The Latino mortality paradox: A test of the "salmon bias" and healthy migrant hypotheses. *American Journal of Public Health, 89,* 1543–1548.

Acevedo-Garcia, D., Pan, J., Jun, H. J., Osypuk, T. L., & Emmons, K. M. (2005). The effect of immigrant generation on smoking. *Social Science and Medicine, 61*, 1223–1242.

Adams, P. F., & Schoenborn, C. A. (2006). *Health behaviors of adults: United States 2002–04* (Rep. No. 10 [230]). Hyattsville, MD: National Center for Health Statistics.

Adler, N. E., Boyce, T., Chesney, M. A., Cohen, S., Folkman, S., Kahn, R. L., et al. (1994). Socioeconomic status and health: The challenge of the gradient. *American Psychologist, 49*, 15–24.

Agency for Healthcare Research and Quality (2006). *2006 National Healthcare Disparities Report* (Rep. No. AHRQ Pub. No. 07–0012). Rockville, MD: U.S. Department of Health and Human Services, Agency for Healthcare Research and Quality.

Alferi, S. M., Carver, C. S., Antoni, M. H., Weiss, S., & Duran, R. E. (2001). An exploratory study of social support, distress, and life disruption among low-income Hispanic women under treatment for early stage breast cancer. *Health Psychology, 20*, 41–46.

Allen, M. L., Elliott, M. N., Morales, L. S., Diamant, A. L., Hambarsoomian, K., & Schuster, M. A. (2007). Adolescent participation in preventive health behaviors, physical activity, and nutrition: Differences across immigrant generations for Asians and Latinos compared with Whites. *American Journal of Public Health, 97*, 337–343.

Berkman, L. F., & Glass, T. (2000). From social integration to health: Durkheim in the new millenium. *Social Science and Medicine, 51*, 843.

Bermudez, O., & Tucker, K. (2003). Trends in dietary patterns of Latin American populations. *Cadernos de Saúde Pública, 19*, S87–S99.

Berry, J. W. (2005). Acculturation: Living successfully in two cultures. *International Journal of Intercultural Relations, 29*, 697–712.

Betancourt, H., & Fuentes, J. L. (2001). Culture and Latino issues in health psychology. In S. Kazarian & D. Evans (Eds.), *Handbook of cultural health psychology* (pp. 305–321). San Diego, CA: Academic Press.

Betancourt, H., Hardin, C., & Manzi, J. (1992). Beliefs, value orientation, and culture in attribution processes and helping behavior. *Journal of Cross-Cultural Psychology, 23*, 179–195.

Betancourt, H. & Lopez, S. R. (1993). The study of culture, ethnicity, and race in American psychology. *American Psychologist, 48*, 629–637.

Burns, E. K., Levinson, A. H., Lezotte, D., & Prochazka, A. V. (2007). Differences in smoking duration between Latinos and Anglos. *Nicotine and Tobacco Research, 9*, 731–737.

Carvajal, S. C., Hanson, C. E., Romero, A. J., & Coyle, K. K. (2002). Behavioral risk factors and protective factors in adolescents: A comparison of Latinos and Non-Latino whites. *Ethnicity and Health, 7*, 181–193.

Centers for Disease Control and Prevention (CDC). (2007). *Health, United States, 2007 with chartbook on trends in the health of Americans* (Library of Congress Catalog No. 76–41496). Washington, DC: U.S. Government Printing Office.

Centers for Disease Control and Prevention (CDC). (2008). Infant mortality statistics from the 2005 period linked birth/infant data set. *National Vital Statistics, 57*(2), 1–32.

Clark, R., & Gochett, P. (2006). Interactive effects of perceived racism and coping responses predict a school-based assessment of blood pressure in black youth. *Annals of Behavioral Medicine, 32*, 1–9.

Cohen, S. (1988). Psychosocial models of the role of social support in the etiology of physical disease. *Health Psychology, 7*, 269–297.

DeNavas-Walt, C., Proctor, B. D., & Smith, J. (2007). *Income, poverty and health insurance coverage in the United States: 2006.* Washington, DC: U.S. Government Printing Office.

Dixon, L. B., Sundquist, J., & Winkleby, M. (2000). Differences in energy, nutrient, and food intakes in a U.S. sample of Mexican-American women and men: Findings from the third National Health and Nutrition Examination Survey, 1988–1994. *American Journal of Epidemiology, 152*, 548–557.

Durazo-Arvizu, R. A., Barquera, S., Lazo-Elizondo, M., Franco, M., & Cooper, R. S. (2008). Cardiovascular disease surveillance in Mexicans and Mexican Americans: A tale of two countries. *Pan American Journal of Public Health, 23*, 119–124.

Espinoza, L., Hall, H. I., Selik, R. M., & Hu, X. (2008). Characteristics of HIV infection among Hispanics, United States 2003–2006. *Journal of Acquired Immune Deficiency Syndrome, 49*, 94–101.

Finch, B. K., Hummer, R. A., Kolody, B., & Vega, W. A. (2001). The role of discrimination and acculturative stress in the physical health of Mexican-origin adults. *Hispanic Journal of Behavioral Sciences, 23*, 399–429.

Finch, B. K., & Vega, W. A. (2003). Acculturation stress, social support, and self-rated health among Latinos in California. *Journal of Immigrant Health, 5*, 109–117.

Flynn, P. M. (2005). Motivated breast cancer screening and its cultural antecedents. *Dissertation Abstracts International, 66*(10), 5730. (UMI No. 3191835).

Gee, G. C., Ryan, A., Laflamme, D. J., & Holt, J. (2006). Self-reported discrimination and mental health status among African descendants, Mexican Americans, and other Latinos in the New Hampshire REACH 2010 Initiative: The added dimension of immigration. *American Journal of Public Health, 96,* 1821–1828.

Gil, A. G., Wagner, E. F., & Vega, W. A. (2000). Acculturation, familism, and alcohol use among Latino adolescent males: Longitudinal relations. *Journal of Community Psychology, 28,* 443–458.

Hayes-Bautista, D. E. (2003). Research on culturally competent healthcare systems: Less sensitivity, more statistics. *American Journal of Preventive Medicine, 24,* 8–9.

Hebert, P. L., Sisk, J. E., & Howell, E. A. (2008). When does a difference become a disparity? Conceptualizing racial and ethnic disparities in health. *Health Affairs, 27,* 374–382.

Hobson, W. D. (2001). *Racial discrimination in health care interview project: A special report.* Seattle, WA: Seattle and King County Department of Public Health.

House, J. S., Landis, K. R., & Umberson, D. (2003). Social relationships and health. In P. Salovey & A. J. Rothman (Eds.), *Social psychology of health* (pp. 218–226). New York: Psychology Press.

Hummer, R., Rogers, R., Amir, S., Forbes, D., & Frisbie, P. (2000). Adult mortality differentials among Hispanic subgroups and non-Hispanic Whites. *Social Science Quarterly, 81,* 459–476.

Katapodi, M. C., Facione, N. C., Miaskowski, C., Dodd, M. J., & Waters, C. (2002). The influence of social support on breast cancer screening in a multicultural community sample. *Oncology Nursing Forum, 29,* 845–852.

Keys, A. (1980). *Seven countries: A multivariate analysis of death and coronary heart disease.* Cambridge, MA: Harvard University Press.

Knight, B. G., Robinson, G. S., Longmire, C. V. F., Chun, M., Nakao, K., & Kim, J. H. (2002). Cross cultural issues in caregiving for persons with dementia: Do familism values reduce burden and distress? *Ageing International, 27,* 70.

Koneru, V. K., Weisman de Mamani, A. G., Flynn, P. M., & Betancourt, H. (2007). Acculturation and mental health: Current findings and recommendations for future research. *Applied and Preventive Psychology, 12,* 76–96.

Krieger, N. (1999). Embodying inequality: A review of concepts, measures, and methods for studying health consequences of discrimination. *International Journal of Health Services, 29,* 295–352.

Lara, M., Gamboa, C., Kahramanian, M. I., Morales, L. S., & Hayes Bautista, D. E. (2005). Acculturation and Latino health in the United States: A review of the literature and its sociopolitical context. *Annual Review of Public Health, 26,* 367–397.

Lillie-Blanton, M., Brodie, M., Rowland, D., Altman, D., & McIntosh, M. (2000). Race, ethnicity, and the health-care system: Public perceptions and experiences. *Medical Care Research and Review, 57,* 218–235.

Marquez, D. X., & McAuley, E. (2006). Social cognitive correlates of leisure time physical activity among Latinos. *Journal of Behavioral Medicine, 29,* 281–289.

McEwen, B. S. (2000). Allostasis and allostatic load: Implications for neuropsychopharmacology. *Neuropsychopharmacology, 22,* 108–124.

McMillin-Williams, K. (2004). Culture and psychological influences on diabetes prevention. *Dissertation Abstracts International, 66* (10). (UMI No. 3191841).

Mendez, M. A., Popkin, B. M., Jakszyn, P., Berenguer, A., Tormo, M. J., Sanchez, M. J., et al. (2006). Adherence to a Mediterranean diet is associated with reduced 3-year incidence of obesity. *Journal of Nutrition, 136,* 2934–2938.

Moy, B., Par, E. R., Feibelmann, S. A., Chiang, S., & Weissman, J. S. (2006). Barriers to repeat mammography: Cultural perspectives of African-American, Asian, and Hispanic women. *Psycho-Oncology, 15,* 623–634.

Mulvaney-Day, N. E., Alegría, M., & Sribney, W. (2007). Social cohesion, social support, and health among Latinos in the United States. *Social Science and Medicine, 64,* 477–495.

National Institute on Drug Abuse (2003). *Drug use among racial/ethnic minorities* (Rep. No. 03–3888). Rockville, MD: U.S. Department of Health and Human Services.

Nieri, T., Kulis, S., Keith, V. M., & Hurdle, D. (2005). Body image, acculturation, and substance abuse among boys and girls in the Southwest. *American Journal of Drug and Alcohol Abuse, 31,* 617–639.

Ortega, A. N., Fang, H., Perez, V. H., Rizzo, J. A., Carter-Pokras, O., Wallace, S. P., et al. (2007). Health care access, use of services, and experiences among undocumented Mexicans and other Latinos. *Archives of Internal Medicine, 167,* 2354–2360.

Panagiotakos, D. B., Pitsavos, C., Arvaniti, F., & Stefanadis, C. (2007). Adherence to the Mediterranean food pattern predicts the prevalence of hypertension, hypercholesterolemia, diabetes, and obesity among healthy adults; the accuracy of the MedDietScore. *Preventive Medicine, 44,* 335–340.

Perez, D. J., Fortuna, L., & Alegría, M. (2008). Prevalence and correlates of everyday discrimination among U.S. Latinos. *Journal of Community Psychology, 36,* 421–433.

Perez-Escamilla, R., & Putnik, P. (2007). The role of acculturation in nutrition, lifestyle, and incidence of type 2 diabetes among Latinos. *Journal of Nutrition, 137,* 860–870.

Pérez-Stable, E., Sabogal, F., Otero-Sabogal, R., Hiatt, R., & McPhee, S. (1992). Misconceptions about cancer among Latinos and Anglos. *Journal of the American Medical Association, 268,* 3219–3223.

Pérez-Stable, E. J., Ramirez, A., Villarreal, R., Talavera, G. A., Trapido, E., Suarez, L., et al. (2001). Cigarette smoking behavior among U.S. Latino men and women from different countries of origin. *American Journal of Public Health, 91,* 1424–1430.

Powe, B. (1994). Perceptions of cancer fatalism among African Americans: The influence of education, income, and cancer knowledge. *Journal of National Black Nurses, 13,* 41–48.

Powe, B., & Johnson, A. (1995). Cancer fatalism among elderly African Americans: Effects on colorectal/cancer screening. *Cancer Nursing Forum, 12,* 65–78.

Ries, L. A. G., Melbert, D., Krapcho, M., Mariotto, A., Miller, B. A., Feuer, E. J., Clegg, L., Horner, M. J., Howlader, N., Eisner, M. P., Reichman, M., & Edwards, B. K. (Eds). SEER Cancer Statistics Review, 1975–2004, National Cancer Institute. Bethesda, M. D., http://seer.cancer.gov/csr/ 1975_2004/, based on November 2006 SEER data submission, posted to the SEER web site, 2007.

Reimann, J. O. F., Talavera, G. A., Salmon, M., Nunez, J. A., & Velasquez, R. J. (2004). Cultural competence among physicians treating Mexican Americans who have diabetes: A structural model. *Social Science and Medicine, 59,* 2195–2205.

Rivera, J. A., Barquera, S., Gonzalez-Cossio, T., Olaiz, G., & Sepulveda, J. (2004). Nutrition transition in Mexico and in other Latin American countries. *Nutrition Reviews, 62,* S149–S157.

Romero, A. J., Martinez, D., & Carvajal, S. C. (2007). Bicultural stress and adolescent risk behaviors in a community sample of Latinos and non-Latino European Americans. *Ethnicity and Health, 12,* 443–463.

Roosa, M. W., Dumka, L. E., Gonzales, N. A., & Knight, G. P. (2002). Cultural/ethnic issues and the prevention scientist in the 21st century. *Prevention and Treatment 5*(1), Art. 5 [Online]. http://journals.apa.org/prevention/ volume5/pre0050005a.html

Rozowski, J., & Castillo, O. (2004). Is the Chilean diet a Mediterranean-type diet? *Biological Research, 37,* 313–319.

Salas-Salvado, J., Garcia-Arellano, A., Estruch, R., Marquez-Sandoval, F., Corella, D., Fiol, M., et al. (2008). Components of the Mediterranean-type food pattern and serum inflammatory markers among patients at high risk for cardiovascular disease. *European Journal of Clinical Nutrition, 62*(5), 651–659.

Schröder, H. (2007). Protective mechanisms of the Mediterranean diet in obesity and type 2 diabetes. *Journal of Nutritional Biochemistry, 18,* 149–160.

Schulze, M. B., Hoffmann, K., Manson, J. E., Willett, W. C., Meigs, J. B., Weikert, C., et al. (2005). Dietary pattern, inflammation, and incidence of type 2 diabetes in women. *American Journal of Clinical Nutrition, 82,* 675–684.

Singh, G. K., & Hiatt, R. A. (2006). Trends and disparities in socioeconomic and behavioral characteristics, life expectancy, and cause-specific mortality of native-born and foreign-born populations in the United States, 1979–2003. *International Journal of Epidemiology, 35,* 903–919.

Smedley, B. D., Stith, A. Y., & Nelson, A. R. (Eds.). (2003). *Unequal treatment: Confronting racial and ethnic disparities in health care* (Committee on Understanding and Eliminating Racial and Ethnic Disparities in Health Care, Board on Health Sciences Policy, Institute of Medicine). Washington, DC: National Academies Press.

Smith, C. A. S., & Barnett, E. (2005). Diabetes-related mortality among Mexican Americans, Puerto Ricans, and Cuban Americans in the United States. *Revista Panamericana de Salud Pública/Pan American Journal of Public Health, 18,* 381–387

Szanton, S. L., Gill, J. M., & Allen, J. K. (2005). Allostatic load: A mechanism of socioeconomic health disparities? *Biological Research for Nursing, 7,* 7–15.

Uchino, B. N. (2006). Social support and health: A review of physiological processes potentially underlying links to disease outcomes. *Journal of Behavioral Medicine, 29,* 377–387.

U.S. Census Bureau (2006). *Nation's population one third minority* Washington, DC: U.S. Government Printing Office.

U.S. Census Bureau (2007). *The American community: Hispanics 2004.* Washington, DC: U.S. Government Printing Office.

U.S. Census Bureau (2008). *Income, poverty, and health insurance coverage in the United States: 2007.* Washington, DC: U.S. Government Printing Office.

U.S. Department of Health and Human Services (USDHHS). (2000). *Healthy people 2010.* Washington, DC: U.S. Government Printing Office.

U.S. Department of Health and Human Services (USDHHS). (2006). *Healthy People 2010 Midcourse Review.* Washington, DC: U.S. Government Printing Office.

Vio, F., & Albala, C. (2000). Nutrition policy in the Chilean transition. *Public Health Nutrition, 3,* 49–55.

Viruell-Fuentes, E. A. (2007). Beyond acculturation: Immigration, discrimination, and health research among Mexicans in the United States. *Social Science and Medicine, 65,* 1524–1535.

Zsembik, B. A., & Fennell, D. (2005). Ethnic variation in health and the determinants of health among Latinos. *Social Science and Medicine, 61,* 53–63.

21

CANCER SCREENING AND SURVIVORSHIP IN LATINO POPULATIONS

A Primer for Psychologists

LYDIA P. BUKI AND MELISSA SELEM

For the past 30 years, advances in medical technology and the aging of the population have fueled interest in the psychosocial dimensions of cancer (Passik, Ford, & Massie, 1998). It is likely that at one point or another, we will all be touched by cancer, whether through knowledge of someone with the disease, by getting screenings for various types of cancer, or by living through a diagnosis ourselves. Psychologists have much to offer, given that individuals affected by cancer benefit from various forms of individual, social, or family support. To be optimally effective, psychologists must be informed about issues pertaining to early detection as well as survivorship.

The number of Latinos with cancer will increase substantially in the coming years. Currently, the Latino population numbers 45.5 million, or 15% of the total U.S. population (U.S. Census Bureau News, 2008). The conservative projection of the Latino population by 2050 is 102.6 million, or 24.4% of the total

population (U.S. Census Bureau, 2005). Using current cancer prevalence rates of 1.88% for 2005, we estimate that at least 855,400 Latinos have been diagnosed with cancer in the last 15 years and that this number will increase to at least 1.9 million by the year 2050 (National Cancer Institute [NCI], 2005b; U.S. Census Bureau, 2005). Therefore, the need to attend to the health-care needs of Latinos is not only a critical issue but in fact will become a necessity and a much greater challenge in years to come.

For certain cancers, Latinos have worse outcomes than the majority of the population. For example, Latinos have a greater chance of being diagnosed with cervical cancer, a greater chance of dying from stomach cancer, and lower chance of being alive 5 years after a breast cancer diagnosis than non-Latino Whites (Jemal et al., 2008; Li, Malone, & Daling, 2003). Because these disparate outcomes arise in a context of social inequalities (Krieger, 2005), in this chapter we focus on psychosocial and institutional issues related to cancer in Latino populations. Attention to these issues is important because psychologists have the tools to intervene and generate psychosocial change (Vera & Speight, 2003).

In the first part of the chapter, we introduce psychosocial and institutional factors that influence cancer outcomes in Latinos. These are broad issues that apply to most cancers. However, not all cancers are the same. Some cancers have screening tests available and can be detected early (e.g., cervical, colorectal), whereas other types of cancer cannot be detected early (e.g., lung cancer). Ideally, everyone who is eligible would obtain the screening exams for cancers that can be prevented or detected early, resulting in better health outcomes and quality of life. For cancers that offer the option of prevention and early detection, it is possible to make the most impact with psychosocial interventions that promote screening. In this chapter, we focus on four cancers that have a great impact on the Latino population and may be prevented (i.e., cervical) or detected early through screenings (i.e., breast, cervical, colorectal, and prostate). Following an overview of these selected cancers, we present information about survivorship that applies to all cancer types, such as barriers to treatment, palliative care (care focused on relieving pain), and end-of-life care. Next, we review successful interventions to promote early detection and to improve quality of life in cancer survivors. Finally, we include suggestions for future research directions, and we close with 10 recommendations for psychologists who work with Latino populations.

FACTORS INFLUENCING CANCER OUTCOMES IN LATINO POPULATIONS

Several psychosocial and institutional factors are related to cancer prevention, detection, and treatment in Latino populations. These include low levels of health insurance, limited proficiency with the English language, low levels of formal education, low income, cultural factors, and institutional racism. Each of these topics is addressed in the following paragraphs.

Lack of Health Insurance

Between 2004 and 2006, the average uninsured rate for Latinos was approximately three times as high (32.7%) as the rate for non-Latino Whites (10.7%; U.S. Census Bureau, 2007a). A substantial literature supports the fact that lack of health insurance coverage, an institutional barrier to care, is possibly the strongest predictor of cancer screening underutilization (e.g., Gorin & Heck, 2005; Ward et al., 2007). Screening underutilization, in turn, leads to late detection of various cancers that are treated more effectively when detected early. Uninsured Latinos are two to three times more likely than those who have health insurance to have cancer diagnosed at a later stage, when the cancer is more advanced and less treatable (American College of Physicians, 2000).

Linguistic Issues

Individuals with limited English proficiency encounter additional barriers in their quest to obtain optimal care. Among adult Latinos, both foreign and native born, 41% are primarily Spanish speaking, 44% are bilingual, and only 15% are primarily English speaking. However, among Latino immigrants, almost two thirds (64%) are primarily Spanish speaking (Hakimzadeh & Cohn, 2007). Therefore, the demand for Spanish-language interventions is high and is likely to continue increasing in the coming years. Latinos who are primarily Spanish speaking are uninsured at higher rates and tend to have more serious health issues (Doty, 2003). Their linguistic barriers are only heightened by the fact that the majority of health-care providers are non-Latino English speakers, creating linguistic and cultural gaps that further affect the patient-provider relationship and the delivery of quality care. In an attempt to address this issue, health-care organizations that receive federal funding are required to provide free interpretation services in accordance with the National Standards on Culturally and Linguistically Appropriate Services (U.S. Department of Health and Human Services, 2001). However, the fact that this mandate is unfunded creates a further institutional barrier to quality care for Latinos with limited English proficiency.

Formal Education and Income

Factors associated with social class also affect cancer outcomes (NCI, 2005a). Latinos have lower levels of formal education, lower incomes, and higher rates of poverty than non-Latino Whites (U.S. Census Bureau, 2005, 2007a). Individuals with lower levels of education and lower incomes are more likely to lack access to quality information and health insurance and thus are more vulnerable in their health outcomes. In the context of competing needs with limited resources, many view expenses for screenings and preventive health care (e.g., Pap smear) as a luxury they cannot afford, a perception that may be reinforced by their cultural health beliefs (Buki, 1999).

Cultural Factors

Latinos in the United States are often conceptualized as being of one culture. It should be recognized that Latinos are a heterogeneous group with different immigration and migration patterns, with roots in at least 21 countries (U.S. Census Bureau, 2007b). Latinos of various ancestries bring with them possible differences in cultural norms, health beliefs, expectations of the health-care system, eating and other health promotion habits, and reasons for immigrating to the United States, among others. All these factors contribute to differences in incidence of chronic illness across groups. As a result, there is also great variation in how Latinos understand and act upon health issues.

To be effective with Latino populations, health interventions must be consistent with the population's cultural explanatory models (CEMs; Kleinman, Eisenberg, & Good, 1978). Individuals' CEMs tend to be based on their sociocultural realities, have emotional meaning, and are dynamic. In contrast, health-care providers' CEMs are based on the biomedical model, which places high value on the empirical, observable, measurable, objective, individualistic, absolute, and rational (Rajaram & Rashidi, 1998). This fundamental difference in the way providers and patients view health and illness contributes to disparate outcomes.

Individuals' CEMs influence a range of health behaviors, from prevention to treatment (Rajaram & Rashidi, 1998). Researchers have found that Latinos perceive their cultural health beliefs as barriers to early detection and timely treatment of cancer (e.g., Buki, Borrayo, Feigal, & Carrillo, 2004; Chavez, Hubbell, Mishra, & Valdez, 1997; Fernández-Esquer, Espinoza, Ramirez, & McAlister, 2003). Therefore, by attending to these beliefs psychologists have a greater opportunity to influence health behavior. For example, Latina women who feel healthy may perceive that they are not experiencing any conditions that would make them likely to have breast cancer, and consequently they may be less likely to get a mammogram (Borrayo, Buki, & Feigal, 2005). To be effective, intervention programs would have to dispel the myth that cancer is always accompanied by symptoms, and would have to provide the information that it is possible to develop breast cancer in the absence of symptoms (i.e., while feeling healthy; ibid.).

Fatalism, the belief and subsequent fear that a cancer diagnosis leads to certain death, has been noted as a barrier to cancer screening and treatment (Borrayo et al., 2005; Borrayo & Guarnaccia, 2000; Buki et al., 2004; Chavez et al., 1997; Matthews-Juarez & Weinberg, 2004). Fatalism also complicates psychological well-being when a diagnosis is received (Ashing-Giwa et al., 2004; Buki et al., 2004) and may result in delays in treatment (Mohamed, Skeel Williams, Tamburrino, Wryobeck, & Carter, 2005). For example, if an individual believes that cervical cancer is fatal, she will have little incentive to undergo screening (Borrayo et al., 2005; Chavez et al., 1997). Also, if someone believes that cancer treatment is worse than the disease (Fernández-Esquer et al., 2003), there is little incentive for the person to begin cancer treatment. Therefore, psychosocial programs that dispel the myth that all cancers are fatal, or that cancer treatment is worse than the disease, are more likely to be effective than those that ignore the existence of these beliefs by simply providing factual information without this context (Borrayo et al., 2005).

Institutional Racism

Institutional racism has been defined as "differential access to the goods, services, and opportunities of society by race" (Jones, 2000, p. 1212). This includes differential access to quality health care and differential knowledge of available resources. Institutional racism can take many forms, from not having an interpreter available for a cancer screening appointment to not having the same treatment options offered once a cancer is diagnosed. It can also include being discriminated against due to one's race or ethnicity. Research has found that second-generation Latinos are more cognizant of discrimination toward them than first-generation Latinos (Viruell-Fuentes, 2007). Second-generation Latinos have reported feeling stigmatized, being looked at condescendingly and with suspicion, and having a salient experience of "otherness" when interacting with systems outside their communities. These experiences of discrimination serve as an additional barrier toward health promoting behaviors. Of growing concern is the issue of repatriation, where hospitals unable or unwilling to provide long-term care to Latino patients, particularly those who lack health insurance or who are undocumented, return them to their country of origin (Sontag, 2008). Thus, patients are being deported by hospitals, the very entities that are supposed to care for them. When experiences of discrimination take place in health-care settings, the information spreads quickly through social networks, having great potential to lower the probability of early detection and timely treatment.

SELECTED CANCERS

For the next portion of the chapter, four cancers were identified for in-depth analysis and discussion: breast, cervical, colorectal, and prostate. Breast and prostate cancer were chosen because they are the cancers with the highest incidence for Latina women and Latino men, respectively. Colorectal cancer was selected because it has the second-highest incidence among Latinos of both sexes, and cervical cancer was chosen because of its disproportionate incidence in Latina populations despite the fact that it is 100% preventable through early detection. In addition, there are exams for early detection of all of these types of cancer, such that by encouraging use of available exams, better health outcomes can result for the population.

Breast Cancer

Incidence and mortality rates for breast cancer are ranked number one for Latinas (89.3 and 16.1 per 100,000, respectively; Edwards et al., 2005; Jemal et al., 2008). The 5-year survivorship rate for Latinas is lower than for non-Latina Whites across the United States. For example, in the state of New Mexico, the 5-year survivorship rate for Latinas is 76%, compared with 85% for their non-Latina White counterparts (Gilliland,

Hunt, & Key, 1998). This difference is due to the disease's being diagnosed at later stages among Latinas (Li, Malone, & Daling, 2003). Late detection may be related to low rates of screening and/or rescreening, but also there is growing evidence that Latinas experience a more aggressive form of the disease at younger ages, which could contribute to late detection of the disease (e.g., Biffl, Myers, Franciose, Gonzalez, & Darnell, 2001; Shavers, Harlan, & Stevens, 2003). Among screening tools for breast cancer, mammography has received the most attention in the literature. The U.S. Preventive Services Task Force (2002a) suggests mammography screening for women over 40 years of age every 1–2 years.

Latinas have reported a number of health beliefs about breast cancer, including (a) that it is not necessary to go to the doctor when one is feeling healthy, (b) that breast cancer is symptomatic, (c) that the exposure to X-rays during screening can cause breast cancer, and (d) that it feels immoral and indecent to expose one's breasts (e.g., Borrayo & Jenkins, 2001; Buki et al., 2004). There is preliminary evidence that women's beliefs may differ by ancestry and that immigrant and Mexican women have more traditional beliefs (e.g., that cancer is fatal; Borrayo & Guarnaccia, 2000; Buki et al., 2004). In addition, studies have found that Latinas have a great deal of misinformation about breast cancer etiology, symptoms, and treatment (e.g., that bumps or bruises can cause breast cancer; Borrayo et al., 2005; Morgan, Park, & Cortes, 1995). The literature also identifies specific factors that have been found to contribute to screening behavior, such as (a) private insurance (Hiatt et al., 2001), (b) awareness of Medicare benefits (Fox, Stein, Sockloskie, & Ory, 2001), (c) receiving a screening recommendation by a physician (see Fox & Stein, 1991), (d) speaking English (Jacobs, Karavolos, Rathouz, Ferris, & Powell, 2005), and (e) previous exposure to cancer education (Buki, Jamison, Anderson, & Cuadra, 2007). Among Latina women, those who are older, who do not speak English well, who do not have a usual source of care, and who are of Mexican descent are least likely to have screened (e.g., Jacobs et al., 2005).

Despite its importance, mammography rescreening has received relatively minor attention in the literature. For example, there is evidence that Latinas have less timely follow-up for abnormal mammograms than non-Latina Whites

(Chang et al., 1996) and that a contributing factor is their lack of understanding about what their results mean (Karliner, Kaplan, Juarbe, Pasick, & Pérez-Stable, 2005). Service providers can ensure timely care by taking an advocacy role and following up with women who have been recently screened to ensure that they understand their results. In addition, having a regular source of care, and thus greater opportunities for a doctor's referral for mammography screening, is associated with higher screening and rescreening rates (Bastani et al., 1995).

The few studies that have examined Latinas with breast cancer suggest that this population encounters more difficulty in adjusting to cancer diagnoses than their non-Latina White counterparts (e.g., Ashing-Giwa, Tejero, Kim, Padilla, & Hellemann, 2007). Latina women of low socioeconomic status are more likely to believe that breast cancer is fatal and to place less trust in the efficacy of cancer treatment, experiencing more pessimism and feelings of helplessness (Ashing-Giwa et al., 2004; Buki, Garcés, et al., 2008; Ell et al., 2005). In addition, Latinas have reported greater concerns about existential, sexual, occupational, and relational/partner issues, as well as greater support needs, than other ethnic minority women (Moadel, Morgan, & Dutcher, 2007; Spencer et al., 1999). Barriers to women's recovery process include financial concerns, lack of cultural competence on the part of healthcare providers, and minimal access to adequate psychological supports, particularly among women who are Spanish speaking (Ashing-Giwa et al., 2004; Buki, Grupski, & Hinestrosa, 2008; Ell et al., 2005).

Cervical Cancer

Incidence for this cancer is ranked number 4 and mortality number 10 in Latina women (13.8 and 3.3 per 100,000, respectively; Edwards et al., 2005; Jemal et al., 2008). Approximately 99.7% of cervical cancers are caused by human papillomavirus infection (HPV; Walboomers et al., 1999). Some Latin American countries have very high rates of HPV infection, whereas others have lower rates (e.g., Muñoz et al., 1996). This variability in rates of HPV infection results in differential rates of cervical cancer by ancestry in the United States. Women of Mexican and Puerto Rican descent, for example, have higher rates of cervical cancer than women of Cuban ancestry

(Trapido et al., 1995). Overall, Latina women have the highest incidence of cervical cancer of all major racial/ethnic groups, up to three times higher than the non-Latina White population (NCI, 2005a; Trapido et al., 1995). Given that cervical cancer is 100% preventable through Pap smears, there is a great need for providers and researchers to empower women to obtain this screening at intervals recommended by the national screening guidelines.

The U.S. Preventive Services Task Force (2002b) strongly recommends cervical cancer screenings through Pap smears at least every 3 years for women who are sexually active or over the age of 21. Much like breast cancer, factors associated with higher rates of screening include younger age (Bazargan, Bazargan, Farooq, & Baker, 2004) and English proficiency (Jacobs et al., 2005). Among Latina women without health insurance, higher levels of formal education and having a child are predictors of screening (Buki et al., 2007). Also, there is evidence that cultural health beliefs (e.g., that cervical cancer is fatal) act as perceived barriers to screening and to timely follow-up of abnormal findings, particularly among Latinas with lower levels of formal education and acculturation (McMullin, De Alba, Chávez, & Hubbell, 2005; Nelson, Geiger, & Mangione, 2002). Some evidence also exists that sexually active Latina college students are not obtaining regular Pap smears and have limited knowledge about HPV (Schiffner & Buki, 2006). For example, in a qualitative study, Latina college students reported that they did not learn much about sex education in the schools because the information they received felt irrelevant to the cultural context of their lives. In addition, participants stated that to have open discussions about sexually transmitted infections with family or partners is not considered culturally appropriate and that this taboo further hinders their knowledge acquisition about sexual health. Participants also felt that seeking such preventive health behaviors as Pap smears would imply that they had been sexually active, which would be detrimental to their reputation in the Latino community and cause family problems (Schiffner & Buki, 2006). This is particularly disturbing because HPV transmission is at its highest among 15- to 24-year-olds, and college students are in that age range (Centers for Disease Control and Prevention [CDC], 1999).

Literature on repeated screening suggests that women who have had exposure to cancer education are more likely to be on schedule with their repeat screenings than those who have not had this exposure (Buki et al., 2007). Research findings also suggest that many Latinas do not keep appointments to follow up on abnormal Pap smear results; in one study, individualized case management increased the probability of follow-up by addressing psychosocial, attitudinal, knowledge, and access problems (Ell et al., 2002). In addition, Pap smear beliefs (e.g., that Pap smears are expensive, that cervical cancer treatment is worse than the disease) appear to influence rescreening behaviors, particularly among women who are less acculturated (Fernández-Esquer et al., 2003).

Although cervical cancer survivors face a plethora of physiological and psychological issues, very little information is available about survivorship in Latina populations. In the most comprehensive study of Latina cervical cancer survivors to date, Ashing-Giwa et al. (2006) found that participants experienced a significant burden from the disease. Physical sequelae included bladder and bowel problems, pain, and sexual health issues. For women who had their uteruses removed, their sense of womanhood was often challenged because of the cultural belief that a woman without a womb is lacking an integral aspect of her female identity; women with supportive partners reported feeling more desirable and better able to cope.

Colorectal Cancer

Incidence of this cancer is ranked number 2 and mortality number 3 for both Latinas and Latinos (32.9 and 11.1 per 100,000 for females, and 47.5 and 17.0 per 100,000 for males; Edwards et al., 2005; Jemal et al., 2008). Evidence suggests that Latinos are at greater risk for this type of cancer, given the changes in diet that take place across generations in the United States (e.g., Menck et al., 1975; Monroe et al., 2003). As Latinos spend more time in the United States, their eating habits become more like those of non-Latino whites, with diets higher in fat and lower in fiber, fruits, and vegetables (Lara, Gamboa, Kahramanian, Morales, & Hayes Bautista, 2005). An issue of concern is that Latinos are more likely than non-Latino Whites to present with tumors that are larger or at more advanced stages of the disease (Chien, Morimoto, Tom, & Li, 2005; Clegg, Li, Hankey, Chu, & Edwards, 2002). Evidence exists that there is some variation in stage of presentation among Latino subgroups; Mexicans/South Americans appear to have elevated risk for Stages III and IV, Puerto Ricans for Stage III, and Cubans comparable to those of non-Latino Whites (Chien et al., 2005). A more advanced stage (i.e., Stage III or IV) is likely a result of late detection, given that in multiethnic studies Latinos have been found to have the lowest screening rates for this type of cancer (Etzioni et al., 2004; Walsh et al., 2004).

Screening for colorectal cancer may involve a fecal occult blood test (FOBT), sigmoidoscopy/colonoscopy, or double-contrast barium enema. Although the U.S. Preventive Services Task Force (2002c) recognizes that these screenings should take place, it does not provide specific screening recommendations. However, according to the American Cancer Society (2007), beginning at age 50, men and women who are at average risk for developing colorectal cancer should have the following screening options: (a) a fecal occult blood test (FOBT) or fecal immunochemical test (FIT) every year, (b) a flexible sigmoidoscopy every 5 years, (c) an annual FOBT or FIT and flexible sigmoidoscopy every 5 years, (d) a double-contrast barium enema every 5 years, or (e) a colonoscopy every 10 years.

Evidence shows that Latinos are less likely than their non-Latino counterparts to have ever received a FOBT or sigmoidoscopy/colonoscopy (Thompson, Coronado, Neuhouser, & Chen, 2005). This may be due, in part, to their low levels of knowledge about colorectal screening exams; in one study, only 57% of participants had heard of colonoscopy, and only 58% had heard of FOBT (Walsh et al., 2004). Being encouraged to screen by trusted peers appeared to facilitate screening behavior, whereas having fatalistic beliefs about screening was a significant predictor of noncompliance (Gorin & Heck, 2005). In comparison with non-Latino Whites, Latinos were more likely to believe that the preparation for colonoscopy/sigmoidoscopy would be unpleasant, to expect that performing an FOBT would be embarrassing, and to believe that they did not need to screen if they were feeling healthy (Walsh et al., 2004). All of these factors contribute to lower rates of screening.

Prostate Cancer

This cancer is ranked number one in incidence and number two in mortality among Latino men (140.8 and 21.2 per 100,000, respectively; Edwards et al., 2005; Jemal et al., 2008). Screening tests include the digital rectal exam (DRE) and the prostate-specific antigen (PSA) test. For prostate cancer, the U.S. Preventive Services Task Force does not advocate screening, because there is a high probability of false positives and mixed evidence about the benefits of early screenings. However, the Task Force recommends that doctors discuss prostate health issues and the need for screening with their patients (U.S. Preventive Services Task Force, 2008). This further places Latino men at risk, given that they are poorly informed about this type of cancer, its symptoms, and screening tests (American Cancer Society, 2003) and are not likely to initiate a conversation about it with their physicians. Specifically, screening for this type of cancer may bring up cultural issues of machismo and embarrassment in Latino men, who may perceive the DRE as an embarrassing procedure that can threaten their masculinity (Chan, Haynes, O'Donnell, Bachino, & Vernon, 2003). In addition, those who believe that prostate cancer is a fatal disease may further refrain from obtaining screenings (ibid.).

Once an abnormality was detected, Latino men appeared to be subjected to "watchful waiting" more often than their non-Latino White counterparts in one study (Shavers et al., 2004). Watchful waiting refers to "medical monitoring with digital rectal exam or prostate-specific antigen testing until the patient becomes symptomatic or has biochemical or clinical disease progression, at which time the patient is offered definitive treatment with surgery, radiation, hormonal therapy or some combination thereof" (ibid.). It is possible that among psychosocial influences, a patient's desire to avoid treatment side effects or to have the cancer removed, or physicians' bias in recommendations may contribute to this outcome (Shavers et al., 2004). In fact, physician bias has been noted to influence clinical decisions when the course of treatment was not clearly guided by clinical presentation (Institute of Medicine [IOM], 2002), which is the case with prostate cancer. Because treatment, palliative care, and end-of-life issues have common threads that run through all cancers, they are addressed jointly in the following section.

SURVIVORSHIP, PALLIATIVE CARE, AND END-OF-LIFE ISSUES

Being diagnosed with cancer can be conceptualized as being faced with a stressor that has the potential to meet or exceed one's ability to cope (Lazarus & Folkman, 1984). Personal coping strategies often change form over the course of an illness (Culver, Arena, Antoni, & Carver, 2002). For example, coping with breast cancer involves dealing with a series of stressful events, beginning with receiving and interpreting the diagnosis, progressing through treatment, dealing with after-treatment concerns, and living life afterward (Lethborg, Kissane, Burns, & Snyder, 2000; Payne, Sullivan, & Massie, 1996). Each of these stages is accompanied by unique challenges which, in turn, call for different forms of support. For instance, when first diagnosed with breast cancer, women need information about medical providers, treatments, and financial resources to pay for treatment. Among Latina women with low incomes who were underinsured, having the ability to pay for treatment was synonymous with a chance for a cure, which was associated with positive mental health outcomes (Buki, Garcés, et al., 2008). After treatment, their concerns included reintegrating into an active social life and coming to terms with changes in body image. Women who adapted to treatment successfully reported family support and also indicated receiving information about prostheses, clothing, and hairstyling to accommodate body changes as a result of treatment (Buki, Garcés, et al., 2008).

The literature on Latinos as well as non-Latino Whites suggests that facing a diagnosis of cancer undoubtedly is a challenge but also offers opportunity for growth. Many individuals experience cancer as a stressor but also as a transitional event, with the potential for positive outcomes (Shapiro et al., 2001; Tomich & Helgeson, 2004). Benefits and meaning derived from cancer experiences include a sense of gratitude and awareness (e.g., Buki, Garcés, et al., 2008; Thibodeau & MacRae, 1997; Tomich & Helgeson, 2004), finding meaning in life (e.g., Buki, Garcés, et al., 2008; Giedzinska, Meyerowitz, Ganz, & Rowland, 2004), and changes in values and priorities (e.g., Buki, Garcés, et al., 2008; Tomich & Helgeson, 2004).

Specific challenges that arise for individuals with advanced cancers include pain management (i.e., palliative care) and hospice use. The literature on pain management, although sparse, shows that there is great complexity in the treatment of pain among Latinos. Culture, family beliefs, and religion influence the way pain is perceived, expressed, and treated by patients (Juarez, Ferrell, & Borneman, 1998, 1999). For example, in a qualitative study with a majority of participants of Mexican ancestry, informants reported being taught to endure pain and not to complain or ask for medication no matter how strong the discomfort. This stoicism could lead physicians to underestimate the pain felt by their patients (Juarez et al., 1998). In addition, institutional issues, such as the availability of adequate pain medication in ethnic minority neighborhoods, influenced palliative care in these patients (Anderson et al., 2002; Morrison et al., 2005). Among Latinos who receive pain medication, many are not given a prescription that is adequate for their pain, and some take less than prescribed because they fear dependence and family members' reactions to their taking the medications (Anderson et al., 2002). Spanish-speaking and less acculturated patients appear to encounter more barriers to adequate pain management (e.g., cannot understand instructions on pain medication bottle) and receive less optimal palliative care than those who are English speaking and have greater access to care (Chan & Woodruff, 1999; Juarez et al., 1998). Regarding hospice use, Latinos have shown the greatest number of access and service problems; many hospices have minimal knowledge and resources to meet the needs of a Latino population (Gordon, 1996). To access hospice services, Latinos depend on Medicaid and charity program services much more than other groups do (ibid.).

Throughout the survivorship continuum, from diagnosis through treatment and end-of-life care, families play a significant supportive role in the cancer treatment and decision-making process of Latino patients, influencing their psychosocial and physical outcomes (Galván, Buki, & Garcés in press; Matthews-Juarez & Weinberg, 2004). In one study, older Latinos of Mexican descent reported a preference for family members to be informed of their advanced cancer diagnoses and to make decisions about their care (Blackhall et al., 1999; Murphy et al., 1996). Unfortunately, these preferences are in sharp contrast with the Western medical model, which is based on patient autonomy rather than a collectivistic orientation to care (Banks, Buki, Gallardo, & Yee, 2007), which further erodes quality care for Latino patients.

CANCER INTERVENTIONS FOR LATINO POPULATIONS

In this section, we report on studies that highlight factors that promote or hinder successful cancer outcomes. We present research conducted with Latino populations whenever it is available. The first part of the section reports on interventions that promote early detection; the second part provides information about interventions directed at individuals who have been diagnosed with cancer.

Early Detection

Considerable research has been conducted on factors that promote and hinder early detection of cancer. Most studies have focused on cancers for which reliable screening methods exist as well as cancers with a greater probability of cure if detected in the early stages. Consequently, the majority of studies have focused on breast and cervical cancer screening. For these cancers, a primary facilitator for screenings is knowledge about the importance of cancer screening. Therefore, research has focused on ways to impart information to individuals who need it.

A growing literature suggests that *promotora* programs (i.e., the use of peer role models) help women obtain needed screenings. *Promotoras* facilitate screening by disseminating information about the importance of early screenings and also by helping women navigate the health-care system to obtain the exams. Moreover, by discussing cancer, a topic that has been taboo in traditional Latino culture, they are helping create a dialogue in the community around cultural issues such as cancer stigma, fatalism, and fear. These discussions, in turn, have the potential to break down barriers to screening. In fact, some promising data have been reported by several researchers (e.g., Fernández, Gonzales, Tortolero-Luna, Partida, & Bartholomew, 2005; Navarro et al., 1998) suggesting that intensive, well-planned, theoretically based and structured programs with peer role models have great potential to increase breast cancer screening rates (Fox, Stein, Gonzalez, Farrenkopf, & Dellinger, 1998). There is evidence that *promotora* programs may increase rates of Pap smear screening as well. The evidence is mixed, however—a likely consequence of methodological shortcomings in the studies (e.g., Davis et al., 1994; Jibaja-Weiss, Volk, Kingery, Smith, & Holcomb, 2003; Navarro et al., 1998; Suarez, Nichols, & Brady, 1993).

The use of computer technology to impart information about screenings also appears to be a promising intervention. Based on Bandura's (1977) social learning theory, Valdez, Banerjee, Ackerson, and Fernandez (2002) developed a multimedia program to educate Latina women about breast cancer. After conducting extensive preliminary research on women's beliefs and mammography use patterns, they designed an intervention to increase knowledge about breast cancer and the importance of early screening. The educational program included interactive modules about breast cancer risk factors, the importance of early detection, the mammogram, the meaning of abnormal mammograms, questions to ask the doctor, and other related topics. The information was presented through a computer kiosk with a touch screen using video, voice, music, graphics, animation, and photographs. Spanish and English versions were available to accommodate participants' language choices. Messages were tailored to women's age ranges such that the recommendations provided conformed to screening recommendations for their age. Results showed that women who participated in the program had higher knowledge levels than those in the control group. Also, women with low incomes and those who had never received a mammogram had higher intentions of asking the doctor about mammography after participating in the program. The benefit of a multimedia intervention is its ability to reach a less literate audience with tailored and consistent educational messages. It also allows cultural adaptation of the information according to women's beliefs such that myths can be dispelled as part of the educational message.

Another popular way of disseminating information about cancer is through print materials. Print materials have been effective in changing individuals' knowledge and behaviors about cancer screening (Paul, Redman, & Sanson-Fisher, 2004) and have been used as integral components of successful community-based interventions (e.g., Navarro et al., 1998). In the development of print materials, two main goals are to make materials culturally appropriate and easy to read for an audience with low levels of literacy (Massett, 1996). In this effort, Buki, Salazar, & Pitton (2008) developed a checklist for the creation of cancer print materials for Latinos with low health literacy. The checklist highlights five design elements to be incorporated into the process of developing materials and five elements related to the content of the materials. For example, in the development of materials, the authors recommend acknowledging the diversity within the Latino population as well as involving the community at various stages of the development process. For the content of materials, they recommend highlighting cancers that can be detected early, as well as addressing cultural health beliefs of the population (Buki, Salazar, et al., 2008). Various stylistic elements (e.g., font size, use of visual aids) also should be considered in the preparation of print materials. The authors provide several recommendations for stylistic elements that can make the material easier to read and more engaging for Latino audiences. Finally, recommendations are given for such linguistic issues as the process of translation and ways to handle Spanish words that may have different meanings for individuals of various nationalities.

To impart knowledge about the importance of early screenings, whether through *promotoras,* computer kiosks, printed brochures, or another medium, requires making trustworthy information available to the population. Some high-quality sources of information about cancer and Latinos include the National Cancer Institute, which has an English Web site (www.cancer.gov) as well as a very complete Spanish-language Web site (www.cancer.gov/espanol); and the American Cancer Society Web site (www.cancer.org), which also has a Spanish-language section on selected cancers (http://www .cancer.org/docroot/ESP/ SP_0.asp).

Survivorship

In a systematic review of studies that examined psychological therapies for cancer patients, Newell, Sanson-Fisher, and Savolainen (2002) concluded that group therapy, education, structured and unstructured counseling, and cognitive behavioral therapy offered the most promise to assist cancer survivors in the medium and long terms. In another systematic review specific to breast cancer, findings suggested that group interventions, as well as interventions that include multiple treatment elements (e.g., relaxation, group therapy) are more likely to be beneficial than narrowly focused clinical services (Bantum, Donovan, & Owen, 2007). Among the many treatment elements identified in the literature are those focused on behavioral coping skills (e.g., guided imagery, visualization, qi-gong, biofeedback), stress management (e.g., relaxation training), cognitive therapy (e.g., reappraisal, problem solving), and support for cancer patients (e.g., professionally led group therapy, informal support from trained peers; Fawzy, 1999).

Some evidence suggests, however, that Latinos with cancer have difficulty finding adequate psychosocial supports (Buki, Grupski, et al., 2008) and feel that language and cultural issues get in the way of their full participation in mainstream programs (Martinez, Loi, Martinez, Flores, & Meade, 2008). To fill this gap, a nonprofit organization with a focus on breast cancer was created to serve Latina women. Nueva Vida, Inc. (www.nueva-vida.org), based in Washington, D.C., provides navigation services for women unfamiliar with the U.S. health-care system and for those who are primarily Spanish speakers. It also offers an extensive array of support services, including individual therapy, a support group in Spanish, and a peer support program. The organization is extensively networked and collaborates with the National Breast and Cervical Cancer Program, to which it refers women for screening, and with other area hospitals that serve women who are uninsured or underinsured. As the largest organization in the United States dedicated to the provision of services for Latina cancer survivors, it fields hundreds of calls a year from all over the country. Unfortunately, most of the survivorship services provided for Latinas across the country are based in small, nonprofit organizations that rely on private grants for short-term services (Buki, Grupski, et al., 2008).

To provide a welcoming, culturally relevant, and supportive environment, Martinez et al. (2008) developed the first cancer camp for adult Spanish-speaking survivors. This camp, which was very well received by participants, included two nights in a beautiful wooded area with cabins, a variety of available activities (e.g., crafts, canoeing), and opportunities for sharing experiences and gaining support from peers facing similar challenges. Although the camp was focused on women with breast cancers detected in earlier stages, we anticipate that this intervention would be beneficial to Latinos with other types of cancer that were also detected in earlier, treatable stages (e.g., cervical, prostate).

For individuals with more advanced cancers, one way to obtain state-of-the-art medical treatment is through participation in clinical trials. However, although many Latinos qualify for treatment through clinical trials, their representation in such studies is low due to various cultural and institutional barriers (e.g., Ellington, Wahab, Martin, Field, & Mooney, 2006). Given these trends, efforts are critically needed to increase Latina/o patients' awareness of the various treatment choices available and possible best options for their situations (Harlan, Clegg, & Trimble, 2003).

DIRECTIONS FOR FUTURE RESEARCH

It is encouraging that the literature on Latinos and cancer has grown significantly in the last few years. However, numerous issues deserve more attention. With respect to early detection, more information is needed about facilitative factors and barriers to screening across geographic regions and for Latinos of different ancestries. In particular, more information is needed about factors that facilitate screening for colorectal and prostate cancers. Regarding mental health treatment and support, the literature on Latinos is grossly inadequate due to the limited number of studies reported for this population. Therefore, additional studies are critically needed that examine mental health needs of Latinos with cancer. For example, emerging data suggest that Latinos may have different treatment needs at different stages of breast cancer survivorship (Buki, Garcés, et al., 2008; Galván et al., 2008). However, studies have not been conducted to examine the relative effectiveness of treatments for each stage. In addition, it is unclear whether Latinos with other types of cancer have different treatment needs depending on survivorship stage. More research is needed to answer this empirical question.

Similarly, more research is needed to understand the needs of Latinos who are facing end-of-life care, as are ways to improve pain management in the population. One possible research project would examine whether a cancer camp like the one created for women diagnosed at earlier stages would be as beneficial to those with cancers diagnosed at an advanced stage.

RECOMMENDATIONS

Based on the information presented in this chapter, we make 10 recommendations to improve cancer outcomes in the Latino population. Some of these recommendations apply to psychologists in various settings, whereas others are more specific to a particular practice setting or type of cancer.

1. Be knowledgeable about resources in your community, such as clinics that offer free screenings, health-care settings that offer interpreters, Spanish-language cancer support groups, and bilingual service providers that can serve as resources.

2. Display culturally relevant pamphlets in offices on the importance of regular screenings, as well as information about where to obtain such services.

3. Adopt an advocacy role for Latinos with limited English proficiency (LEP) by promoting the use of ethical and competent medical interpreters, designing workshops to enhance interpreters' skills, and instructing medical staff on the appropriate use of interpreters.

4. Assist in increasing health literacy of Latinos with LEP by helping them obtain the skills they need to navigate the medical system successfully.

5. Ensure that Latinos have more information about the type of care provided by hospice and the various ways it can be accessed. Similarly, work with hospice care providers to help them develop cultural competence to serve the Latino population adequately (Gordon, 1996).

6. Advocate for patients experiencing institutional racism and discrimination. Make efforts to understand the Latino community's history within local health-care settings. Be aware of differential treatment based on ethnicity, race, or social status, and use your voice as a professional to advocate for patients encountering unfair treatment.

7. Recognize the family as a valuable source of support, and make attempts to keep families involved in the treatment and decision-making processes of patients. Help educate families about cancer, what to expect, and how to support someone with cancer through treatment and survivorship.

8. Be aware of the population's cultural health beliefs and incorporate them into your work. Promote beliefs that are conducive to optimal health and dispel myths, misinformation, and fatalistic beliefs that can limit health promotion behaviors.

9. Develop educational programs for Latino college students; encourage responsible sexual health behaviors and, in particular, regular Pap smear screenings among females. Disseminate this information through the Latino cultural house and other venues where students feel comfortable obtaining and discussing this type of information.

10. Because Latina women experience breast cancer in disproportionate numbers and are more likely to be diagnosed with a type of breast cancer that is more difficult to treat, women under 40 with a family history of breast cancer and/or who present with symptoms should be encouraged to obtain screenings. National guidelines call for women to screen starting at age 40; therefore, younger women with symptoms need additional advocacy to obtain screenings.

CONCLUSION

The number of Latinos in the United States will grow dramatically in the near future. Those individuals who immigrate from Latin American countries, as well as those who reside in the United States, are expected to live longer. With these demographic trends, we can expect that the number of Latinos with cancer will increase dramatically. This brings about an opportunity for psychologists to address the psychosocial issues brought about by cancer, relating both to early detection and to survivorship. Psychologists can contribute to Latinos' optimal health through direct service, program development, advocacy, and consultation with other health-care providers in medical settings. We wrote this chapter to give psychologists and other health professionals a foundation for understanding the psychosocial, cultural, institutional, and medical context of cancer in Latinos. We provided in-depth information about four cancers that have a great impact on Latino health as a whole yet can be detected early through regular screening. We hope that by providing this information, psychologists will increase their awareness of the issues and feel empowered to ameliorate cancer outcomes in Latino populations.

Reference

American Cancer Society. (2003). *Cancer facts and figures for Hispanics/Latinos 2003–2005.* Retrieved March 14, 2006, from http://www.cancer.org/downloads/STT/ CAFF2003Hisp PWSecured.pdf

American Cancer Society. (2007). *Colorectal cancer: Early detection.* Retrieved December 26, 2007, from http://www.cancer.org/docroot/CRI/ content/CRI_2_6X_Colorectal_Cancer_Early_ Detection_10.asp?sitearea=&level=

American College of Physicians (2000). *No health insurance? It's enough to make you sick. Latino community at great risk.* Philadelphia: Author.

Anderson, K. O., Richman, S. P., Hurley, J., Palos, G., Valero, V., Mendoza, T. R., et al. (2002). Cancer pain management among underserved minority outpatients. *Cancer, 94,* 2295–2304.

Ashing-Giwa, K. T., Padilla, G. V., Bohórquez, D. E., Tejero, J. S., Garcia, M., & Meyers, E. A. (2006). Survivorship: A qualitative investigation of Latinas diagnosed with cervical cancer. *Journal of Psychosocial Oncology, 24*(4), 53–88.

Ashing-Giwa, K. T., Padilla, G., Tejero, J., Kraemer, J., Wright, K., Coscarelli, A., et al. (2004). Understanding the breast cancer experience of women: A qualitative study of African-American, Asian American, Latina and Caucasian cancer survivors. *Psycho-Oncology, 13,* 408–428.

Ashing-Giwa, K. T., Tejero, T. S., Kim, J., Padilla, G. V., & Hellemann, G. (2007). Examining predictive models of HRQOL in a population-based, multiethnic sample of women with breast carcinoma. *Quality of Life Research, 16,* 413–428.

Bandura, A. (1977). Self-efficacy: Toward a unifying theory of behavioral change. *Psychological Review, 84,* 191–215.

Banks, M. E., Buki, L. P., Gallardo, M. E., & Yee, B. W. K. (2007). Integrative healthcare and marginalized populations. In I. Serlin (Series Ed.), *Humanizing healthcare: A handbook for healthcare integration: Vol. I. Mind-Body Medicine* (pp. 147–173). Westport, CT: Greenwood.

Bantum, E. O., Donovan, K., & Owen, J. E. (2007). A systematic review of outcomes associated with psychosocial interventions for women with breast cancer. *Journal of Clinical Outcomes Management, 14,* 341–352.

Bastani, R., Kaplan, C. P., Maxwell, A. E., Nisenbaum, R., Pearce, R., & Marcus, A. C. (1995). Initial and repeat mammography screening in a low income multi-ethnic population in Los Angeles. *Cancer Epidemiology, Biomarkers & Prevention, 4,* 161–167.

Bazargan, B., Bazargan, H. S., Farooq, M., & Baker, S. R. (2004). Correlates of cervical cancer screening among underserved Hispanic and African-American women. *Preventive Medicine, 39,* 465–473.

Biffl, W. L., Myers, A., Franciose, R. J., Gonzalez, R. J., & Darnell, D. (2001). Is breast cancer in young Latinas a different disease? *American Journal of Surgery, 182,* 596–600.

Blackhall, L. J., Frank, G., Murphy, S. T., Michel, V., Palmer, J. M., & Azem, S. P. (1999). Ethnicity and attitudes towards life sustaining technology. *Social Science and Medicine, 48,* 1779–1789.

Borrayo, E. A., Buki, L. P., & Feigal, B. M. (2005). Breast cancer detection among older Latinas: Is it worth the risk? *Qualitative Health Research, 15,* 1244–1263.

Borrayo, E. A., & Guarnaccia, C. A. (2000). Differences between Mexican and U.S. older women of Mexican descent on breast cancer screening health beliefs and behaviors. *Health Care for Women International, 21,* 599–613.

Borrayo, E. A., & Jenkins, S. R. (2001). Feeling healthy: So why should Mexican-descent women screen for breast cancer? *Qualitative Health Research, 11,* 812–823.

Buki, L. P. (1999). Early detection of breast and cervical cancer among medically underserved Latinas. In M. Sotomayor & A. García (Eds.), *La familia: Traditions and realities* (pp. 67–85). Washington, DC: National Hispanic Council on Aging.

Buki, L. P., Borrayo, E. A., Feigal, B. M., & Carrillo, I. Y. (2004). Are all Latinas the same? Perceived breast cancer screening barriers and facilitative conditions. *Psychology of Women Quarterly, 28,* 400–411.

Buki, L. P., Garcés, M. D., Hinestrosa, M. C., Kogan, L., Carrillo, I. Y., & French, B. (2008). Diagnosis, treatment, and beyond: Latina women's psychological adjustment to breast cancer. *Cultural Diversity and Ethnic Minority Psychology, 14,* 163–167.

Buki, L. P., Grupski, A., & Hinestrosa, M. C. (2008). *Higher demand, fewer resources: Meeting the psychosocial needs of Latina breast cancer survivors.* Unpublished manuscript.

Buki, L. P., Jamison, J., Anderson, C. J., & Cuadra, A. M. (2007). Differences in predictors of cervical and breast cancer screening by screening need in uninsured Latina women. *Cancer, 110,* 1578–1585.

Buki, L. P., Salazar, S. I., & Pitton, V. O. (2008). Design elements for the development of cancer education print materials for a Latina/o audience. *Health Promotion Practice. DOI: 10.1177/1524839908320359.*

Centers for Disease Control and Prevention. (1999). *Sexually transmitted disease surveillance.* Retrieved March 15, 2006, from http://www.cdc.gov/nchstp/dstd/ Stats_Trends/1999SurvRpt.htm

Chan, A., & Woodruff, R. K. (1999). Comparison of palliative care needs of English- and non-English-speaking patients. *Journal of Palliative Care, 15,* 26–30.

Chan, E. C. Y., Haynes, M. C., O'Donnell, F. T., Bachino, C., & Vernon, S. W. (2003). Cultural sensitivity and informed decision making about prostate cancer screening. *Journal of Community Health, 28,* 393–405.

Chang, S. W., Kerlikowske, K., Nápoles-Springer, A., Posner, S. F., Sickles, E. A., & Pérez-Stable, E. J. (1996). Racial differences in timeliness of follow-up after abnormal screening mammography. *Cancer, 7,* 1395–1402.

Chavez, L. R., Hubbell, F. A., Mishra, S. I., & Valdez, R. B. (1997). The influence of fatalism on self-reported use of Papanicolaou smears. *American Journal of Preventive Medicine, 13,* 418–424.

Chien, C., Morimoto, L. M., Tom, J., & Li, C. I. (2005). Differences in colorectal carcinoma stage and survival by race and ethnicity. *Cancer, 104,* 629–639.

Clegg, L. X., Li, F. P., Hankey, B. F., Chu, K., & Edwards, B. K. (2002). Cancer survival among U.S. whites and minorities: A SEER program population-based study. *Archives of Internal Medicine, 162,* 1985–1993.

Culver, J. L., Arena, P. L., Antoni, M. H., & Carver, C. S. (2002). Coping and distress among women under treatment for early stage breast cancer: Comparing African Americans, Hispanics, and non-Hispanic Whites. *Psycho-Oncology, 11,* 495–504.

Davis, T. D., Bustamante, A., Brown, C. P., Wolde-Tsadik, G., Savage, E. W., Cheng, X., et al. (1994). The urban church and cancer control: A source of social influence in minority communities. *Public Health Reports, 109,* 500–506.

Doty, M. M. (2003). *Hispanic patients' double burden: Lack of health insurance and limited English.* New York: The Commonwealth Fund.

Edwards, B. K., Brown, M. L., Wingo, P. A., Howe, H. L., Ward, E., Ries, L. A. G., et al. (2005). Annual report to the nation on the status of cancer, 1975–2002, featuring population-based trends in cancer treatment. *Journal of the National Cancer Institute Monographs, 97,* 1407–1427.

Ell, K., Sanchez, K., Vourlekis, B., Lee, P. J., Dwight-Johnson, M., Lagomasino, I., et al. (2005). Depression, correlates of depression, and receipt of depression care among low-income women with breast or gynecologic cancer. *Journal of Clinical Oncology, 23,* 3052–3060.

Ell, K., Vourlekis, B., Muderspach, L., Nissly, J. Padgett, D., Pineda, D., et al. (2002). Abnormal cervical screen follow-up among low-income Latinas: Project SAFe. *Journal of Women's Health and Gender-Based Medicine, 11*(7), 639–651.

Ellington, L., Wahab, S., Martin, S. S., Field, R., & Mooney, K. H. (2006). Factors that influence Spanish- and English-speaking participants' decision to enroll in cancer randomized clinical trials. *Psycho-Oncology, 15,* 273–284.

Etzioni, D. A., Ponce, N. A., Babey, S. H., Spencer, B. A., Brown, E. R., Ko, C. Y., et al. (2004). A population-based study of colorectal cancer test use. *Cancer, 101,* 2523–2532.

Fawzy, F. I. (1999). Psychosocial interventions for patients with cancer: What works and what doesn't. *European Journal of Cancer, 35*(11), 1559–1564.

Fernández, M. E., Gonzales, A., Tortolero-Luna, G., Partida, S., & Bartholomew, L. K. (2005). Using intervention mapping to develop a breast and cervical cancer screening program for Hispanic farmworkers: Cultivando la salud. *Health Promotion Practice, 6,* 394–404.

Fernández-Esquer, M. E., Espinoza, P., Ramirez, A. G., & McAlister, A. L. (2003). Repeated Pap smear screening among Mexican-American women. *Health Education Research: Theory & Practice, 18,* 477–487.

Fox, S. A., & Stein, J. A. (1991). The effect of physician-patient communication on mammography utilization by different ethnic groups. *Medical Care, 29,* 1065–1082.

Fox, S. A., Stein, J. A., Gonzalez, R. E., Farrenkopf, M., & Dellinger, A. (1998). A trial to increase mammography utilization among Los Angeles Hispanic women. *Journal of Health Care for the Poor & Underserved, 9,* 309–321.

Fox, S. A., Stein, J. A., Sockloskie, R. J., & Ory, M. G. (2001). Targeted mailed materials and the Medicare beneficiary: Increasing mammogram screening among the elderly. *American Journal of Public Health, 91,* 55–61.

Galván, N., Buki, L. P., Garcés, D. M., & Hinestrosa, M. C. (in press). Suddenly, a carriage appears: Social support needs of Latina breast cancer survivors. *Journal of Psychosocial Oncology, 27*(3).

Giedzinska, A. S., Meyerowitz, B. E., Ganz, P. A., & Rowland, J. H. (2004). Health-related quality of life in a multiethnic sample of breast cancer survivors. *Annals of Behavioral Medicine, 28,* 39–51.

Gilliland, F. D., Hunt, W. C., & Key, C. R. (1998). Trends in the survival of American Indian, Hispanic, and non-Hispanic White cancer patients in New Mexico and Arizona, 1969–1994. *Cancer, 82,* 1969–1783.

Gordon, A. K. (1996). Hospice and minorities: A national study of organizational access and practice. *Hospice Journal, 11,* 49–70.

Gorin, S. S., & Heck, J. E. (2005). Cancer screening among Latino subgroups in the United States. *Preventive Medicine, 40,* 515–526.

Hakimzadeh, S., & Cohn, D. (2007). English usage among Hispanics in the United States. *Pew Hispanic Center.* Retrieved December 20, 2007, from http://pewhispanic.org/files/reports/82.pdf

Harlan, L. C., Clegg, L. X., & Trimble, E. L. (2003). Trends in surgery and chemotherapy for women diagnosed with ovarian cancer in the United States. *Journal of Clinical Oncology, 21,* 3488–3494.

Hiatt, R. A., Pasick, R. J., Stewart, S., Bloom, J., Davis, P., Gardiner, P., et al. (2001). Community-based cancer screening for underserved women: Design and baseline findings from the Breast and Cervical Cancer Intervention Study. *Preventive Medicine, 33,* 190–203.

Institute of Medicine. (2002). *Unequal treatment: Confronting racial and ethnic disparities in health care.* Washington, DC: National Academies Press.

Jacobs, E. A., Karavolos, K., Rathouz, P. J., Ferris, T. G., & Powell, L. H. (2005). Limited English proficiency and breast and cervical cancer screening in a multiethnic population. *American Journal of Public Health, 95,* 1410–1416.

Jemal, A., Siegel, R., Ward, E., Hao, Y., Xu, J., Murray, T., et al. (2008). Cancer statistics, 2008. *CA: A Cancer Journal for Clinicians, 58,* 71–96.

Jibaja-Weiss, M. L., Volk, R. J., Kingery, P., Smith, Q. W., & Holcomb, D. J. (2003). Tailored messages for breast and cervical cancer screening of low-income and minority women using medical records data. *Patient Education and Counseling, 50,* 123–132.

Jones, C. P. (2000). Levels of racism: A theoretical framework and a gardener's tale. *American Journal of Public Health, 90*(8), 1212–1215.

Juarez, G., Ferrell, B., & Borneman, T. (1998). Influence of culture on cancer pain management in Hispanic patients. *Cancer Practice, 5,* 262–269.

Juarez, G., Ferrell, B., & Borneman, T. (1999). Cultural considerations in education for cancer pain management. *Journal of Cancer Education, 14,* 168–173.

Karliner, L. S., Kaplan, C. P., Juarbe, T., Pasick, R., & Pérez-Stable, E. J. (2005). Poor patient comprehension of abnormal mammography results. *Journal of General Internal Medicine, 20,* 432–437.

Kleinman, A., Eisenberg, L., & Good, B. (1978). Culture, illness, and care: Clinical lessons from anthropologic and cross-cultural research. *Annals of Internal Medicine, 88,* 251–258.

Krieger, N. (2005). Defining and investigating social disparities in cancer: Critical issues. *Cancer Causes and Control, 16,* 5–14.

Lara, M., Gamboa, C., Kahramanian, M. I., Morales, L. S., & Hayes Bautista, D. E. (2005). Acculturation and Latino health in the United States: A review of the literature. *Annual Review of Public Health, 26,* 367–397.

Lazarus, R. S., & Folkman, S. (1984). *Stress, appraisal, and coping.* New York: Springer.

Lethborg, C. E., Kissane, D., Burns, W. I., & Snyder, R. (2000). "Cast adrift": The experience of completing treatment among women with early stage breast cancer. *Journal of Psychosocial Oncology, 18,* 73–90.

Li, C. I., Malone, K. E., & Daling, J. R. (2003). Differences in breast cancer stage, treatment, and survival by race and ethnicity. *Archives of Internal Medicine, 163,* 49–56.

Martinez, D., Loi, C. X. A., Martinez, M. M., Flores, A. E., & Meade, C. D. (2008). Development of a cancer camp for adult Spanish-speaking survivors: Lessons learned from Camp Alegria. *Journal of Cancer Education, 23,* 4–9.

Massett, H. A. (1996). Appropriateness of Hispanic print materials: A content analysis. *Health Education Research, 11,* 231–242.

Matthews-Juarez, P., & Weinberg, A. D. (2004). *Cultural competence in cancer care: A health professional's passport.* Houston, TX: Baylor College of Medicine.

McMullin, J. M., De Alba, I., Chávez, L. R., & Hubbell, F. A. (2005). Influence of beliefs about cervical cancer etiology on Pap smear use among Latina immigrants. *Ethnicity and Health, 10,* 3–18.

Menck, H. R., Henderson, B. E., Pike, M. C., Mack, T., Martin, S. P., & SooHoo, J. (1975). Cancer incidence in the Mexican-American. *Journal of* the National Cancer Institute Monographs, 55, 531–536.

Moadel, A. B., Morgan, C., & Dutcher, J. (2007). Psychosocial needs assessment among an underserved, ethnically diverse cancer patient population. Cancer, 109(2 Suppl), 446–454.

Mohamed, I. E., Skeel Williams, K., Tamburrino, M., Wryobeck, J., & Carter, S. (2005). Understanding locally advanced breast cancer: What influences a woman's decision to delay treatment? Preventive Medicine, 41, 399–405.

Monroe, K. R., Hankin, J. H., Pike, M. C., Henderson, B. E., Stram, D. O., Park S., et al. (2003). Correlation of dietary intake and colorectal cancer incidence among Mexican-American migrants: The multiethnic cohort study. Nutrition and Cancer, 45, 133–147.

Morgan, C., Park, E., & Cortes, D. E. (1995). Beliefs, knowledge, and behavior about cancer among urban Hispanic women. Journal of the National Cancer Institute Monographs, 18, 57–63.

Morrison, R. S., Chichin, E., Carter, J., Burack, O., Lantz, M., & Meier, D. E. (2005). The effect of social work intervention to enhance advance care planning documentation in the nursing home. Journal of the American Geriatrics Society, 53, 290–294.

Muñoz, N., Kato, I., Bosch, F. X., Eluf-Neto, J., De Sanjose, S., Ascunce, N., et al. (1996). Risk factors for HPV DNA detection in middle-aged women. Sexually Transmitted Diseases, 23, 504–510.

Murphy, S. T., Palmer, J. M., Azen, S., Frank, G., Michel, V., & Blackhall, L. J. (1996). Ethnicity and advance care directives. The Journal of Law, Medicine, and Ethics, 24, 108–117.

National Alliance for Hispanic Health. (2001). A primer for cultural proficiency: Towards quality health services for Hispanics. Washington, DC: Estrella Press.

National Cancer Institute (NCI). (2005a). Cancer health disparities: Fact sheet. Retrieved September 27, 2005, from http://www.cancer.gov/cancertopics/factsheet/cancerhealthdisparities

National Cancer Institute (NCI). (2005b). SEER Cancer Statistics Review, 1975–2005. Retrieved August 29, 2008, from http://www.seer.cancer.gov/csr/1975_2005/results_single/ sect_02_table.16.pdf

Navarro, A. M., Senn, K. L., McNicholas, L. J., Kaplan, R. M., Roppe, B., & Campo, M. C. (1998). Por La Vida model intervention enhances use of cancer screening tests among Latinos. American Journal of Preventive Medicine, 15, 32–41.

Nelson, K., Geiger, A. M., & Mangione, C. M. (2002). Effect of health beliefs on delays in care for abnormal cervical cytology in a multiethnic population. Journal of General Internal Medicine, 17, 709–716.

Newell, S. A., Sanson-Fisher, R. W., & Savolainen, N. J. (2002). Systematic review of psychological therapies for cancer patients: Overview and recommendations for future research. Journal of the National Cancer Institute, 94(8), 558–584.

Passik, S. D., Ford, C. V., & Massie, M. J. (1998). Training psychiatrists and psychologists in psycho-oncology. In J. C. Holland (Ed.), Psycho-Oncology (pp. 1055–1060). New York: Oxford University Press.

Paul, C. L., Redman, S., & Sanson-Fisher, R. W. (2004). A cost-effective approach to the development of printed materials: A randomized controlled trial of three strategies. Health Education Research, 19, 698–706.

Payne, D. K., Sullivan, M. D., & Massie, M. J. (1996). Women's psychological reactions to breast cancer. Seminars in Oncology, 23, 89–97.

Rajaram, S. S., & Rashidi, A. (1998). Minority women and breast cancer screening: The role of cultural explanatory models. Preventive Medicine, 27, 757–764.

Ramirez, A. G., Gallion, K. J., Suarez, L., Giachello, A. L., Marti, J. R., Medrano, M. A., et al. (2005). A national agenda for Latino cancer prevention and control. Cancer 103, 2209–2215.

Schiffner, T., & Buki, L. P. (2006). Latina college students' sexual health beliefs about human papillomavirus infection. Cultural Diversity and Ethnic Minority Psychology, 12, 687–696.

Shapiro, S. L., Lopez, A. M., Schwartz, G. E., Bootzin, R., Figueredo, A. J., Braden, C. J., et al. (2001). Quality of life and breast cancer: Relationship to psychosocial variables. Journal of Clinical Psychology, 57, 501–519.

Shavers, V., Brown, M. L., Potosky, A. L., Klabunde, C. N., Davis, W. W., Moul, J. W., et al. (2004). Race/ethnicity and the receipt of watchful waiting for the initial management of prostate cancer. Journal of General Internal Medicine, 19, 146–155.

Shavers, V. L., Harlan, L. C., & Stevens, J. L. (2003). Racial/ethnic variation in clinical presentation, treatment, and survival among breast cancer patients under age 35. Cancer, 97, 134–147.

Sontag, D. (2008, August 3). Immigrants facing deportation by U.S. hospitals. Retrieved September 2, 2008, from http://www.nytimes.com/2008/08/03/us/03deport.html?partner=rss userland&emc=rss&pagewanted=all

Spencer, S. M., Lehman, J. M., Wynings, C., Arena, P., Carver, C. S., Antoni, M. H., et al. (1999). Concerns about breast cancer and relations to psychosocial well-being in a multiethnic sample of early-stage patients. Health Psychology, 18, 159–168.

Suarez, L., Nichols, D. C., & Brady, C. A. (1993). Use of role models to increase Pap smear and mammogram screening in Mexican-American and black women. *American Journal of Preventive Medicine, 9,* 290–296.

Thibodeau, J., & MacRae, J. (1997). Breast cancer survival: A phenomenological inquiry. *Advances in Nursing Science, 19*(4), 65–74.

Thompson, B., Coronado, G., Neuhouser, M., & Chen, L. (2005). Colorectal carcinoma screening among Hispanics and non-Hispanic whites in a rural setting. *Cancer, 103,* 2491–2498.

Tomich, P. L., & Helgeson, V. S. (2004). Is finding something good in the bad always good? Benefit finding among women with breast cancer. *Health Psychology, 23,* 16–23.

Trapido, E. J., Valdez, R. B., Obeso, J. L., Strickman-Stein, N., Rotger, A., & Pérez-Stable, E. J. (1995). Epidemiology of cancer among Hispanics in the United States. *Journal of the National Cancer Institute Monographs, 18,* 17–28.

U.S. Census Bureau. (2005). *Facts for features and special editions: Hispanic heritage month.* Retrieved September 22, 2005, from http://www.census.gov/Press-release/www/releases/archives/facts_for_features_special_editions/005338

U.S. Census Bureau. (2007a). *Current population reports: Income, poverty, and health insurance coverage in the United States: 2006.* Retrieved December 19, 2007, from http://www.census.gov/prod/2007pubs/p60–233.pdf

U.S. Census Bureau. (2007b). *Minority population tops 100 million.* Retrieved December 18, 2007, from http://www.census.gov/Press-Release/www/releases/archives/ population/010048.html

U.S. Census Bureau News. (2008, May 1). *U.S. Hispanic population surpasses 45 million now 15 percent of total.* Retrieved June 18, 2008, from http://www.census.gov/Press-Release/www/releases/archives/population/011910.html

U.S. Department of Health and Human Services. (2001). *National standards for culturally and linguistically appropriate services in health care: Final report.* Retrieved August 25, 2008, from http://www.omhrc.gov/assets/pdf/checked/finalreport.pdf

U.S. Preventive Services Task Force. (2002a). *Screening for breast cancer.* Retrieved December 25, 2007, from http://www.ahrq.gov/clinic/uspstf/uspsbrca.htm

U.S. Preventive Services Task Force. (2002b). *Screening for cervical cancer.* Retrieved December 25, 2007, from http://www.ahrq.gov/clinic/uspstf/uspscerv.htm

U.S. Preventive Services Task Force. (2002c). *Screening for colorectal cancer.* Retrieved December 25, 2007, from http://www.ahrq.gov/clinic/uspstf/uspscolo.htm

U.S. Preventive Services Task Force. (2008). Screening for prostate cancer: U.S. Preventive Services Task Force recommendation statement. *Annals of Internal Medicine, 149,* 185–191.

Valdez, A., Banerjee, K., Ackerson, L., & Fernandez, M. (2002). A multimedia breast cancer education intervention for low-income Latinas. *Journal of Community Health, 27,* 33–51.

Vera, E. M., & Speight, V. (2003). Multicultural competence, social justice, and counseling psychology: Expanding our roles. *The Counseling Psychologist, 31*(3), 253–272.

Viruell-Fuentes, E. A. (2007). Beyond acculturation: Immigration, discrimination, and health research among Mexicans in the United States. *Social Science and Medicine, 65,* 1525–1535.

Walboomers, J. M. M., Jacobs, M. V., Manos, M. M., Bosch, F. X., Kummer, J. A., Shah, K. V., et al. (1999). Human papillomavirus is a necessary cause of invasive cervical cancer worldwide. *Journal of Pathology, 89,* 12–19.

Walsh, J. M. E., Kaplan, C. P., Nguyen, B., Gildengorin, G., McPhee, S. J., & Pérez-Stable, E. J. (2004). Barriers to colorectal cancer screening in Latino and Vietnamese Americans. *Journal of General Internal Medicine, 19,* 156–166.

Ward, E., Halpern, M., Schrag, N., Cokkinides, V., DeSantis, C., Bandi, P., et al. (2007). Association of insurance with cancer care utilization and outcomes. *CA: A Cancer Journal for Clinicians.* Published online before print DOI: 10.3322/CA.2007.0011.

22

Substance Use Among Latino Adolescents

Cultural, Social, and Psychological Considerations

Lisa J. Crockett and Byron L. Zamboanga

Substance use and abuse continue to present an important social challenge for the United States. Tobacco use and alcohol misuse are major contributors to such health problems as heart disease and cancer, which are among the nation's leading causes of premature death. Use of illicit drugs, such as cocaine and methamphetamines, also takes its toll, often leading to addiction and crime. The societal costs of substance use and abuse are substantial: In 2002, the estimated economic burden associated with health care, lost productivity, and criminal justice expenditures related to drug use exceeded $180 billion (Office of National Drug Control Policy, 2004).

Studies of drug use, addiction, and treatment show that substance use typically begins in adolescence. National survey data from 2007 indicate that nearly 75% of high school students had used alcohol at some time in their lives, and 26% had engaged in binge drinking during the previous month. Additionally, half of the students had tried cigarettes, and approximately 38% had tried marijuana (Centers for Disease Control and Prevention [CDC], 2008). Although substance use during adolescence is usually sporadic, it can have immediate and long-term effects on health and functioning. Risks associated with the use of alcohol and other substances include accidental injury, poor health, addiction, academic failure, delayed social maturation, and death (Substance Abuse and Mental Health Services Administration, 2001). For example, substance use is associated with automobile accidents, a leading cause of adolescent mortality in the United States (CDC, 2008). Furthermore, recent research on brain development suggests that substance use during adolescence can affect brain structure and function. Because adolescents' brains undergo significant remodeling, they may be especially vulnerable to the effects of numerous substances, and substance use may permanently alter their neural pathways (Chambers, Taylor, & Potenza, 2003).

The significance of adolescent substance use has sparked a plethora of studies on this topic, but relatively few have focused on Latino adolescents. Latinos are the largest ethnic minority group in the United States (Ramirez & de la Cruz, 2003), representing almost 15% of the population in 2006 (U.S. Census Bureau, 2008). They are also the fastest-growing ethnic minority group, accounting for just over half of U.S. population growth between 2000 and 2006; by 2050, it is estimated that nearly one fourth of the U.S. population will be Latino (U.S. Census Bureau, 2008). Not only do Latinos represent a large and growing segment of America's youth and tomorrow's citizens, Latino youth may be at elevated risk for problems related to substance use (for a review, see Prado, Szapocznik, Maldonado-Molina, Schwartz, & Pantin, 2008). Furthermore, some studies indicate that lifetime rates of substance use are increasing among Latinos and that substance use and associated problems place a significant burden on Latino communities (Martinez, Eddy, & DeGarmo, 2003; Vega & Gil, 1999). Taken together, these reports highlight the need to better understand adolescent substance use among Latinos.

Although rates of Latino adolescent substance use generally are not higher than among non-Hispanic Whites, national surveys indicate that Latino adolescents are disproportionately involved in *early* substance use (Johnston, O'Malley, Bachman, & Schulenberg, 2008a). This is significant because early initiation is associated with an increased risk of substance abuse or dependence (e.g., Gil, Wagner, & Tubman, 2004). Latino youth may also be at elevated risk for problems that are associated with substance use, including school dropout, mental health problems, and incarceration; furthermore, early substance use among Latinos may influence rates of HIV, assaults/homicides, intentional harm/suicides, and chronic lower respiratory disease, contributing to health disparities in these domains (Prado et al., 2008).

In this chapter, we review the recent literature on Latino adolescent substance use, examining both the prevalence of substance use and abuse and the processes leading to use. Focusing on alcohol, tobacco, and marijuana use, we consider factors that appear to influence adolescent substance use in general, as well as cultural factors that may be uniquely or especially salient to Latinos. Our review emphasizes research published in the last decade (1998–2007) but draws on other key studies and conceptual models as well. Our goal is to build a road map of what is currently known about substance use among Latino adolescents and to begin to chart directions for future research. In doing so, we point to limitations of the literature, gaps in the knowledge base, and issues that merit attention in coming years.

FRAMING THE QUESTION: ISSUES TO CONSIDER IN UNDERSTANDING LATINO ADOLESCENT SUBSTANCE USE

To understand Latino adolescent substance use, it is important to keep in mind the heterogeneity of the U.S. Latino population. Latinos in the United States differ with respect to a variety of characteristics, including country of origin, nativity, generational status, and length of time in the United States. These differences may affect patterns of substance use as well as the constellation of risk and protective factors in play. Unfortunately, Latinos from different countries of origin are often pooled in studies of substance use and their possible differences ignored. Furthermore, Latinos with the same national heritage have different experiences, depending on their generational status and length of time in the United States. Acculturation (adaptation to another culture) is an ongoing process for individuals and cultural groups alike, and the process may play out differently for immigrant youth than youth from later generations (Prado et al., 2008). Another confounding issue that has received far less attention is race or racialization (Logan, 2003; Parke & Buriel, 2006). Latinos can be of any race, but the race they are perceived to be affects how others treat them, and the race they identify with likely affects their personal norms and expectations, including those related to substance use.

Finally, Latinos vary in socioeconomic status. Although poverty rates are elevated among Latinos as a group, there is substantial variability in economic status between and within groups (Ramirez & de la Cruz, 2003). Some subgroups, such as Mexicans, Puerto Ricans, and Dominicans, tend to come from lower socioeconomic backgrounds than others (e.g., South Americans), which may influence some forms of substance use. Because research on Latinos has frequently confounded ethnicity with socioeconomic status (SES) or neighborhood context, it is often unclear to what extent patterns of substance use and the factors contributing to use among Latinos reflect socioeconomic circumstances as opposed to cultural influences.

Additionally, substance-use patterns may vary regionally and reflect the ethnic composition of the local community (Vega, Gil, & Kolody, 2002). These aspects of heterogeneity need to be considered in conceptual and empirical research on Latino substance use, as they may contribute to inconsistencies in findings. Throughout this review, we identify the specific Latino sub-group(s) comprising each sample whenever possible; we use the term *Latino* to refer to mixed Latino samples or to cases in which particular subgroups were not specified.

PREVALENCE OF SUBSTANCE USE AMONG LATINO ADOLESCENTS

Rates of Substance Use Among Latino Adolescents

Rates of early substance use are elevated among Latino adolescents, compared to most other ethnic groups. In a national survey of secondary school students, Latino 8th-graders reported the highest annual usage rates of most major categories of drugs (except for amphetamines and tobacco), compared to their non-Hispanic White and African American peers (Johnston et al., 2008a). By 12th grade, rates of drug use among Latinos typically fell between those of non-Hispanic Whites and African Americans, though Latinos continued to have the highest reported rates of crack, heroin, metham-phetamine, and crystal methamphetamine use (Johnston et al., 2008a). The change in relative ranking of Latinos and non-Hispanic Whites between 8th and 12th grades could simply reflect the greater rate of high school drop-out among Latinos relative to other groups. Alternatively, it may be that Latinos are more likely to initiate substance use early, but non-Hispanic Whites catch up during the high school years and surpass Latinos by 12th grade (Johnston, O'Malley, Bachman, & Schulenberg, 2008b). Even if the elevated rates of drug use among Latinos are confined to younger adolescents, they are noteworthy because early onset is associated with continued use, abuse, and dependence (Ellickson, D'Amico, Collins, & Klein, 2005; Gil et al., 2004). Early substance use is also associated with unfavorable social outcomes; for example, early marijuana use in adolescence predicted being suspended or expelled from school, being fired, and collecting welfare (Brook, Adams, Balka, & Johnson, 2002).

Not all national surveys find elevated rates of early substance use among Latinos. Analyses of data from the National Longitudinal Study of Adolescent Health (Add Health) indicated that among 7th- and 8th-graders, the rate of cigarette smoking in the past 30 days was higher for non-Hispanic Whites than for either Blacks or Latinos, and the rate of alcohol use in the past 12 months was similar for non-Hispanic Whites and Latinos (and lower among Blacks). Among 9th- to 12th-graders, non-Hispanic Whites showed higher usage rates for both types of substances, with rates for Latinos falling between those of the other two groups (Blum et al., 2000). In national survey data collected by the CDC, Latino high school students were slightly more likely to report having tried alcohol and cigarettes, compared to White and Black students; however, White students were more likely to report current cigarette use and binge drinking (CDC, 2008). Among older adolescents and young adults in the general population, reported rates of drug use were higher among non-Hispanic Whites than Latinos (Substance Abuse and Mental Health Services Administration, 2005), consistent with the notion that although Latinos may initiate substance use earlier, Non-Hispanic Whites eventually surpass Latinos in rates of substance use.

Ethnic differences and similarities have also been observed in age-related patterns of sub-stance abuse and dependence. In a sample of more than 1,000 White, Black, and Latino youth in Chicago, Reardon and Buka (2002) found few ethnic differences in the prevalence of alcohol and marijuana abuse or dependence at age 15; however, from ages 15 to 17, rates of onset increased for Whites and Latinos (with greater increases among Whites) and then declined. These findings point to the need to examine the full spectrum of substance-use behaviors, from initiation to regular use to substance abuse and dependence, to provide a comprehensive picture of ethnic differences in patterns of substance use.

Heterogeneity in Substance-Use Patterns Among Latino Adolescents

Although Latinos are often aggregated in studies of adolescent substance use, there is substantial heterogeneity within this population. Two important aspects of heterogeneity linked to substance use are country of origin (e.g., Cuban, Mexican, Puerto Rican) and nativity (U.S. born vs. foreign born). Using Monitoring the Future survey data, Delva and colleagues (2005) compared 8th-grade Cuban Americans, Mexican Americans, Puerto Ricans, and other Latin Americans on their rates of heavy drinking, marijuana use, and cocaine use between 1991 and 2002. Across the 11-year study period, Mexican Americans reported the highest rates of marijuana use in the past year, and Cubans reported the highest rates of cocaine use. Prevalence rates of heavy drinking (five or more drinks in a row) during the past 2 weeks also differed across Latino groups: Mexican Americans reported the highest prevalence of heavy drinking, followed by Cuban Americans, Puerto Ricans, and other Latin Americans. Interestingly, trend data revealed that from 1997 to 1999, Cuban American 8th-graders had the highest rates of marijuana and cocaine use and heavy drinking of all four groups, although this difference could reflect the smaller sample size of this group as well as actual increases in Cuban substance use.

Drug use patterns among Latinos also vary with nativity. Studies of adolescents and adults indicate that U.S.-born Latinos report higher rates of alcohol and drug use and abuse than foreign-born Latinos (e.g., Gil, Wagner, & Vega, 2000; Vega & Gil, 1998). Immigrant Latino youth also show a delayed progression of substance use compared to U.S.-born Latinos (Vega & Gil, 1998; Turner & Gil, 2002). In a longitudinal study of adolescents from Miami-Dade County in Florida, U.S.-born Latino adolescents showed patterns of onset and progression similar to those of European American adolescents; however, immigrant Latinos lagged behind U.S.-born Latinos in the progression to regular tobacco use and in rates of marijuana and other drug abuse or dependence in late adolescence (Vega & Gil, 2005). Among males in this sample, the strength of the associations between early adolescent substance use and young-adult substance-use disorders varied by ethnicity and nativity, being strongest for African Americans and foreign-born Latinos, two groups that reported relatively low rates of early adolescent substance use (Gil et al., 2004). For foreign-born Latinos, the age of immigration is also influential: Among Mexican immigrant adults, drug use and abuse are more prevalent among those who entered the United States before age 9 (Vega, Sribney, Aguilar-Gaxiola, & Kolody,

2004). Time in the United States is yet another factor: In one study, the risk of drug abuse or dependence was found to be more than six times greater for immigrants who had lived in the United States for at least 13 years, compared to those with shorter U.S. residency (Vega et al., 1998, cited in Martinez, 2006). These results indicate that being foreign born, immigrating at an older age, and living fewer years in the United States are associated with lower rates of substance use and abuse among Latinos. However, foreign-born Latinos who do engage in early substance use appear to be at increased risk for developing substance-use disorders.

The differing onset and progression of substance use by ethnicity and nativity may reflect distinct patterns of risk and protective factors operating for youth from different ethnic groups and different immigrant generations (Prado et al., 2008). Exposure to psychosocial risk factors for adolescent drug use, as well as clusters of risk and protective factors, vary by ethnicity and within ethnic groups (Gil, Vega, & Turner, 2002; Vega & Gil, 2005).

ETIOLOGY OF LATINO ADOLESCENT SUBSTANCE USE: RISK AND PROTECTIVE FACTORS

Identifying risk and protective factors is a common approach to studying the etiology of drug use and abuse. In general, a risk factor is something that increases the likelihood of a negative outcome (e.g., drug dependence); protective factors mitigate the effects of risk factors, reducing negative outcomes among those at risk (Masten, 2001). A number of general risk and protective factors for substance use have been identified (Hawkins, Catalano, & Miller, 1992). To understand adolescent substance use among Latinos, we must consider exposure and vulnerability to these general risk factors. First, stressors and risk factors are not equally distributed in the population and may fall disproportionately on minority youth, especially those with fewer social and economic resources (Prado et al., 2008; Vega & Gil, 2005). Second, general risk and protective factors may be differentially influential for adolescents from different ethnic groups, such that the effects of some factors are stronger and the effects of other factors weaker among Latinos compared to other adolescents. Apart from general risk and protective factors, certain cultural factors may be uniquely salient to Latino adolescents and influence drug use (Beauvais & Oetting, 2002). These might include cultural values and practices that protect against substance use, as well as risk factors associated with immigration experiences, acculturation, and discrimination.

General Risk and Protective Factors

In an early review of the literature on adolescent substance use, Hawkins et al. (1992) identified a host of risk factors operating at different levels, including contextual factors, such as laws and norms affecting substance use and abuse (e.g., taxation of alcohol, laws restricting the sale of substances to minors, availability of substances, norms reflecting tolerance of use); interpersonal factors, such as parent or sibling substance use, poor family management (unclear expectations for behavior, poor monitoring, and inconsistent discipline), early peer rejection, and association with drug-using peers; and individual factors, such as sensation seeking, genetic vulnerability, physiological response to substances, low bonding to family, academic failure or low commitment to school, early and persistent behavior problems, rebelliousness, favorable attitudes toward use, and early onset of drug use. Placed within an ecological framework, these risk factors include individual characteristics and propensities, features of immediate social contexts (e.g., family, peer group, school), and features of the broader community (norms and laws). Different risk factors are influential at different periods of development, and having more risk factors increases the risk of drug abuse. Hawkins et al. (1992) also identified some common protective factors, including strong attachment to parents and parent conventionality. These factors moderated the effect of substance-using peers and also enhanced the effects of other protective factors, such as adolescent conventionality and marital harmony (e.g., Brook, Brook, Gordon, Whiteman, & Cohen, 1990). Many of these risk and protective factors have been supported in subsequent research (e.g., Bahr, Hoffman, & Yang, 2005; Barnes, Hoffman, Welte, Farrell, & Dintcheff, 2006).

The studies cited by Hawkins et al. (1992) were based largely on White samples or mixed ethnic samples and rarely focused on Latinos.

Thus, one question is whether these risk and protective factors operate in the same way among Latino youth. Studies addressing this issue have typically employed mixed ethnic samples and have examined interactions between ethnicity and other risk or protective factors, or conducted analyses within particular ethnic groups. For example, Vaccaro and Wills (1998) reported that the predictors of adolescent alcohol, tobacco, and marijuana use were similar across ethnic groups but that the effects of these predictors were generally stronger among Whites and Latinos than other ethnic groups. Broman, Reckase, and Freedman-Doan (2006) used Add Health data to examine the influence of parental warmth and family acceptance on alcohol and marijuana use for Black, White, and Latino adolescents in grades 7–12. Results indicated that a supportive family climate (defined by parental warmth and family acceptance) was more strongly associated with reduced substance use among Latino adolescents than among White and Black youth. Similarly, an analysis of statewide survey data from Florida (Saint-Jean & Crandall, 2004) revealed that although many risk and protective factors were significant for Whites, Blacks, and Latinos alike (e.g., peer substance use, individual attitudes favorable to use, social skills, and early onset of antisocial behavior), there were also some ethnic differences; for example, the opportunity for involvement in school was significant only for Latino alcohol use. In addition, for Latinos and non-Hispanic Whites, family reward for prosocial involvement and low perceived risk of drug use were associated with current alcohol use, and perceived risk of drug use was also related to current marijuana use; other factors were significant for Whites or Blacks but not Latinos.

Research on peer influences indicates that these effects may be weaker among Latinos. For example, in one study, the influence of friends' smoking on current smoking was weaker for Latinos than for non-Hispanic Whites (Unger et al., 2001), and in a study of 9th-graders, peer smoking was a weaker predictor of smoking among Latino students than among White students (Landrine, Richardson, Klonoff, & Flay, 1994). Finally, a study that focused on the role of substance-use norms indicated that the effect of personal norms on some types of substance use was stronger for Mexican American adolescents than for other Latinos, African Americans, or non-Hispanic Whites (Elek, Miller-Day, &

Hecht, 2006). Taken together, these studies indicate that many general risk and protective factors identified in previous research operate among Latino adolescents as well, although some may have weaker or stronger effects for Latinos (or particular Latino subgroups); additionally, a few risk factors may be uniquely salient to Latinos.

Accordingly, a second question is whether there are additional risk or protective factors specific to Latino youth (or especially salient for these youth). Likely candidates for additional risk factors would be acculturation processes and the associated experience of acculturative stress. Culturally relevant protective factors include such cultural factors as familism and such socialization processes as enculturation, which involves learning about and adapting to one's heritage culture (Beauvais & Oetting, 2003; De La Rosa, 2002; Gonzales, Knight, Morgan-Lopez, Saenz, & Sirolli, 2002). Within the Latino population, the presence and operation of culturally related risk and protective factors may vary depending on other dimensions, such as acculturation level and generational status (Prado et al., 2008).

CULTURE AND ACCULTURATION

Acculturation is defined as a process of change that occurs when culturally distinct groups and individuals come into contact with another culture (Berry & Kim, 1988). Intercultural contact stimulates the acculturation process, which leads to changes in attitudes, knowledge, norms, behaviors, and identity (Berry, 2007). Individuals vary in both the rate and extent of acculturation, depending on age, length of time in the host culture, and exposure to dominant social institutions (Szapocznik, Scopetta, Kurtines, & Aranalde, 1978). For example, acculturation tends to be greater among second- and third-generation Mexican Americans (born in the United States), as compared to first-generation individuals. For immigrants, acculturation involves the gradual incorporation of the language, cultural beliefs, values, and behaviors of the dominant society (Berry, 2006). At the same time, acculturation is a selective process: Individuals adopt some attitudes, values, and behaviors of the host society while also retaining elements of their heritage culture (Perez & Padilla, 2000; Padilla & Perez, 2003).

As such, acculturation encompasses orientations toward both heritage and receiving cultural contexts and practices among immigrants and their descendants (Tadmor & Tetlock, 2006). Lastly, given that acculturation includes cultural values and identifications as well as practices, it is important to consider ethnic identity (i.e., psychological attachment to one's group) as a relevant dimension of acculturation (Phinney, 2003).

Pre-immigration characteristics of U.S. Latino subgroups vary and can significantly impact Latino families' socioeconomic opportunities and acculturation experiences in the United States. Specifically, Latino families who migrate to the United States with considerable English-language proficiency, financial resources, and formal educational backgrounds are less likely to endure economic difficulties. For example, the first wave of Cuban immigrants consisted of highly educated professional elites; they were granted political asylum and helped create a thriving economic and culturally supportive Cuban community in Miami. In contrast, later waves of Cuban immigrants tended to come from lower socioeconomic and educational backgrounds and had to apply for refugee status. In further contrast, many Mexicans cross the U.S. border in hopes of economic betterment for themselves and their families. Those who are undocumented are confronted with the added burden of migrating to the United States without the benefits of "refugee" or "immigrant" status. Their employment and socioeconomic opportunities are therefore limited, placing them at risk for elevated socioeconomic stress and other resettlement adjustment difficulties. Additionally, many Mexicans (and other non-Mexican Latinos) experience discrimination, and some have limited English-language proficiency. These stressors can adversely impact the mental health and well-being of Latino families and place adolescents at elevated risk for substance use and other problem behaviors.

It is also important to consider the local context of acculturation within the United States. The context reflects an array of interrelated factors that influence the acculturation experience and lead to individual differences in levels of acculturation and emerging cultural identity. Portes (1995; cited in Vega & Gil, 1999) referred to this process as "segmented assimilation," which is driven by three primary factors: color, location, and opportunity structure. Skin color affects how easy it is to assimilate: Distinctive physical characteristics associated with race mark an individual as a member of a particular group, reducing the potential to be perceived as a member of the dominant group. Location (e.g., the region and community where the family resides) affects those with whom family members associate and the social norms to which individuals are exposed. Opportunity structure reflects the quality of schools and employment opportunities, which influence individuals' aspirations and expectations. Individuals who differ on these factors will have different acculturation experiences and may develop distinct cultural identities and relationships to the dominant culture (Vega & Gil, 1999). For example, the experience of a light-skinned individual in a middle-class suburb will differ from that of a darker-skinned person in the same community, and their experiences will each differ from those of their counterparts in a poor inner-city neighborhood.

Vega and Gil (1999) argue that segmented assimilation results in different social contexts of drug use and, in some cases, fosters the development of an oppositional "minority group frame of reference," in which experiences related to skin color (or other distinctive physical traits associated with one's ethnic group), residential location, and opportunity structure lead some individuals to see their ethnic group as a target of exploitation and discrimination. Distress and reduced aspirations resulting from this perception may affect inclinations to use drugs. Segmented assimilation thus affects one's cultural identity, including beliefs about the status and treatment of one's ethnic group and one's position vis-à-vis the dominant culture. Low-income, U.S.-born Latino adolescents are more likely than other Latinos to believe that they are discriminated against and have few opportunities, and this belief may increase their risk of substance use.

Acculturation and Substance Use

Traditional Latino values are thought to discourage illicit substance use (De La Rosa, 1998, Vega & Gil, 1998); consistent with this notion, rates of substance use are lower in most Latin American countries than in the United States (Caetano & Medina Mora, 1989; Vega et al., 2002). Among Latino immigrants, length of U.S. residency is positively associated with drug use (Gil et al., 2000; Vega et al., 1998). Furthermore,

U.S.-born Latinos generally show higher rates of substance use than immigrant Latinos; indeed, their usage rates approach the usage rates of the general U.S. population (Vega et al., 1998). Thus, for Latinos, acculturation to U.S. society, or being socialized within it, is associated with an increased risk of substance use, perhaps reflecting the greater availability or acceptability of drugs in U.S. society (Vega & Gil, 1999).

The association between acculturation and substance use among Latino adolescents is well documented (e.g., Delva et al., 2005; Felix-Ortiz & Newcomb, 1999; Gil et al., 2000; Guilamo-Ramos, Jaccard, Johansson, & Turrisi, 2004; Ortega, Rosenheck, Alegría, & Desai, 2000; Ramirez, et al., 2004; Zamboanga, Schwartz, Hernandez Jarvis, & Van Tyne, in press; for reviews, see De La Rosa, 2002; Gonzales et al., 2002). For example, in a mainly Puerto Rican sample, U.S. nativity was positively associated with stage of substance use, whereas Spanish-language preference was inversely associated with substance use (Brook, Whiteman, Balka, Win, & Gursen, 1998). Chappin and Brook (2001) found a significant association between generational status and subsequent marijuana use in a similar sample. Among Latino 6th- and 7th-graders in New York City, adolescents who spoke English with their parents also reported more marijuana use and polydrug use than those who spoke only Spanish with their parents (Epstein, Botvin, & Diaz, 2001). Similar effects have been found for Mexican American, Cuban American, and Puerto Rican adolescents in studies using different measures of acculturation (nativity, generational status, or cultural orientation), indicating a robust effect (Gonzales et al., 2002). However, not all studies find effects. In their review of this literature, Gonzales et al. (2002) cited four studies indicating that more highly acculturated adolescents had higher rates of alcohol and drug use. In contrast, three studies failed to support this association.

The findings for adolescents are complicated by different patterns of acculturation effects for youth born inside the United States versus outside it. Among foreign-born Latino adolescents in South Florida, those with low acculturation levels (as reflected in a primarily Latino cultural identity) reported lower substance-use initiation and usage rates than their bicultural or highly acculturated peers (Vega & Gil, 1998). However, among U.S.-born Latinos, those with low levels of acculturation reported higher initiation and usage rates and had the highest rates among all Latinos. Thus, low acculturation was protective for immigrant youth but increased risk for U.S.-born adolescents.

It is unclear whether the inconsistent findings regarding acculturation effects relate to differences in the samples or to other features of the studies. De La Rosa (2002) suggested that the inconsistencies stem from the lack of an overarching theoretical framework and inadequate conceptualization and measurement of acculturation. Acculturation encompasses multiple factors, such as language use and proficiency, nativity status, behavioral preferences, values, and ethnic identity, which has resulted in diverse measures of this construct (Gonzales et al., 2002). Additionally, acculturation has been (and continues to be) conceptualized by some researchers as a unidimensional continuum ranging from retention of heritage-culture values and practices to acquisition of receiving-culture values and practices (see Flannery, Reise, & Yu, 2001). However, other researchers have adopted "bidimensional" conceptions of acculturation in which orientations toward heritage and American values and practices are considered as separate dimensions (e.g., Ryder, Alden, & Paulhus, 2000; cf. Schwartz, Zamboanga, & Hernandez Jarvis, 2007). A bidimensional approach to acculturation takes into account biculturalism, which represents high levels of endorsement of both heritage and American cultural practices, instead of a midpoint between the two (cf. Schwartz & Zamboanga, 2008). The differences in conceptualization and measurement likely contribute to inconsistent results across studies. Furthermore, studies typically fail to consider the complex nature of the acculturation process within families, which involves acculturation of both parents and children, parent-child differences in acculturation levels, and enculturation, in which parents seek to engage children in their heritage culture. Last, the meaning of acculturation, and hence its effects, may differ depending on age, generational status, and length of time in the United States (Prado et al., 2008). For example, low acculturation for an immigrant Latino youth may be accompanied by such protective factors as family support, whereas among later-generation youth it may reflect limited opportunities, acculturation conflicts, and perceived discrimination.

Parent Acculturation and Parent-Child Acculturation Gaps

Both parents and their children acculturate, and both kinds of changes can affect family processes. Some research suggests that greater parental acculturation is associated with benefits for children. For example, Dumka, Roosa, and Jackson (1997) reported that higher levels of acculturation among immigrant and U.S.-born Mexican American mothers were associated with more consistent discipline, which in turn predicted fewer conduct problems among 4th-grade children. In contrast, other studies indicate that greater parent acculturation is associated with negative youth outcomes (e.g., Vega & Gil, 1998). Driscoll, Russell, and Crockett (2008) found that parenting style differed with nativity: U.S.-born parents of Mexican American adolescents were more likely to be permissive and less likely to be authoritative than immigrant parents. These differences in parenting style, coupled with the heightened negative impact of permissive parenting on third-generation adolescents, helped to explain the higher rates of delinquency and alcohol problems among U.S.-born youth.

Acculturation occurs among all members of the family to differing degrees, and both the rate and extent may vary among family members. Immigrant youth tend to acculturate faster than their elders (Szapocznik et al., 1978), owing perhaps to their greater exposure to the social institutions of the host society, such as schools. The resulting parent-child acculturation gaps are thought to be harmful for family functioning and adolescent adjustment. One theoretical formulation, based on clinical observations of Cuban immigrant families referred for youth behavior problems, posits that acculturation gaps increase the risk of substance use by increasing conflict within the family and disrupting effective parenting (Szapocznik & Kurtines, 1993). Additionally, such core Latino family values as respect for parental authority (Marín & Marín, 1991) may be undermined as youth adopt more individualistic U.S. values. Ultimately, parents who are frustrated in their efforts to manage their adolescents may reduce their level of involvement, thereby increasing teenagers' susceptibility to negative peer influences and substance use (Prado et al., 2008).

Although a number of studies have documented parent-child differences in acculturation, relatively few have linked these gaps empirically to adjustment problems among adolescents (Gonzales et al., 2002). Among these studies, results have been inconsistent, possibly owing to differences in the conceptualization and measurement of acculturation gaps. Some research has supported the original hypothesis that an acculturation gap in which adolescents are more acculturated than their parents would be associated with youth behavior problems. For example, Martinez (2006) found that the difference between Mexican American adolescents' and their parents' levels of Americanism was positively associated with the likelihood of future alcohol and tobacco use as reported by the adolescent. In another Mexican American sample, the father-child acculturation gap predicted father-child conflict and early adolescent internalizing and externalizing problems, but only when father-child relationships were poor (Schofield, Parke, Kim, & Coltrane, 2008); no significant effects were found for mother-child acculturation gaps. Other research has failed to show the expected correlations between acculturation gaps and substance use. Pasch and colleagues (2006) found no association between acculturation gaps and an array of negative youth outcomes, including substance use, among Mexican American adolescents. Similarly, Vega and Gil (1998) failed to find a consistent association between different kinds of parent-child acculturation gaps and adolescent substance use; instead, the results suggested that acculturation of either parent or adolescent increased the risk of substance use.

The mixed pattern of results indicates that the link between parent-child acculturation gaps and adolescent substance use is not straightforward. As Prado et al. (2008) have suggested, the meaning and effects of acculturation (and acculturation gaps) may differ depending on adolescents' age and generational status. Acculturation effects may also depend on the community setting, owing to differences in local norms, neighborhood conditions, and whether the community shares the same ethnic background (Vega & Gil, 1998). Furthermore, it seems clear that multiple processes are involved in acculturation, including the adoption of attitudes and values more favorable to drug use, changes in parenting practices and family dynamics, and stress associated with acculturative conflicts or experiences of prejudice and discrimination. These different strands need to be distinguished and measured

to determine which processes underlie the association between acculturation and substance use in particular samples, including samples that vary by nativity and generational status. We turn next to some of these processes.

Mediators of the Association Between Acculturation and Substance Use

Research on acculturation tends to focus on the direct association between acculturation and some outcome variable (cf. Dinh, Roosa, Tein, & Lopez, 2002); thus, mediational pathways or mechanisms that explain the link between acculturation and youth outcomes among Latinos remain unclear. Conceivably, the effects of acculturation on substance use may operate through family processes, such as reduced parental involvement. Additionally, it is possible that the relations between acculturation and substance use operate through acculturative stress, which represents the negative "side effects" of acculturation. Such a proposition is tenable, for example, in situations where Latino adolescents are criticized by members of their cultural community for adopting the practices of the host society or, alternatively, for retaining their heritage-culture practices (Schwartz, Montgomery, & Briones, 2006). Acculturative stress, in turn, has been linked to increased risk for substance use (Gil et al., 2000). The limited research on this topic suggests that the effects of acculturation on adolescent substance use may be mediated by its effects on these variables.

Family Processes and Parenting Practices. McQueen, Getz, and Bray (2003) examined two aspects of acculturation (language use and generation status) and their relevance to substance use and deviant behaviors in a sample of Mexican American high school students. Results of structural equation models indicated that higher acculturation (as measured by the adolescent's English-language use) was associated with greater emotional separation from parents which, in turn, was associated with increased alcohol and tobacco use for both genders. Additionally, for adolescent boys, higher acculturation was indirectly related to increased marijuana use through greater family conflict. For girls, later generational status was indirectly linked to elevated substance use through its effects on high family conflict and increased separation from parents. Using national data, Mogro-Wilson (2008) found that speaking English at home was associated with lower levels of parental control, which in turn predicted an increase in alcohol use among Latino adolescents. In a longitudinal study of Latino adolescents, greater acculturation was positively associated with language conflicts and acculturative stress; in turn, greater acculturative stress was associated with reduced levels of familism and parental respect, and lower familism predicted higher tendencies toward deviance and more alcohol use the following year (Gil et al., 2000). These studies point to multiple factors—including reduced familism and respect for parents, greater emotional separation from parents, and reduced parental control—as possible processes mediating the link between acculturation and adolescent substance use.

Acculturative Stress. Acculturative stress arises from difficulties in the acculturation process, including challenges related to language differences, perceived cultural incompatibilities, and cultural self-consciousness (Gil, Vega, & Dimas, 1994; Padilla, Cervantes, Maldonado, & Garcia, 1988). The ways in which Latino individuals choose to acquire (or not to acquire) American cultural practices and values, and to retain (or not to retain) traditional cultural practices, may be associated with specific types of acculturative stress. For instance, Latino college students with limited English-speaking skills, and those who do not get involved in American cultural activities, often perceive pressures to do so (Schwartz & Zamboanga, 2008); Latino adolescents may also experience such pressures. In contrast, in such bicultural contexts as Miami, Los Angeles, and border cities in Texas, failing to retain traditional Latino cultural values and practices may also be associated with perceived pressures to improve one's Spanish-language skills and to become more "Latino" (Schwartz, Zamboanga, Rodriguez, & Wang, 2007). Zamboanga and colleagues (in press) examined the extent to which acculturative stress and self-esteem mediated the association between acculturation (as measured by language use and ethnic identity) and substance use (cigarettes, alcohol, marijuana) among Latino early adolescents living in a monocultural community. Results showed that while having a strong sense of ethnic identity was not directly protective against substance

use, it was protective through its positive effect on self-esteem.

These studies of mediating processes provide intriguing clues about the complex array of factors connecting acculturation to adolescent substance use. However, research on these processes is sparse. Possible family processes and their effects on substance use need to be examined among adolescents in different Latino subgroups, among immigrant youth of different ages with different amounts of time in the United States, and among adolescents who differ in nativity and generational status. These studies need to include multiple substances to begin to detect differences related to type of substance. Additionally, the pathways between different aspects of acculturation and substance use appear to differ by gender, further complicating the picture (e.g., McQueen et al., 2003; Torres-Stone & Meyler, 2007).

SOCIAL RELATIONSHIPS: FAMILY AND PEERS

Acculturation and enculturation take place in a social context that includes family, peers, and the local community, as well as the broader society. Local settings provide direct exposure to norms and values, including those of the ethnic and host cultures. They also encompass a community ecology that reflects risks and opportunities for youth. Such factors as the availability of drugs and peers who model drug use, as well as family relationships and practices, can affect Latino adolescents' propensity to use substances.

Family Influences

Traditional Latino family values and child-rearing practices may serve a protective role, limiting adolescents' opportunities or motivation to engage in substance use. Such values as familism and respect for elders may serve this function. *Familism* refers to "feelings of loyalty, reciprocity, and solidarity toward members of the family as well as to the notion of the family as an extension of self" (Cortez, 1995, p. 249). Familism, respect for parents, and family pride have each been linked to lower involvement in substance use among Latino youth. For example, Gil et al. (2000) found that in the context of a larger predictive model, lower familism was associated with a higher disposition to deviance, which in turn predicted greater alcohol involvement 1 year later. Apospori, Vega, Zimmerman, Warheit, and Gil (1995) found that high family pride and support reduced the relationship between deviance and later drug use among Latino adolescent boys, indicating that family factors can play a protective, moderating role. In related work, Vega and Gil (1998) showed that low levels of familism were associated with increased odds of marijuana use among both foreign-born and U.S.-born Cuban adolescents but especially for immigrant youth, suggesting that familism plays a particularly important role among immigrant Latinos. Furthermore, among Latino youth with psychosocial risk factors for substance use, family pride played a protective role against initiating marijuana use regardless of nativity, but other family processes, including family cohesion, family communication, and parental acceptance, were protective only among immigrants, underscoring the enhanced salience of family processes among immigrant Latinos.

As noted earlier, family values and practices may be influenced by acculturation in ways that affect adolescent substance use. For example, greater acculturation may be associated with reduced familism: Low familism is more common among U.S.-born Latinos than among immigrants, and among immigrant Latinos, higher levels of acculturation are associated with reduced familism (Gil et al., 1994; Vega et al., 1993). There is also evidence of acculturation-related changes in other family processes, particularly parenting practices. Among Mexican American adolescents in a national sample, acculturation (indexed by generational status or speaking English at home) was associated with reductions in parental control, which in turn were associated with some forms of substance use (Mogro-Wilson, 2008). More acculturated parents may endorse individualism and grant more freedom to adolescents, which can increase youths' susceptibility to peer influences and to local norms favoring substance use. Acculturation may also affect family cohesion, which has been shown to be a protective factor among immigrant Latinos at psychosocial risk for substance use (Vega & Gil, 1998). In a study of Latino families, lower acculturation and higher enculturation were associated with higher family cohesion, compared to more acculturated or bicultural families (Miranda,

Estrada, & Firpo-Jimenez, 2000); in another study, longer U.S. residency was associated with lower levels of family cohesion and adaptability among Mexican American families (Smokowski, Rose, & Bacallao, 2008). Thus, acculturation and the experience of acculturative stress appear to erode family processes that protect Latino adolescents from substance use. However, the changes in individual family members (and their interactions) that accompany acculturation—and presumably mediate the linkages between acculturation and Latino adolescent substance use—require further exploration.

In addition to cultural adaptations, parenting practices and child socialization are affected by socioeconomic circumstances and other ecological factors that create parental pressures and challenges (Garcia Coll et al., 1996; Parke & Buriel, 2006). Immigrant parents often work long hours, which results in reduced time and energy for direct involvement in their children's daily lives (Pantin, Schwartz, Sullivan, Coatsworth, & Szapocznik, 2003; Smokowski & Bacallao, 2007). Moreover, immigrant parents may be cut off from extended family members who would provide social support and child-rearing assistance (Vega & Gil, 1999). Families may also experience problems in accessing local services and resources, owing to language barriers. Collectively, these factors can decrease effective parenting and parental involvement, leaving adolescents more susceptible to negative peer influences and substance use.

An extensive literature points to the impact of economic stress on family relationships, parenting, and adolescent outcomes (e.g., Conger et al., 2002). Poverty rates are elevated among Latino families, although the proportion in poverty varies considerably between and within Latino subgroups (Ramirez & de la Cruz, 2003). In addition, many Latino families lack economic resources despite being above the poverty line. Research on non-Hispanic populations (Conger et al., 2002; Conger, Rueter, & Conger, 2000) has shown that economic hardship can disrupt family processes and parenting effectiveness, resulting in increased adjustment problems among adolescents. Extending this family stress model to Mexican Americans, Parke et al. (2004) documented links between economic hardship and parental depression and between parental depression, family interactions, and child adjustment in both Mexican American immigrant families and European American families, although there were ethnic differences in the strength of particular associations. These results suggest some commonalities in the effects of economic hardship for European American and Mexican American families, as well as ethnic differences in the relative strength of particular pathways linking these pressures to child outcomes. The connection to adolescent substance use remains to be determined.

Peer Influences

Substantial research supports an association between peer substance use and substance use among adolescents (e.g., Marshal & Chassin, 2000; Urberg, Goldstein, & Toro, 2005; see Hawkins et al., 1992, for a review), including Latino youth (Segura, Page, Neighbors, Nichols-Anderson, & Gillaspy, 2003). A key factor is whether adolescents associate with deviant peers who can provide access to substances and encourage use. It has been suggested that peers may be especially influential for immigrant adolescents, who must look to peers to learn how to negotiate U.S. culture (Prado et al., 2008). In addition, norms regarding substance use in the local peer population may influence substance-use involvement.

The importance of peers has been shown in research linking adolescents' beliefs about peer attitudes or substance-use behavior to adolescents' own use of substances. Several studies have supported the role of peer norms and behaviors in Latino adolescent substance use (D'Amico & McCarthy, 2006; Elek et al., 2006; Olvera, Poston, & Rodríguez, 2006; Segura et al., 2003). In a sample of 170 Latino adolescents, friends' and siblings' smoking were positively related to youth smoking, whereas the reverse was found for maternal support (Olvera et al., 2006). Segura et al. (2003) found that peer alcohol use (descriptive norms) predicted alcohol use among Latino adolescents. Notably, Unger et al. (2001) reported that the influence of friends' smoking on current smoking and susceptibility to smoking was weaker for Latino 8th-graders than for non-Hispanic Whites. However, cross-sectional analyses of a large, predominantly Mexican American sample of 7th-grade students yielded contrasting results (Elek et al., 2006); a comparison of Mexican American and non-Hispanic White students indicated that parent anti-drug norms predicted cigarette use more strongly among non-Hispanic Whites than among Mexican Americans, whereas friend anti-drug norms were more predictive for Mexican Americans. Further analyses suggested that perceptions of peer use (descriptive peer norms) were stronger predictors of marijuana use for Mexican Americans than for other Latinos, but the reverse was true for lifetime cigarette use.

A key limitation of these studies is that they do not separate the effects of actual peer use or approval from those of perceived peer use and approval. Research on other populations has shown that adolescents' perceptions of their peers' behavior may be a stronger predictor of their own health-risk behavior than is their friends' actual reported behavior (Prinstein & Wang, 2005), indicating that adolescents are inferring norms that may not exist. They may be motivated to conform to these standards not because of peer pressure but because they want to be like their peers. Even when adolescents' actual substance use matches that of their peers, it is unclear whether this similarity represents peer socialization into substance use or simply a tendency of substance-using adolescents to affiliate with each other.

Studies of other ethnic groups indicate that such family protective factors as support and monitoring can sometimes offset the effects of association with deviant peers (Dishion, Nelson, & Bullock, 2004; Urberg et al., 2005). Given the importance of familism among Latinos, it seems likely that family protective processes would be especially influential. In line with this contention, Apospori et al. (1995) reported that family pride and support served as a buffer, moderating the relation between adolescent deviance and subsequent drug use among Latino boys. However, as noted earlier, the challenges facing immigrant Latino parents may lead them to reduce their investment in parenting adolescents (Prado et al., 2008). In the absence of parental involvement, adolescents may be more likely to affiliate with deviant peers and use drugs, and weakened family ties may reduce the family's capacity to serve as a buffer against negative peer influences. Unfortunately, few studies with Latino samples have examined the moderating role of parenting on the relations between actual or perceived peer substance use and adolescent substance use.

Community Contextual Factors

The community in which Latino families settle provides a local context for acculturation and the development of cultural identity among adolescents. It is in community settings that the process of "segmented assimilation," or differential acculturation based on color, location, and opportunity structure (Portes, 1995; Vega & Gil, 1999) plays out. Because U.S. society is strongly segregated by race/ethnicity and social class, immigrants filter selectively into particular communities and neighborhoods according to ethnicity and income. In turn, neighborhood characteristics affect a family's exposure to drugs, gangs, and violence, to different levels of social cohesion, and to opportunity structures reflected in school quality and employment patterns (Vega & Gil, 1999). Because they are often of low-income status, Latino families are more likely to live in low-income neighborhoods with their associated problems. Neighbors also matter to the extent that one identifies with and is identified with one's neighbors and adopts their aspirations and social norms (Logan, 2003).

Neighborhood context may also influence parenting (Baldwin, Baldwin, & Cole, 1990; Furstenberg, 1993; Gutman, McLoyd, & Tokoyawa, 2005); for example, restrictive parenting practices associated with low-income families may be an adaptive response to living in high-risk neighborhoods, as they are associated with positive child outcomes in these settings (Baldwin et al., 1990; Deater-Deckard & Dodge, 1997; Furstenberg, 1993; Pinderhughes, Dodge, Bates, Pettit, & Zelli, 2000). However, little neighborhood research has focused specifically on Latino families; hence it is unclear how these ecological pressures interact with cultural values and traditional child-rearing practices to affect adolescent substance use. In one of the few neighborhood studies of Latinos, Frank, Cerdá, and Rendón (2007) explored the association between residential location in Los Angeles County and Latino adolescent risk behaviors (substance use and delinquency). Census tracts in which levels of Latino residents and poverty exceeded the county average were associated with increased odds of risk behavior for Latino adolescents, particularly those born in the United States. Although this is consistent with neighborhood effects on Latino adolescent substance use, the processes involved have yet to be determined.

Another important feature of communities is their ethnic culture: whether the community shares and supports the family's Latino cultural heritage. Local enclaves provide cultural reinforcement and have established structures and systems that facilitate the adaptation of immigrants to U.S. society (Vega & Gil, 1999). Residing in such a community may reduce social isolation and facilitate employment; it may also slow some aspects of acculturation (e.g., becoming bicultural) because parents can operate without learning English or the cultural norms and values of the host society. Where such supports are not available in the receiving community, the challenges of acculturation are likely to be greater, especially among individuals who resist adopting the cultural norms, values, and behaviors of the host society. Together, these forces can give rise to family acculturative stress and increase substance-use risk.

Summary and Conclusions

In this chapter, we have attempted to review the recent literature on Latino adolescent substance use, addressing its prevalence and the factors contributing to drug use and abuse. In general, the empirical literature is sparse and does not match the richness of the theoretical models that have been proposed to explain substance use among Latinos. Both the conceptual issues and the empirical results are complex, and drawing general conclusions is hampered by inconsistent findings. Yet, a general outline is beginning to emerge. There is good evidence that Latinos show elevated levels of early substance use, which increases the risk of negative social and physical outcomes. There is also evidence that many of the general risk factors known to predict substance use in adolescence also generalize to Latino adolescents. Beyond this, acculturation and acculturative stress appear to be salient processes among Latinos, and there is some indication that such family processes as familism, parental control, and support are at least as important among Latinos as in other ethnic groups.

Despite some progress on these fronts, a number of challenges impede the development of a more comprehensive model of Latino adolescent substance use. A basic limitation is the relatively small number of empirical studies, which makes it difficult to draw firm conclusions about differences among Latino subgroups in either patterns of use or etiology and similarly limits conclusions about the factors contributing to use of specific substances. Research on alcohol use is most abundant and may soon permit a more finely tuned analysis of general predictors of alcohol use among Latinos, but even so, we are far from understanding the culture-related correlates of alcohol use among Latino adolescents.

A second limitation is the tendency to study mixed samples of Latinos without sufficient attention to possible subgroup differences. Unless subgroups are analyzed separately, it is impossible to determination similarities and differences in prevalence and etiology. Greater attention should also be given to socioeconomic status. It is important not to assume that findings from low-income samples generalize to Latinos overall or that ethnic differences necessarily reflect cultural differences. Unfortunately, controlling SES statistically can be misleading in cases in which the processes of interest (e.g., parenting practices) in part reflect cultural adaptations to socioeconomic pressures; in such instances, controlling SES can amount to controlling part of what researchers intend to study. Rather, what is needed are comparisons of substance-use patterns among Latinos from the same heritage culture but with different socioeconomic circumstances. To facilitate comparisons across samples, researchers need to describe their samples with respect to Latino subgroup, nativity, generation status, and perhaps community context, as well as age, SES, and family composition.

A third limitation is the relative lack of attention to developmental issues that may affect substance use during adolescence. Studies have focused on Latino adolescents of different ages, and although a number of these studies are longitudinal, there has been little systematic investigation of age-related differences in the predictors of substance use or in the strength of various influences. However, age differences in predictors seem plausible. For example, susceptibility to antisocial peer influence is thought to be greater in early adolescence (Collins & Steinberg, 2006), which indicates the importance of assessing peer substance-use norms and behaviors during that period. Identity development occurs later in adolescence (and early adulthood), and processes related to personal and cultural identity formation may take on increased salience with regard to substance use at the time (e.g., Zamboanga, Raffaelli, & Horton, 2006). Patterns of acculturative stress may also change over adolescence, as young people are increasingly exposed to community influences and face challenges related to postsecondary education and employment opportunities.

Lack of agreement regarding the conceptualization and measurement of such complex constructs as acculturation, acculturative stress, and culturally based family processes presents a major challenge to the field. Although many researchers agree that cultural identity is bidimensional and reflects orientation toward both the heritage culture and U.S. culture, there is little consensus about which behaviors, values, and preferences best capture these orientations. A similar situation holds regarding the conceptualization and measurement of such Latino family values as familism, where few standard measures exist. The lack of agreement regarding measures, combined with the general paucity of research, has contributed to inconsistencies in findings that cannot presently be resolved. In studies of Latinos, these measurement issues compound the standard complexities of assessing substance use, which include consideration of type of substance, frequency and quantity of use, time frame of measurement, and single drug versus polydrug use.

A related challenge is the complexity of the processes contributing to adolescent substance use and the associated burden of measurement. For example, to understand acculturation effects, it is necessary to consider the acculturation level of multiple family members who are acculturating at different rates. The complementary process of enculturation, although rarely studied, should also be measured, as it could protect adolescents from substance use (Gonzales et al., 2002). To capture these simultaneously occurring, mutually influential changes in attitudes and behaviors, it would be necessary to assess the cultural orientation of both parents and children and the discrepancies between them over time, as well as differences related to nativity and generation status, age, and time in the United States. Attention to segmented assimilation adds yet another layer of complexity because the acculturation process for each individual can vary based on physical characteristics, community context, and experiences of prejudice and discrimination.

Furthermore, acculturation processes do not necessarily operate directly to influence substance use, so it is important to identify mediating processes as well as factors that moderate relations between acculturation and Latino adolescent substance use (cf. Zamboanga et al., 2006). Mediating factors identified in this chapter include acculturative stress, adolescents' emotional separation from parents, and reduced familism, parental involvement, and control. Additional mediators may include self-esteem and peer norms. Finally, acculturation takes place in a community context and ultimately in a multicultural society, both of which can condition the process and outcomes of acculturation (Szapocznik & Kurtines, 1993). Examination of the community context should include members of the receiving group as well as the acculturating group. To date, researchers have focused primarily on the latter, but in order to better understand sociocontextual forces and their relevance to acculturation, the attitudes and behaviors of members of the receiving culture must also be examined. For example, social contexts in which members of the host society do not welcome newcomers (or lack cultural sensitivity or understanding of cultural diversity) may contribute to elevated family acculturative stress and general distress, which in turn could increase adolescents' risk for substance use. Recognition of this multilevel complexity, as well as attention to specific intervening processes and mechanisms, is needed in order to develop a more nuanced understanding of acculturation effects that specifies for whom, under what circumstances, and through what processes acculturation influences Latino adolescent substance use. More broadly, attention to multilevel complexity is necessary to understand the web of processes contributing to substance use within a diverse Latino population.

References

Apospori, E. A., Vega, W. A., Zimmerman, R. S., Warheit, G. J., & Gil, A. G. (1995). A longitudinal study of the conditional effects of deviant behavior on drug use among three racial/ethnic groups of adolescents. In H. B. Kaplan (Ed.), *Drugs, crime, and other deviant adaptations: Longitudinal studies* (pp. 211–230). New York: Plenum Press.

Bahr, S. J., Hoffman, J. P, & Yang, X. (2005). Parental and peer influences on risk of adolescent drug use. *The Journal of Primary Prevention, 26,* 529–551.

Baldwin, A. L., Baldwin, C., & Cole, R. E. (1990). Stress-resistant families and stress-resistant children. In J. Rolf, A. S. Masten, D. Cicchetti, K. H. Nuechterlein, & S. Weintraub (Eds.), *Risk and protective factors in the development of psychopathology* (pp. 257–280). New York: Cambridge University Press.

Barnes, G. M., Hoffman, J. H., Welte, J. W., Farrell, M. P., & Dintcheff, B. A. (2006). Effects of parental monitoring and peer deviance on substance use and delinquency. *Journal of Marriage and Family, 68,* 1084–1104.

Beauvais, F., & Oetting, E. (2002). Variances in the etiology of drug use among ethnic groups of adolescents. *Public Health Reports, 117,* 8–14.

Beauvais, F., & Oetting, E. (2003). Drug abuse: Etiology and cultural considerations. In G. Bernal, J. E. Trimble, A. K. Burley, & F. T. L. Leong (Eds.), *Handbook of racial and ethnic minority psychology* (pp. 448–464). Thousand Oaks, CA: Sage.

Berry, J. W. (2006). Acculturation: A conceptual overview. In M. Bornstein & L. Cote (Eds.), *Acculturation and parent-child relationships: Measurement and development* (pp. 13–30). Mahwah, NJ: Lawrence Erlbaum.

Berry, J. W. (2007). Acculturation. In J. E. Grusec & P. D. Hastings (Eds.), *Handbook of socialization: Theory and research* (pp. 543–558). New York: Guilford Press.

Berry, J. W., & Kim, U. (1988). Acculturation and mental health. In P. R. Dasen, J. W. Berry, & N. Sartorius (Eds.), *Health and cross-cultural psychology: Toward applications* (pp. 207–236). Thousand Oaks, CA: Sage.

Blum, R. W., Beuhring, T., Shew, M. L., Bearinger, L. H., Sieving, R. E., & Resnick, M. D. (2000). The effects of race/ethnicity, income, and family structure on adolescent risk behaviors. *American Journal of Public Health, 90,* 1879–1884.

Broman, C. L., Reckase, M. D., & Freedman-Doan, C. R. (2006). The role of parenting in drug use among Black, Latino and White adolescents. *Journal of Ethnicity in Substance Abuse, 5,* 39–50.

Brook, J. S., Adams, R. E., Balka, E. B., & Johnson, E. (2002). Early adolescent marijuana use: Risks for the transition to young adulthood. *Psychological Medicine, 32,* 79–91.

Brook, J. S., Brook, D. W., Gordon, A. S., Whiteman, M., & Cohen, P. (1990). The psychosocial etiology of adolescent drug use: A family interactional approach. *Genetic, Social, and General Psychology Monographs, 116*(2), 111–267.

Brook, J. S., Whiteman, M., Balka, E. B., Win, P. T., & Gursen, M. D. (1998). Drug use among Puerto

Ricans: Ethnic identity as a protective factor. *Hispanic Journal of Behavioral Sciences, 20,* 241–254.

Caetano, R., & Medina Mora, M. E. (1989). Acculturation and drinking among people of Mexican descent in Mexico and the United States. *Journal of Studies on Alcohol, 49,* 462–470.

Centers for Disease Control and Prevention (CDC). (2008, June 6). Youth risk behavior surveillance—United States, 2007. *Morbidity and Mortality Weekly Report: Surveillance Summaries, 57*(SS-4). Retrieved October 8, 2008, from http://www.cdc.gov/yrbss

Chambers, R. A., Taylor, J. R., & Potenza, M. N. (2003). Developmental neurocircuitry of motivation in adolescence: A critical period of addiction vulnerability. *American Journal of Psychiatry, 160,* 1041–1052.

Chappin, S. R., & Brook, J. S. (2001). The influence of generational status and psychosocial variables on marijuana use among Black and Puerto Rican adolescents. *Hispanic Journal of Behavioral Sciences, 23,* 22–36.

Collins, W. A., & Steinberg, L. (2006). Adolescent development in interpersonal context. In N. Eisenberg, W. Damon, & R. M. Lerner (Eds.), *Handbook of child psychology Vol. 3. Social, emotional, and personality development* (6th ed., pp. 1003–1067). Hoboken, NJ: John Wiley.

Conger, K. J., Rueter, M. A., & Conger, R. D. (2000). The role of economic pressure in the lives of parents and their adolescents: The family stress model. In L. J. Crockett & R. K. Silbereisen (Eds.), *Negotiating adolescence in times of social change* (pp. 210–233). New York: Cambridge University Press.

Conger, R. D., Wallace, L. E., Sun, Y., Simons, R. L., McLoyd, V. C., & Brody, G. H. (2002). Economic pressure in African American families: A replication and extension of the family stress model. *Developmental Psychology, 38,* 179–193.

Cortez, D. E. (1995). Variations in familism in two generations of Puerto Ricans. *Hispanic Journal of Behavioral Sciences, 17,* 249–255.

D'Amico, E., & McCarthy, D. M. (2006). Escalation and initiation of younger adolescents' substance use: The impact of perceived peer use. *Journal of Adolescent Health, 39,* 481–487.

Deater-Deckard, K., & Dodge, K. A. (1997). Externalizing behavior problems and discipline revisited: Nonlinear effects and variation by culture, context, and gender. *Psychological Inquiry, 8,* 161–175.

De La Rosa, M. R. (1998). Prevalence and consequences of alcohol, cigarette, and drug use among Hispanics. *Alcoholism Treatment Quarterly, 26,* 21–54.

De La Rosa, M. R. (2002). Acculturation and Latino adolescents' substance use: A research agenda for the future. *Substance Use and Misuse, 37,* 429–456.

Delva, J. D., Wallace, J. M., O'Malley, P. M., Bachman, J. G., Johnston, L. D., & Schulenberg, J. E. (2005). The epidemiology of alcohol, marijuana, and cocaine use among Mexican American, Puerto Rican, Cuban American, and other Latin American eighth-grade students in the United States: 1991–2002. *American Journal of Public Health, 95,* 696–702.

Dinh, K. T., Roosa, M. W., Tein, J. Y., & Lopez, V. A. (2002). The relationship between acculturation and problem behavior proneness in a Hispanic youth sample: A longitudinal mediation model. *Journal of Abnormal Child Psychology, 30,* 295–309.

Dishion, T. J., Nelson, S. E., & Bullock, B. M. (2004). Premature adolescent autonomy: Parent disengagement and deviant peer process in the amplification of problem behavior. *Journal of Adolescence, 27,* 515–530.

Driscoll. A. K., Russell, S. T., & Crockett, L. J. (2008). Parenting styles and youth well-being across immigrant generations. *Journal of Family Issues, 29,* 185–209.

Dumka, L. E., Roosa, M. W., & Jackson, K. M. (1997). Risk, conflict, mothers' parenting, and children's adjustment in low-income, Mexican immigrant, and Mexican American families. *Journal of Marriage and Family, 59,* 309–323.

Elek, E., Miller-Day, M., & Hecht, M. L. (2006). Influences of personal, injunctive, and descriptive norms on early adolescent substance use. *The Journal of Drug Issues, 36,* 147–172.

Ellickson, P. L., D'Amico, E. J., Collins, R. L., & Klein, D. J. (2005). Marijuana use and later problems: When frequency of recent use explains age of initiation effects (and when it does not). *Substance Use and Misuse, 40,* 343–359.

Epstein, J. A., Botvin, G. J., & Diaz, T. (2001). Linguistic acculturation associated with higher marijuana and polydrug use among Hispanic adolescents. *Substance Use and Misuse, 36,* 477–499.

Felix-Ortiz, M., & Newcomb, M. D. (1999). Vulnerability for drug use among Latino adolescents. *Journal of Community Psychology, 27,* 257–280.

Flannery, W. P., Reise, S. P., & Yu, J. (2001). A comparison of acculturation models. *Personality and Social Psychology Bulletin, 27,* 1035–1045.

Frank, R., Cerdá, M., & Rendón, M. (2007). Barrios and burbs: Residential context and health-risk behaviors among Angeleno adolescents. *Journal of Health and Social Behavior, 48,* 283–300.

Furstenberg, F. F. (1993). How families manage risk and opportunity in dangerous neighborhoods. In W. J. Wilson (Ed.), *Sociology and the public agenda* (pp. 231–258). Newbury Park, CA: Sage.

Garcia Coll, C., Lamberty, G., Jenkins, R., McAdoo, H. P., Crnic, K., Wasik, B. H., et al. (1996). An integrative model for the study of developmental competencies in minority children. *Child Development, 67,* 1891–1914.

Getz, J. G., & Bray, J. H. (2005). Predicting heavy alcohol use among adolescents. *American Journal of Orthopsychiatry, 75,* 102–116.

Gil, A., Vega, W., & Dimas, J. (1994). Acculturative stress and personal adjustment among Hispanic adolescent boys. *Journal of Community Psychology, 22,* 43–54.

Gil, A. G., Vega, W. A, & Turner, R. J. (2002). Early and mid-adolescence risk factors for later substance use by African Americans and European Americans. *Public Health Reports, 117,* S15–S29.

Gil, A. G., Wagner, E. F., & Vega, W. A. (2000). Acculturation, familism, and alcohol use among Latino adolescent males: Longitudinal relations. *Journal of Community Psychology, 28,* 443–458.

Gil, A. G., Wagner, E. F., & Tubman, J. G. (2004). Associations between early-adolescent substance use and subsequent young-adult substance-use disorders and psychiatric disorders among a multiethnic male sample in south Florida. *American Journal of Public Health, 94,* 1603–1609.

Gonzales, N. A., Knight, G. P., Morgan-Lopez, A. A., Saenz, D., & Sirolli, A. (2002). Acculturation and the mental health of Latino youths: An integration and critique of the literature. In J. M. Contreras, K. A. Kerns, & A. M. Neal-Barnett (Eds.), *Latino children and families in the United States: Current research and future directions* (pp. 45–74). Westport, CT: Praeger.

Guilamo-Ramos, V., Jaccard, J., Johansson, M., & Turrisi, R. (2004). Binge drinking among Latino youth: Role of acculturation-related variables. *Psychology of Addictive Behaviors, 18,* 135–142.

Gutman, L. M., McLoyd, V. C., & Tokoyawa, T. (2005). Financial strain, neighborhood stress, parenting behaviors, and adolescent adjustment in urban African American families. *Journal of Research on Adolescence, 15,* 425–449.

Hawkins, J. D., Catalano, R. F., & Miller, J. Y. (1992). Risk and protective factors for alcohol and other drug problems in adolescence and early adulthood: Implications for substance abuse prevention. *Psychological Bulletin, 112*(1), 64–105.

Johnston, L. D., O'Malley, P. M., Bachman, J. G., & Schulenberg, J. E. (2008a). *Demographic subgroup trends for various licit and illicit drugs, 1975–2007* (Monitoring the Future Occasional Paper No. 69) [Online]. Ann Arbor, MI: Institute for Social Research. Retrieved September 26, 2008, from http://www.monitoringthefuture.org/

Johnston, L. D., O'Malley, P. M., Bachman, J. G., & Schulenberg, J. E. (2008b). *Monitoring the Future national results on adolescent drug use: Overview of key findings, 2007* (NIH Publication No. 08–6418). Bethesda, MD: National Institute on Drug Abuse.

Landrine, H., Richardson, J. L., Klonoff, E. A., & Flay, B. R. (1994). Cultural diversity in the predictors of adolescent cigarette smoking: The relative influences of peers. *Journal of Behavioral Medicine, 17,* 331–346.

Logan, J. R. (2003, July 14). *How race counts for Hispanic Americans.* New York: Lewis Mumford Center, University of Albany. Retrieved July 19, 2005, from http://mumford1.dyndns.org/cen2000/report.html

Marín, G., & Marín, B. V. (1991). *Research with Hispanic populations.* Newbury Park, CA: Sage.

Marshal, M. P., & Chassin, L. (2000). Peer influence on adolescent alcohol use: The moderating role of parental support and discipline. *Applied Developmental Science, 4,* 80–88.

Martinez, C. R. (2006). Effects of differential family acculturation on Latino adolescent substance use. *Family Relations, 55,* 306–317.

Martinez, C. R., Jr., Eddy, J. M., & DeGarmo, D. S. (2003). Preventing substance use among Latino youth. In W. J. Bukoski & Z. Sloboda (Eds.), *Handbook of drug abuse prevention: Theory, science, and practice* (pp. 365–380). New York: Kluwer Academic/Plenum.

Masten, A. S. (2001). Ordinary magic: Resilience processes in development. *American Psychologist, 56,* 227–238.

McQueen, A., Getz, J. G., & Bray, J. H. (2003). Acculturation, substance abuse, and deviant behavior: Examining separation and family conflict as mediators. *Child Development, 74,* 1737–1750.

Miranda, A. O., Estrada, D., & Firpo-Jimenez, M. (2000). Differences in family cohesion, adaptability, and environment among Latino families in dissimilar stages of acculturation. *The Family Journal, 8,* 341–350.

Mogro-Wilson, C. (2008). The influence of parental warmth and control on Latino adolescent alcohol use. *Hispanic Journal of Behavioral Sciences, 30,* 89–105.

Office of National Drug Control Policy (2004). *The economic costs of drug abuse in the United States, 1992–2002* (Publication No. 207303). Washington, DC: Executive Office of the President.

Retrieved October 15, 2008, from http://www
.whitehousedrugpolicy.gov/publications/
economic_costs/economic_costs.pdf

Olvera, N., Poston, W. S. C., & Rodríguez, A. (2006).
Parental socialization of smoking initiation in
Latino youth. *Journal of Adolescent Health, 39,*
758–760.

Ortega, A. N., Rosenheck, R., Alegría, M., & Desai,
R. A. (2000). Acculturation and the lifetime risk
of psychiatric and substance-use disorders
among Hispanics. *Journal of Nervous and
Mental Disease, 188,* 728–735.

Padilla, A. M., Cervantes, R. C., Maldonado, M., &
Garcia, R. E. (1988). Coping responses to
psychosocial stressors among Mexican and
Central American immigrants. *Journal of
Community Psychology, 16,* 418–427.

Padilla, A. M, & Perez, W. (2003). Acculturation,
identity, and social cognition: A new
perspective. *Hispanic Journal of Behavioral
Sciences, 25,* 35–55.

Pantin, H., Schwartz, S. J., Sullivan, S., Coatsworth,
J. D., & Szapocznik, J. (2003). Preventing
substance abuse in Hispanic immigrant
adolescents: An ecodevelopmental, parent-
centered approach. *Hispanic Journal of
Behavioral Sciences, 25,* 469–500.

Parke, R. D., & Buriel, R. (2006). Socialization in the
family: Ethnic and ecological perspectives. In
N. Eisenberg, W. Damon, & R. M. Lerner (Eds.),
*Handbook of child psychology: Vol. 3. Social,
emotional, and personality development* (6th ed.,
pp. 429–504). Hoboken, NJ: John Wiley.

Parke, R. D., Coltrane, S., Duffy, S., Buriel, R.,
Dennis, J., Powers, J., et al. (2004). Economic
stress, parenting, and child adjustment in
Mexican American and European American
families. *Child Development, 75,* 1632–1656.

Pasch, L. A., Deardorff, J., Tschann, J. M., Flores, E.,
Penilla, C., & Panoja, P. (2006). Acculturation,
parent-adolescent conflict, and adolescent
adjustment in Mexican American families.
Family Process, 45, 75–86.

Perez, W., & Padilla, A. M. (2000). Cultural
orientation across three generations of Hispanic
adolescents. *Hispanic Journal of Behavioral
Sciences, 22,* 390–398.

Phinney, J. S. (2003). Ethnic identity and
acculturation. In K. M. Chun, P. B. Organista, &
G. Marín (Eds.), *Acculturation: Advances in
theory, measurement, and applied research*
(pp. 63–82). Washington, DC: American
Psychological Association.

Pinderhughes, E. E., Dodge, K. A., Bates, J. E.,
Pettit, G. S., & Zelli, A. (2000). Discipline
responses: Influences of parents'
socioeconomic status, ethnicity, beliefs

about parenting, stress, and cognitive-
emotional processes. *Journal of Family
Psychology, 14,* 380–400.

Portes, A. (1995). Segmented assimilation among
new immigrant youth: A conceptual
framework. In R. G. Rumbaut & W. A.
Cornelius (Eds.), *California's immigrant
children: Theory, research, and implications for
educational policy* (pp. 72–76). San Diego:
University of California, Center for U.S.-
Mexican Studies.

Prado, G., Szapocznik, J., Maldonado-Molina, M. M.,
Schwartz, S. J., & Pantin, H. (2008). Drug use/
abuse prevalence, etiology, prevention, and
treatment in Hispanic adolescents: A cultural
perspective. *Journal of Drug Issues, 38,* 5–36.

Prinstein, M. J., & Wang, S. S. (2005). False
consensus and adolescent peer contagion:
Examining discrepancies between perceptions
and actual reported levels of friends' deviant
and health risk behaviors. *Journal of Abnormal
Child Psychology, 33,* 293–306.

Ramirez, J. R., Crano, W. D., Quist, R., Burgoon, M.,
Alvaro, E. M., & Grandpre, J. (2004).
Acculturation, familism, parental monitoring,
and knowledge as predictors of marijuana and
inhalant use in adolescents. *Psychology of
Addictive Behaviors, 18,* 3–11.

Ramirez, R. R., & de la Cruz, G. P. (2003). The
Hispanic population in the United States:
March 2002. *Current Population Reports,*
P20–545. Washington, DC: U.S. Census Bureau.
Retrieved March 22, 2005, from http://www
.census.gov/population/www/socdemo/
hispanic/h002.html

Reardon, S. F., & Buka, S. L. (2002). Differences in
onset and persistence of substance abuse and
dependence among Whites, Blacks, and
Hispanics. *Public Health Reports, 117,* 51–59.

Ryder, A. G., Alden, L. E., & Paulhus, D. L. (2000). Is
acculturation unidimensional or
bidimensional? A head-to-head comparison in
the prediction of personality, self-identity, and
adjustment. *Journal of Personality and Social
Psychology, 79,* 49–65.

Saint-Jean, G., & Crandall, L. A. (2004). Ethnic
differences in the salience of risk and protective
factors for alcohol and marijuana: Findings
from a statewide survey. *Journal of Ethnicity in
Substance Abuse, 3,* 11–27.

Schofield, T. J., Parke, R. D., Kim, Y., & Coltrane, S.
(2008). Bridging the acculturation gap: Parent-
child relationship quality as a moderator in
Mexican American families. *Developmental
Psychology, 44,* 1190–1194.

Schwartz, S. J., Montgomery, M. J., & Briones, E.
(2006). The role of identity in acculturation

among immigrant people: Theoretical propositions, empirical questions, and applied recommendations. *Human Development, 49,* 1–30.

Schwartz, S. J., & Zamboanga, B. L. (2008). Testing Berry's model of acculturation: A confirmatory latent class approach. *Cultural Diversity and Ethnic Minority Psychology, 14,* 275–295.

Schwartz, S. J., Zamboanga, B. L., & Hernandez Jarvis, L. (2007). Ethnic identity and acculturation in Hispanic early adolescents: Mediated relationships to academic grades, prosocial behaviors, and externalizing symptoms. *Cultural Diversity and Ethnic Minority Psychology, 13,* 364–373.

Schwartz, S. J., Zamboanga, B. L., Rodriguez, L., & Wang, S. C. (2007). The structure of cultural identity in an ethnically diverse sample of emerging adults. *Basic and Applied Social Psychology, 29,* 157–173.

Segura, Y. L., Page, M. C., Neighbors, B. D., Nichols-Anderson, C., & Gillaspy, S. G. (2003). The importance of peers in alcohol use among Latino adolescents: The role of alcohol expectancies and acculturation. *Journal of Ethnicity in Substance Abuse, 2,* 31–49.

Smokowski, P. R., & Bacallao, M. L. (2007). Acculturation, internalizing mental health symptoms, and self-esteem: Cultural experiences of Latino adolescents in North Carolina. *Child Psychiatry and Human Development, 37,* 273–292.

Smokowski, P. R., Rose, R., & Bacallao, M. L. (2008). Acculturation and Latino family processes: How cultural involvement, biculturalism, and acculturation gaps influence family dynamics. *Family Relations, 57,* 295–308.

Substance Abuse and Mental Health Services Administration. (2001). Substance Use. *Healthy People 2010* (Conference ed.). Washington, DC: U.S. Department of Health and Human Services.

Substance Abuse and Mental Health Services Administration. (2005). *Overview of findings from the 2004 National Survey on Drug Use and Health.* Rockville, MD: U.S. Department of Health and Human Services.

Szapocznik, J., & Kurtines, W. M. (1993). Family psychology and cultural diversity: Opportunities for theory, research, and application. *American Psychologist, 48,* 400–407.

Szapocznik, J., Scopetta, M. A., Kurtines, W.M., & Arnalde, M.A. (1978). Theory and measurement of acculturation. *Interamerican Journal of Psychology, 12,* 113–130.

Tadmor, C. T., & Tetlock, P. E. (2006). Biculturalism: A model of the effects of second culture exposure on acculturation and integrative complexity. *Journal of Cross-Cultural Psychology, 37,* 173–190.

Torres-Stone, R. A., & Meyler, D. (2007). Identifying potential risk and protective factors among non-metropolitan Latino youth: Cultural implications for substance use research. *Journal of Immigrant Health, 9,* 95–107.

Turner, R. J., & Gil, A. G. (2002). Psychiatric and substance-use disorders in south Florida: Racial/ethnic and gender contrasts in a young adult cohort. *Archives of General Psychiatry, 59,* 43–50.

Unger, J. B., Rohrbach, L. A., Cruz, T. B., Baezconde-Garbanati, L., Howard, K. A., Palmer, P. H., et al. (2001). Ethnic variation in peer influences on adolescent smoking. *Nicotine and Tobacco Research, 3,* 167–176.

Urberg, K., Goldstein, M. S., & Toro, P. A. (2005). Supportive relationships as a moderator of the effects of parent and peer drinking on adolescent drinking. *Journal of Research on Adolescence, 15,* 1–19.

U.S. Census Bureau. (2008). *Hispanics in the United States.* Retrieved October 15, 2008, from http://www.census.gov/population/www/ socdemo/hispanic/files/Internet_Hispanic_in_ US_2006.pdf

Vaccaro, D., & Wills, T. A. (1998). Stress-coping factors in adolescent substance use: Test of ethnic and gender differences in samples of urban adolescents. *Journal of Drug Education, 28,* 257–282.

Vega, W. A., Aguilar-Gaxiola, S., Andrade, L., Bijl, R., Borges, G., Caraveo-Anduaga, J., et al. (2002). Prevalence and age of onset for drug use in seven international sites: Results from the International Consortium of Psychiatric Epidemiology. *Drug and Alcohol Dependence, 68,* 285–297.

Vega, W. A, & Gil, A. G. (1998). *Drug use and ethnicity in early adolescence.* New York: Plenum Press.

Vega, W. A., & Gil, A. G. (1999). A model for explaining drug use behavior among Hispanic adolescents. *Drugs and Society, 14,* 57–74.

Vega, W. A., & Gil, A. G. (2005). Revisiting drug progression: Long-range effects of early tobacco use. *Addiction, 100,* 1358–1369.

Vega, W. A., Gil, A., & Kolody, B. (2002). What do we know about Latino drug use? Methodological evaluation of state databases. *Hispanic Journal of Behavioral Sciences, 24,* 395–408.

Vega, W. A., Kolody, B., Aguilar-Gaxiola, S., Alderete, E., Catalano, R., & Caraveo-Anduaga, J. (1998). Lifetime prevalence of DSM-III-R psychiatric disorders among urban and rural Mexican Americans in California. *Archives of General Psychiatry, 55,* 771–778.

Vega, W. A., Sribney, W. M., Aguilar-Gaxiola, S., & Kolody, B. (2004). 12-month prevalence of DSM-III-R psychiatric disorders among Mexican Americans: Nativity, social assimilation, and age determinants. *Journal of Nervous and Mental Disease, 192,* 532–541.

Vega, W. A., Zimmerman, R. S., Warheit, G. J., Apospori, E., & Gil, A. G. (1993). Risk factors for early adolescent drug use in four racial/ethnic groups. *American Journal of Public Health, 83,* 185–189.

Zamboanga, B. L., Raffaelli, M., & Horton, N. J. (2006). Acculturation status and heavy alcohol use among Mexican American college students: An investigation of the moderating role of gender. *Addictive Behaviors, 31,* 2188–2198.

Zamboanga, B. L., Schwartz, S. J., Hernandez Jarvis, L., & Van Tyne, K. (in press). Acculturation and substance use among Hispanic early adolescents: Investigating the mediating roles of acculturative stress and self-esteem. *Journal of Primary Prevention.*

23

SEXUALITY AND SEXUAL RISK BEHAVIORS AMONG LATINO ADOLESCENTS AND YOUNG ADULTS

MARCELA RAFFAELLI AND MARIA I. ITURBIDE

OVERVIEW

Sexuality is a fundamental aspect of the human experience, representing a potential source of physical pleasure and emotional connection throughout the life span (Christopher & Roosa, 1991; Crockett, Raffaelli, & Moilanen, 2003; Rossi, 1994). During the second decade of life, romantic feelings and thoughts take on intensified significance (Miller & Benson, 1999), and sexual exploration becomes increasingly common (Carver, Joyner, & Udry, 2003). By the end of the teen years, most young people growing up in the United States have engaged in sexual intercourse (Crockett et al., 2003). Despite the fact that it is an integral aspect of human life, sexual activity is potentially risky because unprotected sex may result in negative outcomes, including unplanned pregnancy and sexually transmitted infection. Thus, understanding normative sexuality is an important avenue to gaining an understanding of sexual risk taking.

The focus of this chapter is on sexuality and sexual risk behaviors among Latinos (the term *Latino* is used to refer to both male and female persons of Mexican, Puerto Rican, Cuban, and Central or South American origin or descent, regardless of race; Day, 1996). Because of space constraints, we focus on the experiences of heterosexual adolescents and young adults, who represent the majority of the Latino population.[1] Most Latinos are young (median age of 25.9 years; Guzmán, 2001) and the majority (about 95%) engage primarily in heterosexual activity (Frankowski & Committee on Adolescence, 2004; Rubenstein, Sears, & Sockloskie, 2003).

The chapter is organized into four sections. First, we describe the sexual behavior of male and female Latino adolescents and young adults; next, we discuss factors linked to sexuality, particularly cultural aspects; third, we explore sexual socialization in Latino families; finally, we identify directions for future research and intervention efforts. Although our primary focus is

Manuscript preparation was supported by Nebraska Tobacco Settlement Biomedical Research Enhancement Funds provided by the University of Nebraska-Lincoln to the first author.

on adolescents and young adults, due to data limitations we draw where necessary on findings from studies conducted with older populations.

SEXUAL BEHAVIOR OF LATINOS

National studies comparing the sexual behavior of Latino adolescents and young adults with other ethnic groups reveal differences in behavior patterns and outcomes. According to the national Youth Risk Behavior Survey, Latino high school students are more likely than Whites but less likely than Blacks to have sex, to initiate intercourse before age 13, and to report four or more lifetime sex partners (Centers for Disease Control and Prevention [CDC], 2007b). Among the subset of teens reporting sexual intercourse in the last 3 months, Latinos are less likely than all other ethnic groups to have used a condom the last time they had sex (CDC, 2007b). Pregnancy rates for Latina adolescents are higher than the national average; about half of all Latinas become pregnant before age 20 (National Campaign to Prevent Teen Pregnancy [National Campaign], 2006), and teen birth rates have declined at a slower rate among Latina girls than among girls from other ethnic groups (National Campaign, 2007a). Latino adolescents and young adults are also disproportionately affected by the HIV/AIDS epidemic (Villarruel, Jemmott, & Jemmott, 2006); Latinos represent 14% of the overall U.S. population but accounted for 19% of new AIDS cases diagnosed in 2005 (CDC, 2007a).

It is important to note that although Latinos in the aggregate differ from other ethnic groups in sexual behavior and outcomes, there are also dramatic differences among Latinos from different national-origin backgrounds (Driscoll, Biggs, Brindis, & Yankah, 2001). For example, among Latino 7th- to 11th-grade students who participated in the National Adolescent Survey of Adolescent Health (Add Health), 23% of Cuban Americans, 31% of Mexican Americans, and 44% of Puerto Ricans had engaged in sexual intercourse (Guilamo-Ramos, Jaccard, Pena, & Goldberg, 2005). Unmarried teen pregnancy rates are lowest among Cuban American girls and highest among Mexican American girls (National Campaign, 2006). Additionally, HIV transmission mode varies by national origin, gender, and age. Among adult men, Mexicans and Cubans are more likely to become infected

through male-to-male sex, whereas the main transmission route for Puerto Ricans is injecting drug use; among adolescents and women, heterosexual intercourse is the main mode of HIV transmission (CDC, 2007a).

These statistics indicate that attention should be paid to subgroup differences rather than grouping Latinos into a single category. Unfortunately, this is usually not possible; for example, virtually no studies have explored issues of sexuality among Latinos who are from Central or South America. To the extent possible, in this chapter we specify the focal population when discussing prior research on sexual behavior and risk taking among Latinos.

EXPLAINING SEXUAL BEHAVIOR AND SEXUAL RISK TAKING AMONG LATINOS

A number of theories have been developed to explain sexual behavior, especially behavior that puts individuals at risk of unintended pregnancy and sexually transmitted infections (particularly HIV/AIDS). Many of these theories focus on individual factors linked to sexuality—such as beliefs, attitudes, and self-regulatory abilities—but the importance of social factors has been increasingly recognized (Friedman, des Jarlais, & Ward, 1994). In an influential essay critiquing individual-focused models of sexual behavior, Amaro (1995) noted that these theoretical models do not typically account for the fact that sexual behaviors take place within relationships that are embedded in social and cultural contexts. During the last decade, efforts have been made to develop models of sexual behavior that incorporate contextual factors, including culture (e.g., Gómez & Marín, 1996; Harvey et al., 2004).

Culture has been defined as "the many complex ways in which peoples of the world live, and which they tend to pass along to their offspring" (Lonner & Malpass, 1994, p. 7). Culture encompasses multiple aspects of a group's existence, including its members' values, beliefs, and practices. Through the socialization process, individuals become *enculturated*—they learn cultural rules, internalize values, and acquire behavioral repertoires appropriate to their specific social group (Gonzales, Knight, & Birman, 2004). In any discussion of cultural norms, it is important to recognize that norms define ideals rather than actual behavior, that adherence to norms will vary within cultural groups, and that noncultural factors play a role in explaining sexual behavior (see Fernandez, 1995; Raffaelli & Suarez-al-Adam, 1998). Taking into account these caveats, a good degree of consensus exists regarding traditional cultural characteristics that are thought to shape and influence sexual expression among Latinos, although it must be emphasized that empirical research has seldom explicitly incorporated these constructs. These include gender-related norms and values linked to interpersonal and family relationships.

The complementary gender roles of *machismo* and *marianismo* have been identified as particularly relevant to Latinos' sexual behavior (Marín, 2003; Raffaelli & Suarez-al-Adam, 1998; Scott, Gilliam, & Braxton, 2005). *Machismo* refers to a complex set of beliefs and values regarding what it means to be a man (e.g., Hardin, 2002; Vigoya, 2001). *Machismo* encompasses characteristics that can either increase or decrease involvement in sexual risk taking. For example, *machismo* is typically associated with hypermasculinity, sexual prowess, and bravado (Cauce & Domenech-Rodríguez, 2002; Neff, 2001; Villarruel & Rodriguez, 2003)—characteristics that have been linked to higher levels of sexual risk-taking (e.g., higher number of sex partners, less condom use) in both general and Latino populations (Doss & Hopkins, 1998; Pleck, Sonnenstein, & Ku, 1993). Yet *machismo* is also described as being associated with responsibilities: Latino males are expected to protect, provide for, and represent their family (Cauce & Domenech-Rodríguez, 2002; Villarruel & Rodriguez, 2003). Thus, men who adhere to notions of *machismo* may be motivated to avoid endangering their families and may take precautions during sexual behavior (Villarruel & Rodriguez, 2003). It is unclear, however, whether this is actually true, as linkages between positive aspects of *machismo* and sexual behavior have not been systematically explored. One cross-national study compared the structure of masculine ideology among European American, African American, and Chilean undergraduates (Doss & Hopkins, 1998). Factor analysis revealed one-factor solutions for the two U.S. samples, whereas three factors emerged in the Chilean sample, suggesting that Latino men may hold a more differentiated or more elaborated view of masculinity than non-Latino men. Unfortunately,

this measure included a number of items related to sexual behavior, making it difficult to uncover linkages between different dimensions of masculinity and sexual behavior. In a synthesis of contemporary Latin American masculinities, Vigoya (2001) noted that certain aspects of the masculine role (e.g., being a father) appear to be less salient than others (e.g., having control and power). Because of this, associations between specific dimensions of *machismo* and sexuality remain to be fully explicated.

The corresponding female gender role of *marianismo* suggests emulation of the Virgin Mary (Cauce & Domenech-Rodríguez, 2002). *Marianismo* specifies that women should be silent and self-sacrificing and should subjugate themselves to male authority, including in the arena of sexuality. Adherence to this gender role is thought to be associated with sexual modesty, submission to male partners, and a reluctance to discuss sexual preferences (including condom use). Again, empirical research is scarce on the extent to which Latinas' sexual behavior is directly affected by this cultural value, as researchers have not assessed *marianismo* directly but instead have used it as a *post hoc* explanation of ethnic differences in research findings.

Other cultural values thought to be associated with Latino sexual behavior are *familismo,* an emphasis on family relationships and strong value placed on child-bearing as an integral part of family life; *respeto,* which emphasizes respect and hierarchy in social relationships; and *simpatia* and *personalismo,* a preference for personal relationships and smooth social interactions (Flores, Eyre, & Millstein, 1998; Marín, 2003; Parke & Buriel, 1998; Villarruel, Jemmott, & Jemmott, 2005). Finally, the Catholic religion has been identified as an important cultural influence for Latinos. In a national sample of more than 4,000 Latinos, more than 90% identified with a specific religion (two thirds as Roman Catholics); two thirds of the sample said that religion was "very important" and prayed daily, and 44% attended church weekly (Pew Research Center, 2007).

Attempts to understand the influence of culture on sexual behavior are complicated because cultural norms and values are not static but rather dynamic and subject to change at both the group and individual level (Berry, 2007). As noted earlier, the term *enculturation* is used to refer to socialization into one's culture of origin.

In contrast, the process of *acculturation* describes how immigrants and ethnic minority-group members learn about and adapt to the host or dominant culture (e.g., Marín & Marín, 1991). Acculturation encompasses multiple domains of functioning, such as language, behavior, values, and attitudes (Zane & Mak, 2003), although the vast majority of empirical studies on acculturation and sexuality have used proxy measures of acculturation (e.g., language, nativity) rather than examining cultural values directly (see Raffaelli, Zamboanga, & Carlo, 2005, for review). Much of this research involves adult populations, so we begin by describing this work.

For Latina adults, low levels of acculturation into U.S. culture may be protective because these women tend to have fewer sex partners than women who are more acculturated; however, less acculturated women may be at risk because they have difficulty negotiating condom use with partners (Marín, Tschann, Gómez, & Kegeles, 1993; Sabogal, Pérez-Stable, Otero-Sabogal, & Hiatt, 1995). Acculturation may be linked to an increase in women's power in their personal relationships (Kline, Kline, & Oken, 1992), and relationship power in turn has been linked with higher levels of condom use among Latinas (Pulerwitz, Amaro, DeJong, Gortmaker, & Rudd, 2002). However, condom use is low even among more acculturated Latinas (Marín et al., 1993), and acculturation has been linked to an increase in the number of sex partners among Latinas (Marín et al., 1993; Sabogal et al., 1995).

Research with adult Latino men suggests that linkages between acculturation and sexual behavior differ depending on the specific behaviors examined. Several studies indicate that less acculturated Latino men are more likely to have multiple partners than those who are highly acculturated (Sabogal, Faigeles, & Catania, 1993; Sabogal et al., 1995), although not all studies show this pattern (e.g., Ford & Norris, 1993). Furthermore, in one study lower levels of acculturation were associated with more coercive sexual behaviors among Latino men; this relation held among men who had one sex partner and those who had multiple partners (Marín, Gómez, Tschann, & Gregorich, 1997). Linkages between acculturation and condom attitudes and use have been reported in several studies, such that lower levels of acculturation are associated with lower levels of sexual comfort, less positive attitudes about condoms, and less frequent condom use (Marín et al., 1993; Marín

et al., 1997; Sabogal et al., 1995). In contrast, a recent study revealed that less acculturated Latino men were more likely to have talked about condom use at their last sexual encounter than more acculturated Latinos, although acculturation was not associated with actual condom use (Ibañez, Van Oss Marín, Villareal, & Gómez, 2005). Taken as a whole, the majority of studies indicate that assimilation into the dominant U.S. culture is linked to lower levels of sexual risk taking among Latino men.

In summary, research with adult Latinos has uncovered associations between acculturation and sexual behavior for both men and women, with different patterns of results by gender. It is not clear, however, what underlying mechanisms link acculturation to behavior change. One possibility is that acculturation is associated with changing gender-role beliefs. For example, Marín and colleagues (1997) reported that acculturation was related to holding less traditional gender-role beliefs, which might account for changes in sexual behavior. Another possibility is that acculturation is associated with changes in patterning of sexual partnerships. For example, Ford and Norris (1993) found that highly acculturated men were more likely to have non-Hispanic sex partners than their less acculturated peers, which may account for the observed changes in sexual behavior. Additional research is needed to elucidate these findings and to examine to what extent findings from studies conducted with adult populations are applicable to adolescents and young adults.

There are indications that acculturation influences sexual behavior among young Latinos similarly to adults. In general, Latino adolescents who are low in acculturation wait longer to begin having sex than their more acculturated peers but are less likely to use condoms when they do start having sex (for reviews, see Afable-Munsuz & Brindis, 2006; Jimenez, Potts, & Jimenez, 2002; Villarruel & Rodriguez, 2003). Unfortunately, these studies—like those conducted with adults—have relied primarily on proxy measures of acculturation rather than assessing cultural variables more directly. It is only recently that researchers have begun to examine how specific cultural values are associated with sexuality. For example, a qualitative study examined the extent to which Mexican American adolescents' preferred partner qualities matched cultural values (Flores et al., 1998). For both male and female adolescents, partner preferences reflected the values of *respeto* and *simpatia*. In addition, among girls, family orientation and future ambitions were also important partner qualities (consistent with notions of *familismo*). Boys' partner preferences emphasized physical appearance (e.g., a nice body), which matches cultural notions regarding male sexual pleasure; however, a partner who dressed provocatively was viewed negatively, which accords with notions of female modesty. This study provides suggestive evidence that sociocultural beliefs are linked to partner selection. A quantitative study of 6th- to 8th-grade girls' expectations related to the timing of life-course events revealed that Latinas gave younger desired ages for marriage and first birth than did Black, White, or Southeast Asian girls, suggesting the salience of family roles for Latinas (East, 1998). However, quantitative studies examining relations between different cultural variables and sexual activity and risk taking in various Latino populations have yielded mixed results.

One set of studies indicates that the role of cultural factors differs depending on the specific behavior studied (e.g., sexual initiation vs. sexual risk taking). In a sample of Latina teens attending alternative high schools, Spanish-language use at home was associated with older age at first intercourse (Denner & Coyle, 2007). Among Mexican American adolescents, low levels of religiosity (importance of religion) were a strong predictor of sexual involvement (measured by frequency of sexual intercourse; Liebowitz, Castellano, & Cuellar, 1999). However, in a sample of primarily Puerto Rican male and female adolescents, multivariate analyses revealed links between recent condom use and higher levels of religiosity; gender-role attitudes and familism were not associated with condom use (Villarruel, Jemmott, Jemmott, & Ronis, 2007). Multivariate analyses of data collected from female Cuban American college students indicated that higher levels of sexual risk were associated with both higher levels of ethnic identity (often considered an indicator of cultural adherence) and lower levels of religiosity (Raffaelli, Zamboanga, et al., 2005). Because these studies examined different cultural variables and operationalized sexual outcomes differently, it is impossible to obtain a clear picture of the role of cultural factors. Villarruel and colleagues (2007) speculate that the use of global measures of cultural constructs (as opposed to measures linked to sexuality and condom use) may have contributed to the lack of

associations between cultural measures and condom use in their study (see also Bowleg, Belgrave, & Reisen, 2000). They also note that some of the condom attitude measures that significantly predicted condom outcomes could have tapped into cultural constructs indirectly. For example, girls' condom use intentions were linked to parent approval of condom use and thus may reflect familistic concerns. Research using more precise measures of cultural factors may produce a more accurate assessment of how culture influences sexual behavior among Latino adolescents and young adults.

Indeed, studies that employ specific measures of cultural constructs have revealed significant associations with sexual behavior. In a study of unmarried Latino adult men, Barbara Marín and colleagues examined condom use using a conceptual framework that incorporated cultural factors into a model derived from social cognitive theory (Marín et al., 1997). Results indicated that traditional gender-role beliefs operated through sexually coercive behavior and comfort regarding sexual issues and one's own sexuality on condom self-efficacy. Traditional gender-role beliefs were associated with higher levels of sexually coercive behavior and lower levels of sexual comfort; in turn, condom self-efficacy was positively associated with condom use. In addition, condom social norms were directly associated with both condom self-efficacy and use. Another study predicting pregnancy outcomes reported by male Latino adolescents and young adults found that traditional male gender-role ideology was directly (positively) associated with attitudes favoring coercive sex and number of pregnancies; in addition, there was an indirect path to number of pregnancies from coercive sex via sexual activity (Goodyear, Newcomb, & Allison, 2000). Taken together, these studies indicate that adherence to traditional sex roles makes Latino men more likely to endorse or engage in coercive sexual practices, thus increasing their risk of unprotected sex.

Other evidence of the importance of incorporating cultural factors into models of sexual behavior is emerging from intervention studies. One HIV prevention program for Latino adolescents incorporated cultural factors into an existing theoretically based curriculum originally developed for African American adolescents (Villarruel et al., 2005). The resulting *¡Cuídate!* curriculum is available in both English and

Spanish and draws on cultural values to promote safer sexual behavior. For example, *machismo* is defined in ways that emphasize a man's responsibility for taking care of and protecting his family. The female gender role is depicted as including a woman's responsibility for taking care of her family by taking care of herself, including by carrying and using condoms. Activities with explicit cultural content (e.g., games, music, role plays) are used to modify or reinforce cultural values that hinder or promote safer sexual behavior. The *¡Cuídate!* curriculum led to changes in attitudes and skills related to condom use (Villarruel et al., 2005), and a randomized controlled trial revealed that the curriculum was effective in reducing sexual risk behavior over a 12-month period (Villarruel et al., 2006). At the 12-month follow-up, Latino youth who participated in the intervention were significantly less likely than those in the control intervention to report intercourse (35.7% vs. 40.7%) and sex with multiple partners (10.7% vs. 17.3%), and more likely to report consistent condom use (42.2% vs. 27.6%), during the last 3 months. Other successful prevention programs have been developed for Latina adolescents (e.g., Harper, Bangi, Sanchez, Doll, & Pedraza, 2006) and families (e.g., Coatsworth, Pantin, & Szapocznik, 2002; see National Campaign, 2007b, for review). As results of intervention trials accumulate, it will be possible to identify the role of cultural tailoring in promoting program effectiveness. A recent meta-analysis of sexual risk reduction efforts among adult Latinos showed that intervention efficacy was enhanced when cultural constructs were explicitly considered in the intervention (Herbst et al., 2007).

In summary, information on relations between cultural values and sexual behavior among Latinos is accumulating from research and intervention studies. This work demands considerable effort, as researchers must create and adapt instruments and programs for use with Latinos. Results highlight the value of examining how sexual attitudes and behavior are influenced by cultural processes. However, much of this work has been conducted with adults and does not consider developmental issues that are relevant to adolescents and young adults. The process of developing a healthy sexual identity is multifaceted; youth must come to terms with the physical changes of puberty, adapt to the emergence of sexual desires, make sense of information regarding sexuality from multiple sources, and figure out their sexual identity (see Crockett et al., 2003, for review). Latino youth face the additional challenge of integrating cultural messages that may be in direct conflict with those of the larger society. Thus, additional research is needed to examine how cultural values and attitudes affect Latino adolescents' and young adults' sexuality, and to explore how these relations change during the course of development. One promising avenue for deepening our understanding of Latino sexuality is the study of sexual socialization—how individuals learn about sexuality and come to see themselves as sexual beings. In our discussion of sexual socialization, we draw on the organizational framework of scripting theory.

SEXUAL SOCIALIZATION OF LATINO CHILDREN AND ADOLESCENTS

Scripting theory proposes that sexual behavior results from the interplay between cultural scenarios, interpersonal scripts, and intrapsychic scripts (Simon & Gagnon, 1986, 1987). Cultural scenarios provide the basic framework for sexual interactions, delineating the roles of individuals in a sexual encounter, whereas interpersonal and intrapsychic scripts are the outcome of individual "fine-tuning" through experience and practice. Scholars have examined sexual scripts of adult Latinos and found them to be consistent with cultural norms and values. For example, an ethnographic study of Puerto Rican men living in New York City revealed themes reflecting the *machismo/marianismo* dynamic (Seal, Wagner-Raphael, & Ehrhardt, 2000). The male role reflected the need to be "the man" (to be in control, to perform sexually), whereas views of women encompassed the value of virginity, women as sexual gatekeepers, ambivalence about relationships, and distrust of female partners (Seal et al., 2000; see also Pérez-Jiménez, Cunningham, Serrano-Garcia, & Ortiz-Torres, 2007). A study of ethnically diverse (primarily African American and Latina) urban women indicated that sexual scripts continue to follow "traditional" patterns, with "men being initiators of romantic and sexual encounters and women acquiescent partners" (Ortiz-Torres, Williams, & Ehrhardt, 2003, p. 13). Despite indications of change due to women's changing social and family roles, similar findings have been reported in studies involving Puerto Rican and Dominican women (see Ortiz-Torres, Serrano-Garcia, & Torres-Burgos, 2000). Among adults, then, sexual scripts appear to reflect gender-related norms and values that have been associated with Latino culture.

Given these findings, it is perhaps not surprising that sexual socialization in many Latino families is organized by gender in ways that fit with descriptions of cultural norms and values (e.g., Driscoll et al., 2001; Gallegos-Castillo, 2006; Reid, Haritos, Kelly, & Holland, 1995). For example, Latina adolescents report stricter rules about dating and sex, and more conservative maternal expectations regarding sexuality, than their male counterparts (Hovell et al., 1994). Similar findings were reported in two retrospective studies of gender-related socialization in Latino families (Raffaelli & Ontai, 2001, 2004; see also Harper et al., 2006). Qualitative studies conducted with different Latino subgroups reveal that family beliefs regarding the importance of maintaining daughters' virginity were linked to rules regarding dating and contact with boys for daughters but not sons (Taylor, 1996; Villarruel, 1998). A recent national survey that included more than 200 Latino teens confirms that gender-related socialization differs for boys and girls. For example, three quarters of Latino teens felt that parents give boys and girls different messages about sex, and both girls (68%) and boys (58%) strongly or somewhat agree that "[t]een boys often receive the message that they are expected to have sex" (Vexler, 2007, p. 20). In light of this, it makes sense that Latino boys and girls have different views of abstinence and appropriate dating partners: The majority of Latina girls (87%) stated that it was "very important" not to have sex until after high school, compared to 53% of Latino boys.

It has been proposed that the cultural emphasis on women's innocence may make it difficult for Latino parents to discuss sexuality with children, particularly daughters (e.g., Marín & Gómez, 1997). In the survey described in the previous paragraph over three quarters of Latino teens agreed strongly (42%) or somewhat (35%) that "[w]hen it comes to talking about sex, parents often don't know what to say, how to say it, or when to start"; girls (81%) were more likely than boys (74%) to agree (Vexler, 2007, p. 9). This finding is congruent with findings of an observational study of Latino teens and their mothers that mother-son dyads spent more time than mother-daughter dyads talking about sex

(Romo, Lefkowitz, Sigman, & Au, 2001). In contrast, in both concurrent (Hovell et al., 1994) and retrospective (Raffaelli & Green, 2003) studies of parent-child communication in Latino families, Latinas reported higher levels of communication about sex with their mothers than did their male peers. Given variations in methods used to collect data across different studies, it is difficult to evaluate the extent to which these findings reflect actual gender differences in conversations about sex (see Lefkowitz, 2002). In-depth interviews with Latina mothers and daughters revealed that open communication about sexuality is highly valued but difficult to achieve (McKee & Karasz, 2006; see also Guzmán, Arruda, & Feria, 2006).

In summary, a considerable body of work indicates that sexual socialization in Latino families tends to be consistent with traditional gender norms. It is likely, however, that families differ in the extent to which they endorse traditional gender norms. Identification of factors linked to variations in family socialization (e.g., acculturation, parental characteristics) would be a valuable contribution to the literature.

Sexual scripts are also influenced by actual sexual experiences and partner characteristics. Relationships give young people opportunities to put what they have learned into practice as they experiment with sexuality and develop behavioral preferences. In recent years, information regarding Latino adolescents' early sexual relationships has begun to emerge. This work offers hints about how relationships may contribute to sexual behavior among Latino adolescents.

Partner characteristics that may shape adolescents' sexual behavior include the relative age of the members of the couple. A larger age gap between partners has been shown to increase sexual risk taking (e.g., Manlove & Terry-Humen, 2007; Marín, Coyle, Gómez, Carvajal, & Kirby, 2000). There is some indication that Latina girls are disproportionately likely to date older males (Marín, Kirby, Hudes, Coyle, & Gómez, 2006), a pattern that is described as consistent with Latin American norms (Driscoll et al., 2001). National data confirm that regardless of ethnic group, foreign-born girls had higher odds than U.S.-born girls of having a first sexual partner who was at least 3 years older (Manlove, Ryan, & Franzetta, 2007). Unfortunately, studies have not examined the simultaneous role of ethnicity, partner age, and birthplace, so the interrelations among these factors await elucidation.

Recent studies support the notion that partner ethnicity is an important factor to consider in understanding romantic relationships among Latinos. In a sample of Add Health participants with at least two lifetime sex partners, more Latino adolescents (46%) had a sexual partner from a different ethnic group than either White (13%) or Black (12%) adolescents (Manlove, Franzetta, Ryan, & Moore, 2006). Similar figures emerge from the 1995 National Survey of Family Growth (NSFG): 40% of Latinas had a non-Latino as their first sexual partner, compared to 14% of non-Hispanic Whites and 12% of non-Hispanic Blacks (Manlove & Terry-Humen, 2007). Because early partners represent a socialization context for future sexual behavior, it is important to explore the impact of these experiences.

There is evidence that involvement with older males or Latino partners contributes to Latinas' sexual risk behavior. For example, in a study of 17- to 25-year-old, sexually active Latinas (primarily Mexican Americans), women whose first sexual partner was close in age or non-Latino reported an older age at first intercourse than those who reported a greater age disparity or had a non-Latino partner (Gilliam, Berlin, Kozloski, Hernandez, & Grundy, 2007). In a national sample, Latinas whose partners were non-Latinos were more likely to have used contraception at first intercourse (Manlove & Terry-Humen, 2007). These studies examined partner characteristics as separate variables in multivariate models, but a retrospective study of Latino college students suggests that partner age and ethnicity may be related (Raffaelli, 2005). In that study, just under one fifth of male respondents reported that their first serious romantic partner was Latina; in contrast, nearly two fifths of female respondents said their first boyfriend was Latino. In addition, among young women, partner ethnicity and relative age of the dyad members were associated. In over two fifths (46%) of cases where the male partner was Latino, the age differences between partners was at least 2 years; in contrast, just over one fifth (23%) of women with a non-Latino partner reported an age disparity of 2 years or more. It would be informative to examine whether these patterns are replicated in national data sets and what the implications are for sexual behavior and risk taking among Latinos.

Little is known about how these early romantic and sexual experiences contribute to Latinos'

emerging sense of sexuality. A few small-scale studies have addressed the sexual self-concept of Latina girls and women (Denner & Dunbar, 2004; Gallegos-Castillo, 2006; Faulkner & Mansfield, 2002). These studies provide rich descriptions of how Latinas explore their sexuality and construct a sense of themselves as sexual agents. This body of work highlights that Latinas do not passively accept socialization messages regarding gender-role expectations and appropriate sexual behavior; instead, they select from among those messages to build their sexual self-concepts. One study involving 31 young adult Latinas described them as actively involved in "reconciling messages" received from those around them (e.g., families, friends, partners): "accepting messages that fit their value system, rejecting messages that they feel misrepresent their beliefs, and altering messages to be able to accept their sexual selves and decisions" (Faulkner & Mansfield, 2002, p. 317). For example, the participants identified the cultural norm of female chastity as representing a powerful message regarding acceptable sexuality. Some of the young women decided to stay *señoritas* (virgins), either avoiding all sexual contact or figuring out alternative ways to honor this norm while still exploring their sexuality (e.g., engaging in oral sex but not vaginal intercourse). Others rejected the message but formulated criteria for becoming sexually involved (e.g., only within a relationship that was perceived as stable and meaningful). Findings from these descriptive studies illustrate the active role Latinas play in sexual identity formation.

Less is known about how Latino boys and men make sense of the messages they receive about male gender roles and sexuality. The Puerto Rican men in Seal and colleagues' (2000) ethnographic study (discussed earlier) had clearly absorbed traditional gender messages regarding what it meant to be a man. Among male Puerto Rican college students who participated in focus groups (Pérez-Jiménez et al., 2007), socialization regarding gender roles and sexuality was described as reflecting traditional gender roles (e.g., men should be unsentimental, in control, masculine). As has been found in studies with Latina young women, some of these young Latino men voiced dissatisfaction with traditional roles and questioned prevailing conceptions of masculinity. In a transnational ethnographic study, Hirsch (2000) described both generational and geographic shifts in gender roles and views of ideal relationships among adult Mexican migrants. Whereas in the past the foundation of marriage was *respeto* (respect), younger couples emphasized *confianza* (trust) and aspired to companionate marriages characterized by joint decision making, sharing of household tasks, and emotional closeness. It is unclear, however, whether adolescents are experiencing similar shifts in gender-role attitudes and how their romantic and sexual relationships are affected by these transformations.

Taken as a whole, the findings from studies of sexual socialization of Latino children and adolescents provide evidence that socialization is often organized in ways that are consistent with cultural beliefs about gender-appropriate behavior, although individuals may resist or reframe these messages to incorporate the more liberal sexual mores typical of mainstream U.S. society. Given that traditional Latino gender roles are more restrictive for females than for males, young women are likely to have to work harder than boys to reconcile the contradictory messages they receive from different sources. This may explain why developing a positive sexual self-concept appears to be a challenge for many Latinas. For example, in Flores et al.'s (1998) study of Mexican American adolescents, respondents were asked to sort cards displaying reasons for having sex (or not) into piles based on their similarity. Analysis of the groupings revealed six clusters for boys (3 positive, 3 negative), but eight clusters emerged for girls, two positive (e.g., to express love for partner) and six negative (e.g., being forced by partner). The young women in another study described two options for a sexual persona as "good girls or flirt girls" (Faulkner, 2003). It appears that Latina girls experience more tension and conflict regarding the appropriate expression of their sexuality than do their male peers. However, there are also indications that young people (and their parents and partners) are questioning and reinterpreting traditional gender roles. As discussed throughout this section, many promising avenues for future research on sexual socialization exist.

FUTURE DIRECTIONS

In the process of writing this chapter, we became aware of a number of gaps that remain to be addressed in future research. One limitation—which is shared by the general literature on youth sexuality (Barber & Eccles, 2003; Crockett et al., 2003; Diamond, 2006)—is that research on Latino sexuality has typically focused on a limited set of behaviors (e.g., age of onset of sexual intercourse, number of partners, condom use) rather than examining sexual development in a comprehensive way. Because of this, little is known about how young Latinos think or feel about their sexuality, or what normative sexual development looks like in this population. To balance the picture, future research is needed that examines noncoital sexual experiences and focuses on positive sexual development.

Second, to generate a complete picture of the sexual behavior and attitudes of Latino adolescents and young adults, future studies should examine within-group differences due to the intersections of national/cultural origin, acculturative status, age, and gender. It is worth emphasizing again that most research reviewed in this chapter focused on three groups—Mexican Americans, Cuban Americans, and Puerto Ricans—with little information available on Central or South American and Caribbean youth (Driscoll et al., 2001). Future work should also attempt to parse the influence of such noncultural factors as socioeconomic status (SES), which is usually treated as a control variable in empirical studies rather than examined as a potential predictor of sexual attitudes and behavior. The importance of noncultural variables is illustrated in a study of immigrant Mexican fathers' attitudes about their daughters' virginity (González-López, 2004). Men from rural areas expressed concern about preserving their daughters' virginity, whereas men from urban areas worried that early sexual activity could lead to outcomes (e.g., pregnancy, sexual violence) that would threaten their daughters' well-being and interfere with educational goals. This urban-rural difference would have been obscured in a study that compared "Mexican immigrants" to another group. Similarly, studies that aggregate Latinos into one group may conceal important within-group variations.

Another promising area for future research involves the operationalization and measurement of cultural variables in sexuality research. Common proxy measures of cultural adherence (e.g., language use, generation of immigration, birthplace) are limited because they do not measure cultural variables directly. As noted earlier, language is the most commonly used indicator of acculturation, but language use is of limited utility as an index of acculturation for two reasons. First, linguistic assimilation is typically complete by the third generation; analysis of the census data indicated that 72% of third-generation Latino children aged 6–15 were monolingual English speakers (Alba, 2004). Second, although language is a component of acculturation, it is not a complete representation of the acculturation process; language does not reflect the importance of cultural values, attitudes, and beliefs (Zane & Mak, 2003). Recognizing the limitations of demographic variables as proxies for cultural variables, scholars have started examining the role of culturally relevant constructs directly. This strategy requires confronting the issue of how best to define and measure cultural constructs in sexuality research. There are indications that global measures of cultural constructs are not strongly related to sexual behavior. For example, measures of family financial obligations included in most measures of *familismo* may be less relevant to sexual behavior than items tapping into family obligations relating to sexuality, such as preserving the good name of the family by not becoming pregnant (see Villarruel et al., 2007). Similarly, generic measures of gender-role expectations and attitudes may be less predictive than measures that tap into expectations and attitudes regarding male-female relationships (see Eisenman & Dantzker, 2006; Kulis, Marsiglia, Lingard, Nieri, & Nagoshi, 2008; Pulerwitz et al., 2002). Scholars have pointed out the need to conceptualize and assess culture in more specific and nuanced ways in developmental research (e.g., Guerra & Jagers, 1998; McLoyd, 2004); research on sexuality would benefit from a similar shift.

Additional research on the romantic and sexual partnerships of Latino adolescents and young adults is also warranted. In recent years, developmental scholars have devoted considerable attention to adolescent romantic relationships (see volumes edited by Crouter & Booth, 2006; Florsheim, 2003a; Furman, Brown, & Feiring, 1997; Shulman & Collins, 1997). Despite this, remarkably little is known about normative patterns of dating, romantic involvement, and sexuality among Latino youth (Driscoll et al., 2001; Raffaelli, 2005). There is evidence that the romantic and sexual experiences of male and female Latino teens differ from each other and from those of their non-Latino peers in ways that may be linked to sexuality and sexual behavior. Early romantic and sexual relationships provide an important context for shaping sexual scripts (Driscoll et al., 2005; Florsheim, 2003b; Magana & Carrier, 1991); thus, research on how partner and dyadic characteristics affect the sexual behavior of Latino adolescents and young adults may prove a fruitful avenue for future research.

In terms of intervention, the need is urgent for scholars to continue exploring how best to influence cultural norms and values in ways that promote healthy sexuality while reducing risky sexual behavior. There is evidence that sexual scripts among Latinos continue to reflect traditional cultural values even when acculturation has occurred in other domains (e.g., Espin, 1984/1997). Thus, to foster behavior change, it will be necessary to address issues of gender, culture, and power (Marín, 2003; Raffaelli & Suarez-al-Adam, 1998). Interventions to promote sexual behavior change are increasingly focused on "subverting culture" (Ortiz-Torres et al., 2000) by building on cultural values that enhance positive outcomes and transforming values that increase risk-taking (Harper et al., 2006; Villarruel et al., 2005). It has been demonstrated that shared cultural norms in cohesive Latino communities protect adolescents from teen pregnancy (Denner, Kirby, Coyle, & Brindis, 2001); thus, community-level action may be a key factor in successful interventions.

CLOSING THOUGHTS

A considerable amount of information regarding sexuality and sexual risk taking in Latino populations has been generated in recent years. However, as we hope this chapter has demonstrated, additional attention to the situation of Latino adolescents and young adults is warranted. There are several reasons that Latino youth merit the attention of sexuality researchers. First is the size and projected growth of this population. In 2000, Latino children and adolescents represented nearly one fifth (17%) of the under-18 population (Lugalla & Overturf, 2004), and this proportion is expected to increase to one third by the year 2050 (U.S. Department of Health and Human Services, 2001). Second, due to high rates of ongoing immigration from Latin America to the United States, issues of culture and acculturation will remain salient for Latinos and their children in the future. According to the 2000 census, 14% of Latino youth in the United States were foreign born, more than half had at least one foreign-born parent (56%), and three quarters spoke a language other than or in addition to English at home (Raffaelli, Carlo, Carranza, & Gonzalez-Kruger, 2005). Third, although Latino adolescents are disproportionately likely to experience negative sexual outcomes, only a handful of interventions have been developed for this population (National Campaign, 2007b). Taken in combination, these factors highlight the importance of focusing on sexuality and sexual risk taking among Latino adolescents and young adults. As one scholar noted, "Sexuality and sex roles within a culture tend to remain the last bastion of tradition" (Espín, 1984/1997, p. 93); thus, gaining a full understanding of Latino sexuality will require careful and explicit attention to culture.

Note

1. Sexuality among sexual-minority Latino adolescents and young adults is beyond the scope of this chapter, given the unique issues involved and the lack of research on normative sexuality in this diverse population. Studies of sexual-minority Latino youth have focused primarily on sexual risk behaviors among youth (e.g., Rotheram-Borus, Rosario, Reid, & Koopman, 1995) or in multi-age samples (e.g., Diaz & Ayala, 1999; Diaz, Ayala, & Bein, 2004; Muñoz-Laboy & Dodge, 2007). Thus, there is an urgent need for research exploring normative sexuality among GLBTQ Latino youth; possible topics for such work include adolescent or adult experiences (e.g., Consolacion, Russell, & Sue, 2004; D'Augelli, 1996; Diaz, Ayala, Bein, Henne, & Marín, 2001; Russell & Truong, 2001), sexual identity (e.g., Parks, Hughes, & Matthews, 2004; Rosario, Schrimshaw, & Hunter, 2004), and the variations in experiences among gay, lesbian, bisexual, and transgendered individuals (e.g., Espín, 1999; González & Espín, 1996; Nemoto, Operario, & Keatley, 2004; Rosario, 2004). Given the influence of culture and acculturation on sexual attitudes and behavior, this work should consider how culturally relevant factors affect sexuality and sexual risk taking among young sexual minority Latinos (e.g., Carballo-Diéguez et al., 2004; Greene, 1997; Harper, Jernewall, & Zea, 2004).

References

Afable-Munsuz, A., & Brindis, C. D. (2006). Acculturation and the sexual and reproductive health of Latino youth in the United States: A literature review. *Perspectives on Sexual and Reproductive Health, 38,* 208–219.

Alba, R. (2004). *Language assimilation today: Bilingualism persists more than in the past, but English still dominates* (Working Paper No. 111). San Diego, CA: Center for Comparative Immigration Studies, University of California.

Amaro, H. (1995). Love, sex, and power: Considering women's realities in HIV prevention. *American Psychologist, 50,* 437–447.

Barber, B., & Eccles, J. S. (2003). The joy of romance: Healthy adolescent relationships as an educational agenda. In P. Florsheim (Ed.), *Adolescent romantic relations and sexual behavior: Theory, research, and practical implications* (pp. 355–370). Mahwah, NJ: Lawrence Erlbaum.

Berry, J. W. (2007). Acculturation. In J. E. Grusec & P. D. Hastings (Eds.), *Handbook of socialization: Theory and research* (pp. 543–558). New York: Guilford Press.

Bowleg, L., Belgrave, F. Z., & Reisen, C. A. (2000). Gender roles, power strategies, and precautionary sexual self-efficacy: Implications for black and Latina women's HIV/AIDS protective behaviors. *Sex Roles, 42,* 613–635.

Carballo-Diéguez, A., Dolezal, C., Nieves Rosa, L., Diaz, F., Decena, C., & Balan, I. (2004). Looking for tall, dark, macho man . . . sexual-role behavior variations in Latino gay and bisexual men. *Culture, Health, & Sexuality, 6,* 159–171.

Carver, K. P., Joyner, K., & Udry, J. R. (2003). National estimates of adolescent romantic relationships. In P. Florsheim (Ed.), *Adolescent romantic relations and sexual behavior: Theory, research, and practice implications* (pp. 23–56). Mahwah, NJ: Lawrence Erlbaum.

Cauce, A. M., & Domenech-Rodríguez, M. D. (2002). Latino families: Myth and realities. In J. M. Contreras, K. A. Kerns, & A. M. Neal-Barnett (Eds.), *Latino children and families in the United States: Current research and future directions* (pp. 3–25). Westport, CT: Praeger.

Centers for Disease Control and Prevention (CDC). (2007a). *HIV/AIDS among Hispanic/Latinos.* Retrieved October 23, 2007, from http://www.cdc.gov/hiv/resources/factsheets/PDF/hispanic.pdf

Centers for Disease Control and Prevention (CDC). (2007b). *Youth Risk Behavior Surveillance System: Youth online comprehensive results.* Retrieved October 20, 2007, from http://apps.nccd.cdc.gov/yrbss/HealthTopic.asp

Christopher, F. S., & Roosa, M. W. (1991). Factors affecting sexual decisions in the premarital relationships of adolescents and young adults. In K. McKinney & S. Sprecher (Eds.), *Sexuality in close relationships* (pp. 111–133). Hillsdale, NJ: Lawrence Erlbaum.

Coatsworth, J. D., Pantin, H., & Szapocznik, J. (2002). *Familias Unidas:* A family-centered ecodevelopmental intervention to reduce risk for problem behavior among Hispanic adolescents. *Clinical Child and Family Psychology Review, 5,* 113–132.

Consolacion, T. B., Russell, S. T., & Sue, S. (2004). Sex, race/ethnicity, and romantic attractions: Multiple minority status adolescent and mental health [Special issue]. *Cultural Diversity and Ethnic Minority Psychology, 10,* 200–214.

Crockett, L. J., Raffaelli, M., & Moilanen, K. (2003). Adolescent sexuality: Behavior and meaning. In G. R. Adams & M. Berzonsky (Eds.), *Handbook of adolescence* (pp. 371–392). Malden, MA: Blackwell.

Crouter, A. C., & Booth, A. (Eds.). (2006). *Romance and sex in adolescence and emerging adulthood: Risks and opportunities.* Mahwah, NJ: Lawrence Erlbaum.

D'Augelli, A. R. (1996). Lesbian, gay, and bisexual development during adolescence and adulthood. In R. P. Cabaj & T. S. Stein (Eds.), *Textbook of homosexuality and mental health* (pp. 267–288). Washington, DC: American Psychiatric Press.

Day, J. C. (1996). Population projections of the United States by age, sex, race, and Hispanic origin: 1995 to 2050. *Current Population Reports,* P25–1130. Washington, DC: U.S. Census Bureau.

Denner, J., & Coyle, K. (2007). Condom use among sexually active Latina girls in alternative high schools. In B. J. R. Leadbeater & N. Way (Eds.), *Urban girls revisited: Building strengths* (pp. 281–300). New York: New York University Press.

Denner, J., & Dunbar, N. (2004). Negotiating femininity: Power and strategies of Mexican American girls. *Sex Roles, 50,* 301–314.

Denner, J., Kirby, D., Coyle, K., & Brindis, C. (2001). The protective role of social capital and cultural norms in Latino communities: A study of adolescent births. *Hispanic Journal of Behavioral Sciences, 23,* 3–21.

Diamond, L. M. (2006). Introduction: In search of good sexual-developmental pathways for adolescent girls. In R. Larson & L. Arnett Jensen (Series Eds.) & L. M. Diamond (Volume Ed.), *Rethinking positive adolescent female sexual development: New directions for child and adolescent development, No. 112* (pp. 1–7). San Francisco: Jossey-Bass.

Diaz, R. M., & Ayala, G. (1999). Love, passion and rebellion: Ideologies of HIV risk among Latino gay men in the USA. *Culture, Health, and Sexuality, 1,* 277–293.

Diaz, R. M., Ayala, G., & Bein, E. (2004). Sexual risk as an outcome of social oppression: Data from a probability sample of Latino gay men in three U.S. cities [Special issue]. *Cultural Diversity and Ethnic Minority Psychology, 10,* 255–267.

Diaz, R. M., Ayala, G., Bein, E., Henne, J., & Marín, B. V. (2001). The impact of homophobia, poverty, and racism on the mental health of gay and bisexual Latino men: Findings from 3 U.S. cities. *American Journal of Public Health, 91,* 927–932.

Doss, B. D., & Hopkins, J. R. (1998). The Multicultural Masculinity Ideology Scale: Validation from three cultural perspectives. *Sex Roles, 38,* 719–741.

Driscoll, A. K., Biggs, M. A., Brindis, C. D., & Yankah, E. (2001). Adolescent Latino reproductive health: A review of the literature. *Hispanic Journal of Behavioral Sciences, 23,* 255–326.

East, P. L. (1998). Racial and ethnic differences in girls' sexual, marital, and birth expectations. *Journal of Marriage and the Family, 60,* 150–162.

Eisenman, R., & Dantzker, M. L. (2006). Gender and ethnic differences in sexual attitudes at a Hispanic-serving university. *The Journal of General Psychology, 133,* 153–162.

Espin, O. M. (1984/1997). Cultural and historical influences on sexuality in Hispanic/Latin women: Implications for psychotherapy. In O. M. Espin (Ed.), *Latina realities: Essays on healing, migration, and sexuality* (pp. 83–96). Boulder, CO: Westview.

Espín, O. M. (1999). *Women crossing boundaries: A psychology of immigration and transformations of sexuality.* New York: Routledge.

Faulkner, S. L. (2003). Good girl or flirt girl: Latinas' definitions of sex and sexual relationships. *Hispanic Journal of Behavioral Sciences, 25,* 174–200.

Faulkner, S. L., & Mansfield, P. K. (2002). Reconciling messages: The process of sexual talk for Latinas. *Qualitative Health Research, 12,* 310–328.

Fernandez, M. I. (1995). Latinas and AIDS: Challenges to HIV prevention efforts. In A. O'Leary & L. S. Jemmott (Eds.), *Women at risk: Issues in the primary prevention of AIDS* (pp. 159–174). New York: Plenum Press.

Flores, E., Eyre, S., & Millstein, S. (1998). Sociocultural beliefs related to sex among Mexican American adolescents. *Hispanic Journal of Behavioral Sciences, 20,* 60–81.

Florsheim, P. (Ed.). (2003a). *Adolescent romantic relations and sexual behavior: Theory, research, and practical implications.* Mahwah, NJ: Lawrence Erlbaum.

Florsheim, P. (2003b). Adolescent romantic and sexual behavior: What we know and where we go from here. In P. Florsheim (Ed.), *Adolescent romantic relations and sexual behavior: Theory, research, and practical implications* (pp. 371–385). Mahwah, NJ: Lawrence Erlbaum.

Ford, K., & Norris, A. E. (1993). Urban Hispanic adolescent and young adults: Relationship of acculturation and sexual behavior. *Journal of Sex Research, 30,* 316–323.

Frankowski, B. L., & Committee on Adolescence. (2004). Sexual orientation and adolescents. *Pediatrics, 113,* 1827–1832.

Friedman, S. R., des Jarlais, D. C., & Ward, T. P. (1994). Social models for changing health-relevant behavior. In R. J. DiClemente & J. L. Peterson (Eds.), *Preventing AIDS: Theories and methods of behavioral interventions* (pp. 95–116). New York: Plenum Press.

Furman, W., Brown, B. B., & Feiring, C. (Eds.). (1997). *The development of romantic relationships in adolescence.* New York: Cambridge University Press.

Gallegos-Castillo, A. (2006). *La casa:* Negotiating family cultural practices, constructing identities. In J. Denner and B. L. Guzmán (Eds.), *Latina girls: Voices of adolescent strength in the United States* (pp. 44–58). New York: New York University Press.

Gilliam, M. L., Berlin, A., Kozloski, M., Hernandez, M., & Grundy, M. (2007). Interpersonal and personal factors influencing sexual debut among Mexican-American young women in the United States. *Journal of Adolescent Health, 41,* 495–503.

Gómez, C. A., & Marín, B. V. (1996). Gender, culture and power: Barriers to HIV prevention strategies. *Journal of Sex Research, 13,* 355–362.

Gonzales, N. A., Knight, G. P., & Birman, D. (2004). Acculturation and enculturation among Latino youth. In K. I. Maton, C. J. Schellenbach, B. J. Leadbeater, & A. L. Solarz (Eds.), *Investing in children, youth, families, and communities: Strength-based research and policy* (pp. 285–302). Washington, DC: American Psychological Association.

González, F. J., & Espín, O. M. (1996). Latino men, Latina women, and homosexuality. In R. P. Cabaj & T. S. Stein (Eds.), *Textbook of homosexuality and mental health* (pp. 583–601). Washington, DC: American Psychiatric Press.

González-López, G. (2004). Fathering Latina sexualities: Mexican men and the virginity of their daughters. *Journal of Marriage and Family, 66,* 1118–1130.

Goodyear, R. K., Newcomb, M. D., & Allison, R. D. (2000). Predictors of Latino men's paternity in teen pregnancy: Test of a mediational model of childhood experiences, gender role attitudes, and behaviors. *Journal of Counseling Psychology, 47,* 116–128.

Greene, B. (1997). *Ethnic and cultural diversity among lesbians and gay men.* Thousand Oaks, CA: Sage.

Guerra, N. G., & Jagers, R. (1998). The importance of culture in the assessment of children and youth. In V. C. McLoyd & L. Steinberg (Eds.), *Studying minority adolescents: Conceptual, methodological, and theoretical issues* (pp. 167–181). Mahwah, NJ: Lawrence Erlbaum.

Guilamo-Ramos, V., Jaccard, J., Pena, J., & Goldberg, V. (2005). Acculturation-related variables, sexual initiation, and subsequent sexual behavior among Puerto Rican, Mexican, and Cuban youth. *Health Psychology, 24,* 88–95.

Guzmán, B. (2001). *The Hispanic population: Census 2000 Brief* (C2KBR/01–3). Washington, DC: U.S. Census Bureau.

Guzmán, G. L., Arruda, E., & Feria, A. L. (2006). Los papas, la familia, y la sexualidad. In J. Denner & B. L. Guzmán (Eds.), *Latina girls: Voices of adolescent strength in the United States* (pp. 17–28). New York: New York University Press.

Hardin, M. (2002). Altering masculinities: The Spanish conquest and the evolution of the Latin American *machismo. International Journal of Sexuality and Gender Studies, 7,* 1–11.

Harper, G. W., Bangi, A. K., Sanchez, B., Doll, M., & Pedraza, A. (2006). Latina adolescents' sexual health: A participatory empowerment approach. In J. Denner & B. L. Guzmán (Eds.), *Latina girls: Voices of adolescent strength in the United States* (pp. 141–156). New York: New York University Press.

Harper, G. W., Jernewall, N., & Zea, M. C. (2004). Giving voice to emerging science and theory for lesbian, gay, and bisexual people of color [Special issue]. *Cultural Diversity and Ethnic Minority Psychology, 10,* 215–228.

Harvey, S. M., Henderson, J. T., Thorburn, S., Beckman, L. J., Casellas, A., Mendez. L., et al. (2004). A randomized study of a pregnancy and disease prevention intervention for Hispanic couples. *Perspectives on Sexual and Reproductive Health, 36,* 162–169.

Herbst, J. H., Kay, L. S., Passin, W. F., Lyles, C. M., Crepaz, H., & Marín, B. V. (2007). A systematic review and meta-analysis of behavioral interventions to reduce HIV risk behaviors of Hispanics in the United States and Puerto Rico. *AIDS and Behavior, 11,* 25–47.

Hirsch, J. S. (2000). *En El Norte, La Mujer Manda:* Gender, generation, and geography in a Mexican transnational community. In N. Foner, R. G. Rumbaut, & S. J. Gold (Eds.), *Immigration research for a new century: Multidisciplinary perspectives* (pp. 369–389). New York: Russell Sage.

Hovell, M., Sipan, C., Blumberg, E., Atkins, C., Hofsteter, C. R., & Kreitner, S. (1994). Family influences on Latino and Anglo adolescents' sexual behavior. *Journal of Marriage and the Family, 56,* 973–896.

Ibañez, G. E., Van Oss Marín, B., Villareal, C., & Gómez, C. A. (2005). Condom use at last sex among unmarried Latino men: An event level analysis. *AIDS and Behavior, 9,* 433–441.

Jimenez, J., Potts, M. K., & Jimenez, D. R. (2002). Reproductive attitudes and behavior among Latina adolescents. *Journal of Ethnic and Cultural Diversity in Social Work, 11,* 221–249.

Kline, A., Kline, E., & Oken, E. (1992). Minority women and sexual choice in the age of AIDS. *Social Science and Medicine, 34,* 447–457.

Kulis, S., Marsiglia, F. F., Lingard, R. C., Nieri, T., & Nagoshi, J. (2008). Gender identity and substance use among students in two high schools in Monterrey, Mexico. *Drug and Alcohol Dependence, 95,* 258–268.

Lefkowitz, E. S. (2002). Beyond the yes-no question: Measuring parent-adolescent communication about sex. In W. Damon (Series Ed.) & S. S. Feldman & D. A. Rosenthal (Volume Eds.), *Talking sexuality: Parent-adolescent communication: New directions for child and adolescent development,* No. 97, 43–56. San Francisco: Jossey-Bass.

Liebowitz, S. W., Castellano, D. C., & Cuellar, I. (1999). Factors that predict sexual behaviors among young Mexican American adolescents: An exploratory study. *Hispanic Journal of Behavioral Sciences, 21,* 470–479.

Lonner, W. J., & Malpass, R. S. (1994). When psychology and culture meet: An introduction to cross-cultural psychology. In W. J. Lonner & R. S. Malpass (Eds.), *Psychology and culture* (pp. 1–15). Boston: Allyn & Bacon.

Lugalla, T., & Overturf, J. (2004). Children and the households they live in: 2000. *Census 2000 Special Reports, CENSR-14.* Washington, DC: U.S. Census Bureau.

Magana, J. R., & Carrier, J. M. (1991). Mexican and Mexican American male sexual behavior and spread of AIDS in California. *Journal of Sex Research, 28,* 425–441.

Manlove, J., Franzetta, K., Ryan, S., & Moore, K. (2006). Adolescent sexual relationships, contraceptive consistency, and pregnancy prevention approaches. In A. C. Crouter & A. Booth (Eds.), *Romance and sex in adolescence and emerging adulthood: Risks and opportunities* (pp. 181–212). Mahwah, NJ: Lawrence Erlbaum.

Manlove, J., Ryan, S., & Franzetta, K. (2007). Risk and protective factors associated with the transition to a first sexual relationship with an older partner. *Journal of Adolescent Health, 40,* 135–143.

Manlove, J., & Terry-Humen, E. (2007). Contraceptive use patterns within females' first sexual relationships: The role of relationships, partners, and methods. *Journal of Sex Research, 44,* 3–16.

Marín, B. V. (2003). HIV prevention in the Hispanic community: Sex, culture, and empowerment. *Journal of Transcultural Nursing, 14,* 186–192.

Marín, B. V., Coyle, K. K., Gómez, C. A., Carvajal, S. C., & Kirby, D. B. (2000). Older boyfriends and girlfriends increase risk of sexual initiation in young adolescents. *Journal of Adolescent Health, 27,* 409–418.

Marín, B. V., & Gómez, C. A. (1997). Latino culture and sex: Implications for HIV prevention. In J. Garcia & M. Zea (Eds.), *Psychological interventions and research with Latino populations* (pp. 73–93). Boston: Allyn & Bacon.

Marín, B. V., Gómez, C. A., Tschann, J. M., & Gregorich, S. E. (1997). Condom use in unmarried Latino men: A test of cultural constructs. *Health Psychology, 16,* 458–467.

Marín, B. V., Kirby, D. B., Hudes, E. S., Coyle, K. K., & Gómez, C. A. (2006). Boyfriends, girlfriends and teenagers' risk of sexual involvement. *Perspectives on Sexual and Reproductive Health, 38,* 76–83.

Marín, G., & Marín, B. V. (1991). *Research with Hispanic populations.* Newbury Park, CA: Sage.

Marín, B. V., Tschann, J. M., Gomez, C. A., & Kegeles, S. M. (1993). Acculturation and gender differences in sexual attitudes and behaviors: Hispanic vs. non-Hispanic White unmarried adults. *American Journal of Public Health, 83,* 1759–1761.

McKee, M. D., & Karasz, A. (2006). "You have to give her that confidence": Conversations about sex in Hispanic mother-daughter dyads. *Journal of Adolescent Research, 21,* 158–184.

McLoyd, V. C. (2004). Linking race and ethnicity to culture: Steps along the road from inference to hypothesis testing. *Human Development, 47,* 185–191.

Miller, B. C., & Benson, B. (1999). Romantic and sexual relationship development during adolescence. In B. Brown, C. Feiring, & W. Furman (Eds.), *The development of romantic relationships in adolescence* (pp. 99–121). New York: Cambridge University Press.

Muñoz-Laboy, M., & Dodge, B. (2007). Bisexual Latino men and HIV and sexually transmitted infections risk: An exploratory analysis. *American Journal of Public Health, 97,* 1102–1106.

National Campaign to Prevent Teen Pregnancy. (2006). *Teen pregnancy and childbearing among Latinos in the United States* (Fact Sheet). Washington, DC: Author.

National Campaign to Prevent Teen Pregnancy. (2007a). *A look at Latinos: An overview of Latina teen pregnancy.* Retrieved October 23, 2007, from http://www.teenpregnancy.org/

National Campaign to Prevent Teen Pregnancy. (2007b). *Effective and promising teen pregnancy prevention programs for Latino youth.* Retrieved April 17, 2008, from http://www.teenpregnancy.org/

Neff, A. J. (2001). A confirmatory factor analysis of a measure of "machismo" among Anglo, African American, and Mexican American male drinkers. *Hispanic Journal of Behavioral Sciences, 23,* 171–188.

Nemoto, T., Operario, D., & Keatley, J. (2004). HIV risk behaviors among male-to-female transgender persons of color in San Francisco. *American Journal of Public Health, 94,* 1193–1199.

Ortiz-Torres, B., Serrano-Garcia, I., & Torres-Burgos, N. (2000). Subverting culture: Promoting HIV/AIDS prevention among Puerto Rican and Dominican women. *American Journal of Community Psychology, 28,* 859–881.

Ortiz-Torres, B., Williams, S. P., & Ehrhardt, A. (2003). Urban women's gender scripts: Implications for HIV prevention. *Culture, Health, and Sexuality, 5,* 1–17.

Parke, R. D., & Buriel, R. (1998) Socialization in the family: Ethnic and ecological perspectives. In N. Eisenberg (Ed.), *Handbook of child psychology: Vol. 3. Social, emotional, and personality development* (5th ed., pp. 463–552). New York: John Wiley.

Parks, C. A., Hughes, T. L., & Matthews, A. K. (2004). Race/ethnicity and sexual orientation: Intersecting identities [Special issue]. *Cultural Diversity and Ethnic Minority Psychology, 10,* 241–254.

Pérez-Jiménez, D., Cunningham, I., Serrano-Garcia, I., & Ortiz-Torres, B. (2007). Construction of male sexuality and gender roles in Puerto Rican heterosexual college students. *Men and Masculinities, 9,* 358–378.

Pew Research Center. (2007). *Changing faiths: Latinos and the transformation of American Religion.* Retrieved January 23, 2008, from http://pewhispanic.org/reports/report.php?ReportID=75

Pleck, J. H., Sonenstein, F. L., & Ku, L. C. (1993). Masculine ideology: Its impact on adolescent males' heterosexual relationships. *Journal of Social Issues, 49,* 11–29.

Pulerwitz, J., Amaro, H., DeJong, W., Gortmaker, S. L., & Rudd, R. (2002). Relationship power, condom use and HIV risk among women in the U.S.A. *AIDS Care, 14,* 789–800.

Raffaelli, M. (2005). Adolescent dating experiences described by Latino college students. *Journal of Adolescence, 28,* 559–572.

Raffaelli, M., Carlo, G., Carranza, M., & Gonzalez-Kruger, G. (2005). Understanding Latino

children and adolescents in the mainstream: Placing culture at the center of developmental models. In R. Larson & L. Arnett Jensen (Eds.), *New horizons in developmental theory and research: New directions for child and adolescent development, No. 109* (pp. 23–32). San Francisco: Jossey-Bass.

Raffaelli, M., & Green, S. (2003). Parent-adolescent communication about sex: Retrospective reports by Latino college students. *Journal of Marriage and Family, 65,* 474–481.

Raffaelli, M., & Ontai, L. L. (2001). "She's 16 years old and there's boys calling over to the house": An exploratory study of sexual socialization in Latino families. *Culture, Health, and Sexuality, 3,* 295–310.

Raffaelli, M., & Ontai, L. L. (2004). Gender socialization in Latino/a families: Results from two retrospective studies. *Sex Roles: A Journal of Research, 50,* 287–299.

Raffaelli, M., & Suarez-al-Adam, M. (1998). Reconsidering the HIV prevention needs of Latino women in the United States. In N. L. Roth & L. K. Fullers (Eds.), *Women and AIDS: Negotiating safer practices, care, and representation* (pp. 7–41). New York: Haworth.

Raffaelli, M., Zamboanga, B. L., & Carlo, G. (2005). Acculturation processes and sexuality among Cuban-American college students. *Journal of American College Health, 54,* 7–13.

Reid, P. T., Haritos, C., Kelly, E., & Holland, N. E. (1995). Socialization of girls: Issues of ethnicity in gender development. In H. Landrine (Ed.), *Bringing cultural diversity to feminist psychology: Theory, research, and practice* (pp. 93–111). Washington, DC: American Psychological Association.

Romo, L. F., Lefkowitz, E. S., Sigman, M., & Au, T. K. (2001). Determinants of mother-adolescent communication about sex in Latino families. *Adolescent and Family Health, 2,* 72–82.

Rosario, M., Schrimshaw, E. W., & Hunter, J. (2004). Ethnic/racial differences in the coming-out process of lesbian, gay, and bisexual youths: A comparison of sexual identity development over time [Special issue]. *Cultural Diversity and Ethnic Minority Psychology, 10,* 187–199.

Rosario, V. A. (2004). 'Qué joto bonita!': Transgender negotiations of sex and ethnicity. *Journal of Gay and Lesbian Psychotherapy, 8,* 89–97.

Rossi, A. S. (Ed.). (1994). *Sexuality across the life course.* Chicago: University of Chicago Press.

Rotheram-Borus, M. J., Rosario, M., Reid, H., & Koopman, C. (1995). Predicting patterns of sexual acts among homosexual and bisexual youths. *American Journal of Psychiatry, 152,* 588–595.

Rubenstein, W. B., Sears, R. B., & Sockloskie, R. J. (2003). *Some demographic characteristics of the gay community in the United States.* Los Angeles: University of California. Retrieved May 14, 2007, from http://www.law.ucla.edu/williams institute/publications/GayDemographics.pdf

Russell, S. T., & Truong, N. L. (2001). Adolescent sexual orientation, race and ethnicity, and school environments: A national study of sexual minority youth of color. In K. K. Kumashiro (Ed.), *Troubling intersections of race and sexuality: Queer students of color and anti-oppressive education* (pp. 113–130). New York: Rowman & Littlefield.

Sabogal, F., Faigeles, B., & Catania, J. A. (1993). Multiple sexual partners among Hispanics in high-risk cities. *Family Planning Perspectives, 25,* 257–262.

Sabogal, F., Pérez-Stable, E. J., Otero-Sabogal, R., & Hiatt, R. A. (1995). Gender, ethnic, and acculturation differences in sexual behavior: Hispanic and non-Hispanic White adults. *Hispanic Journal of Behavioral Sciences, 17,* 139–159.

Scott, K. D., Gilliam, A., & Braxton, K. (2005). Culturally competent HIV prevention strategies for women of color in the United States. *Health Care for Women International, 26,* 17–45.

Seal, D. W., Wagner-Raphael, L. I., & Ehrhardt, A. A. (2000). Sex, intimacy, and HIV: An ethnographic study of a Puerto Rican social group in New York City. *Journal of Psychology and Human Sexuality, 11,* 51–92.

Shulman, S., & Collins, W. A. (Eds.). (1997). *Romantic relationships in adolescence: Developmental perspectives.* San Francisco: Jossey-Bass.

Simon, W., & Gagnon, J. H. (1986). Sexual scripts: Permanence and change. *Archives of Sexual Behavior, 15,* 97–120.

Simon, W., & Gagnon, J. H. (1987). A sexual scripts approach. In J. H. Geer & W. T. O'Donohue (Eds.), *Theories of human sexuality* (pp. 363–383). New York: Plenum Press.

Taylor, J. M. (1996). Cultural stories: Latina and Portuguese daughters and mothers. In B. J. R. Leadbeater & N. Way (Eds.), *Urban girls: Resisting stereotypes, creating identities*

(pp. 117–131). New York: New York University Press.

U.S. Department of Health and Human Services. (2001). *Mental health: Culture, race and ethnicity—Supplement to Mental health: A report of the surgeon general.* Rockville, MD: Author.

Vexler, E. (2007). *Voices heard: Latino adults and teens speak up about teen pregnancy.* Washington, DC: National Campaign to Prevent Teen Pregnancy.

Vigoya, M. V. (2001). Contemporary Latin American perspectives on masculinity. *Men and Masculinities, 3,* 237–260.

Villarruel, A. M. (1998). Cultural influences on the sexual attitudes, beliefs, and norms of young Latina adolescents. *Journal of the Society of Pediatric Nurses, 3,* 69–79.

Villarruel, A. M., Jemmott, J. B., & Jemmott, L. S. (2006). A randomized controlled trial testing an HIV prevention intervention for Latino youth. *Archives of Pediatric and Adolescent Medicine, 160,* 722–777.

Villarruel, A. M., Jemmott, J. B., Jemmott, L. S., & Ronis, D. L. (2007). Predicting condom use among sexually experienced Latino adolescents. *Western Journal of Nursing Research, 29,* 724–738.

Villarruel, A. M., Jemmott, L. S., & Jemmott, J. B. (2005). Designing a culturally based intervention to reduce HIV sexual risk for Latino adolescents. *Journal of the Association of Nurses in AIDS Care, 16*(2), 23–31.

Villarruel, A. M., & Rodriguez, D. (2003). Beyond stereotypes: Promoting safer sex behaviors among Latino adolescents. *Journal of Obstetric, Gynecologic, and Neonatal Nursing, 32,* 258–263.

Zane, N., & Mak, W. (2003). Major approaches to the measurement of acculturation among ethnic minority populations: A content analysis and an alternative empirical strategy. In K. M. Chun, P. B. Organista, & G. Marín (Eds.), *Acculturation: Advances in theory, measurement, and applied research* (pp. 39–60). Washington, DC: American Psychological Association.

24

Perspectives and Recommendations for Future Directions in U.S. Latino Psychology

Gustavo Carlo, Francisco A. Villarruel, Margarita Azmitia, and Natasha J. Cabrera

Editing a major volume in the field of U.S. Latino psychology offers an opportunity to reflect on the state of the field and to speculate on the future. In this chapter, we first present some of our observations of the state of the psychological research on U.S. Latinos. Our observations are based on our reading of the chapters and reflect our personal perspectives regarding research in this dynamic, growing area of research. We then look ahead and, whenever possible, highlight specific recommendations for researchers, policymakers, and practitioners that need to be undertaken to further our understanding of Latinos in the United States and to develop more effective programs.

Many scholars have asserted that most extant research on Latinos and other minority groups has been problem focused, resulting in models that emphasized deficits and pathology. Furthermore, such research is likely to focus on low-socioeconomic status (SES) Latinos rather than

on middle- and upper-SES Latinos. Although this research is useful because it can further our understanding of a narrow range of the U.S. Latino population, it is also very limiting. It tells us little about normative developmental trajectories of U.S. Latinos across the spectrum of SES and often does not consider how such factors as generational status might contribute to and influence normative development. Perhaps more troubling is that such limited research might promote the development of intervention and policy programs with suspect validity for use with some Latino populations. In contrast, the scholarship represented in this book highlights U.S. Latinos' personal and social strengths and assets. We believe that an emphasis on strength-based and normative research will likely result in more variation in study topics, which fosters a more holistic and balanced perspective on understanding U.S. Latinos. Based on these observations, we recommend that researchers continue to conduct research with normative populations that highlights strengths, resilience, and well-being. When this research is integrated with problem-focused approaches, it will provide a more comprehensive view of U.S. Latinos, which will contribute to the development of theories and policies that benefit Latinos across SES and generational status.

Many authors acknowledge that Latinos are very diverse in terms of country of origin and geographical location, but to date there is a paucity of research addressing that diversity. Recent research has been conducted with Cubans and Puerto Ricans in addition to Mexicans, but much more work is needed on other Latino groups (especially on peoples from Central and South America). As some scholars have noted, disparities in different health outcomes have been reported among Mexicans, Cubans, and Puerto Ricans (see, for example, Betancourt & Flynn, Chapter 20, this volume; Buki & Selem, Chapter 21, this volume). Some of these disparities are likely due to the different historical, sociopolitical, socioeconomic, and physical characteristics among Latino people from different countries. However, differences in psychological and behavioral outcomes are also likely due to differences among Latinos in the receiving community. Different regions and communities in the United States are likely to make available to Latinos different social support services and resources. Another potential source of variation is mixed-heritage Latinos, whose degree of identification with the Latino part of their heritage, their physical characteristics, and their experiences with prejudice and discrimination are likely to be different from those of Latinos and non-Latinos. We recommend funding support to encourage research efforts with a broad range of Latinos from different origins and SES, as well as in different regions of the United States, and in receiving communities with unique characteristics. We also recommend transnational research that contrasts the experiences, development, and outcomes of U.S. Latinos and Latinos living outside the United States. This research will help us assess the uniqueness of the U.S. experience and will provide further information about changes in Latino cultural values, goals, and practices as the result of immigration and acculturation.

The chapters in this volume represent a wide range of current scholarship on issues related to Latino families' adjustment and adaptation in the United States. Much of the science-based knowledge that psychologists have accumulated on family processes—including parenting, mental health, and adaptation—has been based on samples of convenience, which very often do not represent the demographic diversity of the United States. Consequently, our understanding of how ethnic minority families function and adapt in the United States has been hindered by a lack of representation in the science about how families develop, adapt, and thrive in the U.S. context. More seriously, some of our public policies and interventions aimed at Latino families have been based on science conducted with other groups, and little attention has been paid to its applicability to Latino populations. This volume, then, takes to heart the ecological premise that context is a powerful determinant of individuals' behaviors, motivations, beliefs, and overall well-being. It offers scholarship that acknowledges diversity and complexity, highlights promising lines of research as well as limitations, and offers a view toward the future. To this end, the chapters in this handbook meet multiple goals: (1) They offer an extensive and comprehensive review of what we know about Latinos in the United States, highlighting areas of scientific maturity and other areas where the science is at its infancy and thus provide guidance for the next generation of studies; (2) they advance our understanding of the complexity of issues facing Latinos by moving away from linear and simple models of research, analysis, and interventions to provide a more nuanced and complex picture of the mechanisms by which process occur, of the necessity to disentangle ethnicity from socioeconomic class, of the confounding effects of acculturation on family processes, of the notion that culture is a dynamic concept, and of the meaning of cultural beliefs and values considering the heterogeneity of the Latino population in the United States; and (3) they offer a cohesive and comprehensive analysis of existing interventions aimed at improving the life condition of Latinos. Consequently, the *Handbook of U.S. Latino Psychology* becomes an indispensable tool in the scientific community to advance basic research, policies, and interventions programs for Latinos in the United States.

A comprehensive understanding of Latinos begins with theory and research on child and adolescent development. Thus, several chapters focus on foundational developmental processes. For example, Quintana and Scull (Chapter 6) offer a cognitive developmental understanding of basic processes of cognition among Latino children to understand identity and ethnic formation. Also, Carlo and de Guzman (Chapter 12) summarize and critique traditional and contemporary theories and research in prosocial and moral competencies, with an emphasis on their relevance and applicability to Latino populations. However, to better understand the complexity of behavioral outcomes in Latinos, research is needed that examines the changes across time due to the confluence of biological and socialization-based processes. Moreover, it is our impression that most developmental work focuses on early childhood and adolescence; much more research is needed across other periods of the life span. One specific recommendation that would greatly advance our understanding of Latinos in the United States is to develop and support a large, long-term longitudinal study of Latinos that is representative of the population. There are, for example, a couple of national studies that now include national samples of Latinos (e.g., ECLSB and the Immigrant Survey), but there is no national study that focuses only on Latinos. Thus, although there have been significant advancements in the scholarship involving U.S. Latinos, the opportunity and need still exist for additional focus and attention on developmental issues using culturally relevant theoretical perspectives.

The family is a central context of development, and thus the handbook also covers a range of issues of critical importance to our understanding of Latino families in the United States. For example, Chapter 10, on parenting and family processes (Grau, Azmitia, & Quattlebaum), links Latino children and adolescents' adjustment across the socioemotional, cognitive, educational, and peer domains to their parents' cultural values and socialization goals in the context of immigration and acculturation. Taking a more problem-focused approach, Bernal, Sáez-Santiago, and Galloza-Carrero (Chapter 18) review the state of the science in psychological evidence-based treatments (EBT) for Latino children, adolescents, and families, as well as specific treatments and for "whom and under what circumstances and why" they are most effective. In addition, Chapter 22, on substance use among Latino adolescents

(Crockett & Zamboanga), considers how cultural, social, and psychological factors influence adolescents' substance use. Canino and Alegría (Chapter 3) advance our understanding on psychopathology among adult and child Latino populations by offering an epidemiologic perspective and a review of the literature that examines the prevalence of psychiatric disorders and their associated correlates among Latino children and adults living in the United States and Puerto Rico.

In addition to these central areas of Latino theory, research, and policy, we have included chapters on emerging fields that promise to enrich the field of Latino psychology as well as raise complex ethical issues that must be considered as we move forward. For example, in Chapter 11, on feminist psychology, Hurtado and Cervantez focus on identity and feminism, including feminist theory, and discuss activist scholarship that will result in the implementation of research to policy arenas, a stand that promises to influence areas beyond the academy. Finally, Singer, Fisher, Hodge, Saleheen, and Mahadevan (Chapter 5) focus on ethical issues in conducting research with Latino drug users and examine cultural and linguistic features of the Latino population, as well as several notable social and health disparities that contribute to special ethical challenges in conducting research with Latinos. They report findings from recent research that explores Latino participant perspectives on ethical issues in involvement in health-related research as one strategy for confronting the ethical dilemmas raised by this and other research with Latinos.

While we believe that these and all the other chapters in the handbook advance the field of U.S. Latino psychology, there is one critical issue that all research scientists dedicated to research on U.S. Latinos need to keep at the forefront of their scholarship. This issue is the development of conceptual frameworks that foster research that tests specific hypotheses about expected differences among Latinos and other ethnic groups and why such differences exist. This work would help identify concepts and mechanisms specific to Latinos, as well as those that cut across other ethnic groups. This work would also help develop policies and interventions that benefit Latinos and allow for the integration of findings from different domains and periods of the life span. Finally, this research would help construct transnational models that help contextualize the unique experiences of Latinos in the United States. To date, the literature is piecemeal, and cross talk among scholars working in different fields and different periods of development has been limited. Some conceptual models and theories are available, but research testing aspects of some of those theories is lagging. Based on these observations, we recommend developing new theories and conceptual models, and enriching existing ones, by promoting and supporting multidisciplinary research efforts—efforts across major disciplines (including philosophy, education, medicine, anthropology, political science, sociology) as well as within different areas of psychology (e.g., social, developmental, community, clinical).

One welcome direction that will support the expansion and creation of new theories and policies is scholars' growing focus on methodological challenges in furthering research with Latinos. For example, investigators have begun to examine the psychometric properties of measures used with Latinos and to test the equivalence of models across different ethnic groups. Such research is valuable to ensure that measures are psychometrically adequate and to examine the universality or cultural specificity of psychological and behavioral models. Furthermore, the application of more sophisticated statistical techniques (such as confirmatory factor analyses and structural equation modeling) provides opportunity for more stringent tests of such measures and models, to ensure that measurement error and biases are minimized. To apply these more sophisticated analytical techniques, it will be necessary to design more sophisticated investigations with large sample sizes. However, it is important not to undervalue qualitative and more basic descriptive research, which furthers the accumulation of a rich foundation of knowledge and information regarding Latinos in the United States. Thus, we recommend that qualitative as well as quantitative, descriptive as well as explanatory research efforts are needed to adequately address the gaps in the literature. These more complex quantitative, qualitative, and mixed-methods approaches will require that we review the training of new scholars to ensure that they have the tools to take on this challenge.

Moreover, we believe that the field of scholarship can and should be broader than what is represented in this volume. Numerous issues could not be covered simply due to lack of space; for example, the concept of ambiguous loss resulting from repatriation of law-abiding immigrants, and the psychological impact that this has on family members who may remain in the United States without social support systems; resiliency among laborers who leave their families in their host nation or in different areas of the United States as they seek a living wage; the resilience of U.S. Latino students who attend predominantly white institutions of higher education and cope with the reality of being "*entre dos mundos*"; the stress and resilience associated with seasonal labor, or with labor markets in which U.S. Latinos predominate in the rebuilding of communities after natural disasters; the influence of media on U.S. Latino youth identity formation; and the developmental impact and consequences of child language brokers.

We strongly believe that efforts that follow this and the other recommendations hold much promise for a strong and vibrant future in U.S. Latino psychology, one that will further our understanding of adaptation and adjustment and result in more effective intervention and social policy efforts that improve the lives of all Latinos and move us toward a more equitable and just society.

Author Index

Page numbers with an f or a t indicate a figure or table respectively.

Subject Index

Page numbers with an f or a t indicate a figure or table respectively.

About the Contributors

Margarita Alegría, PhD, is the director of the Center for Multicultural Mental Health Research (CMMHR) at the Cambridge Health Alliance. She is a professor of psychology in the Department of Psychiatry at Harvard Medical School and currently serves as the principal investigator of three National Institutes of Health–funded research studies. Dr. Alegría's published work focuses on the improvement of health-care services delivery for diverse racial and ethnic populations, conceptual and methodological issues with multicultural populations, and ways to bring the community's perspective into the design and implementation of health services. Dr. Alegría also conducts research that will contribute to an understanding of the factors influencing service disparities and tests interventions aimed at reducing disparities for ethnic and racial minority groups. Her other work has highlighted the importance of contextual, social, and individual factors that intersect with nativity and are associated with the risk for psychiatric disorders. In conducting this work, she has actively mentored numerous students and junior investigators. As a result of her contributions to her field, Dr. Alegría has received the 2003 Mental Health Section Award of the American Public Health Association, the 2006 Greenwood Award for Research Excellence, and the 2007 Latino Mental Health Scientific Leadership Award from New York Medical School. In 2008, she received the Carl Taube Award from the Mental Health Section of the American Public Health Association. She is a member of the Institute of Medicine's Public Health Board and recently finished a term as chair of Academy Health.

Edna C. Alfaro is a doctoral student in the School of Social and Family Dynamics at Arizona State University. She completed her undergraduate studies in psychology at St. Mary's University, San Antonio, and obtained a master's degree in human development and family studies from the University of Illinois at Urbana-Champaign. Her research focuses on examining how individual, relational, and contextual characteristics relate to Latino adolescents' academic outcomes.

Anabel Alvarez-Jimenez is currently completing her postdoctoral fellowship at Jackson Memorial Hospital. She received her PhD in clinical psychology from Georgia State University. Her research interests include understanding the positive and negative implications of filial responsibilities on Latino youth's development and the ways in which the field of psychology incorporates and addresses multiculturalism.

Steven R. Applewhite, PhD, MSW, is an associate professor at the Graduate College of Social Work at the University of Houston. He received his doctorate and master's degrees from the University of Michigan and teaches in the areas of gerontology, community development, human behavior and social environment, and cultural diversity. He has published in gerontology and social work and edited the book *Hispanic Elderly in Transition.* His research interests include aging and health-care disparities, Latino mental health, access and utilization of aging programs and services, community and organizational development, and culturally competent systems of care. He serves on national boards and commissions and is a founding board member of the National Hispanic Council on Aging.

Margarita Azmitia, a developmental psychologist and a native of Guatemala, is a professor of psychology at the University of California,

Santa Cruz. Her research focuses on the role of close relationships with family and peers in ethnically and socioeconomically diverse adolescents' and young adults' developmental transitions, educational trajectories, and identity development. Currently, she serves on the Executive Council of the Society for Research on Adolescence and the Executive Committee of the International Society for the Study of Behavioral Development.

Guillermo Bernal, PhD, is a professor of psychology and director of the Institute for Psychological Research at the University of Puerto Rico, Río Piedras. He received his doctorate in psychology (clinical) from the University of Massachusetts, Amherst, in 1978 and is a fellow of the American Psychological Association (Divisions 45, 12, and 27). His work has focused on training, research, and the development of mental health services responsive to ethnic minorities. His current work is on the efficacy of parent interventions in the treatment of depression in adolescents (funded by the National Institute of Mental Health). His most recent books are *The Theory and Practice of Psychotherapy in Puerto Rico* (2008) and *The Handbook of Racial and Ethnic Minority Psychology* (2003). He is the associate editor for research of the journal *Family Process*.

Hector Betancourt received his PhD from the University of California, Los Angeles, and holds positions as professor of psychology at Loma Linda University, California, and Universidad de La Frontera, Chile, where he leads research programs on culture and social inequities in education and health. His research (www.cultureandbehavior.org) has been funded by the National Institutes of Health in the United States and by the Comisión Nacional de Investigación Cientifica y Tecnológica (CONICYT) in Chile). Dr. Betancourt is a fellow of the American Psychological Association and in 2007 was distinguished as Psychologist of the Year by the Chilean Psychological Association. He has served on the boards of the Society for the Study of Peace, Conflict, and Violence; the Society for the Psychological Study of Social Issues; Psychologists for Social Responsibility; and the Interamerican Society of Psychology. He has also served on the editorial boards of the *Journal of Personality and Social Psychology*; *Peace and Conflict*; the *Journal of Community Psychology*; *Revista de Psicologia Social* (Spain); *Interdiciplinaria* (Argentina); and *Psykhe* (Chile).

Joaquin Borrego, Jr., is an associate professor and the associate director of clinical training in the Department of Psychology at Texas Tech University. He received his PhD in clinical psychology from the University of Nevada, Reno. His clinical research focuses on the impact of culture on parenting and discipline practices, and on examining the social validity of parent training programs with Mexican-origin families. He also has an interest in the behavioral assessment and treatment of interpersonal family violence, such as child physical abuse and domestic violence. He is the director of the Parent-Child Interaction Therapy (PCIT) program at Texas Tech University. He also serves on several journal editorial boards and is the associate editor for the journal *Cognitive and Behavioral Practice*.

Lydia P. Buki, a counseling psychologist who grew up in Argentina, is an associate professor in the Department of Kinesiology and Community Health at the University of Illinois. Her main research interest is in the association between health literacy and health outcomes in Latina/o populations, with a special focus on cancer detection and survivorship. As principal investigator of a project funded by the National Cancer Institute, she recently examined immigrant women's health literacy with respect to breast and cervical cancer. Currently, Dr. Buki chairs the American Psychological Association's Committee on Women in Psychology. Her advocacy on behalf of Latina women has been recognized with national and campus awards.

Natasha J. Cabrera, a developmental/educational psychologist, is an associate professor in the Human Development Department at the University of Maryland. Her research focuses on variation in parenting among low-income families, the role of fathers in child development, the mechanism by which mothers and fathers influence their children's cognitive and social development, and the role of culture in parenting and child outcomes. She is the coauthor of *The Handbook of Father Involvement: Multidisciplinary Perspectives.* Her work has been published in *Child Development*, the *Journal of Marriage and Family, Parenting*, and *Sex Roles*.

Carlos O. Calderón-Tena is a doctoral student in school psychology at Arizona State University.

His research and professional interests include the relation between cultural and psychosocial factors, and psychoeducational and health outcomes among culturally and linguistically diverse populations, particularly immigrant children and adolescents. Born and raised in Mexico, Carlos received his undergraduate degree from La Sierra University in Riverside, California. He received his master's degree in social psychology from Arizona State University.

Glorisa J. Canino, PhD, is a professor in the School of Medicine, Department of Pediatrics, and the director of the Behavioral Sciences Research Institute at the University of Puerto Rico. She is presently principal investigator of two grants and co-investigator of three others funded by the National Institutes of Health. Dr. Canino is on the editorial boards of the *Journal of Child Development* and the *Puerto Rico Health Sciences Journal* and serves as an ad hoc reviewer of several high-impact peer review journals. As a leading Latino researcher in the field of psychiatric epidemiology and psychometrics, she has an established history of international collaboration. Dr. Canino has an outstanding track record in the study of Latino health issues. She has been the principal investigator of more than six psychiatric epidemiological studies conducted on the island of Puerto Rico. As the director of a well-established research institute at the University of Puerto Rico and the principal investigator of the UPR/CHA Advanced EXPORT Disparity Center, she is a leading researcher in the fields of mental health and asthma disparities, psychiatric epidemiology, psychometrics, and pediatric asthma and is an international expert on Latino health issues. She has received two president's awards of science and technology and has been named a Distinguished Investigator by the University of Puerto Rico. She was awarded the National Award of Excellence in Research by a Senior Scientist by the National Hispanic Science Network. At present, she is a member of the National Advisory Council of the National Institute of Mental Health and a committee member of two work groups for the development of the *Diagnostic and Statistical Manual of Mental Disorders,* 5th edition (DSM-V).

Esteban V. Cardemil is an associate professor at Clark University. He received his PhD in clinical psychology in 2000 from the University of Pennsylvania. His research focuses on the effects of race, ethnicity, and social class on psychopathology, with a particular emphasis on the development of prevention interventions for depression. Dr. Cardemil has been principal investigator on grants from the National Science Foundation, the National Institute of Mental Health, and the National Alliance for Research on Schizophrenia and Depression. Dr. Cardemil is currently co-investigator of a William T. Grant Foundation award to examine how the provision of parental structure is related to competence, adjustment, and achievement in a sample of Caucasian and Latino adolescents during their transition to junior high school.

Gustavo Carlo is the Carl A. Happold Distinguished Professor of Psychology at the University of Nebraska–Lincoln. Dr. Carlo is a developmental psychologist and a native of Puerto Rico. His main research interest is in the roles of personality, parenting, and culture on prosocial and moral development. His research has been supported by grants from the National Science Foundation and the National Institutes of Health, and he received a Research Excellence Award in Positive Psychology from the American Psychological Association and the John Templeton Foundation. Dr. Carlo also comanages a Latino youth mentoring program and serves on the board of various community organizations.

Karina Cervantez is a doctoral student in the social psychology program at the University of California, Santa Cruz. Her research interests include the social context of education, activism and political identities, and feminist theory. She received her BA in psychology from the University of California, Santa Cruz.

T. Jaime Chahin, MSW, PhD, is a professor and dean of the College of Applied Arts at Texas State University. He has been at the university since 1987, prior to which he served as a senior policy analyst for the Select Committee for Higher Education of Texas. His research interests involve immigrants and cultural and public policy issues that impact access to higher education. His most recent research work involves Caminos, a project for at-risk youth. He also was executive producer of the award-winning PBS documentary *The Forgotten Americans,* which depicts the living conditions and policy issues of *colonia* residents on the U.S.-Mexico border.

Lisa J. Crockett is a professor of psychology at the University of Nebraska–Lincoln. Her research interests include adolescent risk behaviors, especially sexual behavior and substance use, as well as ethnic similarities and differences in the relations between parenting behaviors and adolescents' psychological and behavioral adjustment. Her research has been supported by grants from the National Institutes of Health (NICHD, NIAAA). She is a former associate editor of the *Journal of Research on Adolescence* and currently chairs the Publications Committee of the Society for Research on Adolescence.

Melanie M. Domenech Rodríguez is an associate professor of psychology at Utah State University. She received her PhD from Colorado State University. She was a postdoctoral fellow with the Family Research Consortium–III under the mentorship of Ana Mari Cauce at the University of Washington. Dr. Domenech Rodríguez's primary area of research is the cultural adaptation and implementation of a Parent Management Training Oregon model intervention, *Criando con Amor: Promoviendo Armonía y Superación*. A randomized controlled trial of the preventive intervention was funded by a National Institute of Mental Health K01 award. She has research and applied interests in Latino/a mental health, multicultural competence training, and ethics.

Fairlee C. Fabrett, a native of Mexico, is a doctoral candidate in the clinical psychology program at Arizona State University and an intern at Harvard Medical School/Children's Hospital Boston. Her research has focused on the impact of acculturation on adaptive and maladaptive youth outcomes, including adolescents' academic aspirations, family conflict, and psychological symptoms, and the role of stress and cognitive processes in Mexican American adolescents' risk for depression. Her clinical interests have included the impact of culture on individuals' perceptions and reactions to life events, and the process individuals undergo as they adapt to a different culture.

Celia B. Fisher is Marie Ward Doty Professor of Psychology and director of the Fordham University Center for Ethics Education. Additionally, she is past chair of the Environmental Protection Agency's Human Research Subjects Board. She has been a member of the Department of Health and Human Services Secretary's Advisory Committee on Human Research Protections, the National Institute of Mental Health's Data Safety and Monitoring Board, and the Institute of Medicine's Committee on Clinical Research Involving Children. She has also chaired the American Psychological Association's Ethics Code Task Force and the New York State Licensing Board for Psychology.

Patricia M. Flynn is a postdoctoral research fellow in the Culture and Behavior Laboratory at Loma Linda University in California. She received her PhD in health psychology and her master's degree in public health from Loma Linda University. Her main research interests are the investigation of cultural and psychological factors relevant to health disparities. Dr. Flynn was awarded a research fellowship from the American Cancer Society to investigate Latino women's cultural beliefs and expectations about health-care professionals and the delivery of cancer-related health services. She has also received recognition from the National Institutes of Health through the Health Disparities Loan Repayment Program.

Andrew J. Fuligni is Professor in the Department of Psychiatry and the Department of Psychology at the University of California, Los Angeles. His research focuses on adolescent development among culturally and ethnically diverse populations, with particular attention to teenagers from immigrant Asian and Latin American backgrounds. He received his PhD in developmental psychology from the University of Michigan and was a recipient of the American Psychological Association's Division 7 Boyd McCandless Award for Early Career Contribution to Developmental Psychology. He is a fellow of the American Psychological Association and is currently an associate editor of the journal *Child Development*.

Amarilys Galloza-Carrero is a graduate student in clinical psychology at the University of Puerto Rico, Río Piedras. Her main research interest is in depression in deaf or hard-of-hearing adolescents, and the development of psychometric tests. She has been a teaching assistant for graduate statistics courses and a research assistant for a study that evaluated the efficacy of cognitive behavior therapy and a parental psychoeducational intervention for adolescents with depression. She currently works as a research assistant on statistics in a school-based prevention program for depression in Puerto Rican preadolescents.

Eugene E. García currently serves as vice president for education partnerships at Arizona State University, responsible for the coordination of teacher preparation across colleges and campuses in Arizona as well as the implementation of the university–public school initiative to establish campus schools. Dr. García has published extensively in the areas of language teaching and bilingual development. He served as a senior officer and director of the Office of Bilingual Education and Minority Languages Affairs in the U.S. Department of Education from 1993–1995. He currently chairs the National Task Force on Early Childhood Education for Hispanics, funded by the Foundation for Child Development and the Mailman Family Foundation. He is presently conducting research in the areas of effective schooling for linguistically and culturally diverse student populations, funded by the National Science Foundation.

Mary Jo Garcia Biggs, PhD, LCSW, is an assistant professor in the School of Social Work and an online MSW coordinator at Texas State University–San Marcos. She is co-principal investigator for the Hartford Practicum Partnership and Council on Social Work Education Gero-Ed Initiative grants, as well as co-principal investigator for a $1 million Health and Human Services Rural Distance Education Grant. Dr. Garcia Biggs serves as faculty adviser and mentor for Latinas Unidas (a university student support group). She has more than a decade of experience with Adult Protective Services, and her scholarship activities include publications and presentations (international, national, regional, and state) on aging, online education, Adult Protective Services, and Family Justice Centers.

Nancy A. Gonzales, a clinical child psychologist of Mexican descent, is ASU Foundation Professor of Psychology at Arizona State University. Her program of prevention research focuses on the study of psychological risk and resilience, with particular emphasis on cultural and community factors that impact academic success and mental health of low-income, ethnic-minority children and adolescents. Dr. Gonzales is principal investigator of an ongoing study to test the efficacy of a family-focused intervention to reduce school disengagement and mental health problems for Mexican American adolescents following transition to middle school. She is co-principal investigator of a longitudinal study of cultural, family, and community factors that shape cultural orientation and mental health trajectories for Mexican American youth, and a study focused on the development of postpartum depression in low-income women of Mexican descent. Dr. Gonzales is a fellow of the American Psychological Association and has served on numerous national organizations, editorial boards, and scientific review panels that promote high-quality, culturally informed research and interventions for youth and families.

Josefina M. Grau is an associate professor at Kent State University. She received her PhD in clinical and developmental psychology from the University of Illinois at Chicago. Her research interests include the study of parenting and its relations to social and emotional development in children, with special interest in the roles culture and context play in these processes. She is currently principal investigator of a National Institute of Child Health and Human Development-sponsored grant to study predictors of parenting behaviors and children's socioemotional and cognitive development in Latina adolescent mothers and their 1- to 2-year-old children.

Maria Rosario T. de Guzman is an adolescent development extension specialist and assistant professor of child, youth, and family studies at the University of Nebraska–Lincoln. Her research examines the sociocultural and ecological aspects of development, with particular focus on how culturally structured parental beliefs and children's immediate settings impact the socialization of prosocial behaviors. As extension faculty, she works extensively with various youth- and family-serving organizations.

Angelica P. Herrera, DrPH, is a postdoctoral fellow in the Division of Geriatric Psychiatry at the University of California, San Diego. Dr. Herrera received her doctorate of public health in health education and health administration from Loma Linda University and her MPH in epidemiology from the University of New York at Albany. She is a recipient of the Kellogg Health Scholars Program in Health Disparities and has nearly 14 years of community health experience with ethnic communities. Her research focuses on predictors of long-term care use by Mexican American family caregivers, the relationship between religious coping and Latino caregivers' mental health, and perceptions and patterns of civic engagement in low-income, minority older adults. Her current interest is the development community-based support programs for family caregivers of older, dependent Latinos with type 2 diabetes.

G. Derrick Hodge, a cultural anthropologist, has worked since 1999 with street youth in Havana, Cuba, studying the underground economy and nationalism. He has also worked as a research scientist on two studies funded by the National Institutes of Health, one at Harvard Medical School and the other at the Hispanic Health Council. He is the course director of medical anthropology at the Mount Sinai School of Medicine in New York City.

Aída Hurtado is a professor of psychology at the University of California, Santa Cruz. Her main areas of expertise are the study of social identity and intersectionality, Latino educational issues, and feminist theory. Her most recent books include *Voicing Feminisms: Young Chicanas Speak Out on Sexuality and Identity* (New York University Press, 2003, honorable mention for the 2003 Myers Outstanding Book Awards given by the Gustavus Myers Center for the Study of Bigotry and Human Rights in North America) and *Chicana/o Identity in a Changing U.S. Society: ¿Quién soy? ¿Quiénes somos?* (coauthored with Patricia Gurin, University of Arizona Press, 2004).

Maria I. Iturbide is a doctoral candidate in the developmental psychology program at the University of Nebraska–Lincoln. Her research focuses on understanding factors associated with the well-being of Latino youth. Specifically, her work concentrates on ethnic identity development, ethnic minority parenting, acculturative stress, and their links to adolescent risk behavior. She is an active member of the Latino Research Initiative at UNL and serves on the Society for Research on Adolescence Publications Committee and Emerging Scholars Committee.

George P. Knight, PhD, is a professor in the Department of Psychology at Arizona State University. He received a bachelor's degree in psychology from Macalester College and master's and doctoral degrees from the University of California at Riverside. His research interests

have included the role of culture in prosocial development, acculturation and enculturation processes, the development of ethnic identity, and measurement equivalence in cross-ethnic and developmental research. Dr. Knight has served as an editorial board member for *Child Development*, the *Journal of Research on Adolescence*, the *Journal of Family Psychology*, *Merrill-Palmer Quarterly*, *Personality and Social Psychology Bulletin*, and *Review of Personality and Social Psychology (Vol. 15)*. He has published widely in developmental, cultural, and social journals.

Gabriel P. Kuperminc, a professor at Georgia State University, is director of the community psychology doctoral training program and a member of the developmental psychology doctoral program in the Department of Psychology. He received his PhD in psychology from the University of Virginia in 1994 and served as a research associate and lecturer in the Department of Psychology at Yale University from 1994 to 1997. As a William T. Grant Scholar from 2000 to 2005, he conducted a longitudinal study of changing family roles and resilience among Latino adolescents from immigrant families.

Alexis Lubar is a senior psychology major and special education minor at the University of Maryland. She has assisted in research on low-income Head Start families, child language development, and the Real Relationship project. She is currently working as an intern for the Society for Research in Child Development, Office of Policy and Communication.

Meena Mahadevan, PhD, is a nutritionist whose professional focus has included nutrition education in low-income and ethnic-minority communities. As an adjunct assistant professor of nutrition at Lehman and Queens Colleges of the City University of New York, Dr. Mahadevan has designed course syllabi and taught undergraduate-level courses in food sciences and nutrition. Presently, she is a postdoctoral research fellow with the Center for Ethics Education at Fordham University and is coordinating a study investigating participant perspectives on research ethics practices among illicit drug users.

Esteban L. Olmedo obtained his PhD in experimental psychology from Baylor University but has had a diverse set of experiences in a variety of settings. Shortly after moving to California, he joined the Spanish Speaking Mental Health Research Center at the University of California, Los

Angeles, where he applied his statistical and psychometric skills to the study of the measurement of acculturation, primarily among Latinos in the United States. He then became the first director of the Office of Ethnic Minority Affairs at the American Psychological Association headquarters in Washington, D.C. He returned to California, where he spent the last 16 years of his professional career as professor and senior administrator in several positions at the California School of Professional Psychology (now named Alliant International University). He has published widely, especially on the topic of the psychometric issues involved in measuring acculturation. Dr. Olmedo retired from academia in 2000 to pursue other personal and family interests.

Amado M. Padilla received his PhD in experimental psychology from the University of New Mexico. He is currently professor and chairman of the program in Psychological Studies in Education at Stanford University. Prior to moving to Stanford, he was professor of psychology at the University of California, Los Angeles. A fellow of the American Psychological Association and of the American Educational Research Association, he has published more than 180 articles and chapters on numerous topics, including psychological assessment, ethnic identity, acculturation, second-language learning and teaching, and resiliency of immigrant students. He is the founding editor of the *Hispanic Journal of Behavioral Sciences,* which is currently in its 30th year. He has served as a consultant to numerous regional and national organizations as well as governmental agencies that work with children and families in schools and mental health clinics.

Krista M. Perreira is an associate professor of public policy at the University of North Carolina, Chapel Hill. Her research focuses on the interrelationships between family, migration, and social policy, with an emphasis on racial disparities in health and education. In 2003, she received a national Young Scholar Award from the Foundation for Child Development for her work on the health and education of young immigrant children. Funded by the Russell Sage and William T. Grant foundations, her most recent work combines qualitative and quantitative methodologies to identify how acculturation and migration processes influence the health and academic achievement of Latino adolescents in North Carolina.

Justin Quattlebaum is a doctoral candidate in the Department of Psychology at Kent State University and is currently completing a predoctoral internship at Baylor College of Medicine in Houston. His research interests include the development of emotional regulatory abilities in young children, intergenerational associations of acculturation, and adaptive parenting practices for at-risk families. He is currently investigating the relationship between acculturation, grandmother–mother conflict, and psychological adjustment in a sample of Latina adolescent mothers.

Stephen M. Quintana is a professor of educational and counseling psychology at the University of Wisconsin–Madison. He received a Ford Foundation postdoctoral fellowship and was mentored by Professor Martha E. Bernal. He was a Gimbel Child and Family Scholar for Promoting Racial, Ethnic, and Religious Understanding in America. He has been associate editor for *Child Development* and lead editor for a special issue, *Race, Ethnicity, and Culture in Child Development.* His research focuses on the development of children's understanding of ethnicity and on developing dialogues for elementary, middle, and high schools to promote more social integration and understanding among ethnic groups.

Marcela Raffaelli is a professor in the Department of Human and Community Development at the University of Illinois at Urbana-Champaign. Her current research focuses on development under conditions of extreme poverty, culture and sexuality, and immigrant family adaptation. She holds dual nationality (U.S./Brazil) and collaborates with scholars at the Center for the Psychological Study of Street Youth at the Federal University of Rio Grande do Sul, Porto Alegre, Brazil. She was previously at the University of Nebraska–Lincoln, where she cofounded the Latino Research Initiative, a community–university partnership engaged in outreach scholarship.

Cathy Roche is a doctoral candidate in clinical and community psychology at Georgia State University. She is currently completing her predoctoral internship at Maimonides Medical Center in Brooklyn, New York. Her research interests focus on intergenerational patterns in the transmission of family violence.

Vanessa M. Rodriguez is project coordinator and clinician at Partners Program at St. John's University, New York, where she is currently a doctoral candidate in the clinical psychology program. Her research interests include the treatment of dysfunctional parent-child relationships and parents suffering from posttraumatic stress disorder. She has a special interest in identifying effective therapeutic treatments for multicultural immigrant populations. She has presented her research at various professional research conferences, such as the Society for Research in Child Development, the Association for Behavioral Cognitive Therapy, and Head Start's National Research Conference.

Mark W. Roosa, PhD, is a professor of social and family dynamics at Arizona State University. He received his bachelor's degree from Ohio State University and his master's and doctoral degrees from Michigan State University. His career research interest has been the development of children from low-income families, in particular the etiological processes that place these children at risk and those that protect them from risk. He is particularly interested in the additive and interactive roles of culture (e.g., parent and child levels of enculturation and acculturation) and context (family, community, and school) in influencing child outcomes in Mexican immigrant and Mexican American families. Dr. Roosa has published widely in family, community psychology, and developmental journals.

Emily Sáez-Santiago obtained her PhD in clinical psychology from the University of Puerto Rico, Río Piedras, where she is an Assistant Research Scientist at the Institute for Psychological Research. Her research interests include the prevention and treatment of depression, family environment, emotional adjustment of children and adolescents with diabetes, and culturally sensitive interventions. She has collaborated in several randomized clinical trials for depression with adolescents in Puerto Rico. She has been the recipient of research grants from the National Institute of Mental Health (NIMH) and the National Institute of Diabetes, Digestive, and Kidney Diseases. Currently, Dr. Sáez-Santiago is working on a Career Development Award funded by the NIMH to evaluate a prevention program for depression as part of health classes in middle schools. She has published several articles on depression in Latinos/as, conduct disorders, family environment, coping strategies, and culturally centered interventions.

Hassan N. Saleheen holds an MPH from the University of Queensland, Australia, with an emphasis on epidemiology and biostatistics. As a data analyst at the Connecticut Children's Medical Center, he is working on several studies, including one that assesses physician counseling and practice regarding teen driving safety, and another that analyzes the frequency and patterns of fatal motor vehicle crashes among Connecticut teenagers.

Ingrid A. Sarmiento received her BA in psychology from Skidmore College and an MA in clinical psychology from Clark University, where she is a clinical doctoral student. Her current research is examining the relationships among cultural competence, working alliance, and treatment outcome in a sample of culturally diverse outpatients. Additional research interests include multicultural mental health, mental health disparities, family functioning, and depression. Ms. Sarmiento was the recipient of the 2008 Distinguished Student Research Award presented by the American Psychological Association's Division 45 (the Society for the Psychological Study of Ethnic Minority Issues).

Kent Paredes Scribner is the 17th superintendent of the Phoenix Union High School District. As superintendent of Phoenix Union, Scribner oversees 25,000 students in 17 schools. The student population is 93% minority and 78% Hispanic. Born in Los Angeles, California, Scribner earned a bachelor's degree in Latin American studies from Carleton College in Minnesota, a master's degree in counseling psychology from Temple University, and a doctorate in educational leadership and policy studies from Arizona State University. He began his education career as a high school Spanish teacher in Philadelphia. He moved to Arizona in 1992 as a graduate research assistant at ASU, where he examined issues of quality and diversity in Phoenix Union regarding the district's court-ordered desegregation.

Nicholas C. Scull, MSS, is a doctoral candidate in the Department of Counseling Psychology at the University of Wisconsin–Madison and is currently completing his predoctoral internship at the University of California, Los Angeles, Counseling and Psychological Services. His clinical interests include multicultural and developmental approaches to college student mental health, and he has worked with adjudicated Latino youth. His interests are in international research in Latin America and the Middle East. He is currently working on a study of race relations in Guatemala and on his doctoral dissertation, on forgiveness among survivors of the 1990 Iraqi invasion of Kuwait.

Melissa Selem is a Cuban American doctoral student in community health at the University of Illinois. She earned a master's degree in mental health counseling from the University of Miami. Her research interests are environmental justice, sustainability, and conservation behaviors at the individual and community levels. She is currently working on her dissertation and is a scholar in the Human Dimensions of Environmental Systems program.

Jacqueline D. Shannon is assistant professor of early childhood education at Brooklyn College of the City University of New York. She received her PhD in developmental psychology at New York University. Prior to joining Brooklyn College, she was a research scientist at NYU and a postdoctoral research fellow with the National Institute of Child Health and Human Development. Her research interests include parenting (with a special focus on fathers), young children's cognitive and social-emotional development within families living in poverty using mixed methods (large national data sets, qualitative, and observational), and the use of research in the development of family programs. Recent publications have appeared in *Applied Developmental Science* (2007), *Child Development* (2004, 2006), *Infancy* (2005), and *Parenting: Science and Practice* (2002, 2006, 2009).

Merrill Singer, a medical anthropologist, is a professor in the Department of Anthropology and a senior research scientist at the Center of Health, Intervention and Prevention at the University of Connecticut. He also serves on the Law, Policy and Ethics Core of the Center for Interdisciplinary Research on AIDS at Yale University. His research focuses on health disparities and the political ecology of health. He has been the recipient of research grants from the National Institute on Drug Abuse, the National Institute on Alcohol Abuse and Alcoholism, the Centers for Disease Control and Prevention, and the Robert Wood Johnson Foundation.

Adriana J. Umaña-Taylor, PhD, is an associate professor of family and human development at Arizona State University in the School of Social and Family Dynamics. She received a bachelor's degree in psychology and a master's degree in child development and family relationships, both from the University of Texas at Austin. She received her PhD in human development and family studies from the University of Missouri–Columbia. Her research interests focus broadly on Latino youth and families and, more specifically, on ethnic identity formation, familial socialization processes, culturally informed risk and protective factors, and psychosocial functioning among Latino adolescents. She is currently conducting research on adolescents and families of Mexican origin; one study focuses specifically on Mexican-origin teen mothers, their mother figures, and their infants.

Francisco A. Villarruel, a youth development researcher of Mexican descent, is a University Outreach and Engagement senior fellow and a professor of family and child ecology. His research focuses on Latino youth, juvenile justice systems reform, and afterschool programs. Villarruel serves on the board of directors of the Campaign for Youth Justice and is a consultant for the Children's Center for Law and Policy— two organizations dedicated to addressing inequities in juvenile justice systems throughout the nation.

Natalie Wilkins is a doctoral candidate in the community psychology program at Georgia State University. Her research interests include youth development, mentoring, and examining the role of culture in processes of resilience among adolescents.

Meghan Woo, ScM, is a doctoral student at the Harvard School of Public Health and a research consultant for the Center for Multicultural Mental Health Research at the Cambridge Health Alliance. She received her undergraduate degree from Tufts University and holds a master's degree in social epidemiology from the Harvard School of Public Health. Meghan's doctoral work concentrates on the impact of racial identity, acculturation, and immigration on racial/ethnic health disparities, with a focus on multiracial populations. Her research interests also include health and social policy, focusing on traditionally "nonhealth" policies that impact health.

Byron L. Zamboanga is an assistant professor in the Department of Psychology at Smith College. He received his BA in psychology from the University of California, Berkeley, and his PhD in developmental psychology from the University of Nebraska–Lincoln. He was an active member of the Latino Research Initiative (a community–university partnership engaged in outreach scholarship) at UNL and played a key role in the development and implementation of the Latino Achievement Mentoring Program (LAMP). His research program focuses on alcohol use among adolescents and young adults and on acculturation and cultural identity issues. He is currently conducting several cross-sectional and longitudinal studies on athletics and alcohol use among high school and college students.

Luis H. Zayas is the Shanti K. Khinduka Distinguished Professor and director of the Center for Latino Family Research at the George Warren Brown School of Social Work of Washington University in St. Louis. He is also a professor of psychiatry at the Washington University School of Medicine. A native of Coamo, Puerto Rico, Zayas holds a master's degree in social work and a PhD in developmental psychology from Columbia University. His clinical and research focus has been on Hispanic families and children, with special emphasis on parenting and improving parenting practices. He has conducted intervention research on reducing perinatal depression in Latina mothers, child-rearing values, suicide attempts of adolescent Latinas, and the impact of ethnicity on the diagnoses given by Hispanic and non-Hispanic clinicians to Hispanic patients. Recently, Zayas has addressed the adaptation of extant interventions for Latino children, youth, and families.

Supporting researchers for more than 40 years

Research methods have always been at the core of SAGE's publishing program. Founder Sara Miller McCune published SAGE's first methods book, *Public Policy Evaluation*, in 1970. Soon after, she launched the *Quantitative Applications in the Social Sciences* series—affectionately known as the "little green books."

Always at the forefront of developing and supporting new approaches in methods, SAGE published early groundbreaking texts and journals in the fields of qualitative methods and evaluation.

Today, more than 40 years and two million little green books later, SAGE continues to push the boundaries with a growing list of more than 1,200 research methods books, journals, and reference works across the social, behavioral, and health sciences. Its imprints—Pine Forge Press, home of innovative textbooks in sociology, and Corwin, publisher of PreK–12 resources for teachers and administrators—broaden SAGE's range of offerings in methods. SAGE further extended its impact in 2008 when it acquired CQ Press and its best-selling and highly respected political science research methods list.

From qualitative, quantitative, and mixed methods to evaluation, SAGE is the essential resource for academics and practitioners looking for the latest methods by leading scholars.

For more information, visit **www.sagepub.com**.